DATE DUE

MY 4'00			

DEMCO 38-296

Oil and Revolution in Mexico

Oil and Revolution in Mexico

Jonathan C. Brown

UNIVERSITY OF CALIFORNIA PRESS

Berkeley / Los Angeles / Oxford

University of California Press
Berkeley and Los Angeles, California

University of California Press, Ltd.
Oxford, England

© 1993 by
The Regents of the University of California

Library of Congress Cataloging-in-Publication Data
Brown, Jonathan C. (Jonathan Charles), 1942–
    Oil and revolution in Mexico / Jonathan C. Brown.
        p.   cm.
    Includes bibliographical references and index.
    ISBN 0-520-07934-5 (alk. paper)
    1. Petroleum industry and trade—Mexico—History.   I. Title.
HD9574.M6B7   1992
338.2'7282'0972—dc20   92-25649
                                                                            CIP

Printed in the United States of America
9 8 7 6 5 4 3 2 1

The paper used in this publication meets the minimum requirements of
American National Standard for Information Sciences—Permanence
of Paper for Printed Library Materials, ANSI Z39.48-1984. ⊛

For G. Franklin and Cynthia Ingalls Brown

Contents

Illustrations and Tables

GRAPH

TABLES

Preface

This book may be about Mexico's future as well as its past. After a decade of economic decline, the country's politicians have begun a crusade to integrate Mexico into the world economy and to attract foreign capital. Historians are right to view the new openness with some skepticism. They have, after all, seen it before. At the end of the nineteenth century, Porfirio Díaz once accomplished what Mexico's leaders are now attempting. That exceptional period of economic modernization was succeeded by a revolution. No careful academician claims to foresee the future, but I would suggest that the road the Mexicans travel during the next several decades will be a familiar one. A historical journey over the old route, therefore, would be profitable.

So many persons have helped me in this endeavor that I find it difficult to name them in order of importance. Somewhere near the top of the list would be the late Henrietta Larson, who launched me on this project a decade ago when she sent me her materials on the Latin American operations of the Standard Oil Company (New Jersey). John Tutino deserves credit for telling Larson about me. Together, they helped me return to academia.

My pursuit of the documentary evidence was assisted by Ed Glab, John Oldfield, and L. Philo Maier for Standard Oil; Geoff Jones, A. F. Peters, and Veronica Davies for Shell; Kay Bost and Dawn Letson for DeGolyer; Michael C. Sutherland, Rita S. Faulders, and Msgr. Francis J. Weber for Doheny; Pablo Casanova and Carlos Lomelín for Pemex; and Friedrich Katz with lots of leads.

Student research assistants have been instrumental in collecting (and understanding) much of the material. I have had the capable services of Kurt Weyland, Kevin Kelly, Joe Schreider, Elizabeth Feldmann, Alfredo Poenitz, and Adrian Bantjes.

The researcher also needs financial patronage. I have been assisted by grants from the American Council of Learned Societies and the National Endowment for the Humanities. The University of Texas at Austin has been generous as well: I have received assistance from the Public Policy Research Institute, the University Research Institute, the Mellon research fund of the Institute of Latin American Studies, and the Dora Bonham endowment of the history department.

Numerous persons also gave freely of their material and spiritual encouragement. Jack Womack and John Wirth wrote often and unsparingly, offering advice and letters of support. Others include Mira Wilkins, Alfred Chandler, Laura Randall, Colin Lewis, Jordan Schwarz, Eric Van Young, George Baker, Michael Meyer, and Jim Wilkie. Tina and Freddy Kent gave me shelter in London and took in my family too. Bruce and Jean Wollenberg and Kay Willis put up with us in Santa Barbara; Marty and Carolyn Melosi tolerated us in Washington, D.C., even though they live in Houston. How can I forget Chitraporn Tanratanakul, with her "placas diplomáticas" whisking me through the Mexico City traffic? Both she and Enrique Ochoa collected my microfilm and photocopies long after I had gone. In Mexico, Carlos Marichal, Juan Manuel de la Serna, Jorge Ruedas de la Serna, Cristina González, Víctor Godínez, and María Elena Brady provided hospitality. Pieter and Gesina Emmer and Stan and Ruth Brown offered hospitality in the Netherlands and Germany. I owe special thanks to Max and Ethel Gruber, who helped us during the hard times.

Among those who read and commented on parts of the manuscript were Patrick Carroll, Peter Linder, and Alan Knight (the latter, an inspirational colleague during his tenure as a Longhorn). But Steven Topik saved the book by introducing me to the University of California Press. Editor Eileen McWilliam and two outside evaluators reviewed the manuscript in record time, and now the readers can judge the result.

In the years it took me to research and write this book, the members of my family continued their own quests. Lynore moved with me from Santa Barbara to DeKalb to Austin. While pursuing her own career in education administration, she provided me with the kind of advice every author needs. Each of her suggestions has been right. Jason, who had already survived one book, went from grade-school to university student, and Adam moved from the cradle to grade school. It all proves that time does not stop just because one guy wants to relive the past.

A final caveat is in order. I did not realize until two years into this project that the oilman Edward L. Doheny and I had been born and raised in the same hometown—Fond du Lac, Wisconsin. An old colleague from the *Fond du Lac Reporter,* Stan Gores, had even written about him. Subsequently, my mother and father informed me that Doheny had long ago donated the library at the public high school. How's that for fine irony? One kid goes forth from Fond du Lac to gain wealth and fame, and the other to write about him.

Introduction: Compromising the Forces of Change

Mexicans have a saying: "What would we do without the gringos? But we must never give them thanks."[1] Perhaps the greatest debt Mexico owes to the United States remains the economic modernization of the late nineteenth and early twentieth centuries. Americans contributed capital, materials, and skills to develop the modern railways that reduced the country's long-standing regional and mountainous barriers. Americans brought in steam boilers, ore crushers, pumps, and blast furnaces to resuscitate the decrepit mining industry. They introduced sanitation works, power and light plants, telegraphic services, and trolley systems to cities. They brought in hoists and dredgers to build modern ports. Foreigners also purchased land, contributing new techniques and tools to expand Mexico's production of foodstuffs, tropical products, and hemp.

Finally came the foreign oilmen. First, they developed Mexico's market for imported fuel used in illumination and motive power, converting the economy to this modern source of industrial energy. Foreign oil companies then expanded the country's production and refining of petroleum products for export. Nonetheless, the hosts did not view the petroleum industry developed by foreigners as an unrelieved blessing. Mexicans accused the wealthy companies of financing reactionary political movements, dividing and repressing the workers, extracting the nation's nonrenewable resources, and subordinating domestic needs to international interests. Native oil laborers resented the companies for giving foreign workers the privileges and pay denied to

1

most Mexicans. In 1938, when thousands of Mexicans gathered at the Zócalo to celebrate the expropriation of the foreign oil companies, one of their banners read "Gentle *Patria:* the Christ Child bequeathed you a country and the devil, your veins of petroleum."[2]

How can one explain the Mexican ambivalence toward the fruits of the Industrial Revolution? Did the petroleum industry relegate Mexico to Raúl Prebisch's economic periphery, giving up its wealth to the industrial center because the terms of trade undervalued raw materials and overvalued manufactured goods? Did economic development generate growth and power for the few and poverty for the many, as the *dependentistas* might say? Did it create a Wallersteinian world system in which the local elites sold out to the foreign interests and oppressed the workers? Did "monopoly capital" follow the pattern described by Braverman, rendering the Mexican proletariat a deskilled, hapless lump that could not shape its own world?

This study rejects those scenarios. But it also finds unrealistic the neoclassical analysis that predicts that less-developed countries find salvation in imitating the industrial nations.[3] Those contemporary observers who believe Mexico's current policies of privatization and free trade to be the wave of the future might take heed of that nation's historical experience with the oil companies. There is no doubt that Mexicans desire the benefits of capitalism. But their own history has taught them to be wary of the undesirable consequences that unregulated capitalism might produce when confronted with the country's more rigid political and social structures. The fact is, Mexico cannot travel the shining economic path of the United States. Nor does it want to.

Mexico and other Latin American countries share one commonality: their societies have been born and reared in extreme social diversity. Every Mexican searches for his or her identity amid the social plurality and inequality of the multiracial colonial order. Many racial, ethnic, regional, and even language groups have formed the country's heritage. Octavio Paz has written that Mexico has "a history of man seeking his parentage, his origins."[4] Historically, the problem of maintaining unity among such diverse peoples, from the period before Conquest to the present, has led to the perfection of authoritarian methods of social domination and political manipulation. When the oil companies arrived in Mexico, the elite still formed a narrow minority, jealous of its prerogatives and contemptuous and fearful of its social inferiors. Private schooling and political connections beyond the reach of the "have-nots" enabled the "haves" to reproduce their social superiority from one generation to the next. The middle classes imitated the mores of their superiors and sacrificed to keep from sliding backward into the disreputable working class. Persons with dark skin and native cultures were ridiculed and shunned. They found themselves consistently at the lowest end of the socioeconomic order. Even the working class had its own hierarchy of prerogatives and organization. The skilled descendants of Europeans (in attitudes if not race) maintained a privileged position over the less-educated, less-skilled lumpen proletarians. The peasantry itself, disdained by the elite and urban worker alike, retained the closest ties to the Indian past. For workers and peasants, either religious orthodoxy or nationalism in the Gramscian doses prescribed by the elite had substituted for a healthy distribution of income and opportunities. Paternalism and coercion at all levels contained the various components of this social hierarchy, preventing them from bursting their bounds.

A pluralistic nation may not be able to accept change with equanimity. Economic change disrupts a society made up of many unequal parts to a greater degree than it would threaten a more homogeneous one. Mexico, whose history was richer and more complex than that of most countries, typified the built-in safeguards with which Latin Americans often confronted change. Mexicans attempted to manage change, modernization, or the introduction of things foreign, by rearranging its new social and political relationships according to traditional patterns of behavior. This is not to say that Mexico's twentieth-century corporate state and social inequality perfectly reflect the royal absolutism and caste society of the colonial period. But they have preserved social behaviors developed at that time. It could be argued that social hierarchy accounted for the preservation of political authoritarianism and, subsequently, for the perversion of modern capitalist stimuli in the interests of containing social unrest. As a force for change, economic growth posed a serious challenge to a society that had not been accustomed to dividing property strictly according to economic criteria. In Mexico, social position and political connections had always influenced one's access to economic benefits.

Research in Mexican labor and political documentation as well as in foreign diplomatic and business archives confirms that Mexico's economy cannot be separated from its politics. Yet, the greatest revelation of all has been the primacy of Mexico's social heritage. In few other national histories have the complexities of the preindustrial social order been more evident than in Mexico: the thin, privileged, and fearful

European upper crust; the competitive, vulnerable, and racially mixed middle strata; and the mass of Indian peasants and day laborers, suffering abuses and saving up grudges. This might have been the cauldron in which Barrington Moore prepared his recipe for the social origins of authoritarianism.[5] But it was not. If they study only Western European and North American historical evolution, the theorists hardly account at all for the kind of ethnic and racial complexity encountered in Latin American societies.

Therefore, I have strived to write a comprehensive history. This book analyzes the reasons for and the consequences of the operations of the American and British oil companies in Mexico between 1880 and 1920. More than a business or economic history might acknowledge, those consequences challenged the very political and social order of the host nation. Chapter 1 concerns the entry of foreign entrepreneurs into Mexico. It demonstrates that they had to expand just to survive the growth of international trade in petroleum. Foreign entrepreneurs succeeded because of their earlier experience in oil production, their vast financial resources, their ability to satisfy both domestic and international markets, and the failure of Mexican entrepreneurs to compete on the same level. At the same time, the activities of the foreign companies became inextricably bound to the political and social breakdown that was already leading the country to revolution. Chapter 2 deals with the operations of the foreign oil companies in the first Mexican oil boom. It places Mexico in the international economic context, showing why and how the companies expanded even as Mexico became engulfed in the first social revolution of the twentieth century.

Chapter 3 offers an unusual explanation for economic nationalism. It demonstrates how the unfettered operations of foreign capital in Latin America were incompatible with the historic relationship between the working class and the state. Most studies emphasize the naughty behavior of the foreign companies and the offended sensibilities of national politicians. My analysis suggests that economic nationalism contains social considerations that are too often neglected. Chapter 4 criticizes many trite, oft-repeated misconceptions about the collusion of foreign interests and domestic reactionary forces. The relationship between foreign oilmen and the "counterrevolutionary" caudillo, Manuel Peláez, has stirred considerable conjecture in the historical debate concerning the Mexican revolution. Was Peláez only the political tool of the foreign interests? In fact, the companies fell victim to a local political struggle only tangentially linked to the role of foreign enterprise in Mexico. Nor should one lose sight of the acute social impact of foreign investment. The petroleum industry proved a contradictorily powerful force for both improvement and insecurity in the lives of its Mexican workers. Their collective response, the militancy described in chapter 5, bespeaks the workers' commitment to their own preindustrial values as well as their desire to create their own place in modern industrial society. As each chapter will show, Mexicans of all classes attempted to mold the oil companies to domestic standards—if only to prevent modern capitalism from shattering Mexico's political and social structures.

Returning to the original question: Why cannot the Mexicans show their gratitude? The answer is paradoxical. Every economic benefit that crossed Mexico's northern border also contained its own peril. As the experience of the foreign oil companies makes clear, Mexicans sought to compromise the forces of economic change to a social heritage stronger than modernity itself.

CHAPTER ONE

Not All Beer and Skittles

The Porfiriato, that period of Mexican history dominated by General and President Porfirio Díaz, from 1876 to 1911, was a time of unprecedented economic expansion. Compared to the economic decline and political instability that had plagued Mexico since the beginning of the rebellion for independence in 1810, the Díaz administration seemed to have provided peace and prosperity. Exports grew by 5.6 percent per annum, national income by 2.3 percent, population by 1.4 percent, and per capita income by .93 percent. Foreigners found Mexico so attractive that they pumped an estimated 3.4 billion pesos into the country by 1911. Depending upon their own national economic strengths, foreign investors specialized in different sectors of Mexico's economy. French and Dutch capital financed the public debt. The Germans invested in manufacturing; the Americans, in mining and later petroleum; Britons and Canadians, in public utilities; and the Americans and Britons, in railways. It was said that two-thirds of all capital investment in Mexico, outside of the agriculture and handicraft industries, came from foreign sources. The United States led all investors, but Mexican political encouragement had developed effective competition from British and French capital investments as a foil to U.S. economic dominance. A coterie of immigrant entrepreneurs developed a vibrant domestic manufacturing sector. Political supporters of Díaz often reminded Mexicans of these basic facts. They neglected to mention, however, that the distribution of income remained skewed toward the elite.[1]

Growth of the economy, in turn, generated growth of the Mexican market for petroleum products, lubricants, and illuminants. Railways, mining operations, domestic and export agriculture, industrial and artisan manufacturing, and internal consumption all expanded. In the oil tank car, railways provided an efficient method of bulk transport. The trackage of Mexican railways expanded from 1,073 to 19,280 kilometers between 1880 and 1910. The moving stock of trains needed lubricating oils. So did agricultural processing equipment and the machinery in the mining, textile, and agricultural export industries. In the cities, increasingly prosperous and sophisticated consumers purchased imported lamps that burned kerosene. Kerosene lanterns also became standard equipment in a number of industries, and parlor oil stoves for home heating appeared in the homes of the well-to-do when fuel became more widely available throughout the nation. Even the Irish-made light buoys, equipped with oil lamps and placed by the Mexican government at the entries of the nation's harbors, had tanks large enough to hold fuel for a month of steady light. Nineteenth-century mining operations were starved for fuel, because deforestation hampered the use of wood for the steam boilers of the mines. American investors reopened some colonial mines and applied modern technology to the extraction of silver and gold from low-grade ores. Coal, copper, and lead also came to be mined.[2]

Mexico's domestic market, nonetheless, did little to stimulate Mexican private entrepreneurship in the production of petroleum. Several early Mexican efforts to produce, refine, and sell oil products had failed. To develop the infrastructure of a successful private marketing business in Mexico, the entrepreneur needed capital, management skills, and technological expertise. These commodities, developed in more advanced capitalist economies, meant that only foreigners with prior experience in the oil business could succeed. Their success may have forever blocked effective competition in petroleum from Mexican entrepreneurs. More than that, the foreign entrepreneurs came from another world, not a seignorial but a business world.

American businessmen such as Henry Clay Pierce and Edward L. Doheny found a kind of logical interest in the Mexican marketing and production of petroleum. After all, the United States shared some 1,952 miles of border with Mexico. ("Poor Mexico," Porfirio Díaz supposedly remarked, "so far from God and so close to the United States.") When Standard Oil began exporting Pennsylvania petroleum products, Mexico along with Canada and Cuba represented the nearest foreign markets. A second rationale for American investment in the Mexican oil industry concerned the earlier American investment in the critical element of Mexico's economic modernization, the railways. Nevertheless, American oilmen had competition not from Mexican entrepreneurs, who in any case lacked the capital and technological resources, but from the British—specifically from Sir Weetman Pearson.

These entrepreneurs operated in the half century before the First World War, the initial stage of economic modernization in Latin America.[3] How much of the results of this growth can be attributed to external forces, represented by foreign investment and technology? How much to internal forces, represented by economic policy and sheer political will? Can scholars distinguish the outcomes of policy from those of politics? Mexican politicians struggling among themselves for power have had an important role in shaping their nations' modern economic environment. Foreign entrepreneurs, therefore, owe much of their success and failure not only to their manipulation of production and markets but also to their individual relationships with domestic politicians.

In particular, British success in the Mexican oil industry was willed by influential Mexicans engaged in a nuanced and delicate political contest. They desired to promote economic development to enhance their internal political control without appearing to be dominated (and thereby discredited) by American business. Politicians surrounding President Porfirio Díaz encouraged all foreign oilmen, but they promoted Sir Weetman Pearson's interests above others. Their political support—in combination with Sir Weetman's business acumen—enabled this British entrepreneur successfully to challenge better-placed American competitors. Nonetheless, the new forces of modernization were beyond the capacity of the Porfirians to control. They may have favored the British, but Americans could not be totally eliminated.

Buy Your Lubricating Oils from Us

The Waters-Pierce Oil Company was an American firm with an important mission in Mexico: the development of the domestic oil market. Because of its peculiar niche in the United States petroleum industry, Waters-Pierce came into monopoly control of Mexican petroleum sales during the Porfiriato. Waters-Pierce neither produced nor refined oil products within the United States; it only sold them. A combination of Waters-Pierce's marketing specialization and its connection to the powerful Standard Oil group worked to develop the necessary sales infrastructure and to widen the growth-induced market for petroleum products. But growth of Mexico's consumption of petroleum products, while enlarging Waters-Pierce's profits, at the same time invited competition. (Profits beget competition, as the old capitalist adage goes.) Once it had developed the market in Mexico, by 1900, Waters-Pierce became vulnerable to competition from producers. Only other foreign businessmen—not Mexicans—had the technical and financial resources to break the marketing monopoly that Waters-Pierce enjoyed in Mexico.

It was not as if no one had known that Mexico possessed petroleum resources. In the Huasteca and Tabasco, pre-Columbian Indians had located a number of pools that oozed sulfurous gases and thick pitch, from which they extracted the substance they used for patching canoes, earthen jars, and baskets. Pitch was also used to cover idols and stucco, to stoke cooking and bonfires, and as a curative salve. In the 1540s Bernardino Sahagún noted that Indian merchants were bringing *chapuputli* from the Gulf Coast to marketplaces in the highlands. "This *chapuputli* is odorous," the Franciscan friar reported, "and when it is thrown into the fire, its smell spreads far." Indian women chewed the tar in order to clean the teeth.[4] During three centuries of colonial rule and an additional half-century of troubled independence, both the markets and production of oil in Mexico remained about as limited as these pre-Columbian origins.

Nevertheless, the possibilities of Edwin Drake's 1859 experiment at drilling for crude oil, resulting in history's first oil boom, were not lost upon the Mexicans. The emperor Maximilian gave out a total of thirty-eight oil concessions to Mexicans and Frenchmen in 1865. But nothing happened. After Maximilian fell from power, Ildefonso López had requested the permission of the governor of Tamaulipas to exploit the asphalt bubbling in pools on his Hacienda de San José de las Rusias west of Tampico. He needed a concession from the political authorities, because they had inherited the ownership of subsoil resources— hydrocarbons as well as gold and silver—from the Spanish Crown. What became of López's project is not known. At San Fernando, Tabasco, a priest named Manuel Gil y Sánchez scooped petroleum from what he called a "mine." Apparently thinking of developing an export market, he sent ten barrels of oil to New York. But the Pennsylvania oil boom begun by Drake's discovery had depressed the price of crude to such a degree that no one there was motivated to buy imported oil. Subsequently, Dr. Silmon Sarlat Nava, the governor of Tabasco, bought the San Fernando property. Changes in the mining laws in the meanwhile had reversed the colonial legal traditions and permitted private ownership of oil. In 1894, Sarlat registered his property with the government, also describing it as a "mine." "In a well of three-meters depth, which I ordered to be dug," Sarlat reported, "the petroleum emerges in a fluid and green state, as that of Pennsylvania in the United States."[5] Considering the enormous obstacles to developing these "excavations," the lack of transportation, the isolation and climate of Tabasco, the lack of either domestic or foreign markets, and the limited production of a three-meter well, it is not surprising that none of these native entrepreneurs brought in an oil field.

The Mexicans were not alone in these early production failures. Several foreigners also failed to initiate the Mexican oil boom during the latter quarter of the nineteenth century. In 1876, a Boston naval captain dug some shallow wells at the Hacienda Cerro Viejo near Tuxpan. The climate, vegetation, poor infrastructure, and lack of capital depressed the seaman, and he committed suicide. Cecil Rhodes, of South Africa fame, then joined in a British consortium, the London Oil Trust, that took over the Cerro Viejo property of the deceased. The Britons attempted to bring inland the most up-to-date drilling equipment. The multiple infrastructural problems were daunting, and Rhodes and his associates, none of whom were experienced oilmen, also gave up.[6] In the meanwhile, exploration was also proceeding farther south near Papantla. A Confederate sympathizer of Irish ancestry, one Dr. Adolfo Autrey, in 1869 took over a prospective oil property and distillery close by the ruins of the sixth-century Totonac city of El Tajín. The oil was described as being "as dense a liquid as cooked linseed oil."[7] Autrey displayed the kerosene produced from his small still at the Exposition of Querétaro in August 1882. By then, he had acquired four haciendas near Tuxpan. Containing large lakes of floating oil, the Hacienda Juan Felipe was described as the "fountainhead" of the petroleum supply in the region. A French engineer visited the oil properties near Tuxpan. He was struck by the incessant bubbling of "hydrogen and naphtha" from these oil springs.[8] Despite the good prospects for production (Juan Felipe later became a booming oil field), ultimately the Boston entrepreneur had to give up the property. His problem was transport. Autrey sent his product out of the rain forest on mule-back rather than via pipelines. He finally gave up.[9] Other entrepreneurs with greater financial, technological, and marketing resources would eventually open up production on these very same properties—but twenty years later.

As for pioneer oil sales, a Spanish merchant at Tampico, Angel Sáenz Trápaga, had brought some kerosene and gas oil lamps from New York. He was unable to sustain any kind of volume trade in the new product, for which no market as yet had been developed. Later as a broker, Sáenz aided the American marketer Waters-Pierce. The firm had broken off negotiations with the governor of San Luis Potosí, who had requested a personal fee of 100,000 pesos from the company for a permit to build a refinery there. Sáenz helped Waters-Pierce establish the refinery to process imported crude oil at Tampico.[10] This practical Mexican entrepreneur understood that if he himself could not sell oil products directly, he might as well make what profit he could by assisting the Americans.

No doubt, poor waterways, jungle growth, debilitating climate, torrential summer rains, a lack of roads, and a dearth of experienced laborers worked to disable these attempts by Mexicans and foreigners to open up the Mexican petroleum industry. In truth, there was an even greater obstacle. The capital necessary to put in pipelines, hire drilling teams, purchase equipment and barges, and establish refineries was large. To do these things in a rain forest cost significantly more. But no financier, national or foreign, would be willing to place such large amounts of capital into these oil projects until there existed a market for Mexican petroleum products. The logical place to develop a new market was in Mexico itself, since the United States in the late nineteenth century was awash with petroleum. Only foreigners who had prior experience in the oil business were prepared to undertake such an endeavor. For that, Mexico had to await events elsewhere.

Col. Edwin Drake's discovery in 1859 that oil could be drilled for like water revolutionized the industry. Previously, there existed a very small niche in the illuminant markets for oils distilled laboriously from coal and for kerosene distilled from crude oil skimmed—also laboriously—from pools and creeks. No wonder candles and whale oil remained the primary illuminants of the mid–nineteenth century despite the primitive manufacturing methods in candle making and the declining population of leviathans. Technology and capital had played a role in Drake's breakthrough. He had needed capital for equipment and experienced drillers. Some financiers from New Haven, Connecticut, became interested. With new capital, Drake hired a team of experienced water and salt drillers, adopting the existing technology to search for crude petroleum. The Drake well was hardly a gusher. It was only sixty-nine feet deep and flowed at a rate of 25 bd (barrels per day). But it did prove that oil could be produced in commercial quantities by drilling for it.[11] Before too long, petroleum illuminants replaced candles and whale oils, first in U.S. markets, then in markets elsewhere in the world.

Standard Oil had become the most successful business organization in the world within just one generation of Colonel Drake's first oil well in Pennsylvania. Previously associated with a New York mercantile house, John D. Rockefeller in 1865 became a partner in one of Cleveland's oil refineries. By 1870, he had created the Standard Oil Company (Ohio) in order to combine several specialty oil companies into a multi–million-dollar concern. Standard next worked to secure a monopoly of oil transport to the eastern seaboard via rail and pipeline. In 1882, Rockefeller's associates organized the first vertically integrated company. The Standard Oil Trust created a business structure in which each subsidiary company carried out a different, specialized economic function. A leader in export, Standard's East Coast refineries soon handled about 90 percent of U.S. petroleum exports.[12] Standard accomplished its expansion into and domination of oil markets in the American Southwest and in Mexico through an affiliate, the Waters-Pierce Oil Company of St. Louis.

Ironically, Henry Clay Pierce had once been a successful competitor of Standard Oil. The year 1867 found the twenty-two-year-old Pierce in St. Louis distributing oil products for one of the first marketers west of the Mississippi River. He became the oilman's son-in-law and eventually bought out the business. In 1873, Pierce formed a partnership with William H. Waters, who helped him keep the growing Rockefeller interests out of the Southwest.[13] But Pierce needed capital for further expansion and to buy out Waters. His powerful competitors provided it. In 1878, Pierce sold majority interest in his company to Standard in order to get capital for expansion. Together they bought out Waters, Standard taking a 60 percent controlling share of the stock and Pierce the remaining 40 percent.[14] As president of the company, Henry Clay Pierce then became signatory to the famous Standard Oil Trust agreement in 1882. He helped the trust standardize products regularly adulterated by independent jobbers and speculators. Standard's components, the Standard Oil Company (New Jersey) and the Standard Oil Company (New York) handled most of the nation's export of petroleum on the East Coast whereas the Standard Oil Company (California) eventually engaged in exporting from the West Coast. By the 1880s, petroleum ranked as the nation's fourth largest export.[15]

The tie to Standard Oil defined the powers and limits of Waters-Pierce. It only marketed oil products produced and refined by other Standard Oil subsidiaries and affiliates. In turn, Waters-Pierce expanded as Standard's exclusive agent in the states of Texas and Arkansas, Oklahoma and Indian territories, parts of the states of Missouri and Louisiana, and all of the Republic of Mexico. Pierce's company already had sales in these territories, but now its volume sales grew appreciably. Other marketing companies in the Standard group did not operate in Waters-Pierce territory, and it did not operate in theirs. Waters-Pierce did not own a single oil well or refinery in the United States. This relationship to Standard Oil made Waters-Pierce at once a powerful, prosperous, but dependent oil company.

Its experience in Texas bears examination, for Waters-Pierce's vulnerability there presaged its later demise as a monopoly firm in Mexican oil sales. Before the nineteenth century was out, Waters-Pierce had expanded its sales and competed with a tenacity that gained Henry Clay Pierce some enemies among competitors and politicians within his marketing area. In 1889 and 1895, the state of Texas passed antitrust laws requiring licensing of all firms that engaged in interstate business. State statutes outlawed any business combination that fixed prices or restricted competition. At the time, before oil was discovered anywhere in the state, Texas consumers depended upon petroleum goods—mostly kerosene and lubricants—imported in boxes and tins via ship and rail. Pierce controlled 95 percent of this Texas market. His agents charged prices that were 10 to 25 percent higher than those in other marketing areas.[16] Normally, Waters-Pierce extended sixty-day credit to their jobbers on a long line of axle greases, lubricants, and engine oils. "We hope that you will continue to buy your lubricating oils from us," the company would write to Texas merchants. "[We] are willing to make contracts with you for one year at lower prices than you could purchase the same quality of oils for from any of our competitors."[17] The Waters-Pierce agents gave rebates of 15 percent to Texas merchants who signed exclusive contracts with the company.

Merchants in various parts of the Pierce marketing area sometimes broke the exclusive agreement and began to sell the illuminating and lubricating oils of competitors. Waters-Pierce responded by dropping prices in that locale until the jobbers reconsidered. "Stringent methods were usually followed to keep out competition," reported a long-time Waters-Pierce employee, "and wherever a small concern endeavored to invade the territory occupied by the Pierce interests prices were lowered until the smaller concern was driven out of business."[18] To create the appearance—if not the substance—of competition, Pierce bought out firms like the Eagle Company and the Texas Oil and Gasoline Company of San Antonio and kept them in operation as "apparent" competitors. The state's attorney general remained skeptical. In a popular and widely publicized trial, Waters-Pierce was convicted of acting as a "trust" to fix or manipulate prices and restrain competition. Waters-Pierce in 1898 lost its license to operate in Texas.[19] The Texas case represents the continuing efforts of government bodies in the United States to regulate the volatile competition in the petroleum industry and to prevent the consumers from getting fleeced.

Henry Clay Pierce, however, soon recovered his lucrative market by colluding with Standard Oil to reorganize Waters-Pierce. As he later told a Missouri court, he wanted it to appear that he was managing and controlling the company "absolutely free from the dictation and direction of the Standard Oil Company."[20] In 1900, he took back all Waters-Pierce stock from Standard Oil but secretly returned two-thirds of the shares. The stock strategy—and a timely loan to a Texas congressman—enabled Pierce to apply for a new Texas license. Waters-Pierce thought it was back in business as before.

In any case, the second license had not returned Waters-Pierce to its monopoly position in Texas for long. Discovery of the Spindletop oil field in 1901, ushered in with Anthony J. Lucas's 100,000–bd gusher, abruptly transformed the state's petroleum market. Large new consortiums that combined production, refining, and sales, like the Gulf Company and The Texas Company, came to dwarf Waters-Pierce. The latter, after all, had remained a marketing concern. Just a few acres at Spindletop in 1902 now produced about 20 percent of the nation's petroleum.

Several of the new Texas refineries would have exported to Mexico, if Waters-Pierce had not already had a refinery in place at Tampico. When these first Texas wells began to flow to salt water in 1903, the wildcatters opened up new booms elsewhere in Texas and, by 1907, in Louisiana and Oklahoma as well. By 1902, Texas produced more than 18.5 million barrels of oil, second only to the new boom state of Ohio. As other companies—such as Joseph Cullinan's The Texas Company—expanded refining capacities along the Gulf Coast from 700 bd in 1902 to 200,000 bd in 1905, Waters-Pierce was left out.[21] In the fullness of time anyway, the company's reorganization had come to seem the fiction it actually was. The state of Texas filed another lawsuit in 1907, resulting in a second revocation of Pierce's license. The continuation of Waters-Pierce's exclusive relationship with Standard Oil had violated the 1903 Texas statute against unfair competition. The Texas courts found that even after the breakup of the Standard Oil Trust in 1892, the Standard Oil Company "controlled, managed and directed" Waters-Pierce.[22] Its connection to Standard Oil that had once made the sales company such a powerful business entity in the American Southwest now, after 1901, relegated Pierce's firm to second-class citizenship within the booming industry. Waters-Pierce would be condemned to repeat the same cycle of power and vulnerability in Mexico.

Shipped Down from New York

It is unclear exactly when Waters-Pierce began exporting, but American petroleum products had found a small market in Mexico relatively early. Soon after the U.S. Civil War, production in the Appalachian field had expanded so rapidly that the classic capitalist syndrome of overproduction and falling prices motivated the petroleum exports. Crude oil's first valuable product, kerosene, rapidly replaced tallow candles and whale oil as the world's foremost illuminant. In addition, the manufacture of kerosene also produced the by-products of naphtha (gasoline), lubricants, paraffin wax, and tar. The wealthiest of Mexico's consumers were already using imported oil during the empire of Maximilian in the mid-1860s. Their kerosene lamps and cans of illuminating oil arrived on consignment through merchant houses in New York and Mexico City. The Standard Oil Company in the 1870s exported such products worldwide through rather conventional mercantile organizations that traded in a variety of merchandise besides oil. Waters-Pierce also sold through jobbers in Mexico as part of its marketing in the American Southwest. It is certain that Pierce established a permanent and specialized sales force in Mexico soon after Standard Oil purchased the company. In 1887, Waters-Pierce had three salaried agents, a traveling salesman, offices in Mexico City and Monterrey, and a small refining operation in Mexico.[23] Here Pierce managed the market differently from his United States market areas.

Assisted by Standard Oil, Waters-Pierce built and operated oil refineries in Mexico. J. J. Finlay and Company, a subsidiary of Waters-

Pierce named for Pierce's brother-in-law, operated a refining company in Mexico City called La Compañía de Petróleo. Waters-Pierce began construction of a second refinery in January 1887. Each invested approximately $60,000 in their ventures, paying duties on the imported crude oil they processed and claiming to have from the government an "exclusive privilege." Without mentioning his connection to Waters-Pierce, Finlay therefore protested vigorously when a certain Gilberto Crespo y Martínez obtained a concession to import crude petroleum duty free from the Department of Public Works. Despite the fact that the government refused to revoke Crespo's concession, nothing came of this domestic competition. The Tampico plant had a refining capacity of 450 bd; Veracruz, 250 bd; and Mexico City and Monterrey, 100 bd each.[24] Nowhere else did Waters-Pierce also handle the refining end of the business.

In Mexico, the refineries processed crude obtained from Standard Oil–affiliated terminals on the mid-Atlantic coast and, later, the Gulf Coast of Texas. At first, the crude was transported in five-gallon tin cans. The tins were then washed out with gasoline and filled with refined kerosene. So ubiquitous had petroleum marketing become in Mexico that visitors traveling over the Sierra de Ajusco south from Mexico City noticed Indian huts roofed with cut-up oil tins bearing Standard Oil brand names.[25] As Pierce explained, "[W]e shipped nearly everything that went into the upkeep of refineries in Mexico from New York, and the tin for the manufacture of cases went from there and iron for tanks, in fact everything that entered into the manufacture of oil down there was shipped from New York."[26] The company's best grade of oil, *Eupion,* was refined in the Mexican plants, whereas the *Eupion* that Waters-Pierce sold in the United States originated in refineries controlled by other Standard companies. Its small refining plants processed Pennsylvania crude shipped from Philadelphia. After the Texas oil discoveries, crude was shipped from Corsicana and Beaumont. Pierce transported it to Veracruz and Tampico aboard Waters-Pierce's own bulk steamers. When Standard Oil's California refineries came on line, Waters-Pierce obtained kerosene and other finished products in San Francisco.[27] Mexico's west coast would thenceforward be supplied from California refineries.

Certainly not all of Waters-Pierce's success in Mexico derived from the quality of his three Mexican refineries. Apparently, the distillation they performed on the imported crude oil was quite minor—really a subterfuge to evade the higher import duties on refined products. "The

Company made a practice of bringing in 'crude oil' which, as a matter of fact, contained perhaps 90% of the refined product, but was colored by the crude, so as to pay the lower import duty," explained a manager of the Waters-Pierce refinery at Tampico. "The small amount of crude was then refined out, and the whole product sold by the Company at a much less cost than if it had been entirely crude," the manager continued.[28] At the height of its operations in 1902, Waters-Pierce maintained twenty tank-distribution stations and additional sales agencies in Mexico. It owned 104 tank cars and leased another 148 tank cars for transporting oils on the rail lines. In Mexico City, the largest of the marketing areas, Pierce's distribution plant maintained twelve two-horse tank wagons manufactured in St. Louis, ranging in capacity from 160 to 398 gallons each. Pierce sold kerosene-burning heaters in the biggest cities.[29] The company's operations in Mexico had developed unimpeded by competitors since its entry into the country.

Growth of petroleum sales responded to the expansion of the Mexican economy, and the profits of Waters-Pierce expanded accordingly. In order to stimulate Mexico's consumption of imported kerosene, the company sold as many as fifty-five thousand small glass lamps per year—nearly at cost. Its exports to Mexico accounted for 60 percent of all Standard's exports of crude to Latin America and 20 percent of the conglomerate's total crude exports. Saying that he maintained no division of his business between the United States and Mexico, Pierce declared that his total oil sales for 1902 amounted to 2,677,362 barrels. United States trade statistics for the fiscal year ending 30 June 1902 indicate that 287,369 barrels of petroleum products were exported to Mexico. Assuming that all the exports belonged to the monopoly marketer, therefore, Mexico accounted for just ten percent of Pierce's volume sales.[30] (See table 1.) Presumably, the Mexican market provided more than 10 percent of the company's fiscal sales, since his monopoly permitted Pierce to charge higher prices than in its U.S. sales area, where it competed with non–Standard Oil marketing companies. In 1906, Pierce admitted that he had competition of other "tank wagon companies" in its United States territories but not in Mexico.[31]

Certainly, there was no lack of profits. Waters-Pierce Oil Company's capital stock in 1911 was just $400,000, identical to its capitalization when it joined the Standard group in 1878. Still, Pierce paid yearly dividends amounting to 600 percent of its capitalization during the first six years of the twentieth century. One contemporary author placed Waters-Pierce profits at $1.8 million in 1900, $2.0 million each

Table 1. *Exports of U.S. Petroleum Products to Mexico, 1880–1911*
(*in gallons per fiscal year, 1 July to 30 June*)

Year	Crude Oil	Naphtha	Illuminants	Lubricants	Tar and Residual Products
1880	—	—	27,400	2,950	4,200
1881	429	1,669	1,128,155	12,418	—
1882	38,556	40,335	1,472,766	56,995	—
1883	11,100	66,990	1,755,835	20,509	—
1884	15,790	35,756	1,444,002	21,047	210
1885	550	14,226	1,623,770	24,877	1,722
1886	2,214	106	1,266,943	29,136	1,512
1887	3,556	5,155	2,173,677	31,410	2,646
1888	1,000,459	1,546	1,154,775	62,507	1,302
1889	1,881,398	6,952	2,123,532	77,343	1,218
1890	2,217,846	9,120	1,754,748	125,505	2,688
1891	3,854,176	4,455	2,168,834	98,921	2,898
1892	3,499,514	333	1,094,474	164,775	840
1893	5,508,769	250	913,645	322,656	462
1894	8,026,189	2,541	388,847	318,848	84
1895	5,229,983	1,241	257,842	464,343	210
1896	6,779,059	1,540	241,061	388,546	546
1897	7,090,850	6,905	335,692	494,031	5,376
1898	7,713,859	8,705	550,544	547,604	19,026
1899	7,969,871	73,405	581,222	605,249	6,510
1900	8,002,845	4,327	282,160	769,566	840
1901	8,356,258	7,158	225,172	610,923	64,764
1902	10,844,913	9,774	371,421	679,510	163,884
1903	9,859,154	10,717	342,000	798,282	3,528
1904	10,938,448	21,308	409,266	695,308	54,012
1905	14,036,517	56,555	461,266	697,382	1,218
1906	14,366,495	100,674	2,095,939	1,097,746	966
1907	19,992,434	133,147	2,495,070	1,255,991	530
1908	17,523,440	79,686	746,067	839,966	3,716
1909	27,554,581	73,819	511,276	1,165,272	5,446
1910	41,202,787	61,550	740,615	1,376,321	3,692
1911	24,398,337	363,101	200,252	1,308,964	1,023,559

SOURCE: Treasury Department, *Annual Report on the Foreign Commerce and Navigation of the United States,* from Executive Documents, House of Representatives (Washington, D.C., 1881–1912).

in 1901 and 1902, $2.3 million in 1903, and $2.8 million in 1904. The latter figure represented 672 percent of capitalization.[32] Considering that Henry Clay Pierce was the only other stockholder besides Standard Oil, his personal income must have been considerable.

When he faced a rash of litigation in the first decade of the twentieth century, Pierce claimed that he alone controlled the destinies of the Waters-Pierce Oil Company. Indeed, if one surveys the top management of the company, dominated by family and long-time associates, his claim seems convincing. Pierce, in his mid-fifties, was the chairman of the board. His brother-in-law, Andrew F. Finlay, had been the manager in Mexico and in Galveston before 1890, at which time he became one of the directors of Waters-Pierce. Finlay served as the company's president from 1900 to 1905. Clay Arthur Pierce, the chairman's son, began working for the company in 1898 as assistant treasurer. Serving from 1900 to 1904 on the executive committee, he helped set prices throughout the sales area. Clay Arthur succeeded to the presidency in 1905. The secretary and treasurer of the firm, Charles M. Adams, who had been with the firm since 1878, was responsible for coordinating crude-oil requisitions between Mexican refineries and New York exporters.[33] The management arrangement seems to have given Henry Clay Pierce a measure of autonomy despite the fact that Standard Oil directors were controlling 60 percent of his stock.

In actuality, Standard Oil Company managed the operations of Pierce's company rather closely, a fact that ultimately became a source of some contention. Day-to-day direction of operations from 1900 to 1908—especially for Mexico—resided in Waters-Pierce's New York representative, Robert H. McNall. McNall was, in fact, an employee of Standard Oil. The address appearing on his Waters-Pierce letterhead, 75 New Street, was actually the rear entrance of Standard's legendary headquarters at 26 Broadway. McNall coordinated Mexican transactions through Standard's export committee, whose offices were also at 26 Broadway. Not even bothering to seek prices and supplies elsewhere, he arranged for the delivery of crude oil to Tampico and Veracruz from Standard affiliates like the Atlantic Refining Company of Philadelphia. McNall also arranged for shipment of Standard California refined oil products from San Francisco to Mexico's west coast ports of Acapulco, Manzanillo, La Paz, San Blas, and Guaymas. He also helped maintain the Waters-Pierce refineries. McNall spent much time ordering pipes, engines, valves, and "a thousand and one articles that are used in a refinery." Refining experts were always nearby for consultation at 26 Broadway.[34]

Standard Oil established a normative and unitizing management over Waters-Pierce, as it did over other affiliates, and coordinated the company's Mexican operations into its all-inclusive information-gathering system. Branch managers routinely dispatched reports from Mexico City to St. Louis, thence to 26 Broadway. Those reports were made on the organization's standard forms, which McNall obtained directly from Standard's refining, transportation, and export departments. He sent the reports to the operating companies. Mexico dispatched forms to fill out to St. Louis on deliveries of naphtha and refined oils, on refinery performance, and on sales. These completed reports eventually returned to McNall. In this manner, Standard Oil even had semi-annual statements as to the bad debts charged to the profit-and-loss statement of the Mexican division.[35] Most telling of all, Standard Oil accountants regularly audited the books that Waters-Pierce maintained in St. Louis.

In fact, McNall's authority extended beyond the duties of coordination and information gathering. He and others at 26 Broadway not only evaluated reports of all kinds and audited the Waters-Pierce books but also approved of personnel matters. Concerning Mexico, he once wrote Finlay, the Waters-Pierce president:

I beg to acknowledge receipt of your favor of the 21st. inst., enclosing list showing suggested changes in salaries of Mexico employés. I have been over this matter with Mr. Van Buren [of Standard Oil], and as I telegraphed you today he agrees with your suggestion that these changes be made effective as of January 1st.[36]

Clearly, the Standard Oil Company and its managers retained a large measure of control over the operations of the Waters-Pierce Oil Company both in the United States and in Mexico. The connection accounted for the early success of Waters-Pierce in Mexico—and its ultimate failure.

Although Waters-Pierce dominated the Mexican market as an importing petroleum company roughly from 1880 to 1905, the company did not have to exert its market muscle to subdue either Mexican entrepreneurs or North American competitors. No Mexicans had sufficient expertise or capital. No other U.S. company had business patronage as powerful as that of Standard Oil. Yet competition did finally arrive in 1901, first in the person of a California-based oil prospector, Edward L. Doheny, then in the person of a British engineering contractor, Sir Weetman Pearson. Each had access to technology and capital—and Mexican political support, as we will see below—to discover,

refine, and market domestic petroleum resources. Siege of the Waters-
Pierce monopoly in Mexico would ultimately produce a breach between Pierce and his Standard Oil associates.

To meet this new competition in the first decade of the twentieth
century, Henry Clay Pierce and Standard Oil initially resorted to price
cuts, to flooding the market with competitive products, and to personnel changes in Mexico. Although Mexican petroleum prices were
higher than in the United States, Waters-Pierce dominated a market in
which consumer prices were actually falling from the moment that the
company had begun refining domestically. From 1886 to 1911, petroleum prices declined steadily, and competition provoked more price
cutting after 1901.[37] Doheny's oil discovery at El Ebano in 1902
brought domestic supplies of tars and residual products into the market. Because Pierce enjoyed the status of monopoly oilman in Mexico,
the figures for U.S. petroleum exports to Mexico in table 1 accurately
reflect Waters-Pierce's response. Waters-Pierce increased its imports of
residual products from 20 barrels in 1899 to 3,902 barrels in 1902.
Likewise, the monopoly importer greatly increased the lighter ends. In
order to offset the expected production from Pearson's new refinery on
the Isthmus of Tehuantepec, Waters-Pierce expanded the imports of illuminating oils from 461,266 gallons in 1904 to nearly 1.5 million gallons in 1906. Eventually, the company had to shut down its inefficient
Monterrey and Mexico City refineries and expand the Tampico facility
to 5,000 bd. Pierce even began to buy and process Mexican crude in
limited quantities.[38] These initial tactics, however, proved insufficient
to arrest the competition of Doheny and Pearson.

Next, the oil monopoly tried reorganizing its management in Mexico. In 1904, an employee from the Standard Oil comptroller's office,
R. P. Tinsley, came to St. Louis to serve as Finlay's vice-president. He
also brought a Standard-appointed comptroller. In Mexico, meanwhile, the resignation of Thomas Ryder, a manager there, shook the
organization. He took many Waters-Pierce employees with him to
work for the competing British Pearson firm. In 1905, Tinsley forced
out President Finlay, Pierce's brother-in-law, who departed immediately for Europe "to restore his health." Tinsley himself took over as
president and immediately proceeded to make personnel changes, dis-
missing directors selected by Pierce and replacing many of the managers in the field. Pierce later expressed some bitterness about Standard
Oil's meddling in his company's personnel management. The chairman
of the board complained that Tinsley sent a Standard Oil general man-

ager to Mexico "who was entirely unfamiliar with Mexico, its customs, people, languages or the business of the company. The effect of that was to cause the very efficient manager of the company to resign his position."[39] Tinsley apparently replaced old Waters-Pierce men in as many as three hundred positions. Pierce protested vigorously. He ultimately succeeded in getting Standard Oil to withdraw Tinsley. Pierce's son, Clay Arthur, became the new president. Yet the company's position in Mexico as well as in the United States continued to erode.

From this point onward, Waters-Pierce and Standard departed in their policies over Mexico. Waters-Pierce, after all, was involving Standard Oil in a number of state antitrust suits that would eventually reach the United States Supreme Court. The Standard officials did not hide their dislike of Pierce. One executive confided that when Henry Clay Pierce got into a jam, he became nasty: "He was the meanest fighter you ever saw."[40] In addition, the sheer weight of the antitrust litigation undertaken by Texas and Missouri began to sap the business initiative of Waters-Pierce. In 1908, a two-year trial in Missouri terminated in Pierce losing his charter to do business in his home state. The Missouri court had found that Waters-Pierce and another Standard affiliate, Republic Oil Company, headed by a young Walter J. Teagle, had colluded to divide the market territory.[41]

Further troubles remained in store for Waters-Pierce in Mexico. It was Texas all over again. By 1908, one of the competitors, Sir Weetman Pearson, had established a refinery and a sales organization in place in order to challenge Pierce for the Mexican marketplace. "Mr. Pierce thought himself so strongly entrenched in the oil business that he 'went to sleep' on the job," his Tampico refinery manager reported later. "The competition [with Pearson] for a number of years was of the cut-throat variety, and there was no love lost between the two companies."[42] Nonetheless, a market for specialty oil imports would survive the onslaught of domestic production. Foreign miners continued to buy foreign oil as late as 1908, even though they had to pay import duties. "The reason why we ship these goods from the states," confided a Philadelphia mining capitalist in Etzatlán, Jalisco, "is on account of the very inferior grades that we obtain in Mexico, which will not do our work. . . . [The oils] that are used for machinery purposes cannot be obtained in that country, as the quality that is sold is so inferior that it had almost ruined our machinery."[43] But of course Waters-Pierce wanted to remain more than just the Mexican marketer of specialty imports.

In November of 1908, the increasing strength of Doheny and Pearson brought Clay Arthur Pierce to Mexico City. Mexican newsmen sensed a great struggle in the making. They found Clay Arthur at the Palace hotel. "Of course you cannot expect me to discuss future plans regarding our business in Mexico," the president of Waters-Pierce told the Mexican reporters, "but I can call your attention to the fact that a company, with as much capital invested as that which the Waters-Pierce Oil Company has in Mexico, and with as many years of activity as it has had here, cannot but be prepared to meet whatever situation may come up." Clay Arthur Pierce detailed a litany of services that his company had provided for Mexico over the past three decades. He said that he doubted that another company would be able to organize its marketing in order to give the Mexican public equally as good service as Waters-Pierce. "Where it has been found necessary to cut the price of oil against competitors' initial cuts," Pierce concluded, "the Waters Pierce company has necessarily done so but it has kept up the standard of its products and service. Consumers of our materials get the product of the Pennsylvania fields, which is the very finest oil found anywhere." Pierce refused to respond to reporters' queries about when his company would begin to develop Mexican oil fields.[44]

The younger Pierce's sometimes inopportune comments to the Mexican press illustrate another of Pierce's weaknesses. Like many other American entrepreneurs, he did not consider it to be absolutely essential to be a business diplomat in Mexico. It was enough that the Americans were bringing the fruits of capitalism to this backward country. "The American 'generally tries to hog the whole thing' and is often short-sighted in his dealings with the Mexican people," a former Pierce employee observed later. "The English and the Germans, on the other hand, are much more considerate, and in this way gain very considerable business advantages over the American."[45] Such would be the case with Pierce's adversary, Sir Weetman Pearson.

Having lost its market dominance in the southwestern United States, Waters-Pierce was preparing to defend its last lucrative monopoly sales area—not from Mexican entrepreneurs but from other foreigners. The long-time monopoly importer was vulnerable. Initially, Henry Clay Pierce had concluded a contract with Standard Oil that bequeathed him enormous advantages. He had access to as much refined petroleum as he needed, and no other Standard-affiliated firm could enter Pierce's market area. The Mexican market fell into his lap. The profits of Waters-Pierce were very high in Mexico, where it had little competition. But the Standard Oil contract prevented Waters-Pierce from diversifying. It could neither produce nor refine crude oil. The refining capacity of Waters-Pierce depended upon Standard's patronage, which did not extend at all to production in Mexico. Consequently, new sources of production—such as Spindletop, Oklahoma, and Kansas—flooded Waters-Pierce's territory with cheap crude oil out of Standard's control. New refining centers along the Gulf Coast in Louisiana and Texas encouraged the development of powerful and fully integrated competitors. Moreover, growing U.S. legal problems were also poisoning the working relationship between Standard Oil and Waters-Pierce. The American business environment had already humbled Waters-Pierce. Soon thereafter, competition in the Mexican marketplace would do the same.

Drilling to the Source

The early history of the petroleum industry, as most capitalist breakthroughs, abounds in willful, driven men. John D. Rockefeller, who consolidated the first oil trust, and Henry Clay Pierce, who dominated Mexico's market, were such men. So was Edward Laurence Doheny. Doheny personified a type of American business entrepreneur who abandoned family and security in search of wealth on the American frontier. His discovery of oil in California seemed to have been accomplished by chance. Doheny built that opportunistic discovery into a worldwide organization that pioneered in the production of Mexican crude oil. He capitalized on the rapid expansion of markets for petroleum and even contributed in the process to developing additional uses of the substance in Mexico. Doheny succeeded in Mexican production because he had superior resources of capital and technology. One might also observe that he entered Mexico in 1901, during a period of intensive domestic economic growth partially attributable to, among other things, Pierce's having promoted the use of petroleum products. No contractual limitations to a superior organization inhibited Doheny's entrepreneurship. If pluck contributed to his California oil success, it played no role in Doheny's far superior achievements in Mexico. He was a willful, wealthy, competent, and now oil-experienced entrepreneur. Almost until the end of his life, Doheny thought himself a man capable of molding destiny.

Doheny's thirty-year journey from his youth in Wisconsin to Mexico resembles the classic Greek odyssey. It combined both caprice and fate. In 1892, after two decades of mine prospecting in New Mexico and Arizona, Doheny and his partner, Charles Canfield, arrived in Los Angeles with scarcely $1,000 between them. Doheny noticed that the local ice plant obtained pitch for fuel from the La Brea tar pits at West Lake Park. As Doheny later explained:

> Without ever having seen an oil district or an oil derrick, as I had never been east of Chicago in my life, my natural prospecting instinct told me that these tar exudes bore the same relation to the petroleum below that the resin on the outside of a pine tree bears to the more limpid sap within. I felt sure that by drilling to the source of these exudes I would develop a supply of petroleum.[46]

Doheny and Canfield had begun the Los Angeles oil strike with a seven-barrel-per-day, hand-bailed well that was only 170 feet deep. Within five years, however, experienced well drillers from Pennsylvania moved into the area, opening up some three hundred wells within a 160-acre area. Well riggings stood "as thick as the holes in a pepper box" among residential homes in the West Lake Park suburb of Los Angeles. To compete with rival oilmen attracted to California, Doheny learned the technology and hired drillers from back east. He expanded into the Fullerton, Bakersfield, and Kern River oilfields.[47] The Los Angeles discovery ultimately directed his entrepreneurial talents to Mexico, where some of Doheny's U.S. buyers already had investments.

Perhaps years of prospecting had prepared Doheny to survive the rigors of intense competition in the U.S. petroleum industry. The new oilman refused to depend entirely on selling his production to existing marketing companies like Union Oil and the growing Standard Oil Company of California. Doheny organized the Producers Oil Company and began to build his own marketing apparatus. He approached the Southern Pacific Railroad. Collis P. Huntington's company ran its locomotives on coal and wood obtained in the East and Northwest. The California crude was heavy, especially suitable as fuel oil. It prepared Doheny, in a way, for the even heavier oil he would discover in Mexico. The prospector-turned-oil-businessman set up a demonstration oil-burning steam boiler. He introduced a force-fed jet to a locomotive fuel system that had been burning petroleum in Peru.

He then approached other western railroad men. The Atchinson, Topeka, and Santa Fe Railroad was always on the lookout to buy oil close to its operations. Coal was more expensive to ship, and created

much waste.[48] Doheny's California properties produced enough petroleum to supply the Santa Fe Railroad with one million barrels of oil per
year for use on its ferry steamers and yard engines in California and for
sprinkling the railway roadbed through the Mojave Desert to San
Francisco. The contract was worth $1 million in sales.[49] Doheny was
following destiny.

His California oil business led Edward L. Doheny directly into
Mexico. The Santa Fe Railroad's A. A. Robinson, builder and president of the Mexican Central Railroad, informed Doheny that his line
running between San Luis Potosí and Tampico had been depending
upon imported Alabama coal of "indifferent quality." Moreover, Robinson had just constructed the spur line to Tampico under pressure
from the Díaz government; development of a new industry in the territory would provide revenues for his beleaguered line. Therefore,
Robinson asked the enterprising Doheny to investigate rumors of bubbling pits along the railroad's right-of-way. Canfield and a California
railway man, A. P. McGinnis, accompanied Doheny in May 1900 as he
traveled in a private Pullman car, complete with cook and porter. They
stopped thirty-five miles west of Tampico. The party descended from
the luxurious Pullman, were stunned by the stultifying humidity of
Mexico's hot lands, plunged into the lush underbrush behind a Mexican guide, and found some exudes.[50] The *chapopotes,* as the residents
called them, were ponds of brown pitch through which gas bubbled
from deep underground. The inhabitants for years had maintained
fences around these oil pools to keep the livestock from disappearing
into them. Doheny concerned himself, however, with the industrial potential of the exudes.

The American entrepreneur next turned to assembling the necessary
capital and technology from his own economy that could be used in the
Mexican venture. Returning to Los Angeles, Doheny, now forty-four
years old, absorbed himself in establishing a home for his twenty-five-
year-old second wife and in organizing a Mexican production company. He collected capital from a group of investors and railway men in
California and formed the Mexican Petroleum Company.

Back in Mexico in August 1900, Doheny and Canfield announced
that they would pay five pesos to any inhabitants who led them to a tar
pit.[51] He acquired his first property along the eastern border of the
state of San Luis Potosí. Mariano de Arguínzoniz was offering for sale
283,000 acres of the Hacienda del Tulillo. Arguínzoniz was difficult.
Doheny and Canfield were unknown, could not speak Spanish very

well, and were without means of establishing their credibility. "I wired to the City of Mexico, to an attorney whose name had been given to me by a friend of mine in Chicago, and asked him to meet us at Aguascalientes," Doheny explained later. "The attorney we wired was the Hon. Pablo Martínez del Río, since deceased. He was, perhaps, the most prominent English-speaking Mexican attorney in the City of Mexico."[52] Martínez del Río served as Doheny's legal representative in Mexico and introduced him to the heads of various government departments. Because Doheny was establishing a new industry, he obtained certain rights to import machinery duty free for ten years. This was to be an exclusive privilege, but Doheny discovered that a British oilman later received the same rights. Of Pearson, Doheny said that he was "placed on even a better footing than us—getting a 50-year concession— although our efforts to discover petroleum were eminently successful and his efforts, commenced several years afterwards, were based upon our success."[53] As soon as he learned that these Yankees were oilmen, however, Arguínzoniz raised the price from $250,000 to $325,000. Doheny then purchased the Hacienda de Chapacao of 150,000 acres next to Tulillo.

The Chapacao property gave him access to existing rail lines and to the Tamesí and Pánuco rivers leading to the port of Tampico. For his assistance in closing the land deals and serving as Doheny's retainer in Mexico City, attorney Martínez del Río received 600,000 pesos (approximately $300,000). But Doheny insisted that the previous owners sign over the mineral rights, a clause Doheny had included in all his land purchases in the United States.[54] After all, Mexican mining laws since 1884 had copied Anglo-American precedents. Doheny and other foreign oilmen obtained subsoil rights through lease and purchase directly from the Mexican landowners. Foreigners were quite comfortable with this arrangement, because it paralleled the legal practices of private property in the Anglo world.

The Mexican government welcomed Doheny's new petroleum venture, providing encouragement and tax breaks. The U.S. minister to Mexico, Gen. Powell Clayton, introduced Doheny to President Porfirio Díaz. Mexico's chief executive said that domestic petroleum production would save a country already deforested and dependent upon imported fuel. At the time, as Doheny explained later, "I was very busily engaged in denying rumors published in Mexican periodicals to the effect that we were an agent of the Standard Oil Company or a subsidiary of that organization." Díaz, no doubt aware of Pierce's association with Stan-

dard Oil, did not want the infamous oil trust to capture Mexico's petroleum. The president secured Doheny's promise to sell his oil properties to the Mexican government before offering them to Standard
Oil. President Díaz was also interested in the demonstration effect of
foreign capital. "He told us that his greatest desire for our prosperity in
Mexico," said Doheny, "was the example which our workmen would
present to the Mexican workmen of how to work, how to live, and how
to progress."[55] In the meantime, attorney Martínez del Río assisted
Doheny in securing all the lawful tax breaks from the government. Despite the political support he received, Doheny was convinced that
none of the Mexicans—Díaz and Martínez del Río included—thought
that his oil venture would succeed.

By February 1901, Doheny's men were preparing to open Mexico's
first oil field—at El Ebano. Some experienced oilmen from Spindletop
in Texas may have come to look over Doheny's properties. Walter
Sharp, who along with Howard Hughes, Sr., would later develop the
Hughes drill bit, went to Tampico and Matamoros in 1901. "The
Standard and Water's Pierce [sic] Oil Company are fighting the oil
business very hard," Sharp wrote, "and it will take every bit of energy
and good business plans or they will own it all."[56] Doheny's men established an oil camp at KM 613, a marker denoting the distance in kilometers from Aguascalientes along the right-of-way for the rail and
telegraph lines to Tampico. The Mexican Central Railroad constructed
a four-hundred-foot siding so that freight cars could unload imported
equipment. Herbert G. Wylie came from Los Angeles as the general superintendent at Ebano. He immediately set three thousand Mexicans to
clearing the "impenetrable jungle," making roads, building wood-
frame houses, and constructing a small refinery. In an incident that
portended future problems, Wylie had to fire an American foreman
who displayed impatience toward the Mexican laborers. From Pittsburgh, Doheny brought in the equipment for the ice and cold-storage
plant, water distillery, electrical plant, sawmill, machine shop, boiler,
and blacksmith shop. Boilers were disassembled, hauled into Ebano on
boats, then transferred to pack animals and reassembled at the well
sites.[57]

North American drillers began the first well in May, and within two
weeks the night crew struck oil at a depth of 525 feet. "Oil had come
into the hole in such quantity as to lift the tools off the bottom and interrupt drilling," Doheny wrote later. "[The driller] immediately put
out the fire under the boiler and shut down, to await daylight and our

inspection."[58] These first shallow wells produced about 10 to 50 bd of heavy, viscous crude oil. Measured at 10 degrees to 12 degrees Baumé, the crude oil of El Ebano was as "thick as cold honey." It served as a heavy fuel oil and asphalt but contained little of the valuable lighter ends such as kerosene. As they began to drill deeper in search of a lighter crude oil having greater rates of flow, Doheny's men used cable tools manufactured in Pennsylvania. Drilling crews first sank an eight-inch pipe into the soil until it struck bedrock. After dropping some two tons of drilling tools into the pipe, they engaged the machinery that raised and dropped the drill bit forty to fifty times per minute. The bit turned on each blow and pulverized the rock. Injected water mixed with the pulverized rock and was pumped out of the well as the drill worked downward. On average, the drilling teams could bore about one hundred feet per day into the earth.[59] Exploration proceeded slowly, and the oil proved disappointingly heavy.

Doheny's subsequent explanations of the El Ebano oil strike under-estimated the technological obstacles of the Mexican strike. Doheny tended to exaggerate his own entrepreneurial role, great as it already was. To a financial writer years later, and in his appearances at congressional hearings, Doheny depreciated the value of trained geologists. "Geology profs don't find oil," he used to say.[60] Nevertheless, he was a smart enough businessman to make use of available knowledge. Doheny hired Mexican geologist Ezequiel Ordóñez, who had written an optimistic report on Mexico's oil prospects for the Mexican Geology Institute. His report had become so controversial that Ordóñez was forced to resign from that organization when he encountered the wrath of the powerful finance minister, José Yves Limantour. The Mexican geologist found the American entrepreneur optimistic, domineering, unable to accept being contradicted, and strangely lacking in original ideas. Ordóñez located Doheny's prolific well at the base of Cerro de la Pez (Pitch Hill) at El Ebano. Pez No. 1 came in on 3 April 1904, flowing at a rate of 1,500 bd. Several years later, a Stanford University geologist would remark that all the successful Ebano wells had been put down practically on the seepages. Other geologists and engineers also served Doheny by mapping all the oil exudes on the El Ebano properties.[61] For the moment, the larger well that Ordóñez brought in permitted the pioneer oil producer to continue his operations.

Establishing a commercial oil producing venture in the wilderness at El Ebano proved a daunting task. Armed with capital, technological experience, a reasonably developed infrastructure, and access to growing

Fig. 1. An El Ebano well blows in, c. 1904. One of the first oil wells in Mexico, this El Ebano gusher blows out gas and thick crude petroleum shortly after being drilled in. The workmen next disassemble the remainder of the wooden derrick, remove the equipment, and place a valve over the well casing. From the Estelle Doheny Collection, courtesy of the Archive of the Archdiocese of Los Angeles, Mission Hills, California.

domestic and foreign markets, Doheny was the first oilman equal to the challenge. First, the land was cleared. "A narrow gauge railroad had to be built," the superintendent, Herbert Wylie, reported, "and the whole region opened up before oil could be produced."[62] Moreover, a pipeline for the heavy oil was undesirable. "The continued heating of the oil, especially to a temperature that would enable us to pump it through a long pipe line, would render this oil unfit for fuel," Wylie observed. A railroad spur was absolutely necessary to get the oil out. The porous adobe soil prevented wagon traffic during the rainy season.[63] Then the managers needed to secure an adequate supply of water for drilling operations and for the workers. A neighboring hacendado would charge $500 for allowing the company to run a water line across his land from the Pánuco River. Besides, the Pánuco water had an unpleasant odor. Wylie favored water pumped from the Tamesí River.

The Mexican Petroleum Company had a difficult time selling Doheny's heavy petroleum. Wylie approached foreign railway men, but many as yet had no way of transporting the fuel. Worst of all, the Mexican Central Railroad reneged on its promise and refused to purchase the thick stuff from Doheny. Just nine months before its first strike, the management of the Mexican Oil Company had concluded a sales contract with the Mexican Central. The oilmen were to convert the Central's locomotives at their own expense and keep those locomotives supplied with fuel at set prices of 90 cents to $1.20 per barrel. Financially strapped in 1902, the old board, dominated by Doheny's associate Robinson, sold out to new investors led by rival oilman Henry Clay Pierce. Apparently, Pierce used his influence to cancel the oil purchases.[64] The Doheny interests were disheartened.

In the midst of the depression of 1902, when oil prices were depressed and Ebano oil had few buyers inside or outside of Mexico, the Doheny interests considered selling Mexico's first producing oil field. "In my judgement," board member R. C. Kerens wrote, "we should, if possible, sell a half interest (of Mexico Petroleum Co. [*sic*]) to Standard or Pierce Co. . . . If we could make satisfactory contract & price with Pierce for our product I should favor that." Kerens even offered to close the deal with Pierce during a hunting trip. "Pierce is the most accomplished sportsman in America," he said.[65] Within six months, Pierce's managers came to inspect the operations at El Ebano. Wylie took Thomas J. Ryder, Pierce's supervising manager in Mexico, to the Pez oil wells. He demonstrated the quality of the Pez crude by burning it under a drilling boiler. "I had great pleasure in demonstrating to them that the fire was under perfect control," reported Wylie. Other officials of the Pierce group were inspecting a run of crude oil at the Ebano refinery. They arranged to have sixty barrels shipped from Pez No. 1 to the Tampico refinery of Pierce. Wylie was enthusiastic about their visit. "From the investigations and inquiries of these gentlemen, I would judge that they had in mind the purchase of the property, rather than the production."[66] As it turned out, however, Pierce was really not interested. He would have had to contravene his contract to buy crude from Standard, on whom he was hopelessly dependent.

Doheny had little choice but to bring in a small refinery at El Ebano and organize his own asphalt paving company in Mexico City. The paving business introduced a young man to the oil business who would become a long-time associate of Doheny. Harold Walker was a graduate of Columbia Law School. His father, Aldice F. Walker, was chairman of the Atchison, Topeka, and Santa Fe Railroad "when I induced them to commence the use of fuel petroleum," as Doheny explained.[67] The elder Walker became a stockholder in the Mexican Petroleum Company. He had once served in the administration of President Grover Cleveland, and Doheny was also a lifelong Democrat. Young Walker had come to Mexico to check on his father's interests. Doheny made him manager of the paving company and his principal agent in Mexico City. The Cía. Mexicana de Pavimentos de Asfalto y Construcciones had a board interconnected with the Mexican Petroleum Company.[68]

Selling to a government agency in Mexico, however, flung the fledgling foreign company into the maelstrom of domestic politics. The Mexico City *ayuntamiento* (municipal government) held up some of Doheny's first paving contracts. His Mexican associate, Ezequiel Ordóñez, suspected that some of the council members were in the employ of the Pierce interests. "Unfortunately the President of Ayuntamiento has changed. It is now Mr. F. Pimentel, director of Central Bank who, I supose [*sic*], has been engaged with the P. Co.," speculated Ordóñez. Ordóñez said he would have to go directly to the minister of finance, José Yves Limantour. Without outside intervention, he wrote, "the Council will entertain me with evasives everytime [*sic*]."[69]

The paving business did not provide great profits, although it did keep Doheny in business. Municipal paving contracts paid half up front and the rest over ten years. The company eventually paved streets in Mexico City, Guadalajara, Morelia, Tampico, Durango, Puebla, and

Chihuahua. By 1906, the Doheny group had laid 44,000 square meters of asphalt paving in the capital alone.[70] The asphalt business had grown to the extent that the Cia. Mexicana de Asfaltos could not meet all the internal demand. Moreover, much of that demand was still governed by domestic politics. As the Centennial celebration of Hidalgo's call for Mexican Independence from Spain approached, Governor Enrique Creel insisted that the streets of his capital city be paved immediately. Walker had not scheduled Chihuahua's paving until the following year. It would require three hundred tons of asphalt and six hundred tons of flux, Walker explained, and he would need to build a plant for the job. Anyway, the company was busy sprinkling oil on the dusty streets of Mexico in preparation for the celebration. "I think that on the strength of the Tlalpam Calzada work, we can land a lot more sprinkling jobs before the Centennial," Walker wrote Doheny. By this time, the Doheny interests and others were also putting in gas pipes for public street lighting.[71] Asphalt sales, therefore, paid Doheny some early dividends in domestic sales and staffing.

Exporting Ebano oil was even more problematic than developing the domestic market. The Spindletop discovery in 1901 increased the supply of crude throughout the gulf region and drove prices down. Between 1900 and 1905, the average price of a barrel of crude oil "at the well head" dropped from $1.07 to 65 cents. By 1910 the price was 61 cents. (See graph 1.) Thick Ebano oil could not compete with the lighter Texas crude. Doheny had sent the biggest potential buyer, Stan-

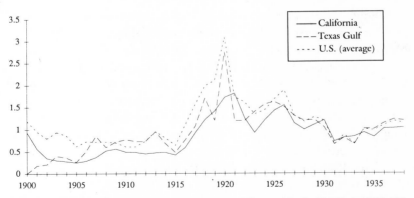

Source: American Petroleum Institute, Petroleum Facts and Figures (9th edn, New York, 1950), 170.

Graph 1. Yearly Average Price per Barrel of Crude Oil at the Well, 1900–1938 (in U.S. dollars)

dard Oil, three different samples of Ebano crude. Standard Oil refused
to buy any of it because it contained high amounts of pitch and asphalt
and low increments of kerosene and gasoline. Doheny subsequently admitted that these early rebuffs had embittered him.[72] Lack of markets
left Doheny in a vulnerable position. For the moment, greater production of heavy crude oil, the long-term uses for which Waters-Pierce's
pioneer marketing had done nothing to develop, would only bring
Doheny greater problems in selling it.

Nonetheless, Doheny relied on his contacts in the western United
States to enable him to export Mexican asphalt into a market heretofore dominated by Trinidad and California paving materials. As early
as 1902, Doheny sent a sample of the Ebano product to an asphalt
pavement contractor in San Francisco. The man raved about the sample's bitumen content (98 percent) and its temper and toughness.
"[A]fter the most rigid tests we are able to report that your refined asphaltum is without question, equal to or better than any refined asphaltum which has come under our notice for many years."[73] Eventually,
the Mexican Petroleum Company also began to export asphalt to the
United States. Doheny benefitted from the fact that the U.S. oil fields
produced very little heavy petroleum. For a number of years, Pitch
Lake in faraway Trinidad had been the exclusive supplier of asphalt for
the U.S. market. Consequently, the value of Mexican asphalt exported
to the United States expanded from 2,234 pesos in 1908 to 9,050 pesos in 1909.[74] Soon Doheny was receiving inquiries as to the FOB
price of his product. "[I]f there is a chance to handle it," one St. Louis
sales agent inquired, "I would like to have the opportunity of so
doing."[75] In no time, Mexican tar was paving the streets of Pierce's
hometown.

Contempt for Our Efforts

Those first years in Mexico began to consume Doheny's
capital. His backers lost heart in the financial depression of 1902.
Doheny and Canfield had to buy back much stock, raising their ownership from 8 to 40 percent. The Mexican Petroleum Company, incorporated in California and capitalized at $6 million, had spent $2.8 million just on the asphaltum refinery and paving business. Although
Doheny's operations were in a fledgling state, the prospectus of 1905

expressed enthusiasm about new properties he had acquired at Cerro Viejo and Cuchillo del Pulque near Tuxpan. He obtained a pipeline concession exempt from state and municipal taxes. He had every expectation of selling kerosene to fifteen million Mexicans—cutting into the Waters-Pierce market. Doheny also had visions of exporting to Great Britain—cutting into another Standard Oil market.[76] As of 1905, these were but expectations. Reality had forced Doheny to expend $750,000 of his own money between 1902 and 1905 merely to attract other investors and remain in business. Harold Walker claimed that $6 million had been sunk in the Mexican Petroleum Company before the first barrel of Mexican oil was exported in 1911.[77] Nevertheless, 1906 rewarded some of the optimism.

Doheny's persistence yielded results when railways and other industries began to convert to oil. Mexico's economy had been growing on the energy source of coal and coke. By 1900, 2.7 million tons of this hydrocarbon were used by railways and steamships (67 percent), metal smelters and mining mills (22 percent), and the iron and steel foundry at Monterrey (10 percent). The opening of a coal field in the state of Coahuila lessened somewhat the need to import coal. But Mexico still depended upon annual imports of 1.1 million tons of coal and coke from Great Britain, the United States, and Germany.[78] Finally and characteristically, Doheny solved his marketing problem by equipping his own locomotive with an oil-burning boiler. He proved that his heavy Ebano oil could be burned as fuel. In 1905, Doheny negotiated a fifteen-year contract to sell oil to the Mexican Central Railroad, despite the fact that Henry Clay Pierce was still its board chairman. By now, the price per barrel was about half of the original contract, but the Central was soon taking 6,000 barrels per day.[79] By 1906, the Mexican Central operated fifteen locomotives on El Ebano petroleum; the remaining fifteen still burned coal from West Virginia and Alabama. Large earthen reservoirs along the rail lines dispensed the "heavy molasses" oil to the Central's engines. The Central saved about 150,000 pesos per year using domestic sources of fuel—perhaps one of the reasons that the oil importer and Central chairman, Henry Clay Pierce, had little choice but to cooperate with Doheny. Railroad engineers found that oil burned cleaner and with less residue than coal. Ton per ton, oil saved railway managers 3.02 pesos over coal. Even the mining industry, like the smelters of ASARCO, began to convert their boilers to use Ebano oil.[80]

Moreover, the Mexican government's purchase of the nation's railways, beginning in 1902, opened up additional prospects for domestic sales of Ebano fuel oil. His Mexican associates especially were exuberant about being able to circumvent Pierce's obstacles. As Ordóñez observed, one of the government's reasons for gradually taking over the railways concerned the protection of new industries like Doheny's oil-producing company. All Mexicans assumed that freight rates would be lowered. "I cannot explain [to] you fully the advantages you got with the acquisition of the Interoceanic RR by Mexican Government," Ordóñez wrote to Doheny, "because the product of Mexican Petroleum Co. will come to Mexico at better conditions of freight than before."[81] Mexico's oldest railway, the Interoceanic ran between Veracruz and Mexico City. It too was considering the substitution of fuel oil for imported coal. Doheny's attorney in Mexico, Pablo Martínez del Río, approached one of its officials, who agreed to accept one hundred barrels of Ebano oil for testing in their locomotives. The Interoceanic was also importing fuel from Texas for experimentation. "This shows that they are very seriously endeavoring to use petroleum," said Martínez del Río. But he also warned, "This road, belonging principally to the Government, can perhaps import its fuel without paying duties. This circumstance must be borne in mind in making the charge of this shipment and at the time of negotiating the whole supply."[82]

At first, the National Railways did not become the sales solution for the Ebano production. A. W. Cockfield, a machinery superintendent for the Veracruz–Mexico City line, cornered the Mexican patents on eight different kinds of oil burners for locomotives. Doheny's representatives in Mexico thought that Cockfield was a Pierce agent. He could rig those burners not to operate on Ebano oil. "Evidently if Mr. Pierce has control of the oil business," they wrote Doheny, "Mr. Cockfield has control of its use for fuel."[83] Up to this moment, nothing that Doheny had accomplished in Mexican production threatened very much the established sales monopoly of Waters-Pierce. The Standard Oil affiliate had never imported fuel oil for Mexican railways nor sold much imported asphalt. Doheny merely introduced new oil products and diversified Mexico's consumption of petroleum.

Meanwhile, Doheny was also engaging in a wholesale process of expanding production. His agents and prospectors had been searching for exudes in the Huasteca Veracruzana. Stretching from Tampico and El Ebano to Tuxpan and Papantla, the region had remained relatively uncharted. American and Mexican leasing agents surveyed the territory on yachts, motor launches, canoes, horses, donkeys, and foot. George J. Owens, who had drilled for Doheny in Peru, found some lands west of Tuxpan in the Casiano Basin. The Barber Asphalt Company of New

York acquired properties known as Cerro Azul and Juan Felipe, and the London Oil Trust (Rhodes's old company) still retained properties called Cerro Viejo and Chapopote. Owens led an inspection team consisting of Doheny, Wylie, and Dr. Norman Bridge to the properties. "The lighter character of the exudes we also noted with much satisfaction," Doheny wrote.[84]

Within two months, the Mexican Petroleum Company acquired the oil properties. Many local landowners such as the simple herdsmen and subsistence farmers preferred to sell their land for cash rather than to lease it for promises of future royalties. As Doheny observed, few had faith that oil would be found. Larger landowners, having greater investments and profitability in their estates, generally preferred the lease and royalty arrangements. So Doheny created the Huasteca Petroleum Company to hold the fee-simple lands and the Tamiahua and Tuxpan Petroleum companies to hold the leased properties. He also created the Pan American Transportation Company in Delaware to provide for the tanker fleet by which he was planning to export Mexican oil.[85] All four were wholly owned subsidiaries of Mexican Petroleum of Los Angeles. Ever hopeful, Doheny not only persevered but expanded his operations.

The potential for land-title problems also existed in the sparsely and informally settled area along Mexico's Gulf Coast. Doheny had his share. In 1901, Mexican Petroleum purchased lot no. 2 along the Tamesí River from Paulino Morate. A problem arose because the previous owner, Amado Garabaldi, had sold the same parcel a second time. The second buyer was the Tampico Sugar Company, a local agricultural company employing seventy workers in the area. Tampico Sugar put up a fence across the property, denying access by the drilling crews. Jacobo Váldez of Mexican Petroleum called in the *rurales* to tear down the fence and protect the oil workers. The Mexican courts subsequently decided that the sugar company and the original owner, Garabaldi, had conspired to defraud Mexican Petroleum. Garabaldi spent six months in jail.[86] More serious title disputes were to arise once the oil industry became very wealthy—disputes that the Mexican judicial system would be incapable of handling.

Mexican politics, meanwhile, could not be discounted. By the time that Doheny formed Huasteca and applied for government concessions to build three pipelines to connect the oil wells of the Faja de Oro to Tampico, Doheny changed Mexican attorneys. "Mr. [Martínez] del Río being attorney for the Railway Company could not continue to act for us, we being customers of the Railway Company," Doheny explained, "and we employed in his stead, [the] Hon. Joaquín de Casasús," a former ambassador to the United States.[87] In fact, Martínez del Río suggested that Doheny hire Casasús. The latter had more influence in the government, because President Díaz had not forgotten that Martínez del Río's father had served in Emperor Maximilian's cabinet.

Doheny's managers informed the Díaz government about everything his companies did in Mexico. They needed political protection in these formative years. The 1905 depression produced something of a nationalist reaction against foreign investors. Doheny's leases and sales were investigated, though the committee upheld the Mexican laws that had adopted the Anglo-American concepts of private property. Clearly, some influential Mexicans were getting nervous about the rapidity and direction of the Díaz-era economic development. Doheny identified Finance Secretary José Yves Limantour as one of those who, suspicious of Americans, attempted to discourage Doheny by disputing the wealth of his properties in official Finance Department reports. Limantour also may have exerted influence on Mexico's Geological Institute to produce an unfavorable report on El Ebano.[88] Doheny's managers also suspected that Limantour (prompted by agents of Pierce) had prevented Doheny from obtaining the right to export Mexican oil duty free.[89] As Doheny later said, Limantour tried "to create an atmosphere of dislike, almost contempt, for our efforts." Díaz himself was said to have favored Doheny. But several powerful men serving Díaz "considered our interests as being inimical to theirs," Doheny stated; they were suspicious that the American oil companies would become an active competitor to the government itself.[90] Doheny seemed to take a kind of perverse pride in the "open hostility" and obstructionism he encountered from some Mexican politicians. It made his ultimate success that much sweeter. It confirmed he was a man of destiny, and they were among the unbelievers. Yet Mexican opposition did exist in the highest political circles.

Consequently, Doheny reinforced his companies' expansion with all the proper concessionary contracts with the government. Huasteca negotiated a concession in 1908 to explore and exploit the whole of the Faja de Oro and adjacent Tamaulipas and San Luis Potosí regions wherever Doheny's companies already had private rights. The government approved of Huasteca's plans to build a refinery at Mata Redonda, across the river from Tampico, and to construct pipelines through the Huasteca to the refinery. The company, which was obliged to invest 500,000 pesos ($250,000) on the project within five years, had to submit to the ministry of development all plans for construction. It could import the equipment duty free. The contract also specified that "the concessionary company could export free of all taxes or duties the natural or refined products that come from the exploitations referred to in this contract."[91]

Additional contracts such as Huasteca's concession to pump water from local rivers established a number of considerations that later governments, less lenient to the foreigners, were to use to increase taxes. According to the contracts, for example, the government retained the right to review oil company activities. The companies signing the contract were to be regarded as Mexican, subject to the laws of the Republic and having no rights of recourse to foreign diplomats. The first of many tax hikes also came during the Díaz presidency. In 1910, the government raised the bar duties collected at ports to fifty centavos per ton of oil.[92] In effect, this was to become a tax on all exports of petroleum as well as a tax on crude oil brought by barge from Tuxpan to the Tampico refineries. Some of the oil could be taxed twice, coming in and going out. If it went to another Mexican port, it might be taxed thrice.

The precedent for future government-company conflict was already in place before Díaz even fell from power. Yet, Doheny later claimed that his visits with various presidents of Mexico and heads of different departments never led him to conclude that bribes were necessary to accomplish business in Mexico. "I can testify that the treatment was uniformly courteous, considerate," he said. No "other means were necessary to obtain the rights and privileges which we were requesting, than the statement of a good reason therefore."[93]

Other evidence seems to bear out Doheny's assessment. In Chihuahua, state officials were so eager for oil investments that they were prepared to pay. Governor Creel of Chihuahua, who had leased some of his own extensive properties to American drillers, in 1908 offered a prize of 10,000 pesos ($5,000) to the person who brought in the first well producing 60 bd or more. At the time, imported coal cost as much as 18 pesos per short ton; kerosene, 68 centavos per gallon; and gasoline, 93 centavos per gallon. "It will thus be seen," reported the U.S. consul in Chihuahua, "that the matter of fuel makes the cost of manufacturing so high as to offer very little encouragement to such industries."[94] Meanwhile, Doheny's search for production continued—not in Chihuahua but in the Huasteca.

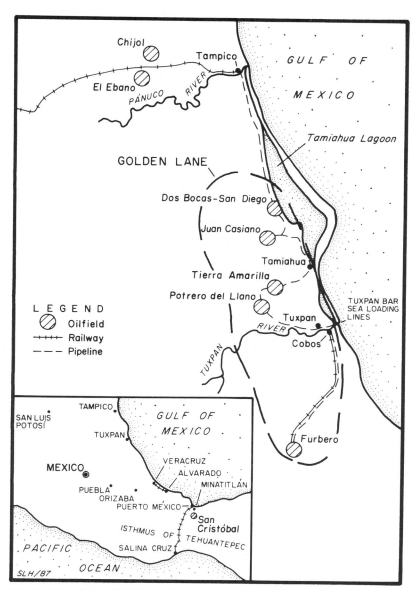

Map 1. The Major Oil Fields of Mexico

Doheny was gambling over a ten-year period that he would be able to produce a lighter grade of Mexican petroleum—and in sufficient quantities to justify pipelines, refineries, and tankers. Doheny found it in the Huasteca. By 1906, he had leasing agents traveling through the tropical forests seeking out leases on the larger haciendas. It was here, in the region just north and west of the small port of Tuxpan, fifty miles south of Tampico and connected only by water, that Doheny's producing interests first began to compete with those of the British businessman, Sir Weetman Pearson. In fact, Doheny entertained the local gentry lavishly, bringing them to his oil camp of El Ebano by boat and his private rail car for the 1906 Christmas celebration. On this social occasion, Doheny did buy the La Pitahaya Hacienda of 5,000 acres—and its mineral rights—from Manuel Saldívar, for $49,000. Afterwards, Doheny traveled by train to the capital, where he saw Martínez del Río, visited the bank, lunched at the American Club, and visited American and Mexican friends. "Everything is progressing favorably," he wrote to his wife, Estelle; "Inform Canfield and Bridge."[95]

Confident of the potential of the properties he acquired in 1906, crews immediately began constructing the pipeline from Casiano to Tampico. They built 125 miles of eight-inch pipeline, ten pumping stations, and twelve 55,000-barrel steel tanks. But a recalcitrant landowner prevented them from extending a seven-mile section through his hacienda. Evidently no geological work preceded the exploratory drilling at Casiano. Doheny's men relied on the principles that Ordóñez had taught them at El Ebano. The first five holes were dry.[96] Even before the pipeline came on line, drilling crews at the nearby Casiano properties had brought in wells 6 and 7. The first had a flow-rate exceeding 15,000 bd, filling all available storage tanks. Casiano no. 7 proved to be the big one—flowing uncontrollably at the rate of 60,000 bd. In September 1910, crews attempted to cap no. 7, but its pressure of 285 pounds-per-square-inch forced oil out through cracks in the casing and through a fissure in the earth three hundred feet from the derrick. Before they could control the flow, crews lost thousands of barrels of crude, which flowed into a creek and had to be burned off. Because no. 7 defied capping, employees reduced the flow to 23,000 bd, enough to stop the leak through the fissure. They then worked feverishly to construct a 750,000-barrel earthen reservoir and more than a hundred storage tanks. President Díaz himself finally interceded with the recalcitrant landlord so that the oilmen could complete their pipeline to Tampico.[97] To his advantage, Doheny's company had discovered a light oil. Measured at 20 degrees Baumé, the Mexican crude of the Huasteca region yielded kerosene, fuel oil, lubricating oil, and gasoline.

The new discoveries pressed Doheny for funds to pay for the infrastructure needed to market the vast supplies of crude oil. Pipelines, storage tanks, oil loading terminals, expanded refining capacity, oil tankers, and buyers were needed. Once again, he turned to U.S. financial circles. Doheny contacted the successful Pittsburgh-based wildcatters Joseph C. Trees and Michael Benedum. They were partners in the South Penn Oil Company. Trees toured the Mexican properties and was impressed by the tar pits and the new wells. Together, Trees and Benedum invested $500,000 and received 5,000 shares of preferred stock, plus an additional 2,500 shares of common stock in the Mexican Petroleum Company. Two other Pittsburgh financiers invested lesser amounts.[98] Doheny used the money to pay for the pipelines and loading facilities. Then Mexican Petroleum required additional funds to develop a marketing system within the United States. William Salomon and Company, a New York financial house, agreed to purchase $5 million worth of the company's securities, guaranteed by a mortgage on the Mexican properties. Two American geologists evaluated the Mexican oil holdings. Stanford University's Ralph Arnold appraised the oil fields at El Ebano and Casiano and the undeveloped Cerro Azul properties at $20 million.[99]

Doheny took special exception to Arnold's appraisal, which he considered far too conservative. Some of his prejudices toward geologists were revealed in his critique of Arnold's estimate. He accused Arnold of certain erroneous conceptions of the facts. "[W]e not only do not accede to one approximate valuation given to the properties," Doheny complained, "but we do not agree with the opinion of the geologist as to the area of land, at the different localities, which will prove to be oil-containing." Doheny never again hired Arnold. He had another evaluation completed by I. B. White, whose evaluation of $62 million Doheny approved. (In 1912, Arnold went on to work for Shell Oil Company in accomplishing the first evaluation of Venezuela. Here, Arnold would identify the potential of the Maracaibo Basin, which within fifteen years would supplant production in Mexico.)[100] In the meanwhile, Doheny received his loan and began constructing tank farms, pipelines, and terminals.

Building so large a marketing organization also took time; the Mexican Petroleum Company had a lot of oil in its tanks right now. The disposition of the enormous quantities—at least 40,000 bd from just

Table 2. *Contract Sales of Crude and Refined Petroleum by the Mexican and Huasteca Petroleum Companies, 1911*

Buyer	Seller	Term (years)	Barrels per day	Price per barrel (cents)
National Railways	Mex. Pet.	8⅓	6,000	49
National Railways	Huasteca	8½	4,000	42
Waters-Pierce Oil Co.				
Commercial	Huasteca	3	2,900	66
Refinery	Huasteca	—	700	93
Fuel	Huasteca	—	300	50
Standard New Jersey	Huasteca	3[a]	6,000	39
Mex. Natural Gas Co.	Huasteca	10	250	50
Mex. Asphalt Paving[b]	Mex. Pet.	10	800	50
Gulf Refining Co.	Huasteca	2	2,000	44
Atchison, Topeka and Santa Fe RR	Huasteca	3	2,500	46
			Total: 25,450 bd	

[a]With option to renew for five years.
[b]Company affiliated with Mexican and Huasteca Petroleum companies.
SOURCE: Herbert G. Wylie, "Contract of Mexican and Huasteca Petroleum Companies" [1911], Arnold, box 201.

two wells—had to be sold to someone with established marketing networks. In 1911, the Mexican and Huasteca Petroleum companies did have market contracts with a diversified set of institutional buyers. They had long-term sales contracts for some 25,450 bd of crude and processed petroleum at prices fixed between 39 cents and 93 cents per barrel. The problem was that the Mexican market was somewhat inelastic. It could not absorb even at low prices the vastly increased domestic production, and Doheny's companies still relied upon these domestic consumers for 60 percent of its sales (see table 2). Doheny needed to break into the North American market if he wanted to survive the flush production of the Faja de Oro, "the Golden Lane," as the prolific oil zone just west of Tuxpan came to be known.

As the largest transporter, refiner, and marketer of petroleum in the country, Standard Oil remained the logical buyer of Mexican crude. Doheny requested that his new stockholder, Mike Benedum, negotiate a sales contract with Standard. Benedum concluded a tentative agreement for the sale of 12,000 bd of Mexican crude at 52 cents per barrel. Doheny, who was himself dealing with the Gulf Oil Company, however, allowed the Standard negotiations to lapse inconclusively. Annoyed, Benedum subsequently broke with Doheny and began to sell off his Mexican Petroleum stock. Benedum and his partner made a nice profit on one year's investment.[101] Then the Gulf negotiations also broke down. Mexican Petroleum Company appeared on the brink of drowning in its own flush production. The United States Supreme Court in 1911, however, had just dissolved the giant Standard Oil Company. The centerpiece of the old organization, Standard Oil New Jersey, inherited refineries, oil tankers, and marketing apparatus—but no oil-producing subsidiaries. Both Jersey Standard and Waters-Pierce used the dissolution as an opportunity to sever their formal if strained ties. Thereafter, Jersey Standard was receptive to Doheny's need to sell a lot of crude oil, and quickly. It is no exaggeration to say that the Standard company saved the Mexican Petroleum Company in 1911 when it contracted to purchase 2 million barrels of Mexican crude per year for a period of five years.[102] At least, Doheny could maintain that he had kept his word to President Díaz. He had not sold his oil properties into Standard Oil's control, although Jersey Standard was purchasing Mexican crude petroleum. (Control would follow in due course—in 1932, to be precise.)

Doheny at last was able to compete in growing United States markets. He supplied oil-fueled steamships and gasoline-powered automobiles as well as traditional kerosene and lubricating markets. The first regular export cargo of crude oil left Tampico in May 1911 on the steam tanker *Captain A. F. Lucas,* named for the discoverer of Spindletop. The tanker delivered 30,262 barrels of Huasteca crude to the Magnolia Petroleum Company's refinery at Sabine, Texas.[103] One historian estimates that after the oil strikes in the Faja de Oro, Doheny began to earn about $10 million a year on his Mexican ventures. Another places the fortune at $75 million.[104] In the meantime, Mexico had become a net exporter of petroleum.

By 1911, the Mexican Petroleum Company had survived the vicissitudes of Mexican geology and the competition of the oil business. Not a little of the success is attributed to Doheny's entrepreneurial spirit and tenacity, attributes he no doubt developed while prospecting in the American West. Yet, several other factors also contributed to his achievements in opening up Mexican petroleum production. First of all, Mexico's economic development had created demands for a cheap, domestic source of efficient fuel. To Pierce goes the credit for developing demand in Mexico for sufficient petroleum products to support a domestic oil industry. Second, the political will of the Díaz regime had

Fig. 2. Doheny at the site of an El Ebano well, c. 1904. When the wells
came in, the gas pressure splattered the thick oil over the vegetation
in the immediate vicinity. Edward L. Doheny (third from left) leads
a delegation of oil executives to the well site. Mexican geologist Ezequiel Ordóñez stands to the left, and Herbert Wylie is the heavyset
man at center right. From the Estelle Doheny Collection, courtesy
of the Archive of the Archdiocese of Los Angeles, Mission Hills,
California.

created an atmosphere in which long-term investments could be nur-
tured. Third, Doheny's prior experience in California oil production
had given him access to the capital and technological resources needed
to organize an advanced industry such as petroleum. It was simply beyond Mexico's ability in the first decade of the twentieth century to accomplish what the foreign entrepreneurs were able to do. Without foreigners, Mexico would have had no oil industry this early. Indeed, the
country would have had little demand for petroleum. It was natural, in
a way, that a successful American oilman should follow successful
American railroaders across the border to the south. The Mexican journey of the third great foreign oil entrepreneur, Sir Weetman Pearson,
differs not only in particulars but also in substance. That he was British
made all the difference.

Looking to Strike Oil at Any Moment

As an oil pioneer in Mexico, Sir Weetman Pearson's career could not have contrasted more starkly to that of Doheny. Pearson had no previous experience in the oil business at all. As grandson of the founder of a modest British construction firm, S. Pearson and Sons, young Weetman grew up in comfortable circumstances.[105] He attended a public boarding school but eschewed training in engineering and the sciences at Oxford or Cambridge. Instead, Pearson entered his grandfather's firm. His family believed that sons should "learn their business in the business," as the saying went. By the age of twenty-three, Pearson had become a partner and was managing the construction of the main drainage system at Ipswich and a dock at King's Lynn. Pearson moved the firm to London in 1879 and competed for construction contracts throughout the world: docks and harbors in Egypt and Canada, rail lines in Spain, and the Hudson Tunnel in New York City. Taking over construction from less capable companies became Sir Weetman's specialty. He tried to save the Hudson Tunnel project by introducing the Greathead shield, complete with hydraulic jacks and segment erectors, to protect men and equipment from cave-ins during digging. He also engineered a recompression chamber that prevented workers from getting the bends as they emerged from their subterranean work. Pearson's company already had an international reputation in engineering before he came to Mexico.

Porfirio Díaz himself was responsible for bringing Sir Weetman to Mexico, where the Englishman proved himself a worthy champion. In 1889, the Mexican president sent emissaries to New York in an effort to interest the famous engineer in salvaging Mexico's Grand Canal.[106] An American firm had floundered in attempting to construct the Mexico City drainage system, abandoning the poorly placed capital city to its centuries-old problem of flooding. Pearson drove a hard bargain, obtaining in negotiations with Díaz much autonomy in the work. To complete the twenty-nine-mile-long Grand Canal, Pearson brought in giant steam-powered dredgers from the German firm of Lobnitz, whose equipment had widened the Suez Canal. For most of the financing of the drainage project, Pearson depended on his partner, the Mexican government, which at the time enjoyed budget surpluses and quantities of silver provided by the American mining companies.

Díaz's administration had an impeccable rating in European credit markets. Mexico was one of the few countries to be able to borrow at the preferential rate of 5 percent, and after 1905 at 4.5 percent. Pearson also had independent sources of capital. His company at any one time had contracts worth from £5 million to £10 million, and London bankers and the stock market provided Pearson additional capital.[107] Pearson thus was able to buy the forty-one-mile-long Veracruz-to-Alvarado railway and build and operate various Mexican tramworks and utility companies. His connections in England were impeccable. The wealthy businessman in 1895 had won a seat in the House of Commons, where he was known as "the Member for Mexico."

Indeed, success with the Grand Canal also earned Pearson an unassailable reputation in Mexico. The president personally made contacts with Pearson, and Pearson's direct link to Díaz—he entertained Porfirio Díaz, Jr., on the son's tour of Europe and England—also insulated the British engineer from having to submit to the corruption of the bureaucrats surrounding the Mexican president. Díaz willingly used the British engineer as a foil to the Americans, who already dominated the smelting and railway businesses. Pearson was the logical choice to construct the modern harbor and port at Veracruz. He also hired American medical technology and built a new water and sewage system to control the perennial scourges of *el vómito negro* (yellow fever), malaria, and cholera. Sir Weetman, the world's foremost engineering contractor, had won the implicit admiration of a Mexican president suspicious of Americans.[108] As a foreigner and British gentleman, Pearson may also have been politically more trustworthy to Díaz even than most Mexican businessmen.

In the meanwhile, the Tehuantepec railway was turning out badly. Díaz had given the concession to another British firm in order to break the American-owned Panamanian Railroad's monopoly of transisthmian transport. Once completed, however, the 190-mile line was plagued with frequent breakdowns, roadbed washouts, insufficient port capacities, and undersized rail cars.[109] Díaz summoned Pearson to the rescue. The Díaz government provided the capital, often paying Pearson in silver bars. But the British company retained managerial control. Once completed, the company would operate the entire complex as managing partner, sharing with the government one-half the loss and one-third the profit. Finance Minister Limantour, who had been in Europe when the Tehuantepec contract was signed, criticized the liberal terms and autonomy given to the foreign capitalist. But Díaz supported Pearson. Nevertheless, a second contract, renegotiated in 1902, tightened the restrictions. Article 106 of that contract stipulated that after seven years, Pearson had the right to transfer his contract to another company, which could be organized in Mexico, Great Britain, France, Belgium, or Germany—but not the United States.[110] Sir Weetman benefited from anti-American political sentiments.

By now, Pearson had an experienced staff in Mexico. J. B. Body had served as assistant manager of the Grand Canal and was chief of the Veracruz harbor construction. Since 1889, he had come to speak fluent Spanish, often translating at meetings between Díaz and Pearson. Body took charge of rebuilding the transportation complex. Pearson's isthmian project involved survey and construction of a new roadbed through the lowlands of Tehuantepec, flood control, extensive bridging, breakwaters and docks at the Pacific terminus of Salina Cruz, and dredging and dockwork at the gulf terminus of Coatzacoalcos. The latter river port was rechristened as Puerto México. Body supervised the work of two thousand to five thousand Mexican workers recruited from the highlands and provided with housing, medical care, and food. J. N. Galbraith, the new general manager of the Tehuantepec National Railroad, estimated that about twenty-four trains a day would pass over the two-hundred-mile route. When he inaugurated the Tehuantepec complex with a train ride in 1907, Díaz was effusive in his praise. "Portions of the Isthmus have been literally remade," the Mexican president said.[111] "Flourishing new towns with pretty and comfortable houses and contented inhabitants owe their existence to the energy and courage of Sir Weetman Pearson, whose name will endure and be held in honour in this historic region of Mexico, long after the rails on which our party has glided so smoothly have become eroded by age."

Sir Weetman was no less effusive in his praise of Díaz. In his speech, Pearson said, "It was only owing to great hardships and personal sacrifices, ungrudgingly made, the exercise of unvarying patience and the determination and courage which have had for their inspiration the glorious example furnished by the career of General Díaz that the results you have seen and are to see have been arrived at." He had good reason to thank Díaz. The Mexican government had provided up to 85 million pesos to complete the Tehuantepec project.[112] Pearson owed his success in Mexico to his worldwide business experience, his access to the engineering technology of the day, his financial resources among London bankers, and the capital and patronage of President Díaz. All these factors enabled S. Pearson and Sons, engineers and contractors,

Fig. 3. Lord Cowdray (formerly Sir Weetman Pearson), c. 1915. In Great
Britain's House of Lords, he was known as the "Member for Mexico" because of his varied business interests in that country, including the Compañía Mexicana de Petróleo El Aguila. From the Pearson Photograph Collection, British Science Museum Library,
London, courtesy of Pearson PLC.

to become oilmen as well. All except one: Díaz provided no capital for oil projects. His government would help Pearson in other tangible ways.

Pearson's decision to exploit Mexico's oil resources, although it proved sound from a business standpoint, had come to him in a roundabout fashion. Body had come upon tar pools at San Cristóbal and mentioned them to Pearson as another oddity of the tropical environment. Later, in 1901, as he was traveling by train between Mexico and New York, Pearson stopped over in Laredo, Texas. Lucas had just brought in the oil strike at Spindletop. Everyone on the Texas Gulf Coast was in the grip of "oil fever." Pearson made inquiries about this new oil business, spending time in San Antonio as well. He learned that prospectors had been attracted to Spindletop by the occurrence of tar pools. Pearson immediately wired Body to "secure option not only on oil land, but all land for miles round" in the Isthmus of Tehuantepec. Pearson added, "move sharply, and be sure that we are dealing with principals."[113] By the end of 1901, he had men exploring the isthmus and in Tabasco. They began immediately to buy and lease land. Pearson's general manager in Mexico City, J. B. Body, gained an education—like Doheny and Pearson themselves—on the job. He negotiated for purchase of numerous large estates in the isthmus, rejecting some after a "visual look for prospects" and buying others for as little as 6,000 pesos. He took out leases with important elite families such as that of the Rubio Romero, in-laws of President Díaz. Doña Carmen Rubio de Díaz, in fact, became lessor to Pearson on contracts that provided for royalties of two to five centavos per barrel [of 150 liters] of crude produced in the San Cristóbal fields. By 1903, his Mexican managers were moving drilling equipment from the Veracruz docks to the isthmian oil properties.[114]

At the same time that work progressed on the transisthmian project, Pearson's agents in Mexico also assembled an experienced team to make their Mexican oil properties productive. Body hired Thomas Ryder away from Waters-Pierce and engaged drillers who had worked for Doheny at El Ebano. Pearson had even traveled to Washington, D.C., to hire Capt. Anthony F. Lucas, discoverer of Spindletop and later called the first petroleum engineer. Lucas spent two years as a consultant, investigating Pearson's isthmian properties. After an exhaustive survey, he recommended drilling at Jaltipan, San Cristóbal, Los Tigres, and El Chango. Lucas spoke enthusiastically of their prospects on the isthmus. In the conclusion of one report, he considered that his client would soon be able "to change oil for coal on all of your locomotives, dredges on both oceans, and any motive power, with perhaps plenty to spare not only for refining and for the Republic's consumption, but for the export trade as well."[115] A heady appraisal. Unfortunately, of the sites Lucas investigated, only San Cristóbal ever yielded oil in commercial quantities. In time, however, other oil fields outside of the isthmus would fulfill Lucas's prophecy.

Early work did not prove at all promising. Many wells blew out gas, mud, and water but little in the way of crude petroleum. The first Tabasco wells produced oil in such insufficient quantities that the Pearson managers used it in its crude state as fuel oil; it did not warrant expensive refining. Yet the expectations remained high. Those wells that did produce yielded a high grade of crude suitable for fuel oil, lubricants, illuminants, and naphtha. Body, therefore, expressed confidence, as in this account in 1905 of a trip to the isthmian fields:

> Ryder has just returned from the Lucas field, and he tells me that No 3 started to gas just before he arrived there, and to such an extent that they were not able to get anywhere near the well, and that they heard the noise whilst on the river when approaching San Cristobal landing. Yesterday morning the gas subsided, and they recommenced drilling, but only to break through into another big gas pocket, and they are still stopped from working. The drillers are looking to strike oil at any moment, after they resume operations. Ryder tells me this gas was coming out with terrific force, carrying mud and water with it several hundred feet in the air.[116]

Body's letter represented greater expectations than, in fact, the foreign interests were ever to realize in southern Veracruz, Tabasco, and Campeche, where the Pearson group owned 600,000 acres of oil lands and leased an additional 300,000 acres. The Lucas well soon played out. Despite Pearson's financial ability to hire the best managerial talent, drilling expertise, and legal and political minds available in Mexico, his company was incapable of opening up the area that in the mid-1970s would become the prolific Reforma oil fields. They could not drill deep enough. Rotary tools in 1905 seldom penetrated three thousand feet below the surface. Drillers for Petróleos Mexicanos (Pemex, the national oil company of Mexico) in the 1970s perforated on and offshore to thirty thousand feet.[117] Had they lived long enough, Pearson and Body might have been gratified that their initial optimism was borne out. Back in 1905, however, the geology confounded them.

Gambling that the slight production of the isthmus would soon increase, the Pearson interests undertook to construct a refinery at Minatitlán. At the time, Minatitlán was just a small commercial town of four thousand persons forty kilometers inland on the Coatzacoalcos River. In 1905, the Pearson group laid a pipeline from the San Cristóbal oil field to the new refinery at the same time that it brought the 3,000–bd facility on line. Obtaining experienced refinery personnel, not merely good mechanics, proved to be a more difficult problem than acquiring good drilling crews. Waters-Pierce had always relied upon the expertise of Standard Oil. Pearson acquired at least some of the technology and expertise of Standard Oil by hiring Thomas Ryder and other managers from Waters-Pierce. Otherwise, Pearson had to settle for businessmen of no special oil experience. John Purdy, a long-time railroad contractor and shipping manager for Pearson, helped build the Minatitlán Refinery.[118] Then Pearson proceeded to make a contract with Bowrings and Company, a marketing company, for the distribution of Mexican oil products throughout Great Britain. Pearson's confidence tended to get ahead of both his Mexican production and his ability to refine it. In 1908, a fire shut down the Minatitlán plant, providing Pearson the opportunity to correct certain processes and improve the quality of the product.[119] Ultimately, Pearson wanted to enlarge the refinery to a capacity of 40,000 bd, supply fuel oil to the Mexican railways, and export to Great Britain.

Yet up to 1908, the British businessman was still losing money. Pearson sank £5 million of his own capital in the oil venture. The Díaz government did not become his financial partner as it had for the Grand Canal, ports, and railway. Optimistically, Body expected to be able to make at least £5,000 a month selling fuel oil to the railways but admitted that such sales were not yet possible. He did not have the product. Construction of the refinery had been expensive. By 1907, Body had already overseen the expenditure of 630,000 pesos for American machinery, dock- and brick-works, machine shops, power station, warehouse, pipelines, staff housing, and a hospital.[120] If he was going to stay in the petroleum business, Pearson had to make some sales and make them soon. Of course, that was something he could not do until he had crude oil.

Pearson, nevertheless, pressed forward in the oil business. The Minatitlán refinery commenced operation in March 1908 and in August, the first shipment of refined oil departed via tanker to England. By that time, a pipeline had been completed to Pearson's newly constructed oil terminal at Puerto México, alias Coatzacoalcos. But Pearson was not yet exporting Mexican petroleum. Poor production results on the isthmus motivated the Pearson group to purchase 400,000 barrels of crude oil from Texas.[121] Thus far, Pearson was not very different from Waters-Pierce—he was refining imported oil—except that Pearson had more political friends in the Díaz regime.

Sir Weetman Pearson, by dint of long engineering service to the Mexican government, had come to practice a sort of business diplomacy meant to create a favorable climate for his enterprise. In order to keep from appearing to be overrun by the Americans, Mexican politicians found much political expedience in supporting British interests. The government encouraged all foreign capital but Pearson's in particular. In fact, Secretary Limantour complained constantly that the government concessions were far too favorable to the British engineer. Pearson defended the generosity. "Unless special facilities had been given by the Government and subventions," Pearson wrote later, "no railways in Mexico could have been constructed."[122]

The British engineer continued to solidify his friendships in Mexico through favors and gifts. When he came to visit, Pearson brought valuable European objets d'art for Secretary Limantour's home; he lent Emilio Velasco 20,000 pesos so that he could purchase a house; and Body made his home in Veracruz available to traveling notables like the Rubio Romero family. Díaz himself stayed at Body's home at the Mexican port before boarding a German liner for exile in 1911. Lady Annie Cass Pearson established a well-appointed home in Mexico City in a colonial mansion that had once been the British legation, giving large parties for Mexican society. The Pearsons donated £100,000 to found the Cowdray Hospital. Pearson considered it expedient to "lean over backwards" to favor the Mexicans in all his dealings with them.[123]

To counter a bad press in some Mexican newspapers, Body used company funds to advertise, to print the company's views on certain issues, and to gain the cooperation of newsmen. Body was also careful to apprise President Díaz personally of all his company's activities. During the depression of 1905, when a flare-up of nationalism motivated the Academy of Jurisprudence to criticize the proposed oil law of 1905 as being too liberal and unrestricted, President Díaz himself calmed Body. The president personally assured him, Body reported, that the Pearson group could "devote a lot more time to the direct work of the fields, instead of spending so much time and worry on legal matters and titles to protect ourselves in and around our fields of exploitation."[124] While Díaz remained in charge, the British and other oilmen too were able to concentrate on business.

Pearson's close relations with members of the Díaz regime paid a large dividend in 1906, when the engineering company received the biggest government oil concession to date. The fifty-year contract, which did not challenge the existing mining laws nor invalidate any contracts between oilmen and private landholders, covered all national land, lakes, and lagoons in the state of Veracruz. The national government was to receive a royalty of 7 percent of all production. Veracruz state obtained a royalty of 3 percent. In return, the government granted the company duty-free import of machinery and free export of oil found on subject lands. One final obligation existed: the oil company was to be incorporated in Mexico, not abroad.[125] None of the concessionary lands were to yield any major oil discovery. Once Díaz left power, nonetheless, succeeding Mexican governments were to repudiate this generous oil concession.

Such political influence contained its own limitations and dangers to Pearson. Secretary of Finance Limantour proved a difficult man for the Pearson interests to control. While he vowed to assist Pearson against competition from Standard Oil, the nemesis of all the Mexicans, Limantour was careful to collect all taxes due the government. Occasionally, this meant taxing domestic petroleum twice, once when Pearson brought Tabasco crude oil destined for the refinery into Puerto México and then again when the refinery shipped the refined product out again.[126] Despite occasional toughness, government favoritism toward Pearson's oil interests gained many political enemies, as will be seen. Americans resented the "conspiracy" between Díaz and Pearson, whereas Mexicans who opposed the Díaz regime also came to resent the Pearson connection.[127] To the extent that capital investment was a political act in Mexico, foreign capitalists became involved in domestic politics—whether intentionally or not.

A Flame Seen for Thirty Miles

In Mexico, the oil companies developed differently than had the big petroleum firms in the United States. Standard Oil began as a refinery group that integrated forward and backward into sales, transport, and production. Gulf and The Texas Company had started out in Texas as producers, then became integrated by acquiring refining and sales divisions. Perhaps such techniques of organization building

were denied the firms in the less-developed Mexican marketplace precisely because they had to compete with the more dynamic, integrated
U.S. firms. Both Pearson and Doheny from the beginning attempted to
form integrated oil firms in Mexico. Doheny set up a small refinery at
El Ebano and developed his own sales network, which was limited,
however, by having available only heavy crude. Unable to challenge the
Waters-Pierce monopoly on sales of lighter oil products such as kerosene and lubricants, Doheny's company used El Ebano's heavy oil as
paving asphalt and as fuel for the nation's steam locomotives. In similar
fashion, Pearson built a refinery and acquired a transport and sales organization at the same time that he was trying to develop production.
Because part of his sales organization, Bowrings, was in England, perhaps the fledgling foreign oil company in Mexico might qualify as a
multinational corporation.[128]

Waters-Pierce did not participate in simultaneous integration at all.
The marketing company developed oil field production very slowly, because its long-term contract committed Waters-Pierce to purchase petroleum products only from other Stardard Oil–affiliated companies.
Although the parent firm permitted Pierce to have refineries in Mexico
in order to avoid import tariffs on refined products, Waters-Pierce had
no refineries of its own in its larger southwestern U.S. markets. Therefore, Waters-Pierce was destined to lose its monopoly sales position in
Mexico to the two fully integrated companies belonging to Doheny
and Pearson.

The difficulty of discovering Mexican crude oil initially created a
bottleneck in the simultaneous integration within both Doheny's and
Pearson's organizations. Sir Weetman's immediate solution was to buy
crude. After his refinery at Minatitlán came on line, Pearson contracted
to purchase crude oil from Percy Furber, another British oilman. Although Furber lacked the financial and technological backing that
Doheny and Pearson were able to muster, he had found a modest deposit of high-grade crude oil at a wilderness location about seventy-five
miles southwest of Tuxpan. He named the place Furbero, for Percy
Furber was not as modest as his assets, and anyhow the natives could
not pronounce Furber. Drilling began in 1904, and six wells were completed. According to his own account, Furber's small production, coming in around 1905, attracted the interest of both Henry Clay Pierce
and Standard Oil. Colonel Weller of the 26 Broadway headquarters
traveled by donkey into Furbero in order to test the production. The
Standard Oil man found Furber's crude to contain a high degree of sul-

fur, which emitted the odor of rotten eggs. Furber claimed that the Standard Oil chemists concluded that the sulfur easily could be separated from the oil. Furber claimed that Standard Oil offered to buy his oil field but he turned the big company down. Furber's account, however, differs from the one found in Standard Oil's documents, which reveal, as we shall see below, that Standard Oil was reluctant to enter Mexico.

Furber and whatever financial backers he could find thus had to bear the extra costs of operating in Mexico, if they were going to be oilmen at all. Furber's oil field manager, Arthur C. Payne, was not an oilman but an investor in Mexican real estate and tropical products. He noted that the cost of drilling was more expensive in Mexico than in the United States. All supplies and equipment had to be imported from the United States, incurring heavy freight costs. American drillers demanded U.S. wages plus traveling and living expenses. The jungle had to be opened, and a camp infrastructure had to be erected, of which sanitation was the most important.[129] Furber looked for a wealthy partner, but the Mexicans were opposed to having Standard Oil enter into domestic production. Afraid that the giant "trust" might buy out Furbero, the Díaz regime brought Furber together with Pearson. The Mexican government agent in London, Luis Camacho, introduced Pearson to Furber, and the two signed a contract, as Furber claimed, just before a second Standard Oil offer arrived, which he had to reject. At any rate, Pearson's group contracted to purchase from 2,000 to 6,000 bd of Furbero crude.[130]

Unlike Doheny's property at El Ebano, Furber's holdings lacked a preexisting infrastructure, a problem that Pearson's engineers now worked to correct. The plan was to expand production in order to justify a new six-inch pipeline and two pump stations. First, they constructed a narrow-gauge railway into the jungle, complete with three iron bridges. Rail cars facilitated the delivery of equipment for drilling, storing, and pumping the crude oil. A team of six American surveyors, assisted by a crew of Mexican *macheteros* to clear jungle paths, began work in February 1908. They promptly set out to locate a route along the high ground so as to avoid arroyos, rivers, and steep grades. The Americans had experience in handling the survey equipment and mapping routes. As the survey chief wrote in his field book, "Nibbi ran check levels, Bittle X-sectioned, Anderson worked on profiles, while I went on locating."[131] The difficulty of the jungle terrain and not a little sickness—one of the Americans died—slowed the completion of the survey until the summer rainy season. American construction engineers followed. Supervising crews of local peons and some three hundred workers from Cuba, they completed the narrow-gauge line and necessary bridges between Furbero and Tuxpan in April 1910. Furber also acquired drilling experts through an agent in the United States.[132] This independent oilman used foreign capital in order to buy foreign equipment and hire foreign technicians. Many common laborers were also foreigners.

Furber gained more from the Pearson contract than Pearson himself. As producer, Furber used his long-term sales contract in order to expand—a direction his drilling program did not sustain. He eventually bought another six hundred square miles from landowner Pedro Tremari, thus avoiding offset wells from competitors. In the process, Furber acquired what would be Mexico's most prolific oil field of the 1930s, Poza Rica. The Pearson-Furber contract provided for the delivery of 2,000 to 6,000 bd, but Furber was unable to produce this much. His American drillers simply failed to discover a large well. On one exploratory well begun in April 1908, oil flowed at the rate of 120 bd at only 432 feet. The manager was hopeful. "I would venture to say," he wrote in the well log, "it is absolutely proved that there is oil-bearing sandrock below this show, and the oil must have come up through fissures and cracks into this strata."[133]

But the second well prophesied a different outcome. After showing only slight oil flows at numerous levels, the drill bit struck salt water at 2,608 feet. The crew abandoned the well. "This is a great dissapointment [sic]," noted the driller, "as the striking of salt water is a very favourable indication, as it frequently overlies the Oil strata." The American drillers working at Furbero, used to working in the oil sands of Spindletop, did not understand that they were drilling in limestone formations. Mexico was the oil world's first experience in the more porous limestone. Salt water lay under the crude, not over, as the drillers believed. As they frequently drilled far below sea level, salt water promised eventually to invade even the most productive wells. Further well-testing at Furbero yielded more disappointments. By 1910, Furber's properties were producing not more than 600 bd. Nine of seventeen wells did not produce anything at all. Guillermo de Landa y Escandón, director of Pearson's new oil organization, suspected that Furber might have been telling his workers to hold back production.[134] Clearly, buying crude oil from so unreliable a source provided no solution to the production needs of Pearson the refiner and marketer.

Because Mexico's oil industry, like its general economy, was linked to that of the United States, Pearson did not have to rely exclusively on Furber for supplies of fuel oil. Low prices, especially on the Gulf Coast, encouraged Pearson to buy Texas crude, refine it at Minatitlán, and sell it throughout the country. In a way, Mexico's nascent oil industry benefited from low U.S. oil prices in the first decade of the twentieth century. Pearson was able to break the Waters-Pierce sales monopoly with cheap imported oil before the even cheaper Mexican production had come in.

If Furber did extend to the Pearson group a short-term benefit, it came in directing their attention to the Faja de Oro. Pearson's agents were in the Huasteca Veracruzana as early as 1906, competing with Doheny's agents over the purchase and leasing of potential oil properties. Once again, the unstructured nature of land titles in an area of only limited agricultural development caused some problems. The Pearson and Doheny interests moved into what would be a prolonged conflict over the estate of the widow Gorochótegui. The first prospector, A. R. Skertchly of the undercapitalized London Oil Trust, acquired the original oil lease on Cerro Viejo. Skertchly sold the lease to Doheny. The widow Gorochótegui proceeded to contract a second lease to Theodore Gestefeld, who represented the Pearson interests. The widow thereupon brought suit against the London Oil Trust to invalidate the first lease. A judge in Tuxpan placed Skertchly in jail for failing to vacate the property. Meanwhile, Doheny arrived in Tuxpan, for he had a number of leases with the local *jefe político* of Chapopote. Apparently, Doheny threatened the Pearson agent, Gestefeld. Both parties appealed to the American consul in Tuxpan, who declined to be involved in a legal dispute that ought to have been settled by the Mexican legal system. Doheny and his Mexican lawyer appealed to Veracruz state authorities in Jalapa. Gestefeld, a Prussian who had lived for a time in Chicago, wrote to the secretary of state, Elihu Root, that Doheny was flaunting his American citizenship in Mexico.[135] Pearson's lawyers worked for years attempting to untangle the titles to oil properties both in the isthmus and the Faja de Oro. Ultimately, Pearson arranged leases with a second influential family in Tuxpan, the Peláez. Pearson concluded a lease for the family's estate at Tierra Amarilla and even retained the eldest son as one of his Mexican legal consultants.[136] Competing foreign oilmen, representing an infusion of wealth into an agrarian society, became inextricably involved in local alliances and disputes so politically tangled that the Mexican courts had little capacity to settle them. Both the Cerro Viejo dispute and the Peláez family would affect subsequent oil operations in the Faja de Oro.

Meanwhile, in the spring of 1908, Pearson was growing despondent about his failure to make a breakthrough in the oil business. He lamented having relied more on the commercial knowledge and hard work of his own organization than on outside expertise. Yet Pearson remained the consummate business manager. "The oil business is not all beer and skittles," he wrote to his son Clive. "Far-seeing provisions have to be made to ensure success. Wise principles have to be followed. Much detail should hour by hour be gone into to avoid all waste. Everyone, on an oil-field that has been proved, is naturally inclined to be extremely wasteful as it is considered to lead to untold wealth. And beyond all, it is essential to know the business."[137] Pearson was learning the business while in the business, as his family's adage had directed.

Pearson's move toward Doheny's oil properties in northern Veracruz proved a momentous setback and spur—all at the same time. Pearson had drilling crews who were putting down wildcat wells at the Haciendas San Diego and Dos Bocas in the region west of Tuxpan. In the spring of 1908, a 2,000–bd well came in at San Diego. It was Pearson's first oil production outside the isthmian region. In July, a crew of Americans using the standard cable drilling tools of the era had already reached a depth of 1,800 feet in a second exploratory well, named Dos Bocas. The American consul at Tampico described what happened next:

The oil was struck on July 4th at a depth of 1832 feet. . . . [W]ith a terrific roar of gas and oil and a clap not unlike thunder, which shook the earth violently, a solid stream of oil began to pour out with such a force that the drill and the pieces of casing over thirteen hundred feet of which were hurled hundreds of feet into the air while pockets of oil were formed in all directions.

The workmen immediately put out the fire underneath the boilers but the oil, which the immense pressure had forced up along the outside of the casing and through fissures over the surface, ignited from the red-hot pipes, which were impossible to cool quick enough, and, within a few minutes, the well and surroundings was [sic] a seething roaring conflagration beyond all control and from which the manager and laborers on the ground saved their lives only after great difficulty.

The heat was so intense that it is impossible to go nearer than several hundred feet. Considering the great quantity of oil coming out, there is little gas. The internal pressure is tremendous. The height at which the oil first ignites is forty feet. The steady height of the column of oil is 850 feet while gusts of wind are constantly deflecting the main flame and portions of the burning air to an immense height, oftentimes exceeding fourteen hundred feet. The flame itself is visible at thirty miles distance while the light, under favorable atmospheric conditions, can be seen two hundred miles.[138]

Veteran Pennsylvania oilmen claimed that the Dos Bocas blowout, which had created a crater one hundred meters wide, was the largest blaze they had ever seen.[139] The government sent two hundred army sappers to help the foreign engineers, who tried blowing steam, water, and dirt into the flames with centrifugal pumps. Nothing worked. The giant torch burned so hot that workers were unable to get near enough to start capping the enormous hole through which the crude oil continued to blow at the rate of 100,000 bd. Later, Pearson's rival, Edward L. Doheny, was to call Dos Bocas a "freak well." He claimed that it was basically a blow-out of gas, the well yielding not more than 10,000 to 15,000 barrels of oil. "[A]ll of the oil and gas flow . . . was burned in the air, without a drop of it striking the ground."[140] It burned like this for two months, leaving Dos Bocas a gaping, bubbling crater of salt water and sulfur gas.

Pearson now decided to move against the Waters-Pierce sales monopoly. He grew confident that he would ultimately discover a large oil field in Mexico, and he was encouraged by his own modest production and what he purchased from Furbero and Texas. In fact, much of Pearson's negotiations with Waters-Pierce were proceeding simultaneously with his crude oil purchases and exploratory programs. Sir Weetman had approached Henry Clay Pierce at the end of November 1907. The British engineer speculated that Pierce's profit margins—calculated at 100 pesos per ton—were too high. He proposed that together the two oilmen reduce those margins closer to the break-even point of 25 pesos per ton. What Pearson suggested was a combination between the two companies that would keep out other competitors. In other words, they should form a cartel. In New York, the British capitalist proposed that his company provide Pierce with Mexican crude oil (even though Pearson did not have much of it yet) and receive one-third of Pierce's total profits. Pearson estimated that, at any rate, Pierce would be saving some 150,000 gold pesos per year over the import of foreign crude oil. Waters-Pierce was to serve as Pearson's exclusive marketer in Mexico. Pearson would be the sole producer.[141] Pearson proposed to imitate Standard Oil's initial relationship to Waters-Pierce. Limantour agreed to the proposal beforehand, as long as Mexican oil prices did not rise.

The two oilmen came to a deadlock over fuel oil, however, which promised to be the most important Mexican product. Pearson wanted to include only traditional Waters-Pierce products, like lubricants and

Fig. 4. The Dos Bocas well after the blowout, c. 1911. Geologist Ralph
Arnold photographed the crater and wrote the following caption:
"At present this is a lake of about 1,000 ft. in diameter, around
which numerous hot water springs flow, from which emanate deadly
gas. Notice the desolation of the country around the well." From the
Ralph Arnold Photo Collection, courtesy of the Huntington
Library, San Marino, California.

kerosene, in the cartel agreement. But Pierce, who had never had any
fuel oil sales in Mexico, wanted to make fuel part of the deal. As the
British learned later, Henry Clay Pierce was at the same moment negotiating to buy Doheny's surplus production at El Ebano.[142] At the
time, a second round of court battles in Texas was distracting Pierce,
and rumors said he was "racked with illness." Pearson suspected that
Pierce was delaying for time. He ordered Body to begin buying railroad tank cars and distribution depots in the ten largest Mexican market centers. Offering petroleum products at a 20-percent discount,
Body was to enter Mexico's retail trade.[143] Nevertheless, negotiations
continued. Believing that Pierce and Standard Oil were not on speaking terms, Pearson established contact with the directors at 26 Broadway. Pearson did not desire Pierce to "use us as [a] pawn" in settling his
differences with Standard Oil. President John D. Archbold of Standard
Oil informed Pearson that because it was facing its own court litigation, Standard Oil was momentarily unable to do anything in
Mexico.[144] Pearson was pleased. With Doheny stuck in his heavy oil,

and Standard Oil preoccupied by court proceedings, the Pearson and Waters-Pierce groups were left to struggle over the Mexican market.

The Great Mexican Oil War

Negotiations broke down in June 1908, signaling the beginning of "the great Mexican oil war." Pearson consulted with President Díaz and Secretary of Finance Limantour. Both had distrusted the negotiations between Pearson and Pierce. Limantour especially feared that Sir Weetman's combination with Henry Clay Pierce would only encourage Standard Oil to buy them both out and gain direct control of Mexican oil retailing. Pearson finally made a momentous decision. "After full consideration I have decided to form a Mexican Company to take over all our oil interests north of Veracruz," Sir Weetman wrote. "This Company will trade only in Mexico and I want Mexican capital to be interested. Then the Oil interests at San Cristobal and the Refinery would remain ours and be devoted to export business."[145] In April 1909, therefore, Pearson formed the Compañía Mexicana de Petróleo 'El Aguila,' S.A. (The Eagle; Sociedad Anónima, or Corporation). The new incorporated company absorbed all of the oil properties of S. Pearson and Son, Ltd., the engineering firm. The parent firm remained the primary stockholder, but going public facilitated the expansion of stock value from £100,000 to £2,550,000. On the board of directors sat many prominent members of Mexico's governing class. Guillermo de Landa y Escandón, governor of the Federal District, served as president. Other board members were Enrique Creel, governor of Chihuahua and former Mexican ambassador to the United States; Pablo Macedo, board chairman of the National Railways of Mexico; Fernando Pimentel y Fagoaga, president of the Central Bank; and Col. Porfirio Díaz, Jr.[146] Creation of a "national" company mollified the Mexican politicians.

The organization of El Aguila provided Pearson the wherewithal to attack the Waters-Pierce monopoly, for now it became expedient for politicians to help him. The government had already raised duties on oil products traditionally imported by Waters-Pierce, placing tariffs of three centavos per kilo of crude oil and eight centavos per kilo on refined petroleum. The government stated it intended to impart "a moderate degree of protection to certain Mexican industries which are capable of easy and vigorous development."[147] Friends in high places also secured for El Aguila a National Railways contract to supply one-third of its lubricating oils. Before, Pierce had been the sole supplier. The cooperation between the government and Pearson did not escape the notice of Waters-Pierce either. From this point onward, Henry Clay Pierce began a publicity campaign to discredit the political connections of El Aguila. Waters-Pierce's first press salvos in Mexico were defensive:

> We have created a new industry in Mexico and for Mexico. Over 90 per cent. of the employees engaged in this work are Mexicans. We have taught them a new trade, and built refineries in which they can follow it. We believe that these acts constitute as just grounds for our claim to be in essence a Mexican concern as would the assumption of a Mexican name that would simply be a veil to thinly conceal foreign ownership. . . . We are a commercial concern: we do not propose to meddle in finance, politics or religion if we can avoid it.[148]

Other salvos were deliberately offensive. Bureaucrats in Limantour's Treasury Ministry were not amused when news stories suggested that Waters-Pierce alone had been responsible for the nation's budget surpluses. Limantour told Body in 1906 that if Standard Oil increased its influence in Mexico, the government would assist the Pearson group in competing against the American oilmen. Moreover, rumors spread through the American community in Mexico. Díaz was a silent partner in Pearson's enterprises. They conspired to compete with Standard Oil and to raise import duties on the crude that Waters-Pierce refined in Tampico.[149] When the Revolution broke out, Waters-Pierce continued to disparage the reputation of the Pearson interests, linking them to the discredited Díaz regime.

At the time that news of the Dos Bocas blowout sent shock waves throughout Mexico, in July 1908, Pearson went public with his marketing plans. His company announced that it now had fifty forty-ton tank cars to carry fuel oil from its 6,000–bd refinery at Minatitlán to bulk storage installations in ten Mexican states. (The refining capacity at Minatitlán was only 3,000 bd; perhaps the other figures too were exaggerated.) Newspaper reports stated that El Aguila, the new "Mexican" company, by cutting prices by 20 percent, would break "Standard Oil's control of Mexico" once and for all. "The domestic consumer of Mexico will at once enjoy the luxury of cheaper oil than they have ever known before."[150]

Within months, the war became more vicious. Thomas J. Ryder, the former Waters-Pierce agent and now chief of Pearson's oil department, began to expand Pearson's retail distribution throughout Mexico by hiring experienced agents away from Pierce. By the end of October 1908, Pearson had seventy-two distribution agencies in Mexico. Newspaper advertising touted El Aguila's lubricating oils and greases as "the best ever sold in Mexico." Pearson began to take satisfaction in Pierce's helplessness. Pierce had tried to hire Pearson's best employees but failed. "It shows that the man must be losing his balance and becoming irresponsible for his acts," observed Sir Weetman.[151]

Mexican oil prices, which once had been four times greater than U.S. retail prices, begin to tumble beyond the initial 20-percent cut. Kerosene fell from 13 centavos to 7 centavos, and gasoline fell from 35 centavos to 11 centavos. The newly nationalized Mexican railways in November concluded a contract in which Pearson was to supply fuel oil for about 920 kilometers of line for a seven-year period. Plans also went forward to construct an oil terminal at the port of Veracruz.[152] At this point, the president of Waters-Pierce and son of the board chairman, Clay Arthur Pierce, made his heralded trip to Mexico.

The "great oil war" in Mexico, because it lowered prices, tended simultaneously to widen the consumption of petroleum products. El Aguila agents noted that nationwide sales of illuminating oil and naphtha had risen from nine million gallons per month in 1906 to twelve million gallons in 1909. In fact, Pierce's volume sales and imports had not decreased. The oil war had only diminished the Waters-Pierce profits at the same moment that it eroded Pierce's market domination.[153] The final decline of the Pierce monopoly and creation of the Mexican oil industry as an oligopoly (control of the market by a few large companies) came with Pearson's giant oil discovery at Potrero del Llano.

Drilling Themselves In

Having failed to tame the Dos Bocas blowout, Pearson in 1909 decided to bring in even more expertise. He hired Dr. C. Willard Hayes, director of the United States Geological Survey, to direct the field work. Hayes had met Pearson the year before while the geologist was visiting the site of the famous Dos Bocas blowout. Pearson subsequently convinced Hayes to enter the oil industry as a highly paid consultant without giving up his position at the U.S. Survey. Hayes was to engage field geologists and inspect their exploratory work once a year. In a preliminary survey, Hayes concluded that

Mexican demand for oil still exceeded supply, that heavy Mexican crude was not competitive with lighter American crude, and that the average cost of production was high. What Mexico needed was a big discovery of light crude.[154] Hayes brought in a bright young geology student from the University of Oklahoma. C. Everitt DeGolyer needed no passport or visa to take the train down to Tampico. Mexican immigration officials merely asked if he were an "anarchista." Tampico was not yet an oil boom town, although El Aguila already occupied the five-story building across from the Imperial Hotel. The American geology student joined a company whose superintendent was a Scot; the bookkeeper, a Dutchman; and the manager of launches and transportation, an Englishman. The other American field geologists included Chester Washburne and Edwin B. Hopkins. DeGolyer traveled with them to the El Aguila properties west of Tuxpan. He mapped the Hacienda Tierra Amarilla, home of one of the company's Mexican lawyers. A younger brother, Manuel Peláez, was managing the hacienda. Twenty wells drilled at Tierra Amarilla were to produce only moderately. At nearby Tanhuijo, another small producer was struck.[155] The search continued for the big gusher that would put Mexico on the world's oil maps.

At an hacienda named Potrero del Llano, young DeGolyer, who had just turned twenty-four, helped to choose the drilling sites for four exploratory wells. The American geologists mapped the upthrusting rock strata for indications of subterranean rooflike domes that trapped the oil deposits. Since Pennsylvania, the Americans were trained in the *anticline* theory of oil detection. Capt. Anthony Lucas had used the anticline theory to bring in the first Spindletop gusher. So had Pearson's geologists in Veracruz. DeGolyer later recalled how the first well at Potrero del Llano came in:

[W]e were all in the mess hall having dinner when there was a terrific roar, like the blowing off of a boiler. Nobody could think what could cause such a noise, so we all rushed out. Potrero del Llano #1 had drilled itself in. It had been drilled to a point so close to the rock holding oil that the oil finally just broke through and finished the job.... This discovery well, located by Geoffrey Jeffrey [a British geologist], was a small well that flowed by heads and made three or four hundred barrels a day. There was no difficulty in stopping the free flow of a well of that size, just a matter of closing a valve.[156]

As 1910 drew to a close, Sir Weetman Pearson was reasonably satisfied with his geologists. They had begun Mexican domestic production in the region west of Tuxpan known as the Faja de Oro, the "Golden Lane." The region derived its name from the fact that the crude discovered here was much lighter than that found farther north around Tampico. At 28 degrees Baumé, the Golden Lane crude contained valuable components of fuel oil, gasoline, and kerosene. With his geologists and drilling crews working on additional prospects, Pearson felt assured he would soon have enough domestic crude so that he would be able to cancel the purchases of Texas oil. He wanted a big well that would not stop with the mere turn of a valve.

DeGolyer located the fourth well site at Potrero del Llano. Drilling commenced in April 1910 and was suspended in June at a depth of 1,856 feet. Drilling crews then awaited completion of the pipeline, returning to the well two days before Christmas. On 27 December 1910, after the drillers had penetrated another fifty-five feet into the Tamasopo limestone, they stopped for the night. Since no gas emission had warned them that the drills were about to strike oil, the drillers had not placed a drilling valve over the wellhead. Potrero No. 4 came on its own at 2 A.M. The bailer, a long cylinder used to scoop out samplings from the well, was blown clear out of the well. A black plume of crude petroleum rose 250 feet into the air with a deafening roar and commenced to lay a coat of oil over all the vegetation—and human and animal life—for a radius of a mile around the well. The chief driller on duty scrambled through the underbrush in the darkness in order to extinguish the fires in the boilers. That the boilers had been placed some distance from the drilling platform prevented Potrero del Llano No. 4 from becoming another conflagration like Dos Bocas.

As it was, the Potrero well, flowing wildly, presented its own technological challenges. Lord Cowdray, as Sir Weetman Pearson was to be known after his elevation to the peerage in July 1910, was in Mexico City that December, introducing his sons Clive and Harold to the Mexican enterprises. DeGolyer was on horseback with Dr. Hayes, introducing the new general manager of El Aguila, Robert Stirling, to the Furbero field. Sterling left immediately for Potrero, but Hayes and De-Golyer were summoned to Mexico City. Yet before they arrived, Lord Cowdray himself had left by train for Potrero to take charge of capping the wild well. Lady Cowdray, the British ambassador, and Governor Landa y Escandón took charge of several days of social affairs toasting the young American geologist's success. DeGolyer did not arrive at his runaway well until a week had passed. He took the train through San Luis Potosí to Tampico and a launch through the Tamiahua lagoon.

Potrero del Llano had become bedlam itself. Accompanied by a large quantity of gas, the oil spewed out of the well at the rate of 100,000 bd, the pressure heating the oil to a temperature of 147 degrees F. Everyone was caked with oil, and the Buena Vista River was filled with so much oil that one could not see the water underneath.[157] The crude flowed into the Tuxpan River and out onto the beaches of the Gulf Coast of Veracruz. Eventually, oil washed ashore on the beaches at Tampico, two hundred miles to the north. DeGolyer and a Mexican civil engineer surveyed a route for the urgently needed second pipeline to Tuxpan. Local *jefes políticos* ordered ranch foremen to bring in their peons to build earthen reservoirs to catch and store the flow. Thousands of Mexican villagers worked at Potrero at one time or another, most leaving after getting their first paycheck. They had to be replaced by others. Mexican women organized kitchens under oil-soaked canvas shelters. Never had the casual population of these livestock and agricultural districts been so mobilized.[158] Indeed, the oilmen enlisted the support of local authorities to apply some coercive measures to get them to stay.

In the meantime, the immediate task was to prevent the spread of oil. Workers set fire to the crude on the river in an effort to minimize the damage to crops and farmland. The conflagration started five miles downstream from Potrero, lifting great billows of black smoke and soot into the humid air. Men constructed flumes, troughs that carried the oil swiftly downriver to the fire, and built a dam farther downriver to catch the crude that escaped the flames. Some of the oilmen's experience in the Baku oil fields of Russia contributed to the tactics used during the Potrero crisis.[159]

The second task remained to control the ferocious plume of oil that spewed directly out of the well casing. Experienced engineers devised an elaborate valve dubbed the "Bell Nipple," after a design that an American driller had seen used on much smaller Texas gushers. The device, lying sideways, was attached to one side of the well casing by means of extended ratchets. The men worked slowly. They were beset by gas fumes that burned the eyes (a slice of potato held over the eyelids was found to provide relief), by the gusher's noise, and by sheets of oil constantly falling around the well. Eventually, they winched the bell nipple upright and over the blasting spout of crude. It was not until 25 January 1911 that the crews had tightened the bell nipple over the casing, but the valve device proved unable to control the flow and had to be replaced by a second, larger bell nipple in March. Then workers constructed a mound of concrete and pipes over No. 4. Gradually, they diverted the flow into valves, earthen reservoirs, and the hurriedly constructed pipeline.

The work of El Aguila's geologists made hollow Doheny's boast that geology professors had not been successful at finding oil. Moreover, the fury of Potrero No. 4 challenged experienced British and American oilmen to devise additional technological solutions to problems peculiar to Mexican production. Best of all for El Aguila, the crude oil at Potrero No. 4 had an American Petroleum Institute rating of 21 degrees gravity. Unlike the heavy crude produced at Doheny's El Ebano in the north, the wells in the Faja de Oro contained large increments of fuel oil, kerosene, and gasoline—the valuable products of oil.[160] El Aguila no longer had to import crude from Texas but, in fact, began to export to Texas and elsewhere.

The Britons and Americans who had directed the Potrero operation eventually gathered enough knowledge of geological conditions in the Huasteca to realize how fortunate they were to have saved the giant well. For the first time in petroleum history, they were exploiting deposits lying in limestone rather than a sandy formation. Holes drilled into the mare and limestone seldom collapsed, and the fierce flow of oil did not disturb the strata. They learned that the oil sands tended to plug fast-flowing wells in places like the Baku and Trinidad. If a well having the force of Potrero No. 4 had flowed uncontrolled in oil sands, it would have destroyed itself within days. It was rarely safe to allow a well sunk in oil sands elsewhere to produce at a rate faster than 2,000 bd, whereas Cowdray's men in Mexico had harnessed a well that, once it was pinched back, produced at the rate of 30,000 bd.[161] These oil engineers also did not know on 31 March 1911, when they had definitely brought Potrero on line, that this well's future was to be equally as eventful as its discovery. Nor did they understand yet the long-term weakness of oil production in limestone formations.

El Aguila had other concerns in 1911. Finding itself suddenly awash in oil production, the company now had to move quickly to provide transport and markets. J. B. Body devised a floating loading dock in the shallows before the river port of Tuxpan, so that gulf tankers could take on crude oil approximately one-half mile from shore. Eventually, the Tuxpan terminal accommodated four tankers at once, loading at the rate of 120,000 gallons per day.[162] The drilling crew at Potrero del Llano slowed down while others built a pipeline that carried the modest production of Tierra Amarillo and the first Potrero wells down to the Tamiahua lagoon. From there, barges ferried the crude oil over to Tampico. Pipelines were completed from Potrero first to Tuxpan then to the deep-water port of Tampico. Almost immediately, El Aguila purchased land along the Tampico ship channel and began to build a second refinery. Shipping traffic in the Tamiahua lagoon and along the coast multiplied as El Aguila shipped oil in barges to Tampico and Veracruz. Potrero del Llano crude was shipped to Puerto México and pumped to the Minatitlán refinery. Lord Cowdray's son, Clive Pearson, as chairman, expanded the new Anglo-Mexican Petroleum Company into an eight-hundred-person firm distributing Mexican oil throughout Great Britain and the Continent.[163]

Steam tankers began to arrive from the United States, and Lord Cowdray laid plans to build his own fleet to carry Mexican oil to Europe and Canada. Now, the prolific wells of both Pearson and Doheny had made Mexican oil competitive on the U.S. market, even though prices softened a bit. Mexican production burgeoned from 3.6 million barrels in 1910 to 12.6 million in 1911 (see table 4). Armed with technological superiority, financial wealth, access to foreign markets, and the political favor of Porfirio Díaz, the foreign businessmen had at last made Mexico not only a consumer of hydrocarbon energy but also a major producer. The oil industry was a powerful force for social change as well.

Poorly Defined Boundaries

Foreign investment in Mexico's economy contained profound social consequences. The oil boom severely disrupted the society of Mexico's Gulf Coast, and for a simple reason: prior economic development of the region around Tampico and on the isthmus, having been rather lethargic, had not conditioned the people's social relationships to change and mobility. Despite being the second largest port on the east coast and home of the Mexican Central Railway and the Waters-Pierce refinery, Tampico lacked the infrastructure of a modern economy. Few exports had yet integrated the gulf port either with the Atlantic economy or the Mexican economy. Stockraising, subsistence agriculture, and fishing were the leading economic pursuits in the area—as they had been since colonial days. Just at the time Doheny arrived to prospect for oil, however, the rural population of the Mexican Gulf Coast was beginning to grow behind a migratory flow from the highlands.

These recent arrivals tended to fill in the empty land as subsistence squatters rather than as commercial farmers. American farmers grew cash crops, hired wage workers, and introduced efficient production methods. The isthmus did not share even this modest development. The inhospitable and isolated Tehuantepec region lay deserted except for rustic squatters and large, unproductive estates when the Pearson interests constructed the railway. At the turn of the century, economic development in Mexico's future oil zones had been quite weak. The majority of the rural population was illiterate, unskilled, and socially differentiated by race, income, and prospects for advancement. The educated, property-owning commercial class remained quite small.

Although modernizing, society in the Mexican oil zones was unprepared for the rapid pace of change to which the oil boom subjected it. The state of Veracruz, dominated by the port city of Veracruz and the highland cities of Córdoba and Jalapa, was growing during the Porfiriato. In-migration increased. Typical of migrant populations, Veracruz had several thousand more males than females. The Huasteca and isthmian regions, however, were among the least populated in the Veracruz state. Of the future refining cities and oil ports, Tampico had a population of 17,500 persons in 1900; Tuxpan, 13,000; and Minatitlán, 6,100. Puerto México, Pearson's gulf oil terminal on the isthmus, known as Coatzacoalcos up to 1903, was a town of 4,487.[164] Many of these cities counted farmers in their populations. In fact, the largest category of the working population in and around Tampico consisted of farmers and field workers (*peones del campo*). Although 855 *tampiqueños* were in commerce, only 49 worked in industry. The port had a relatively mobile population: only 9,000 were natives, more than 1,000 were foreigners, and 7,000 had migrated from other Mexican locales. Nearly half of the natives of Tampico older than twelve years of age were also illiterate. Tuxpan was even more rustic. In the entire Canton (county) of Tuxpan there was but one industrial worker; 14,000 of the residents of Tuxpan were farmers or rural peons, and more than 90 percent of the adult population was unable to read. Only 123 natives in these four oil zones had a working knowledge of metals.[165] Mexico's future oil cities at the turn of the century had greater administrative than commercial importance, and they completely lacked any manufacturing base whatsoever.

Moreover, the Gulf Coast was isolated from the more populous highlands. In Mexico, railways had begun the process of economic development. Although the Veracruz-Mexico railway was complete in 1877, when Díaz came to power, primitive conditions at the port of

Veracruz limited the rail traffic on the line. The rail boom of the latter half of the nineteenth century benefited Mexico's north central plateau. There old silver mines were reopened by foreign companies. Lacking mining resources, the Gulf Coast north and south of Veracruz languished in comparison.[166] They served as underpopulated livestock and agricultural zones attractive to modest numbers of foreign immigrants and *mestizo* migrants. Spaniards and Mexicans from Hidalgo and Puebla came to Tuxpan; *potosinos* and *tamaulipiqueños* migrated to Ozuluama; and Americans, Spaniards, and *potosinos* came to Tampico. In the city of Tampico, in fact, only half the residents had even been born in the state of Tamaulipas. Seven thousand had migrated from the other states of Mexico; another 1,100 were foreigners. Lethargic coastal vessels served as the only link between Veracruz and the future oil towns of Tampico, Tuxpan, and Minatitlán.

The Eastern Sierras effectively prevented large-scale commerce between these places and the more prosperous and populated highlands. During much of the nineteenth century, local trade at the port of Tampico suffered from a lack of suitable roads to draw produce from the towns and villages. Foreigners were unwilling even to build rail lines to the Gulf Coast. Initial construction was abandoned in 1873. A. A. Robinson of the Mexican Central Railway finally agreed to construct the spur line from San Luis Potosí to Tampico only under government pressure. The Mexican Central began construction in 1881 and completed it in 1889, extending the line beyond San Luis Potosí to Aguascalientes for a total of 654 kilometers. Nevertheless, traffic remained light, and the Central Railroad had to spend an additional four million pesos ($2 million) on port construction at Tampico. Part of the problem of the delay in rail construction had to do with the importation of materials. Rails, bars, bolts, switches, cars, and locomotives came from merchant specialists in New York and New Orleans, who first had to order these items directly from the American steel mills.[167] Soon, Tampico became a center for the distribution of fuel throughout the nation. Welsh and West Virginian coal cost twelve pesos per ton at the port, but after transport by rail to the highlands, it cost nearly thirty pesos per ton. Its high price somewhat inhibited the use of coal. West Indians were brought in to work in the coal and coke piles at the docks, because Mexicans refused to do this work.[168] It is little wonder that expensive imported coal would soon yield to domestic petroleum.

At the beginning of the twentieth century, great variation existed in the landholding patterns and social organization of the future oil zones. Although land was widely distributed, the population nonetheless lived a dispersed but clearly hierarchical lifestyle. Traditionally, Veracruz society for centuries had blended the descendants of the colonial black slaves to Spaniards and to native Indians. Except for a narrow elite of mostly white Europeans (many of whom were recent Spanish immigrants), the majority of the population consisted of racially mixed mestizos. Migrants from the highlands too were mestizos. Few ethnic Indian groups remained in the future oil zones. The Pánuco region at the northern extremity of Veracruz had no Indian-language speakers at all, the only census category of 1900 that indicated preservation of Indian ethnicity. Ozuluama, midway in the Huasteca between Tampico and Tuxpan, still had four thousand persons who spoke *huasteco* and *mexicano*. The latter groups represented just 12 percent of the area's mostly rural population. Approximately eight hundred residents near Minatitlán also spoke *mexicano*. In the Tuxpan region, especially south near Furbero and what later would be the Poza Rica oil field, Indian speakers were found in larger numbers. Nearly one-third of the inhabitants of the Canton of Tuxpan spoke *huasteco, mexicano, totonaco,* or *otomí*.[169] If the Indians of these areas were like their highland brethren, they probably remained isolated from the neighboring mestizo society except to sell their labor. Spanish-speaking, hispanicized mestizos looked down upon those who spoke an Indian dialect and wore Indian clothing.

Besides race and ethnicity, additional social distinctions divided the rural society of Mexico's Gulf Coast. The first oil maps of the 1910s noted the rather wide distribution of land into modest family holdings that the Mexicans call *ranchos*. The trend in the Veracruz lowlands was quite distinct. Agricultural settlement, especially of vacant land, had contributed to the growth of large estates, the well-known Mexican *haciendas*. Where wild cattle once foraged in the dense undergrowth, stockmen began to specialize in cattle raising. Mexican markets for beef opened up to the Huasteca via the railway passing between Tampico and the central plateau. Nevertheless, individual small holdings expanded much more rapidly. Small holders specialized in goats and pigs.[170] In numbers of population involved, the ranchos were statistically significant. Growth of small holdings were appreciable compared to haciendas, according to these figures:[171]

	1877	1900	1910
No. Haciendas	237	360	536
No. Ranchos	652	1,733	1,807

If the social position of the *rancheros* from other areas of Mexico provide any indication, these independent landowners formed a kind of rural bourgeoisie. They were indistinguishable in dress and speech from the mestizos who owned no land and served as hacienda and itinerant peons in the area. Yet the rancheros also hired landless workers, thus functioning as a middle-level mechanism for social welfare and control.[172]

In a sense, the economic and social power to occupy land substituted for precise titles along the Gulf Coast. Legal boundaries meant little to illiterate squatters who settled on terrain of little value for short durations and who were anyway beholden, in one way or another, to their social superiors. Undoubtedly, many of those listed by the census of 1900 as *peones de campo* were squatters who worked as rural proletarians while still having access to vacant land. The situation delayed the legal process of land transfer, even between the new American buyers. Numerous clouded titles and overlapping claims for land only complicated the delays normally caused by a deliberate Mexican court system characterized by the required certificates, stamps, fees, and "all the siestas between times."[173] Americans never understood that local courts practiced a tradition of accommodation and compromise rather than outright decision. Mexican geologist Ezequiel Ordóñez explained how ill prepared such a society was for the legal exigencies of free-market capitalism based on private property rights:

> The boundaries were not well defined [and] no one bothered to measure or to fence his property; the transfer of ownership was done from fathers to sons, almost by tradition and [transfers] done by sales or exchanges followed a vague and at times uncertain specification of the boundaries. In other cases, the actual extension of land was hid in order to escape the tax collector and finally, as the majority of the land remained uncultivated and covered by virgin jungle, the proprietors did not actually know the size of their [properties].[174]

The oilmen who came seeking leases desired precise legal titles. Common enough in American oil fields, fraud and litigation also accompanied the rapid escalations of land values in the Mexican oil zone.

One should not conceive of this rural society as existing in a state of democratic egalitarianism. By virtue of their family background and economic leverage, the few large landowners exerted a measure of decentralized control over the rural population. Among the hacendados of the Huasteca were numbers of Spaniards who had immigrated during the Porfiriato. The Peláez, who owned the Hacienda Tierra Amarilla west of Tuxpan and whose eldest son served as El Aguila attorney, were such a family. So strong was the Spanish presence that Tuxpan harbored intense hostility toward Americans residing there during the Spanish-American War of 1898.[175] Despite their recent arrival, Spaniards used strong family ties and educational and capital resources (all of which the mestizos lacked) to form a narrow elite. Racially European, religiously Catholic, lingually Spanish, and there to stay, these immigrants easily worked their way into the upper and middle bourgeoisie of the multiracial society. The larger estates owned by Spaniards specialized in cattle production as well as agriculture. Here, as in northern Mexico, the opportunities enjoyed by these immigrants occasionally caused resentment among the mestizo lower bourgeoisie and workers. As Andrés Molina Enríquez noted, "These Spaniards . . . , if you scratch the modern man, you discover beneath the skin an old Conquistador."[176]

The easy movement of the Spanish immigrants into positions of social prominence indicates a measure of fluidity in Mexican Gulf Coast society. Indeed, mestizos emigrating from the highlands also found opportunities in modest landownership, as rancheros, in the sparsely settled region. Such opportunity might have been denied these newcomers had the land already been more densely populated—or its products more valuable. Rancheros probably worked the land more intensively, producing more agricultural products than livestock. In the more sparsely settled Ozuluama region, many rancheros were small cattlemen, but they must have been beholden to the elite for short-term credit and for sales of agricultural products in local marketplaces. At any rate, the larger number of landless and squatters who served as *peones de campo* were dependent on both hacendados and rancheros for employment. The number of landless persons was by no means small. This fact unified the interests of the hacendado and ranchero, socially separated as they might have been, in protecting the rural status quo from being overrun by a rootless rural proletariat. All three social groups were united in their disdain for the Indians. In 1900, the future oil zones had a rural society organized in the following fashion:[177]

	Tampico	Ozuluama	Tuxpan	Minatitlán
cattle-raisers	16	285	15	13
farmers	153	45	1,259	189
rural workers	3,631	9,227	13,112	1,494

Additional characteristics probably worked against mobility for the landless. In the first place, these were the inhabitants most apt to be illiterate. Second, the informal family structure—that is, only one in five females in Ozuluama and one in seven in Tampico were married—provided little support for a sibling attempting upward mobility. Single men and women outnumbered married persons in the adult population of the Gulf Coast oil zones by a factor of five to one. The census of 1900 also suggests that spatial mobility in Mexican society might also have undermined the possibilities for family units among the rural and urban working classes. Only 1,344 out of 6,247 adult women in Tampico were married, which testifies to the fact that a formal family structure was even less prominent in this migrant town than in the rural areas of the Gulf Coast.

Society on the Mexican Gulf Coast was not a yeoman democracy. Although its sparse population and relatively open land provided a measure of social opportunity, the future oil zone displayed many of the social divisions and rigidities that characterized other parts of Mexico. In the absence of egalitarianism, one found clear lines of social distinctions and hierarchy. In the absence of democracy, one found authoritarianism at all levels of society. Personal service of one kind or another was quite prominent. This postcolonial society, in particular, degraded the position of women, who vastly outnumbered men in positions of subservience such as household servants and homemakers. Shut out of jobs as farmers, cattlemen, *peones de campo,* merchants, artisans, and public employees, women dominated only as laundresses and seamstresses. They formed a majority of the school teachers but a minority of the students. There were more *quehaceres de la casa* (homemakers) than married women in this society, an indication that informal conjugal relationships were the norm. In this, the periphery of Mexico was much the same as the core of the nation.

Not Satisfied to Go in Peace

The expanding agrarian society of the Veracruz lowlands assumed a more rapid pace of change when the impact of the economic revolution began to reach the Gulf Coast. Both the southern and northern ends of Veracruz state lagged behind the central corridor in the development of a commercial infrastructure.[178] But they did develop. First the railway link and then the petroleum exploration began to transform the northern port of Tampico. Channel dredging, a crew of boat pilots, and new lighthouses somehow always seemed insufficient to handle the modest foreign trade. Captains of foreign ships complained of long waits (in capitalism, time is money) for a Mexican pilot to guide the ship up the Pánuco River to Tampico. Incomplete and submerged jetties made the trip dangerous. Longer ships, now able to pass over the dredged sandbar at the mouth of the river if they did not draw more than twenty-two feet, nonetheless could not come about at the docks before the city because the channel remained too narrow. The Díaz regime accomplished what it could to encourage the development of the transportation infrastructure. In 1908, canal construction for intercoastal shipping between Tampico and Tuxpan was only half complete. The government awarded an American engineer the $2 million contract to finish the final sixty miles of the waterway. The crew of two hundred laborers lived and worked on a flotilla of five large dredges, two colliers, a ninety-foot material barge, a machine-shop barge, and a number of houseboats. Mexican officials intended the completed five-foot-deep, forty-foot-wide channel to benefit agricultural development in the area.[179] The waterway would soon facilitate exploration, supply, and transportation in the fledgling oil industry.

The ports of Tuxpan and Coatzalcoalcos developed rather more lethargically. Coatzalcoalcos received a new lighthouse at the harbor in 1890. Navigational aides, featuring a fixed light visible sixteen miles from the coast, made safer the arrival of coastal vessels to this slumbering southern Veracruz port. Foreign contractors stimulated much activity here in the 1890s when construction of the first Tehuantepec railway got under way. Pearson's reconstruction of the railway and his building of port complexes at Coatzalcoalcos and Salina Cruz brought heightened activities to the isthmus, beginning in 1900. Improvements at Coatzalcoalcos, renamed Puerto México, included jetties, railway tracks, a terminal station, warehouses, and three steel piers.[180]

Tuxpan's development came last. Its poor harbor remained the largest drawback to Tuxpan's becoming another important gulf freight terminus, after Veracruz, Tampico, and Puerto México. Although the channel had a depth of twenty-five feet for thirty miles up the Tuxpan River, the sandbar at the mouth of the river was just four to seven feet deep. The Tuxpan region too was racked with tropical illness, sustaining from five to seven deaths per week in a population of 14,000 persons. In an age of few tourists, Tuxpan had a magnificent two-hundred-mile beach—until fouled by local oil activity. Located 230 kilometers from Veracruz and 125 from Tampico, the city remained on the itinerary of American steamers trading in hides and tropical products.

Coastal steamers obtained no coal at Tuxpan. Spanish and Mexican merchants collected the export products at the port, and a U.S. consul there helped them prepare the customs invoices for entry at New York.[181] Although the Mexican authorities established a lighthouse and buoys at the mouth of the river and maintained a customshouse and pilot services at Tuxpan, the port was not considered important enough to support the trunk line that the Mexican Central Railway once had planned between Mexico City, Tuxpan, and Tampico. Nor did the government float bonds in European money markets in order to finance port improvements at Tuxpan.[182] No one here had the political clout necessary to obtain such largesse from the government.

Then came the foreigners. Drifters from the United States passed through Tampico looking for work on the railways and seeking land to buy for farming. Like the natives, they too fell sick to the yellow fever and malaria, as in the epidemics of 1898 and 1903. Mexicans discovered an additional measure of modern economic opportunity with American colonists. In 1865, a number of ex-Confederate soldiers had emigrated from the American South to Tuxpan with their families. They produced vanilla on plantations, occasionally importing West Indian blacks to harvest the crops.[183] Attracted by government propaganda, cheap land, and even cheaper labor, farmers also came from Wisconsin, Nebraska, Iowa, Illinois, and Texas. They imported the machinery to which they had been accustomed in the states, raised hogs and mules, grew corn and onions, and employed Mexican peons. American ranchers imported short-horned stock such as the Hereford from the American Midwest.

Like many Spaniards who settled around Tuxpan, the Americans came with capital and families. They hired their American countrymen as administrators. Assisted by American real estate firms based at Tampico, some colonists paid a down payment of as much as 30,000 pesos ($15,000), taking mortgages on the balance.[184] American land speculators purchased large Mexican cattle estates, such as the Hacienda Atascadero, and broke them up into smaller lots for resale to other Americans from Texas and Oklahoma who wanted to plant corn, wheat, and other crops. Even some Chinese immigrants, having made capital in various business ventures, were buying ranches near Tampico.[185] Just as the big oilmen dealt with lawyers influential in the federal government, so too American land purchasers used the services of Mexican lawyers in Tampico who looked up land titles and dealt with municipal officialdom.[186] Not all these immigrant farmers found prosperity. American land companies, whose activities often bordered on fraud, exaggerated the rumors of success in their "misleading" circulars. "There are a few American colonies in the vicinity of Tampico," the American consul warned a prospective American immigrant. "Their prosperity to date has not been a remarkable success. Unremitting work and hardship have been their portion."[187]

If the Americans had spoken Spanish and been Catholics, they might have fit perfectly into the pattern whereby Mexican society since the Conquest had absorbed European immigrants into positions of privilege. Mexican authorities certainly treated American landowners the way they did their own countrymen. Local officials in Tuxpan were motivated by the traditional nonchalance that permitted the rural workers subsistence in the face of economic change, all for the sake of social peace. They refused to remove squatters and defaulted renters from American-owned properties. Confronted by indignant protests from American landowners, the *jefe político* and the *rurales* at Tuxpan responded with inactivity. Occasionally, there was land fraud perpetrated by Mexicans and Americans alike on potential American buyers. Americans from time to time bought land from those unable to transfer legal title or from others who charged inflated prices for "improved" land still covered with tropical vegetation.[188] Despite setbacks, during the first decade of the twentieth century, American owners and American administrators were hacking back the rain forest and planting vanilla and rubber trees and other tropical products.

In addition to the big plantations owned by foreigners, small foreign family farmers could also be found in the area. Most of the farms belonging to the American colonists—as opposed to those belonging to planters—consisted of an American-sized farm of 250 acres, less than an hacienda but larger than most ranchos. Their productivity supported higher wages among the peons. In 1919, one of these American farmers testified about the changes brought to Mexican labor relations:

Question: What did [the American farmers] do in reference to exploiting the Mexican peon?
Answer: Well, their first effort to exploit the Mexican peon was to raise his wages from 25 or 30 cents up to one peso, Mexican dollar.[189]

When, in 1890, an American landowner arrived to begin a banana plantation near Tampico, the common peon was receiving a daily wage of twenty-five centavos. Agricultural expansion and construction of the Mexican Central Railway raised wages to fifty centavos by the time the first oilmen arrived. As the demand for labor increased, Mexican hacendados petitioned the government to hold down wages. Wage stabilization was impossible to enforce, however, and the oil boom soon lifted wages to one peso and more per day. Although American landowners never resorted to debt peonage (or so they claimed), a banana plantation operator in Tampico never had any trouble securing workers. The Mexicans preferred to work among the bananas. There was shade, water, and the right to eat all the bananas they wanted.[190] And, of course, higher pay. Good wages improved the material life of the Mexicans. Shoes replaced the sandals called *huaraches,* and the peons began to wear better clothing. American oil managers noted that the Mexicans soon began to demand the same clothes worn by the Americans and to imitate their ways. Not all Americans were pleased by the imitation. "Mexicans demanded these things too quickly," commented one employer.[191]

Mexico's Gulf Coast was not completely immune to the economic development represented by American farmers. Still, these stimuli occurred late and in isolated forms. But the slight development did not so much raise pay levels as it brought more persons into the wage labor system. Dampened by inflated prices for necessities, real wages on the Gulf Coast rose from only twenty-five to thirty-three centavos between 1885 and 1908.[192] The Huasteca region lay outside and somewhat isolated from the main regions of economic transformation in Porfirian Mexico. Yet, the entire state of Veracruz led the rest of Mexico in the population explosion. A zone of in-migration, Veracruz enhanced its population from 854,000 inhabitants in 1895 to 1,133,000 in 1910. It moved from sixth to the second most populous Mexican state.[193] Even so, the railways and shipping merely embellished—but did not change—the multiracial and multiethnic social order that had developed there since the Conquest.

Nevertheless, Mexican workers had never been hapless victims of the economic system. They continued to manipulate the world in which they lived. American landowners found themselves the object of insults and abuses of their own peons, especially when the latter became drunk. They stole the landlord's cattle, killed steers merely for the tongues (a prized delicacy), and tore down fences. Then, complained one American landowner near Pánuco, the local authorities would free the disorderly peons. "I firmly believe these depredations would not have occurred," he complained, "had the early offenders been properly punished."[194] Although the local authorities enjoyed considerable license to deal with the recalcitrant rural workers, inertia and lassitude often prevented the social control system from becoming truly draconian. Village *caciques* around Ozuluama and Pánuco often rounded up the "vagrants, those with bad inclinations, or whomever was around" for service in the Mexican army. After some assignments sweeping the streets, however, the new recruits ran away, adding to the Americans' concern about lawlessness and danger in the countryside.[195]

It is difficult to know just how much this underclass assertiveness contributed to banditry in Mexico. Yet bandits, especially in the Huasteca Mountains of San Luis Potosí, had never succumbed completely to the government's pacification of the countryside. In 1906, rural Mexicans identified as "bandits" and "Revolutionists" by American landowners preyed on foreign-owned haciendas and threatened the lives of American managers.[196] And woe to the foreigner who could not pay his workers. One hacienda manager at Ciudad del Maíz in 1905, when he neglected to issue the pay, found himself surrounded by one hundred armed peons demanding horses, money, and food. A desperate cablegram prompted the state governor to dispatch a unit of the *rurales* by special train. The *rurales* did not shoot the peons but resolved the problem peacefully. Whenever foreigners violated certain accepted standards of reciprocity, the "moral economy" of Mexican rural society, the peons knew how to gain justice.[197] Certainly little in this social and economic organization prepared the Mexicans of the Gulf Coast to manage the oil boom that descended upon them like a sustained hurricane when in 1910 the Casiano and Potrero wells came in.

Like the American miners and railroaders, the first oilmen imported much of their skill from the United States and Europe. Mexican workers were needed only as peons and gang laborers. Local personnel who could handle machetes and teams of mules sufficed to clear the jungle for wildcat wells, pipelines, and small-gauge railways. If not cut back every six months by the *macheteros,* tropical vegetation soon grew over buildings, installations, and equipment. "The breaches that were cut especially for the automobile roads and pipelines," wrote geologist Ordóñez, "had to be widened to at least twenty or thirty meters in order to prevent the shade of the trees from retaining the moisture in the soil, forming great quagmires during the rains."[198] Additional unskilled Mexicans loaded, unloaded, and carried equipment. Permanent workers who learned skills and mechanical procedures were needed only in limited numbers. The first Mexican boiler workers, carpenters, and mechanics came from the highlands, where shopwork in mines and railroads imparted to them some limited familiarity with the new job requirements.

Foreign oilmen satisfied their initial needs for semiskilled and unskilled workers through the *enganche* system. Literally translated as "hookers," the Mexican *enganchadores* established themselves in the plazas of Tampico and Ciudad Victoria and in the towns of the Bajío surrounding Guanajuato. These labor contractors offered bonuses and transportation to workers who were attracted by the adventure, status, and high pay of working in the foreign oil sector. The first wages for these jobs were seventy-five centavos per day. Doheny brought workers down from Cerritos, located in the highlands along the Mexican Central railway line. Both the hacendados and the railway men protested that Doheny's high wages were spoiling the workers. "We usually got our native workers from the little towns in the sierras," recalled pioneer oilman Percy Furber. "I would send up a letter to the jefes mayors [*sic*] and negotiate for a hundred or more men for a month or two at a time for a special piece of work. At the height of our work at Furbero we had from four to five hundred native workers."[199] Yet neither the lowlands nor the mountain villages entirely supplied Furber's early labor needs. He still had to bring in three hundred Cubans, many of whom were blacks and mulattoes. In a way, the early oil industry contributed additional diversity to an already pluralistic Mexican Gulf Coast society.

Porfirio Díaz had been hoping for the transformation of the Mexican worker. Doheny himself offered a poignant glimpse into the president's intentions. In 1903 Doheny and several other American businessmen paid their respects to Díaz. The president turned to the subject of Mexican workers:

He told us of his early hopes with regard to the bettering of conditions of his own people, and in the midst of his conversation about the futility of his endeavor to alleviate the working conditions of his own people he stopped, choked up with emotion, and the tears rolled down his cheeks. He begged our forbearance, and later proceeded to apologize for his emotion by saying that he never contemplated the failure of his design in bringing good conditions to the working people of Mexico without being overcome as we had seen him. . . .

He told us that we must be patient with the ignorance and the lack of initiative in the Mexican workman. He called our attention to the fact that they could not learn by instruction, that they must be taught by precept, by example; that they were very imitative, that anything they saw others do they could learn to do, and do well; that they would be faithful to those whom they worked for if they were treated well. He told us that his greatest desire for our prosperity in Mexico was the example which our workmen would present to the Mexican workmen of how to work, how to live, and how to progress.[200]

At first, the oil managers at El Ebano had great difficulty in finding workers in order to carry out Díaz's plans. The locals worked in agriculture or owned their own small-holdings. Wylie engaged *enganchadores* to bring the men down from the central plateau for a week. Gradually raising wages from thirty-five to seventy-five centavos and finally from one to two pesos, Wylie induced many Mexicans to stay and work regularly for the company. They were trained at the same time. "These boys were put first into the copper works," Wylie said, "then advanced to the machine shops and carpenter shops as they showed special aptitude and faithfulness in their work." Shifts lasted ten hours, and the work was done under the *tarea* (piece-work) system. Unlike some of the American mining firms, the oil company did not have to resort to bonuses to exhort their workers' steady performance. Wylie said he was able "gradually to weed out the undesirables and more shiftless."[201] Doheny believed that El Ebano's relative isolation contributed to the absence of the kind of prejudice and dislike between Americans and Mexicans found along the border. He noted with pride that few racial frictions had occurred in the Ebano camp, despite the fact that the local people were "primitive."[202]

Living conditions in the first oil camps were also as primitive as some managers regarded the native Mexicans. The oilmen had to build warehouses, sawmills, electric light plants, ice plants, and provide for sanitation, hospitals, and nurses simply to maintain the work efficiency of both Americans and Mexicans. American roustabouts could not rough it in the tropics as they did in the Texas and Oklahoma oil fields—without regard for sanitary conditions. The first foreigners at El Ebano developed sores and fevers. Superintendent Wylie had to order the burning of dirty blankets, bedding, and clothing of the sick men. Their laundry was washed every week and their rooms kept well aired and cleaned. As a result, only two Americans died, one from peritonitis and the other from smallpox. The company attended to the health needs of the Mexican labor as well, maintaining a hospital at El Ebano and a doctor at Tampico. Normally, workers regularly suffered from a swamp fever. Yellow fever appeared at El Ebano only once, forcing the company to take a greater interest in the housing of the Mexican workers. Wylie instituted a system of quarantine, had lime scattered and distillate sprayed throughout all the houses. Many Mexican huts, built with earthen floors "in defiance of company regulations," had to be torched. Those residents who refused to vacate were forcibly removed. Meanwhile, the company erected houses with wooden floors and organized a "sanitary gang" to inspect them. Wylie was not adverse to using coercion. He noted without apology that the violator of these sanitary laws was taken before the local magistrate, fined, and jailed for a few days.[203]

Social relationships in the early oil industry also tended to retard skill transfers from foreign to native workers, no matter what Díaz had hoped. Mexican workers were accustomed to short-term agricultural work. They treated the oil industry as the same kind of employer. Workers hired on for a month or two, then went back to their native villages, to a plot of land, or to the next job. The element of coercion traditionally found in Mexican labor relations also remained. Furber had thought nothing of placing a worker prone to drink in the stocks overnight. The leg-stocks had been set up by a Mexican labor contractor.[204] The *jefes políticos* contributed toward work discipline in the early oil fields by extending hacendado-like authority to the foreign managers. Company officials could have men arrested and expelled from the camp. The old system of decentralized social control worked effectively in the oil fields, where the workers were isolated and dispersed, almost as if they were working on a large hacienda. Managers easily dealt with disorders. Few serious disciplinary problems actually arose, according to Manager Payne of Furbero, who exerted hacendado-like powers over American workers as well. For several months, Payne would not allow three disgruntled California oil workers to leave camp until they had repaid their travel advances. They complained that Furbero was like a tropical prison. The company prevented escape because it owned all the land, operated the only railroad, and had all the horses "a round this place." Even the *rurales* helped the management, so the Californians claimed.[205] Sir Weetman Pearson relied on local political authorities to discipline workers to stay on the job longer during the blowouts at Dos Bocas and Potrero del Llano. None of these practices were particularly new to Mexico. As the foreign employer discovered, higher wages at first did not provide sufficient incentives for Mexican workers to change their traditional work habits. Therefore, foreign management accepted corporal punishment as a method of "teaching" the benefits of progress, as if the Mexicans were children.

Foreigners mixed the disdain they harbored toward Mexican workers with an equal portion of paternalism. Doheny's camp at El Ebano held Christmas parties complete with games and presents for the children. The boss himself financed the technical education in the United

States for the son of one of the Mexican engineers working for the dredging company at Tampico.[206] At El Ebano, the resident manager, Herbert Wylie, prided himself on the loyalty that the peons developed for the Mexican Petroleum Company. He was personable and a man of his word (if we may believe Wylie's own testimony), which contributed to his ability to gain the men's respect. Wylie had an imposing, bulky figure, joked with the men, knew their names, and gave a "pat occasionally on the back." Wylie claimed that they treated him with deference, saying "Si él dice, está bueno." Despite their regard for Wylie, the Mexicans were very reluctant to leave El Ebano when in 1910 he ordered them to move south to the new operations in the Huasteca. Wylie had to give them extraordinary assurances. Finally, the men and their families boarded the three large barges that transplanted nearly the entire camp to the south.[207]

The Pearson interests developed this same kind of noblesse oblige in order to attract labor as they began building the railway across the Isthmus of Tehuantepec. The region was notoriously short of workers and the climate inhospitable; the Pearson group was beset with high labor turnover on the isthmus. By 1905, Pearson approved the construction of company housing for the *cargadores* (carriers or porters). As he noted, the government would not build houses at Salina Cruz and Coatzacoalcos, the two terminals of the Trans-Isthmian Line. "[T]here is very little time to lose," Sir Weetman wrote to his superintendent, J. B. Body.[208] Generally, company housing was reserved for semiskilled Mexican workers rather than peons. Such accommodations built at company expense seldom housed all the skilled workers and later was to be a matter of contention when it became apparent that even better housing was made available to foreign personnel. Nonetheless, the promise of such solid company housing contrasted sharply with the earth-floored, thatch-roofed *jacales* common to the tropical lowlands. Moreover, the demand for labor in the advanced, foreign-owned industries and in the inhospitable, isolated, and infectious lowlands pushed common wages to two to four times the average agricultural wage.[209] Mexican workers approved of these benefits of modernization, although the high rate of turnover indicated that Mexican workers accepted them on their own terms and not on those of the foreigners.

Other characteristics of the modern petroleum industry proved less pleasing. In a nation not yet distinguished for safe working conditions, Mexicans soon discovered that work in the "modern" sector contained its own element of danger. By 1905, Waters-Pierce already had a congregation of 350 workers and their families living near the phosphorus fumes of its Tampico refinery. Their homes had no sanitation or lights; pigs, chickens, and children ran freely through the yards. Yellow fever, malaria, and dysentery crippled many Mexicans from the more agreeable highlands. Americans and foreigners too suffered these maladies, but companies provided more health care for foreign employees. Employers provided no benefits and showed little responsibility for Mexican unskilled day workers. Sooner or later, everyone would get one form of *vómito* or another.[210]

But gas explosions confirmed in the new industrial worker his occasional helplessness and fatalism before the forces of modern technology. On 8 December 1908 one of the stills at the Minatitlán refinery exploded in flames. Soon the conflagration spread to four other stills and five storage tanks. Apparently only a foreign chief of the guards was killed and eight injured. Workers and their families fled their homes, which had been built close to the oil storage tanks, in terror. Even the small refinery hospital had to be evacuated.[211] Then there were the great conflagration at Dos Bocas and the enormous loss of crude from the wells at Potrero del Llano and Casiano. Oil fouled the rivers and beaches and seeped into the fields. Life in Mexico, whether in the highlands or lowlands, seemed fickle enough. But the Minatitlán refinery fire and the Dos Bocas blowout proved that modernization had introduced a kind of technological savagery.

Racism—another feature of the foreign-controlled oil industry that soon became manifest to every Mexican connected to the business— also tended to retard technology transfer. This is not to say that Mexicans were new to racism. But Mexican racism was subtle. It noted gradations of race mixture and permitted movement from one category of race and ethnicity to another. Indians could become mestizos by speaking Spanish and donning mestizo clothing. American racism, however, was crude. Formed in the crucible of a majority European society, American racism recognized all gradations of color as equally tainted. To some Americans, the proud, educated, but olive-skinned Mexican bourgeois was the same as the swarthy, illiterate peon. It mattered very little that Mexicans may have served as legal advisers and even as board members of the foreign companies. Everyone who spoke Spanish was a "spic" or a "greaser." "Would a man have to bring his own labor," inquired an American driller, "or could he find 'greasers' with enough sense to operate machinery?"[212]

Foreign workers occupied the privileged supervisory and skilled positions. The technological expertise, the knowledge that ran the industry day in and day out, resided in the foreign workers and supervisors. Sir Weetman Pearson and Percy Furber, although British, hired American drillers and even experienced workers from the Baku oil fields in Russia. Such practices did not assure uniform excellence, for even the so-called skilled foreigners occasionally drilled a crooked well hole and had to be relieved of their duties.[213] Doheny relied exclusively on American skilled workers. Take Charley Sackett. He was white, a native of Parkersburg, Wood County, West Virginia, and had traveled to the oil fields near Beaumont, Texas before moving to a place he spelled "Lampasopa Mexico." Like his fellow American workers, Sackett looked down on the darker-skinned people who spoke "spic lingo" and wore sandals and cotton "pajamas."[214]

Neither the Europeans nor the Americans, as a group, were enlightened, understanding supervisors. First of all, American workers who held the skilled jobs were very mobile. They never remained at any one job in the oil zone to establish more than just casual relationships with the Mexicans whom they supervised. In the second place, those from Pennsylvania as well as the Southerners were racists. They valued the Mexican mestizos about as little as the African Americans back home. In the Texas refineries and oil fields, for instance, the dirtiest and most menial tasks were reserved for blacks and Chicanos. African and Mexican Americans did not work directly in the oil fields of West Texas at all in the 1920s. They did the hot, dirty, and unskilled jobs: clearing land, doing laundry, cooking and washing, cleaning buildings, and carrying equipment.[215] Multiracial hierarchy was not new to Mexico. Nor racism, nor privileges based on birth. But Americans and other foreigners did nothing to break down these social traditions. In fact, these "agents of modernization" reinforced them. They compelled the Mexicans to overlook their own subtle racism whenever confronted with the blatant prejudice of the Americans and Europeans.

The social distance that race, language, and culture established between the foreign industrial "teacher" and the Mexican "student" worked to reduce the amount of skill transfer. One American's daily work log reveals this disdain for the Mexican employees. Surveying the route for Percy Furber's rail line in 1908, the American complained frequently of the lethargic work habits and delays of the Mexicans. He encountered trouble among the forty peons of his survey party. "Fifteen

Fig. 5. Doheny's drilling crew at El Ebano, c. 1902. The Mexican Petroleum Company imported the equipment and management expertise
to open up Mexico's first oil field. A steam tractor driven by an
American worker hauls well casing and a boiler to the wooden derrick in preparation for drilling. A crew of seven Mexican workers
assist, supervised by a second American on horseback. From the Estelle Doheny Collection, courtesy of the Archive of the Archdiocese
of Los Angeles, Mission Hills, California.

of the peons announced their departure on account of poor eating arrangements," he wrote in the log book. "Not satisfied to go in peace
they tried to get all the peons to leave and ended up by two of them
coming out 2nd best in a row, one with several loose teeth to remember
me by. After that most of them begged to be taken back and I let 3 stay.
May live to regret it. Am probably foolish to put any confidence in
these animals." Such morally inane sentiments flowed easily from the
pen of this ambassador of the American way of life. At another point,
he proposed in his notebook that a "nigger is a colored person who had
no money." Nevertheless, his prejudices did not prevent this American,
during a village celebration of Cinco de Mayo, the national holiday of
"this detestable nation," from dancing all night with "a Mexican
princess."[216] Back in the States, these men willingly taught the oil field

business to their white brothers who had come off the farms. They did not teach the skills of modernization, however, to those whom they considered racially or ethnically inferior.

As long as expanding production provided continued employment opportunities in the oil zone and as long as nothing threatened their higher incomes, the new Mexican oil workers tolerated these petty vexations of working in the foreign-owned oil industry. In fact, they welcomed the opportunity. There were no strikes in the oil zone during the Porfiriato. Unlike their brethren in the older railway and mining industries, Mexicans working for the foreign oil companies did not organize or agitate to reduce the numbers and privileges of the skilled foreign workers. They did not participate in the great strikes of 1906 and 1907. They did not engage in the campaign of "Mexico for the Mexicans" that in 1906 disconcerted American employers and skilled workers in other industries in Mexico. The quiescence of Mexican oil workers would change after 1911. In the succeeding decade, more Mexicans would be attracted to the industry, other work opportunities would shrink, and the Revolution would create the machinery for unionization. This is not to say that, later, these oil workers would become revolutionary. They were not to attack capitalism, per se. But they would seek, and succeed to a certain degree, to change how capitalism operated, according to Mexican standards. But for now, 1910, the petroleum industry and the nation poised on the cusp. Mexico was about to have simultaneously an oil boom and a revolution. The two phenomena were bound to influence each other—even before Díaz fell from power.

The Incomplete Liberal Revolution

The Mexican economy had always been profoundly politicized. In colonial days, businessmen cultivated contacts in the royal bureaucracy in order to secure licenses to sell goods to the Indians, obtain export licenses, or settle labor disputes. The colonial government set prices, regulated employer-employee relationships, and ran monopolies on mercury and tobacco. The liberal state's prominent role in seizing and reselling Church-owned properties during the reform era of the 1850s hardly diminished the political nature of economic activity in Mexico.

Thus it was, at the end of the nineteenth century, that foreign investment also became a political act. The foreigner needed government concessions, import licenses, export permits, tax exemptions, rights of way, and notarized contracts and bills of sale. An investor was required to make reports to the appropriate sections of government ministries. Railway builders purchased contracts from Mexican concessionaires. Survey companies obtained government contracts that conferred ownership of public lands in exchange for dividing the parcels for sale. By necessity, foreigners involved themselves with local, state, and national officials. Above all, they needed Mexican representatives capable of securing the necessary documents from the byzantine world of Mexican bureaucracy. No foreign businessmen could operate in Mexico without having agents represent them before the various government offices.

Therefore, foreign investors and Mexican politicians attempted to influence each other at the end of the nineteenth century—albeit in contradictory ways. Foreign investment in Mexico promoted the economic development that lent sanction to the *continuismo,* or "continuance," of Porfirio Díaz in power. This may not have been their intention, because foreigners were motivated more by profit, yet they willingly supported the administration. Foreign businessmen very soon realized that profits and politics were inseparable. For their part, Díaz's supporters used the product of the foreigners' activities, namely economic prosperity, as justification for the dictator's indispensability to the nation. Díaz wanted Mexicans to believe that he alone was responsible for their economic prosperity, and he wished foreigners to think that he was indispensable to their profits. Moreover, foreign capitalists selected those Mexican representatives who could advance their interests in the country with a degree of effectiveness. Numerous political insiders began to base their individual influence in the regime upon their relationship to the foreign interests. As a result, this mutually reinforcing process between foreigners and the influence-peddlers tended, over time, to unbalance the political equilibrium. It enhanced the power and wealth of one fraction of the elite over others. Over the long haul, foreign capital tended to discredit those native politicians whom it most benefited, because *continuismo* meant that those who felt excluded from the largess grew more numerous each year.

To say that the foreign capitalists became involved in Mexican politics is not the same as giving the foreign interests a primacy in the direction of Mexico's internal political affairs. One interpretation of the relationship between the center and periphery maintains that the industrial power manipulates the internal affairs of the "dependent" country. Military intervention, diplomatic and economic pressures, destabilization, and playing domestic factions against each other, it is said, are some of the tactics the great powers such as Britain and the United States use as they compete against each other in the periphery. The process is sometimes described as involving the active collaboration of the domestic elite—a comprador bourgeoisie—that controls politics and oppresses the proletariat in the interests of the foreigners. A corollary issue pertains to the impact of international capital. Several analysts question its ultimate utility, emphasizing that it injured long-range economic development by stifling middle-class entrepreneurship, by keeping prices high, and by exaggerating the power of the traditional elites.[217] It is said that developed nations benefit more from modernization and the periphery becomes more underdeveloped.

Such views underestimate the relationship between politics and the economy in Mexico. During the Porfiriato, Mexicans did not subordinate themselves to foreigners. Yet, the domestic politicos promoted the foreign interests for their own political and economic reasons, making the very entry of foreign capital an intimate domestic political issue. Association with foreign interests enhanced the short-term ability of one domestic political faction to dominate others. Economic growth provided the dominant politicians with the resources they needed to mollify political competition and to widen the patronage to accommodate larger numbers of supporters. In other words, during the Porfiriato, Mexicans retained the capacity either to manage or to mismanage their own economy. In any case, it was the Mexicans who set the ground rules for foreign investment—not the other way around.

All foreigners were involved, and the oilmen were no exception. After all, they entered a Mexican economy in the 1880s that despite the professions of nineteenth-century classical liberalism and free-market capitalism was nonetheless an economy in which political fiat determined profit and loss.[218] The result was the undermining of domestic entrepreneurship, an excessive dependence on foreign capital and entrepreneurship, the continued maldistribution of new wealth, and an ultimately divisive competition at the highest level of government over the spoils of political power. Foreigners were inextricably involved. It was almost the universal practice, said one American businessman, "for the companies doing business in Mexico to secure favors through the control of men influential in the Government." They granted stock to Mexican officials, appointed them as legal counsels, and made them outright gifts. Laws and procedures did not matter much. "The local officials did not often have to be dealt with if the Governor of the State or others high in the Federal Government favored the company's operations," the informant concluded.[219]

In fact, the Mexicans subordinated economic policy and the economy itself to their needs to provide a measure of political peace and social stability. What this meant was that the economy would not develop in an unfettered fashion. The government's hand was involved in every economic decision, and the railway, financial, and land policies were determined by their ultimate contribution to the political process. Gershenkron notes that late-developing economies like Mexico's always reserved a larger role for the state in the effort to "catch up" to the industrialized world. But hitching the economy to the political wagon was also important to the Mexicans.[220] For reasons relating to the consolidation of political power, the Díaz regime never permitted the free operation either of economic liberalism, of foreign capital, or of Adam Smith's "invisible hand." To a degree, liberal capitalism was what the Mexicans made of it.

If government tended to dominate the economy for political reasons, Finance Secretary José Yves Limantour's secret of success came in enhancing that control. Limantour became Mexico's economics czar by virtue of having produced the first budget surpluses since Independence. The finance secretary of Porfirio Díaz inspired the confidence of the foreign capitalists.[221] It cannot be said, however, that Limantour was a patsy or agent of the foreign interests. He was no "comprador bourgeois." Limantour often acted as a nationalist, believing that even the subsoil wealth—the products of mines and wells, including petroleum—belonged to the nation. Yet, the state would not be able to tax minerals and petroleum unless entrepreneurs with capital first started to exploit it. Domestic entrepreneurs could not and would not do it. Therefore, politicians swallowed the bitter medicine and changed the laws in order to encourage foreign investment. The laws making minerals and petroleum subject to private ownership were passed in 1884 and 1892, before Limantour began to exact his influence on the economy.

These changes, reflecting the quite revolutionary ideas of free-market capitalism, had overturned long-standing Hispanic legal traditions. From colonial times, the underground wealth such as gold, silver, and bitumens belonged to the royal patrimony. The king granted the mines to certain of his subjects under conditions that the monarch determined, meaning a tax of one-fifth (changed in the late eighteenth century to one-tenth) of the mine's production. If the grantee failed to meet the conditions, the king canceled the mining grant. At Independence, the sovereign's patrimony transferred to the government of Mexico, and colonial mining laws continued to obtain until 1884. In that year, the liberals in Congress attempted to overcome the reluctance of foreigners to invest in their mining industry by adopting an Anglo-American conception of property rights. The mining code of 1884 granted ownership of the subsoil wealth to the surface owner. A second law in 1892 further stipulated that the owner of the soil could exploit the subsoil wealth freely without any special concessions from the government. The laws were intended to encourage foreign investment rather than to remove mining and the future oil industries from direct government control.[222] Thenceforward, the foreign oilmen needed only to arrange contracts and leases from landowners in order to drill their wells. At least, this is the interpretation that many foreigners chose to give Mexican laws.

Acknowledgment of private property rights only appeared to have been a significant liberal reform.[223] In truth, mining and petroleum laws always contained a number of ambiguities, inconsistencies, and contradictions that permitted the politicians some leverage over the use of these properties. The official policy of the later administrations of Díaz, undoubtedly under Limantour's influence, recovered some measure of supervision of the economy. The law of 1901 gave power to the federal executive to issue concessions for the exploitation of mineral deposits on national lands, lakes, and lagoons, in addition to concessionary rights to import machinery duty free. A 1902 law referred to mineral deposits as eminent domain belonging to the nation. In response to the first spasms of the 1905 economic collapse, a number of congressmen proposed making the petroleum industry a public utility, requiring of oilmen that they obtain permits from the development ministry before exploiting their own private properties. The law did not pass. To deepen the legal muddle, a 1909 mining law returned to the original language of the 1884 law.[224]

No doubt, the existence of contradictory laws affecting petroleum deposits contributed to some legal uncertainties in the oil business. A state of legal imprecision was characteristic of the authoritarian regime. Power was the absolute arbiter of conflict. The Porfirian judiciary hardly provided legal interpretations, for it lacked the necessary degree of independence. The president appointed judges, and he dismissed them. The elected Supreme Court was also beholden to Díaz, because he controlled the electoral processes, even to the degree of deciding the candidates.[225] In the case of Mexico, the state under Díaz and Limantour was beginning to consolidate political and economic power—indeed, the two were often indivisible. But in a new industry in which the government wished foreigners to invest, some autonomy resided with the investor. British and American oilmen, therefore, operated in Porfirio's Mexico as if they were exploring for oil in a private property jurisdiction. They misunderstood completely that the state's reaction against free-market capitalism was already apparent in Díaz's time.

In his memoirs, written with much hindsight after the fall of Díaz, Limantour expressed reservations about these mineral laws. He claimed they led to wasteful, unregulated usage of national resources. In petroleum, for example, Limantour claimed that he had tried to avoid the most wasteful aspects of free competition in oil production—that is, offset wells. "When they began to exploit the petroleum wealth in the nation," he wrote, "the secretariat of Finance proposed and sustained the idea that to avoid the waste of this precious liquid, as happened in certain parts of the United States, it ought to be assured that discovery and exploitation occur in a large enough area to protect against the greed of those who would drill wells at the side of those already opened."[226] In other words, he had proposed a unitary method of exploitation, in which the oil companies shared production at a reduced rate to conserve oil reserves. What was ultimately to occur in Mexico's oil fields was quite the opposite of what Limantour said his vision had been. A fearsome campaign of offset drilling would lead to wasteful exploitation of Mexican petroleum in the 1910s. Limantour never did take on the oilmen directly. Others would do that later.

Nothing Causing Greater Harm

If the actions of Mexican politicians had influenced the operations of the oil companies, how did the foreign interests influence domestic politics? Did the foreign interests meddle decisively in Mexican affairs during the Porfiriato? Foreign oilmen, intent as they may have been to stick to business, became involved intimately in domestic Mexican politics. Because economics was so thoroughly politicized, anyone engaging in business, ipso facto, also assumed a political role. Pioneer oilmen were no exception. Percy Furber's Mexican lawyer was Francisco de la Barra, whose brother was to become the interim president in 1911. With the assistance of Pablo Martínez del Río, De la Barra introduced Furber directly to President Díaz. In 1897, when Furber's purchase of oil property near Papantla was contested by American interests in the Veracruz State Supreme Court, Furber paid a personal visit to Díaz and Governor Dehesa. The court subsequently decided in Furber's favor.[227] Little information exists on the political connections of American oil importer Henry Clay Pierce. His company imported products and equipment, bought land for tank farms, pioneered the new industry of oil refining, and hired Mexican workers. Moreover, from 1903 to 1907, Pierce served on the board of directors of the Mexican Central Railway, which operated under government permits and concessions. A document from the files of his competitor, Pearson, claims that the lawyers Pablo Macedo and Pablo Martínez del Río served as Mexican legal counsel for Waters-Pierce.[228] The evidence is more specific concerning the political connections of Doheny and Pearson.

Doheny's principal Mexican legal counsel came from Martínez del Río and Joaquín de Casasús, two Mexico City–based lawyers and politicians. Martínez del Río was born of the social pedigree to which Díaz, the successful general of modest background, had to marry. His father at midcentury had been a conservative moneylender and financier in the risky business of lending to bankrupt Mexican governments. Educated at Stoneyhurst in England, Martínez del Río spoke four languages and was seen in the society that surrounded Limantour. He served the regime as deputy from Puebla, which was not his home state.[229]

On the other hand, the attorney Joaquín de Casasús was from a humble Campeche family. Although not an early partisan of Díaz, Casasús cultivated elite connections and a liberal political image. By 1888, Casasús was using his gifts of oratory in the Chamber of Deputies to praise President Díaz for the economic prosperity of Mexico. He soon gained a reputation as an economist and businessman. Casasús served on the board of directors of the Mexican Central Railroad with Doheny's friend, A. A. Robinson, and later, also with Pierce. Casasús ultimately acquired such influence that he began to determine who served as governor of his home state of Campeche.[230] Both Martínez del Río and Casasús belonged to the political faction called the

Científicos. Known for their "scientific" methods of public administration, the Científicos were the supporters of Díaz who gathered around Limantour. They wielded great influence and therefore were indispensable to foreign businessmen.

Clearly, Sir Weetman Pearson enjoyed the most substantial connections among the Científicos, once again because the Mexicans themselves promoted such intimacy. Porfirio Díaz desired a British counterweight to the preponderant influence of the American economic interests. Guillermo de Landa y Escandón, board chairman of El Aguila, had been brought into the president's inner circle in 1886 after he joined the effort to amend the constitution and reelect Díaz. Landa's home in Mexico City became the center of numerous banquets in honor of don Porfirio and doña Carmen. He attracted a wide clientele of professionals, bankers, railroaders, entrepreneurs, merchants, and foreigners. After 1900, Landa y Escandón served periodically as Mexico City municipal president, governor of the Federal District, and senator from Chihuahua.[231]

The foreign oilmen may have been involved in politics through association, but they recognized that a more direct foreign intervention would be counterproductive. Little documentary evidence exists to support the notion that the oilmen were willing to marshal the foreign interests in order to save the toppling regime of their Mexican patron. In April 1911, as the rebellion against Díaz was spreading, Sir Weetman Pearson (now elevated to the peerage as Lord Cowdray) visited President William Howard Taft in the White House. At the moment, American Ambassador Henry Lane Wilson had been urging direct U.S. interference, emphasizing as an excuse the adverse effects of the unrest upon foreign investments. But the oilman took issue with the "misstatements" of the U.S. ambassador. Lord Cowdray attempted to dispel the rumor that American mining interests were suffering. Since none of the rebellions against Díaz occurred in the Huasteca, the oil interests remained unaffected by the breakdown of the Porfirian regime. British diplomats also wished to temper the overreaction of Ambassador Wilson. His Majesty's envoy to Mexico, T. B. Hohler, thought little of the American ambassador's suggestion that the foreign residents arm themselves against the rebels.[232] E. L. Doheny, who appreciated Díaz despite having experienced some friction with Limantour, was more blunt in counseling against rash action. Just three weeks before Díaz lost power, Doheny cabled President Taft, urging him *not* to send United States troops. He wrote:

Rumors have reached us that great pressure is being brought to bear in favor of intervention in Mexico by United States Forces. We are in daily telegraphic and mail communication with our agents in Tampico, Mexico City and other parts of the Republic and are certain that no situation exists which requires such intervention at present time. Only gainers thereby would be British and other foreign interests. Nothing could cause greater harm to Americans and American interests in Mexico than intervention at present time. If matter is receiving serious consideration respectfully and earnestly solicit opportunity to present the facts to you in full. Our interests in Mexico are the most important American interests next to the railways.[233]

The Standard Oil Company would be implicated to a much greater degree than other oil companies in the rebellion against the Díaz regime. Accounts of Standard Oil's favoritism for the revolt of Francisco I. Madero appeared widely in the world press. Vice President Corral on a trip to Spain denounced the American foreign interests for aiding the enemies of the Díaz regime. The Standard Oil Company denied "all interference in the affairs of the Mexican Republic, with which it has no connection moral or material."[234] Despite its denial, Standard Oil became drawn into Mexican affairs through mystery and intrigue. A man identifying himself as C. R. Troxel and claiming to be the representative of Standard Oil Company, in April 1911 attempted to make contact with the Madero forces at El Paso. Obviously the man wished to be noticed. Pretending to act in secrecy, he asked to be introduced to the Madero officials, revealing to his go-betweens that he wished to offer the rebellion up to $1 million in order to secure oil concessions. The agent made it a point that Standard no longer wished to work in Mexico through the Waters-Pierce Oil Company, on whom the Díaz government had imposed "unreasonable taxes." Troxel sought to draw up a formal contract, take it to Madero for his signature, and then deliver it to New York for the approval of Standard's president, John Archbold. Within days of the connection, the U.S. attorney general in Washington, D.C., had a full report of Troxel's meetings in hotels, Turkish baths, and massage parlors.[235]

Soon a whole covey of intermediaries became involved, four men with English names and four with Hispanic names. At least one was an El Paso attorney. Several bragged about knowing Alfonso Madero, brother of Francisco. Then the intermediaries decided with Troxel to charge Standard Oil a 5 percent commission, while also obtaining from the Madero *insurrectos* an exclusive privilege to sell their cowhides in El Paso. For good measure, the intermediaries also formed a company to sell arms and ammunition to Madero, in violation of U.S.

neutrality laws.[236] Troxel negotiated the loan for oil concessions with Gustavo Madero, uncle of the rebellion's leader, in an El Paso public park. The Maderos reportedly wanted to be able to cancel the concessions if they should be able to repay Standard Oil before the due date. Troxel compromised, agreeing that the Maderos could cancel but only after a five-year time lapse. All of this information Troxel freely related to a man whom he had not known previously but who was an informant for the U.S. attorney general.[237] Apparently, Troxel was less interested in obtaining a deal agreeable to Standard Oil (oilmen detested short-term contracts) than in gaining maximum exposure of his "secret" negotiations.

The Department of State was concerned about the authenticity of these reports and wished to dissuade Standard Oil from intervening in Mexican political affairs. Secretary of State Philander C. Knox detailed the entire story to John D. Archbold, cautioning him not to violate neutrality laws. At the time, Standard Oil (New Jersey) was in the process of regrouping following the Supreme Court's antitrust decision of 1911. It was also severing its relationship with Waters-Pierce. For some years, the company remained very reticent about tempting the federal prosecutors and refrained from new foreign ventures. Archbold disavowed any involvement in the Madero rebellion. He had known of Mr. C. R. Troxel, however, as Archbold informed Knox. Once, in January of the previous year, Troxel had attempted to interest Standard Oil in the purchase of an oil concession in Chihuahua. He claimed his partners were Alberto Terrazas and the latter's son-in-law, Governor Enrique Creel. Standard had declined.[238] Troxel was willing to deal with Porfirians one year and *insurrectos* the next.

In reality, Standard Oil was not yet ready to enter Mexico and stood to gain nothing from having Troxel negotiate a concession on its behalf. When the company did go into Mexico, as we shall see, Jersey Standard would not seek an oil concession that no Mexican politician dared give to the world's most notorious trust. It would, instead, lease lands directly from landowners and buy out an established company. Could it be, then, that Troxel acted for an unnamed competitor? A vengeful Henry Clay Pierce perhaps? Pierce certainly knew of the Mexicans' pathological fear of the oil trusts. As one whose stormy but profitable relationship to Standard Oil was nearing an end, he was certainly interested that Jersey Standard not take up a rival position in Mexico by buying out the Pearson or Doheny interests—whether Díaz fell or not. After all, Pierce was not about to leave the Mexican market just because

he lost his connection to Jersey Standard. The American consul at
Tampico suggested that the Pearson interests in London had originated the allegations.[239] But the charge does not fit the style of Lord
Cowdray's organization. At any rate, very soon he would attempt to interest Standard Oil in buying his own properties. What would it profit
him to defame the company he hoped would buy out his own interests?
Troxel did not provide any answers, for he quickly disappeared from
the annals of oil history. Yet, his crude machinations were to generate
a whole decade of hostility and suspicions between Mexican politicians
and foreign oilmen.

Although he had asked for the neutrality of the United States during
the Madero rebellion, Lord Cowdray was not about to forsake his
benefactor Porfirio Díaz. When Díaz resigned, Lord Cowdray offered
Díaz an English estate for retirement. Apparently, he and other foreign
businessmen cooperated to get Díaz safely out of Mexico City and on
the ship to Europe. Díaz expressed his thanks for the offer but refused
to stop in England. He too retired in Paris.[240] This loyalty to his old
friends prevented Cowdray from eliminating any of the old Porfirians,
neither his directors nor his attorneys, from his organization. It was to
cause him some embarrassment later.

The politicians surrounding President Porfirio Díaz bore direct responsibility for the success of British interests in the nascent Mexican
oil industry. Mexican liberals had adopted a commitment to modernizing and strengthening the nation by encouraging the entry of foreign
capital. Díaz himself supported economic expansion. It provided him
with the resources to enhance federal power and assure his own continuance in office. Yet the Mexican politicians, for historical reasons,
could not appear to allow the economy to be dominated by American
interests. The administration therefore showed considerable favoritism
toward the work of European businessmen. Díaz himself invited Sir
Weetman Pearson. Deliberately contributing to Pearson's engineering
and business triumphs in the country, the government agreed to liberal
contracts and financially underwrote many of his projects. Although
it declined to offer capital for Pearson's oil business, the government
did provide other kinds of favoritism. Tariff protection, access to political insiders, tax benefits, generous concessions, and fuel sales to the
National Railways helped Pearson maintain his business momentum
for an entire decade while he competed against more experienced
American oilmen in Mexico. Pearson's astute creation of managerial

organization and development of technological expertise accomplished the rest.

Mexican politicians contributed significantly to the manner in which capitalism developed within their own country. Porfirio Díaz's reputation has been much diminished by the Revolution, yet his economic policies had an enduring impact. El Aguila survived to become the largest foreign oil concern in the country. Furthermore, the dichotomous ownership of the oil industry promoted by Díaz's political requirements later weakened the foreign oilmen's resistance to the economic nationalism soon to be generated by the Mexican Revolution. Successive Mexican administrations after 1912 increased taxation and worked to erode the property rights of the foreign oil companies. American and British oilmen may have originated in another world, but no sooner had they arrived than Mexican elites began to refine the impact of their presence. The working class too would apply its own imperative to the activities of the foreign entrepreneurs in Mexico. But for now, the oil boom was on.

There is a final irony of the Porfirian age. On the very day that the foreign oilmen shipped out the first volume exports of petroleum—25 May 1911—their leading benefactor, President Porfirio Díaz, fled into exile.

CHAPTER TWO

The Great Mexican Oil Boom

They were like the proverbial locusts. Once the news spread that the wells Potrero del Llano No. 4 and Juan Casiano No. 7 came in, the oilmen, drillers, lease-takers, and fortune seekers swarmed into Mexico. They came singly and in groups. They arrived at Tampico by boat and on the train. Encouraged by strong demand for petroleum products and prolific discoveries of oil, they continued developing Mexican production for a decade, searching the *monte* (tropical rain forests of the Veracruz lowlands) for oil leases and drilling wells. These foreigners worked right through the Revolution. By the end of the decade, more than 155 separate companies and 345 individual entrepreneurs and partnerships were operating in Mexico. For many, this was just another oil boom. These men had previously participated in the Ohio, Illinois, Kansas, and East Texas oil strikes. Their work had been speculative, sometimes wasteful, and occasionally rewarding in individual wealth. Then they would move on to other oil booms in Oklahoma and West Texas. When the swarm of opportunists departed, the big companies—and the Mexican oil workers—would inherit what was left.

One thing was certain: foreigners were making the oil boom as if they were operating in the United States. They operated in Spanish only when it was necessary to notarize an oil lease or hire domestic labor. Most of the time, they interpreted Mexican property laws as if they were carbon copies of U.S. statutes. They resisted Mexican interpretations and resented any meddling in their business affairs. At a time

101

when the federal and state authorities in the United States were tightening the regulation of business and busting the trusts, the expatriot American oilmen viewed Mexico as the new frontier of deregulation. Mexican officials could not do much about it. Perhaps the Díaz regime might have been able to staunch the breakneck speed with which the foreigners were constructing the oil industry during the great Mexican oil boom. But Díaz and his clique had been swept away by a hurricane that would not abate for ten years.

During the Revolution, those with a tenuous hold on federal power desperately needed the tax revenues provided by oil exports. All other sectors of the economy lay prostrate. Those who fought for political power, and there were many, sought to deny the federal authorities control of the oil fields. The result was a buildup of government resentment toward the freewheeling, powerful foreign interests, threats of drastic action against the oil companies, but little governmental influence on how the nation's oil business was being conducted. A booming foreign market and anemic domestic consumption of Mexican oil production gave many advantages to the foreign oilmen. They proceeded to create an Anglo-American capitalist haven out of the Huasteca.

In the popular mind, the scramble for oil leases involved cutthroat tactics, lawlessness, duping of naïve landholders by greedy foreigners, assassination of Mexican notaries, and company thugs known as *guardias blancas*.[1] To a degree, the era of exploration and oil boom in Mexico did have its distinctively "Wild West" character. It was a capitalistic, free-market free-for-all. But much has been exaggerated. Mainly, the foreign oilmen can be accused of attempting to Americanize a portion of Mexico. The great Mexican oil boom almost overwhelmed a country distracted by revolution. Almost.

Contracts in Very Poor Condition

One of the principal reasons contributing to the creation of an unregulated Anglo-American business world was the growth of international demand for oil and the decline of domestic Mexican demand in the second decade of the twentieth century. Heretofore used principally for illumination, crude petroleum was gaining additional versatility and demand. Oil's use in fueling railways, ships, and industries gained momentum, and oilmen pioneered the conversion of railway locomotives to fuel oil, substituting for wood and coal. This conversion occurred as early as 1889 in Russia. In the 1890s, Doheny introduced petroleum to the locomotives of California.

Railway men in Mexico too converted their locomotives to fuel oils, dispensed in 10,000-gallon tanks along the rail lines, effecting savings and improving performance. With oil, the railways saved approximately 40 percent on their fuel bills. Doheny estimated that three and one-half barrels of oil, costing $2.60, accomplished the work of one ton of coal, which cost between $3.45 and $4.00.[2] Fuel oil weighed less and was more efficient. Mexico's locomotives consumed only sixty-two pounds of domestic fuel oil per kilometer compared to ninety-one pounds of imported and domestic coal. Fuel oil performed better over flat terrain. On the 189-mile Tehuantepec railway, stretching from the Atlantic port of Puerto México to the Pacific terminal of Salina Cruz, oil fuel improved the speed of the locomotive by 16 percent over coal.

Other sectors of the Mexican economy were also in the process of increasing their usage of domestically produced petroleum. El Aguila produced inexpensive fuel oil with a low flash point of 80 degrees Fahrenheit through preliminary distillation at its "topping" plants. It sold the oil for use in sugar mills, electrical light and power stations, breweries, steel works, cement works, and brick factories. Moreover, the Mexican government refitted its coastal vessels with boilers that burned petroleum.[3] However, Mexican fuel oil gained greater usage outside of the country in the second decade of the twentieth century.

Owing to its abundance and low price between 1911 and the First World War, Mexican petroleum lent itself to expanded uses in the United States and throughout Latin America. Railways and dredgers used in building the Panama Canal were equipped with oil-burning boilers. Once the interoceanic canal was opened to shipping in 1915, Doheny's tankers delivered petroleum to the Chilean nitrate and copper industries.[4] In England and the United States, industries adapted fuel oil to annealing furnaces, making nuts, and distilling zinc. Even biscuits came to be baked in petroleum-fueled ovens. The manufacturers of oil burners and furnaces multiplied, and at the end of the war, apartment buildings and homes converted their heating systems from coal to oil. Business was brisk. "We have been literally swamped with requests for our [oil-burning] installations in buildings here," reported the president of the Petroleum Heat and Power Company of New York. "Our ability to meet this demand depends upon an uninterrupted Oil supply from Mexico."[5] Markets for asphalt, for which heavy Mexican crude petroleum was particularly appropriate, also expanded. United States refineries increased their production of Mexican asphalt from 114,000 tons in 1914 to more than 674,000 tons in 1919. In the same year, Mexican crude yielded more asphalt than did domestic American crude oil. Great Britain and Europe had few asphalt roads before World War I. But following the war, Shell's refineries in the Netherlands produced bitumen from Mexico's heavy crude oils for that purpose.[6]

The second decade of the twentieth century was one in which the world's fighting ships began to be converted from coal to fuel oil. As First Lord of the Admiralty, young Winston Churchill laid plans to provide twelve super Dreadnoughts, twelve cruisers, and forty destroyers of the British navy with oil-burning equipment. However, the British Admiralty used little Mexican oil. Its sulfur content was too high, its flash point too low, and it smoked excessively. In January of 1914, the Admiralty attempted to purchase some two hundred thousand tons per year of Mexican fuel oil. Cowdray used his very best oil to fulfill this contract, but it was not good enough. British warships ran mostly on the lighter, sulfur-free, American fuel oil.[7] Doheny too suffered from the British Admiralty's exclusion of Mexican oil. He once told a Senate hearing on the matter that he believed there existed a conspiracy between Shell and the Russian companies (before the Bolshevik Revolution) to provide for the British navy. "I went over there [to England] two years ago, at the solicitation of English capitalists, to talk about selling oil from Mexico," Doheny testified. "I found that their specifications were very ingeniously contrived by people who were selling oil from other places. The arrangement was such as to exclude Mexican oil." Doheny also harbored hostility toward the U.S. Department of the Navy for not buying Mexican fuel oil.[8] But the product was just not good enough.

Not only were navies of Europe and the United States converting their ships to fuel oil but so too were the merchant marine and well-known steamship lines. Overseas transport and passenger firms like White Star Line and Cunard Company completed the conversion before the war. Many smaller steamship lines put off converting from coal to oil-burning engines during the time of high oil prices—during World War I—but began conversion again when prices began to decline in 1919.[9] In any case, fuel oil was rapidly replacing coal.

That Mexican oil did not serve the needs of British warships did not bode ill for exports. After the war broke out in August 1914, Mexican

oil poured into U.S. markets. It formed the oil stocks for industrial usage and replaced the finer U.S. fuels being diverted to American and
British warships. The New York office of Anglo-Mexican negotiated a
number of sales contracts with the larger American companies such as
The Texas Company, Standard Oil of New Jersey, and Gulf, which were
selling their U.S. production to the British Admiralty.[10] Attempting to
produce a nonodorous kerosene, chemists of El Aguila in 1920 had
tried various methods of removing the sulfur from the oil. They ran the
crude through lead salts and heated the product in order to decompose
the sulfuretted hydrogen. It was no use. "The remaining kerosene still
contained sulphur," they reported. The same was true of the fuel oil.
The United States provided a total of 85.2 percent of British petroleum
supplies in 1917; Mexico contributed a mere 6.3 percent.[11]

Given the expansion of markets, exports of Mexican production to
the United States and other foreign destinations increased dramatically
throughout the second decade of the twentieth century. Mexico provided the United States market with a mere 1 percent of its petroleum
in 1911. But by 1919, Mexican oil satisfied 14 percent of a vastly expanded American consumption of petroleum products. Mexico's petroleum was shipped to refineries on the Gulf Coast and in the North
Atlantic states. By the end of the decade, well over 80 percent of Mexican crude oil headed for U.S. ports. The remaining 20 percent or less
of exported Mexican petroleum was destined for Latin America and
Great Britain.[12]

Mexican production expanded up to 1916 because of the flush production of its major wells—only half of the story of the great Mexican
oil boom. Price trends made up the other half. The heavier weight and
location of Mexican production made it a part of the Gulf Coast market, where it competed and mixed with Texas, Louisiana, and (later)
Oklahoma crude oils. It was priced consistently lower than the lighter
Appalachian crude of Pennsylvania. The heavier Mexican crude oils
were classed similarly to the heavy California crude oils. The former
served Atlantic Coast markets and the latter served Pacific Coast demand. Between the discovery of Spindletop in 1901 and Potrero del
Llano in 1910, oil prices in the gulf hovered around forty cents and
seventy cents per barrel. Those prices rose above one dollar per barrel
during the First World War, as demand rose and U.S. exploration declined. By 1919, prices stood at nearly twice their prewar levels. (See
graph 1.) High prices meant that Mexico, or more precisely the foreign
oil companies there, reaped profits in greater ratio than their expanded

output. Domestically, prices for bunker fuel also rose.[13] Few oil-producing nations in the twentieth century ever again would benefit, as Mexico did from 1917 to 1920, from the simultaneous rise of production and prices.

For the most part, Mexican governments permitted the export-led oil development. During the Revolution, it was the only economic bright spot and contributed to scarce public revenues. Mexico's peculiar petroleum geology, however, imposed some of its own limits on how it yielded up its treasures. Never before had oilmen encountered oil deposits in limestone formations. The gulf plain of northern Veracruz averages a width of thirty miles inland from the coast. It is bounded on the west by terraces, valleys, and the irregular foothills of the Eastern Sierras. "Scattered over the plain are characteristic cone-shaped hills which seldom rise over one hundred feet," Ralph Arnold, a Stanford geologist, reported in 1911. "These hills are made up chiefly of basalt, and play a very important role in the oil accumulation of the region, most of the oil seepages occurring at or near their bases."[14]

The Tamasopo limestone, a stratum some 3,000 to 7,000 feet thick, held the principal petroleum deposits in its uppermost reaches. The limestone began anywhere between 1,000 to 2,500 feet below the surface. It was both porous and cavernous. Located well below sea level, the limestone formations permitted relatively free circulation of both oil and water. Usually, water underlies the oil because it is denser. The mixture remained under great pressure from gas and thus both the oil and the water were quite hot. The oil pouring forth from the well head, however, reached very high temperatures, up to 149 degrees F., not because it was that temperature underground but because of the heat created by the friction of being rapidly forced through the well casing by gas pressures. Wells pinched back, purposely slowing the rate of natural flow, sufficed to lower temperatures of the crude.[15] The thicker oil would have been difficult to force through the casing had not the gas pressure heated the oil, rendering it less viscous. Once on the surface, the heavier oil cooled to the consistency of cold honey. It had to be heated artificially in order to force it through pipelines and terminal lines.

Once the oil boom was on, the lease-takers and speculators arrived in number. The East Texas boom was about over and the Mexican border provided no barrier to the speculative oilmen. To them, a boom was the same anywhere. Or at least, they would attempt to make it so. Some, like Michael A. Spellacy, were veterans of the Alaska gold rush. Others might have participated in the brief Spanish-American War;

still others had experience in the U.S. oil booms of Texas and Kansas. Spellacy arrived in Mexico in 1908 as a driller. Then he enlisted his brokers and some American financial backers in securing leases near Tuxpan and Tampico. Aided by the changes in Mexican mining laws dating from the 1880s, these pioneer lessors made oil leases with the fee-simple private-property owners. As in the United States, no government concession was necessary to start drilling. They usually paid the landowner an up-front fee, an annual rental fee, and perhaps a percentage of future production. By law, no royalties were due the government. None were offered. Mexican attorneys and U.S. lawyers who knew Spanish (William Buckley is a good example) established themselves in Tampico and specialized in perfecting oil leases. These leases usually obligated the lessee to drill within a certain amount of time and offered the lessor or landowner an annual rental, say six pesos per hectare, and a royalty, say ten centavos per barrel of oil produced.[16]

Then, the lease-makers would sell their leases to a drilling or producing company for development. The mestizo and mulatto smallholders and squatters and the Spanish hacendados of the coastal plain north of Tuxpan willingly cooperated. They operated within the American private-property system. But the Indian villagers south of Tuxpan were very suspicious of these first lease-takers. They had deep memories of being exploited by Mexicans and believed the Americans equally nefarious. Besides, they operated under corporate, village ownership of land, not individual. Therefore, lease-takers who did succeed in making a number of oil leases with these villagers had to specify that all village residents, collectively, were to receive royalties of any oil production.[17] This was not the only Mexican wrinkle in an otherwise American fabric.

The peculiarly Mexican conditions of private-property ownership in the Huasteca also created some problems to the lease-takers. Possession of isolated land was often quite informal; family lineages and inheritance records were not well maintained; and legal marriages were not generally practiced among the humble folk of the rural Huasteca. The lease "pioneers" who passed through the *monte* looking for prospects had to go to Tuxpan and other towns to check the civil records for proper titles. This was called "perfecting the title." Still, the possibility of competing leases and lease jumping was quite real. As one not-so-broad-minded lease-taker from Oklahoma put it: "There is no title down there that is any good because there are so many illegitimate children."[18] El Aguila attorneys, when they acquired the Horcones hacienda, discovered that numerous branches of the Suara family had divided up ownership of the property into 1,200 shares. Between 1912 and 1920, the company's lands department acquired 1,109 and 1/36 of the shares and were still pursuing the purchase of the 90 and 35/36 remaining shares from six family members. Their information on the remaining owners was as follows: "Refugia Sanchez is the concubine of Felicitos Suara and Maria Margarita, Sinforlana, and Adela are his sisters. The heirs of Cirila are minors (6) who live with Maria Margarita, their aunt and with Donato Marquez. These shares will be very difficult to procure. The remaining 5⁵/₉ shares are owned by Sara Carballo y Suara whose whereabouts are unknown."[19]

Mexican landowners did not take much time in learning that they could manipulate the leasing system to their advantage. All one needed was a Mexican attorney. Soon oilmen had to tighten up the legal clauses of the leases so as to reduce the opportunities of landowners to find them in default of the lease contract. "Lic. Rodríguez [of the El Aguila legal staff] stated he has had in mind for some time recommending that all of our subsoil contracts stipulate a period within which exploration work should be commenced, in order that the land owner could not allege the contract was null and void due to our not having undertaken any exploration work during a given period."[20] Of course, El Aguila was complaining that landowners were eager to find any breach in old leases so that they could make new leases at higher rentals and royalties. They were catching on to the American system of oil boom.

These leases were to give the oilmen trouble. The complicated leases and multiple claims served as a source of conflict which the government could resolve by imposing its own regulations. Some Mexicans were motivated to "jump" a lease held by a company whose wells had already proven the property. Thus, the claimant and his backers, whether Mexicans or Americans, could drill a risk-free well.[21] Huasteca, one of the earliest entrants into the oil-leasing business, ultimately had to revise its initial nonchalance toward its leases. A competitor described their problems:

[T]he Huasteca Company, who had formerly never taken any steps to perfect their subsoil contracts but had left them in their original state and expected everybody else to respect them no matter what their legal situation might be, had lately changed their tactics and started a campaign of curing the defects. [T]hey have considerably increased their activities in that direction, having taken new and larger quarters for their legal and lands departments and having

engaged a very capable young attorney from Mexico City, who is working together with their American lawyer. Some of their contracts are in very poor
condition legally, but they are working energetically and apparently now fully
realize that their old policy . . . will not be sufficient to protect their interests.[22]

As the oil boom got started, leasing of oil lands became more common than buying them outright. Land in the Huasteca had been relatively inexpensive before the Dos Bocas blowout. The first oil entrants
like Percy Furber, Doheny, and the Pearson interests could buy large
tracts of land. Once the oil boom got under way, land prices shot sky-
ward. Consequently, the early comers like Huasteca and El Aguila
owned most of the land held in fee-simple status in the oil zones, and
the perhaps four hundred other companies and individuals who arrived
later leased most of the remaining hectares held by the oil interests. In
1919, the total amount of leased and owned oil lands amounted to
nearly 2.7 million hectares. Seventy-five percent of the prospective oil
lands were leased. A latecomer like the Tal Vez Oil Company, a name
that certainly expresses the speculative character of the industry, held
rights to thirty thousand acres of oil land in 1919 but owned only five
thousand acres outright.[23]

Companies that arrived late to a particular oil district, however, discovered the best prospects were gone and the remaining lands cost a
great deal. This was the case when El Aguila attempted to expand into
the northern zone. In 1917, its agent reported that the rental and commission charges on leases around Pánuco had skyrocketed after several
big wells had come in. "Practically all the land in the area . . . has been
leased," they reported, "and any acquisitions we make will have to
be sub-leases or transfers, and hence will cost us more than if we had
gone into the field years ago."[24] Lease prices rose and fell according to
the success of drilling activity nearby. "The average rental paid by the
companies amounts to $1.92 per hectare [1 hectare = 2.47 acres],"
one report stated, "but the rentals paid by the different companies vary
greatly. One company pays as much as $4,166 per hectare, three com-
panies pay about $2,000 per hectare, and many pay from $500 to
$1,000 per hectare, while other companies pay only a nominal rental or
none at all."[25] Not more than 10 percent of all these properties would
ever yield any oil at all. But this was how the lease-takers made money.
They effected leases with landowners and sold them for a windfall to
producers. Naturally, some leases never got bought. Others went for a
fortune. It was the same in Mexico as it had been in East Texas and
Ohio before that and western Pennsylvania before that.

Throwing Cable over the Derrick

Naturally, the whole object of securing leases was to drill wells that produced oil. Drilling attracted a second classical character of the industry—the oil driller. As in the United States, drilling was accomplished on several legal bases. The large firms hired North American drillers, nearly all of whom had prior experience on a monthly salary. Usually these drillers were also given opportunities to share a percentage of the production. Many drillers served as wildcatters, working purely on the speculation that a property in which they had some financial interest, or for which they worked without a wage, would yield production. This could be very risky. Most wells—probably 75 percent—were dry holes. But wildcatters might also gain great individual wealth. Much of the drilling work in Mexico, like growing carrots, was seasonal. Rigging and equipment could be moved easily only during the dry season. From June to September, the rains prevented mules, horses, and the five- and ten-ton Caterpillar tractors from hauling the equipment over the muddy roads.[26] The Mexican oil boom occupied many drillers, all foreigners. Few Mexican workers ever participated in this aspect of the business. The technology was alien to them, known only to the American or European drillers, who were loath to transfer it to any Mexican.

The drilling crews in Mexico had come down from East Texas. These Texans, Oklahomans, and Midwesterners had learned their craft from the Pennsylvanians, who had taught the oil industry to others around Beaumont and Corsicana. They behaved very much as they had in East Texas, except in coping with the enormous gas pressures of the Tamasopo limestone. That required some innovations. W. M. Hudson, who in 1906 had come to Tampico with some farmers from Llano, recognized this element of danger in Mexico. He and a partner had bought the Santa Fe Ranch, which had twenty-one kilometers of frontage on the Pánuco River at Topila Estero. Having witnessed the Dos Bocas blowout from afar, Hudson knew that the gas pressure in the limestone formation was ferocious.

Shortly after Potrero del Llano had come in, Waters-Pierce agents from the refinery at Tampico came to lease Santa Fe, forty miles upriver. As owner, Hudson was to receive 20 percent of production. "We'll agree in this contract to drill as many as three wells," the Pierce agent told Hudson. "If it's oil, we'll punch the ground full of holes."

They drilled the wells with standard percussion tools, the rig having been hauled up the Pánuco River on a barge. At two thousand feet, the sudden release of gas in the well blew the drill stem out through the derrick. A shower of rocks then followed from the well casing. Within five minutes, the rocks destroyed the timbers 110 feet atop the derrick and oil began to flow out at a rate of 17,000 bd. The manager had a dam placed across a creek below the well, and the flow of crude collected in this makeshift earthen reservoir. Hudson later inspected the rocks that had been blown out through the well. They looked like "creek boulders," round and smooth but coated with asphalt. Almost all the rocks were larger than the diameter of the pipe out of which they had passed! Hudson and two partners made about $25,000 apiece in selling their well to Pierce.[27]

When Pierce took over Santa Fe, they brought in Clinton D. Martin. Martin had dropped out of college, where he had acquired little scientific education to begin with, and entered the oil business in 1901 in Kansas. In the next twelve years, Martin worked for a pipeline company and three different refining firms. Then he came to Mexico for the Compañía Mexicana de Combustibles, Waters-Pierce's new production company. As soon as Pierce took over the Santa Fe wells, however, they all went to salt water. Martin eventually drifted out of Mexico and returned home.[28]

El Aguila had obtained some of its early drillers from the European oil fields. E. J. Nicklos learned his trade as a teenager in Galicia, a part of the Austro-Hungarian empire, in the 1890s. His father had helped build a refinery. As a young student, Nicklos broke into the business by rolling barrels around the refinery's yard. In 1907, he was hired through the auspices of the Pearson's business office in London. His crew consisted of Canadian drillers and an English bookkeeper and carpenter. They used the Canadian pole-tooled derricks, which operated on the same principle as cable tools except that the drill was suspended on iron rods instead of cables. Little scientific knowledge was involved in site selection. Dr. Orchesky, a geologist with experience in Galicia, directed the crews to drill near the oil seepages. The Pearson group set Nicklos to drilling with two rigs in Chiapas. He gathered together an eighty-man Mexican crew to drag a forty-horsepower boiler through the rain forest, hacking away the foliage with machetes as they went. Guy wires held up the smokestacks. He struck oil at five hundred feet, but it was no gusher. About 120 bd flowed gently through the ten-inch casing and slowed considerably after several days. The creek into which

Fig. 6. Preparation of an oil drilling site, c. 1913. Mexican workers clear the dense rain-forest vegetation of the Golden Lane in preparation for well drilling. From the Eberstadt Photo Collection, courtesy of the Barker Texas History Center at the University of Texas.

it flowed was dammed up, and the crude set afire so it would not seep into a nearby village. The Pearson group could not find enough crude in Chiapas to justify pipelines, storage tanks, and export terminals.

Nicklos later moved to Tampico, where he performed some drilling for the Shell Company of Corona, formed in 1912. "I got some [cable] tools together and started contracting," he reminisced. Corona gave Nicklos one-half interest in the wells that he brought in near Pánuco. There the gas pressure continued to present the drillers with problems and dangers. Nicklos recalls bringing in a well in 1920:

> [A]s soon as you'd hit . . . the oil, why, the water would start coming out first and the oil was behind it. Well, as soon as the water started boiling over we'd start getting the tools out as quick as we could, but we never did get them out all the way. The last three or four hundred feet of the cable was thrown right back over the top of the derrick, then land, perhaps a hundred, two hundred feet away from the hole. But we had all of our steel and iron and everything covered up with big heavy logs or timber or planks and also the gate valves, so that if the tools did come and happen to hit then wouldn't set off a spark and . . . [start] a fire.[29]

In December of 1921, Nicklos pulled out of Mexico and deposited his considerable earnings in the Houston National Bank.[30]

These early drillers later learned to cope with the extraordinary gas pressure. During drilling, they set the heavy casings in concrete cellars with elaborate tubing configurations beneath the derrick floor. Thus, the drillers could pinch back the well almost immediately after the oil was struck.[31] When the well was flowing, the crews separated the gas from the crude oil. Huasteca's veteran geologist, Ezequiel Ordóñez, in 1932 estimated that the oil companies had vented or flared a total of one billion cubic feet of gas from the wells of Mexico during three decades of oil production. Very little gas was used beyond the energy needs of the isolated oil camps. A gas pipeline to Mexico City's urban population could have been five hundred kilometers long just to negotiate the passes of the Sierra Oriental. At one of Doheny's big wells, a tube was attached to the well head, separating the gas from the crude and shunting it to a nearby hilltop, where it was flared. The torch at this site burned continuously for ten years.[32]

Among the drillers and field personnel who worked for competing companies, there was great camaraderie. They lent each other fishing tools to get the drilling tools out of the wells. Another drilling contractor once lent Nicklos a boiler in Pánuco until another drilling rig could be shipped out from Tampico. The cooperation extended to the geologists as well. Everette DeGolyer, who had become the head geologist for El Aguila, collected extensive records of the activities of other companies. He even had copies of their well logs and drilling records.[33] DeGolyer traded information with others. The fact that C. Willard Hayes and DeGolyer were employed by El Aguila did not prevent them from sharing their knowledge and experiences with geologists like Stanford University's Ralph Arnold and V. R. Garfías and others, like Mr. Cummings, who was employed by East Coast Oil.[34]

Some drillers attempted to wildcat on their own accounts. Although it remained speculative, drilling did have a certain logic. "Drilling, in practically every case, has shown that no commercially productive well has been drilled farther than ¼ mile distant from some sort of surface evidence, such as seepages, asphalt deposits, or gas emanations," explained Arnold, "and in many instances negative results have been obtained much nearer than this to good surface indications."[35] Outside of these areas, drilling would be more or less hit or miss, usually miss. Drillers and geologists located wells by "walking or going over the country and noticing the general contour and the surface layout."[36] As yet, no one used sophisticated instruments to find oil.

The many wildcat drillers who failed did not leave a record of it. A few who did strike it rich wrote about it later. Mordelo L. Vincent told of his successful drilling at Tepetate in 1914. There he and a partner had discovered an important oil field, but the blowout had forced the casing back up through part of the derrick and a plume of oil and gas roared out. Vincent's inexperienced crew fought unsuccessfully for days to place a valve on the runaway well. Finally, an agent for Gulf Oil arrived. "I know the spot you are in," he told the partners, "and I know you can trade if you want to. Gulf Oil is prepared to give you one million smackers for this lease, plus 33⅓ royalty, and we will move our experienced crews in here, plug this wild bastard, and drill another well right beside it." "Shake hands with a millionaire," replied Vincent.[37] Some of these oilmen, like Vincent and Nicklos, left Mexico wealthy and others, penniless. Yet, together they developed the Mexican oil industry during the great boom much as they and their peers had accomplished in Pennsylvania, Ohio, Illinois, California, Texas, and Oklahoma.

Along the coastal plain from Chiapas to the Pánuco River, these men set down more than seven hundred oil wells during the great Mexican oil boom. One-half of those wells produced crude petroleum in commercial quantities.[38] Despite the large number of producing wells, Mexico's major production was really taken from a small number of prolific wells. They had been drilled to depths of between 1,700 and 3,000 feet, at which point the men would stop if the well flowed to salt water or nothing at all. The producing wells were allowed to flow of their own pressure, without pumping. In 1914, for example, most producing wells were yielding from 15 to 200 bd. Every company relied upon one or two great wells. El Aguila had Potrero del Llano No. 4, which ran 37,000 bd; and Alazán No. 4, yielding 17,000 bd. Huasteca had Juan Casiano No. 7, flowing at 12,000 bd.[39] Wildcat drillers working speculatively on their own accounts merely rounded out production. They were hoping to drill a well that could be sold to the bigger companies or to find that one "gusher," against all odds, that would make them a big company. It had been the same in U.S. oil booms.

A Few Hundred Meters Distant

The drill bits of innumerable rigs ultimately delineated three distinct zones of Mexico's oil fields. Each zone had definitive geographic boundaries, yielded distinctive crude oils, and presented different problems and possibilities of exploitation. At the northern extremity of the coastal oil region lay the so-called northern fields. Doheny's El Ebano in the state of San Luis Potosí had been the cornerstone of this zone. But between 1910 and 1920, other foreign interests challenged Huasteca's supremacy here and opened up production on both sides of the Pánuco River, centering on the town of Pánuco and the district of Topila. An independent firm named the East Coast Oil Company, apparently connected to the Southern Pacific Railroad, opened up production on the Pánuco River in 1911. Its crude oil was identical in density and asphaltic content to that of El Ebano. Soon, other companies started production in the northern zone, but problems of transport (the oil was too thick to pipe), quality (it was expensive to refine), and leases (the area had small producers) combined to retard the full development of the Pánuco-Topila fields.[40] Once shorn of its ties to Standard Oil, the Waters-Pierce interests moved upstream, as the saying goes. From its refinery at Tampico, it developed modest producing properties along the Pánuco River. The Royal Dutch/Shell established its new Mexican subsidiary, La Corona, in the producing fields near the town of Pánuco. The Texas Company of Mexico, Gulf, and eventually Standard Oil would also secure important leases in the northern fields. Only El Aguila among the large firms would have no presence at all in the north.

One characteristic of production tended to make the northern fields distinctive. The crude petroleum found here was very heavy and viscous, yielding abundant tars and asphalt but little kerosene and gasoline. At El Ebano, the oil averaged about 12 degrees Baumé, a standard measure of specific gravity. The lower the specific gravity, the thicker and heavier was the oil. Pánuco and Topila crude measured from 10 to 15 degrees Baumé. These heavier oils had to undergo a rudimentary refining called topping before being converted into fuel oil. In general, the wells flowed more slowly here. One also found few pipelines in the northern fields. Only the East Coast Oil Company and La Corona had pipelines, but they were not lengthy, the longest covering the twenty-four miles from the east coast wells to the Pánuco River. The oil had to be heated before it would flow properly. Two pumping stations were also needed to push it through the pipe. Most crude petroleum in the northern fields was transported to tank farms, refineries, and export terminals at Tampico aboard river barges. Five of the larger producing companies had Mississippi stern-wheelers to carry the barges down to Tampico. By 1914, three independent barge companies had also been established to carry the crude from Pánuco to Tampico.[41] Generally, the lower returns on oil exploration and refining rendered the northern fields somewhat less attractive than those oil lands near Tuxpan to the south. In the 1920s, however, the north would remain the foundation of the Mexican oil industry after the more prolific and productive wells in the south became exhausted.

Still, the northern fields west of Tampico shared one characteristic of the fields farther south—portions of the production came from leases on small-holdings. The valley of the Pánuco River had become an important agricultural zone before the oil boom. In the absence of Indian-village agriculture, the *campesinos* had divided up the land into modest family-sized holdings. In the areas of Pánuco and Topila especially, the lease-takers had made individual leases with the numerous landholders and then resold them to competing drilling and producing companies. Few big companies, therefore, held contiguous leases and none of the oil reservoirs were developed on the unitary system, at least during the oil boom. If one wildcatter successfully brought in a big well on his small lease, the discovery would set off a scramble to secure the small leaseholds next door. Competitors then drilled offset wells before the first rig could drain the entire reservoir. Along the river, many separate interests had competing wells in close proximity to each other. Agents of El Aguila acquired two leases in the Pánuco area in

1917. Both properties were less than ten hectares. "Across the river and only a few hundred meters distant [from our leasehold]," reported the agents, "is a six thousand barrel well, controlled by the Cia de Petroleo de 'La Universal,' S.A., and close to that well the Penn-Mex. Fuel Co. are [sic] now drilling."[42] The only thing that prevented the early exhaustion of the northern fields, many of which are still producing today, was the nearly intractable consistency of the crude here. The heavy oil simply refused to come out of the ground quickly and easily.

Only in the more arid cattle lands north of the river could the oilmen buy and lease land in large quantities. Thus, Doheny was able to purchase just two ranches to make up the large El Ebano field. Yet the larger haciendas like the San José de Rusias and others that lay in the southern part of the state of Tamaulipas were not as productive as the smaller holdings in the basin of the Pánuco River.

The southern fields, which came to be known as the Faja de Oro, the Golden Lane, lay west of Tuxpan and shared only a few similarities with the northern fields. Here one also found production on larger haciendas, although, as in the north, several farming districts in which offset drilling proliferated could be found within the Golden Lane. But the differences were much more important. The crude oil of the southern fields was lighter; impressive single- and double-looped pipelines stretched across the tropical landscape; few river barges plied the smaller Tuxpan River; exploration here was positively frenzied; and oil field exhaustion came sooner.

The firstcomers like Furber, Doheny, and Cowdray had already secured fee-simple title and leases on the larger properties when the oil boom began in 1911. At the southern extremity of the Faja de Oro, about forty miles southwest of Tuxpan, Furber owned the large property to which he gave his name, Furbero. He acquired additional large haciendas next door, most notably the property of Trapani, a factor that was to loom large beginning in the late 1920s. Its oil was the lightest and most valuable of the Faja de Oro, measuring 24 degrees Baumé. During the great Mexican oil boom, however, Furbero's wells were not very productive. Doheny, of course, had secured title to the Cerro Azul and Juan Casiano haciendas. The Pearson interests of Cowdray owned Potrero del Llano and had leases on several larger cattle haciendas, like Tierra Amarilla of the Peláez family. Of course, their companies, La Huasteca and El Aguila, were locked in a legal dispute over competing leases on the hacienda property of Cerro Viejo. Production continued anyway.

Still, there existed areas in which small-scale farming had predominated before the oil boom and where lease taking, well drilling, and production were much more competitive—even frenzied. Tanhuijo, Los Naranjos, Amatlán, Tepetate, and Chinampa were farming areas. Here the independent wildcatters, smaller producing companies, and late-arriving larger companies gained entry into the Mexican oil boom. The Texas Company, Gulf, and eventually Jersey Standard established important wells in this region. Lesser-known firms like the Penn-Mex also got their start here. Eventually many of the smaller firms either exhausted their wells or sold out to the bigger companies. Yet during the period of rising oil prices, from 1915 to 1920, these smaller interests engaged in a dash for leases. Oil strikes flashed across the landscape like lightning, gaining instant recognition and majesty, then fading quickly. Independent wildcatters and company drilling teams moved first to Chinampa, then to Los Naranjos. They produced oil prolifically, like the tropical rainstorm, from closely placed wells, leaving the ground exhausted, then moving on to the next site. The strike at Amatlán in 1919 and 1920 culminated the boom. There the big companies, even Jersey Standard, had encouraged their drilling crews to share in the flush production. They worked overtime. On the smaller holdings, each well owner felt pressured to empty the common reservoirs of crude oil before his competitor next door. Conservation was impossible. Exhaustion was inevitable, especially given the property of the oil here in the southern fields.

It was not called the Golden Lane for nothing. The oil of the southern fields was light, valuable, and flowed quickly. When it burst from the well at Dos Bocas, the oil had a temperature of 165 degrees F., compared to 105 degrees F. for El Ebano's heavier crude. The gas and water pressures in the southern fields were considerable. Engineers measured it at 285 pounds per square inch in the Casiano well and 850 pounds per square inch at Potrero del Llano. Its specific gravity measured 19 to 22 degrees Baumé, the oil yielding about 12 percent illuminants and 20 percent gasoline with the refining technology of the day. It also produced good lubricants. Topped off, that is, after a preliminary distillation, the crude could be used for fuel oil.[43] The latter was the growth product.

The lighter, more viscous crude of the southern fields also lent itself to being transported from well to refinery via pipeline. Huasteca had three major pipelines. The longest one, covering sixty-five miles, went from Juan Casiano to Tampico, and two smaller ones connected the eight miles between Cerro Azul and Juan Casiano. El Aguila also had numerous eight-inch pipelines, two hundred miles of pipe in all, connecting Potrero del Llano east to the Tuxpan bar, Potrero north through Tanhuijo to Tampico, and Los Naranjos to Tuxpan. Mexican Gulf laid a sixty-two-mile, eight-inch pipeline from Tepetate to Tampico. The Cortez, the Texas Company, and Island Oil built smaller pipelines from the Tepetate-Chinampa oil fields to Port Lobos, a small oil terminal and topping complex at the southern end of the Tamiahua Lagoon.

Port Lobos and Tuxpan, however, did not develop into important oil refining complexes. Neither had good deep-water ports; nor did they have existing rail connections to the Mexican markets of the highlands. Port Lobos and Tuxpan had pipelines hoisted into floating loading hatches stretching two miles offshore, where steam tankers could load crude petroleum in bulk. The crude was then refined elsewhere. El Aguila sent Potrero crude to be refined at Minatitlán, while North American companies transported the crude to refineries on the Gulf and Atlantic coasts of the United States. The propensity of the Golden Lane crude to be transported on pipeline motivated the larger companies to continue the development of the oil region's major deep-water port, Tampico, as the principal Mexican refining center. Tampico surpassed Minatitlán as a refining town and Puerto México as Mexico's bustling oil terminal. In 1918, Tampico was exporting more than 5.3 million tons of petroleum; Tuxpan and Port Lobos, 2.6 million tons; and Puerto México, 149,600 tons of mostly reexported oil. Coastal barge and steam transportation served to transport equipment and personnel; few of the inland waterways of the Tamiahua Lagoon ever had as much traffic of oil barges as one found on the Pánuco River.[44] Oil moved exclusively in pipelines there.

The third zone of oil production was the Tehuantepec-Tabasco-Chiapas coastal lowlands, known merely as the isthmus. Isthmian crude was the highest quality of all (25 to 32 degrees Baumé), had a paraffin base, contained less sulfur, and yielded larger proportions of illuminating oil. Its deposits lay very close to the surface, sometimes at only 150 feet. El Aguila was the most active company to work here, and its leases and fee-simple properties were held in large haciendas, not on small-holdings, which were not found here in great numbers. The environment and petroleum would have been conducive to a large company's great success, and in fact, a large company, El Aguila, had been here since 1901. It built a refinery at Minatitlán and a railway and port terminal at Puerto México. The only problem was, El Aguila never could drill a gusher on the isthmus. Those wells that did produce abundantly soon tapered off and sooner or later were capped. Their leased properties there might have been the oilman's dream. They were huge. El Aguila's option on the hacienda belonging to José Yves Limantour, then in a Parisian exile, covered ten thousand hectares. El Aguila might have developed this property over a long period of time, unmolested by offset wells of competitors. But it had no oil at all. "[T]he Limantour [property] has no desirability as a subsoil lease," reported El Aguila's agent.[45]

As export prices climbed to unprecedented heights, oil exploration proceeded not only in the three principal zones of production but elsewhere as well. Successes were hardly notable. Seven British capitalists had obtained the oil rights to more than one hundred thousand acres near Saltillo. Some U.S. interests were attempting to secure permits to drill on lands south of the Río Bravo (Rio Grande), on the opposite side of the border from some Texas oil fields. Farther west, on the Pacific Coast, Japanese, American, British, and Dutch agents were investigating oil-bearing lands near Ensenada and also in Sonora. Nothing worthy of drilling was found.[46] American prospectors were attracted to the southern parts of the Mexican Gulf Coast by El Aguila's abandonment of exploration there. An oil field explorer reported on oil seepages in the lowlands of Oaxaca, Chiapas, and Tabasco. "The San Andres–Tuxtla section is especially promising," he stated.[47] The explorer was wrong. American entrepreneurs were planning to bring drilling equipment to a site fifteen miles west of Hecelchakan, Campeche, where they had discovered evidence of petroleum and asphalt deposits. One drilling team also sank a well to three thousand feet near Progreso, Yucatán, before they abandoned it. On the opposite side of the isthmus, following the war, German entrepreneurs had returned to prospect for oil near Pochutla, Oaxaca.[48] Crude was not discovered in sufficient quantity, however.

During the great Mexican oil boom, the characteristics of the southern fields near Tuxpan encouraged foreign oilmen to develop them more rapidly than either the northern or the isthmian zones. The value of the product, the rapid rate of flow, and the ease of transport motivated a burgeoning rise in production of the oil fields of this zone. By 1921, more than three-quarters of Mexican production came from the southern fields, a fifth from the northern fields, and the remainder from the disappointingly impoverished fields of the isthmus (see tables 3 and

Table 3. *Total Oil Production in Mexico by Fields, 1901–1920*

	Year First Produced	Total (no. of barrels)
Northern Fields		
El Ebano–Chijol	1901	22,933,224
Pánuco	1910	102,570,244
Topila	1910	8,374,990
San Pedro–La Labor	1912	5,859
Chila-Salinas	1913	189,134
Total (Northern Fields)		134,073,451
Southern Fields		
Tepetatate-Casiano	1910	116,342,997
Potrero-Alazán	1910	97,126,054
Furbero	1910	1,099,663
Tanhuijo–San Marcos	1910	357,371
Tierra Amarilla [abandoned 1916]	1911	259,426
Naranjos	1913	103,128,560
Alamo-Chapopote	1913	33,628,745
Tierra Amarilla [only 1 yr.]	1914	789
Cerro Azul–Toteco	1915	48,657,603
Zacamixtle	1919	75,716
Total (Southern Fields)		400,676,924
Isthmian		
San Cristóbal-Capoacán	1907	1,369,075
Concepción	1909	3,792
Soledad	1910	167,546
Sarlat (Tabasco)	1910	4,695
Ixhuatlán	1911	446,122
Tecuanapa	1911	250,500
Total (Isthmian)		2,241,730
Grand Total		536,992,105

SOURCE: E. DeGolyer, "Production of the Mexican Oil Field, 1901–1920," n.d. DeGolyer, File 5300.

4). El Aguila's ambitious refinery at Minatitlán processed more crude from Potrero than the nearby Tehuantepec fields, and its new terminal at Puerto México served almost exclusively to funnel in Potrero crude and funnel out the products refined from this crude.

Table 4. *Yearly Production of Mexican Oil in the Northern and Southern Fields,*
1901–1924

Year	Northern Crude (barrels)	Southern Crude (barrels)	Total (barrels)
1901–1917	17,990,725	—	—
1901	—	—	10,345
1902	—	—	40,200
1903	—	—	75,375
1904	—	—	125,625
1905	—	—	251,250
1906	—	—	502,500
1907	—	—	1,005,000
1908	—	—	3,932,000
1909–1913	—	49,106,444	—
1909	—	—	2,713,500
1910	—	—	3,634,080
1911	—	—	12,552,788
1912	—	—	16,558,215
1913	—	—	25,696,291
1914	7,076,544	19,158,859	26,235,403
1915	3,848,398	29,062,010	32,910,508
1916	12,088,397	28,458,518	40,546,915
1917	20,502,300	34,790,470	55,292,770
1918	19,857,361	43,970,965	63,828,326
1919	31,836,581	55,236,373	87,072,954
1920	42,880,275	120,158,708	163,038,983
1921	44,641,849	158,120,678	202,762,527
1922	46,538,664	137,881,021	184,419,685
1923	88,352,774	63,374,796	151,727,570
1924	100,493,754	40,119,101	140,612,855

NOTE: The southern fields include the production of Tehuantepec, which was negligible.

SOURCE: Charles A. Bay, "Review of the Petroleum Industry in Tampico, 1924," Tampico, 5 Feb 1925, State Dept. Decimal Files, 812.6363/1558.

Wading in Oil up to the Knees

It is not known exactly how many different companies and oil interests came to operate in Mexico during the great oil boom, but they were numerous. Much depends upon what is counted: leaseholders, drilling and production, or exporting. One source mentioned that 400 companies owned Mexican oil rights in 1916, 75 percent of which were American. A second source places the number of companies drilling wells in 1919 at 155. "Of the total investments in the oil industry of Mexico," the U.S. Department of Commerce reported in 1920, "97 percent is held by foreigners. . . . Of the total of 63,828,326 barrels produced in Mexico in 1918, the American interests produced 73 percent, British 21 percent, Holland 4 percent, and Spanish-Mexican 2 percent."[49]

These companies came in all varieties, all shapes. Lord Cowdray's El Aguila company was not the only British oil interest in Mexico. In 1916, the Foreign Office compiled a list of twenty-three other companies, whose capitalizations ranged from £100 (for the Mexican Selected Oil Estates, Ltd.) to $1 million (for the Tuxpam Oil Company). Other lists abound with the names of individuals and small companies. By the end of the boom, most big U.S. companies had at least some representation in Mexico. The Texas Company, Sinclair, Gulf, and Standard Oil of New Jersey existed alongside the big producers like Huasteca and El Aguila, the host of small firms like the Cortez Oil Corporation and Lot Seventeen Oil Company, and individuals like Charles Rathbone and Mr. Carrie Yates.[50] Given the high prices during the First World War, small companies could get started by virtue of one or two good wells. The Port Lobos Petroleum Company (an oil transport company) and Cortez Oil Corporation (a producer) together owned one hundred thousand acres of leaseholds in 1916 but had only two wells. In 1917, The Texas Company was completing construction of its refinery at Tampico. The Gulf group of Pittsburgh began exploration in 1913. Mexico was to remain this company's only source of foreign crude supplies until it entered Venezuela in 1925.[51] Naturally, the competition among so many interests was bound to be keen. In 1912, The Texas Company had applied to Mexico's Chamber of Deputies for a pipeline concession to carry crude oil from Tampico to Texas refineries. Apparently, the Doheny interests fought the measure, successfully raising the specter of the Standard Oil trust, for whose benefit the pipeline was attributed.[52] The important companies in Mexico were not transporters nor refiners, but producers of oil.

Several medium-sized firms also began operations in Mexico by combining capital, experience, and contacts from numerous U.S. sources. The Penn-Mex Fuel Company is a fitting example. Its founders, J. C. Trees and M. L. Benedum, had once contributed critical financial support to Doheny but fell out with the owner of Mexican Petroleum and Huasteca. They made a considerable profit when they sold their stock in "Mexican Pete" and decided to reenter Mexico on their own account. From Pittsburgh, they sent John Leonard and Eddie Gilmore, both Pennsylvanians with experience in the oil industry, to look over the Alamo Hacienda twenty miles west of Tuxpan. Wined and dined by the Núñez family, Leonard and Gilmore eventually secured options from them for their twenty-thousand-acre estate. Benedum traveled up the Tuxpan River and liked what he saw at Alamo. "You could see oil everywhere," he said later. "There were places where you could have waded in it up to your knees."[53] The partners of Benedum and Trees put up the $450,000 to exercise their options.

Back in Pittsburgh, Benedum and Trees organized a new corporation, the Penn-Mex Fuel Company, in 1913. They secured the backing of Pennsylvania oilmen and financiers and buyers in Jersey Standard. As soon as the Pennsylvania drillers brought in the oil at Alamo, the Penn-Mex became plagued by the same difficulty experienced by the other independent producers, Doheny and Cowdray: the need for capital. Penn-Mex constructed a pipeline to the Gulf Coast. They also built a railway, wharfs, warehouse, roads, and camps to support the entire operation. But the cost was beyond the means of Benedum and Trees. Just as the prices began to rise in 1916, therefore, Benedum and Trees sold out. They were never sure, but they suspected that the buyers had acted for the South Penn Company of Pennsylvania.[54] They were correct. But they also thought that the South Penn belonged to Standard Oil Company of New Jersey. That was wrong: it was then part of Socony, Standard Oil New York, but Jersey Standard would eventually absorb it.

Nonetheless, despite the rapid rise of Penn-Mex and other one- and two-well firms, the Doheny and Cowdray interests remained very much the leaders of the Mexican petroleum industry. Their success, of course, attracted many companies to challenge the near monopoly on oil production they had enjoyed in 1911. Other companies were drilling more oil wells in 1920 than were El Aguila and Huasteca.[55] Other companies also combined to wrest some 50 percent of production from the early arriving Doheny and Cowdray interests (see table 5). Yet, Huasteca and El Aguila were the largest and most important enterprises.

The flurry of activity sufficed to elevate Mexico, by war's end, to the second largest producer of petroleum in the world. It had surpassed Russia, whose oil production in the Baku had suffered from war, revolution, and Bolshevist expropriation. The United States remained the

Table 5. *Oil Production in Mexico by Company, 1918*

Company	Production (no. of barrels)
Huasteca (Doheny)	20.2 billion
El Aguila (Cowdray)	16.9 billion
Penn-Mex	6.9 billion
East Coast	3.5 billion
Cortez Oil Corp.	2.2 billion
Mexican Gulf	1,728.2 million
La Libertad	1,550.9 million
Mexican Petroleum	1,446.0 million
Texas Company	1,280.0 million
Tal Vez	1,152.1 million
International Petroleum	609.7 million
Tampascas	578.5 million
Pánuco-Boston	531.5 million
Transcontinental (Jersey Standard)	382.0 million
La Corona (Shell)	337.6 million
Mexican Combustible	300.1 million
La Petrolera	91.3 million
Vera Cruz Mexican Oil	51.7 million
Oilfields of Mexico (El Aguila)	29.9 million
Chijoles	25.3 million
Monterrey Petroleum	25.0 million
Mexico & España	5.5 million
Hispano-Mexicana	4.2 million
Mexican Oil	3.5 million
La Universal	3.1 million
Panuco	2.7 million

SOURCE: J. Vázquez Schiaffino, "Mexico," *Petroleum* 7, no. 4 (August 1919): 104.

premier oil producer, responsible for more than two-thirds of the world's production. In 1919, Mexico produced nearly 16 percent of the world's oil, a dramatic increase during the war years, according to these figures (in millions of barrels) on the world's leading producers:[56]

	1914	1919
World production	407.5	555.9
United States	265.8	378.4
Mexico	26.2	87.1

Russia	67.0	31.7
Dutch East Indies	11.4	15.5
Persia	2.9	10.1
Romania	12.8	6.6
Poland (Galicia)	6.4	6.0

The oil boom was one of the few growth industries during the Mexican Revolution. Tax collections on the production of Mexican petroleum, and after 1921 on its export as well, came to be the mainstay revenue producer of the fragile governments of revolutionary Mexico. Under the circumstances, the domestic authorities did not ignore the formation of a most American-like industry in Mexico, but there was little they could do about it. In the meanwhile, the oil boom fostered the growth of some large foreign interests.

A Great Flow of Gas

The combined properties of Edward L. Doheny, the Mexican Petroleum Company in the northern fields, and Huasteca in the southern fields came to form the largest single oil interest developed during the great Mexican oil boom. Doheny's men in 1901 had brought in the first Mexican production at El Ebano, and in September 1910, they drilled the fabulous Juan Casiano No. 7 in the Golden Lane, which became the mainstay of the Huasteca company for nine years following its discovery. It would eventually yield a total of between eighty and eighty-five million barrels of crude, one of the single most productive wells in the world—after Potrero del Llano No. 4.[57] Based upon Casiano's initial production of 100,000 bd, Huasteca completed the pipeline to Tampico, made important sales contracts, began construction of a refinery at Tampico, and expanded its tanker fleet. It even supported the first efforts of Doheny to create a refining and marketing network of his own along the Gulf and East coasts of the United States. In appreciation, Doheny named his private yacht the *Casiano*.

Nonetheless, Doheny's lease-takers and drillers were not idle during the frenzied period of Mexico's oil development. They continued to explore and keep up with the competition in both the northern and the southern fields. Doheny did not speculate as heavily in the smaller leaseholds of the Pánuco, Tepetate, and Alazán districts. As one of the early arrivals, he relied on developing the larger haciendas that he had purchased or leased in the final days of the Porfiriato. By 1911, the Doheny companies had acquired more than six hundred thousand acres of land, 85 percent of which was held in fee simple. They already had under contract haciendas that would later serve as new oil fields, such as Juan Felipe, Cerro Viejo, Chapopote Núñez, Zacamixtle, and Chinampa. But its properties in the northern fields were showing signs of anemia.[58] Salt water was showing already at El Ebano. No Doheny drilling crew ever ventured into the isthmus, which was El Aguila's domain, nor into other areas of exploration. Doheny's exploration concentrated now on the southern fields for one reason: Casiano crude yielded higher profits than did El Ebano crude. Geologist Ralph Arnold calculated that the heavier crude, more expensive to bring up and transport, made a profit of only five cents per barrel when sold at Tampico, while the lighter and easier to transport Casiano crude made Doheny's companies a profit of forty-one cents per barrel. As his field manager stated, "Topping Casiano oil you would get about 13% gasoline; from Ebano or Panuco oil, you would get 3 or 4%."[59]

Although Doheny was inclined to belittle the contributions of geologists, they nonetheless had helped him to establish a working geological model of oil exploration. Doheny had hired Stanford geologist Ralph Arnold and the former West Virginia state geologist I. C. White. Moreover, the most renowned Mexican geologist of the period, Ezequiel Ordóñez, had been an employee of the Mexican Petroleum Company since 1903. Ordóñez was instrumental in distinguishing between the oil exudes that indicated large underground accumulations of oil and those seepages that indicated isolated dissipations.[60]

Doheny, Ordóñez, and other Huasteca employees developed a hypothesis. The size of the surface oil pool was not crucial, nor did a bubbling oil seepage indicate that a sizeable oil deposit lay directly beneath. They concluded instead that the oil had collected in the underground crevices and caverns formed by old volcanic explosions that forced basaltic plugs up through the sedimentary strata. Therefore, the exudes found in areas of contact between basaltic plugs and the limestone were the most important indicators of oil. This was the case when Doheny's crews, advised by Ordóñez, had brought in production at the base of the Cerro de la Pez at El Ebano in 1903. Such low-lying hills were also found at the Huasteca properties of El Chapopote, Juan Felipe, Cerro Viejo, and Cerro Azul. The drillers would sink the wells on the largest fracture radiating outward from the plug.[61] This was the geological theory that brought drilling crews to the hacienda of Cerro Azul in 1916.

As Doheny's Casiano well had made his company one of Mexico's largest, the Cerro Azul discovery would catapult his organization into one of international importance. Doheny had acquired the property of Cerro Azul, known for its numerous oil pools, as early as 1906. Huasteca delayed the development of this solid prospect. After the Juan Casiano discovery, other necessities intervened: the pipeline, market contracts, storage facilities, and the refinery. In addition, work crews built a narrow-gauge railway from San Jerónimo, a small port on the Tamiahua waterways, to Cerro Azul and numerous roads in order to transport equipment to the property. The first two perforations at Cerro Azul were begun in 1914. The third well, completed in 1915, yielded a continuous but minor flow of oil. Crews then sank Cerro Azul No. 4 "in the middle of a small esplanade," Ordóñez explained, "partly surrounded by hills, that is to say, a situation similar to that of the Casiano wells."[62]

Like many of the wells of the Faja de Oro, Cerro Azul No. 4 had "drilled itself in." Once the cable tools had struck through to a pocket of gas, the rush of gas out through the well casing tended to deepen the well to the level of crude oil.[63] The first emission of gas on the night of 10 February 1916 blew out the drilling equipment. It destroyed the derrick in the classic fashion of Mexican gushers. After seven hours, the transparent gas turned to black crude oil. The well ran wild for nine days. By that time, the well was exploding at the rate of 260,000 barrels per day, throwing a jet of crude oil three hundred meters straight up. When they finally placed a valve over the well and shunted its crude into a pipeline, the well head maintained a pressure of 1,035 pounds per square inch.[64] Such wells as the Cerro Azul did not need to be pumped. On the first day, the well flowed unchecked at 152,000 bd and by the fifth day, it was flowing at 160,858 bd.

News of the Cerro Azul discovery spread rapidly among competing foreign oilmen. J. B. Body reported to Lord Cowdray that the gas noise could be heard at El Aguila's Naranjos camp nearby.[65] Cerro Azul No. 4 made oil history for being the most productive shallow well ever. Its depth was 1,792 feet, or 1,351 feet below sea level in the nearby Gulf of Mexico. Its total production to 1932 had been eighty million barrels.[66] Cerro Azul No. 4 elevated Doheny into the position of largest producer and exporter of oil during the great Mexican oil boom. His company now surpassed Cowdray's El Aguila by a large

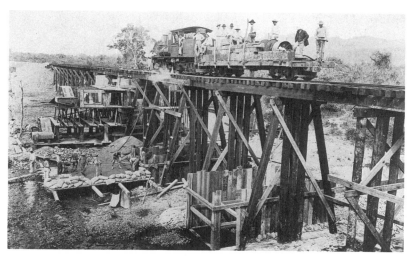

Fig. 7. Bridge building near Cerro Azul. The Huasteca Petroleum Company constructed a narrow-gauge railway to its new oil fields in the Golden Lane in order to deliver equipment and supplies to its oil camps. Here, Mexican laborers and their American supervisors complete the pilings of a railway trestle over an arroyo. From the Eberstadt Photo Collection, courtesy of the Barker Texas History Center at the University of Texas.

margin. But he also suffered the problems of flush production: how to transport the oil to market and how to sell it. To solve these problems, Doheny had to expand his operations outward from Mexico until he had created a multinational business enterprise.

The nightmare of every independent producer was to have discovered enormous quantities of crude petroleum with no means for transporting it to buyers—and then having no buyers. Doheny's discovery of Juan Casiano No. 7, followed within four years by Cerro Azul No. 4, placed Doheny in such a dilemma. He sold asphaltum and fuel oil in Mexico and also exported asphalt. But, being a Californian oilman, he had few outlets in the eastern United States. Nor, in September 1910, did he have the financial resources to rapidly develop the kind of infrastructure needed to transport the oil to tidewater and deliver it to refineries in the Gulf and Atlantic states. Therefore, his first phase of expansion entailed a simultaneous and desperate search for customers and capital necessary to build transport and storage. The second phase of expansion, commencing with the discovery of the Cerro Azul well, propelled him into the development of his own refining and retail networks in the United States.

The first phase of expansion found Doheny quite successful in completing the pipeline from Juan Casiano to Tampico and in finding buyers. He secured the capital from a combination of independent Pennsylvania oil speculators and from a New York investment bank, William Salomon and Company. Apparently, the sum amounted to $12 million from Salomon.[67] The pipeline was completed in 1911. A terminal station and tank farm was constructed at Mata Redonda, on the southern bank of the Pánuco River opposite Tampico. Tank steamers anchored just three hundred feet from the nearest storage tank, one of thirty-five at the terminal's tank farm. The company owned twenty-two other large (55,000-barrel capacity) steel tanks elsewhere and numerous smaller storage facilities. On any one day in 1911, the company might have more than 2.5 million barrels of oil in storage, including earthen reservoirs. On the Pánuco River, Doheny operated three oil barges, a river steamer, and two steel freight barges. The latter would become increasingly important to deliver imported equipment from Tampico.[68] By 1917, nine tankers with a capacity of 60,450 tons were in the Pan American fleet, even though the United States had commandeered five and Great Britain one for wartime service. The English-made tankers (or "tank steamers," as they were sometimes called) were carrying crude oil from the Huasteca terminal at Tampico to U.S. ports from Texas to Massachusetts. His work gangs were also building the roads and rail lines through the Huasteca lowlands from Tuxpan to Tampico.[69] Although he borrowed capital to construct, quite rapidly, an impressive transportation infrastructure, Doheny still depended upon the big U.S.–based refining and marketing companies to buy his crude oil.

The Mexican market for petroleum came into crisis beginning in 1911. The fall of the Díaz government and the outbreak of revolutionary violence from Chihuahua to Morelos eroded Doheny's established markets for petroleum products. Mines shut down, railway tracks were breached, trains destroyed, and street paving stopped. Mexican Petroleum Company had had a contract with the Mexican Central Railway since 1905, since assumed by the National Railways, to buy 16,000 bd of fuel oil for a period of fifteen years. In order to compete on the domestic market with El Aguila, Waters-Pierce had stopped importing crude oil. It concluded a contract to take 2.5 million barrels of Huasteca's lightest crude oil from 1911 to 1915 for its Tampico refinery.[70]

Once the Revolution struck, the National Railways took less than half of what it had contracted to buy from Doheny. Even so, it was seldom able to pay cash for it. The Huerta government in 1914 and then Carranza in 1916 paid for fuel oil by giving Mexican Petroleum, and El Aguila too, certain tax credits instead of cash. The cessation of street paving motivated Doheny's men to carry on this business elsewhere. Harold Walker was in San Salvador in 1912 in order to make a bid for the paving of the streets of that Central American city.[71] None of these activities helped Doheny sell his new production.

For that, he turned to the large refining and marketing companies that dominated the U.S. oil market, especially Standard Oil of New Jersey. This must have involved some swallowing of pride for an independent oilman. Curiously, the new alliance between Doheny and Standard Oil now set Doheny against the interests of Jersey's former associate, Henry Clay Pierce. Early in 1911, E. L. Doheny had met with Jersey Standard's H. C. Folger, Jr., at 26 Broadway, New York. Standard Oil and Huasteca agreed to a five-year contract by which several of Jersey's refineries would purchase a total of two million barrels of oil per year from Mexico. Best of all, Jersey paid in advance, much to the relief of the Doheny organization.[72] For its part, Jersey Standard's move to deal directly with a producer of Mexican crude oil was its strategic reaction to the 1911 Supreme Court dissolution. In that decision, Standard Oil New Jersey, a refining and marketing giant, was separated from nearly all of its producing subsidiaries. Standard New York, Ohio, Indiana, and California were broken off, forming separate entities from Jersey. The Supreme Court also separated Standard from Waters-Pierce. Thereafter, Jersey Standard was free to develop refining and marketing in the Lower Mississippi Valley and Texas, previously part of the Waters-Pierce territory. Jersey was also free to move into Mexico.

Soon, tankers owned by Jersey Standard began delivering stocks of crude oil to the refineries of its new affiliate in Corsicana and Beaumont, the Magnolia Petroleum Company. What Mexican production Magnolia could not absorb, Magnolia sold off to other refineries and marketing companies from Texas to Missouri. Apparently, the contract enabled Doheny to draw on a $400,000 loan from the U.S. marketing company that Doheny used to develop his infrastructure in Mexico. The entrance of the Magnolia Company into the Texas market provided a very direct assault on the monopoly that Pierce had enjoyed in selling Standard Oil brands exclusively. Armed with inexpensive

Mexican crude oils acquired from the Huasteca Company, Magnolia's refineries began putting out Standard-brand gasolines, naphthas, and kerosenes at reduced prices. Magnolia's sales agents then began to undersell Pierce's products by as much as 20 percent. Pierce complained bitterly.[73] All this was, of course, of no concern to Doheny. He needed to sell a great deal of petroleum, and the Standard contract allowed him to do just that.

Rights of Citizenship and Accumulation

No sooner had Doheny settled into these arrangements than the Cerro Azul gusher brought additional marketing problems and strained all of Huasteca's new transportation facilities. From that moment onward, Doheny began to build his own refining and marketing facilities at ports along the coast from Louisiana to New England. This second phase of expansion lasted from 1916 to 1921. Doheny created a holding firm, the Pan American Petroleum and Transport Company, incorporated in Delaware. Pan Am came to hold the stock of the Mexican producing subsidiaries, Huasteca and Mexican Petroleum, as well as his California oil fields and the plethora of new facilities on the Gulf and Atlantic coasts of the United States. Pan Am established distribution depots in Portland, Maine, Boston, Providence, Fall River, New York, Baltimore, Norfolk, Jacksonville, Tampa, New Orleans, and Galveston. It built a 25,000–bd refinery at Destrehan, Louisiana. Abroad, the new Doheny interests established additional depots in the Canal Zone, Pará, Pernambuco, Bahia, Rio de Janeiro, Santos, Montevideo, and Buenos Aires. In Great Britain, Pan Am opened up distribution centers in Southampton, Liverpool, Avonmouth, South Shields, and Glasgow. Bunker and fuel oils continued to be the principal products sold at these points. The opening of the Panama Canal in 1914 permitted the Mexican oil, for the first time, to be sold on the west coast of South America. Doheny in 1917 was selling crude to Union Oil of California and to Chilean mining companies. Despite some problems with sea transport during the war, Pan Am came to own thirty-one tankers, amounting to 272,493 total tonnage, by 1921. It chartered many others. As the third decade of the twentieth century began, Doheny's companies had the capacity of selling some twenty million barrels of oil per year.[74] Moreover, it was attempting to wean itself from dependence upon the large U.S. marketing firms like Jersey Standard.

The rapid expansion also created a need to expand Doheny's refining capacity. Beginning in September of 1916, Huasteca laid plans to convert its Tampico topping plant into a larger and more sophisticated refinery. While its capacity to produce fuel oil was expanded, stills and equipment to manufacture kerosene, gasoline, and lubricants were also installed. Within a month, Huasteca received the government permits. The contract stipulated that the company was to obey Mexican laws, permit government inspections, and provide certain services and benefits for refinery workers.[75] By the end of the decade, the Tampico refinery had the capacity to refine 140,000 bd.

Pan Am appeared to maintain a solid profitability during the great Mexican oil boom. Its sales—and dividends—mounted. By 1918, sales revenues rose to $17 million, and net profit to nearly $5 million. In 1920, its total assets were $103 million.[76] By any measure, Pan American Petroleum was becoming a successful multinational company.

The expansion of his oil enterprise motivated Doheny to promote his experienced employees and bring in new officials. His old partner from the Los Angeles oil rush, C. A. Canfield, remained as a vice-president but died in 1919. Herbert Wylie, who opened up production at El Ebano and in 1910 directed the Mexican operations from Tampico, moved to New York as general manager of Pan American Petroleum. Wylie had accomplished much in Mexico without ever having learned Spanish at all.[77] Harold Walker left his duties as manager of the paving operations in Mexico to assume the vice-presidency of Pan Am with responsibility for public relations. Walker soon became Doheny's political alter-ego.

New men soon rose within Doheny's Mexican operations. Capt. William H. Green in 1916 took over as general manager of Huasteca at Tampico and had charge of oil fields and refineries of both Mexican "Pete" and Huasteca. Green knew Spanish, having served with the U.S. Constabulary in the Philippines.[78] Weighing 250 pounds, Green was an imposing, dominating figure. He dealt with Mexican labor disputes and with local Mexican officials. José López Portillo y Weber, a young technician for the government petroleum office in Tampico in 1919 (and father of a future president), did not like Captain Green. He thought that Green, who could speak Spanish quite fluently, purposely maintained a strong English accent, because "he was convinced of the efficacy of humor to attract sympathy."[79] Green was also considered a

Yankee jingoist, believing the Americans were great and the Mexicans were lucky to be so close to such greatness.

In Mexico City, Hilarión Branch became the chief political trouble-shooter and public affairs official of the Doheny interests. Born to British citizenship in the Antilles, he lived for many years in Mexico, learning to speak Spanish grammatically and elegantly. He had polish where most American oilmen were somewhat coarse. Branch studied Mexican law and became an *abogado*. "He knew and understood us [Mexicans] very well," said López Portillo of Branch.[80] Branch's job was to deal with the diverse functionaries of the government. Mexican officials appreciated foreigners like Branch more than those like Green.

The whole of the Pan Am organization bore the imprint of Doheny. An optimistic and driven man, of rigid puritanical character, Edward L. Doheny did not easily accept criticism. It was rumored that his first wife, who died, was an alcoholic, and he suffered no one to drink or smoke in his presence. Together with his second wife, Estelle, Doheny became a great philanthropist and patron of the Catholic Church in Los Angeles. His Mexican geologist, Ezequiel Ordóñez, described the personal traits that led to executive success:

Two things were characteristic in the active business life of Doheny. The first was a slow and almost completely discussed resolution, but once taken, indeed, he had to carry it out promptly and decidedly. The second was that he was not a creator of great ideas. The primordial idea of a thing had to come from outside, from others, but once placed in his mind, he could develop and calculate its consequences with astonishing precision.[81]

Nevertheless, the successful, self-made American oilman in Mexico also had an Achilles' heel, a fatal flaw that was soon to mar his career and leave him a retired recluse who would die a vilified and embittered man. Doheny began to feel he was superior. Against those who opposed him, crossed him, or questioned him, Doheny could be a tireless fighter. "He could spend entire hours speaking about only one negotiation, trying always to dominate his listeners," observed Ordóñez. "Generally, he did not admit objections to his conversations and in the best epoch of his work, if someone dared contradict him, he would start to shout, pound his fists, his eyes irritated and his face reddened."[82] His arrogance and his growing profile during the war led him on a collision course in the political arena. What he saw as President Woodrow Wilson's bumbling responses to the Mexican Revolution and his wrongheaded domestic oil policies soon converted his political sympathies from the Democratic to the Republican party.

As the scion of an immigrant, working-class Irish family, Doheny had always been a Democrat. He gave money to Democratic candidates and to the Wilson campaign. But as a westerner and businessman, he came to resent the conservationist attitude of the East Coast Democratic establishment. He soon became an outspoken witness in Congressional hearings. In 1917, he appeared before the Senate Committee on Public Lands and clashed with the administration over its decision to withdraw the naval oil reserves at Elk Hills, California, and Teapot Dome, Nevada, from private exploitation. Doheny also objected to the U.S. Navy's refusal to burn high-sulfur Mexican bunker oil in its warships. Questioned about the excessive smoking of Mexican oil, Doheny retorted that various senators were intimating "that I lied about it."[83] Josephus Daniels, the secretary of the navy, spoke against exploiting U.S. naval oil reserves. "We would prefer to buy the oil, all that we can get, from foreign countries, if we can, and hold our own supply as long as possible," he told the Senate panel.[84] Doheny held a grudge upon which he would act later, becoming involved in the Teapot Dome scandals. Daniels later was to serve as U.S. ambassador and witness the Mexican oil expropriation. Needless to say, Daniels would not be known as a friend of American oilmen in Mexico.

The next year, 1918, Doheny returned to Capitol Hill to protest wartime policies of the U.S. Shipping Board. Pan American Oil representative, attorney Frederick R. Kellogg, claimed that the government had commandeered five Pan Am oil transports from the company's Tampico run. He asked for 100 percent compensation for the loss of the ships and not merely payment for the use of these ships. The argument stressed that Pan Am tankers were not carrying Huasteca's product to war but transporting the oil from competitors on the East Coast to France. The competition, not Pan Am, was therefore reaping the profits from the government's shipping policy.[85] Doheny's own testimony to the Senate committee seemed both condescending and whining. When war was declared, he said, he had offered all his ships and five million barrels of Mexican oil to President Wilson. Instead the government "commandeered" five of his vessels and paid him a charter fee amounting to $3.65 per ton for moving the petroleum of other companies. His companies could have been earning $16 per ton if those ships carried Mexican oil. Clearly, Doheny was forming the opinion that the Wilson administration was persecuting him. As the largest producer of oil in Mexico, if not the world, Doheny said he deserved better.

The world's greatest oilman continued this kind of political action during the remainder of the Wilson administration. Doheny commissioned a special panel of scholars to study Mexico and propose to the government a more appropriate U.S. policy toward the Mexican Revolution. The Doheny Research Foundation, featuring the investigative research of some fifteen prominent American academicians, may have been one of the first conservative think-tanks in U.S. politics. He also commissioned newspaper attacks against U.S. policies, and he supported one book, *The Mexican Problem,* by Clarence W. Barron. Among that book's profoundest convictions are the following:

> The redemption of Mexico must be from the invasion of business, forcing upon the natives—the good people of Mexico—technical training, higher wages, bank accounts, financial independence, and the rights of citizenship and accumulation.[86]

The opinion reflected Doheny's ideas perfectly.

The Senate's investigation of U.S.–Mexican relations, however, was Doheny's most prominent public forum to express a policy alternative that was to be known as the "interventionist" lobby. Doheny's old friend from his prospecting days in New Mexico, now senator, Albert B. Fall, was an influential member of that committee. Moreover, Fall had become the Republican party's chief critic of the administration's Mexican policy. When the Senate began its hearings on Mexico in 1919, Doheny served as the first witness. Two giant wells in Mexico and a new marketing presence on the East Coast of the United States had taken Edward L. Doheny so far that he felt justified in influencing U.S. policy toward Mexico.

Selling the Surplus Oil

The second great oil producer in Mexico, El Aguila, shared several similarities and some differences with the combined Huasteca and Mexican Petroleum companies. During the last years of the Porfiriato, El Aguila had gained an early lead in production by combining political favoritism from the Porfirian regime with the early purchase and leasing of oil lands. After some frustrations exploring in the Isthmus of Tehuantepec, Sir Weetman Pearson's crews brought in the biggest Mexican oil well of all. Potrero del Llano No. 4 formed the basis of all subsequent development. But unlike Doheny's companies, El Aguila did not bring in a second great oil well during the great Mexican oil boom; nor did it ever enter into production in the heavy crude of the northern fields. Thus, it was destined to lose its lead to Doheny's Huasteca in the 1910s.

As a major independent producer, El Aguila confronted the same problem as the Doheny group: it suffered from having insufficient marketing of its own. The Pearson group survived by selling large quantities of oil to refining and marketing companies in the United States and Great Britain and developing its own marketing apparatus in South America and England. Nonetheless, El Aguila never shook its market vulnerability. The reason: as a British company, El Aguila was much more inhibited by the ravages of war, because of capital shortages and transportation interruptions, than its American competitors. A closer relationship to a sympathetic British government did not assuage Lord Cowdray's feeling of vulnerability. In fact, the home government would not aid this British entrepreneur in Mexico. And so, in the end, El Aguila became the first of the large Mexican independent oil firms to merge with a giant international oil company.

Having acquired most of its oil properties before the rush of the lease-takers, El Aguila did not have to scramble for the marginal and risky oil prospects. It could have been quite expensive for El Aguila. Landowners and other lease-takers inflated their prices when dealing with the wealthy El Aguila. Much the same thing happened to El Aguila when it sought to construct pipelines. The property owners, whether Mexican or foreign, had to be given "substantial personal interests" to assign the rights-of-way. Many landowners would hold up the negotiations with El Aguila's Mexican lawyers in order to get more from the company. Mexican landowners were not stupid. They knew how to defend themselves and, according to the oilmen, to make "exorbitant claims."[87]

Often, El Aguila had to acquire additional oil lands in order to protect existing wells. In the midst of the lease-taking frenzy, geologist Everette DeGolyer purchased shares of the Horcones hacienda for El Aguila in order to protect the nearby Potrero wells. El Aguila also dealt in oil leases, subletting and selling its leases of doubtful prospects to other companies.[88] Keeping track of its oil leases and payments of royalties and rental fees occupied a team of company lawyers. The company in June 1912 inadvertently neglected to pay a certain Sánchez his monthly royalty on a lease in Tanhuijo. Sánchez immediately declared the leasehold null and void because of El Aguila's breach of contract. Embarrassed attorneys rushed to confer with Sánchez, who refused at first to renew the lease to El Aguila, which already had two producing wells there and was drilling another. Sánchez was now free to sell the proven property to the highest bidder. Eventually, he signed a new lease with El Aguila—for a much larger royalty.[89] Mexican landowners were learning how to deal with the big companies.

As in the United States, lease and contract disputes in Mexico often embroiled the big companies in complicated litigations. El Aguila was no exception. The American independent oilman Ralph Culliman in 1912 assigned to El Aguila the lease for Lot 113, Amatlán. Immediately, El Aguila's acquired rights were set upon by what it called "parasitical speculators," who searched for imperfections in titles in order to sell contested rights to competing companies. Lots with clouded titles that yielded oil were especially attractive. Although El Aguila's lawyers had investigated the title with the Chinampa public notary when they purchased the lease, the company was later sued for royalties by a competing leaseholder. Although the Mexican Supreme Court eventually upheld El Aguila, the company in the meanwhile had to support a staff of Mexican attorneys to fight the suit.[90]

The greatest legal contest over a valuable leasehold concerned two big companies. Both El Aguila and Huasteca had acquired leases dating from 1909 for the same prolific property, the Cerro Viejo hacienda. Huasteca had moved its drilling crews onto the property first, in 1912. El Aguila's J. B. Body asked for an injunction against Huasteca. Yet, the legal department moved slowly. It took Licenciados Blas Rodríguez and Peláez five months to obtain a Supreme Court injunction against Huasteca. By that time, Doheny's company had brought in production on the estate and refused to leave.[91] Once the war broke out, the Foreign Office wanted to resolve the dispute amicably and offered to reconcile the two companies. In Washington, Sir Cecil Spring Rice, who shared an Irish heritage with Doheny, opened negotiations. Sir Cecil and Doheny got on famously, but the latter and his staff proved less forthcoming to El Aguila's representatives. El Aguila proposed to share production from Cerro Viejo on a fifty-fifty basis. But "[Doheny] was not willing to make any transaction with us," Body reported.[92]

When litigation over Cerro Viejo entered its eleventh year in 1917, Huasteca was taking approximately 60,000 bd from the seventeen-thousand-acre property. All things being equal, Doheny would have profited by prolonging the litigation. But all things were not equal. By

1918, regulatory pressure by the Mexican government of President Venustiano Carranza forced Doheny to make concessions with a business competitor in order to form a united front of foreign companies. Huasteca finally gave in. It created a new company, giving El Aguila a half share, in order to exploit Cerro Viejo production from that point onwards. But Huasteca kept everything it had gained since 1912.[93] Such leasing problems, hardly absent in U.S. oil development, added a measure of instability to Mexican oil development. Although theoretically falling within the jurisdiction of Mexican courts, such lease disputes nonetheless involved foreign diplomats. Their resolution was as apt to be hammered out in Washington, D.C., and London as in Mexico City.

In exploration and production, El Aguila lived off its early entrance into Mexico. The British company exploited some new fields but never discovered another well as significant as its Potrero No. 4, which had made El Aguila strong in the southern fields. In a way, the company became victimized by its early entrance too. El Aguila continued on a fruitless quest for production in the disappointing isthmian area and neglected, or nearly so, the northern fields. In 1913, the managers were shocked that its old rival, Waters-Pierce, had brought in a 50,000–bd well at Topila, on which they had commented unfavorably.[94] Instead, El Aguila expended much effort on the isthmus, where it remained the monopoly foreign concern and where it had (perhaps unwisely) completed its first refinery in 1906. DeGolyer and other geologists were working in 1916 to locate additional drilling rigs even though its old wells there were showing signs of decline. In the Faja de Oro, El Aguila accountants calculated that their net profits amounted to 6.4 million gold pesos, but in the isthmian fields, a mere 134,000 gold pesos.[95] The company finally decided to hold its isthmus properties without wasting more money on their development.

El Aguila remained the second largest producer in Mexico because of its work in the southern fields. The first order of business was to protect its most prolific well, Potrero No. 4. (By 1930, this one well had produced more than 115 million barrels of crude oil, more than several Texas oil fields combined.)[96] Recognizing the potential damage by fire, the managers first sought to make the great well fireproof. In 1914, lightning actually struck Potrero No. 4, setting the well head ablaze. Before workers could build up an earthen embankment around the fire and fill it with quenching water, the conflagration consumed a million barrels of crude oil and melted the valve casings. In reviving the well, El Aguila's crews encased the new well head in a mountain of concrete

Fig. 8. Putting out an oil fire. Workers construct an earthen wall around
this minor blowout—which still produced a thick, acrid smoke—in
a flow line from one of El Aguila's wells. Then the roaring torch was
smothered by filling the temporary reservoir with water and mud.
Major well fires, like that of Potrero del Llano No. 4 in 1914, were
extinguished in the same fashion. Courtesy of the DeGolyer Library
of Southern Methodist University.

and pipes. The hollow cavity of the concrete mound was filled with water during thunderstorms. Thereafter, the men reduced the risk of fire
to all the wells. They cleared and burned off the *monte* (tropical vegetation) around each well and earthen reservoirs, covered over the seep-

ages, and sunk flare pipes into fissures in the ground that leaked dangerous gases.[97]

Meanwhile, El Aguila spent its remaining energies holding off the competition in the southern fields. In 1912, the company had moved its oil rigs into Alazán, where they had brought in Alazán No. 4, flowing at 1,200 bd. They were also sinking numerous wells at the hacienda of Tierra Amarilla, belonging to the family of its attorney, Peláez, although production here never met expectations. By 1914, the company had expanded into the area of Amatlán and Naranjos, buying leases and studying the geology.[98] The major interest of competitors had shifted to Tepetate in 1917. Therefore, the British firm suspended its drilling activities at Naranjos to work on its Tepetate leases. The Vincent well at Tepetate had just come in at 12,000 bd, and The Texas Company immediately began drilling an offset well on a nearby lot, not more than one hundred meters away. "So many companies are drilling around us at Tepetate," said J. B. Body, "and we must take steps at the earliest possible moment to secure our share of this pool."[99]

When El Aguila opened up the first well in the Los Naranjos field, it could not pause even to congratulate itself. The field manager fully expected competitors like Mexican-Sinclair, Agwi, Mexican Gulf, International, and Union Oil Company to begin drilling on their small leaseholds. Consequently, El Aguila was motivated to open the well heads on small leaseholds in the Los Naranjos district and allow them to flow at maximum capacity. "I think Mr. DeGolyer's arguments in favour of our selling as much crude as we can get out, in excess of the requirements of our own Refineries, are entirely sound," reported the general field manager at Tampico. "As I see it the whole thing comes down to this: whether we shall take out this surplus oil, selling it as crude and making a good profit on it, or whether we shall let our competitors do so."[100] The answer was obvious to the capitalist businessman: produce as much as possible before it was too late.

Movement of drilling crews was not accomplished easily in the dense tropical rain forests of the Faja de Oro. One American driller described what it was like:

Of all the plain damned misery we had [moving to a new drilling site]! We moved everything; I don't mean we just picked us up a tent and a skillet and some little things like that and set out for a weekend camping trip; no sir! We packed every damned thing we'd need to drill a well—boilers, wrenches, picks and shovels, pipe, casing, rope, steel, timbers for the rig floor, tin for the boiler house and the belt house, everything—and packed 'em on burros. . . . We had a string of 'em several miles long. . . . There was more'n two thousand

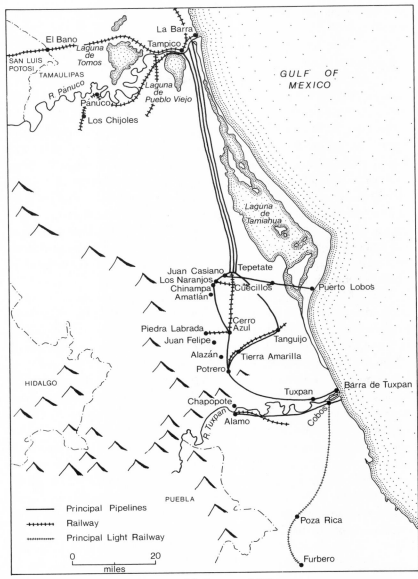

Map 2. The Northern Veracruz Oil Zone, c. 1920

Mexicans—teamsters, roughnecks, roustabouts, hands for the picks and shovels, and some of them that was not supposed to work but just come along for the hell of it.[101]

Even at the height of the boom, there were harbingers of things to come. Drillers were always aware that in the prolific southern fields, where the sweetest crude and highest gas pressures were found, the oil reservoirs were located one thousand to two thousand feet below sea level. Many "dry holes" did not get their name because no liquids at all came up out of the well casing. Most wells yielded gas and salt water. Approximately one-half yielded commercial quantities of crude petroleum. Only a few wells, however, lasted more than one to two years. The best geologists, Everette DeGolyer for example, who knew the southern fields as well as anyone, understood that salt water underlay the petroleum deposits of the Potrero and other wells. "Mr. De" (as he came to be known) and his geologists would turn out scientific treatises on "A New Cretaceous Rudistid from the San Felipe Formation of Mexico" or "Notes on Lithology and Paleontology of the Sedimentary Formation of Eastern Mexico."[102] DeGolyer met regularly with paleontologists and geologists at academic meetings in the United States and reported on his Mexican work. The business managers of El Aguila, especially J. B. Body, were furious. They were afraid the geologists were giving away trade secrets; but Body gave in to these scientific inquiries when El Aguila's entire geology department threatened to resign en masse.[103] As early as 1916, DeGolyer warned of rising temperatures of the crude oil. High temperatures, he said, usually signified the approach of the underlying salt water. He suggested that production be pinched back at such wells, in order to preserve the underground oil reservoirs.[104]

In 1918, salt water invasion first began to appear in the previously productive wells at Alazán. El Aguila's men also perceived that the exhaustion of the wells at Tepetate had resulted from the competitive offsetting. Still, production here had been beyond expectations. However briefly the Alazán and Tepetate wells had flowed, they had nevertheless filled the earthen storage pools with more than 400,000 barrels of crude. The Potrero well had also created a giant lake with 2,500,000 barrels of crude before the pipelines had been connected. This reservoir would wait for a decade to be used.[105]

There was also another portent, this one fortuitous for El Aguila and for Mexico. Since 1908, the Pearson interests had been purchasing crude from the Oil Fields of Mexico properties of Percy N. Furber. In

June of 1914, Furber offered to sell his properties, and El Aguila acquired 51 percent of Oil Fields of Mexico stock. It was El Aguila's last effort at expansion before the war broke out.[106] Having acquired such a large oil property did not mean that El Aguila would strike out in a pell-mell effort to develop it. Its policy had always been to develop the smallest properties first. "Having been able to select from the pick of the petroleum lands before its competitors were in existence," its prospectus bragged in 1921, "the Mexican Eagle is reserving for later development the large zone where it is the sole owner."[107] And what a deal: the combined properties of the Oil Fields of Mexico had included the old Trapani hacienda, site of the future Poza Rica oil field.[108] The most immediate problem remained how to get rid of the oil already drawn from the ground. For this, the company with very large production needed to develop transportation, refining, and storage capacity.

No Discrimination against Best Customers

Once the pipelines linked the Potrero field to Tampico in 1911, El Aguila thereafter worked to integrate the other wells of the southern fields into the system. Discoveries in new fields like Alazán, Naranjos, and Tepetate necessitated the laying of trunk lines feeding into the main pipeline. When Naranjos came in, crews rushed to connect it to the main pipeline with four "Prescott" pumps, a pumphouse, and a double eight-inch line running to Potrero, thirty-four kilometers away.[109] El Aguila's legal department acquired the rights-of-way from local landowners. Often, the pipeline would pass through a property owned by a rival company. Huasteca and El Aguila had a reciprocal agreement to allow the passage of each other's pipelines. But Huasteca officials always seemed to be "unavailable" when El Aguila wished to complete an auxiliary pipeline in a hurry. Finally, in 1913, El Aguila returned the petty vexation by obstructing the passage of a Huasteca pipeline through one of its properties.[110]

Like its rival, the Huasteca, the British company bought land at the river ports of Tampico and Tuxpan to build wooden and steel storage tanks and loading wharves. By 1914, the company had a total storage capacity in steel tankage of two million barrels. Such storage was essential, because the lighter and more valuable ends of the crude quickly evaporated in open earthen storage, reducing the remainder to a mass of thick tar.[111] At Tuxpan, where it already had an offshore loading terminal of pipelines laid out into the surf, El Aguila constructed a new topping plant. The Tuxpan plant would never be a great success. Technical problems forced its shutdown in 1917, and inspections by the new Mexican Petroleum Office delayed repairs and alterations. Finally, the replacement furnace failed to heat the crude petroleum properly for primary distillation.[112]

El Aguila had greater refining advantages in the isthmus. The Pearson interests had already developed deep-water port facilities at Puerto México when they constructed the Tehuantepec Railway. The Minatitlán refinery, completed in 1906, had a daily capacity of 1,400 tons of crude. But even the Mexican oil it refined was imported, so to speak. It came not via pipeline from nearby isthmian oil fields but via tankers from Tuxpan, three hundred miles up the coast. The refined products had to be exported again through Puerto México even to Mexican markets. For these reasons, the management never invested much to improve the Minatitlán refinery during the great boom. General manager Body reported in 1916 that he "was disappointed to find that the Refinery Plant had not been kept up to the high state of maintenance that it had been formerly."[113] Once again, fire stalked the isthmian facilities. The Minatitlán refinery, which had suffered severe damage in the 1908 blaze, suffered a second major fire in 1916. The asphalt loading wharf and a barreling shed were destroyed. Five months later, a third fire broke out at the tank farm in nearby Puerto México.[114]

El Aguila's greatest manufacturing achievement was neither its maiden refinery at Minatitlán nor its ne'er-do-well topping plant at Tuxpan. The Tampico refinery, begun in 1912, was the greatest of all Mexican refineries. When it came on line in 1914, the Tampico refinery could run four thousand tons of crude per day. Built in Doña Cecilia, the industrial park between Tampico and the mouth of the Pánuco River, the Tampico refinery underwent nearly constant alteration and improvement. The facility manufactured a full range of products, such as lubricants, waxes, coke, and kerosene. The Tampico refinery was the pride of El Aguila. "The success of our Refineries should be such," Lord Cowdray ordered, "as will compare most favourably with any up to date Refinery controlled by the [Standard Oil] Co. or any other existing Refinery."[115] Still, the war interrupted refining developments too. Prices of imported machinery rose throughout the war, and finding technical personnel became difficult. The management constantly sought draft exemptions to retain its best British personnel. The war with Germany also brought into question the continued status of Dr. Weinstein, the German-born refinery manager. Cowdray had to use his influence at the Foreign Office to get permission for Weinstein to stay on. Indeed, Weinstein did remain with the company to supervise in 1920 the expansion of the Tampico refinery, involving expenditures of several million pounds.[116] Indeed, the El Aguila refinery at Tampico, the biggest in Mexico, became the most advanced, state-of-the-art oil facility in all the land. It would also become the center of labor militancy.

Ultimately, El Aguila the great producer also had to develop its capacity to transport petroleum to foreign markets. It recognized that a sizeable fleet of its own steam tankers would increase profits and enable the producing company to sell at the best prices in New York and London. El Aguila in 1911 spun off a separate shipping company, the Eagle Oil Transport Company, Ltd., and purchased its first tanker, the nine-thousand-ton *San Dunstano*. Quickly, the transport firm ordered the construction of other, and larger, steam transports. The *San Fraterno* came on line in 1912.[117] It was 548 feet long and had a total dead weight capacity of 15,700 tons of oil stored in twelve holds. Steam heating coils were installed in the holds to facilitate discharge at the rate of 1,200 tons per hour. These tankers ran on their own cargoes. On sailings to Great Britain, they consumed 13 percent of their fuel oil cargo. Cowdray's organization calculated that each of its ships made profits of between £23 and £76 per day.[118] By 1914, the company had seven tankers in operation and more on order in British shipyards. Cowdray was hoping soon to have twenty tank steamers carrying Mexican oil to Europe and South America.

The war interrupted all plans. Shipyards cancelled Cowdray's orders in order to build warships for the Admiralty. In addition, the Admiralty took over four of the tankers of Eagle Oil Transport for wartime duty, for which the company received a rental fee.[119] Just as Doheny had complained of his sacrifices for America's war efforts, Cowdray also chafed under Britain's draconian wartime measures. His company's activities in Mexico suffered because the Admiralty did not assign the commandeered ships to move Mexican oil. Feeling unfairly treated, Cowdray made proposals to increase the sales of his Mexican oil to the Admiralty in return for the use of one of his tankers. No deal. British naval commanders did not like the smoke. The German submarine campaign in the North Atlantic also took its toll. The company reported that all four commandeered El Aguila tankers had been torpe-doed and sunk in 1917.[120] No American competitor in Mexico had suf-fered from the war as did El Aguila.

The battle for the Mexican market between El Aguila and Waters-Pierce did not end when the former began exporting. Pierce continued to plant news stories in Mexican newspapers about how cozy the Pear-son group had been with the Díaz administration. Indeed, El Aguila still retained its directors from the Porfirian clique, Enrique Creel and Guillermo de Landa y Escandón. Lord Cowdray corresponded with José Yves Limantour, who had retired in Paris. The Pearson group in Mexico continued raiding the Pierce organization for personnel.[121] El Aguila still retained some advantages of low prices over Waters-Pierce's imported products. But now Waters-Pierce was buying domestic pro-duction from Huasteca and also got into production, especially in the northern fields. Its small refinery at Vera Cruz was running Mexican crude to the still.[122]

Be that as it may, El Aguila sought a formal market agreement with Waters-Pierce. Cowdray preferred a fifty-fifty market share on each item, except for fuel oil, which was El Aguila's strength. In this way, Cowdray hoped that the low prices might be lifted somewhat, in order to improve marketing profits. He knew that both companies were suf-fering from defaulted domestic accounts. During the Revolution, the Mexican economy had been so disrupted that rail lines and mining companies owed Waters-Pierce about one million pesos and Pear-son, approximately six hundred thousand pesos. Many accounts were described as "absolutely bankrupt."[123] Finally, the two old enemies reached a satisfactory market agreement. The fight was over. The news articles condemning the Pearson interests stopped appearing, and prices were raised on gasoline.[124] El Aguila's problems, in any case, had shifted from domestic to international markets.

The tendency to raise prices in Mexico in concert with world price trends during the war was also tempered somewhat by the competition and by Mexican nationalism. Also, many El Aguila subagents had been guilty of selling El Aguila products at higher than scheduled prices, cutting down on sales. In 1914, price hikes engendered domestic pro-test, and the company became somewhat circumspect about raising do-mestic prices too high. "I am afraid it would be detrimental to our in-terests to increase the price of our products," general manager Body decided, even though they still remained below import costs.[125] Under the circumstances, the company was making its profits in foreign markets now. In 1912, Cowdray reported that the new export trade was making approximately £2 million a year, while his domestic Mexican trade was garnering only £120,000.[126] The great oil boom had, quite suddenly, diminished the importance of the domestic market for the existence of the Mexican-based companies.

As it developed its refining and transporting capacities, El Aguila also had to build a world marketing organization. This was a paradoxical period in El Aguila's existence. The Mexican-based production company worked feverishly to make itself independent of the large marketing firms like Standard Oil Company of New Jersey. At the same time, however, it depended on Jersey Standard to buy its surplus crude oil. Cowdray himself had traveled to New York to arrange the sale of his crude oil to the big American companies. He negotiated secretly with Jersey Standard—and The Texas Company too—with a view to organizing his entire Mexican operations under one international company. In effect, he was offering to sell shares of his holdings to the Americans. After all, they had the markets—Cowdray only had oil. In 1911, Jersey's president, John Archbold, informed Cowdray that the company would soon be disassociating itself from Henry Clay Pierce and would be in a position then to deal with him.[127]

Ultimately, Jersey Standard declined purchase into El Aguila, but it did bail out the company by buying its crude. In 1912, Jersey concluded a five-year contract in which it promised to purchase a total of ten billion barrels of oil. To El Aguila, the contract was a lifesaver. Jersey Standard was not merely being magnanimous; it had been separated from its American production companies by the Supreme Court in 1911 and needed to find oil supplies to keep its marketing contracts filled. Using its own tankers, Jersey Standard obtained El Aguila's crude at preferential prices of fifteen cents to thirty cents (f.o.b. Tampico) for its refineries in Galveston, Sabine, Baton Rouge, New Orleans, Tampa, Baltimore, Philadelphia, and New York.[128] The price was well below Gulf Coast benchmark prices.

Yet El Aguila executives did not complain. Instead, they raised hosannahs. The agreement functioned well until 1914, when Standard Oil lost some of its shipping fleet to the government. After having taken 3.9 million barrels of El Aguila crude, Standard Oil technically had to breach the contract.[129] But during the war, Standard was still buying from El Aguila, albeit at higher prices, thirty-seven cents to forty cents per barrel, f.o.b. Tampico. Hoping to effect some wartime savings, Cowdray once suggested separating the highest quality crude oil from its deliveries to Standard Oil at Tampico and Tuxpan. General Manager Body dissuaded him. "It is not considered that it would be good policy," Body wrote diplomatically, "to discriminate in such a way against our best customer." In the end, Cowdray had to concur. The Jersey Standard sales agreements had been crucial to the company's survival. "[I]f we had given the oil away," said Cowdray, "we could not have disposed of any greater quantities than we have sold [to Jersey Standard]."[130]

However, the Jersey Standard contracts came with a catch—or perhaps with an uneven exchange. El Aguila agreed not to develop a marketing organization in the United States, and Standard Oil accepted El Aguila's market encroachment in South America. These agreements were not at all contractual ("We have an unwritten understanding with regard to trade in South America," said Cowdray in 1912 after attending a New York banquet given in his honor by John D. Rockefeller, Jr.), but they were nonetheless effective.[131] Unlike the Doheny interests, which expanded into marketing in the United States, the business interests of Lord Cowdray expanded elsewhere. The Standard Oil contract had prevented El Aguila from direct participation in the more lucrative U.S. market.

Nevertheless, the British company moved briskly on developing its own marketing apparatus in the United Kingdom and South America. In 1911, it bought out the Bowrings Company and formed Anglo-Mexican Petroleum Products Company, Ltd., for marketing in the United Kingdom. El Aguila's strength remained in fuel oil, where the Mexican-based company provided half of the United Kingdom's needs. It had fuel oil installations at the English ports of Manchester, Hull, Avonmouth, and Thames Haven, and an inland distribution system of river barges, rail tank cars, and road wagons. Its outlets for "spirits" (gasoline) and lubricants in England and Wales (there were none in Scotland and Ireland) numbered 229. Anglo-Mexican was not a dominant source of these products. On the London market in 1913, Anglo-Mexican provided only 6 percent of the city's kerosene consumption, 1.2 percent of its lubricants, and 2 percent of its "motor spirits." Anglo-Mexican also had depots in Canada, Tampico, Veracruz, St. Thomas (West Indies), Pará, Rio de Janeiro, Santos, and Buenos Aires. Interoceanic and coastal vessels on the east coast of South America and river craft on the Amazon and Paraná river basins operated on Mexican fuel oil.[132] By the end of the war, El Aguila was a major supplier of fuel and bunker oils in the Atlantic world—except for the United States.

Despite the wartime disruption, El Aguila had emerged from the great Mexican oil boom as a great multinational oil enterprise. In 1915, Cowdray claimed a capital investment of £12 million and employment of three thousand to four thousand persons outside of Mexico. Its profits reached figures of 6 million gold pesos in 1915 and 10.3 million in 1916. At its height in 1921, El Aguila was producing nearly 38.3 million barrels of crude oil per year and making profits of nearly 82 million gold pesos.[133]

The Paradox of Rapid Expansion

Although his business was profitable and growing, Lord Cowdray felt continually preoccupied with pinching pennies and paying dividends to stockholders at the same time that he built an expensive, giant oil company quickly. Cowdray grew increasingly weary of the oil business. In 1916, he wrote to Body:

> We have to be all the time remembering that the many demands that are being made for capital expenditure upon the Aguila Co. cannot take priority over the dividends that have to be paid. What with our dividend programme and our big capital expenditure programme it will, I know, take us all our time to provide the moneys they require. Of course, we cannot stand still but we have to keep the tightest grip possible on all expenditure.[134]

The wartime exigencies only made manifest his many financial vulnerabilities. Although production and profits had doubled during the war, his company's degree of business independence in terms of refining capacity, transportation, and marketing had not much advanced. Cowdray perceived correctly that he could not compete effectively with the truly great international oil companies: Royal Dutch–Shell, any of the Standard Oil groups, The Texas Company, and Gulf. Its high profits surely would be in jeopardy when prices declined again.

Why? The reason was that El Aguila was imperfectly integrated. Its production far surpassed the firm's capacity to transport, refine, and sell it. In 1919, for example, the British company was producing about 100,000 bd but refining and topping only 28,000 bd. Its fleet could not carry very much of the crude oil that it sold abroad.[135] Other Mexican-based companies faced the same dilemma. Production had expanded so rapidly that the companies had not been able to construct enough capacity to refine it all. In 1918, consequently, more than two-thirds of Mexican oil was exported in its crude state. About one-quarter was reduced by a process of primary distillation, called topping, so that it could be used for bunker and fuel oils. Only 6 percent of the Mexican production was distilled further for the lubricants, illuminants, and waxes and sold on the domestic Mexican market.

But El Aguila was worse off than the Doheny group, which also remained somewhat imperfectly integrated. The difference was that El Aguila suffered more from wartime interruption, and it had a tacit agreement with Jersey Standard not to enter the biggest market of all, the continental United States. The great Mexican oil boom had confronted Cowdray with the paradox of rapid expansion: as it grew, El Aguila became an ever-more-imbalanced oil firm. The choice for Cowdray was simple: either he had to purchase refining and marketing capacity to match his production or he had to sell his production company to a refiner and marketer. His decision was always clear. He wanted to sell out. But to whom?

One logical buyer was the Standard Oil Company of New Jersey. For six years, Cowdray and Jersey's executives carried on a coquettish, on-again, off-again courtship. It occurred to Jersey officials to purchase El Aguila and/or Huasteca as early as 1911. In September 1911, shortly after Cowdray paid a visit to New York in order to sell his crude oil, Arthur Corwin led a party of Jersey men to inspect Mexico. He recommended: (1) that a customs pipeline should not be built because it was not yet justified; (2) that Jersey should not enter Mexico to lease for development ("Based on the seepage showing, by far the richest seen in any oil fields, the cream of the territory has been taken," he wrote); and (3) that Jersey attempt to acquire "at a fair price" the Huasteca Company (preferred) or El Aguila, or both.[136] What constituted a fair price was subject to judgment. Neither Doheny nor Cowdray were willing to give away their Mexican properties. Standard Oil had also been quite leery of the political problems that El Aguila had been having with the Madero government. Jersey executives noted, "We have seen newspaper clippings to the effect that the Madero Government is going to try and if possible cancel some of the concessions granted to the Pearson interests."[137] Anyway, Jersey was not terribly motivated at the end of 1911. Standard Oil executives were busy reorganizing following the dissolution, and they bought crude from their own domestic suppliers and from Mexico too. So for the moment, Jersey Standard decided not to purchase any Mexican properties.

In the spring of 1913, Jersey Standard began to change its mind again. It asked to see all of the assets and balance sheets of El Aguila. Cowdray complied. Jersey President Archbold even traveled to London and discussed the purchase of El Aguila with Lord Cowdray. Then, Cowdray noticed that Archbold's ardor suddenly blew cold again. Archbold said that his legal department had advised against purchase of any new ventures until the dissolution matters were fully sorted out.[138] Perhaps Cowdray did not know, but Jersey Standard at that very moment was pursuing a second attractive British firm. And in 1913, it secretly bought the Peruvian oil properties of the London and Pacific, a mercantile group. Apparently, the matter was one of price. A Jersey inspection team had evaluated the Peruvian properties to be worth four times what they would have to pay for them under their option agreement.[139] Having successfully bought a Peruvian oil field, its first in Latin America, Standard Oil declined to enter the more expensive Mexican industry as a direct producer. Yet Jersey executives couched their objections in political terms, not economic. "[I]n view of existing conditions, political and legal," wrote Archbold to Cowdray, "we are not in position to pursue [the purchase of El Aguila] at this time."[140]

Once again, beginning in November 1916, Lord Cowdray and Jersey Standard resumed their transatlantic courtship. Lord Cowdray continued to think of selling El Aguila because it would relieve him of the endless—though fascinating—details of the business. He would have preferred to sell a majority of his shares to a knowledgeable oil enterprise, and Standard Oil New Jersey certainly qualified. Jersey Standard's new president, Walter Teagle, declared again that the asking price was too high by about 50 percent. The negotiations continued into 1917.[141] In the midst of wartime, when His Majesty's government was concerned about oil supplies, the Petroleum Rationing Committee decided not to allow British-controlled oil properties in Mexico to pass into U.S. hands. A final appeal was rejected by His Majesty's government in 1918. The Lords Commissioners of the British Treasury "do not feel able to give the instructions you suggest, to the Board of Trade to permit the transfer of your shares to an American citizen."[142] Pearson interests finally brought the affair with Standard Oil to an end. Neither oil firm was anxious to move against the displeasure of His Majesty's government. By that time, Jersey Standard had moved into Mexico by purchasing another, smaller British-controlled company, anyway. Although Cowdray was close to British political authorities, that proximity did not always give him the business freedom he may have desired. They prevented him from selling out to the Americans.

The Pearson interests were not averse to an all-British solution to its paradox of rapid growth. This had been one option that Cowdray had always pursued. In his quest for access to superior capital resources, he had conferred often with government officials about an amalgam with Anglo-Persian or the Burmah Company. He had also been negotiating, apparently fruitlessly, with Anglo-Persian officials for marketing the products of El Aguila in England and on the Continent.[143] Cowdray had also suggested the formation of an all-British "Imperial Oil Company," in which His Majesty's government was to purchase shares of El Aguila, providing capital for expansion. Cowdray was hopeful of government aid. After all, unlike Doheny and the U.S. government, Lord Cowdray remained on close terms with His Majesty's government. He was consulted about major decisions on Mexico and on petroleum matters, even if the government did not always heed his advice. For the best part of 1917, moreover, Lord Cowdray became minister of aircraft, receiving a new title of Viscount Cowdray of Cowdray in the process. He had a falling out with Prime Minister Lloyd George at the end of the year and resigned his government post.[144]

But the government was reluctant to form an Imperial Company. It worried about political conditions in Mexico during the Revolution, and it did not want to provoke the United States by violating its Monroe Doctrine.[145] With considerable pique and exasperation, Lord Cowdray lashed out at the government's opposition of a sale to Standard Oil and its simultaneous refusal to form a government-supported oil company. "We find it difficult to believe," he wrote diffidently in 1918, "that the Lords Commissioners [of the Treasury] intend to tie our hands, without providing us with a remedy."[146] Disappointed by his own government, Lord Cowdray had to find a different suitor altogether. Was El Aguila to be left standing eternally at the altar?

Deals Made in Foreign Fields

Inevitably, the large multinational oil companies such as Standard Oil New Jersey, Royal Dutch–Shell, The Texas Company, and Gulf became interested in the great Mexican oil boom. Why? One long-standing view holds that the modern world had become a battleground for the control of petroleum resources between Shell and Standard Oil. Each capitalist organization, so the argument goes, attempted to monopolize the world's oil resources—not for immediate development to benefit the host countries but to be able eventually to strangle the world's consumers with high, monopoly prices. This view has had a particular appeal to Latin American intellectuals and politicians. It has justified the regulation of foreign interests and the state's nationalization of oil resources in the twentieth century.[147] However appealing, the viewpoint lacks a basis in fact. One might state more accurately that the big international oil companies had to expand into Latin American and world production or decline as competitive business entities.

In a world in which the oil business was booming, the development of independent firms actually eroded the market dominance of great companies like Standard Oil. Standard Oil exporting companies like the Waters-Pierce and West Indian Oil companies had dominated oil sales in Latin America since the 1880s; the opening up of production by independent companies in countries threatened to reduce Jersey Standard's sales through the process of import-substitution. Private British investors began developing the oil fields of Peru's northern coast in 1887. In the lucrative market of Argentina, a government water-drilling crew discovered oil in 1907.[148] And finally, the independent oil producers, E. L. Doheny and Sir Weetman Pearson, discovered oil in the Faja de Oro of Mexico in 1910. These discoveries threatened not merely to eliminate Standard's export markets in the specific countries of discovery but also to encroach upon markets shares in neighboring countries as well. By 1912, both Doheny and Lord Cowdray were establishing storage depots and arranging petroleum sales in Rio de Janeiro and Buenos Aires and in Europe and the United States as well.

Expansion into Mexico was more a question of survival than of domination. The biggest companies had to expand into foreign production or be excluded and absorbed by more aggressive competitors. The oil industry found economic advantages in vertical integration— controlling all assets of the business from production, transportation, refining, marketing, and sales. Vertical integration assured outlets for crude, for a steadier and more efficient planning of output over time. It made possible more efficient operation of expensive refineries as a result of a secure and managed flow of crude oil. It allowed a flexible adjustment to short-run changes in demand of different products in different areas and cushioned, as much as possible, disruptive price fluctuations that would raise costs to producers and consumers.[149] For this reason, neither of the two biggest international oil concerns of the twentieth century, the Standard Oil Company of New Jersey and the Royal Dutch–Shell Company, could afford to ignore the great Mexican oil boom. They had to participate in it or be diminished by it. They chose to participate.

Jersey Standard, after all, faced a rather imbalanced integration in the 1910s too. Unlike Huasteca and El Aguila, Standard did not have enough production. The Supreme Court in 1911 had taken away its U.S. producing companies. Overseas, where it had always been, until the expansion of foreign production, a dominant supplier of export U.S. petroleum, Standard Oil faced aggressive competition. Thus, the second decade of the twentieth century marked a time of great transition in the company. It too expanded vigorously into foreign production.

Two men dominated this transition at the Jersey Standard corporate offices at 26 Broadway. Both had early foreign experience, one in production and the other in sales. Together, they fashioned a policy in which foreign sales would have been impossible without foreign production. Walter C. Teagle, an Ohio-bred oilman who had foreign experience in Britain and Canada, became president of Jersey Standard in 1916, representing a new postdissolution generation of Jersey executives. He was still a young man and although a part of the legal controversies that separated the Standard Oil companies in 1911, he was not inhibited by the experience.[150] Teagle's background in European sales, Canadian production and sales, and exporting disposed him toward foreign production as well.

He was not entirely alone. Everett J. Sadler also served as a catalyst directing the company toward foreign production. He had been manager of Standard's production company in Romania, where in 1917, he witnessed the German army's occupation of his company's assets. Returning to New York, he urged the company aggressively to pursue foreign production elsewhere. "I feel," he wrote, "the real source of power in the oil business is control of production, and it does not seem that our company is sufficiently fortified in this respect. Foreign production is almost exclusively in the hands of our competitors. In the last ten years many big deals have been made in foreign fields as in Japan, Persia, Russia, Galicia, Egypt, Mexico, Romania, Venezuela, Dutch Indies, etc."[151] Sadler suggested a long-term, comprehensive program for Jersey Standard. The firm should be at the forefront of collecting data about development work and transfers of oil properties throughout the world. He warned against depending on only a few localities.

"[P]olitical events, government monopolies, freight rates, or many other causes can shut particular sections out from competition."[152] Sadler became a persuasive proponent of overseas production in several Latin American areas.

Moreover, the company's foreign marketing expanded appreciably throughout the second decade of the twentieth century. In 1912, Latin American earnings amounted nearly to $1.5 million, 16.7 percent of Jersey's total overseas sales. By 1918, the total earnings had risen to more than $7.9 million, and Latin America constituted 43 percent of all Jersey's international sales. Its Latin American sales subsidiary, West Indian Oil Company, had marketing depots throughout the Caribbean Islands, the Dutch and British Guianas, Bolivia, Colombia, Ecuador, Venezuela, Chile, Panama, Guatemala, Argentina, Paraguay, and Uruguay.[153] Increased sales in Latin America dictated a more open policy at Jersey Standard concerning foreign production. Ultimately, Jersey Standard responded to Sadler's admonitions: they sent him to Mexico for additional foreign experience. When the foreign production department was created in 1919, Sadler was placed in charge. Sadler's clout within the company appreciated again the next year when he was made a member of Jersey Standard's board of directors. By this time, the operations of Standard's recently acquired properties in Peru (1913), Mexico (1917), and Colombia (1919) as well as the properties in Indonesia all came under Sadler's operational control. It was not long, however, until Sadler's organization was exploring and seeking concessions in additional countries, such as Argentina, Bolivia, Venezuela, and the Middle East. "[O]ur first efforts should be to obtain crude for our existing refineries," Sadler wrote, "and to supply our European and South American marketing organizations."[154] Latin America was the principal theater of Jersey's foreign activities in the 1910s and the 1920s. Mexico was the testing ground.

The enmity between Jersey and its erstwhile affiliate, Waters-Pierce, came to a climax in 1911. The Supreme Court dissolution of 1911 separated thirty-seven companies from the Standard Oil Company (New Jersey). It lost its major producing fields, pipelines, and refineries, except for the Bayonne, New Jersey, plant. Nonetheless, Jersey Standard remained the largest oil company in the world and retained most of its foreign-marketing apparatus. Most, that is, except for the Waters-Pierce Oil Company, Standard's link to the Mexican market. The Supreme Court dissolution also removed Henry Clay Pierce from the Standard orbit. What remains ironical about the dissolution of Standard Oil is that the petroleum industry worldwide had been expanding so rapidly that the Standard Oil group had been becoming less of a monopoly.[155] Every oil boom like the one in Mexico had created new rival oil companies and had reduced Standard Oil's market shares.

The new aggressive foreign policy of Teagle and Sadler, however, took time to coalesce. On the one hand, Jersey Standard's older executives, those like Bedford and Archbold, had grown cautious after long years of fighting domestic lawsuits. They were also apprehensive about the Mexican Revolution. On the other hand, it was convenient to arrange long-term contracts for the purchase of Mexican crude from independent producers, as the company did in 1911 and 1912 when prices were low. It was not that Standard Oil was asleep in Mexico, as one Jersey attorney put it, but the company was able to buy large amounts of oil cheaply. Under the circumstances, its geologists questioned the wisdom of developing production in Mexico in 1911 when you could buy someone else's oil at ten cents a barrel.[156]

In 1914, Jersey Standard established its first asset in Mexico, a small skimming plant on the south bank of the Pánuco River near Tampico. The plant separated Huasteca and El Aguila crude into fractions meeting the varying needs of Jersey's scattered refineries and those of other refiners.[157] Change was coming, however slowly. "Standard men [had] a way of saying that the Dissolution was one of the greatest things that ever happened to Standard," commented Burton Wilson, an American attorney for Jersey Standard in Mexico. "It was great because Standard had become [so] over-centralized . . . at 26 Broadway that the men in the outlying offices were afraid to take any initiative."[158]

Henry Clay Pierce did not want Jersey Standard to enter Mexico. But neither did very many Mexican-based companies. Pierce whipped up Mexican fears of the foreign trusts and monopolies whenever it appeared that Standard might buy El Aguila or Huasteca. In 1912, Shelburne Hopkins, a New York lawyer said to be in the employ of Henry Clay Pierce, accused Standard Oil of controlling Mexico's entire production of crude oil. "About four months ago," Hopkins told Congressional investigators,

that company purchased some 400 acres of land, surreptitiously at Tampico, and the Standard Oil Co. sent down its own men to go over the land and survey it and purchase it for the Magnolia Co., all the while denying that they had any interest in it. They were to erect, and will erect, on that land an immense refinery, and with that as a base and with the possible consolidation with the Aguila Oil Co. they will endeavor to monopolize the oil business in Mexico, precisely as they did in this country until recently; all of which I think will be bitterly opposed by the Madero administration and the Federal Government of Mexico.[159]

One competitor, at least, appealed to extraeconomic stratagems to keep a rival out of the petroleum market.

Taking Advantage of Opportunities

Nevertheless, Jersey agents began to participate in the search for prospective oil lands and leases. So as not to attract attention or to force up prices, the agents always took out the leases in their own names. The first was James W. Flanagan. A flamboyant Texan of Irish descent, Flanagan claimed to have been a conductor on the Mexican Central Railroad and, later, to have fought with the rebels in the Cuban war for independence. He earned the title of captain in the Spanish-American War. Flanagan was an unusual Standard Oil man. He had no particular education nor experience in the oil business, and he was a Catholic in something of a white Anglo-Saxon Protestant organization. Good with languages and having a charming personality when the occasion called for it, Flanagan became the confidential employee of Walter Teagle. He was tapped for special and secret missions, often having to do with making political connections, as he did later in Peru and Colombia. His tie to Teagle and Standard was never to be admitted, seldom even to Standard's top men in the field. Flanagan was a man made for legend and intrigue.

Armed with introductions to important men of different revolutionary groups, Flanagan entered Mexico in June 1914. He arrived at a moment when the revolutionary turmoil of the highlands had just descended upon the tranquility of the oil zone. "It is impossible to convey to you in an intelligent manner the extreme chaotic conditions that exist in this country," he reported to Teagle.[160] The rebels were assessing forced loans and fines on the oilmen. The Americans had just occupied Veracruz, and some armed groups harbored hostility to the gringos. He reported that he had to talk himself out of one holdup. On a trip to Tuxpan, he said, he was "taking no arms whatever, believing that I had best take my chances talking than fighting through any difficulties."[161] Nonetheless, he persevered in a search for oil properties that took him, by foot and by dugout canoe, into the *monte*.

It may be that Flanagan was more flamboyant than effective, more flimflam and boastful than successful, at his work. He constantly wrote to his benefactor Teagle of his multiple difficulties. One American engineer pretended to offer Flanagan an "unbiased" professional opinion on a property that the engineer himself was secretly selling. The Cuban war veteran, however, did provide useful intelligence to Teagle, informing him of the problems of obtaining safe titles to properties in an area where the complexity of ownership was extreme. The Hacienda Moyutla near Tuxpan, for example, had been so hopelessly divided among heirs that proof of ownership was nearly impossible to establish.[162] And Flanagan waxed eloquently about the graft and corruption of Mexican politicians and public officials. But as far as the documents show, Teagle never authorized Flanagan to offer graft money nor did Teagle advance him any funds for that purpose.[163] In truth, Flanagan had very little to show after two years in the country. Teagle finally sent him on a mission to obtain an oil concession from the Peruvian government (in which he did not succeed) and brought in John Kee of the Carter Oil Company. Within a year, Kee had obtained thirty-three leases in such promising areas as Zacamixtle, Chinampa, and Amatlán.[164] So much less flamboyant than Flanagan, Kee nevertheless was a more fitting Standard Oil man: quiet, unassuming, low profile, but effective.

Yet up to 1917, Standard Oil for all practical purposes had not been a party to the enormous development of the Mexican oil industry. Besides a small topping plant and a few leases, Jersey had no production in Mexico at all. Not only were Huasteca and El Aguila expanding into Standard Oil markets in the United States and South America, but others of the fabled Seven Sisters (the seven largest oil companies of the world) already had operations in Mexico. Shell had established a production company in 1912, at the same time that it obtained the largest oil concessions in Venezuela. Mexican Gulf of the Mellon group and The Texas Company also entered Mexico, and Standard Oil Company of New York had just acquired the Penn-Mex concern through its South Penn subsidiary. "[A]ll of our principal competitors are more strongly entrenched in Mexico than we," said Sadler. "They were earlier in the field and bought their property under more advantageous conditions than will probably ever exist again. They are all in shape to make deliveries from the moment that steamers will be available for the purpose."[165] These big competitors were developing their own refineries and marketing organizations. The danger was that soon none of the producers in Mexico would have to sell their crude petroleum to Jersey Standard. Then what?

Almost as a matter of self-defense, Jersey Standard finally relented and purchased a Mexican producing company. It was not Huasteca or El Aguila, properties found to be too expensive or politically inexpedient to acquire. Late in 1917, Jersey Standard bought the Compañía Petrolera de Transcontinental, a British company with American stockholders. For nearly $2.5 million, Jersey Standard acquired a Mexican charter, valuable leases, permits to construct pipelines and storage tanks, import tax-exemptions, one producing oil well in the northern fields, and no refinery.[166] Why late 1917 and not sooner? By that time, Teagle and Sadler were making their opinions known among Standard Oil executives. Now that the United States had entered the war, the British government was no longer adverse to allowing a small company, at least, to pass into the hands of an ally. Furthermore, the strategic importance of petroleum supplies during wartime had tempered the hostility of the U.S. government toward Standard Oil. Jersey thus decided to go ahead with a direct purchase of Transcontinental.

The architect of Jersey's new foreign production, E. J. Sadler himself, assumed the head of Transcontinental. His plans for the new Standard Oil subsidiary were ambitious. Sadler wanted Transcontinental to purchase new production and leases from other small firms that because of the war could borrow capital only at high rates of interest and had difficulty finding transport. "We will not fail," he hoped, "to take advantage of the opportunity which is now presented to equal and surpass the greater number of our competitors in Mexico." He planned for Transcontinental's delivering 100,000 bd of Mexican crude between the northern and southern fields.[167] Article 27 of the Mexican Constitution, which claimed national ownership (as opposed to private ownership) of all subsoil wealth, had gone into effect on 1 May 1917. Sadler did not indicate that it caused him the slightest concern when, shortly afterwards, he took up his new assignment in Mexico.

Sadler arrived at a time when world oil prices were rising to record heights. Transcontinental's expansion followed in short order. The first wells were exceptionally productive. One well in the Pánuco district was gauged at 76,000 barrels per day, and the first two producers in the southern fields reached a combined capacity of 60,000 bd.[168] Sadler was directing an extraordinary expenditure on transportation, refining, and terminal facilities. In 1920, Transcontinental acquired the La Barra refinery near Tampico. The number of employees in Mexico rose from

751 in 1918 to 3,313 in 1920. Jersey Standard raised its direct invest-ment in Mexico from $730,000 to more than $5.2 million. By 1922, the dollar investment in Transcontinental amounted to $32.6 million. New leases had been acquired on the Isthmus of Tehuantepec and in northern Mexico.[169] As a parent company, Jersey Standard had the ability to draw earnings from many subsidiaries and lend large amounts of capital to designated companies. It had a great reservoir of its own investment capital. As of December 1912, Jersey's ledgers recorded loans of $110.8 million to affiliates.[170] The war did not much inhibit the growth of these internal capital transfers. At a time when Lord Cowdray and his British-owned El Aguila were strapped for capital, Standard Oil of New Jersey poured money into Mexico.

Like others, Transcontinental's managers also began to notice the exhaustion of its new oil wells, particularly those in the southern fields, as salt water rose to replace the crude oil in the hastily exploited oil pools of Zacamixtle. The decline of some wells began in 1919. By then, Transcontinental had only two wells in the southern zone; they pro-duced abundantly but were beginning to flow to salt water. A plan was considered to decrease the rate of flow. Representatives of Transconti-nental, El Aguila, and The Texas Company met late in 1920 to discuss a joint conservation program for the Amatlán, Zacamixtle, and Chi-nampa. In these fields, the wells were driven by hydrostatic pressure, and the keen competition multiplied the number of wells. The under-lying salt water, consequently, rose in the wells faster than if the wells had been pinched back. Yet none of these oilmen understood exactly how much retardation of flow rates would have prolonged the wells. They did not agree on any conservation policy at all. In fact, the man-agers decided to drill even more wells to make up for dwindling production.[171] Dealing with the problem of salt-water encroachment was put off, although not exactly ignored, as long as total production continued rising during the great oil boom.

There was little doubt, however, that Jersey Standard had finally en-tered the Mexican oil industry, even though its long-expected entry had been delayed. The company did not exactly enter Mexico in order to capture all the country's oil production or to strengthen its command of the world's oil resources. Instead, Jersey Standard entered Mexico for the same reason that ultimately drove it to enter every major oil boom in the United States from 1859 to 1910. It expanded in order *not* to lose any more market shares than necessary to the new companies cre-ated by each new boom. When oil production went international in the

twentieth century, Jersey Standard too had to go international. If it did
not enter Latin American production, Jersey stood to forfeit its lucrative markets there to upstarts like El Aguila and Huasteca. It was the
same for other big companies.

Pulling Together Makes Strength

If Jersey Standard was becoming more directly involved
in the great Mexican oil boom, was not its arch rival, Royal Dutch–
Shell, close behind? In fact, the competition of the one tended to drive
on the other, and together, Jersey and Shell were driven by the success
of the Pearson and Doheny groups. Unlike the image presented by
many observers at the time—and by some historians since—Shell and
Jersey Standard were not engaging in some sort of death struggle
to wrest control of world markets and oil supplies from each other.
The Mexican oil boom created El Aguila and Huasteca, potential competitors. So, like Jersey Standard, the Royal Dutch–Shell had to get
into Mexico.

The Royal Dutch had its beginning in oil production in the Dutch
East Indies (today Indonesia). By the end of the nineteenth century, the
Royal Dutch had built up markets in the Far East supplied by production and refining in Sumatra. Standard Oil once, in 1897, attempted to
buy out the company, an offer the Dutch directors refused to take, and
in 1907, the Royal Dutch combined with the British company Shell
Oil Transport, widening its access to markets in Europe, Great Britain,
and especially throughout the British Empire.[172] The Royal Dutch–
Shell was not averse to using its special national privileges in a Dutch
colony and did what it could to keep Standard Oil from developing in
the Dutch East Indies. At least this was the view of Standard's executives; actually, Standard established production on the island of Sumatra despite the best efforts of the Royal Dutch.

Shell's interest in Latin America came through its imperial connection. As a half-British, half-Dutch company, it explored the possibility
of producing oil amidst the numerous pitch lakes of the British island
colony of Trinidad. Before World War I, Shell was selling petroleum
products in many of the larger markets of Latin America. According to
the "straight-line" theory of the president of the Royal Dutch–Shell,
Sir Henri Deterding, the expanding company needed to find produc-

tion close to its new markets. As Sir Henri explained, "[Shell's] business has been built up primarily on the principle that each market must be supplied with products emanating from the fields which are most favorably situated geographically. . . . In order, however, to maintain our position in the world market it is not sufficient to be satisfied with the advantages already obtained. We must not be outstripped in this struggle to obtain new territory."[173]

Deterding directed his crews from Trinidad to Venezuela. Shell acquired options to several huge but quite neglected Venezuelan oil concessions. The Mexican oil boom having just begun, no Americans were interested in developing any more production—at least, not yet. So Shell had a free hand in Venezuela for a decade. By 1912, crews of American geologist Ralph Arnold had selected drilling sites, and the first small production for Shell came in 1916 in the Maracaibo Basin. Here it built a small refinery whose products soon undersold those imported into the country by Jersey's West Indian Oil Company. Shell finally brought in a gusher in 1922, and the Venezuelan oil boom was on.[174] By that time, the American oil industry had become quite interested in finally shifting its attention from Mexico to the great Venezuelan oil boom. A decade earlier, however, Mexico was the biggest name on the international oil map.

In the very same year that Shell sent geologists to Venezuela, 1912, it established its first subsidiary in Mexico. The Royal Dutch–Shell saw its Mexican—and to a lesser extent, its future Venezuelan—production as a method of getting into the domestic United States market. At the time, Shell was setting up marketing outlets in California for its Sumatra production. It could use Mexican and Venezuelan production for markets on the East Coast of the United States.[175] Having shunned an opportunity to purchase Furber's Oil Fields of Mexico, Shell rushed into the swarm of lease prospectors, obtaining an option on 150,000 acres in the northern fields. The N. V. Petroleum Maatshappij La Corona was formed in the Netherlands in December of 1912 in order to funnel five hundred thousand guilders into the Mexican enterprise. Seven wells were drilled on various properties in Topila. Only the fifth well, in January 1914, came in a gusher, initially producing 100,000 bd of the thicker crude of the northern fields.

La Corona would have preferred working on a larger, more secure oil field of its own. It acquired the 1.25-million-acre hacienda north of Tampico, San José de las Rusias, and purchased 820,000 acres of the El Cojo hacienda. Neither yielded much oil. La Corona had also purchased land for a tank farm and oil terminal at El Rodeo on the southern bank of the Pánuco River, just four kilometers from the mouth of the river. Upriver, at Chijol, La Corona constructed a river terminal in order to dispatch its oil downriver by barge. By 1914, the Dutch colony in Tampico numbered nearly one hundred people, mostly employees of La Corona and workers from the Dutch colony of Curaçao.[176] Expansion was cut back during the war as a result of the parent company's lack of cash.

Like El Aguila, La Corona could not expand at the very moment that Jersey Standard's subsidiary, Transcontinental, was growing rapidly. La Corona suffered from the multiple transport, marketing, and capital problems then afflicting war-torn Europe. Although oil had been exported from the El Rodeo terminal before the war, La Corona's dependence on European tankers curtailed exports during the four years of the European war. At any rate, the heavy quality of the crude from the Pánuco area required much refining before it could be used for motor oil and fuel oil. La Corona had shut in its Pánuco No. 5 well, which lost much of its high flow rate as a result.[177] Production rose, but slowly, from 553,000 barrels in 1916 to 737,000 barrels in 1917, but only because La Corona was buying out smaller companies. The 20,000–bd refinery that La Corona planned had to await construction until after the war. Production rose following the war when its wildcat crews entered the southern fields as well, opening up Cacalilao in 1920. Thereafter, Corona's production rose from 4.2 million barrels in 1920 to 17.5 in 1922. By then, the encroachment of salt water was greatly reducing La Corona's potential.[178] This small firm would remain part of Shell's entree into Mexico, but La Corona could hardly be termed, by itself, a great success. It was not Shell's ticket into American and other Latin American markets.

Following the war, therefore, Deterding moved quickly to expand in Mexico in other ways. He negotiated to purchase El Aguila. Apparently, this suitor had approached Lord Cowdray as early as 1914, but Deterding rejected a purchase at the time because El Aguila lacked long-term sales contracts for its great production. In 1918, however, Shell wanted to create a larger "all British" oil concern in Mexico. Deterding had wanted to buy 51 percent of El Aguila's shares. Since the Royal Dutch–Shell was already half British, then El Aguila would have remained very much a British entity, thus overriding some of the concerns of the British government.[179] The two companies entered into formal contract in March of 1919. The Royal Dutch–Shell paid the

Pearson group a reported £10 million. By agreement, Shell's share actually was less than 50 percent but the Pearson group, contractually, turned over managerial control to Shell, permitting it a majority of members on the board of directors. Shell's managerial control would last for twenty-one years—until 1 January 1940.[180] In this way, Deterding was acting on another of his business maxims: "Pulling together makes strength." That is to say, large business enterprises succeed not when they engage in cutthroat competition and price wars but when they combine through alliance and partnership.[181]

Cowdray had wanted a market pooling agreement to be included in the sales contract. El Aguila would thereby gain access to Shell's worldwide markets for all its excess Mexican production, none of which thereafter would be in danger of going unsold. But Shell resisted. "I shall consider it my duty," Deterding wrote to Cowdray, "even if no Pooling Agreement is entered into, to safeguard the interests of the Mexican Eagle shareholders in every way."[182] Cowdray bought it. So did the British government, which had been advised of the negotiations and did not raise the same objections it had to a Standard Oil–El Aguila combination.

Lord Cowdray finally solved his paradox of rapid growth. The merger with Shell increased the refining and marketing capacity available to handle El Aguila's vast production, which he considered necessary for the continued and unimpeded growth of El Aguila. Also, by this time, he had become quite annoyed at the obstacles placed in his path by the British government. El Aguila now benefited from Shell's superior access to capital for expansion and to petroleum technology for future exploration. Shell also benefited. It jettisoned the small La Corona refinery at Tampico and expanded the El Aguila refinery into Mexico's largest. In 1920, the Shell-Mex Company was established in order to combine its own marketing organization with that of the Anglo-Mexican Company in England.[183] Moreover, in Mexico, Shell became the second largest producer, surpassing the growing Jersey Standard subsidiary, Transcontinental. This must have provided Deterding no end of satisfaction. In one fell swoop, Shell had obtained at least one-quarter of all Mexican production and one-half of the Mexican market.[184]

Production now proceeded at full tilt, in part because of the relaxation of wartime disruptions and the availability of capital. Rising prices spurred the entire process. Having sold for as little as 40 cents before the war, a barrel of Gulf Coast crude oil had climbed to $1.80

Vista general de la Refinería "El Aguila" en 1917. Tampico.

Fig. 9. Panorama of the El Aguila refinery at Tampico, 1917. This was already Mexico's largest refinery, and construction was still continuing. Nearly one thousand men worked here. Courtesy of the Rama del Trabajo, Archivo General de la Nación, Mexico City.

in 1918 and reached a peak of $2.50 in 1920 before falling again. (See graph 1.) El Aguila's production overcame its ceiling of less than seventeen million barrels per annum during the war years to reach nearly thirty-three million barrels in 1920 (see table 6). Remarkably, this advance in production came about just as the cornerstone well of the entire company, Potrero No. 4, was beginning to show signs of exhaustion. On 3 December 1918, company officials received word from the field managers that the well showed emulsion. Additional indications of hot salt water in the oil caused the well to be pinched back and finally shut in. Potrero No. 4 had yielded nearly 104.8 million barrels of crude oil in its nine years of existence. Some of its past production remained to be used. More than 9.8 million barrels of Potrero's crude remained stored in huge, open-air earthen reservoirs.[185]

As regards direction of the company, El Aguila's former officials, all of whom had been recruited over the years by Lord Cowdray, continued operating the company's business. J. B. Body would eventually leave the general managerial position in Mexico City and take up an office in Shell's London office, where he coordinated the Mexico activi-

ties. T. J. Ryder remained in the New York office until he retired early in the 1920s. Two assistant managers in Mexico would eventually move into the direction of El Aguila's affairs in Mexico. J. A. Assheton replaced Body as general manager and A. E. Chambers acted as his deputy. Most supervisors of oil fields and refineries remained at their posts. The continuity of company policy was significant, as was the deference that Shell headquarters gave to this experienced team to run the oil operations in Mexico and deal with local labor and political conditions.

Salt-water intrusion, a signal of the impending exhaustion of the oil field, was not easily dismissed. Geologists, drillers, and their employers had been aware all along of the relationship between the salt water and the oil in the limestone reservoirs. Two wells that Pearson had drilled near the Dos Bocas blowout had produced little else but hot water. As early as 1911, numerous wells in the El Ebano field, Mexico's oldest, had begun to yield "large quantities of hot water with the oil." Several wells at the Hacienda Santa Fe, near Topila, which Pierce had acquired, had also gone to salt water as early as 1913.[186] Now that the truly prolific wells of the southern fields were flowing emulsion, Shell was confronted with having paid £10 million for declining oil fields. The company moved to reassure its stockholders. In its 1920 annual report, El Aguila said: "Particular emphasis is drawn by the directors to the fact

Table 6. *Production, Profits, and Dividends of El Aguila, 1911–1920*

	Production (no. of barrels)	Net Profit (in pesos)	Dividend Rate (% per share)
1911	3,813,827	437,086	8[a]
1912	5,228,675	2,131,521	8[a]
1913	11,274,540	4,083,258	8[a]
1914	10,879,898	4,844,487	8[ab]
1915	16,145,989	5,607,750	8[ab]
1916	16,425,292	8,532,000	16[ab]
1917	16,906,251	9,935,329	20[ab]
1918	16,892,918	14,117,720	25[ab]
1919	18,740,000	18,597,213	45[ab]
1920	32,931,572	29,726,786	60[ab]
Total	149,238,972	98,014,150	206%[a] 182%[b]

[a]Preferred stock.
[b]Ordinary stock.

SOURCES: "Production Mexican Eagle," n.d., DeGolyer, File 5300; *Mexican Eagle Oil Company, Ltd.* (New York, 1921), 3.

that the appearance of salt water in some of the more heavily exploited fields need cause no anxiety to the shareholders, in view of the company's large reserve territories."[187] But the annual report was wrong. The great Mexican oil boom had already reached the beginning of decline.

What was the difference between the great Mexican oil boom, one may ask, and those oil booms that had preceded it in the United States? Just in terms of the economic structure of the industry, there were few. Lease-takers searched for prospective oil properties, dealing directly with landowners and local property records as they did in the United States. The entire industry was based on the private-property contract. Thanks to those mining laws changed by nineteenth-century Mexican liberals in 1888 and 1892, the oilmen acquired land by purchasing or leasing it directly from the landowner. The ranchero and hacendado's sale of the oil underneath their houses, fields, pastures, and forests did not come under the purview of the state at all. As in the United States, therefore, the oilmen's exploitation of the oil deposits could be brutal and wasteful in areas dominated by small property owners and many companies. Their exploitation could be more conservationist in areas dominated by large landholdings and few oil companies. Offset campaigns were just as prominent a feature of the Los Angeles oil boom of the 1890s, where rigs were placed as close to each other as "holes in a salt shaker." Offset wells could also be found at Topila, Pánuco, Alazán, Amatlán, Zacamixtle, and Los Naranjos.

In the United States, the oil industry of the twentieth century was becoming ever more integrated into the world economy. This was even more true in Mexico. The major market for Mexico's oil was the United States and, secondarily, Latin America and Europe. When the world's price for petroleum rose and fell, so did the prices for Mexico's crude oil. Profits grew during times of strong demand. They slowed down during times of excess worldwide production. Each boom in the United States fostered the development of a large number of individual companies, a few of the fortunate first-comers usually emerging into significant business organizations. Some of these boom-created entities thrived and expanded their production, refining, and marketing outlets in order to survive the boom that created them; many competed with the existing multinational oil companies. The same was true in Mexico. Moreover, the tendency of a maturing oil boom had been to consolidate and integrate the larger companies through acquisition of complementary assets downstream and upstream. El Aguila and Huasteca were Mexican-based companies that best typified this economic behavior.

Finally, one is struck with the tendency of the entrenched great companies to move into an area of oil boom. In the United States, Standard Oil had had a long history of moving out of western Pennsylvania in order to follow the oil booms west, into Ohio, Indiana, Illinois, Iowa, Kansas, East Texas, Louisiana, Oklahoma, West Texas, and California. From its base in Sumatra, the Royal Dutch–Shell worked its way east toward California and west toward Europe and Venezuela in a global process of consolidating both markets and production. For those reasons, Jersey Standard and Shell inevitably felt a need to enter Mexico. They could no longer ignore the Mexican oil boom that was fostering such intense competition for market shares in the United States, Europe, and Latin America. Also, during World War I, the Americans had the advantage of being able to expand internationally, while British companies were set back.

What was different about the oil boom in Mexico? The oil was found in limestone, not oil sands, and produced a lot of gas. This was merely a matter of technological adaptation to oil drillers. But it mattered not at all to the basically Anglo-American structure of the oil industry.

The important differences were cultural and political. This was Mexico, after all, not the United States. Neither the Mexican politicians nor the native work force were satisfied with the way in which the capitalistic industry was developing. No doubt, some Mexican landowners were reveling in their newfound wealth. But the Mexican state worried about its ability to control the industry as a source of tax revenue and as a threat to state power. Only the distraction of the Revolution and the strength of international demand prevented the Mexican state from intervening in the affairs of the oil companies. Furthermore, the workers wanted an economic institution that provided security and dignity to their lives. Mexican laborers would organize to resist those aspects of modern capitalism that threatened their culture and their security. Even as the foreign companies developed the Mexican oil industry according to strict capitalistic and market considerations, the politicians and the workers, each in their own way, were preparing to reclaim the Huasteca Veracruzana as their own.

CHAPTER THREE

Revolution and Oil

The Mexican Revolution abounded with rumors of conspiracies. How could it have been otherwise? The mercurial politics of revolution dictated that domestic politicians had to choose sides. The wrong choice often meant exclusion and exile, loss of property, or death. Foreign businessmen also felt pressure to be swept into the rumor mongering, to prevent a competitor from gaining advantage with the political regime of the moment. Often, the deeds of foreign businessmen did not substantiate the charges and rumors, as few actually felt they could really influence a revolution that appeared to them to be a strictly Mexican affair. Inasmuch as revolutionary factions were struggling over who would deal with foreign interests, the foreigners themselves had to deal with the truly byzantine power struggles.[1] Therefore, many Mexican power contenders easily believed in the machinations of the powerful, distant forces of Wall Street and The City. How else can the success of unworthy enemies be explained?

The problem for the foreigners was that they became coconspirators in the game of innuendo and unsubstantiated allegation. After all, the mere change of government signaled an enormous adjustment in the political involvement of foreign interests. Old power brokers became excluded from influence, while new aspirants took command of the perquisites of office. The changeover at the top invalidated the oilman's connections to the Científicos. Now *maderistas, huertistas, convencionalistas,* and *carrancistas* replaced each other in bewilderingly quick succession. The foreign businessmen themselves succumbed to the rumor mongering. Hoping to gain some business advantage for themselves, either the foreign oilmen were quick to anticipate a competitor's political maneuver or they propagated rumors to prevent a rival's maneuver. In essence, the foreign business community was divided against itself, company against company, and Americans against the British.

The continuation of the Mexican Revolution more than inconvenienced the foreigners. The longer the struggle continued and the more actively the Mexican peasants and laborers became involved, the greater the economic destruction and the disruption of business-as-usual. While licenses for pipelines and refineries languished at the top, the oil companies became susceptible to paying double taxation, forced loans, and bribes to competing revolutionary factions. No capitalistic organization, least of all these penny-pinching oil competitors, desired to dole out that kind of money to every passing army general and bandit straggler. But the oil companies did just that. Moreover, the competition for military superiority made its way from the central plateau down into the hot-lands. The longer the revolutionary violence lasted—roughly from the Orozco rebellion against Díaz in January 1911 to the successful rebellion of General Obregón against President Carranza in May 1920—the more inviting the oil industry became to the competing factions. It was the only sector of the economy that boomed during this period. Therefore, the oil industry was seen increasingly as a revenue source for penurious revolutionary governments and their political opponents.

Ultimately, the revolution enhanced economic nationalism in Mexico. Revolution created in the state a severe need for monies with which to reestablish control over the social furies unleashed by revolution. The state sought the essential revenues from the prosperous foreign interests. When those foreigners resisted, the politicians would accuse them of complicity in creating the conditions of revolution in the first place. All in all, control and ability to tax meant about the same thing to revolutionary politicians. Other Latin American countries, in time, would achieve economic nationalism without revolution. But always, a domestic environment of political and social stress underlay the creation of economic nationalism.[2] In Mexico, that stress became dramatically extreme.

Their inevitable political involvement in the Revolution itself—either through rumor of their own making or through coercion by contending factions—rendered the foreign companies susceptible to heightened exactions by successive governments and rival factions. No one was immune from the political struggle. Therefore, even as the industry itself grew according to the market dictates of the great Mexican oil boom, the revolutionary process and the oilmen's complicity in it were subjecting the industry to political intervention. The fact is, state control and regulation increased; Mexican politicians willed it; the Revolution sanctioned it; and the foreign oilmen, despite their accumulated wealth, were too divided to stop it. Economic nationalism in Mexico had a social base, and that is why the social revolution of 1910 to 1920 also produced an economic nationalism bent on reducing the power of the foreign oil companies.

The Smaller the Better

The rumors began to surface as soon as the initial rebellion of the Mexican Revolution succeeded in sending President Díaz into exile and placing the green, white, and red sash of executive office across the torso of Francisco I. Madero. Reports appeared in London newspapers that Waters-Pierce had financed the rebellion in order to obtain important oil concessions from the victorious Madero. Mexican newspapers recounted the rumors. Along the northern border, conversations among Americans and Mexicans turned to the conspiracy of Standard Oil to provide Madero with a one-million-dollar loan. Again, important oil concessions from the Madero regime were to be the payoff. Nearly everyone recounted stories to each other of the support of Lord Cowdray for the Díaz regime and how Doheny and Standard Oil desired and worked for the overthrow of the Anglophile *porfiristas*.[3]

Perhaps historians will never be able to document who started which rumor, but little evidence exists that any company willingly gave money to any Mexican faction. Even the circumstantial evidence is very spurious. By the same token, there is no doubt that the oilmen themselves engaged in the rumor mongering because they half-believed the political malevolence of their rivals. As they had been involved in the politics of the Porfirian regime, so the oilmen became involved in the machinations of the Madero regime too. Perhaps a distinction should be made between involvement and intervention. To be involved in Mexican affairs, all the oilmen had to do was be present and be a source of income for Mexican politicians and revenues for the state. They had to depend to a degree on political support for obtaining licenses and economic privileges. Thus, the rumors were testimony to the involvement of the foreign oil companies in domestic Mexican politics during the Revolution. To intervene in politics, however, the oilmen had to voluntarily direct their resources to influencing the outcome of disputes between Mexican politicians. Involvement was vastly more common among oilmen than intervention.

The rumor that the Standard Oil Company of New Jersey had financially supported the successful Madero rebellion would not die. As the story went, American oilmen resented the Díaz government for having supported the British oil interests of El Aguila. Everyone had heard some version of C. R. Troxel's alleged negotiations for Standard Oil (see chapter 1). Both Mexicans and Americans continued to repeat these rumors. They did so in newspapers and political proclamations and under oath in U.S. Senate hearings. Therefore, a Mexican attorney who once served some foreign oilmen could calmly testify to Standard Oil's financing of John Kenneth Turner's book *Barbarous Mexico,* which had vilified the Díaz regime for an otherwise adoring American public.[4] An American agriculturalist in Mexico claimed that "a brother of my cashier" had seen a check from the Madero government made out to Waters-Pierce. The check had overpaid for a government purchase of kerosene in order to repay Pierce for his loan to the Madero rebellion. When erstwhile ally Gen. Pascual Orozco broke with the Madero government and condemned Don Francisco for having accepted "FOURTEEN MILLION dollars from Wall Street millionaires," Orozco pointed to the Waters-Pierce Oil Company, which had hoped to widen its petroleum sales to the Mexican National Railways. A second rumor immediately arose: Lord Cowdray was financing the Orozco revolt because Madero had revoked El Aguila's Díaz-era concessions. In fact, the concessions had not been revoked.[5]

Lord Cowdray was convinced that Henry Clay Pierce was behind many of the malicious stories. When *El Diario* broke the news in 1912 that Standard Oil, "that great oil octopus," was about to purchase El Aguila, Cowdray suspected that the news items were the work of Pierce. "He employed Press men, unscrupulous but able, to attack us, day by day, in the American and Mexican Press," Cowdray wrote confidentially. "[Pierce] issued a pamphlet which was sold on the London bookstalls. He accused us of having bribed and corrupted the Díaz Government and of doing the same to each of the revolutionists that for the moment, were in disfavour. I was shadowed when in America."[6]

One who did know rather more about the connections—or lack thereof—between Madero and the foreign interests was Madero's American consultant. Shelburne Hopkins was a confidant of the Maderos, acting as their counsel on retainer for American affairs. He had even been in a position to know a bit about Waters-Pierce. The company employed Hopkins in 1912 to "get evidence" against the Standard Oil Company in Mexico. Hopkins claimed that Madero had received no money at all, whether from Standard Oil or Waters-Pierce. Although the American oil importer wanted to "make it hot" for El Aguila, Waters-Pierce obtained no advantages at all from the Madero rebellion. Hopkins claimed that much of Pierce's animosity derived not from the oil business but from the Porfirian consolidation of the railways. As principal stockholder of the Central Railways, he had approved of Limantour's railroad stock purchases and consolidation of the Mexican National Railways. What Pierce distrusted was those Mexican notables—Creel, Landa y Escandón, Pablo Macedo, Luis Elguera, and even Porfirio Díaz, Jr.—who subsequently joined Limantour's new board of directors of the National Railways. They were all Pearson men. Therefore, Pierce approved of Madero's removal of these *porfiristas* from the directorate of the National Railways although, said Hopkins, Madero had not consulted Pierce about these replacements.[7] If Don Porfirio's economy had been politicized, so was Don Francisco's.

In 1913 and 1919, the United States convened public hearings into allegations of American interference in the affairs of Mexico, as well as to propose U.S. policy alternatives toward the Revolution. Senator Albert B. Fall had interviewed witnesses in El Paso and Los Angeles. He found that, although rumors abounded as to the American oil interests' financing of the Madero rebellion, "very few persons had any definite knowledge upon the subject." He concluded that the Maderos had supported themselves substantially from family funds. Other revolutionists "largely supported themselves by killing and rustling cattle and sheep, by looting stores, and by securing forced contributions." The American oil interests, therefore, "should be exculpated of the charge that they incited or promoted the revolution against the Díaz Government," Fall wrote in 1913.[8] Fall's judgment may be trusted. His closest ties to American oilmen were not to Standard Oil or Pierce. They were to Doheny and Harry Sinclair, neither of whom were involved in the controversy. Nevertheless, few Mexicans and Americans along the border paid much attention to the conclusions of Senate hearings. The rumors persisted and were believed.

While Madero was in power, from 1911 to 1913, the actual relations between the oil company representatives and the government continued to be formally correct. Foreigners still needed political insiders in order to accomplish official business, as in the old regime. Only one oil-man's archive, that of Lord Cowdray, is extant to provide a glimpse of the important art of business diplomacy. The Pearson interests had the most arduous task with the Maderos. They had to quietly shed the im-age of having been cozy with the discredited Porfirians. It was not easy. Nasty little reminders always cropped up in newspapers in Mexico and the United States, thanks, said Cowdray, to his rival Henry Clay Pierce. The Pearson group also sensed the urgency of a rapprochement with the Maderos when Manuel Calero, described as Doheny's representa-tive in Mexico City, joined the government as minister of development. Fortunately, J. B. Body knew Ernesto Madero, the uncle of the incom-ing president. But Ernesto admitted hostility toward the Pearsons, ac-cusing them of attempting to influence American policy in favor of Díaz during the revolt.[9]

Nonetheless, Francisco I. Madero and Lord Cowdray met in August 1911. Responding to Cowdray's primary concern, Madero said that he intended to respect all Díaz-era contracts and concessions. He also as-sured Cowdray that he had never had any ties to Standard Oil; all the money for the rebellion had been raised by Mexican donors. Madero's own father had raised $350,000, using his properties as collateral. Cowdray informed Madero that he believed Pierce to be behind the scurrilous press attacks. Cowdray said he had never meddled in Mexi-can politics. It appeared a frank meeting, based upon the notes of Body. Cowdray informed the future Mexican president that he needed funds to expand El Aguila's markets, perhaps combining with a larger oil company. Madero replied that he would "look with suspicion" on the sale of El Aguila to Standard Oil, and Cowdray quickly added that he was considering The Texas Company or Gulf.[10] Perhaps the Madero government would not be so bad for the Pearson oil interests, after all.

At any rate, the early political breakdown of the Madero regime did not permit the Pearson group to develop a lasting, profitable relation-ship. El Aguila's pipeline permits for Bustos-Tancochín were held up in the secretariat of development by the influence of the Doheny interests, Body thought. Rising political tension may have been more at fault. When the battle between Madero's federal army and Orozco broke out at Torreón, Body wrote that it was becoming "most difficult to transact any business in the Government Departments, and I fear we shall be at a stand still until things change."[11]

Still, Cowdray found himself working on behalf of the Madero gov-ernment in March 1912. While in the United States, Cowdray spoke to the brother of President William Howard Taft about the need to prevent the sale of arms across the border to Orozco's rebel forces. Eventually, the executives had to devise a code so that they could discuss the political turmoil in Mexico so that, if compromised, its correspondence "might [not] be viewed unfavourably by other parties."[12] Despite the cordial relations, the British managers were ever suspicious that the Americans might have more influence with Madero.

Body in Mexico City thought that the Doheny representatives had obtained major political advantages with the Madero government. Near panic derived from two Porfirians still on El Aguila's staff, Enrique Creel and attorney Riba. "We must prepare action to counteract," Body cabled to Cowdray. Cowdray agreed.[13] None of the documents reveal what issue concerned the Pearson group, whether pipeline rights-of-way or fuel oil sales. The crisis passed quickly—or at least was overwhelmed by Madero's mounting political problems. When he had to make a cabinet change in November 1912, Madero's foreign affairs secretary asked Lord Cowdray to wire a note of his "satisfaction" with the new appointees. The Pearson representatives were willing to comply, although privately they said they would have preferred it if the brief rebellion of Félix Díaz, nephew of Don Porfirio, had been successful.[14]

As the fortunes of the regime sank, the Maderos turned to the foreign interests for money. Ernesto Madero devised a scheme to buy the opposition newspapers in Mexico City and asked J. B. Body to contribute $100,000 toward this end. Cowdray was put out. He felt obliged to contribute something so that Madero would not consider a refusal to be an "unfriendly act." "[W]e ought to subscribe whether we like it or not," he wrote Body, "of course, the smaller the better."[15] The fall of Madero and his assassination within a month relieved the Pearsons of this obligation. Yet, they had succeeded in gaining a degree of cooperation from the Madero government despite the persistent rumors.

Rumors and Wise Precautions

Much of the animus that developed between the various revolutionary governments and the oil industry was a matter of both principles and finances. It was a fight between advocates of alien concepts of free enterprise and state control. Foreign oilmen subscribed to Adam Smith's ideas that the pursuit of private interest will contribute to the general wealth. For example, Doheny never felt any embarrassment about how rich he had become on Mexican oil. He did not exploit anyone, he said. He paid "honest prices" for his land, and the Mexican landowners who leased to him were the envy of their neighbors. Doheny's attorneys, he said, were constantly decrying the high prices that he paid for his leases.[16] The revolutionary state, on the other hand, wished to control and direct national life in a way that would avoid the causes of revolutionary outbreaks. For the twentieth-century state to do this—as for the colonial royal government to have done it—revenues were required. In the colonial period, the silver mines provided the resources. In the twentieth century, the oil and other advanced industries provided those revenues. The difference was that the industry of early twentieth-century Mexico was owned by foreign capital.

The Madero regime, pressed for funds, began to look to the oil industry soon after coming to power. The Díaz-era budget surpluses dwindled—but did not yet disappear—as Madero attempted to satisfy old Porfirian families and new political players. The federal army and the *rurales,* for instance, augmented the numbers deliberately shrunk by Porfirio Díaz. Some old *insurrectos* like Emilio Madero, Pascual Orozco, and Pancho Villa were brothers in arms with Generals Reyes, Blanquet, and Huerta. The army payroll nearly doubled. Military expenditures mounted when the *zapatistas* continued their rebellion, and Orozco and others followed suit. How to raise money? Congressman José María Lozano introduced a bill to tax all oil lands, because their export of petroleum was contractually tax-free for fifty years. Lozano said he wanted to free Mexico from the clutches of Standard Oil, which was attempting to take over El Aguila. To Lozano, taxation was an instrument of control.[17] In Veracruz, the state legislature considered a proposal to impose a state tax of fourteen centavos per ton on crude oil. Both El Aguila and Huasteca sent their Mexican attorneys to confer with the state governor, who anyway was unwilling to press forward until President Madero and Minister of Development Calera approved. They did not. They were preparing their own federal tax increases. Meanwhile, the representatives of twenty oil companies organized a coordinated protest against the state deputies.[18] Oil company protests were often couched in predictions that any increased taxation would undercut economic growth and the country's tax base. "It is possible that this [tax increase] might cause the cancellation of otherwise profitable contracts and thus greatly reduce the amount which the Government desires to realize," Harold Walker of Huasteca warned.[19] In the end, the oilmen settled for a compromise, getting the state government to reduce its tax demands. Yet, taxes did rise from their previous level.

What oilmen feared most was any break with an 1887 Mexican law which stated that petroleum was subject only to the stamp tax. But by this time, the break had already been made. The Porfirian regime had imposed bar taxes at Tampico, the proceeds of which ostensibly financed the dredging of the harbor. The oil companies agreed to pay the modest tax just to avoid higher taxes. The tax exemption of Huasteca as a pioneer company also expired in 1911. Thereafter, it could no longer import new equipment duty free.[20] Then, late in 1912, Madero proposed to increase the bar tax to thirty centavos per ton. Once again, the oilmen pooled their resources, protested in unison, sent their attorneys to speak with congressmen, and wrote pamphlets about how Mexican oil would be priced out of international markets. Again, the big companies effected a compromise, agreeing to pay one-third of the increased tax. Representatives of the smaller companies were disgusted. William Buckley later pointed to these Díaz- and Madero-era compromises as the beginning of "the troubles of the oil companies."[21] Ever cognizant of its need for government goodwill, El Aguila always seemed to be in the vanguard of compromise. Ernesto Madero later praised the company for not meddling in Mexican politics.[22] Yet Buckley was essentially correct. The Mexican state had begun imposing some new rules on the oil industry even as it began to boom. The process would intensify.

The Madero revolution and its political problems also began to erode the sense of security that the oil operations had enjoyed during the Díaz era. When Orozco revolted in March 1912, the "rumors" of impending trouble motivated the sometimes isolated oil managers to arm themselves. At the Minatitlán refinery, A. E. Chambers requested that he be permitted, as a "wise precaution," to import 20 rifles and organize a force of volunteers. Foreign diplomats soon entered into the action. The British minister at Mexico City acquired 160 rifles from the Mexican government for distribution to the British "defence committee" in the capital. It was reported also that the U.S. ambassador had 1,500 rifles imported for the protection of his countrymen.[23] In Tampico, the Waters-Pierce refinery obtained rifles and ammunition, as did El Aguila, which imported 90 carbines and 9,000 cartridges. The Americans working for J. A. Sharp of the Petroleum Iron Works Company, constructing tank farms at Topila, requested 20 guns and 400 cartridges. The arming of frightened foreign oilmen was done with the consent of government authorities. The governor of Tamaulipas and the local military commander assisted in arming the foreign community at Tampico.[24] This arming of foreigners was a waste. No foreigners in the oil patches were any match for even the smallest military patrols. Various revolutionary factions would soon disarm the foreigners, who were also relieved of much else.

If foreign businessmen were inextricably involved in domestic politics, then their greatest need was for stability. Only in an atmosphere of political calm could the oilman establish the long-term relationships with insiders so essential to obtaining construction permits, oil concessions, tax exemptions, and domestic sales. The extent of state control of industry in the second decade of the twentieth century was just this modest. As yet, the Mexican state did not regulate drilling, production, oil exports, or domestic prices. It had not yet gained control of oil property. Therefore, the oil business proceeded in full boom, despite the political tribulations of the Mexican Revolution. Still, the political disruption did affect the oilmen. This was true for two reasons. During the revolution, fiscal deficits grew, motivating each succeeding government to seek new taxes on the booming oil companies. Also, competing politicians became increasingly inclined to blame the foreign interests for their own political problems—and for the nation's, as well.

Therefore, the fall of the Madero government, although first welcomed by foreigners already weary of political turmoil, proved to be the beginning of their considerable vexations in Mexico. When Madero fell from power, the oilmen scrambled to establish friendly relations with the new regime, whichever it was to be. J. B. Body of the Pearson group rushed immediately to see Gen. Félix Díaz, nephew of the former president. Body and Lord Cowdray were thinking that Díaz would be the next president. (Privately, they preferred Díaz to General Huerta.) Cautiously, Body refrained from making "real propaganda" with any faction, except to cultivate them all. Then news broke like a thunderclap that Madero and his vice-president, Pino Suárez, had been assassinated by their jailers. Body was horrified.[25]

Nevertheless, the new provisional government headed by Gen. Victoriano Huerta had to be cultivated. Body paid courtesy calls on all of the new ministers. The new cabinet already understood how the game worked. The minister of justice asked Body for information regarding Huasteca. Then the foreign minister requested that Lord Cowdray use his influence to obtain British recognition of the Huerta government. On both requests, Body said he would try. Body subsequently called on the British ambassador, whom he convinced that British recognition of Huerta would be appropriate if only to counteract the American ambassador's enthusiasm for Huerta. Huerta even asked Lord Cowdray to use his influence with the British government to retain the British ambassador, Sir Francis Stronge, whom Huerta liked. Stronge was replaced anyway.[26] Other foreigners also interceded with their home governments for recognition of the Huerta government, but the Americans did not have any success with President Wilson.[27] Still, they discovered that this inexpensive aid was a way of ingratiating themselves with the new regime.

Men in and out of government continued to court favor with the oilmen, and vice versa. How could oilmen not do otherwise when today's outcast might well become tomorrow's minister? On learning of Félix Díaz's arrival in London, Lord Cowdray sent a motorcar for his use and invited his old friend's nephew to dinner. Meanwhile, the surviving Maderos were also treated with respect. From his exile in San Sebastian, Spain, Ernesto asked Lord Cowdray to intercede with the Foreign Office in order to dispatch a cable of protest over Huerta's imprisonment of three other Maderos. Cowdray again complied and requested to meet Madero whenever he might be in London.[28]

Occasionally, these petty courtesies became burdensome, as in the case with Aurelio Melgarejo. The Pearson group in Mexico had been retaining attorney Melgarejo, who in February of 1914 received President Huerta's appointment to serve as the Mexican minister to Colombia. Melgarejo had already forced a doubling of his retainer, saying that he could influence oil legislation. Now, however, he asked Lord Cowdray to cover the entire cost of his post in Colombia. Cowdray was embarrassed by the request but felt compelled to comply "without too great a tax," if only to prevent Melgarejo from becoming an enemy. The Pearson group later were relieved when the fall of the Huerta government allowed them to dismiss Melgarejo's services completely.[29]

The oil companies were soon drawn into Huerta's fiscal problems, for he had to fight against *zapatistas* in the south and *constitucionalistas* in the north. As a consequence, the Madero federal army of fifty thousand troops grew under Huerta to more than two hundred thousand. Counting the rebel armies of Obregón in the west, Villa in the north, Pablo González and Aguilar in the east, and Zapata in the south, Mexico now had a lot of men—and some women and children, if the Casasola photos are to be believed—under arms. These struggles began to extract a greater economic toll than had the (comparatively) parochial rebellions of the Madero period. The deteriorating economy did not provide the revenues for burgeoning federal expenditures. Moreover, the peso was losing its value. It slid from a conversion of fifty centavos to thirty-six centavos to the dollar within five months of Huerta's taking power. Prices rose, and government employees and federal troops experienced delays in receiving their pay. President Wilson's refusal to recognize his government prevented Huerta from securing a loan in the United States.[30]

Thus, Huerta turned to Europe for a loan, and it occurred to him that Europeans with businesses in Mexico ought to be delighted to help him. The foreign minister asked Body to seek Cowdray's assistance in securing a one-hundred-million-peso loan. It was suggested that a number of businessmen could help with one million pesos each. Cowdray replied that he would be willing to underwrite a million pesos provided that banks would take up one-half of the loan. Cowdray then contacted José Yves Limantour in Paris, who already had considerable contacts in European banking circles. Eventually, Huerta secured a loan of £20 million with the Banque de Paris, of which £6 million was dispatched immediately. Limantour's old financial associates at Spreyer acted as brokers, earning a handsome commission. Cowdray later admitted to having participated in 3 percent of this Mexico loan, meaning that the Pearson group purchased several thousands of pounds sterling of Mexican bonds.[31]

Such "requests" by unstable Mexican governments placed the foreign businessmen in a dilemma not inconsistent with their involvement in domestic politics. Should Cowdray have saved precious capital by refusing to subscribe to the loan and risk incurring the wrath of the Huerta government? Was a politically unstable Mexico really a good risk for additional investment? A Pearson group memo on the Mexican foreign debt listed £39,481,800 in government loans and £190,940,700 in railway bonds and direct foreign investment (see table 7). Cowdray did the right thing: he equivocated. He contributed just enough support not to "make enemies," as he so often said of his business diplomacy.

The reluctant contributions of the foreign businessmen, however, did little to satisfy Huerta's financial problems. He was still forced to increase taxes. His "friends" in the foreign business community were forced to pay them. Huerta doubled the stamp tax and increased the import tax by 50 percent. Apparently, he even assessed a forced loan of 7,500 pesos on Waters-Pierce, whose chairman, Henry Clay Pierce, had been having difficulty getting close to the Huerta regime. Huerta

Table 7. *Lord Cowdray's Estimation of the Foreign Debt and Investment of Mexico, 1913*

Creditor	Loans or Credits	Amount (pounds sterling)
Morgan, Grenfell	1899 Federal Govt. loan @ 5%	10,029,600
Speyer Bros.	1904 Federal Govt. loan @ 4%	7,661,300
Speyer Bros.	Mex. Irrigation Co. 4½% bonds	5,144,000
Morgan, Grenfell	1913 Federal Govt. 6% T-bonds	1,450,000
Glyn, Mills, Currie	Federal Consolidated 3% internal loan	4,333,000
Glyn, Mills, Currie	Federal Consolidated 5% silver loan	9,105,000
Trustees Executors	Mexico City 5% loan	1,385,500
Antony Gibbs	San Luis Potosi state loan	189,700
Dresdner Bank	Oaxaca City 5% loan	183,700
Subtotal (government loans)		39,481,800
Speyer & Schroder	National Railway of Mexico bonds	60,798,100
Various	Privately Owned Railways	53,663,300
Various	Banks, Tramways, and Industrial Companies	46,390,200
Various	Oil Companies	20,325,500
Various	Mining and Kindred Companies	9,763,600
Subtotal (railway bonds and direct foreign investment)		190,940,700
Total		230,422,500

NOTE: Exchange rate: 1 British pound sterling = $5 U.S. = 10 Mexican pesos.
SOURCE: "Memorandum re: Mexico. Schedule," 14 Jan 1914, Pearson, A3.

then "fined" Huasteca $400,000. American diplomats suggested that Doheny's company not pay it, and Huasteca resisted at the risk of jeopardizing its business. The fine was pending throughout Huerta's term of office.[32] All the foreign businessmen resisted these new exactions. Cowdray cabled his protest to proposing a 10 percent tax hike, which the Mexican Senate approved anyway. Oilmen at Tampico calculated that Huerta's tax increases, amounting to seventy-five centavos per ton of exported oil, now equaled 50 percent of the oil's price at the well head, according to these calculations:[33]

Old Tampico bar dues	20 centavos per ton
Huerta bar dues increase	30 centavos
Old stamp tax	06 centavos
Huerta stamp tax increase	20 centavos
Madero-era Veracruz state tax	10 centavos

To add insult to injury, Huerta's customs officials insisted on collecting these duties in U.S. currency rather than the deteriorating Mexican peso. Months later, the Huerta government decreed additional tax increases, raising the bar dues to one peso per ton. Perhaps stung by U.S. diplomatic hostility, Huerta even suggested that the oil industry, which exported so many Mexican resources without benefit to the nation, ought to be nationalized. Incensed American oilmen converged on Mexico City to protest the tax increase. Even Secretary of State William Jennings Bryan dispatched a stiff protest to a Huerta government he did not recognize.[34]

The increased taxation failed to solve Huerta's financial problems. Ultimately, he suspended payment on the national debt, as the peso slipped to a value of twenty-nine cents.[35] These fiscal maladies tended to dampen the ardor of the foreign community toward Huerta. They also motivated an essentially reactionary Huerta regime to propose nationalizing the Mexican oil industry.

Huerta did nothing to discourage the continuation of the bickering and rumor mongering among the oil competitors. Waters-Pierce did not see any advantage at all in Huerta's ascension to power and mounted a relentless press campaign to identify Cowdray as the chief patron of "the Usurper." American and Mexican newspapers reported a litany of spectacular charges:

that Lord Cowdray helped Huerta overthrow Madero;

that Cowdray had brought about the British recognition of Huerta;

that he had arranged the loans for Huerta's government;

that he had placed his man, Sir Lionel Carden, as ambassador to Mexico;

that Sir Lionel, as Cowdray's surrogate, criticized Wilson's policy toward Mexico;

that Huerta gave El Aguila new oil and railway concessions;

that Cowdray was about to sell his interests to Standard Oil; and

that Huerta was to nationalize Mexico's oil lands in order to transfer them to Cowdray for $50 million.[36]

Cowdray personally countered the rumors by writing corrections and protests to editors, but much of the damage had already been done.

Fig. 10. Concrete mound protecting Potrero No. 4, 1916. Following the nearly disastrous fire at this prolific well, El Aguila constructed a concrete mound over the well head and drained off the volatile gases. The cavity of the mound could be filled with water and steam during thunderstorms to prevent another bolt of lightning from igniting the gases. From the Pearson Photograph Collection, British Science Museum Library, London, courtesy of Pearson PLC.

The State Department was certain that Cowdray's influence had obtained British diplomatic recognition for Huerta and that the British oilman was reaping great material benefits from Huerta.[37] Pierce became enraged when in November of 1913 he had not been reelected to the board of directors of the National Railways bondholders in New York. An article in the New York *Herald* recounted how Lord Cowdray had used his influence in the new government to deny this post to his old rival. Cowdray was at his wits' end. "[U]nless [Henry Clay Pierce] is prepared to be friends all round," Cowdray warned, "we will break the [sales] arrangement now existing—which was made at his request—and go for as much of the Domestic Trade as it is possible for us to obtain." Lord Cowdray suspected that Pierce's agents in Mexico were Shelburne Hopkins, who later admitted as much, and José Vasconcelos.[38] Their own economic competition seemed to draw the foreign interests into the whirlwind of Mexican revolutionary politics.

The Most Difficult Moment

The problem was that oilmen were forced to choose between so many conflicting authorities during the Revolution. The military factions that controlled certain areas of Mexico always took it upon themselves to collect the taxes and issue permits, denying jurisdiction to other domestic powers, no matter which of them happened to occupy the national palace in Mexico City. Oilmen who sold to the internal market had to deal with different factions in each sales area. In the fields, they often had to treat with two factions at once, one collecting export taxes at the ports of Tampico and Tuxpan and the other controlling the oil patches. The oilmen reacted as best they were able.

The confusion of authority began soon after Huerta took power, when the Constitutionalist forces loyal to Venustiano Carranza first invaded the oil fields. In May, General Lárraga and two hundred troops appeared at El Ebano. He arrested the superintendent, helped himself to supplies, exacted a "loan" of five thousand pesos, and went away with all the rifles in camp.[39] Gen. Cándido Aguilar arrived in the southern fields in November and ordered the cessation of drilling and pipeline operations. He demanded the payment of two hundred thousand pesos to the new military authorities. Within three days, Aguilar permitted oilmen to resume pipeline operations, so long as they did not sell oil to any of the Mexican railways within federally controlled areas. Local managers were forced to shut in their prolific wells at Potrero del Llano, Alazán, and Naranjos. Around the mighty Potrero No. 4, the gas pressure soon broke fissures through the ground. It was this damage, oilmen said, that led to the three-month conflagration that nearly destroyed El Aguila's great well.[40]

Aguilar also demanded a tax payment of fifty thousand pesos from the Huasteca oil fields, although he later accepted a payment of ten thousand pesos. Huasteca's operations had not been interrupted, although the Aguilar forces confiscated all the arms in the Huasteca camps. Still, Huasteca was not a company that relished paying taxes to two authorities. Harold Walker suspended tax payments to the federal government at Tampico, a tactic justified by the U.S. failure to recognize Huerta. Subsequently, when Walker was in Mexico City on business, Huerta threatened him with death. Walker promptly signed a draft for one hundred thousand pesos to cover the unpaid federal taxes.

Once Walker was safely out of the city, the company then canceled payment on the draft.[41]

Most of the Waters-Pierce assets remained in Tampico, still controlled by Huerta's troops. Therefore, Pierce was worried when the Constitutionalists ordered him to discontinue fuel oil deliveries to Huerta's troop trains. Knowing of Washington's attitude toward Huerta, Pierce asked for U.S. protection, going so far as to notify the State Department of the location of his refinery, storage tanks, pipelines, oil wells, and floating craft. Was he expecting—or hoping for—a U.S. invasion? Upriver at Pánuco, Shell's employees of La Corona Company had strict orders not to meddle in Mexican politics. Yet, now La Corona too was confronted with a problem of knowing to whom to pay oil taxes. Should it pay to the Constitutionalists, whose troops occupied Pánuco after December 1913, or to Huerta's troops still in Tampico?[42]

All of the oilmen had to use their best diplomacy in order to placate all the parties. They also had to avoid alienating competing political factions but at a reasonable cost. El Aguila's managers desired to operate with both the Constitutionalists and Huerta. Therefore, they decided to pay Huerta's new taxes—even though existing contracts gave them tax exemptions. Meanwhile, El Aguila, Huasteca, and Waters-Pierce all acceded to General Aguilar's orders not to sell fuel oil to Huerta's railroads.[43] To complicate matters, Huerta's federal troops retained control of the isthmus, where El Aguila had a refinery and several minor oil fields. General Aguilar, a Constitutionalist, summoned J. B. Body to his headquarters at Tuxpan to pay a $120,000 tax bill on the isthmus properties. Body sent his vice president, Ryder, to temporize with the Constitutionalist commander. Body also saw fit to leave Tampico just before the arrival of Carranza, after that city had fallen to the Constitutionalists. He did not wish to arouse Huerta's suspicions. At the same time, when it appeared likely that the Constitutionalist rebellion was going to succeed, the oilmen scrambled to sell fuel oil to Carranza, so as not to appear partisans of Huerta. Then Carranza ordered El Aguila to halt deliveries of oil from Tuxpan, held by *constitucionalistas,* to its refinery in Minatitlán controlled by the *huertistas*. In response, the *huertistas* prevented the refined products of the Minatitlán refinery to pass into Constitutionalist-held territory.[44] Few companies were immune from this domestic struggle for power during the Revolution. The National Petroleum Company of Richmond, Virginia, had been leasing land from the National Railways of Mexico. When the rent came due, the Constitutionalists demanded payment be made to them. So did the Huerta government. The dilemma was short-lived, however, as the Constitutionalists soon took complete control of the National Railway system.[45]

Such problems for oilmen even outlasted Huerta, because the Constitutionalists did not recognize any contracts that oilmen had made with the *huertista* government. Both Jersey Standard and Shell officials had built riverside storage and terminal facilities while Huerta controlled Tampico. After the Carranza troops took over, both companies had to present their "illegal permits and contracts" to Tampico's new officials.[46] In the meanwhile, Huasteca had made an agreement with the Constitutionalists to supply their fuel oil needs during their struggle with Huerta. The value of these supplies was to be used to defray the future payment of taxes to Carranza. Carranza's need for funds became acute soon after Huerta's fall, when Villa and Zapata occupied Mexico City. Carranza's agents ordered Huasteca to pay them 665,000 pesos in back taxes. Huasteca declared that it had already provided the Constitutionalists with 685,000-pesos-worth of fuel oil, essentially paying these taxes in advance. Cables passed from Huasteca's New York attorney F. R. Kellogg, the secretary of state, and the British ambassador in Washington. Their diplomatic intervention helped resolve the matter.[47] Once they realized that the Carranza victory did not end the domestic political conflict (for Villa and Zapata immediately rebelled against the new government), the oilmen openly expressed nostalgia for a simpler time—the era of Porfirio Díaz.

The longer these conflicts continued, the more the oilmen sought refuge with a new ally, the diplomatic community. They did so in violation of their Mexican government contracts and permits, almost all of which treated the companies as if they were Mexican entities. In disputes with the government, the companies were to seek remedies in Mexican courts, not with foreign governments. Of course, the Mexican court system was deteriorating as rapidly as the domestic political situation. Oilmen naturally turned increasingly to their home governments. Diplomatic support had been nearly nonexistent during the Díaz regime. Indeed, it had been unnecessary. Revolutionary times provoked more diplomatic activities in defense of the oilmen. Domestic factions least in favor with the foreign governments were encouraged to wrap themselves in the cloak of nationalism. It was a refuge of sorts for an increasingly beleaguered Victoriano Huerta. American, British, and even Dutch gunboats appeared off the shores of Tampico and Tuxpan in order to "defend" the lives of foreigners. Some managers of the

Dutch company, La Corona, began to live aboard the Dutch cruiser *Kortenaer.* Dutch marines and the ship's crew worked for La Corona, because many of the skilled workers had fled.[48]

Without having been asked, the Dutch even attempted to mediate between the Constitutionalists and Huerta. One Dutch businessman laid before Huerta a plan for immediate elections approved by the American secretary of state. President Huerta was indignant. He cursed the American president and his new diplomatic representative in Mexico. He also deplored the presence of foreign naval vessels at Veracruz and Tampico. "No one has the right to intervene in our domestic politics," Huerta shouted, "and if the United States continues to do so—then *I* will defend the honor of Mexico as long as one Mexican is still alive." Reported the chastised mediator to the Dutch foreign minister: "That, Excellence, was the most difficult moment I have experienced in my life."[49]

More and more, the petty vexations aroused a desire among oilmen for some diplomatic or even foreign military solution. Other companies had followed Waters-Pierce's example of informing the U.S. government of its valuable installations, presumably so that these would become an integral part of the military plans should an American invasion come. Even the British and Dutch were half expecting U.S. intervention. Given President Wilson's disgust for the Huerta regime, British and Dutch businessmen felt that the United States was obliged to protect non-American properties too. Everyone wanted to avoid in Tampico the kind of looting of the foreign community that had occurred after Villa's troops took Torreón. The Dutch and British ambassadors in Washington said they held the United States responsible for any damage the Constitutionalists might inflict, since Wilson and Bryan were backing Carranza and Villa. El Aguila began to take precautions. "My dear Hugh," Cowdray wrote to the commander of the HMS *Essex,* introducing him to Body in Mexico, who was to "tell you the nearest way to our oil fields in the event of trouble arising, so that they can be adequately protected."[50]

Clearly, the demand was mounting for some kind of resolution of the unsettled situation in Tampico. But the oilmen were hardly of one mind about what should be done. "Does not the situation appeal to you as one in which our Government should see that its citizens should not be despoiled of their property?" the National Petroleum Company asked Secretary Bryan.[51] But El Aguila looked upon military intervention with horror. "We know that if the United States decides upon intervention as one way of dealing with the situation," Body observed, "no foreign life or property will be safe."[52] Intervention is what they got; but it was to be intervention of the American government's choosing—not the oilmen's.

Seize the Custom House

Tension had been mounting between the federal troops of President Huerta in Tampico and the Constitutionalist forces operating in the surrounding environs. The British government recognized Huerta. The American administration openly supported the Constitutionalists. Foreign oilmen became involved insofar as they needed to operate with all parties and as they represented an increasingly substantial source of revenues for contending factions. Perhaps an explosion was not inevitable, but the revolution in the Huasteca Veracruzana was as volatile as some of the belching oil wells. A local spark (struck by a nervous foreign manager) or a bolt of lightning (sent down by diplomatic misstep taken thousands of miles away) might have been enough to set off a political conflagration consuming the entire oil industry. The Tampico incident was almost it.

For several months before the spring of 1914, Constitutionalist and federal troops had engaged in sporadic skirmishes around the city of Tampico. To protect foreign property and life, the gunboats of the United States, Great Britain, and the Netherlands cruised up and down the Pánuco River among the oil barges, tank steamers, and federal gunboats. The battleship USS *Virginia* had been stationed two miles off the entrance to the harbor.[53] By November of that year, the Navy Department had been making contingency plans. Rear Admiral Frank F. Fletcher had reported no fighting or disruption of the oil industry as yet but estimated that the Constitutionalists had 4,000 men in the district while the Federalists had a force of 1,500 men at Tampico. Fletcher had drawn up plans to place 3,500 American servicemen with machine guns, field guns, and one-pound mortars into the field to protect the oil installations. On one occasion, the Americans had even ordered the evacuation of its citizens. In December 1913, when three thousand troops under General Aguilar took up positions on the Pánuco River opposite Tampico, approximately five hundred evacuees, including two hundred Chinese, gathered for evacuation. Gunboats ferried the first refugees to the battleships *Virginia, Rhode Island,* and *New Jersey* lying offshore.[54] The action turned out to be somewhat precipitate, and the Americans soon returned to work.

The Constitutionalist siege of Tampico began in earnest on April 7. A force under Gen. Luis Caballero probed, somewhat desultorily, the federal defenses at the railway trestle just north of the city. Meeting resistance, the Constitutionalists fell back. Federal gunboats also fired back at rebel positions in the southern industrial suburbs of Doña Cecilia and Arbol Grande. Their shells landed near the Pierce refinery, setting fire to two oil tanks and a warehouse. Some foreigners were brought aboard British and American naval craft, and the German cruiser *Dresden* arrived to protect German nationals. Meanwhile, Aguilar apparently had menaced El Aguila's oil fields because of Lord Cowdray's alleged support of Huerta.[55] To this point, no group of foreigners had as yet been singled out for reprisals by any of the combatants. But the situation was tense.

The feverish activity of the American naval vessels had consumed their supply of petrol. As the city lay nervously under siege, the U.S. gunboat *Dolphin* dispatched its paymaster and a crew aboard a small whaleboat flying the American flag. The American refineries were now closed for business, and this crew rowed along the river and up a small canal to the wharf owned by a German merchant in order to buy gas. They landed within blocks of the northern railway bridge, where the Federalist forces were expecting a Constitutionalist advance. Once onshore, the American sailors were arrested by federal troops and held at gunpoint for one hour. American naval officers notified the federal commander, Gen. Ignacio Morelos Zaragoza, who promptly released the men with his profound apologies about the misunderstanding of his subordinate officers. The American sailors returned to their gunboat with a cargo of gasoline.[56]

Cables passed between the American naval commanders at Tampico and Veracruz and their superiors in Washington. Admiral Henry T. Mayo demanded that General Morelos Zaragoza order his forces to fire a twenty-one-gun salute to the offended American flag. The American government also demanded that President Huerta compel his commander to comply. To some in Mexico City, Huerta almost seemed to welcome U.S. intervention as the only way he could rally enough support to shore up his weakening government. Huerta's defiance motivated the secretary of the navy, Josephus Daniels, whose assistant secretary at the time was young Franklin D. Roosevelt, to dispatch six

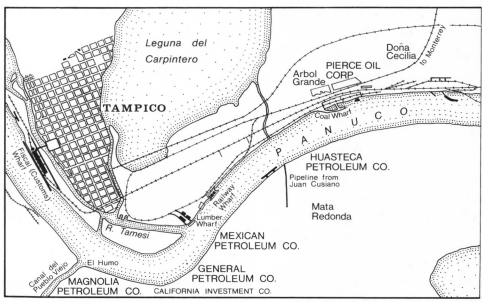

Map 3. Tampico in 1918

more battleships to Tampico.[57] Were Daniels and Roosevelt recreating
the momentous decision of Uncle Theodore Roosevelt, who as assistant navy secretary in 1898 and on his own authority sent Admiral
Dewey's fleet to Manila? Apparently not. The decision to "get tough"
with Mexico had come from President Wilson himself. At the time,
Wilson told his personal physician and golf partner: "I sometimes have
to pause and remind myself that I am president of the whole United
States and not merely of a few property holders in the Republic of
Mexico."[58] Cooler heads did not prevail. It soon became clear that no
one was thinking at all about the oil industry in Mexico nor about the
Americans who worked there.

    An armed invasion of Mexico was ordered. Instead of having the
marines storm ashore to protect the oil fields of the Huasteca Veracruzana and the refineries of Tampico, the Wilson administration
sent the expeditionary force to the port of Veracruz. Naval planners
had contemplated an invasion or at least a bombardment of Tampico. But their inability to sail their battleships across the sandbar
at the mouth of the Pánuco River deterred them. Admiral Mayo worried that his smaller gunboats and cruisers on the Pánuco River would
be susceptible to Mexican artillery fire. American policymakers had
chosen Veracruz because Huerta still obtained arms and supplies

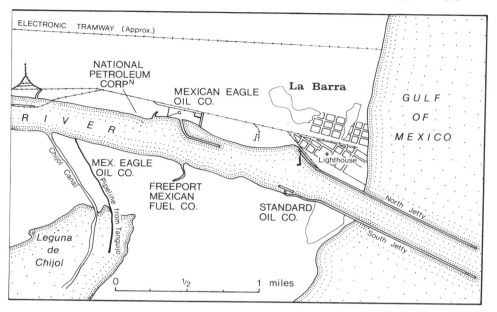

through the port. An American interdiction of the Veracruz port—although not invited by Huerta's principal adversary, Carranza—was intended to rid Mexico of this "tyrant" and "assassin" once and for all. A report that the German cargo vessel *Ipiranga* was nearing Veracruz sealed the decision. The Americans did not want Huerta to obtain arms.[59]

In the haste of decision making, officials in Washington dismissed the danger that armed intervention posed for U.S.–Mexican relations or for the relationship between Americans working in Mexico and their hosts, the Mexican people. No one, for example, had queried the American consul at Tampico, Clarence A. Miller. He would have warned that a troop landing at Tampico or Tuxpan would lead to the Mexicans' destroying all the oil fields, tank farms, pipelines, and refineries in the district. "A war of American intervention would be a great calamity. All other nations will stand to reap all the advantages; whatever the result might be," he warned; "our country would bear all the expense and reap all the crop of resulting hatred and vengeance. Americans will be unable for many years to come to work in the outlying districts in the oil fields and other parts of Mexico."[60] Miller had not even considered what would happen in the oil zone if American troops landed at Veracruz instead.

The navy's plans to protect the oil fields remained on the shelf. Instead, Daniels cabled his admirals: "Seize custom house [at Veracruz]. Do not permit war supplies to be delivered to Huerta government or to any other party."[61] By the second day of the invasion, by which time the Congress had approved Wilson's action, more than 3,300 American troops were ashore at Veracruz. The German merchant vessel *Ipiranga* was indeed detained by the American occupation of Veracruz. But the invasion forces, not being at war with Germany, could not confiscate the cargo. Once allowed to depart, the *Ipiranga* headed for the federally held port of Puerto México, where the arms were off-loaded for Huerta's troops.[62] The Americans could not even prevent the shipment of arms to Huerta, which had been the ostensible excuse for seizing Veracruz.

As soon as the news spread along the Mexican Gulf Coast that the United States had declared war on Mexico (which was not true), all American gunboats pulled out of the Pánuco River and sailed to Veracruz. The Americans at Tampico were stunned. Within hours, refugees with white skin began descending on Tampico from the oil fields. Englishmen, Dutchmen, and Germans accompanied the Americans. Europeans had little faith that the Mexicans, at the moment, cared about the differences between the nationalities. As the American workers saw it, "Brown howling mobs, armed with clubs, stones and pistols, immediately congregated all over the city, parading the streets and howling for 'Gringo' blood. To a Mexican everything with a white face is a hated 'Gringo.' "[63] The fearful Americans gathered at the Southern Hotel, where they bolted the doors against a mob of Mexicans who had gathered to wreck Sanborn's American Drug Store. No doubt, the Mexicans were not calmed by the sight of the American flag waving above the Southern Hotel. Finally, the German commander of the *Dresden* and a detachment of German marines marched on the hotel, where the Americans were trapped. The Germans gained the cooperation of the federal commander and escorted 150 Americans to the waterfront, where they were evacuated. The Americans credited the Germans with having saved them from being overrun by Mexican "mobs."[64] It was a curious exchange for the U.S.'s presumption of having intercepted a German merchant vessel during peacetime.

The American naval commander, Admiral Charles T. Badger, later considered this withdrawal of the gunboats from Tampico to have been a grave error. If the gunboats had subsequently returned to save the Americans, they would have come under fire by both federal and rebel forces, because the navy's reappearance at Tampico would have been a provocation.[65] Indeed, the British and German commanders cautioned the American vessels not to return. They requisitioned the barges and tankers belonging to the Huasteca and El Aguila oil companies, raised the German and British flags over them, and evacuated Americans as well as their own citizens.[66] In any case, the withdrawal of U.S. gunboats from Tampico had had the approval of the Navy Department. Secretary Daniels stated that he did not want the Mexicans to think that the United States was at war, he did not desire to endanger all foreigners at Tampico, and anyway the British naval commander had agreed to protect American citizens. Indeed, the commander of the *Kortenaer,* which arrived in Tampico to take on the Dutch citizens from the *Dresden,* was certain the Mexicans would have destroyed the oil industry if the American forces had reappeared in the river. In fact, he was concerned that the Constitutionalists might destroy the wells anyway.[67]

Glad Enough to Get Out

In the meantime, panic had spread among the American and European workers. American drillers at Pánuco heard rumors of an imminent landing of U.S. troops and did not want to be caught upriver. The Texas Company sent "a big stern-wheeler" steamboat to Pánuco. Coming downriver with a load of Americans, the British pilot, flying the Union Jack, warily floated past the federal gunboat. The Mexican gunboat did not fire. The Americans on board had been expecting to see Leathernecks scampering along the riverbanks to rescue them. None came. The Chinese employees who stayed behind at Pánuco packed up the tools and took them to the British consular office for safekeeping.[68] Many left their personal effects behind. A blacksmith working for Mexican Gulf at Pánuco left behind his own set of tools, valued at $165. Not choosing to return, he later sent for them, only to discover that the tools had been pilfered in his absence. "At the time all the Americans were glad enough to get out themselves," the worker later wrote to the U.S. consul.[69] The American evacuees boarded a mixed flotilla of merchant vessels and oil tankers off the coast. Naval officers came on board to draw up passenger lists, and the entire group was dispatched to Galveston. Apparently only one American had died. Weston Burwell was killed while en route from Pánuco to

Ozuluama, carrying four thousand pesos to purchase mules in order to build an earthen reservoir for La Corona. In all, some two thousand oil workers and family members had clambered aboard the ships bound for Galveston.[70]

The recriminations began immediately. Those refugees who had either returned to their hometowns or stayed for a month at Galveston complained of the shabby treatment they had been accorded by U.S. forces in Mexico. President Wilson and Navy Secretary Daniels came under special criticism. The oil field and refinery workers grumbled about the navy's retreat from Tampico just when U.S. forces were attacking Veracruz. They felt their lives had been endangered and their personal property lost because of their government's perfidy. The refugees certainly were not philosophically against the notion of U.S. intervention in Mexico. In fact, many would have welcomed the marines at Tampico; they even demanded that U.S. military forces protect them on their return to the oil fields. Somewhat defensively, Daniels asked why these Americans were protesting a policy that had saved their lives. They had gone to Mexico to get rich, he suggested, and now expected the country to raise an army of five hundred thousand men to protect them.[71] Perhaps no one reflected the sentiment of the American petroleum workers in Mexico better than William F. Buckley. He continued to be a bitter critic of the Wilson administration. At the 1919 Congressional hearings on Mexico, he claimed that the American troop landing at Veracruz had needlessly endangered lives at Tampico.[72] Thereafter, the American workers in Mexico, as well as the owners, were to form a vocal lobby against what they considered Wilson's inept foreign policies.

For the moment, however, the owners of oil companies withheld their criticism, needing diplomatic support to protect their abandoned properties in Mexico. The big question concerned the oil leases. The American companies would not be able to make their rental and royalty payments to landowners during their exile. Lack of timely payment often meant breach of contract, and they feared that the British and Dutch would jump American claims. Some Americans even feared that the British gunboats might collude with British oilmen to prevent the return of the Americans. They looked to the secretary of state for help.[73] Secretary Bryan conferred with British and Dutch diplomats in order to prevent the breach of American-held leases. The Dutch and British oilmen, as it turned out, were quite willing to agree to a policy of *status quo ante*. They too had evacuated Tampico and were not will-

ing to return until the Americans did. Their leases were in the same
danger of being breached. The British government queried Lord Cowdray, who disclaimed any interest in taking advantage of the Americans'
plight. The Dutch government also agreed to withhold any diplomatic
support to Dutch citizens who sought to jump American leaseholds.[74]
Once again, the fate of the Mexican oil industry was decided outside
the country.

The owners of oil properties in Tampico, of course, expected the
worst. They were certain that the evacuation and lack of U.S. military protection would mean the destruction of the oil fields. A representative of the East Coast Oil Company painted a mental picture of
Mexicans looting the oil fields, runaway wells catching fire, and destroyed and burning oil camps.[75] "The oil field of Mexico is gusher
country," said a representative of The Texas Company, who warned
of the danger of "unsupervised" wells filling up the storage pits and
then "spreading over the lands and streams." The danger of fire grew
with the oil spills. "Such a fire would burn the entire oil country
and doubtless a multitude of its inhabitants," he said. Conflagration
would also melt the valves of those wells that were pinched in, causing
additional losses.[76] Of course, these owners were asking, rather indi-
rectly, for an American military escort so that the oilmen could return
to Mexico.

Destruction of neither the oil wells nor the oil camps ever took
place. Some oil managers had stayed on their properties. William
Green of Huasteca later bragged that once ordered out to sea, he returned by boat to the oil wells in the Faja de Oro, which he managed
for thirty days until the U.S. government permitted the return of the
American workers.[77] Indeed, the feared looting consisted of only a few
mules and automobiles taken by Constitutionalist troops. For the most
part, the refineries were untouched, and the Mexican workers in the oil
fields prevented the wells from overflowing the storage capacity. The
American consulate reopened in Tampico on 4 May, just thirteen days
after the evacuation, protected by the forgiving attitude of the federal
troops still in the city.[78] The State Department had sought to minimize
the danger to the oil zone but not by dispatching U.S. troops to protect
the wells. Instead, Bryan attempted to negotiate separately with the
Constitutionalists to declare the oil zone a neutral area in its revolutionary struggle with the federal forces. Carranza's answer was somewhat noncommittal. The neutrality of the oil zone, he said, depended
on Huerta's leaving.[79]

Once again, the Pearson group attempted to make friends on all sides. "I have maintained very cordial relations with [American forces at Veracruz]," said J. B. Body, "but not to such an extent as to run the risk of being called to account by our Mexican friends at some later date."[80] All El Aguila coastal craft struck their Mexican colors and hoisted the Union Jack so as not to be captured as war prizes by the American navy. Meanwhile, the British naval officers at Tampico traveled into the oil fields, speaking to both Constitutionalist and Federalist commanders about protecting the volatile oil wells. The English managers remained in most of the oil camps; El Aguila's pipelines continued pumping crude oil, which its fleets carried to the refinery at Minatitlán. The only Pearson asset in transition during the aftermath of the Tampico incident was its Tehuantepec National Railway (TNR). Huerta's federal army took control of the TNR, which Mexican workers had operated when American workers evacuated.[81] Operations of the British company continued.

The Americans, however, were out for most of May, during which time the Federalists had surrendered Tampico to the Constitutionalists. They began to return on 20 May, just a month after they had left, and within five days, the steam tankers resumed loading petroleum at the Huasteca terminal.[82] In Tuxpan, June was another record-breaking month for oil exports. General Aguilar maintained order in the city for Americans and occupied himself with collecting a 15 percent tax on all Mexican properties. In Pánuco and Topila, however, in the absence of Constitutionalist troops, the local citizens greeted the returning Americans with anti-American meetings and insults. Several citizens of Pánuco demanded that Americans turn over their weapons and be treated as spies.[83] Many Mexican citizens in the Huasteca remained hostile while the American troops still occupied Veracruz. They did not leave Veracruz until November 1914, fully four months following the collapse of the Huerta government. Like the Americans earlier at Tampico, Huerta fled to safety aboard the German cruiser *Dresden*. The Constitutionalists and the Federalists had shown great forbearance while American troops occupied Tampico. Both Mexican factions had found it in their interest not to destroy the oil industry, because as Navy Secretary Daniels was fond of saying, it was "the goose that laid the golden egg." Both sides needed the revenues provided by the oil fields. As for the American intervention at Veracruz, it did not seem to have accomplished very much at all except to promote the resentment of Mexican combatants toward Americans. The oil zone would never return to normal following the Tampico incident. One colonist from Tampico said later that until the Veracruz occupation, Americans on the Gulf Coast had experienced some inconveniences.[84] Thereafter, all foreigners were molested aplenty.

Showing Signs of Unrest

Although the oil companies had already suffered from their inevitable involvement in Mexican politics, the American invasion of Veracruz marked the beginning of wholesale depredations in the oil zone. Before April 1914, disruptions had been sporadic and isolated. Thereafter, conditions approached anarchy. Prolonged civil conflicts rendered the booming oil industry the object of attention by a penurious new government, ascending army chieftains, and destitute military deserters. Although these depredations caused countless vexations for the foreigners and Mexicans running the oil industry, little real damage occurred to the oil assets themselves. From 1914 onward, the prices increased at the same time that new drilling yielded record flows of crude oil. Most leases had been taken before that date anyway; most pipelines and oil terminals had already been well established. Refining and exporting continued almost unimpeded by the civil turmoil, except (as we shall see in chapter 5) for brief moments of labor unrest. The depredations took place primarily in the countryside. Both foreigners and local Mexicans working in the oil fields suffered robberies, holdups, insults, intimidations, indignities, ravages, forced loans, and assassinations. These were not part of a revolutionary program but a result of the breakdown of law and order in the Huasteca. Although revolutionary depredations made life insecure in the oil fields, they hardly affected the performance of the foreign-owned industry.

After the fall of Tampico, there were just two more pitched battles in the oil zone, both at El Ebano. No sooner had Huerta fallen than the combined forces that had brought about his government's demise began to break up. The old federal army of Porfirio Díaz and Victoriano Huerta was destroyed. Now the victorious Constitutionalist forces broke into competing factions. *Villistas* and *zapatistas* fell out with *carrancistas* and *obregonistas*. Meanwhile, Carranza made Veracruz his capital while the *zapatistas* and *villistas* occupied Mexico City. Constitutionalist forces loyal to the first chief held the Huasteca region and

Tampico. In November 1914, a force of *villistas* under the command of Gen. Tomás Urbina descended from the central plateau along the San Luis Potosí–Tampico rail line. They were met at El Ebano by Constitutionalist forces under Gen. Jacinto Treviño. The battle was joined in the midst of Mexico's oldest oil field. One hundred cannon-balls and countless bullets pierced the oil storage tanks. Smokestacks of the topping plant were shot off. Water and oil pipelines were broken, and the crops and livestock were looted. Doheny's Mexican Petroleum Company lost eight hundred thousand barrels of oil, none of which had caught fire because it was so thick. Mexican Petroleum also had to buy foodstuffs from Texas to make up for the loss of agri-cultural production.[85] The *villistas* did not abandon the area until a sec-ond battle, this time fought near but not in the oil camp. In April 1915, a Constitutionalist force of 1,500 men under General Lárraga, a local landowner, cut the railway line between the *villistas* at San Luis Potosí and General Urbina. Then they pushed Urbina's forces north out of the region.[86]

While in the oil zone, the *villistas* attempted to wield some influence over the industry, adding to the administrative confusion. A certain E. J. Eivet of the Conventionalist (Villa's) Railway was having difficul-ties securing fuel oil from the Constitutionalist-held oil fields. The *vi-llistas* had been forced to purchase fuel oil in Texas. In Mexico City, Eivet called Frederick Adams of the Pearson organization on the car-pet. He demanded a fifty-thousand-peso "loan" in exchange for good treatment when the Convention triumphed. The Pearson group de-clined to pay the loan; it pleaded neutrality in political conflicts. Eivet threatened that Pancho Villa himself would be interested in knowing who his enemies were.[87] Even after the second Ebano battle, General Urbina menaced the oil zone once again. "We are not all dead, but hav-ing a good time," he was reported to have said during a banquet. Ur-bina boasted that he could capture Ebano, and Pánuco too, anytime he wanted. Perhaps he wanted the Constitutionalists to divert troops from Celaya and Aguascalientes, where they were pressing the *villistas,* to de-fend Tampico.[88] Perhaps Urbina was merely posturing, mocking defeat with characteristic bravado. In any case, the *villistas* soon abandoned the oil region to the *constitucionalistas* during the weeks that Gen. Al-varo Obregón drove Villa's army north through the central plateau.

Only one other time, besides the Veracruz invasion, did the foreign-ers have to evacuate the oil fields en masse. This occurred in 1916, dur-ing the second U.S. armed intervention in Mexico, when a detachment of U.S. forces was sent into Chihuahua to punish Pancho Villa for his raid on Columbus, New Mexico. Unlike the first crisis, this one lingered at low intensity during the eleven months that U.S. forces were in Mexico. At the time, labor unrest was building tensions within the city of Tampico. The Constitutionalist military authorities, in their disgust for the presence of U.S. troops on Mexican soil again, now had a perfect excuse to make common cause with the Mexican working class. A rumor passed through the city that the police chief was planning to have all the Americans killed or captured before they could reach the safety of U.S. gunboats, which had quietly returned to the Pánuco River. Once again, Americans were disarmed at roadblocks throughout the oil zone, and Mexican soldiers around Tampico mounted guns on the jetties and railway flatcars. Shortly after midnight on 15 May 1916, soldiers surrounded the refinery of the Standard Oil Company. While Mexican officers positioned themselves at the gangplank of the oil tanker *John D. Rockefeller,* then docked at the terminal, soldiers were seen on launches in the river. A night watchman feared they were laying mines. Then at 4 A.M., according to Standard Oil executives, "Three whistles were sounded from the opposite side of the river, and the Mexican soldiers immediately took to their boats and crossed to the other side."[89] The troops did not commit any destruction of the refinery. Some foreign workers, nevertheless, were so spooked by the incident and the rising level of tension, that nineteen men, eight women, and two children left with the *John D. Rockefeller* the very next day. The indignant refinery manager, J. A. Brown, claimed that "they stampeded."[90]

As usual, the oil companies prepared themselves as best they could against the political hurricane over which they had no control. El Aguila planned to place the Mexican supervisors in charge of the oil fields if the Americans invaded. The British managers feared that the American troops would be content to secure the refineries and oil terminals on the coast and not the great oil wells just thirty miles inland. Ryder's chief Mexican assistant, Múñoz, was to take charge at Potrero, and other oil companies planned similar contingencies.[91] British citizens were carrying translations of their passports to identify themselves to Mexicans unable to differentiate a London accent from a Texas twang. Although local commanders assured the Britons that no British-owned property would be harmed in the event of an American invasion, the Carranza government notified the diplomats that *all* oil wells would be destroyed. The British, of course, were concerned to prevent any disruption to the world's supply of petroleum during the world war. The new American secretary of state, Robert Lansing, responded to British concerns. He promised that his government had no intentions of invading the oil fields.[92] In Tampico, British officials had effected a less tense relationship with the local commander, Gen. Emiliano Nafarrete. The commander calmed the labor upheavals of the first three months of 1916, and he assured British citizens that he would protect them.[93]

By this time, everyone suspected that U.S. troops might also be dispatched to the oil zone. The Constitutionalist authorities now moved their offices out of Tampico. General Nafarrete warned the American consul that he would burn the oil fields if U.S. troops landed at Tampico. Mexican troops covered the lighthouse at Tuxpan bar with black sacks and posted troops at the entrance to the river. All available foodstuffs from the oil camps of El Aguila were ordered to be delivered to Tuxpan. Consul Dawson was a cautious man. He immediately ordered all Americans, with their families and handbags only, out of the oil fields. They were to assemble for evacuation at the Bergan Building, at the Colonial Club (a provocative name for a social club catering to foreigners), and at the Victoria Hotel. Within a week, some 1,200 Americans and a few Britons left Tuxpan for Tampico. Others stayed. Doheny claimed that his ships alone had evacuated 900 Americans. He graciously refused reimbursement from the U.S. government, which as far as records show had offered him none.[94] The 1916 evacuation was brief; the foreigners soon returned.

The British consul at Tuxpan despaired of saving the dangerous situation. He feared that a landing of U.S. troops would certainly mean the destruction of the oil fields. Already reeling from a shortage of foodstuffs, the rural population in the Faja de Oro were made more destitute by this second exodus of Americans. "[T]he people are shewing [sic] signs of unrest at being without work on account of the Oil Companies having shut down, and do not hesitate to express themselves against the threats made by various commanders to destroy property, etc.," observed British Consul Hewitt. "The people realize that they are dependent in everything on the foreign interests in this section. There are many thousands now without employment and the exodus of Americans is a sore blow to them."[95] Perhaps Hewitt may be faulted for sharing the view of his fellow Britons in Tuxpan—not necessarily that of the Mexican residents themselves. Yet, there is no denying that Mexicans suffered along with the foreigners—indeed more so.

The British Foreign Office, Lord Cowdray, and even some American owners were relieved that the United States did not intend to land troops at Tampico. For one thing, such an invasion would have had to be "whole hog or nothing," as one British diplomat put it.[96] Cowdray had pressured the Foreign Office to take up his concerns with the State Department. In the event of an invasion, which he counseled against, Cowdray wanted to be able to export through any naval blockade of the Gulf Coast. He also desired American troops to protect El Aguila installations and not to molest company vessels flying the Mexican flag. Nor did Cowdray want his Mexican merchant seamen captured as prisoners of war. As a precaution, nevertheless, El Aguila protected their wells with "armoured mounds"; Penn-Mex next door also placed concrete blocks over the valves of their well heads.[97] If the foreign oilmen avoided getting foreign troops, they did have to contend with the presence of increasingly unruly Mexican government soldiers.

Applying Deleterious Epithets

The presence of troops in the oil zone, as in the rest of the country, contributed to the insecurity of economic and human life in Mexico. Troop depredations began and intensified with the Revolution itself. In the 1911 rebellion against Díaz, marauding bands of armed men operated in the oil zones. They came down the rail line from Tuxpan to sack the oil camp at Furbero, burning railway bridges on the way. Farther north, the El Aguila managers worried about the effect of an armed attack on Potrero del Llano No. 4. Ominously, someone had cut the telephone wires to the camp at Potrero. Cowdray acted prudently. He took out fire insurance, at a premium of 2.5 percent, on 2.5 million barrels of oil per year.[98] Cowdray even suggested that the owner of the Hacienda Potrero del Llano, Crisóforo B. Peralta, who was receiving substantial royalties from the company, ought to organize its defense. "[T]he Peraltas are so largely interested in the Potrero field that they ought to be extremely alert in doing all they can to assist in ensuring its safety."[99]

The series of revolts against Madero, commencing in 1912, brought additional problems of oil-camp security. At the time, El Aguila and other companies were engaged in expanding their pipeline and terminal facilities. None of the companies deemed the political disturbances to be sufficiently dangerous to abandon their construction plans. On the other hand, the oil companies would have suffered more if they had not been able to get rid of their oil. In August 1912, armed "bandits" attacked the oil camp of Ixhuatlán on the Isthmus of Tehuantepec. Because the American drillers were getting edgy, El Aguila's general manager, J. B. Body, protested to the Madero government and asked for protection. Gen. Félix Díaz then led a rebellion in the Huasteca region and captured the virtually undefended port of Tuxpan. Only a few others supported the Díaz rebellion, his first of many, and government troops soon arrested and transported him to a military prison in Mexico City.[100] In February 1913, Díaz conspired with Generals Bernardo Reyes and Victoriano Huerta to produce La Decena Trágica, the ten tragic days of bombardment in Mexico City between army forces in the National Palace and rebel army forces in the Ciudadela. That particular rebellion cost Reyes his life and Madero first the presidency, and shortly afterward, his life too.

Within a year, as the rebellion against Huerta took shape, the oil zone became even more involved. Rebel raids indicated to the foreigners that federal troops were ineffective at protecting the countryside. In May 1913, a Constitutionalist force plundered La Corona's camp at Pánuco.[101] The Constitutionalist troops under General Aguilar began to occupy the southern fields. They besieged a small garrison of federal troops at Tuxpan during November 1913, eventually sending them fleeing to Tampico. Thus far, the oilmen were much relieved to report no damage. "I strongly consider that our relationship with the natives from the district between Tuxpam [*sic*] and Tampico is such that our property will not be generally attacked," said Lord Cowdray, optimistically.[102] Thereafter, only Tampico would remain under federal control for the rest of the year. The rebels controlled the countryside.

But conditions in the countryside only worsened following the American occupation of Veracruz and the victory of Carranza over Villa. Manuel Peláez led a local rebellion against the Constitutionalists in the oil zone. Constitutionalist officers lost control of their troops; pay was scarce, liquor was not; and rivalry between fellow officers exacerbated the depredations in the oil zone. Troops often entered the oil camps for supplies. They ate the camp's food, confiscated the livestock, and fed the camp's fodder to their own animals. The Penn-Mex Fuel Oil camps reported total losses of $84,252 and 594,544 pesos during the Revolution; Doheny's Mexican Petroleum Company set its losses at 1.6 million pesos; Transcontinental's losses of equipment and food amounted to $45,866.[103] The officers courteously scattered about receipts and chits for the goods they took. In June 1914, El Ebano camp lost three thousand pesos in cash and four thousand pesos worth of fodder to a visiting Constitutionalist force. The oil men preferred that the Constitutionalist troops remain in the towns of Topila and Pánuco rather than be stationed among the oil camps. Under the influence of alcohol, the soldiers became uncontrollable, dangerous, insolent, and "very obstreperous."[104] Operations were disrupted on many mundane levels. Reported William Green of Huasteca:

> I have many of the annoyances to which we are subjected by these Constitutionalists, such as the commandeering of our launches, demands on our commissaries, the holding up of emissaries between one station and another where the telephone lines are down. We are practically without mules at Casiano at present.[105]

Moreover, the officers, each of whom recruited and paid for their own troops, displayed a good deal of friction and rivalry among themselves. A hierarchy of command hardly existed among Constitutionalist officers like Generals Millán and Alemán (father of the later president Miguel Alemán); Colonels Alberto Herrera, Adalberto Tejeda (later governor of Veracruz), Agapito Barranco, Tito Hernández, and Enrique Hernández; and Lieutenant Colonel Luis Ramos. In the southern fields, Constitutionalist officers were said to be recruiting oil workers by bragging about the abundant opportunities for looting and the violating of girls.[106] Most of the time, the many armed groups composing rival forces went about avoiding each other and aggrandizing themselves.

The refining and exporting cities, like islands of rock in a churning and frothy sea, were only seldom threatened by contending armies. Tuxpan was calm under Aguilar, as was Tampico after the Federalists surrendered. In 1917, Generals Alvarado and Maycotte led three thousand government troops into Minatitlán to clear out the rebels who under Gen. Cástulo Pérez had threatened the Tehuantepec National Railway. The Constitutionalist generals conferred with A. S. Gulston, manager of the Minatitlán refinery, about garrisoning the oil camps at Filisola and San Cristóbal. Gulston became very apprehensive. He did not wish to antagonize the opposing armed faction on the isthmus. "[I]t is somewhat difficult not to appear as taking a prominent part in connection with advising them what operations they should undertake," Gulston admitted.[107] In the countryside, no area was permanently cleared during the Revolution. Yet another rebellion by Félix Díaz in southern Veracruz and Oaxaca preyed on isolated, small garrisons of Constitutionalists. In May of 1918, a band of six hundred men under Pafnuncio Martínez raided Minatitlán, killed twenty soldiers of the local garrison, threw their bodies into the barracks, which they set on fire, and took 45,000 pesos in currency and 25,000 pesos in goods from the El Aguila refinery. "I had no idea that so many as 600 rebels in one gang could exist in the Isthmus," exclaimed Lord Cowdray.[108] The government troops swept through the area again, apparently finding few of the rebels.

The depredations and demands of armed troops in the oil zone were unsystematic and arbitrary. In the process, the oil camp managers became veritable diplomats. They learned to deal with the demands of the different factions, giving in here, resisting there, and making every general feel important. For the Huasteca company, William Green handled these chores in the southern fields. His description of one day, 1 March 1918, in the life of a supervisor is instructive of this diplomacy, as well as of Green's contempt for the Mexican officers with whom he was dealing:

> On my return to Tampico from my last trip, General Acosta, who is in Tampico at present, sent for me to say that General de las Santos [sic] had instructions to pay me the money I advanced them when we first met at Ojital. [S]ince the $1000 [pesos] I gave to Pruneda and the $1500 [pesos] I gave to Acosta, I gave $2000 [pesos] to Robinson, Jefe de Armas, Tampico, for rations for Acosta's troops; in all I have receipts for $4500 [pesos], and I will receive that as soon as the pay of Acosta's troops becomes due again. Instead of paying this to the soldiers General de las Santo [sic] will pay it to me. . . .
> Acosta tells me that many companies have made bitter complaints both against him and General Pruneda, and he informed me that he had taken pains to let his command know this, and he has especially recommended the Huasteca Petroleum Company to the consideration of all his subordinates. . . . He thanked me most effusively for not having made reports against him to [President] Carranza or [General] Dieguez, and told me that he would show his appreciations for this consideration on my part. Of course, I cannot vouch for Acosta, as this undiscopline [sic] mob is very hard to handle, but taking into consideration our helplessness I believe it to our interests to lead him through these paths, on the theory that you can catch more flies with molasses than you can with a shot gun.[109]

Such diplomacy, if indeed this is the word that describes Green's dealings with the local commanders, occupied a great deal of time. Their local problems multiplied considerably as new military commanders were assigned and reassigned throughout the oil zone. Generals Acosta, Pruneda, and De los Santos were replaced by other commanders from outside the district, who brought in their loyal troops.

Bribery Becoming So Customary

The military activities in the Huasteca Veracruzana had some very serious consequences. At once, transportation for foreigners and natives alike became very problematic. Troops placed barriers on the roads, stopping cars and travelers and examining the luggage. They commandeered the trains and little flatcars, called *cucarachas* ("cockroaches"), used by the oilmen for traveling on the narrow-gauged railways. The railway was the transport of choice among Constitutionalist troops. Rebel troops such as those of Gen. Manuel Peláez, the *pelaecistas,* therefore, blew up the trains and destroyed the railway bridges.[110] River and coastal craft of the oil companies were taken continually by the troops. Soldiers once helped themselves to barges and boilers belonging to an American marine company in order to salvage a sunken gunboat, returning them when they had finished. Some Constitutionalist officers commandeered company yachts to go fishing. "The Aguila has carried over 1500 passengers during the past year," reported the company's navigation department in 1916. William Green lamented, "There have been days when we have not had a single launch in our hands for work on the laguna."[111]

Secondly, the depredations of Mexican troops destroyed the agricultural base of the northern Veracruz economy. One American claimed that 3,500 American colonists, in addition to the Mexican rancheros and hacendados, had once produced in small farms around Tampico. Only 150 remained in 1919, the rest having been driven out after the American invasion of Veracruz. T. E. King had been a prosperous farmer in Tampico until "the government (Carranza) troops took all of my horses, mules and a great number of other live stock to[g]ether with a great quantity of grain and provisions, besides turning loose their horses in a young grape fruit orchard destroying five or six hundred trees."[112]

Clearly, the armed bands did not single out only the Americans. Mexicans as well suffered. On a seventy-kilometer mule ride through the oil districts of the southern fields in 1917, British Consul Hewitt found the countryside outside the oil camps overgrown with weeds where a few years before cultivated fields had predominated. He noted that the few remaining people in the towns took to the bush when the Constitutionalist forces drew near. The foreign companies began to import foodstuffs from Texas in order to feed their workers.[113] It is difficult to ascribe these depredations to the land hunger of the lower classes, or to local peasants exacting punishment on the landlord class for past injustices. The Constitutionalist troops were underpaid, unmotivated, poorly trained soldiers from outside the Huasteca who stole from foreigner, hacendado, and small-holder alike. Social revolution in the Huasteca had become pillage, pure and simple.

One thing led to another. Small rebellions against Díaz and Madero gave way to the militarization of the oil zone. The military competition between Constitutionalists and Federalists led to double taxation on the oil industry. The American interventions contributed to the resentment of the foreigners. The Constitutionalist victory led to a struggle with the *villistas* and the local rebellion of Peláez in the Huasteca Veracruzana. The military depredations and requisitions led to a breakdown in transportation and agriculture. Then, the poor military pay and high cost of foodstuffs contributed to the breakdown of discipline among the Constitutionalist garrisons. By the end of 1917, the final scourge of revolution visited the oil zone: robbery and murder. The perpetrators were easily identified but not easily apprehended.

The oil camps attracted this final stage of revolution largely because they represented, for the individuals caught up in the confusing political and military campaigns as well as for the government, one of the last remaining sources of income. All the individual crimes that broke out between 1917 and 1920 had to do with robbery. The payrolls for workers and the rental payments to lessors provided the targets of opportunity. Small groups of armed bandits, usually numbering between seven and twenty, preyed on oil camps and traveling gringos. Isolated pump stations on the major oil pipelines became easy pickings, such as the robbery at the Tepetate pump station of The Texas Company that resulted in the murder of the Mexican cashier in July 1918. A month before, a band of *ladrones* (thieves) engaged in a series of robberies by passing leisurely through every pump station on the Huasteca pipeline.[114] The oil camps themselves were easy, stationary, and inviting targets. Insecurity affected the foreign workers, who began to leave the country. "[A]s misery loves company their leaving might be the first step in a general exodus," reported Green of Huasteca. "The morale of the men is at the lowest possible ebb."[115]

Mexican landowners also suffered. Company officials who were dispatched to pay them their monthly rental fees and royalties were held up. The companies resorted to calling the owners into Tampico to receive their monies. Roadways and rail lines became the favorite haunts of small groups of robbers. The Chijol Canal, the narrow dredged passage between Tampico and the Tamiahua Lagoon, was another favorite area for bandits. They would ambush the oil company launches passing by, order them to shore, and take payroll boxes and personal valuables. Every now and again, a company paymaster was killed.[116]

The holdup was always a harrowing experience. An exalted oilman like E. J. Sadler, president of Transcontinental and Jersey Standard's foreign production expert, was not safe in Mexico, as this report of a robbery on the Chijol Canal testifies:

> Mr. Sadler was ordered ashore by these Mexicans and directed to walk along a path into the bush. Having no other recourse or any adequate means of self protection, he proceeded as commanded. He was continuously beaten upon the head and shoulders with the barrel of a cocked rifle and was told that he would be killed by a Mexican who followed him along the path. Mr. Sadler's response to this abuse was that it would be of no use to kill him. Another Mexican intervened and Mr. Sadler was allowed to return to the launch.[117]

Not even the ports were safe. Armed robberies occurred at the Tuxpan terminal and once aboard a Tampico tugboat that was carrying the Transcontinental payroll just across the river.[118]

There was precious little that the oilmen could do. Most of their arms had been taken from them, and those few who had arms were no match for the bandits. Every now and again, as in the case of the Americans' retaliation for the rape of the superintendent's wife, they mounted vigilante parties. On other occasions, if their phone lines had not been cut, they might lay an ambush in the oil camp on the expected arrival of bandits. William Green once noted that "our own rurales," by which he must have meant the armed watchmen (vigilantes), with a few shots scared off a group of bandits lingering on the road. Payroll men hid their money in the ashes of fireplaces, and others attempted to send the payroll from Tampico out to the camps by placing it in plain boxes among the general supplies, without any guard whatsoever. The latter stratagem was not successful. "How the matter leaked out, nobody knows," exclaimed the frustrated manager.[119] But the oilmen did keep statistics on their victimization. In the eighty-three robberies that occurred in the twelve months following 15 August 1917, no suspects were ever apprehended. In the cases of 168 Americans who were killed in the Tampico oil district during the entire Revolution, not one killer was brought to justice.[120] The explanation is not hard to find.

No one was apprehended for these robberies and murders because the perpetrators were the very officers charged with keeping law and order: the Constitutionalist troops themselves. The evidence was everywhere. Robberies and outrages occurred while Constitutionalist forces were in the area. They occurred near their garrisons. Often, bandits presented themselves in their military tunics. At other times, robbers asked for the precise amount carried by paymasters who had first reported their travel itineraries to Constitutionalist commanders. Said a field report from Transcontinental: "No serious effort has been made to prevent them or to apprehend the guilty parties who are generally small bands of Carranzista [sic] soldiers."[121] Sometimes, in the midst of a robbery, they would say that they were *villistas*. But the oilmen knew better. At one point, the representatives of the companies requested that the Tampico military commander, General Magaña, send military escorts with the paymasters. "I cannot do that," he informed the oilmen. "The officers and men might steal the payrolls."[122] William Green, ever a caustic observer of the Mexican outback, did not find it difficult to ascertain why the Constitutionalist troops were engaged in robbery. These men did not come from the Huasteca Veracruzana itself. Moreover, "[t]hey are underfed, rarely clothed, and more than one-half of their pay is stolen from them by their officers," he said.[123]

Indeed, perhaps the decay of moral authority had started at the top. At any rate, the practical parameters of moral degeneracy meant that bribery and extortion became rampant at all levels of the oilmen's activities. In Tampico, Americans began to loathe and scorn the Mexicans on this count. They noted that, unlike Porfirian times, when only the highest official had to be paid for this license or for that infraction of the regulations, now it had become necessary to pay each subordinate official. Occasionally, a particular company, especially the larger and more powerful ones, was able to resist some new exaction. Then, it discovered that a competitor had benefited in some way by yielding to bribery. The Huasteca company began to equate resistance to bribery with resistance to each new exaction of government taxation.[124] Perhaps the reason why corruption became something of an absolute condition at Tampico at the end of the Revolution was the unsettled state of politics. Even Carranza's own military commanders and civil authorities came and went with frequency. Did they and their retainers have to secure their incomes quickly, before they fell from favor or were ordered elsewhere?

The temptations were great for small Mexican entrepreneurs to use the influence of powerful Constitutionalist generals. One Jesús Herrera attempted to entice Gen. Pablo González, the highest Constitutionalist military officer in northeast Mexico, into buying shares of his Mexican petroleum company at Pánuco. Herrera appealed to nationalism: if Mexicans do not buy shares, the foreigners will exploit the country's oil wealth. González declined.[125] Nonetheless, General González soon heard of unscrupulous "Spaniards," aided by the local military chief, Capt. Armando García, forcing landowners to sign unfavorable oil contracts. González ordered the captain's dismissal. Then the general learned that a prospectus circulating in New York had attached his name as part owner of an oil firm promoted by an American. "We are in a position to get anything we ask for," such as oil concessions, said the flyer.[126] Little in the unsettled political and military life of the oil zone prevented such frauds, which already had a long history.

At any rate, each new regulation of the industry became the excuse for another fee. When the law was passed to prevent the use of oil storage tanks with wooden tops, thought by Mexican officials to be the cause of fire, the oilmen paid their fines of five hundred pesos for each tank and went on using them as before. When oil steamers landed at Tampico, up to thirty customs officers descended on each vessel. Only five of the customs officers actually had commissions—the others were retainers—but the ship's bursar had to pay them all. Americans cooperated with the system of graft, encouraging the Mexican officials with their eager compliance but with disdain and contempt. "I believe my report will show that there is not as much diplomacy and courtesy and straightforwardness on the part of the foreigns [sic] in Mexico as high ethical ideas would demand," wrote one U.S. naval officer in Tampico.[127]

As an oil-leasing attorney in Tampico since 1911, William F. Buckley was in a unique position to know of such things. "[Bribery] has become so customary," he wrote, "that the Carrancista officials demand it and feel no gratitude toward the companies when they get it; they feel that the companies pay it to them because they are afraid of them and not because they like them, which is of course the truth."[128] On the other hand, some of the larger, more powerful oil companies might have been able to withstand the pressure to pay bribes because of their superior resources. "It should perhaps be noted," wrote a Jersey attorney, "that the Standard Oil Company, on going into Mexico, adopted the policy, as a matter of principal [sic] of declining to pay any 'graft' or protection money, to anyone, and that this policy has been followed, without exception."[129] Notwithstanding this commendable resolve, Tampico and Tuxpan had become a revolutionary Sodom and

Fig. 11. Early rebels in the oil zone. Identified as the men of "Col. Zuig," these mounted irregulars were typical of those few bands of rebels operating among the oil fields against the governments of Porfirio Díaz and Francisco I. Madero. They would take a few rifles and horses from the oil camps. The systematic despoliation came later, after 1914, when larger groups of troops and rebels operated in the Faja de Oro. Courtesy of the DeGolyer Library of Southern Methodist University.

Gomorrah to some foreigners. And the hinterlands of these cities became the rookery of thieves.

The True Interests of the State

Why did the popular uprisings and the participation of the masses in the Mexican Revolution impel the state to increase the regulation of the foreign-owned petroleum industry? The official answer, proposed by the politicians and thereafter by scholars who took them at their word, concerns the intolerable power of the companies. The foreign interests meddled in internal political affairs; they bribed public officials; they supported some unpopular faction or another during the rebellion; they were not interested in Mexican economic development; they exploited native workers; they used up domestic resources; and they made lots of money. Yet, the real reason why the Mexican revolution turned on the oil industry in particular was fiscal and social. The oil industry was wealthy and the state, indigent. An impecunious polity cannot discharge its social obligations, and in revolutionary Mexico, those social obligations grew enormously.

In Mexico, the state had always assumed the mission of controlling the tensions of a social order composed of groups with unequal opportunities and privileges. Politicians knew that their right to rule was predicated on their ability to mediate and ameliorate social antagonisms inherent in a diverse society. No matter how powerful Díaz had been, his successors faulted him for nurturing a government that did not or could not contain these social tensions. The politicians and generals who participated in the Revolution knew firsthand the dangers of the breakdown of social control. Architect of the Mexican constitution and Carranza's cabinet minister, Pastor Rouaix, expressed it succinctly: "The revolutions have been the unavoidable consequence of an intense popular discontent provoked by the inequality of rights between the components of the conglomeration that forms the nationality, and inequality which has been exacerbated more and more in the passage of time."[130] The first priority of the revolutionary state was to reestablish public order. Depending historically upon paternalism and coercion to maintain social control, the state badly needed the funds to fulfill popular demands and to support the vastly bloated revolutionary army. Thus, the centralization of power in revolutionary Mexico, as in the early days of the Díaz regime, necessitated broadening the state's fiscal base.

But in 1915, the economy was prostrate. The prolonged revolutionary fighting and military exactions had crippled internal transportation, ruined agricultural production, and reversed economic growth. The rail lines were cut and the rolling stock destroyed. Mining production, so dependent upon the rail industry to carry ore from mine to smelter, also diminished. As the peasant armies directed so much of the revolutionary violence toward the properties of the hated hacendados, agricultural production and exports tumbled. In the north, Villa's administrators confiscated the great cattle estates of the Terrazas family and exported the breeding stock through El Paso in order to purchase arms. Indeed, famine broke out in many parts of the country in 1915, especially Mexico City.[131] Only the oil industry boomed.

In time, a new generation of politicians labored to reestablish the state, eventually moving beyond the mere political centralization of Díaz himself. They came to blame all the social unrest of the Revolution on the rapid, uncontrolled capitalist development of the Porfirian age. They lost sight of the fact that the reason for opening the economy to foreign investment in the first place also concerned an earlier generation's desire to strengthen the state's capacity to control the masses. Now in 1915, the men around Carranza sought to strengthen the state's power to pacify the masses, by reform or by force. They cast about for sources of revenue. Taxing imports and exports no longer sufficed; the state had to create new taxes. To do it, the state was willing to resurrect older, colonial doctrines of the public good overriding, if necessary, the Díaz-era contracts protecting individual rights. The foreign-owned oil industry became the battleground for the state's vigorous imposition.

Venustiano Carranza was to be the agent for Mexico's economic nationalism. He was philosophically unprepared to change the status quo, yet under him, because of the extraordinary popular mobilization of the Revolution, the process of social reform began. It was not as if the first chief was motivated to seek political power because he had a blueprint for the kind of social reforms that Mexico needed. He was not a man of revolutionary spirit or ideology. But one thing Carranza was prepared for: he had the indomitable drive to dominate Mexican political life. If he had to legitimize himself in politics by taking those steps that enhanced the state's social controls, he was prepared to do that. If he needed new sources of revenue as a means to that end, then Carranza would take those steps too. Carranza fell into economic nationalism, despite himself. To the first-chief-turned-president of Mexico, political domination was the end—economic nationalism, merely the inevitable means.

Carranza did not initiate the fiscal onslaught on the oil industry. Díaz had raised the bar duties in 1909; Veracruz state increased production taxes in 1911; and Huerta raised the federal bar dues and stamp taxes in 1913. The Veracruz revolutionary general Cándido Aguilar initiated the Constitutionalist fiscal exactions. Aguilar had campaigned as a rebel military leader against the federal forces in the Huasteca Veracruzana region as early as November 1913. Soon he began collecting taxes at Tuxpan, which he held for the rebels during most of Huerta's tenure in office. General Aguilar became governor of Veracruz when the Constitutionalists triumphed. As governor and general, he faced the very same fiscal problems as his fellow revolutionary politicians. Less than three weeks after he became provisional governor, Aguilar issued Decree No. 3 of the State of Veracruz. This is what it said:

Whereas (1) petroleum lands have been sold and rented under disastrous circumstances for the owners and at "enormous profits" for oilmen;

(2) foreign companies prosper while Mexico suffers and the former ought to accept the same losses as nationals;

(3) the predominance of foreign capital poses a danger, inasmuch as it demands protection from foreign armed forces; and

(4) progress ought to benefit native Mexicans without being dangerous to our integrity.

Therefore (1) all oil contracts are to obtain authorization from the state government;

(2) no contract is legal without said authorization; and

(3) disregard of the above will be punished by confiscation of land involved in the "unauthorized" contract.[132]

That was not all. Part of his animus toward the oil companies had to do with hatred of Huerta and the rumors that some oilmen had supported Huerta's government. Governor Aguilar declared null and void all contracts and oil leases made during "the Usurper's" tenure in office. The oilmen were stunned. To them, the language was hastily contrived and vague as to whether Aguilar referred to private leases or those made on public lands.[133]

The oilmen operating in the Huasteca became concerned. Not only did they have to pay fees for the governmental inspection and authorization of their contracts, but there remained many questions about the clarity of their titles. "The oil people anticipate a great amount of trouble from these decrees," observed Admiral Mayo, still standing off the coast in support of the Veracruz landing, "as some of [the original land] titles are over one hundred years old and the surveys naturally more or less inaccurate."[134] The decrees plainly seemed retroactive and contrary to the land laws under which they had operated in Mexico since the time of Porfirio Díaz. Replied Aguilar, Huerta had illegally usurped political power and all contracts executed during his regime were also illegal. He did not quite clear up whether he referred to contracts executed on publicly or privately owned land—or both. Ultimately, the first chief, Venustiano Carranza himself, provided some corrective backtracking, declaring that all concessions of the Department of Petroleum during the usurper's (Huerta's) regime were nullified.[135] Aguilar's brand of economic nationalism anticipated Carranza's.

January 1915, the month that the Constitutionalists took back Mexico City from the forces of Zapata and Villa, turned out to be a busy time for Carranza regarding new oil policies. The first chief learned of the outbreak of an anti-Carranza rebellion in the Huasteca Veracruzana led by General Peláez. Also, the Constitutionalists were discovering the extent of the famine in the capital, although Carranza himself kept the provisional government in Veracruz. General Obregón, meanwhile, was proceeding with the equipping of an army to challenge Villa in northern Mexico. Consequently, one of Carranza's first decrees of the new year was directed at the oil companies. All oil development not having the permission of the Constitutionalist government was to come to a halt, Carranza declared, until a new oil law was written. Construction of pipelines and the drilling of wells were to be suspended immediately. Moreover, the decree stated, any company's appeal to the diplomatic representation of its home government invited foreign interference.[136] Once again, the company lawyers were puzzled. Did Carranza's decree apply to wells already in operation or just to new wells?

In the midst of the confusion (but not inaction, for the companies continued to export), Carranza lobbed another bombshell. In mid-January, he ordered an embargo on the exports of Huasteca and El Aguila petroleum, this over a tax dispute. Those two companies had been delivering fuel oil to the Constitutionalist railways without recompense on the understanding that the value of those oil deliveries would be deducted from future Constitutionalist taxes. Huasteca owed 375,000 pesos in taxes. Within a week, the companies were forced into a settlement. Thomas Vaughan of El Aguila went to see Carranza in Veracruz and agreed to pay a production tax to the Constitutionalists, if Carranza would acknowledge ten thousand pounds worth of oil already delivered to his railways. El Aguila then turned over fifty thousand dollars to Carranza's financial emissaries in New York.[137] Carranza had collected.

But was that all? No. Before January 1915 was out, additional demands were made on the oil companies. "Threatening [a] close down of export shipping," Governor Aguilar imposed a fifty-thousand-dollar fine on El Aguila for polluting the Tuxpan River. Then the Constitutionalists increased the production tax to thirty cents per ton, which would have collected eight thousand pounds per month from El Aguila alone. Then Luis Cabrera, the Constitutionalist minister of the treasury, ordered a suspension of all oil-field work pending government inspection of the company's statistics. The companies were to turn over data on cost per barrel, leased and owned properties, and capitalization.[138]

Why? So that the government could claim its share of the exploitation of this national resource.

The Carranza regime visited still other small vexations on the oil companies in January 1915. They included: a fine of £500 on El Aguila for filing its accounts after the deadline; delaying the departure of steam tankers at Tuxpan on technicalities; the removal of many items for pipeline and refining facilities from the duty-free list, despite existing contracts; and the issuance of no new permits for drilling and construction until companies signed statements subjecting themselves to petroleum laws not yet formulated.[139] This latter requirement was to assume greater importance as Carranza's oil policy matured. For the moment, the government was quite incapable of enforcing its own decrees.

At the end of this eventful month, customs officers finally lifted the export embargo. But permits for pipeline and refinery construction were not forthcoming, and American skilled workers began to leave Mexico while their work was suspended.[140] The companies reasoned that the new decrees were unjust and meant as simple harassment. They had been operating in Mexico for years under certain agreements that Carranza now wished to amend. These amendments, they argued, were unworkable, unreasonable, and an infringement of prior government contracts and of their private contracts with landowners.[141] In the end, the oilmen complied just enough to continue their activities free of outright government crackdown.

In truth, a total crackdown, such as a halt to all oil exports, was not in the Constitutionalists' interests. After all, Carranza had bills to pay, and the oil industry remained among the few sources able to contribute to his treasury. The year 1915 was pivotal. The main Constitutionalist army under Obregón was adopting the tactics and equipment of European warfare—barbed wire, trenches, machine guns—to defeat Gen. Pancho Villa. Harassment of the oil industry occurred only intermittently after an eventful January. The Constitutionalists attacked El Aguila, claiming that the British company was responsible for all of Mexico's international difficulties. As for the American companies, Carranza threatened that Constitutionalist troops would set fire to their oil wells if the marines landed again in Mexico. Another decree again descended upon the industry in mid-November. Reiterating earlier stipulations, Pastor Rouaix ordered all oil companies to file inventories listing capitalization, properties, leases, number of wells, and other information with his new Petroleum Technical Office.[142] The Constitutionalist government was now creating a new bureaucracy to monitor and keep statistics on the oil industry. For the companies, this was ominous.

Meanwhile, Mexico's fiscal problems did not abate, and 1916 brought additional government constraints on the oil industry. Once again, Cándido Aguilar provided the dynamism. So far as he was concerned, there was no such thing as a private contract in Mexico. The state was a legitimate party to all contracts between individuals and between Mexicans and foreign companies. Governor Aguilar again proposed an inspection of company contracts:

> The State Government shall refuse its authorization if the contract shall appear unjust or prejudicial to any of the partisans thereto, when the development to be carried on thereunder redounds exclusively to the benefit of the unnationalized [*sic*] companies to the prejudice of the Mexican citizens, when [the contract in question] tends to solidify the predominance of foreign capital constituting a menace to the integrity or the progress of the nation, or in other cases when the contract is against the true interests of the State.[143]

What constituted a "prejudice" to Mexican citizens? Precisely what menaced "the integrity or the progress" of Mexico? Exactly when was a contract against the "true interests" of the state? Needless to say, the state was to collect a fee for each contract it "inspected." Aguilar's proposal seemed to subject all oil contracts to political criteria.

During the rest of 1916, the provisional government of Carranza seemed to grapple with these questions. There were plans and discussions about the return of oil lands that the companies had purchased or leased from Indian communities. Government officials contemplated granting a concession for a common-carrier pipeline in Tuxpan, open for public use and breaking the control of the big foreign companies. More decrees nullified laws, permits, leases of oil lands, and previous decrees. Some came from Governor Aguilar, others from the Petroleum Office. An order to public notaries required that all foreign signatories of oil charters must agree to renounce "their national rights and privileges of appeal to their [diplomatic] representations."[144] The provisional government flexed its muscles in confronting a small company. It rescinded the oil rights that the Compañía Petrolera Marítima (CPM) had acquired under Madero. Although owned predominantly by American capital, the CPM had a Mexican charter. Therefore, all American diplomatic protests on behalf of the CPM were brushed aside by Carranza's foreign minister. "The Government of Mexico," he replied, "is surprised that the Government of the United States should make the representation transmitted when only the interests of Mexican citizens appear concerned."[145] Nevertheless, foreign oilmen appealed to their home governments each time a new decree came down.

The year 1917 was also critical for the oil companies in a number of respects. The Constitutionalists had written a new constitution, Carranza was running for president and Aguilar for Veracruz governor in national elections, Villa was hiding in the Chihuahua mountains, Zapata was still operating in Morelos, Obregón had retired to his chickpea farm in Sonora, and Manuel Peláez eluded government forces in the Huasteca Veracruzana. Oil prices and oil exports continued to rise. In the midst of all this, Venustiano Carranza issued a new decree, establishing a 10 percent *ad valorem* tax on the export of all petroleum.[146] Previously, the state had taxed only documents, bar crossings, imports of selected equipment, and the stamps affixed to all legal documents. Now its customs officers were to collect revenues on the export of petroleum as well. The oilmen once again refused, stating that their existing contracts exempted them from export taxes. This decree fell by the wayside, but even more economic nationalism was on the way.

Plans to Suit a Mexican Engineer

State formation in revolutionary Mexico brought in its train the creation of a professional bureaucracy that studied the technical aspects of the oil industry. This bureaucracy would ultimately provide the continuity in state policies that Carranza and his successors could use to bend industry to the needs of the Mexican polity. Rather than working to promote industry, to foster oil development in Mexico, this body of public-service technocrats sought, above all, to control the existing foreign-owned industry. The oil bureaucracy had its beginnings while Carranza was in Veracruz. There he attracted "many young professionals with revolutionary ideas," such as engineers Pastor Rouaix, Modesto Rolland, Manuel Urquidi, Salvador Gómez, and Alberto Langarica. In March of 1915, Carranza formed them into the Comisión Técnica del Petróleo, under the political leadership of none other than Cándido Aguilar. They were to study the industry and propose laws for its regulation.[147]

Pastor Rouaix received the portfolio of the secretary of industry and created the Department of Petroleum within his ministry. José Vázquez Schiaffino and Joaquín Santaella became its directors. Eventually, the petroleum department established branch offices in Tampico, Tuxpan, and Minatitlán. Engineers José Colomo and Gustavo Ortega staffed these offices with petroleum inspectors. In the meanwhile, the finance secretariat of the provisional government, headed by Luis Cabrera, also established a new tax-collection unit specializing in petroleum affairs, the Petroleum Fiscal Agencies. Under the direction of Leopoldo Vázquez, it began to formulate methods for taxing petroleum exports.[148]

The Petroleum Department in 1916 inaugurated its own *Boletín del Petróleo,* a journal devoted to the history of Mexican oil and the technical aspects of the industry. The tenor of the articles remained somewhat critical, not the sort of praiseworthy pieces one finds today in Pemex literature. For example, these technocrats would write about well-drilling accidents, uncontrolled fires, oil spills, and pollution. The overarching editorial policy supported increased governmental oversight of the industry. In case the readers missed the point, editorials in the *Boletín* helped them to focus. "Mexican petroleum ought to be considered like a great, but exhaustible, national wealth," stated the first issue, "and for that reason, the State ought to care for its conservation and best utilization."[149] The petroleum department adopted a second long-range policy concerning oil. That is, that Mexico's production ought primarily to serve the domestic market, to promote national industry and public utilities rather than be subservient to external markets. Thus, the department pushed for the construction of a pipeline from the oil zone across the Sierra Oriental into Mexico City, where a refinery was to be built.[150] These oil bureaucrats remained rather visionary. Many of these policies eventually would come to pass. The *Boletín* also promoted development of Mexico's technical knowledge. The Department sent delegations of bureaucrats on inspection trips to the United States. There they visited oil fields and conferred with regulatory agencies such as the Texas Railroad Commission, which, despite the misleading name, increasingly had come to oversee that state's oil industry.[151] They wrote articles on refining technology and the cementing of well casings. These "technocrats" gleaned information from the U.S. oil journals and reproduced the petroleum laws of U.S. regulatory agencies.

Philosophically, the new generation of bureaucrats, even while resurrecting essentially colonial traditions of intervening in the economy, rejected the colonial order. They did not conceive of Mexico's colonial heritage as having been a system of internal social domination—a social hierarchy defined by race, ethnicity, and differential privileges. To these bureaucrats, colonialism had been a foreign monopoly of the economy. Spain forbade the development of Mexican industry, Santaella wrote. Therefore, the foreign domination of the oil industry was but a new form of colonialism. It stifled Mexican entrepreneurship and extracted Mexican resources for the benefit and wealth of other nations. "Industry remains in the hands of foreigners, especially Anglo-Saxons," Santaella said. "Economic savings are destroyed, that is, invested savings; the economic independence of Mexico is delayed, its industry being set back, and our race remains with the stigma of slavery, voluntary death."[152] Plainly, the technocrats were perfecting the justification for regulating the foreign interests, even though the actual reason for doing so may have been otherwise.

Subsequent to the election of 1917, the secretariat was taken over from Rouaix by other technocrats and politicians, but the petroleum department endured and expanded. The petroleum department busied itself with technical matters. Among its first acts was to study the distance between wells, which the technocrats thought was too close in certain areas of Pánuco, Topila, and Tuxpan. They considered that offset drilling on small, contiguous properties would lead to premature exhaustion of the oil fields. The department directed that the companies operate these fields as a unity, apportioning production between them and reducing the flows. The companies ignored them. It was also the Department of Petroleum that required the companies to place steel tops on the oil storage tanks in order to prevent explosions. Huasteca representatives William Green and Hilarion Branch protested the order vehemently. They also wrote to the State Department, greatly annoying the oil bureaucrats.[153]

It was not so much that the new members of this bureaucracy were imbued with oil expertise or with revolutionary principles but that they served the state. In turn, the state served larger interests, which consisted of ameliorating social tensions. To Mexican politicians in 1915, the reestablishment of civil order and the gaining of control over the economy were one and the same thing. Unfettered capitalist expansion, after all, had brought about the social dislocations producing the Revolution. At any rate, their personal politics were those of many Mexicans at the time—having to do with survival. Take José López Portillo y Weber, for instance. From a distinguished landowning family of Jalisco, his father had been an anti-científico governor of the state under Porfirio Díaz and minister of foreign affairs for Huerta. Young José graduated from the military academy in 1913, serving as a officer in Huerta's federal army before it collapsed. In 1919, López Portillo was offered a position in the petroleum department "through the influence of my brother-in-law." He admitted that he knew nothing about oil. His supervisor at the Tampico office sent the new technocrat on his first inspection trip to the oil camps of the Golden Lane. López Portillo's assignment: to ascertain if the storage tanks at the wells had been properly placed.[154]

The oil managers looked somewhat askance on these neophyte inspectors—and the Mexican officials returned the contempt. A typically unenlightened view of the bureaucrats came from William Green of Huasteca, who was annoyed that "Senor Shafino" (his name was Vázquez Schiaffino) had depreciated the expense and risk of producing oil in Mexico. "The *Mexican's knowledge of the oil industry,* in common with his education and culture, is *superficial,*" wrote Green, not a man to mince words:

> He is sent from Mexico City to size up the oil situation, and he rides up and down the Panuco River in our launches and sees our ships being loaded, as well as those of other companies, and he knows that oil is going into them and being exported, and that is just about the extent of his knowledge. He has *no idea of the time and expense necessary to arrive at that point of development.*[155]

For their part, the bureaucrats rejected the American capitalist's notion that private contracts benefited the Mexican landowner. "[I]t depended on the morality and the rectitude of the industrialists," said López Portillo. "Among the [Yankees], it was improbable because one only found among them either employees or imitators of Rockefeller. . . . All were entirely adverse to the interjection of the government into the industry. Among the Englishmen, it was because they had to be employees or imitators of Deterding."[156] Needless to mention, the managers and bureaucrats were taking adversarial positions.

The creation of such a formal bureaucracy, leavened by a growing gaggle of young technocrats who learned the technical side of the industry while on the job, diluted the old influence of the foreign entrepreneurs. During the Porfiriato, attorneys such as Pablo Martínez del Río and Pablo Macedo had entrée into the highest circles of government. The owners met with Presidents Díaz and even Madero. No longer. Like a flood, the Revolution deposited a thick layer of inspectors, government engineers, and lawyers between the foreigner businessmen and the nation's politicians. The power over policy now became diffused. Foreign companies still retained Mexican attorneys belonging to the Mexican Academy of Jurisprudence and even others who had served in Madero's cabinet. One senator, José J. Reynoso, worked closely with the companies during the Carranza presidency.[157] The old influence was gone, however. During the Revolution, the companies' communication with government increasingly got absorbed and deflected by a phalanx of appointed officeholders.

Creation of the petroleum bureaucracy also forced the companies to deal at mundane levels with government functionaries in a manner that consumed managerial time and expense. Company accountants now busied themselves in assembling statistics of individual well production and figures accounting for losses of oil because of fire, spillage, and evaporation. All statistics were required to be converted from the English system of weights and measures to the metric system. Signs at the installations had to be in Spanish.[158] The petroleum inspectors now issued the permits for repairs and improvements to refineries and other installations. The requirement to submit detailed blueprints, even topographical maps of entire estates, if oil field work was contemplated, multiplied the *tramitaciones* (paper shuffling) and delayed work schedules. It no longer sufficed to cultivate powerful insiders—Alberto Pani, for example. Executives of the Pearson group treated Pani royally when this urbane official went abroad—all to no avail. " 'Government' business still takes up a large proportion of everyone's time," commented an El Aguila manager. "[I]t appears to increase."[159]

As usual, William Green formed an opinion about the bewildering welter of requirements. "The God of all engineers could never make a map or plan of any kind that would suit a Mexican engineer connected with the Petroleum Department," wrote the Huasteca field manager, "and they would usually return them several times to be amended, with the result that when the plan is finally approved by the Inspector's office, it is neither what we want nor is it understood by any one."[160] On the surface, the Revolution as yet had done little to influence the production and export business of the foreign oil companies in Mexico. For the moment, their performance was merely the visible one-tenth of the proverbial iceberg. Radical changes were taking place in the submerged portion of the industrial glacier floating on a sea of high-priced oil. There, beneath the waterline, beneath the optimistic statistics, the iceberg was melting.

The Limitations of Public Interest

The story of the Mexican Constitution of 1917 bears repeating if only to link the fate of the oil companies in Mexico to the pervading social and political conditions of that nation. Petroleum was not a dominant issue during the constitutional convention. Yet, as the *constituyentes* (those who collaborated to write the constitution) discussed basically domestic issues, they were also deciding the future of the foreign interests in their nation. Venustiano Carranza himself, however, was not a part of those discussions.

Wishing to confirm himself in power, Carranza, as first chief of the Constitutionalist Revolution, proposed a new constitution for Mexico that was essentially political. His draft provided for elections, delegated the powers of the executive, Congress, the courts, and the states, and expressed the rights and duties of citizenship. Carranza thought that all demands for social reforms could be handled by legislation, rather than by constitutional provision. In this respect, the first chief was ignoring strong precedents in Mexican constitution-writing. That of 1824 sought to acknowledge the widespread participation of the common people in the independence movement. Therefore, it removed the legal disadvantages—slavery for some blacks, head taxes for Indians and *castas*—borne by the nonwhites during the colonial period. Written by conservatives dismayed at the continuation of social unrest, the charter of 1836 sought to reestablish basic social controls by restoring privileges to the military and the Church. The Constitution of 1857 prominently profiled the program of the resurgent liberals, restricting the role of the Church in landowning, education, and society. This reform movement, in fact, mounted a massive land redistribution program, using some of the very same notions of state dominion over property that colonial authorities had used in reassigning peasant villages in the sixteenth and seventeenth centuries and in confiscating Jesuit holdings in the eighteenth. It was already well established that Mexico's basic political charter would also reflect the social agenda of the era in which it was formulated. Owing to the massive mobilization of peasants and labor in the revolutionary struggles, the compulsion of the *constituyentes* to respond to these popular demands overrode Carranza's narrow viewpoint.

As the constitutional convention convened, the delegates clearly went beyond Carranza's instructions. For one thing, the assembly was held in Querétaro, in December of 1916 and January of 1917. Carranza, in the meantime, carried out the executive duties of the provisional government in the capital. A coalition of reformist politicians, encouraged by General Obregón, who was not a member of the assembly, and young attorneys and bureaucrats, soon gained control of the Querétaro convention. The critical articles of the new document were written in committees dominated by the forty-two-year-old Pastor Rouaix, who represented the technocracy of the new revolutionary state, and by the thirty-two-year-old Gen. Francisco Múgica of Michoacán, who represented the reformist elements of the Constitutionalist army.[161] This coalition hammered out three reformist elements. Article 3 restricted the role of the Church in education, making the state supreme. Article 123 established the rights of labor, the obligations of employers, and the authority of the government to mediate the first two. Finally, Article 27 dealt with the ownership of property.

In essence, Article 27 reversed the late-nineteenth-century property reform laws that had moved toward vesting in private individuals absolute dominion over property. The laws of 1884 and 1892, as mentioned in chapter 1, had adopted English common-law concepts of private property so as to attract foreign capital to Mexico. The *constituyentes* now rejected both the property reforms and the results of foreign investment. The rapid economic development was thought to have created intense social antagonisms that spilled over into revolution. "The financial prosperity the country acquired with the dictatorial regime of General Díaz," said Pastor Rouaix, "only served to deepen even more that abyss that separated the plutocracy from the proletariat and to augment the animosities that were impregnating the popular soul with the constant abuses suffered by the disinherited classes, which formed 90 percent of the Mexican population."[162] The object at the end of 1916 was to reapply the state's traditional obligations. Harking back to prerogatives (nay, duties) that the Crown had assumed in the colonial period, the twentieth-century Mexican state was to take a more active role in economic affairs in the interests of social stability. These reformist articles revived colonial precedents. Some lawyers for the oil companies recognized them as such. W. E. McMahon called the state's ownership of subsoil rights "a relic of absolute monarchy," a phrase that conveyed his view of its applicability to the modern age.[163]

Article 27 had two principal objectives. First, it was to provide the juridical basis for a massive land-reform program. Among some of the *constituyentes*, there was a general feeling that the hacendados' monopoly of land had goaded the peasants into rebellion. Revolutions in Mexico would end once and for all, Luis Navarro told his fellow delegates, if the peasants were to own their own land, for they would never leave it to follow some revolutionary leader.[164] The article's second purpose was to increase the state's dominion over the mining and petroleum industries. As drafted by Rouaix's committee, Article 27 read:

> Ownership of lands and waters within the boundaries of the national territory is vested originally in the Nation which has had, and has, the right to transmit title thereof to private persons, thereby constituting private property.
>
> Expropriations shall only be made for reasons of public utility and by means of indemnification.
>
> The Nation shall at all times have the right to impose on private property such limitations as the public interest may demand. . . .
>
> In the Nation is vested direct ownership of all minerals . . . such as . . . petroleum and all solid, liquid, or gaseous hydrocarbons.[165]

Naturally, in and of itself, the wording is open to interpretation. What was the precise meaning of "public utility," for example? One's exclusive enjoyment of property could be abridged by the state in the interests of the public. But what were the public's interests? Who interpreted those interests? These were political, as opposed to constitutional, questions and remained to be defined primarily through political processes and only secondarily through legal means.

Article 27 affected the oil industry in several ways. It declared that the direct ownership (dominion) of petroleum and all hydrocarbons in the subsoil was vested in the nation. Water, and the beds and banks of inlets, bays, lakes, and rivers and even intermittent streams and ravines were likewise vested in the nation. The Constitution of 1917 prescribed that the subsoil hydrocarbons and minerals and national lands were inalienable and imprescriptible. They could be granted to private parties or corporations only as government concessions, not as private property. Only Mexicans by birth or naturalization or Mexican companies had the right to acquire ownership of the lands and waters or to acquire concessions to develop mineral mines and petroleum wells. Aliens could develop minerals and hydrocarbons only if they agreed to become Mexican with respect to that property and not to invoke the protection of their own government. Otherwise, non-Mexicans would forfeit their rights. Perhaps the greatest expression of the state's reemergence as an economic arbiter was found in the provisions for expropriation. Article 27 established a justification (that is, public utility) for the state's revocation, with indemnification, of an individual's use of land and mineral rights.[166]

Besides the questions of public utility and who defines it, the private companies wondered about the retroactive aspects of Article 27. Did the new constitution revoke private contracts over subsoil rights that the oil companies had already acquired directly from landowners? Could those persons who had acquired land under the Porfirian-era laws, thus having private use of the subsoil wealth, still lease those rights to second parties even after 1917? Of course, the foreign oilmen believed that Article 27 should have no retroactive effect. They interpreted that they would be able to continue in the exclusive privilege of developing their pre-1917 leases, as if the Constitution did not exist. Many of them also believed that they still had a right to acquire the exclusive use of subsoil rights by continuing to make new leases on land acquired by Mexican owners under the 1884–92 laws. Why? Article 14 of the constitution specifically stated that no law should be given retroactive effect to the prejudice of any person whatsoever.[167] As was to be expected from a charter written by two hundred individuals in just two months, the Constitution of 1917 contained a few contradictions.

The constitutional provisions concerning national lands presented another conundrum. On land contiguous to the Pánuco, Tuxpan, and other rivers, many an oil company had sunk productive wells that could easily be offset if the state conceded the riverbanks as well as the beds of intermittent streams to second interests. For example, Potrero del Llano No. 4 was located just twenty-five yards from the bank of the Buena Vista River. If the government were to give a concession on that bank to a competing interest, an offset well could be drilled nearby.

Much depended upon interpretation. Carranza himself, who was elected in August under the provisions of the 1917 Constitution, had not pushed for such a constitutional revision of the property laws. Nevertheless, he accepted it, along with the other reformist provisions, which, after all, the executive could choose to ignore, much as Porfirio Díaz had allowed the anticlericalism of the 1857 Constitution to remain unacted upon. But the bureaucrats were of a different mind. Clearly, they believed that Article 27 could be considered retroactive in its effect. "So, whatever may be the rights established by a prior constitution," said Vázquez Schiaffino, of the petroleum office, "the new basic law could abolish them without hindrance." Vázquez Schiaffino even ventured a definition of public utility. The idea behind the constitutional reform, he said, was the welfare of the greatest number of

Mexicans. Private patrimony of a few great companies had been detrimental to Mexico, because those interests had not given "any more than an insignificant part of their enormous incomes" to the Mexican people.[168] Plainly, Article 27 was conceived in the notion that property rights in Mexico, as so much in life, could be reduced to fiscal proportions. Pastor Rouaix justified the reestablishment of colonial mining laws because the oil industry had created enormous profits for the foreign companies and little for Mexico. "But it was through drastic measures of the triumphant Revolution that the privileges of capitalism were not recognized and that obliged the companies to leave a part of their enormous profits to the Public Treasury."[169]

Having been a *constituyente,* although often absent from the working sessions, Cándido Aguilar understood very well the clash between the Anglo-American conception of property and the Hispanic tradition now being revived in the 1917 Constitution. He also recognized its financial parameters. "It concerns an application of a simple principle," he wrote; "along with the right to collect taxes, the Government now has an efficacious mechanism to make the petroleum industry contribute its part to the necessities of the Nation." Aguilar also understood the unavoidable union between foreign investment and domestic affairs. Social reforms could not be brought about in Mexico without, at the same time, transforming the rights of foreign investors. "If it is declared that Article 27 is not applicable to the oilmen," he said, "it will harm the application of the social and economic reforms contained in the Constitution. Agrarian, labor and other issues will not be carried into action except by overcoming major obstacles. Those Mexicans interested in agricultural and other businesses will take delight that the foreigners are in a privileged position."[170] And the reforms could not wait, Aguilar warned his father-in-law, the president of Mexico. He quoted the dictum of Justo Sierra, "Si no se paga, la revolución se apaga." If one does not pay, the revolution will perish.

Clearly, the Mexicans felt themselves under pressure from the extraordinary events of the Revolution to reestablish control over the foreign interests, a situation of which some of the oilmen were well aware. Early in 1917, when the provisions of Article 27 became known, the British managers of El Aguila decided to put off all plans for expansion. They resolved to acquire no new leases and to undertake no new work. Capital expenditures were to be cut back, and managers would proceed only with ongoing construction projects. "[N]either Carranza nor any other leader of the Revolution is at the present time strong enough even if they were willing to try, to reverse the decrees of the Party embodied in the new Constitution, and directed against capitalists and foreigners," wrote Frederick Adams of El Aguila, "and any alliance with foreign interests at the present moment would have dangerous if not fatal consequences upon their political life."[171]

For the moment, the foreign governments took a guarded view of the new constitution. Neither the British Foreign Office nor the United States State Department initiated any comment whatsoever on the questions raised by Article 27. They waited instead for specific instances of enforcement that might impinge upon the rights of the oil companies. Perhaps the Dutch took the most enlightened view of the situation. They realized the new constitution was dangerous, threatening to push out the Dutch, American, and English companies and possibly allow the Germans in. But the Netherlands was also a colonial power. In the Dutch East Indies it too held the *dominium directe* of the subsoil, much like the Spanish Crown had held in colonial Mexico. If the oil industry is now in trouble, said the Dutch consul-general, it was the fault of Wilson and U.S. intervention, which created the present chaos anyway.[172] Rather than clarifying the issues, Article 27 of the Constitution of 1917 merely contributed to the fiscal and legal uncertainties. The questions raised by the constitutional charter, in time, would be settled via the political process. The remainder of the Carranza regime was but the initiation of that political settlement.

Taxation Versus Principles

The Carranza government spent much of the rest of 1917 addressing itself to political and military matters. The Constitutionalist army still had to deal with rebellions in the periphery of Mexico, such as those of Emiliano Zapata in Morelos, Félix Díaz in Oaxaca, Pancho Villa in Chihuahua, and Manuel Peláez in the Huasteca Veracruzana. Coping with the economic crisis and low agricultural productivity forced Carranza to reconsider his monetary experiments (his pesos *infalsificables* [unfalsifiable] had become practically worthless in 1916) and to halt land reforms. He even returned some confiscated land to the original owners, hoping that these hacendados would invest capital and produce the foodstuffs that Mexico desperately needed. In the Huasteca Veracruzana, many landowners who had become wealthy leasing land to the oil companies also complained about the new Constitution. Their spokesman was the rebel *caudillo* General Peláez. Many *carrancistas* dismissed such opposition as the machinations of the powerful oil interests. "Behind these individuals," a confidant of Cándido Aguilar wrote about the hostile landowners of the Huasteca, "are the vicious foreign petroleum companies and all our enemy elements. . . . In these complaints, you will not see the attitude of Mexican landowners but of the oil companies."[173]

Indeed, it was Cándido Aguilar, now the elected governor of Veracruz, who began to apply Article 27 to the oil companies. One of his first postconstitution acts concerned the revocation of some of the Díaz-era concessions granted to El Aguila. The British company had known that these concessions were going to be troublesome. Given the prevailing nationalism among the revolutionary leaders, Lord Cowdray had thought of relinquishing these extensive concessions covering state and national land but only in exchange for $2 million in tax rebates. Governor Aguilar did not give him the opportunity. In December 1917, he decreed the cancellation of the 1906 Pearson concessions of Veracruz state lands.[174] The federal land concessions were not yet affected. (Actually, the federal government attempted to cancel Díaz-era federal concessions shortly after the sale of El Aguila to Shell. Mexican authorities, however, did not succeed because they had predicated their revocation on the incorrect supposition that Shell was part-owned by a foreign government.)[175] Aguilar was also among the first to propose an organic petroleum law, which he submitted to the Veracruz state legislature in February 1919.[176] At the federal level, by way of contrast, the bureaucrats were planning tax packages.

Carranza's government thought in terms of taxing first and settling the constitutional polemics later. In 1917, the federal government contemplated assessing a 5 percent federal royalty on each hectare of oil land, as if the state had originally offered these lands as concessions to the oilmen and landowners. Such a package ignored the fact that the oilmen had acquired these oil lands not as concessions but under private contract. Nonetheless, the bureaucrats dreamed of tax revenues. Joaquín Santaella of the petroleum commission calculated that had the tax been in force during the entire year of 1917, the federal treasury would have been richer by three million pesos. For good measure, Santaella also calculated the possible proceeds of a contemplated federal tax on the rents paid by lessees to landowners, which would have amounted to 3.2 million pesos in 1917. Why the tax increase? The state considered that it had a constitutional right to impose these fiscal contributions on an industry exploiting resources over which the nation now had direct dominion. Also, the economic emergency demanded the state use all its resources to save the nation.[177] Prompted by his oil bureaucrats, Carranza would not be long in acting to extract more from the booming oil industry.

The first important, postconstitution oil decree came on 19 February 1918. Exactly as the bureaucrats had planned, Carranza assessed an annual rental fee and a 5 percent royalty on all petroleum lands developed by the surface owners or their lessees. It also required, once again, the registration of oil properties. If not registered, or "manifested," as the saying went, within three months, third parties could "denounce," or lay claim to, the oil lands. The response was immediate. Oil companies accused Carranza of confiscating their properties through illegal taxation and enlisted the protests of their governments. The United States responded at once, saying that it "could not acquiesce in any procedure . . . resulting in confiscation of private rights and arbitrary deprivation of vested rights."[178] The big American companies of Huasteca and the recently arrived Jersey Standard, owner of Transcontinental, resisted the Mexican government. They and others refused to register their oil lands. "The desire of the Mexican Government to enforce article 27 of the constitution, practically confiscating the subsoil rights," said E. J. Sadler, "has been demonstrated during the last six months by the promulgation of a decree on February 19th and the subsequent efforts to nationalize the industry, including a radical increase of the export tax on crude and its products."[179]

Lord Cowdray and El Aguila likewise found much to fault in the new tax proposal. El Aguila had five hundred thousand hectares in oil leases and would have had to pay 2.5 million pesos per year for them. Most were not in production at all, although the company still paid rents to the landowners. El Aguila management decided to refuse to pay the new taxes and attempted to convince others to resist as well. Nearly all companies complied. The government calculated that although they were collecting 11.1 million pesos in production taxes, some twenty-four companies were not paying the 2.6 million pesos in royalties.[180] The dilemma was pretty clear. In order to collect 2.6 million pesos, Carranza could ill afford to shut down the companies that refused to pay. He stood to lose a far greater amount in production taxes. Even among the bureaucrats and Mexican politicians, there was a feeling that the land tax, or royalty, was not equitable. Mexican citizens bore the brunt of such decrees, and the tax was hardly progressive. It fell equally upon poor property-holders whose land did not yield a prolific well as on the lucky landowner whose property contained flush production. One government functionary wrote that the decree even ran the danger of "confiscating" the property of the poor landowner, just as the companies were claiming.[181]

Nonetheless, the government still attempted to exert its new powers in order to enforce this and other decrees. It began to give out unregistered claims to Mexican citizens (most of whom were politicos, so the companies claimed). Several new claimants took up land along the Pánuco and Tuxpan riverbanks, defined as federal property by the new constitution. These claims lay astride oil pools already proved by El Aguila and other companies.[182] The Texas Company experienced some typical difficulties. The government refused to issue drilling permits to the company until it had complied with the decree of 1918. When The Texas Company drilled three wells anyway, the government threatened to take them over. Moreover, the company soon discovered that rival claimants acquired government leases on lands in Zacamixtle, where The Texas Company already had production, and on the Isla de Potrero, where it was about to drill.[183] There the matter stood at the end of 1918: a stalemate between the Mexican government and the companies.

The standoff continued throughout the following year too, as both prices and exports rose and the oilmen began to notice the omens of impending salt-water encroachment in the wells. Government bureaucrats developed three different vises for squeezing the companies: well permits, third-party denouncements, and government troops. Out in the field offices, petroleum inspectors routinely denied drilling permits to those companies failing to accept Article 27, to pay their rental taxes, or to "manifest" their titles.[184] In support of the oil companies, the Department of State suggested that shipments of U.S. arms and ammunition be halted until the Carranza government relented in its pressure on the oil companies. The strategy did not deter the Mexicans in the least. The government immediately reminded oilmen that all decrees issued after 7 January 1915 were still in force and that unauthorized drilling would result in government confiscation. Sure enough, the denial of drilling permits continued.[185]

Meanwhile, third parties continued to "denounce," or lay claim to, properties that the oil companies had been exploiting. A Mexican group acquired drilling rights from the government on several pre-

1917 leases of the Scottish Mexican Oil Company.[186] When the oil companies induced the State Department to complain, the Mexican government responded testily. "The American companies have ill advisedly failed to comply with the laws which the Mexican government issued on the exploitation of petroleum," responded the Mexican Foreign Affairs Secretariat. ". . . [C]onsequently, if the situation of the petroleum companies is complicated by the denouncements made by third persons, the companies are doubtless[ly] the only ones blamable."[187]

For a time, the Carranza government even attempted to play its German card against the vested interests of the Americans, Dutch, and British. The Mexicans sought—or at least, threatened—to involve German capital in the oil industry. The Allied powers could be positively paranoid about the Germans. As early as 1916, the British managers of El Aguila had heard rumors that the Germans had been enlisting the aid of Mexican labor unions to blow up British oil installations. El Aguila placed extra watchmen on duty and asked the Foreign Office for some German- and Spanish-speaking detectives. In 1917, they set up a four-inch gun at Tuxpan for use against German submarines.[188] None appeared. The Dutch company of La Corona, in the meantime, had heard wild rumors of German sabotage as well, even that the Germans had burned twelve million barrels of El Aguila's oil at Minatitlán, which of course was apocryphal. Under the circumstances, the Dutch government had little choice but to dismiss its German-born vice-consul at Tampico, Richard Everbusch. Other ludicrous rumors hinted that the Germans were paying bandits to destroy Waters-Pierce tank cars and that twenty-five thousand Mexican troops paid by the Germans would end oil exports at Tampico.[189] As improbable as these scenarios seemed, it was a Mexican pretext that brought the United States into the European struggle. President Wilson declared war on Germany after having intercepted a note from Foreign Minister Zimmerman offering German support if President Carranza declared war on the United States. Mexico's reward was to retrieve the territory it had lost to the Americans in 1848. Obviously, Germany did not entirely understand the Mexican situation either.

The German card was so patently feeble that the Mexicans did not get around to even using it until months after the European armistice. In 1919, German citizens were awarded some denunciations of so-called federal lands. Japanese interests too had been reported in Tampico looking for oil possibilities.[190] Germany clearly was not the kind of alternate foreign power that Mexican nationalists could use against the United States, for example, not like Soviet Russia would be for the Cuban Revolution of 1959. Díaz had had to play off the British against the Americans, a game having many limitations, and Carranza too was left with a deck pretty much loaded in the same way.

Still, Carranza did have an army, and the Mexican government was not unwilling to intimidate the companies through the surgical use of force. This option seldom produced anything but antipathy. The State Department once again took exception to government threats to deploy army units to stop unauthorized drilling and construction. American diplomats feared for American lives.[191] Carranza did occasionally order his war department to use force in ending "illegal" drilling. When the Atlantic Company announced that it would not shut down its operations in the Pánuco region because compliance to government orders would imply that company's recognition of Article 27, Gen. Ricardo González dispatched troops to the Atlantic's oil field.[192] The government obviously could not win a total victory. It needed production earnings and declined to go after the big companies like El Aguila, Huasteca, and Transcontinental that were leading the industry's resistance. Carranza settled for a degree of fiscal success, giving up the principles for the moment.

Besides confronting rebellion and economic problems, the various actors of the Mexican state hardly recited from the same philosophical script. Carranza and his bureaucrats placed taxation ahead of state ownership. Governor Aguilar counseled the reverse order. The Supreme Court indicated that it might not uphold the retroactive interpretation that the above parties were applying to Article 27. When the government revoked some of its leases, the East Coast Oil Company sought an *amparo* (legal injunction). Cándido Aguilar took especial interest in the court case. He corresponded with Justice A. M. González of the Supreme Court and had a subordinate meet personally with him. "Thank you for the attention that you have lent to the affair," the Constitutional army general, Veracruz governor, one-time foreign minister, and now son-in-law of the president wrote to Justice González, "and I hope that the Supreme Court passes sentence in justice, which without any doubt whatsoever is part of the general interests of Veracruz state."[193] Nonetheless, the Supreme Court suspended the order, ruling against the government and Aguilar's position. Thereafter, government ministers attempted to delay the Supreme Court's consideration of the other *amparo* cases that the companies had brought against it.[194] The hard-line nationalists evidently could not entirely erode the position of the companies until they had concentrated the full weight of the Mexican state behind them.

The government had always intended to codify its interpretation of Article 27 into concrete legislation. The Petroleum Department, in fact, had produced a draft petroleum law as early as July 1917. It was sixty-six typewritten pages in length. But President Carranza apparently had objected to the radical interpretations that bureaucrats such as Alberto Pani and Vázquez Schiaffino had given the proposed legislation. Subsequently, a special commission adopted some of Carranza's objections.[195] Therefore, the draft legislation that emerged from this process by 1918 did not embody the strictly retroactive aspects of previous government decrees. But to be on the safe side, C. O. Swain of Standard Oil New Jersey made some recommendations on several articles of the new bill.[196] Oil representatives met with Pani. Some oilmen thought the government wanted to trap them in a labyrinth of regulations in order to confiscate their assets. "Mexican government officials were fully advised verbally and in writing of the exact position of the American Oil Companies and that they did not approve of law as presented to Congress," reported the oilmen.[197] Nonetheless, an exasperated Pani ultimately repudiated the intransigence of the oil representatives and submitted his draft anyway.

When the Congress considered the legislation late in 1919, however, it could not reach a consensus. Some conservative members, encouraged if not supported financially by the oil companies, proposed countermeasures. Word also circulated among the government's supporters that Carranza himself did not wish the legislation to pass at this time. Others waited for Aguilar, who had gone off to represent Mexico in the Paris Peace Conference. The Senate passed the bill, minus two important articles, and the Chamber of Deputies failed even to consider the measure.[198] By this time, December 1919, the political life of the country was preoccupied with the coming presidential election. Carranza was known to oppose a military candidate for the office, which appeared to foreclose the chances of the popular Gen. Alvaro Obregón. The result of all this: no petroleum legislation passed. In fact, it would have to wait until 1926.

In the meantime, the executive powers were attempting to fashion some face-saving compromise that might result in higher revenues. The new minister of industry, Gen. Plutarco Elías Calles, brought about an effort to reach an interim accord. He announced that the government would issue "provisional" drilling permits, if only the companies would agree to be bound by future Mexican oil legislation.[199] Naturally, the companies were no more willing to comply with future legislation, whose provisions they feared, than to pay royalties on land they already held under private contract. Of the companies, Transcontinental in particular refrained from applying for these drilling permits. The Department of State responded to the companies' complaints. Mexico's requirements as to drilling permits, it said, constituted "an admission of the correctness of the contention of the Mexican Government in the matter of the ownership of oil deposits."[200] Herein lay the nub of the problem. The oil companies were concerned principally about the validity of their preconstitutional private property rights and only secondarily about fiscal exactions. But the *carrancistas* were preoccupied with the short-term problems of bringing the Revolution to an end and reestablishing political and economic stability. These were fiscal concerns. They could not await a definitive settlement of the constitutional issue.

Oilmen did not wish to accept higher taxes in lieu of property revisions. They complained, often bitterly, about how higher production and bar taxes were raising the cost of Mexican oil on world markets. Some applied the word "confiscatory" equally to the government's tax increases and to its retroactive interpretation of Article 27.[201] Therefore, both the petroleum office and the companies drew up numerous cost estimates per barrel of exportable petroleum. Mexican bureaucrats wanted to show that the companies could sustain higher taxes and still make substantial profits. The companies wished to show how tax increases could not be supported. The differences between the two estimates were naturally quite startling. Note the 1916 estimates of El Aguila compared to the 1919 government estimates (see table 8). But as long as prices rose (they did not reach their zenith until mid-1920), the oil companies were able to sustain the higher taxes. So, they paid up. Federal revenue collections from the oil industry had risen nearly one-hundred-fold throughout the Revolution. The per-barrel tax receipts had quadrupled (see table 9).

Since the companies rejected paying more fees to get the drilling permits, the government again ordered the troops into the oil camps. In November of 1919, petroleum inspectors directed Mexican soldiers to shut down drilling operations on eight wells of Transcontinental, Island Oil, Sinclair, Amatlán, Union Oil, and The Texas Company. Additional diplomatic protests burned the telegraph cables between Washington and Mexico City. In the meantime, J. A. Brown and

Table 8. *Estimated Cost of a Barrel of Oil, 1916, 1919*

El Aguila Estimate, 1916 (centavos per barrel)		Government Estimate, 1919 (centavos per barrel)	
Office expenses	5	Administration	12
Pumping and storage	10	Rent and royalties	4
Drilling and exploration	17	Depreciation	15
Camp expenses	1	Transport	6
Royalties	5.2	Terminal costs	5
Rentals	1.5		
Production tax	9		
Bar duties	1.3		
Total	50	*Total*	42

SOURCES: "Estimated Cost of a Barrel of Oil," March 1916, Pearson, C45; Secretaría de Industria, Comercio y Trabajo, *Documentos relacionados con la legislacion petrolera mexicana* (Mexico City, 1919), 141.

Table 9. *Mexican Federal Production Tax Revenues Collected from the Oil Industry, 1913–1920*

Year	Output (barrels)	Production Tax (total in pesos)	Tax (cents per barrel)
1913	25,696,000	767,043	
1914	26,235,000	1,232,931	2.9
1915	32,911,000	1,942,687	3.8
1916	40,546,000	3,088,368	6.8
1917	55,293,000	7,074,968	6.8
1918	63,825,000	11,480,964	9.4
1919	87,073,000	16,690,622	9.9
1920	157,069,000	45,479,168	16.3

SOURCES: Santaella to Hacienda, 15 Jan 1926, Thomas A. Lamont Collection, Baker Library, Harvard University, Boston, 197-15; George Philip, *Oil and Politics in Latin America: Nationalist Movements and State Oil Companies* (Cambridge, Eng., 1982), 17.

Arthur Corwin of Jersey Standard traveled to Mexico City in order to interview Luis Cabrera about the stoppages. The finance minister informed them of the cabinet's resolve to withhold drilling permits until the companies complied with its decrees.[202] The stalemate seemed interminable.

In the meanwhile, El Aguila was one of the only companies that had obtained government permits to drill new wells. Had it made its own compromise with the government independent of the other private companies? Did it make a deal in order to get new production to make up for the expected salt-water encroachment of its older wells? Was Carranza playing one foreign national against another? It was to avoid such an eventuality that the companies as early as 1916 had formed a united front and urged strong diplomatic action. But El Aguila had always been a maverick.

In Defense of Vested Rights

In the beginning, Carranza's political faction appeared to have found favor with the oilmen—at least few harbored any outright hostilities. His victory at least offered hope. The American community in Tampico turned out to welcome the first chief in 1914, on his first (and only) trip to the newly liberated port city. The American consul hosted a dinner and reception in Carranza's honor. Carranza thanked the Americans for their neutrality during the revolution against Huerta. Fair and equal treatment would be accorded those who lived under the laws of Mexico, he assured guests at the reception. Obviously Carranza harbored no grudges toward the American community for the invasion of Veracruz, and the Americans did not hold Carranza responsible for having been forced by enraged mobs to abandon Tampico. Some of the Americans only noted that although charming enough, Carranza had a rather "unmagnetic personality" and tended to numb his listeners when he spoke.[203] All in all, it was a not inauspicious beginning.

As all honeymoons, this one between Carranza and the Americans at Tampico was over too soon. The depredations in the countryside increased to a point that banditry and pillage became the universal order of the day. Moreover, a nationalist onslaught appeared on the verge of taxing the oilmen and removing their property rights. Such pressures could hardly be expected to go unchallenged. In order to defend themselves, the foreign oilmen strove to overcome their national and competitive instincts. They organized protective associations. They lobbied the governments. They mounted a publicity campaign to state their case. They coordinated their resistance. In the final analysis, the foreign oilmen were only partially successful in defending their privileges and rights in Mexico.

Certainly, oilmen were motivated to unite so that the government could not continue the Díaz tactic of playing off one nationality against the other and one company against another. Luis Cabrera, as minister of finance, had attempted to do just that in December of 1915. When General Manager Body protested the government policy of inspecting El Aguila's books and operations, Cabrera regretted Body's objections. Walker and Galbraith of Huasteca had just seen him in order to give their enthusiastic support to the Constitutionalist policies, he said, and they even disparaged El Aguila while they were at it. On the other hand, the personnel of Standard Oil, he continued, always refrained from criticizing other companies and were entirely neutral in their negotiations with the government.[204] Cabrera and other Mexican officials would have preferred to deal with each company separately, whittling down their resistance to new taxes and laws.

Apparently, the impetus for a collective organization of oilmen came from below, so to speak. In May of 1916 it had become clear that the Constitutionalist army in the Huasteca was the primary cause of the insecurity of foreign personnel. A mass meeting of all American oilmen took place in Tampico. The assembly directed William F. Buckley, a local lease lawyer and oil speculator, to draft a letter to President Wilson, expressing the dissatisfaction of the oilmen with conditions in Mexico. Several months later, the company executives got together in New York and drew up a charter for an oilmen's association. No one from El Aguila was present, but Percy Furber, who had become a stockholder when El Aguila absorbed his Oil Fields of Mexico company, represented the Britons.[205] The large British firm soon joined. The American companies, especially Huasteca and Standard Oil New Jersey, tended to dominate the new Association of Foreign Oil Producers in Mexico. Harold Walker of Huasteca's New York office was elected president. Although the oil producers' association concerned itself principally with petroleum issues, several oilmen participated actively in a second lobbying group, the National Association for the Protection of American Rights in Mexico, also headquartered in New York. The National Association represented broader business interests—taking in banking, mining, and the railway bondholders. The board in fact was made up primarily of oilmen: Amos Beaty of The Texas Company, E. L. Doheny of Pan-American, Chester O. Swain of Jersey Standard, and Thomas W. Lamont of the J. P. Morgan banking firm.

First and foremost, the oil producers' association served to coordinate the resistance of all foreign companies toward the Mexicans.

Although willing, in general, to give in to modest tax increases, the association attempted to prevent concessions eroding any of the companies' prior contractual prerogatives. Consequently, they were hostile to the retroactivity of Article 27. They relied on another article of the constitution: Article 14 guaranteed all existing Mexican contracts against retroactive application by any of the other articles. The companies, therefore, considered that any contracts they had acquired before 1 May 1917 were absolutely valid. When Jersey Standard's Swain rejected the attempted compromise of "provisional" drilling permits in 1919, all companies did the same.[206]

The oilmen were convinced that there would be no change in Mexican policies, nor in the insecurity in the oil zone either, unless forced by Washington. Consequently, the oil companies began a campaign to pressure the American and British governments to intervene on their behalf. But President Wilson had tired of their incessant weeping and gnashing of teeth. He suspected that the oilmen supported the Republicans anyway. All the companies had was the diplomatic corps. Patrician, elitist, out-of-favor with the White House, American diplomats took over the technical (read petroleum) aspects of Mexican foreign policy. With much forbearance, Secretary of State Robert Lansing and his Latin American section received endless legal briefs from oilmen. Members of the oilmen's association dropped into Foggy Bottom—sometimes unannounced—to pester the diplomats. British diplomats too received their share of "documents relating to the attempt of the government of Mexico to confiscate foreign-owned properties," all generated by the verbose attorneys of the association.[207] The pressure of the oilmen was relentless. When Mexican troops halted well drilling, oil executives, their attorneys, and friendly senators like Morris Sheppard of Texas inundated the Department of State with letters inquiring what it intended to do about it.[208] Increasingly, the association's propaganda tended to become anti-Wilson and anti-Democratic.

Nonetheless, the oilmen felt perfectly justified in placing pressure on the State Department. Once the United States entered the European war, the oil producers' association increasingly took up the excuse that Mexican restrictions threatened to cut off this vital source of supply.[209] Once the war ended in November 1918, the continuing rise of oil prices lent credence to the oilmen's new position that Mexican oil was necessary for American industries and the merchant marine. "[I]n this critical time we must look to our Government not only to protect the oil companies themselves and the thousands of their stockholders," Jersey's C. O. Swain wrote to the State Department, "but also to take effective measures to secure to all the people and industries of the United States the supplies of fuel oil, gasoline and lubricants necessary to meet the demand."[210] Indeed, the supply of fuel oil was critical in 1919. The U.S. Geological Survey encouraged the oil companies to begin exploring in the Middle East and South America. The National Association, in the meantime, was writing to remind U.S. government officials of the 427 Americans who had been killed in Mexico during the decade of 1910.[211]

So what did the State Department do for the oil interests? It protested to the Mexican government. American diplomats responded to every new Mexican measure and nearly every paymaster robbery and death in the oil zone. There were fifty-eight different diplomatic protests between 1914 and 1919. But many oilmen suspected that the protests had become mere formalities, that the American diplomats were delivering them as if they were routine communications between friendly governments. "[Henry P.] Fletcher is not altogether the right man," an El Aguila executive said of the new U.S. ambassador. "He is doing what [former Ambassador John R.] Silliman did; that is to diminish and explain away inconvenient notes or communications he is ordered to make."[212] In reality, the Department of State did not have much leverage to back up those protests. The government was reluctant to halt arms shipments to Carranza, fearing that a victory of his enemies could be much worse for U.S. interests. Finally, there was no longer any will in the Wilson administration to contemplate another armed intervention—especially to save the investments of some of the wealthiest men in America.[213] Had not the first two interventions turned out badly enough?

So what did the oil companies do? They went public. The oilmen took their case to the newspapers and to Congress. They wanted to show that the Wilson administration was weak in its responses to revolution in Mexico. More than any other oilman, Doheny made himself a relentless publicist. He had always been a Democrat and had donated to Wilson's presidential campaigns. But he became increasingly critical of administration inaction. He wrote a pamphlet in which he posed the following question: Will Carranza succeed in depriving Americans of their oil supplies, "or will the people of the United States lend their encouragement and approval to the Administration in insisting upon and compelling the Carranza Government to fulfill its international obligations?"[214] At one point, Doheny donated one hundred thousand dollars to fund an *ad hoc* think tank. The fund supported twenty university professors from Princeton to Berkeley. "Each investigator is also expected to make suggestions of policy for improvement in the Mexican situation," Doheny instructed them. "In this he is to consider the problem from the point of view of 'Mexico for the Mexicans.' "[215] Very little came of this effort. Anyway, Doheny wanted immediate results, and the academicians had a habit of dithering and pondering. Wanting decisive action, Doheny made himself available to newspapermen. In fact, he became something of a media celebrity, never ceasing to produce a good quote.[216]

His access to newspapers made Doheny's trip to the Paris peace conference in 1919 highly visible. If he wanted to gain the attention of the American, British, and Mexican governments, he succeeded. Even Carranza received press accounts of his trip. "The new constitution of Mexico is intended to confiscate or attack many vested rights of foreigners," he told the Los Angeles *Herald*. [217] Of course, the Paris peace conferees, among them Doheny's nemesis, Woodrow Wilson, found more pressing things to discuss than the problems of foreign businessmen in Mexico. British diplomats refused to help Doheny because they suspected Doheny of helping the Irish Republican movement.[218] Doheny left Paris empty-handed.

More than any other company official, Doheny was willing to carry his message to Congress. The oil producers' association and its members deluged senators and congressmen with its propaganda and viewpoints.[219] But few oil executives were willing to subject themselves to congressional hearings. Doheny welcomed the opportunity. His testimony at three congressional hearings caused sensations, as he warned of Mexico's seizure of U.S. property and sparred with Democratic senators who dared question his views. His biggest audience came during the famous Mexico hearings of the Fall committee in 1919. Albert B. Fall, the Republican senator from the new state of New Mexico, and Doheny were old friends, having prospected together in the 1880s.[220]

But many active oilmen, fearing reprisals from the Mexican government, shied away from appearing before the Fall committee. Doheny was the star witness, testifying for several days. From the oil industry, only three other company representatives appeared (Beaty from The Texas Company, Williams from Pánuco, and Buckley from Island Oil), and no current oil workers.[221] Most men testifying before the committee were former lease-takers and colonists, despite the fact that the oil producers' association had attempted to select sixty oilmen and forty colonists from Tampico to come to the hearings. But they balked. "The oil companies have for so many years impressed these men with the danger of criticizing the Carranza authorities in public or private," Doheny wrote later, "that this has been accepted by the employees as the settled policy of the oil companies." Apparently, the managers in Mexico in particular sabotaged Doheny's efforts to organize a truly massive protest during the hearings. Doheny was incensed at the lack of nerve of his fellow oilmen. He sent them a stinging rebuke. "I should like to call the attention of the Association to the fact that in the investigation of Mexican affairs lasting for a period of several months which was brought about largely through the influence of the oil companies, in which the oil companies have taken such a prominent part, and in which they have such a vital interest," he wrote scathingly to Swain of Jersey Standard, "no man connected with the oil business who lives in Mexico, or who lives in the states and goes to Mexico occasionally, has testified and taken any risk except myself."[222] Obviously, there were limits to how much the oil producers' association could narrow the differences between and among the oilmen.

A Weak and Vacillating Policy

What did oilmen want from the U.S. government, anyway? The largest question then and now pertains to whether the oilmen really wanted a massive military intervention; whether they wanted American marines garrisoning the oil camps and patrolling the pipelines. There were perhaps as many answers to that question as there were oilmen in Mexico. What did Americans in Tampico want? Here are some of their answers:

support from the home government (Frederick R. Kellogg, Pan American attorney);

U.S. support short of armed intervention (Rev. Dr. Bruce Baker Corbin of Tampico);

"a just application of international law" (Ira Jewell Williams of Pánuco);

intervention from Allied creditor nations and aid to Carranza government to put down rebels (Lord Cowdray);

aid to Carranza, as "best hope in Mexico for straightening the affairs without intervention" (Commanding Officer, USS *Annapolis*, Tampico);

withdrawal of U.S. recognition of the Mexican government, so that its reestablishment would be the reward for better treatment of U.S. companies (Harold Walker, Huasteca);

a threat of force that would cause the Mexicans themselves to clean house (an anonymous oilman);

withdrawal of diplomatic representatives and dispatch of warships to Mexico (C. O. Swain, Standard Oil Company of New Jersey);

an invasion of Mexico if necessary to keep oil flowing (Commander James O. Richardson).[223]

For one thing, there was no consensus among those who criticized U.S. inactivity. For another, few of these men were willing to go completely public with their most draconian suggestions. Of those offering their opinions in various forums, Lord Cowdray was one of the few who did not hector officials, publicly or privately, with his ideas. He expressed them once in a very private meeting with the American ambassador in London. Cowdray said he was convinced that unilateral U.S. intervention in Mexico would result in a protracted guerrilla war and additional unrest.[224] Other top executives were equally chary about suggesting armed intervention. For example, not once did the voluble Doheny publicly recommend the dispatch of U.S. Marines. Both the oil producers' association and the National Association for the Protection of American Rights in Mexico denied that they were agitating for armed intervention.[225]

But the lower one went in the hierarchy of the companies, the more one found greater support for intervention. Those in the field were like colonialists. They despised the Mexicans. They thought them weak and bumbling, incapable of resisting American fighting men, and in great need of being bossed around by the Anglo race. In the field, the social attitudes of the Americans were not much different at all from those of Spaniards who had come earlier to dominate the mestizos and *indios*. William Green seemed to speak for these American supervisors, drillers, and skilled workers in the oil industry:

Our Government does not encourage us in any way to stand up for our rights, and if we do stand up for our rights, we run a good chance of being deported. This condition could be changed in twenty four hours. . . . There are

6,000 fairly well armed Mexicans awaiting the opportunity to co-operate, and
nine tenths of the Mexican population are praying for intervention—any other
statement, from whatsoever source to the contrary, notwithstanding. Every
Mexican with a dollar to protect desires intervention, as he knows that sooner
or later it will be stolen from him unless it is protected by our Armies. That is
the truth.[226]

Another critic of the big oil companies did not charge them with being too rigid but with compromising too much. William F. Buckley,
the American attorney and owner of the Island Oil Company, held that
small compromises hurt the American oil workers. It was to protect
these workers, many of whom had "invested all their savings, and were
then robbed and driven out" of Mexico, that Buckley formed yet a
third group, the American Association of Mexico. The Americans in
Mexico, he said, had been abandoned not only by the government but
by the companies too.[227] Buckley excoriated the corporation lawyers
like Chester Swain who were giving in to the Mexicans. He charged the
heads of the oil companies in the United States and their managers in
Tampico with having a "weak and vacillating policy very similar to that
followed by the American Government in handling the general Mexican situation."[228]

Others within the oil industry differed from the difficult-to-define
mainstream. On the left bank, so to speak, were a number of small
firms and independent oilmen who resented the economic power of
the big companies. A few were Mexican. They might look to Carranza
for special privileges, pleading, like J. B. Yzaguirre, that Mexican engineers like him ought to develop national resources "with respect for the
laws."[229] Small independent American companies would do the same.
Managers of the Tal Vez Company declared that Carranza's taxation of
the big companies was not at all excessive. "[T]he oil companies' objections to the new oil taxes has [sic] little foundation," they wrote to
Senator Sheppard of Texas.[230] Joseph F. Guffy of the AGWI Company
showed extraordinary independence from the other foreign oil producers. In interviews with *El Universal* and *Excélsior,* Guffy praised the
Mexican Revolution and said that Doheny was responsible for 90 percent of the troubles between Carranza and the oilmen.[231]

Then there was the rustic wildcatter from Houston, Texas, who
wanted to reduce foreign oil imports. "Every Independent producer
of crude in Txas and Ok. would like to see a prohibitive duty on
Mexican Crude into Txas," he wrote to the secretary of state. "Impor-
tation of Mexican oil into Txas has almost put the little fellows out

of business."[232] In truth, the competitive nature of the oil business contributed a centrifugal force, reducing the cohesion for which the oil producers' association was created. Oil companies that otherwise competed against each other around the world could not find perfect unity in Mexico. "In fact, they enter into an agreement to find shortly after the agreement has been entered into," reported one observer in Tampico, "that one of them has secretly gone to the Mexican officials and violated the agreement in order to gain a certain psychological advantage for his company."[233] Despite the work of the oil producers' association, there remained a surprising diversity of opinion and a divisive spirit among the foreign companies.

The British government had always been less forceful in its protestations. When Carranza first raised taxes, the Foreign Office refused to relay Lord Cowdray's objections because El Aguila had been registered in Mexico, and, besides, it was already paying taxes it did not have to according to its existing contracts. "In the circumstances, I do not see how we can take up the case very strongly," a British diplomat replied.[234]

The Foreign Office's indifference was evident in its attitude toward recognizing the Carranza government. On this issue, the oil companies and governments seemed hopelessly at cross-purposes. His Majesty's Government did not recognize Carranza, a policy increasingly favored by many American oilmen. In the meanwhile, the American government recognized the Constitutionalists in a way that pleased Lord Cowdray. The evolution of Cowdray's attitude toward Carranza merits some consideration. At first, his general manager in Mexico, J. B. Body, suggested the British government ought not to recognize the Constitutionalists until Carranza promised to respect the rights of foreigners and promised to repeal those illegal taxes. Lord Cowdray overruled him. He counseled the Americans and Britons alike to recognize Carranza in order to gain more protection of foreign businessmen there and to prevent retaliation against them. Cowdray also held Mexican bonds and wanted diplomatic pressure to fix a repayment schedule for the Mexican debt.[235] The British government, however, acted as Body would have wished, holding out for guarantees before it recognized Carranza. So the Foreign Office was startled when in 1915 the Wilson administration extended recognition to Carranza's provisional government. By that time, Great Britain had more important problems in the European war and simply washed its hands of Mexico. British diplomats relied on the Americans to watch over their interests. The British did not think Carranza would last in power.[236]

Cowdray bristled privately at the lack of support from the Foreign Office. He had asked for a strong British protest against the adoption of the Mexican constitution. British diplomats put him off. They said they would protest when the government passed some specific legislation rather than objecting to general constitutional principles. All of Cowdray's protests had to be conveyed by the State Department in Washington.[237] Cowdray never tired of seeking British recognition for Carranza. To that end, he organized a meeting of British businessmen with interests in Mexico. "In the event of disastrous British losses occurring in the Oil Fields," he pleaded, "shall we not have placed the United States Government in a position to be able to disclaim all responsibility to the British Government, owing to the latter having held aloof from Carranza and refused him recognition?"[238] Lord Cowdray opposed his government's policy in Mexico, and the American oilmen opposed their government's opposite policy.

Once the European war was over, the Foreign Office's objections to regularizing the relations between Mexico and Great Britain diminished. There was still some sentiment within the British diplomatic community that recognition at long last would display a certain weakness on the British part and would confirm Carranza in his onslaught of foreign rights in Mexico.[239] By now, the argument was becoming very shallow, inasmuch as those Britons whose rights were under attack very much desired British recognition of Carranza. Some overtures were attempted.[240]

No diplomatic initiatives were ever consummated. Some American oilmen began to think that British diplomatic obstinacy actually extracted more concessions from Carranza. Early in 1920, the oil producers' association suspected that the Mexican government was giving preferential treatment to El Aguila in order to obtain British diplomatic representation. Harold Walker suggested that the United States withdraw recognition of the Mexican government to protect American oilmen equally.[241] All of this controversy was leading, seemingly illogically, to a compromise of sorts.

The reconciliation came early in 1920 because Carranza needed it as much as the oilmen did. The president of Mexico was facing a period of difficult political transition. Suspicious of the power of the military, Carranza ignored the presidential aspirations of his most successful general, Alvaro Obregón, and was about to impose the election of the relatively unknown ambassador to the United States, Ignacio Bonillas. He certainly did not need to be distracted by oil problems at the moment. Moreover, news of the salt-water invasion (in December 1918, El Aguila's Potrero del Llano No. 4 had been shut in) caused him alarm. If the oil companies did not drill more wells soon, production would decline along with tax revenues. The companies themselves were faced with declining production. El Aguila had its greatest production in the Faja de Oro, exactly where the salt-water problem was the most severe. Beginning in mid-1919, El Aguila began to receive the drilling permits that the government had been denying to the other companies. Joseph Guffy of AGWI also obtained drilling permits, largely because having arrived after May 1, 1917, he was willing to observe Article 27 of the constitution. But El Aguila had followed the oil producers' association's policy and refused to comply with the retroactive aspect of the Carranza oil decrees.[242] Why did El Aguila finally get the drilling permits? Was it because the Mexican government wanted to reward El Aguila for favoring diplomatic recognition? Did Carranza hope, thereby, to change the policy of the British Foreign Office? Did Carranza wish to split the united front of the oil companies? For whatever reason, the favorable treatment of the British company, now an affiliate of the Royal Dutch–Shell Company, raised suspicions among American diplomats, and especially among American oilmen.

Once El Aguila received drilling permits, the united front of the oilmen could no longer hold out. Some members were becoming restive under Carranza's restrictions on their drilling. Mexican Gulf, The Texas Company, and Island Oil (Buckley) were about to withdraw from the association and make their own deals with the Mexican government. To hold the line, the association's executive secretary, Frederick Kellogg, had proposed a pooling arrangement. Those companies not losing production because of their adherence to association policy would receive oil from those companies not injured by their compliance with association policies.[243] Few companies, El Aguila included, wanted to be on the giving end.

For that very reason, El Aguila used its favored position to benefit its sister companies. A representative of El Aguila, Rodolfo Montes, met with President Carranza shortly after New Year's day in 1920. Worried about the salt-water problem (perhaps the election even more), Carranza announced that he was willing to compromise with the companies. He would grant them their "provisional" drilling permits, if they would accept them as temporary—without regard to future oil legislation. The deal was to be consummated between the companies and the Mexican chief executive. "I consider diplomatic pressure by foreign governments inopportune," said Montes.[244] (Later, some rancorous American companies would spread the rumor that El Aguila had negotiated this compromise in order to get out of the pooling agreement. Managers of El Aguila saw their leadership role as "unselfish.")[245] Within ten days of the Carranza-Montes meeting, forty-six member companies of the oil producers' association cabled the Mexican president of their willingness to receive provisional permits, as long as their titles were not thereby prejudiced. Snatching victory from a draw, Carranza announced that the oil companies had given in and that they would submit to future oil legislation.[246] The orders went out from Carranza to his petroleum inspectors to issue the provisional permits.

The compromise that Carranza fashioned directly with the oil companies has subsequently come under censure. His critics accuse Carranza of giving in to the companies and for not holding out steadfastly for the principles outlined in Article 27. Writing long afterwards, petroleum inspector López Portillo y Weber condemned the issuance of provisional permits. Part of his resentment centered on the fact that he learned of the compromise from Theodore River, manager of The Texas Oil Company. "They were going to formally initiate the ravaging, enormous and stupid, of the Faja de Oro," he wrote.[247] Actually, Carranza did not compromise any principles. He did not bind subsequent governments to the provisions of his agreement. He may, in fact, have released the companies from some of the pressures, but Carranza had been motivated by short-term Mexican political considerations. Carranza had to attend to the transition of government and, financially, he could not afford the loss of petroleum revenues. Because he was determined to deny power to Obregón, his choices were otherwise quite limited, especially taking into account that oil revenues in 1920 broke previous records—by a wide margin (see table 9). In a moment of political crisis, Carranza could not antagonize any source of income.

Despite the renewed surge in production, the oil companies continued to operate with much uncertainty. Once drilling resumed, oil production, already high, rose by 40 percent in 1920. The full impact of the salt-water invasion, thereby, was put off until the next year. As for the uncertainty, Standard Oil's Transcontinental Company found itself in a particularly vulnerable position. It had arrived in Mexico after the promulgation of the constitution. Some of its best oil prospects were not pre-1917 titles, to which the compromise plainly applied, but contracts Transcontinental had made since 1917. Acquiring new leases directly from landowners after 1917 was risky, but Transcontinental had been willing to take the risk because its best wells in the southern fields were beginning to flow to salt water.[248]

Yet Carranza had one last hurrah in his assault on the oil companies, one that did not endanger his production revenues at all. He continued to give out concessions for the so-called federal lands that, according to Article 27, ran along riverbeds and shorelines. In March and April, his last months in office as it turned out, Carranza issued concessions along arroyos passing through the prolific Los Naranjos field. Other federal grants were also made. The oilmen were bitter, accusing Carranza of giving out these proven oil prospects to his political cronies as well as to cooperating oilmen like Guffy. The Dutch company La Corona protested that federal-lands concessions amounted to virtual confiscation of a substantial portion of its oil rights. The oilmen called it "iniquitous poaching."[249] Clearly, Carranza had not given up all his prerogatives under the Mexican constitution. Despite the short-term financial expedience of his compromise over drilling permits, succeeding Mexican governments would again take up the struggle to substitute property laws inherited from the colonial epoch for those from the more recent liberal capitalist age.

How did the Revolution, a manifestation of popular outrage and rebellion from below, advance the cause of economic nationalism? No doubt, there had always lingered an opinion in Mexico that free-market capitalism must be handled circumspectly. The Mexican Revolution, with its peasant armies, its demands for social reforms, its brigandage and barbarism, led the new political elites to blame the foreign interests for bringing about the conditions that provoked rebellion. They were convinced in this belief by the mass participation in the armies of Villa and Zapata and in their own Constitutionalist forces, often under the command of powerful military *jefes* who gained popularity by promising land and labor reforms. The revolutionary elites, therefore, sought to reestablish old social controls. They wanted to tame the demands of the peasants, the Indians, the less fortunate of society, without impinging very much on their own newfound privileges.

The new leaders looked to the state. They demanded that the state in revolutionary Mexico create increasing capacity to control the populace, through the time-honored dual strategies of repression and paternalism. Therefore, the state desperately needed resources during a time of revolutionary disruption of the economy, when those sources of revenues were being destroyed by the very popular wrath they hoped to contain. The foreign interests seemed the logical source of funds to re-establish the state's suzerainty over the popular classes. If, in the mean-time, one had to sacrifice the potential for economic growth, so be it. Social control took precedence over economic dynamism. Therefore, new political elites attempting to consolidate the social revolution tended to become economic nationalists. Economic nationalism was no alternative to—no diversion from—social reform. The economic nationalists, in truth, were the indispensable coconspirators of the so-cial reformers. They sought to reestablish control over the foreign in-terests, over capitalism, and over the economy so that assets could be diverted to the larger public good, that of managing social antago-nisms. By virtue of their wealth and the growth of their assets during the Revolution, the oil companies became the logical target of such po-litical antagonism.

A second, perhaps more startling conclusion of the above analysis concerns the severe political limitations of the otherwise powerful com-panies. Quite often, scholars find it difficult to address the limitations of the foreign interests. These Wall Street organizations were far-off yet omnipresent; they were specialized yet omniscient. They are depicted as giant octopi, tentacles reaching out, suction cups holding fast to some valuable asset. We have reviewed the record with respect to the foreign oil companies in Mexico. Their representatives suborned with bribes, entertained lavishly, wrote to senators, had meetings with dip-lomats, published their views in newspapers and books, testified before congressional hearings, contributed to political campaigns, organized protective associations, protested, complained, and lobbied. What did it get them? Higher taxes and the beginnings of state infringement of private property rights in Mexico. They had been abandoned by their home governments and left to cope as best they could. Despite Her-culean efforts, they remained divided and competitive amongst them-selves. The only things upon which they were able to rely during the great Mexican oil boom were the strength of external demand and the fecundity of the wells. As long as prices rose and nothing interrupted the flow of oil through the well heads, the companies retained enough economic strength to absorb the exactions of the Mexican revolution-ary state.

Only one political factor favored the companies in delaying the ero-sion of their power: the weaknesses of the Mexican governments. No president during the Revolution had benefited from social peace and a healthy economy. Incessant rebellions by would-be presidents ruined the economic base and drove the state deeper into debt. The petroleum industry escaped the worst of the economic decay because it was off to one side of the main fighting. The construction of its pipelines and terminals had been completed before the period of pillage, and it depended on outside markets. Moreover, Carranza's government and the bandits too, to a certain degree, would not have profited if the industry had been completely shut down. So they did not stop it. Yet, under the circumstances, the Mexicans acquitted themselves successfully in extracting greater amounts of the "surplus value" of "international monopoly capitalism."

There was a final tragic note. Carranza succumbed to a domestic rebellion in May of 1920. While escaping through a small town in the mountains of Puebla, high above the Huasteca, he was assassinated. His killers were identified as having ties with the rebel general Manuel Peláez, who was said to have been "in the pay" of the oil companies. These circumstances bring up an issue that this analysis so far has cast aside: being relatively unsuccessful in their other political activities, did the oil companies then engage in fomenting internal rebellion? Did they support counterrevolution? If so, perhaps the early rumors they spread about each other contained the germ of verisimilitude. If not, perhaps it provides additional proof of the limited power of wealthy companies—like leaves in the storm of the Revolution, as Mariano Azuela would say.

CHAPTER FOUR

Law, Morality, and Justice

On Sunday, 15 November 1914, following the Constitutionalist victory, a lone horseman rode into the El Aguila camp at Potrero del Llano. He identified himself as Maj. Luis A. Ruiz and demanded thirty thousand pesos in the name of Gen. Manuel Peláez. The
manager refused. Major Ruiz returned the next day with fifty armed
men and instructions from General Peláez to collect the thirty thousand pesos or take it by force. The manager, T. H. Vaughan, explained
that the money he had on hand was for the payroll of one thousand
men who would riot if they did not receive their wages. After some negotiations, Ruiz agreed to take fifteen thousand pesos, leaving the manager enough for the next payroll. The major made out a receipt. As they
left, the partisans of Manuel Peláez also took seven horses and saddles.
The rebels displayed a certain commitment to equity in their new
movement. The men of Peláez also stopped by the Huasteca oil camp at
Casiano, where they obtained ten thousand pesos and all the rifles the
American workmen had.

Word soon spread that a local landowner had risen in rebellion. He
called himself a *villista,* the principal elements of whom under Pancho
Villa then occupied Mexico City. The Constitutionalists remained in
possession of the ports: Tampico, Tuxpan, and Veracruz. In the following two weeks, these local *villistas* relieved the survey camps of more
horses and saddles, sometimes giving receipts and other times not.
It embarrassed El Aguila that Peláez led this rebellion, because the
British oil company maintained a small oil field on his hacienda, Tierra

253

Amarilla. Soon, the Peláez group involved El Aguila more deeply in local affairs. They commandeered the company's engine and seven railway cars, in order, they explained, to take their horses to Tierra Amarilla. Instead, they picked up additional men and horses, traveled by El Aguila's train down to the coast, seized one of its motor launches, and raided the small town of Tamiahua on the lagoon. The Constitutionalists took offense. Colonels Zumaya and Benignos confronted Vaughan and accused El Aguila of supporting the enemy *villistas*. Vaughan assured them such was not the case. "[W]hen armed men rode into the camps, and commandeered trains or launches, we were perfectly helpless," he told the Constitutionalist commanders. He requested their protection for the camp at Potrero del Llano, but the Constitutionalists said they had insufficient troops.

In December 1914, events took a more ominous turn. Another Peláez officer demanded an additional thirty thousand pesos. When refused, he returned to deliver a note from Peláez himself that El Aguila was to turn over one hundred thousand pesos within eight days. Meanwhile, the Constitutionalist forces appeared at El Aguila's terminal camps and rail stations, searching warehouses and cabins for arms and ammunition. They found nothing. They also stopped and searched the company's launches on the Tamiahua lagoon, opening up the mail sacks. The Constitutionalists helped themselves to corn and gasoline. At Tuxpan, the departure of three tankers from the offshore loading terminal was delayed by Constitutionalist port authorities. On 16 December, a town merchant, Alfonso Sánchez, attacked the Constitutionalists at Tuxpan, claiming to have rebelled with General Peláez because of government *atropellos* (insults or abuses). Sánchez died in the raid, and the local authorities assessed punitive fines on those of his relatives who happened to live in town. A British resident who worked for El Aguila was arrested after he complained that Constitutionalist troops had robbed his house.

Meanwhile, the British consul at Tuxpan advised the company's managers to "temporize" with General Peláez and to settle his demands "at the cheapest possible price." Finally, from his headquarters at the Hacienda Temapache, General Peláez delivered a proclamation to El Aguila. He claimed to be the representative of the First Division of the East of the nationalist army, whose chief was Pancho Villa and whose government was in Mexico City. From then on, the company was to pay their taxes to Peláez, not to the Constitutionalists.[1] Above his signature appeared the motto, "Law, Morality, and Justice."

Aside from Victoriano Huerta and the assassins of Madero and Zapata, no participant of the Mexican Revolution has received such consistent vilification as Manuel Peláez. He is portrayed as the quintessential reactionary, a local *terrateniente* who formed an army of dependent oil workers and hacienda peons in order to protect the oil companies from Carranza's economic nationalism. On the face of it, the evidence seems incriminating. Peláez consistently fought the troops loyal to the Carranza government and encouraged others to do so as well. Obtaining financial resources from the oil companies, particularly El Aguila and Huasteca, he ran a well-financed and exceptionally disciplined movement in the Tuxpan area. But the *pelaecistas* did not establish a following or cast much of a shadow in Tampico and the northern fields. His political program fit that of the companies: an end to the 1917 Constitution and especially Article 27, support for the Allies in World War I, and peace and security in the oil zone. His movement endured through the entire Constitutionalist period, that is to say, until the end of the violent phase of the Mexican Revolution. Peláez went into something of a political retirement once Carranza fell. His movement split up. One might easily surmise that with the Constitutionalists out, the companies no longer needed this surrogate opposition and ended it.

Certainly the relationship between Peláez and the oil companies raises some salient questions about foreign investment in Latin America. The coincidence between the oil companies' troubles with Carranza and the Peláez rebellion in the richest oil fields has engendered some juicy interpretations. The tendency has been to use Peláez as a demonstration of the power—and the willingness to manipulate it—of the foreign interests in Mexico.[2] Was not Peláez a creation of the avaricious companies? Did they not willingly provide him arms and money? Did they not conspire with foreign governments to support Peláez in order to combat the economic nationalism and social reforms of the Mexican Revolution? In 1938, when he expropriated the oil industry, President Lázaro Cárdenas cited the companies' alleged support of Peláez as an example of their political meddling.[3]

There is no doubt whatsoever that the oil companies supported Peláez. That is to say, he obtained money, if not arms, from them. Even if the Peláez rebellion were not part of an oil company plan but presented them an opportunity to operate politically and militarily through a surrogate, which opportunity they accepted wholeheartedly, then the foreign interests, indeed, were guilty of political meddling. On the other hand, if the companies were dragged unwillingly into the political fray as a source of "forced loans" for competing domestic factions, then the judgment should not be so severe. We have already established that the companies were inevitably involved in Mexican politics, even though they may have fancied themselves neutral. Therefore, political involvement will be the least one can expect. Finally, the analysis of the Peláez rebellion should address itself to its actual impact, with a view to ascertaining whether it contributed to the conduct of the oilmen's Mexican business. A final issue also suggests itself. Was Peláez the new Mexican politician, willing to break with backward patterns of behavior? After all, he proclaimed that what Mexico needed most was economic progress, not social reforms. Would Peláez in power have been the sort of man to set Mexico on the road toward unfettered, free-market capitalism? Rule of law? Even electoral democracy?

An Educated Mexican
of Spanish Appearance

Manuel Peláez Gorróchtegui, twenty-nine years old when he began his movement, was a member of a prominent family among the Spanish immigrant community in the Huasteca Veracruzana. As one American wrote later, "Peláez is a pleasant mannered educated Mexican of Spanish appearance."[4] In a region made up of mixed-raced inhabitants, the majority of whom were mestizos with some admixture of Negro features, his appearance and family heritage counted for much. Among the non-Anglos, the Spaniards and their (legitimate) progeny had always dominated the commercial, skilled labor, and estate overseer positions. They also owned the largest haciendas in the Huasteca. Land made the second generation of Peláez men—Ignacio, Manuel, and Alfredo—a notable family. Their father had owned Tierra Amarilla, an estate twenty-seven kilometers west of Tuxpan. Their mother, Ana Gorróchtegui de Peláez, may have come from a more distinguished family, also Spanish. The Gorróchtegui owned the Cerro Viejo, whose competing leases to both El Aguila and Huasteca in 1906 had sparked a lengthy dispute, ending in the 1918 compromise.

Manuel grew up amidst all the privileges the local gentry had acquired during the long and peaceful reign of Porfirio Díaz. He and his brothers were educated. His schooling commenced at the academy of Dr. Mariano Molina in Tantoyuca and continued at the Escuela Preparatoria of San Ildefonso in Mexico City. On the death of his father, Manuel returned home to manage the family's estates, eventually marrying Hermila Florencia of Tamiahua, a town that Peláez would later sack and burn several times over. He produced cattle and tropical products that were marketed through the auspices of the immigrant and Mexican-born Spaniards at Tuxpan. The family leased its oil rights to El Aguila in 1909. The British company annually paid the Peláez family five pesos per hectare for 6,881 hectares of oil claims at Tierra Amarilla, Paloma Real, Llano Grande, and Cuchillo de la Cal. Manuel also used his distinguished position in the community to serve as a labor contractor, when in 1911 and 1912 the companies put in their pipelines. He contracted as many as five thousand peons from the local area, who worked as day laborers in the oil camps.[5] Meanwhile, his elder brother studied for the Mexican bar and in 1909 joined El Aguila's legal staff, concentrating first on perfecting the titles to the company's leaseholds and freeholds. Later, Ignacio graduated into some political work, being dispatched by the company to confer with the state governor, legislators, and bureaucrats about the new regulations and taxes.

Apparently, Manuel was a restless sort. No sooner was construction of the pipelines and railways under way than he organized a local group to fight for Madero against the Díaz regime. The national success of the rebellion gained Peláez some local benefits. He was elected municipal president of Temapache within weeks of Díaz's going into exile. But Peláez soon fell out with the Madero regime. He disliked having his followers mustered out of the national army, and like General Huerta, he resented the continued social unrest and banditry that seemed to proliferate as the Madero regime approached political paralysis. Manuel eventually joined the anti-Madero rebellion of Félix Díaz. His brother Ignacio was said to have been a longtime *felicista*. In October 1912, Manuel participated in the occupation of Río Blanco and Orizaba. The *felicistas* operated briefly in the oil zones, making some forced loans, appropriating supplies and transport, and even threatening to take Tampico. Peláez had as many as eight hundred men under his command.[6] Although Díaz was captured and went on to engage in the events of the Ten Tragic Days, Manuel fled to the United States, where he took up residence in San Antonio until Madero fell.

Peláez and his fellow citizens entertained strong sympathies in favor of Huerta. Given his experience and leadership ability, Peláez was elected by his colleagues to organize a home guard of irregular troops in order to provide for the security of the Huasteca Veracruzana. He traveled to Mexico City and secured arms and ammunition from Huerta's war ministry. He also received a military commission as major of irregular forces. Peláez, however, was no match for the rebels of Gen. Cándido Aguilar. These Constitutionalist outsiders quickly overran the countryside and took Tuxpan. The collapse of the Huerta government again sent Peláez into exile. He boarded a steamer for Galveston and resumed residence at San Antonio. With the victorious anti-Huerta coalition breaking up, Villa moving toward Mexico City, and Carranza preparing to vacate the capital in October 1914, Peláez had his chance to return to the field. In October he took a steamer to Veracruz, then in its last days of American occupation. He traveled secretly to his home, gathered his men once again, and attacked a small Constitutionalist patrol.[7] Back in business as a *cabecilla,* a local military leader, Peláez sent Major Ruiz to the El Aguila camp at Potrero del Llano for his first "tax collection."

In the meanwhile, the Tierra Amarilla oil field was heading for early exhaustion. El Aguila crews had drilled eighteen wells on the Peláez estate, of which eleven were still producing in 1916. The early production merited Tierra Amarilla's connection to the main pipeline going down to the Tuxpan and to the company's telephone line to Tamiahua. El Aguila's light railway to La Peña on the coast, however, passed through the neighboring estate, the Hacienda Horcones. For Tierra Amarilla, the Peláez family had been receiving ten thousand pesos annually, paid on 24 March of each year, in rental fees. If the Peláez received the standard royalty fees, which the private property provisions of the 1884 law permitted, then they were receiving an additional income of ten centavos per barrel of oil produced. The only problem for the family was that Tierra Amarilla's production had peaked in 1913. It fell by 75 percent throughout 1914, at the end of which Peláez took to the field. According to Everette DeGolyer's figures, Tierra Amarilla had yielded the following production:[8]

1911	5,709 barrels
1912	64,680
1913	49,345
1914	34,531
1915	5,161
1916	0

The Peláez family did not rely entirely on Tierra Amarilla for its oil income: other properties were also leased. The renegotiation of these leases in 1918 was a tortured process. By then, the lessor was the head of a very important armed movement in the oil zone, but his main property of Tierra Amarilla was practically devoid of petroleum. Thomas J. Ryder and Licenciado Robassa spent much time drafting and redrafting the contract, the details of which are not found in the correspondence.[9] There is no doubt, however, that this *cabecilla* was a wealthy man. When he began his rebellion in 1914, he had already displayed a penchant for local power and military adventure.

If we take Peláez at his word, he began his uprising in the Huasteca because of the depredations and violence brought there from outside—especially in 1913 and 1914 by the forces of General Aguilar. "[T]he aggressions of which the peaceful and hardworking inhabitants of this region were victims," he later stated, "obliged us to resort to force to protect us from violence."[10] Although Manuel Lárraga holds the distinction of being the first general to take money, rifles, and horses from the companies—in May 1913 at El Ebano—Aguilar introduced the system to the Huasteca Veracruzana. He brought an army composed of Santa María Indians, Totonac-speaking inhabitants of the Canton of Papantla, fifty miles south of Tuxpan. In December 1913, while Huerta's troops still held Tuxpan, General Aguilar's troops took command of the countryside. He extracted forced loans of ten thousand pesos from both Huasteca and El Aguila. To convince the manager of El Aguila it was in his interest to cooperate, he stopped the pumps that provided water for the steam that drove the boilers of the pipeline pumphouses. On the advice of American diplomats, Huasteca met Aguilar's demands.[11] Apparently the Constitutionalist forces extracted similar contributions from the Spanish landowners and mestizo smallholders of the region. The documents speak of an especial resentment in the area toward the Santa María Indians, who may have used their military positions on occasion to humble aloof Spaniards and superior mestizos. Oilmen reported Indian raids on small towns. The Santa María troops sacked Tancoco, Amatlán, San Antonio, and Chinampa. By May, Aguilar's troops moved into Tuxpan, where they collected customs duties in a manner that may have annoyed the local Spanish merchants.[12] A man of swarthy visage and an outsider, General Aguilar must have resented the cold treatment the local notables gave him as their Constitutionalist liberator. No doubt these light-skinned Spaniards were all closet *huertistas*.

The high-handed behavior of poorly trained and ill-paid troops from outside the region—especially Indians—should not be discounted as a factor in bonding big landowners (mostly white) and small-holders (mostly mestizo). Many of the officers personally loyal to Peláez were called "Spaniards." It is clear that Peláez led a multiclass movement supported by local residents outraged at the incursions of unwanted, detested outsiders. As Peláez himself said, "Several hundreds of residents of this region confided to me the command of the forces organized to defend the flag of law and order from the outrages of those false revolutionaries whose ends and aims are destruction, murder and personal mistreatment."[13] The *pelaecistas* were not merely an army of dependent hacienda peons led by officers who were also their employers. Many rather independent small-holders, rancheros, were also loyal partisans.

Although Peláez appeared to have had remarkable control over the operations of his troops, there still occurred in the oil zone those seemingly senseless acts of violence for which the Mexican Revolution, indeed any revolution, is known. On 6 June 1915, a band of two hundred *villistas* belonging to the Peláez group attacked the camp of the La Peña pipeline pump station, located at the mouth of the Tuxpan River. Thirty-two Constitutionalists were garrisoning the site. Before retiring from the engagement, the *villistas* bombed the wireless station, killed two Mexican pumphouse workers and two tank builders, and escaped with 5,000 pesos from the company's payroll. Vaughan of El Aguila speculated that the money was the reason for the attack. Four British citizens also died, among them a woman and a baby, and several were wounded. Caught in the cross-fire, they had been shot in their homes. Colonel Guillermín of the Constitutionalists immediately apologized for his men having shot at the homes and also for their pillaging.[14] But General Aguilar denounced El Aguila for the attack. He claimed that several employees had assisted in the attack and that the *villistas* had fired the volleys that killed the British citizens. "El Aguila employees [were] solely responsible for the affair," Aguilar said, "as they had communicated to the Villistas our movements by telephone." Our employees were instructed to be politically neutral, replied El Aguila executives, on penalty of dismissal. British authorities protested the incident to Pancho Villa, who immediately promised prompt reparations to the families of those British subjects killed in action. But as for this Peláez fellow, Villa said, he knew nothing about him.[15]

In the meanwhile, His Majesty's Government ordered its consul at Tuxpan to investigate the incident. Consul George Hewitt found that one El Aguila employee, Santos Travieso, a Spaniard, had led the *villista* forces. Santos had been engaged as a peon, an "unimportant position," by El Aguila for two or three years. Furthermore, a British employee injured in the attack, who had lost his wife and child, gave evidence that the *villistas* could not possibly have fired the shots that killed them. He claimed the Constitutionalists were culpable. El Aguila mustered evidence from a Constitutionalist naval officer to the same effect and made much of Colonel Guillerín's prompt apology.[16] J. B. Body concluded that the Constitutionalists had fired on the company houses in retaliation for the *villista* raid—even though no *villistas* were around at the time. The British consul tried to obtain an agreement between Generals Aguilar and Peláez to consider the oil camps a neutral zone. But the effort failed.[17] Already the Peláez rebellion was costing El Aguila time, money, property, and the lives of Mexican workers and British citizens.

In the next few years, rebels once again wrested the southern fields from the government troops. First it had been the *maderistas* taking control from the *porfiristas,* then the *felicistas* from the *maderistas,* then the *constitucionalistas* from the *huertistas.* Now the *pelaecistas* constituted the formidable guerrilla force among the oil camps and haciendas of the region. They seldom engaged the better-armed Constitutionalists in open battle, contenting themselves to raid small patrols and garrisons. When pursued, they fled to the bush or into the nearby Sierra Oriental. Constitutionalist troops, stationed at the small ports along the Gulf Coast, traveled among the oil camps at will. Usually, they commandeered the launches and trains of the oil companies, motivating the guerrillas to destroy the rail bridges on the Huasteca and El Aguila lines.[18] The oil field managers were constantly repairing the rail lines.

At first, the managers at El Aguila asked the Constitutionalist troops for guarantees—to protect the oil camps and keep the *pelaecistas* from cutting the water lines. The limitations of such a strategy made themselves manifest very early. In January 1915, two months after Peláez began his rebellion, Potrero del Llano No. 4 caught fire, burning for three months. While the company's workmen were busy extinguishing the raging blaze, members of the camp's Constitutionalist garrison robbed the store and warehouse. When manager Vaughan complained, General Aguilar accused El Aguila of supporting the "revolutionists."[19] In the meantime, the raging well caused some burnt oil to foul the Buena Vista River. General Aguilar assessed the company a fine of fifty thousand pesos for pollution. The men of El Aguila considered Aguilar responsible for the fire. His closing of the water pumps had caused the well to be closed in and the gas pressure to break through fissures in the ground, making the well vulnerable to the lightning that eventually set it ablaze.[20] El Aguila's Vaughan grew exasperated with Peláez too. His troops constantly cut the company's water lines, usually after a demand for money, and threatened the great well. On one occasion, Peláez himself came with his troops to the Potrero camp "uninvited and unwelcome," as Vaughan put it. Returning from an unsuccessful raid on Tuxpan, Peláez was in a foul mood. He snarled when Vaughn handed him only 7,500 pesos instead of the 10,000 he required.

The conflict in the southern fields also disrupted the water communications network that the companies had established between Tuxpan and Tampico. Each time the *pelaecistas* raided a coastal garrison, such as the 1917 sacking and burning of Tamiahua, the Constitutionalists stopped water traffic on the Tamiahua lagoon for days at a time. Normally, they merely detained the motor launches and rifled through the mail sacks for messages to Peláez.[21] All the Constitutionalist officers were convinced the foreigners were aiding the enemy. How else could Peláez be so successful? Every government commander had a tendency to take out his failures on the foreign oil companies. British consul Cummins at Tampico recounted one such instance:

> So far as we can make out [Major] Zumaya made an attack on Saladero and Pelaez gave him a licking and it appears that some Govt. troops under Zumaya also visited San Geronimo and did damage to the Oil Camp there. Zumaya then seems to have taken all the launches he could find and to have retired to Toro Island in the lagoon whence he sent a message to the Camp Supt. at Tanjuijo [sic] to say that he would allow nothing to pass and would shoot any [expletive] "Gringo" who came near.[22]

These games of tit-for-tat continued for years, and the ugliness and brutality of civil war often rose to the surface. Two direct confrontations were recorded at Potrero del Llano in 1916. On 31 January, Peláez sent a raiding party of three hundred men against the forty Constitutionalists stationed at the El Aguila camp. The attack drove out the government forces, who abandoned their arms and ammunition to the rebels. It also set the Mexican employees to flight. Meanwhile, the *pelaecistas* helped themselves to horses, mules, saddles, and two hundred pesos from the El Aguila paymaster. "During the last two months," lamented one manager, "it has been almost impossible to keep our men, more especially Mexican labour, such as line-riders, telephone line-riders, and watchmen."[23]

In October, 160 green Constitutionalist troops set up defensive positions around Potrero under Major Ruescas. On 12 October, Peláez called Ruescas on the camp phone and told him to get out. Ruescas re-

fused. The *pelaecistas* attacked next morning, routing the Constitutionalists. Eighty government troops were killed, and Peláez lost only sixteen men. The rebels hung or stabbed to death the Constitutionalist
prisoners; they were not shot because Peláez was short of ammunition.
One of the foreign workers, who had a box camera, took snapshots.
The rebel leader, an educated man, after all, apologized to the management for the massacre. It was necessary to make an example to the *carrancistas*. He had refrained from such barbarity early on, Peláez said,
but he was getting a reputation for being soft because he was "letting
prisoners go."[24] So much for Peláez as a humanitarian.

In Tuxpan, a city of less than five thousand inhabitants, there existed
deep sympathy for Peláez and loathing for the Constitutionalist troops.
The government had a garrison there, numbering from five hundred to
eight hundred men, five or six machine guns, and two three-inch cannons. The town's civilian authorities did not like the military commanders, and the poorly paid, undisciplined troops were shunned.
Even the school mistresses begrudged the government, which owed
them several months back pay. "There are a great many Pelaezistas [*sic*]
in this town," reported British consul Hewitt, "as he is connected by
marriage with most of the families." The Constitutionalist authorities
in Tuxpan had become quite paranoid, ordering the British consul not
to speak, interview, or treat with Peláez at all.[25] At the time, the Spanish community in Tuxpan was dominant (and still is). The aspect of
darker-skinned, underfed Constitutionalist troops panhandling on the
streets was certainly not very savory to them.

A number of hometown oil field workers also supported the *pelaecistas*. Often they served as reserves rather than with the strike forces
and provided intelligence for Peláez, even telephoning him at Tierra
Amarilla on oil company lines. The managers noted how their Mexican
workers scattered when a Constitutionalist patrol approached. Early
on, the *carrancistas* suspected the Mexican oil field workers. They once
executed three natives after a skirmish at Potrero del Llano and took
away two timekeepers and eight pipeline workers as hostages. A sudden demand for local labor, such as the discovery of Doheny's second
giant oil well at Cerro Azul in 1916, enforced a calm over the oil zone.
Many *pelaecistas* were said to have gone to work building pipelines and
earthen storage for Huasteca.[26]

Within the home district, where the rebels were able to keep the
Constitutionalists at bay from 1915 to 1917, the military discipline
maintained by Peláez gained him a broad base of support. It was said

that the farmers were able to attend their crops relatively unmolested. Americans who worked at the oil camps within the territory also grew to appreciate the tranquility, despite its cost to the companies that employed them. Everyone knew that 90 percent of the robberies in the region occurred in the zones controlled by the Constitutionalists.[27] In this period of time, Peláez eliminated the Constitutionalist leadership of many of the towns in his district, appointing his own men to the civil administration. He instructed them on such things as cutting back the undergrowth along the sides of the roads. Peláez warned that if they did not obey, he would return and destroy their property—an oddly autocratic method of encouraging civic pride, to say the least. There is a firsthand description, by an ostensible *carrancista* correspondent, of the peace reigning in the Huasteca region. It fairly reeks of nostalgia for the *pax porfiriana*:

> Frankly, I tell you that these people [of Peláez] are very orderly and disciplined and after so many years as guerrilleros, they are to be taken very much into account. Commerce flourishes in the territory that they dominate, and life has returned to its old normality. I attended a dance to which whole families went, and there was not a single discordant note. Money circulates, because the companies pay tribute monthly.[28]

The reality of the civil war in the Huasteca Veracruzana was not so idyllic as the *pelaecista* paradise portrayed here.

Undoubtedly, the incursion of the Santa María Indians played a major factor in uniting the people of the Huasteca behind Peláez. The Indians were feared and hated. The *carrancistas* such as Aguilar were resented because they had introduced Santa María troops to the area. The Indians of the villages to the south were led by Constitutionalist officers, whites, or like Aguilar himself, mestizos, and occasionally by their own *jefes*. Some reports mentioned that the Constitutionalists did not pay these Indian troops at all, a strategy that enhanced a certain penchant among them to pillage. The Indians also got some very bad military assignments. When most government troops had withdrawn from the countryside back to the city, they left a few small garrisons, mostly Santa Marians, numbering five to thirty men each in small hamlets like Chicontepec.[29] They became special targets for the *pelaecistas*. During 1916, Peláez led his men several times into Santa María territory to punish the Indians. His forces sacked Tepezintle, forcing the Indian leader, Enrique Cristóbal, and most of the residents to flee. The *pelaecistas* killed seventy "male Indians" in that raid, certainly a far larger toll in human life than the Indian troops had ever exacted in the

Huasteca.[30] Obviously, the *pelaecistas* were observing the differential privileges of the multiracial society: it was acceptable for a lighter-skinned Hispanic to exact especially savage revenge on the Indian. Instead of an eye for an eye, it was two or three eyes for one. To a degree, that also applied to persons from outside the home districts. The rebel attacks north to Pánuco were also very destructive.

The King of Paper

Like all guerrilla forces, the strength of the *pelaecistas* varied considerably. Foreigners who reported on the Peláez rebellion also had their own estimates, all of which differed. Obviously a biased source, Peláez himself in 1916 told the British consul at Tuxpan that his men numbered four thousand. He also said he had five machine guns and "plenty of ammo." He could take Tampico, if he wanted, even though Constitutionalist reinforcements could retake it "within a month."[31] Evidently Peláez wished to exaggerate his strength—and his intentions—hoping that the Constitutionalists might overrate his capabilities. If his forces were well armed and numerous, the Constitutionalists would not want to patrol and garrison his territory. His boasts that he could take Tampico, which would have been a real blow to the government, implied that all available Constitutionalist troops in the area ought to be stationed there. Later, when he was persecuting Germans in hopes of getting British arms, Peláez claimed that he could raise twenty thousand men "if he had the support." The British diplomats in Mexico thought this an exaggeration.[32] Clearly, Peláez was not a reliable authority on his own military strength.

Other sources said his forces were much less numerous. Hewitt in 1917 placed them at two thousand "perfectly armed" and many more as reservists who were "fairly" armed.[33] Equipping his irregulars was always a great problem for Peláez. In 1918, American military intelligence estimated that he had six thousand men, of which less than half were under arms. To quote the intelligence estimate: "The majority of [the *pelaecistas*] is armed with machetes. They somewhat resemble a 'home guard,' working their little farms and reporting for immediate duty when called to 'arms.' "[34] An oilman from the Penn Mex camp at Alamo estimated that Peláez had only one thousand men under arms and two or three times that many subject to call.[35]

Like so many armed men during the Revolution, Peláez's guerrillas were organized in a patriarchal fashion. They looked to Peláez as the nominal chief of the rebel movement. *Pelaecista* bands numbering in the tens and hundreds operated in the oil zone under the orders of men who had recruited them. Many of the five thousand adherents that Peláez also claimed to be under his leadership were more like allies, commanded by eleven leaders, some of whom were identified as *felicistas* or as partisans of Guillermo Meixueiro (both groups were operating in Oaxaca and southern Veracruz).[36] No matter the true number of Peláez's forces, they were numerous enough to deny the Constitutionalists from physically securing the southern fields. A British correspondent from Tuxpan estimated that ten thousand "well-armed" Constitutionalists posted in the oil camps would have been necessary to control the Peláez rebellion in its home district.[37]

Typical of guerrilla forces everywhere and at all times, the tactics of the *pelaecistas* consisted of laying ambushes, concentrating forces for lightning raids, disappearing into normal occupations, but never challenging the full force of the enemy. Peláez and his lieutenants would form up his troops only when they were about to carry out an operation. Otherwise, they dispersed and behaved as *pacíficos*, "noncombatants," going about their daily business. The Mexican geologist Ezequiel Ordóñez witnessed one *pelaecista* ambush:

> One morning, a numerous cavalry force was unexpectedly attacked by soldiers of [Peláez] posted in the jungle growth on both sides of a pipeline right-of-way. The surprise of that group of cavalry could not have been greater before the relentless fire of the *pelaecistas*. In a matter of minutes, the government soldiers suffered numerous casualties, the inopportune attack causing a great confusion among men and horses.[38]

Generally speaking, the *pelaecistas* were reasonably disciplined and motivated troops, perhaps sharing a common belief that they were defending *su tierra*, their "rural homeland," from rapacious outsiders. The following description by a visiting American, who regarded Spanish surnames with great casualness, is instructive of the general state of the *pelaecistas* in 1919:

> All troops that I have ever seen of the Pelias Estas [*sic*] outfit are fairly well mounted and armed, considering the class of arms and mounts that obtains in this country. Every man carries a belt full of ammunition furnished by Pelias Esta [*sic*]. Rifles are also furnished by Pelias Esta. . . . Condition of troops— much better as to personnel and morale, arms and equipment, comparitively [*sic*] speaking, than the Carranzista [*sic*] troops in this district.[39]

Fig. 12. The Peláez forces in 1917. On Christmas day, the *pelaecistas* paid a visit to the oil camp of the Mexico Gulf Oil Company for a feast and a round of speeches. Said the military intelligence officer at Fort Sam Houston, Texas, to whom the photograph was delivered: "It was not known whether this [hospitality] was dictated by affection or policy." From the National Archives, Record Group 165, Military Intelligence Division, Washington, D.C.

Within the Huasteca, the *pelaecistas* seldom engaged in pillaging. No one in the home district paid tribute to Peláez nor were the merchants and hacendados subject to *pelaecista* demands. His troops did not ride onto the haciendas to demand food, money, and eventually the hacienda itself, as so often happened in Tlaxcala, San Luis Potosí, and Morelos.[40] But Peláez was being more than a little disingenuous when he claimed his young rebellion represented "two years and a half of struggle and of bloody encounters—years during which not one single act of brigandage can be imputed to us."[41] When operating outside the district, *pelaecistas* behaved much as the Constitutionalists did in the Huasteca: Peláez allowed his subordinates to direct the looting. His troops' behavior when in the Pánuco region and in the Santa María villages cannot be said to have been chivalrous.

The financial strength of the *pelaecista* movement—over the long-term it was the wealthiest rebel group in the country—contributed to the discipline and its moderate, even reactionary program. The financial liquidity of the Peláez rebellion was good for the individual *pelaecista*. "The pay of a soldier is one dollar American currency a day, and each morning they are paid in actual cash. The pay of a Captain is four dollars a day American currency," reported an American visitor. "The leaders . . . seem to have all sorts of money and indulge in drinking and gambling to an extent which seems excessive."[42] There were other pay-offs for Peláez's troops too. The periodic forays into Santa María territory or the sacking of Tamiahua and Pánuco provided opportunities for acquisition. Right at home, the oil camps provided perquisites, mounts and meals, to be enjoyed without disrupting the local gentry. "We cannot keep any horses," lamented Lord Cowdray.[43] *Pelaecistas* were perhaps the best-paid soldiers of the Mexican Revolution.

The method of securing the funds, taking them from foreigners, saved Peláez from having to resort to more revolutionary notions to satisfy his constituents. He did not have to attack large landowners or divide up their land as the price of securing the loyalty of his followers. He did not have to resort to economic nationalism like the Constitutionalists, bewailing the suffering of the common people while the companies enriched themselves. No one was out of work here. Despite liking the *pelaecista* program, the British consul half-hoped that a Constitutionalist expedition against Peláez would succeed in making the men "lay down their arms, and seek work, of which there is plenty with the oil Companies right now."[44] Obviously, the men and especially the officers were wallowing in the good life, enjoying the *rescate*, "the taking of material goods," without having to suffer the scarcity that impelled some other movements to lurch leftward to satisfy the desperate masses. The *pelaecistas* took all they needed without affecting oil production, in itself an unusual feature of the Revolution. Elsewhere in Mexico, of course, revolutionary activities caused severe economic deterioration.

The contributions that the oil companies made to the Peláez rebellion were not voluntary. They did not willingly hand over anything, even to a local movement that promised to protect property. Of course, the *carrancistas* found it convenient to allege that the companies paid Peláez voluntarily. The allegations demeaned the Peláez rebellion outside the oil zone at least and justified certain other of the government's nationalist policies. Their very first reaction in 1915 to the forced loans demonstrates how unprepared the oilmen were to handle the initial demands of Peláez. In New York, Harold Walker of Huasteca cautioned against payment. "Don't know what Aguila or Penn Mex are taxed. Latter camp looted on first stop," Walker cabled to Doheny. "My fear is danger from other side if we pay, as Pelaez is now an outlaw, but Carranza unable or unwilling drive Pelaez out permanently. Also Pelaez now desperate and apt to take vengeance on Americans. Believe advisable shut down all developments for present until we are guaranteed protection from Washington."[45] But General Manager Wylie differed and brought Walker around to the importance of not shutting down production. Besides, who knew when Washington would "guarantee protection?" Wylie wired Doheny his recommendation: "Walker and I have discussed your message from Yacht. Do not believe we can do otherwise than pay Pelaez. Not in favor of abandoning camp and anxious to get new developments soon as possible."[46]

Peláez entertained few doubts that he deserved the money he got from the companies. He said he provided them security. "The Country is in a state of anarchy and the fall of the Govt. is imminent," Peláez told the British consul:

> I have been able to maintain order in this District and the Cos. have not been molested by me or my men. The paymasters can travel about with all the money they like in perfect safety, a condition that is not to be found in any other part of the Country. The monies I have received from various sources including the oil Cos. have been spent on my men and I have not taken it for myself as so many have done. I could have been a millionaire had I so desired. When the Govt. falls I propose taking charge of this District but it will then become necessary for the oil Cos. to provide me with what I shall need in the way of arms, ammunition, money and supplies.[47]

Note that he was not asking the oil companies (1) if he should continue his rebellion, (2) if they would care to pay him for these services, or (3) how much those donations should be. In the Huasteca, Peláez decided what was in the best interests of the foreign companies.

The companies never made public—nor did they tell each other—how much they were paying. Huasteca manager Green spoke to newspapers in general terms, saying in effect, "We pay Peláez all right, but he receives this money in the form of forced loans."[48] Each time the armed men came calling at Casiano, Green and Doheny were scrupulous to notify the State Department, the Mexican ambassador in Washington, and the Carranza government. Carranza was aware of the payments and the circumstances under which they were made. Since

Huasteca was paying far higher government taxes at Tampico, Ambassador Arredondo in Washington said it was a "good thing" Huasteca paid Peláez, so that the oil flow would not stop.[49]

How much Peláez demanded each month was well known. How much was paid was another matter. Early on, Huasteca and El Aguila adopted a program of strict secrecy—not to inform each other or their governments how much was actually handed out. The only indication of the quantities involved come from what the companies later declared to the claims commission. According to the terms of the 1924 debt agreement, all Americans were to submit their claims of damages and losses due to revolutionary activity. Here is where one learns that Transcontinental paid out a total of fifty-nine thousand dollars in protection money to Peláez.[50] This money represented only the years 1918 to 1920, for Peláez's unique form of tax collection (that is, the cutting of water lines) worked only on those companies that had production that was to be pumped through pipelines. Transcontinental's production in the southern fields—Peláez had no power to tax the northern fields at all—did not commence until February of 1918. El Aguila and Huasteca's payments began in January 1915. The Penn Mex also began paying Peláez shortly after he rose in rebellion, but the managers did not specify how much. They did recount the Peláez threat: "If you don't pay, I will raid your company and destroy your property." The former Penn Mex managers also recalled the words of Constitutionalist General Alemán two days later: "If you do pay, I will shoot you."[51]

The oil companies did reveal the amounts demanded by the Peláez tax collectors. At first he had demanded ten thousand pesos, then twenty thousand. Finally the standard payment came to be thirty thousand pesos each month from each producer. On occasion, when military activity intensified, as in the springs of 1918 and 1920, Peláez assessed additional surcharges and ordered the payments in advance.[52] Col. Daniel Martínez Herrera, a Peláez officer, in 1916 notified Huasteca of his chief's formal communiqué, that henceforward the tax would be increased to thirty thousand pesos monthly. Peláez was courteous enough to point out the reasons:

[I]n view of the fact that for one year and four months the forces under my orders have given ample protection to the different companies that are located in the zone controlled by my forces without paying any contribution to their support, and that the said companies have been paying big sums to the cause of the Constitutionalist Government, I have thought it best in order to save the poorer classes of people from suffering any damage that the said companies contribute every month to the support of said forces, I have assigned to the Huasteca Petroleum Co. the sum of 30,000 pesos every month, which should be paid without any excuse.[53]

Peláez had first approached the Penn Mex company with the same demand. El Aguila management suspected that he would come to them next with a demand for fifty thousand pesos. Eventually, Peláez asked them for one hundred thousand pesos payable twice monthly, a demand that was forwarded immediately to the Mexican foreign minister. The British company wanted Carranza to know of its handicap.[54] Peláez apparently believed in progressive taxation—the richer companies paying more. When The Texas Company brought in its modest production in the Faja de Oro in December of 1917, the vigilant Peláez taxmen dropped by its camp, assessing two thousand pesos monthly, which was doubled after two months.[55]

How much was the Peláez exchequer getting? In September 1917, Harold Walker said it totaled less than fifty thousand dollars per month. He calculated that El Aguila was paying ten thousand dollars in this protection money, and Penn Mex ten thousand. A number of other companies paid less. He did not state how much Huasteca paid, only what he "calculated" others paid. If Walker based this on what his company actually paid, say ten thousand dollars, or twenty thousand pesos, this represented two-thirds of what Peláez demanded. But Doheny claimed that all the companies combined paid less than "$30,000 per month."[56] At any rate, the companies never paid the entire Peláez tax bill. They successfully dodged his taxes while giving full measure to government customs agents in Tuxpan and Tampico. Doheny's standing instruction to William Green, his field manager, specified: "Pay only what is unavoidable to save property of company and lives of employees."[57]

It is difficult to ascertain the exact extent of Peláez's taxation. One estimate suggests that one company, Huasteca, paid Peláez more and more money as production and exports increased, although not at the same trajectory:[58]

1916	40,000 pesos
1917	260,000
1918	325,000
1919	380,000
1920 (first half)	230,000

"The arrangement was not satisfactory to the oil companies," as one report said, "but was probably the best that could have been made under the circumstances."[59] This was an exceptionally well-financed movement. If the oilmen were correct, they gave Peláez approximately thirty thousand dollars per month and he was receiving up to 40 percent of what the companies paid Carranza. Assuming that he had one thousand full-time troops, Peláez could have paid up to twenty-five dollars per month to each of his followers and still have one thousand dollars left for "discretionary" expenses. Small wonder his troops were able to stay in the field for six years without demanding social reforms. Peláez gave them a redistribution of income, thereby avoiding a redistribution of property, which the popular forces in other areas had sought when the income ran out. Peláez was the perfect caudillo—his largesse never ran out. The oil companies were the perfect tax base. Their economic growth, at least during the Revolution, never gave out.

Democracy Must Rule

Although they served as the reluctant financial base of the Peláez rebellion, the oil companies found nothing in the political program of their tax collector with which to find fault. His was the blandest, most noncommittal, and shallowest program of any of the revolutionary caudillos. First and foremost, Peláez stood against Carranza, whom he called a usurper, dictator, "farcical liberator," and "false revolutionary." The lives of the people of the Huasteca had been tranquil and peaceful until the Constitutionalists came along. Therefore, Carranza was identified as the person who brought pillage and destruction to the Huasteca Veracruzana, and Peláez was the defender of "the sacred rights of the people against spoilation." What would he substitute for Carranza? A peaceful, democratic rule of law, of course. "As we are convinced that the country must be ruled by the Law and that its progress must not be obtained by violence, and as we are also convinced that the public power must be an institution for the benefit of the people, and that the latter must designate its commanders," he proclaimed, "[then] democracy must rule our country."[60] The general signed this particular proclamation below the motto "Liberty and Constitution."

In other words, the *pelaecistas* qualify as belonging to Alan Knight's concept of the *serrano* revolt: reactive to outside intervention and commanded by local notables and landowners. The *serrano* revolt involved the participation of the rank-and-file as members of a rigid social hierarchy led by their local social superiors. The guerrilla troops of the *serrano* revolt are not often led by their own popular leaders and do not necessarily act upon their grievances against the local landowners and bourgeoisie.[61] By "tranquility," for instance, the *pelaecistas* meant strict law and order and the *status quo ante*. They did not want to be molested by outside "liberal" authorities bringing in Indian troops. They advocated no redistribution of property.

Politically, Peláez sought a restoration of the Constitution of 1857. In this, Peláez even claimed once to have been a brother-in-arms to Carranza, when the latter was proclaiming the Constitution of 1857 in the fight against Huerta. (This was factually wrong, of course; Peláez had been a *huertista*.) Naturally, the earliest proclamations made no mention whatsoever of the constitutional issues involved. Peláez had been in the field for three years before the Constitution of 1917, but beginning that year, comments about its "idiocy" and "insane foolishness" began to leaven the political loaves of Peláez. His denunciation of Article 27 pleased the oilmen exceedingly. Yet, it should not be forgotten that Peláez represented those local landowners who were leasing and selling their subsoil rights as they pleased according to the 1884 legislation and whose property rights were circumscribed by Article 27. Peláez was doubtlessly influenced by the economic interests of his own class as well as by the arguments of his brother, Ignacio, formerly of the El Aguila legal staff.

Meanwhile, he appended to the constitutional questions several general thoughts reflecting nineteenth-century Mexican liberalism. One concerned education: that the masses ought to be uplifted through the magical qualities of literacy. Not that he was the sort of man who established schools for the children of his hacienda peons, but Peláez said the unrest in the country perpetrated by the *carrancistas* prevented the orderly civil administration from establishing schools. "Public instruction has not been given the attention which a branch of such importance demands," his 1915 proclamation says:

> Mexico needs schools in her cities, towns and country; schools to teach reading and writing, cultivation of land and the trades and industries which will develop with the country. Only in this way can the living conditions of the native population be bettered, now rendered worse each day by their pretended redeemers; and prepare them to fulfill their duties as the best means to make their civil and political rights respected.[62]

In other words, education was a substitute for social reforms. Peláez did not suggest that peons be liberated from the tyranny of landowners, only that they be allowed to go to public schools. Obviously, such rhetoric appealed to his fellow landowners, who knew exactly what he inferred—no social reforms—and to the Americans, who held high the banner of public education. The other nineteenth-century liberal ideal he espoused was that of progress. Economic prosperity was touted as the solution to all problems and the harbinger of the peace and administration of the early Porfirians, although Peláez was careful to give the obligatory (but brief) denunciations of Porfirio Díaz. He welcomed the foreign investor to Mexico (what *terrateniente* with oil exudes on his land would not?) and also the immigrant (what son of a Spaniard would not?). Such proclamations summoned up the *juarista* liberals of the 1870s.

As far as his foreign policy was concerned, Peláez criticized Carranza for his pro-German stance. He kicked out all Germans, which probably were not many, and relieved the oil camps of worry about "German sabotage." Peláez said that he was a strong backer of the Allies in the European war. He wanted Mexico to be "absolutely neutral" in the struggle but provide the Allies with all the petroleum they needed to press on to victory. (Apparently Peláez never realized how contradictory his own ideas were.) He also thought that his movement was the best substitute for an American invasion. This last was a malleable idea, as many others also appear to be. While desperately seeking arms, or under Constitutionalist attack, Peláez would have his brother, Ignacio, serving as his emissary to Washington and New York, proposing a joint military occupation of the oil zone. The foreign diplomats might have scoffed at these grandiose plans, but at least they trusted that Peláez would not destroy the oil fields.[63] He couched his support of foreign businessmen in Mexico in terms of the Allied cause:

> We do not abandon the interests which the belligerents have in the region which we dominate, and that these interests will be defended by us whoever may be their owners, and that we will permit no one to attack them, not only because it is our duty as Mexicans to grant protection and give hospitality to all foreigners who, attracted by the liberality of our institutions and the richness of our land, have come with their wealth, labor, capital and civilization to take part in our life.[64]

This was language the foreign investor understood. Yet, even Peláez's foreign policy commitments are suspect. Once, in October 1917, because of Wilson's recognition and support for the Carranza government, Peláez was reported to have met with a German agent. He threatened to deal with Germany if the United States did not change its policy.[65]

The historian, basking in the sunshine of hindsight, would do well not to make too much of this *pelaecista* ideology. His actions spoke louder than his words; that is why he "proclaimed" so infrequently and ruled above the law rather than under it. Anyway, his pronouncements (I have found four) were all alike. In fact, Peláez had been in the field for nearly three years before he bothered to make so much as a "proclamation." He said lamely that he did not want the Mexican people to confuse him with those others who have enriched themselves in rebellion "by exercising the many forms of pillage."[66] This, of course, was not the Mexican tradition. The best and brightest of his class always began their rebellions with high-sounding, fulsome, suitable-for-publication proclamations, usually named after the location where the peripatetic rebels penned them. Madero had his Plan of San Luis Potosí; Zapata had his Plan of Ayala; there was a Plan Orozquista; Carranza wrote the Plan of Guadalupe; and Obregón would have his Plan of Agua Prieta. The Mexican revolutionary landscape was littered with numerous other plans but not with a Plan of Tierra Amarilla.

What mattered most to Peláez was power. And money was power. Even if he did not extend the justice and rule of law he proclaimed to the foreign oil companies, Peláez did support their policies. After all, the oil companies formed the basis for the well-being of his real constituents, the Huasteca landowners, large and small. Peláez vilified the Constitution of 1917, because it removed his property rights and because it had been Carranza's.[67] Also, the timing of his proclamations are most suspect. Peláez was very quiet when his rebellion was going well. On the other hand, the most complete discussion of the *pelaecista* program comes in his two and one-half-page document of December 1917. Here is where Peláez was most effusive in his praise of the oil companies and the Allies. Why? The Constitutionalists had just announced an all-out offensive against his forces, and brother Ignacio was in Washington and New York meeting with oilmen and diplomats in an attempt to get arms. Peláez was also pro-Allies because he wanted their arms.[68] He touted education, foreign investments, and economic progress because his fellow landowners believed these were preferable to—and substitutions for—the redistribution of property and prerogatives. All of these things, in the true *serrano* tradition, would keep the central authority out of the Huasteca Veracruzana.

If the Peláez political program, the very antithesis of radicalism, made his alliances appear purely opportunistic, they were. A movement favored by landowners and dominated by sons of Spaniards certainly could not have been enthusiastic about the program of the *villistas,* the *zapatistas,* and their allies in the 1915 convention. Villa had dispossessed some of the biggest landowners in Chihuahua, such as the Terrazas; Zapata was unabashedly dividing up the land of the hacendados; and much of the discussion at their convention in Aguascalientes concerned the need for agrarian reform. Moreover, Villa was self-consciously anti-Spaniard, even going so far as calling his followers *indios,* in contradistinction to the overbearing immigrant Spanish merchants and overseers of North Mexico. When his troops took Chihuahua and Torreón in 1913, the Spanish residents of the city were persecuted—along with the Chinese, who were massacred as well.[69]

Yet Peláez identified himself as a *villista*—though not as an *indio.* The reason is that Villa had broken with the hated Constitutionalists, and his occupation of Mexico City at the end of 1914 appeared to be Carranza's demise. What better way was there for Peláez to be in a position to claim political suzerainty of the Huasteca, of Tuxpan (where many of his relatives lived), and of Tampico—maybe even all of Veracruz—than to climb aboard the Villa train? Did Villa count on Peláez? When American and British diplomats protested to Villa that the *villista* war taxes on the oil companies in the Huasteca were too high, Villa said he did not know anything about the Huasteca. He did not know Peláez.[70] Peláez became a *villista* because Carranza was their common enemy, not because *villismo* attracted a large following in the Huasteca Veracruzana. Wanting autonomy above all, Peláez gambled that Villa would win. His was not the first calculation to go awry during the Revolution.

There was a weakness of the Peláez movement. Once Villa's star had fallen in the north, Peláez could not gain a great deal of allegiance beyond his *patria chica,* his "little homeland" in the southern fields. As we have seen, he did not espouse a program (protection of property and the foreign interests) that had much appeal in other areas. Only the *felicistas,* sometimes operating in southern Veracruz, indicated interest in the Peláez program. Félix Díaz, however, always considered that he had rank on the younger Peláez. The two caudillos corresponded. They negotiated, bartered, and planned for the Díaz forces to land on the coast and join with those of Peláez. Constitutionalist gunboats dissuaded Díaz. Rebel leaders wanted arms and ammunitions from Peláez, but he offered them only money, which, of course, was acceptable. Among the anti-Carranza generals of the Eastern Sierras and Gulf Coast, who conferred together in October 1916, Peláez became know as *El rey de papel,* the King of Paper, the banker.[71]

Despite sharing their common hatred of Carranza, Peláez did not get on with those other anti-Constitutionalists who entered his territory. Early in June 1917, a *villista* band numbering eight hundred men, lead by a Colonel Reyes, mounted a raid on the oil districts, passing through *pelaecista* turf and collecting forced loans at Potrero, Alamo, and Papantla.[72] Peláez would have nothing to do with allies tapping his financial resources. Soon thereafter, his old leader, Félix Díaz, brought two hundred of his men to Tierra Amarilla. The British consul heard that Díaz had requested to be given command of the Huasteca. When the rebellion placed Díaz in the presidency, he then would allow Peláez to be in charge of the entire oil district from Furbero to El Ebano. Peláez reported later that they had come to no agreement, and Díaz withdrew his troops.[73] The money that the "King of Paper" had once been sending Díaz was now withheld. In the final analysis, Peláez did not find any particular advantage to serving as financier to a decrepit *felicista* movement.

His later alliances were much the same—informal, uncoordinated affairs with other anti-Carranza rebels, most of whom had radically different programs. In November of 1917, Peláez concluded an agreement to affiliate with the Cedillo brothers, the land-reforming caudillos of San Luis Potosí. The Cedillos' area of operations began just west of El Ebano. Curiously, the more traditional caudillos of that region, like the De Los Santos and Lárragas, with whom Peláez should have had an ideological affinity, joined the Constitutionalist movement. The popular caudillos such as Saturnino Cedillo joined with Villa. In contrast to Peláez, Cedillo ran a very Spartan operation.[74] Between the *cedillistas* and *pelaecistas* were many *carrancistas,* so that these first two groups promised to fight the third. Ideological differences were ignored.

Alliances between local, independent guerrilla chieftains being a sometime kind of thing, Manuel Peláez exaggerated more than a little in his 1918 manifesto. He claimed then to be the recognized leader of thirty-nine different generals in eastern Mexico, commanding 30,450 troops called the "National Guard." Most of the leaders were definitely of the second rank among the pantheon of the Mexican Revolution. General Meixueiro had the largest contingent of troops, five thousand; Peláez claimed four thousand, and the other thirty-seven generals commanded fewer than six hundred men each. This idea of a national guard led by Peláez expanded (mostly in the mind of the commander himself) in 1919. In a letter to President Wilson denouncing Carranza, Peláez boasted of having another former leader, Pancho Villa, under his command, as well as Felipe de Angeles, the *zapatista* Gildardo Magaña,

Meixueiro, and Félix Díaz. The document praised the Constitution of 1857 and liberty and property and urged Wilson to cast Carranza aside and favor Peláez's National Guard.[75]

This *zapatista* alliance too was a bit of a fiction. Emiliano Zapata had declined to join Peláez in 1918 when the latter, through intermediaries in Puebla, had promised to obtain the recognition and a sizable loan from "the White House." But Zapata had been assassinated in April 1919, and Peláez attempted to pick up the pieces. In vain did he offer finances for alliances to several surviving Zapatista chiefs.[76] At this time, Peláez, having been unsuccessful in the field, was actively seeking that the United States lift the arms embargo it had imposed on everyone but Carranza.

A Neutrality Perfect as Possible

Peláez had made himself a fact of life in the oil zones. The question now before the oilmen and their home governments was "What are we going to do about it?" In general, the debate centered on whether to support Peláez or the Constitutionalist government. Among those wishing to support Peláez, there remained specific questions about what kind of support: money, arms, or military intervention? Those actively involved in the debate included the governments of Great Britain and the United States, the top executives of the foreign oil companies, and the local field managers. But we have already seen the great difficulties of fashioning any kind of policy for the foreign interests. The companies themselves were competitive; the U.S. government had a general policy toward the Mexican Revolution that irked the American oil companies; and the British policy of nonrecognition of Carranza differed from that of the United States and the major British oil interest in Mexico. The number of options available and the number of persons concerned, each from their own perspective, endangered the formation of a coherent policy. What resulted was a perfect muddle.

The arrival of Gen. Manuel Peláez on the Mexican revolutionary scene both delighted and consternated the British. On the one hand, the diplomatic community was happy that there existed a challenge to Carranza, at least in the oil zone. His Majesty's Government wished no cessation of oil supplies needed for the war effort and worried that the

Constitutionalists might shut down the industry in order to enforce Article 27. On the other hand, Lord Cowdray and the managers of El Aguila found themselves bankrolling the Peláez movement and having to live daily with military activity among the oil wells. Between the two British perspectives, there developed one shared conclusion: that foreign military invasion of the oil zone would be a disaster. Right away the British eliminated any talk of a U.S. or a British military operation. "The danger to the oil fields has long been known," observed one diplomat at the Foreign Office,

> but no one has devised any means of safeguarding them as they could easily be destroyed long before an expeditionary force or land party could drive off the local Mexican forces. The oil district is even now the scene of constant skirmishes between the followers of Villa & Carranza & other stray freebooters. The oil companies have done the best they can do to avert danger by means of arrangements with the local leaders.[77]

Besides, there was doubt about whether Peláez could be relied upon to protect British subjects. In 1916, when there appeared a danger of U.S. invasion during the Pershing expedition, Peláez had told British citizens they would have to leave. He could not guarantee their safety even from his own men. Anyway, the British armies just at that moment were engaged elsewhere, and the Americans did not seem to favor a military solution, although they did have contingency plans. Indeed, J. B. Body of El Aguila had conferred with the American State Department about invasion plans. If the Americans were going to intervene militarily, he wanted to make sure they knew where El Aguila's wells were located. Body only hoped that Peláez could hold his men in check and not allow them to "run amuck."[78] As far as the British were concerned, an armed invasion to protect the oil fields was quite undesirable.

The second issue concerned money; that is, whether to commit British resources to support Peláez. If yes, the Foreign Office would have to secure the permission and cooperation of the Exchequer, involving another participant in the decision making.[79] Among the diplomats, there was much support for this. But Lord Cowdray reminded them that providing Peláez with money would be a waste of British resources. He said that El Aguila was already subsidizing Peláez but that it had yielded no protection at all. Constitutionalist forces still passed through his oil camps at will.[80]

In the final analysis, Lord Cowdray came to loggerheads with his own diplomatic representatives over the very idea of a pro-Peláez policy. Cowdray told his friends at the Foreign Office that he would be pleased if the *pelaecistas* retired from the field, as the military uncertainties among the oil wells would be very much relieved. Moreover, Cowdray held out for British recognition of the Carranza government. The diplomats were quite defensive about the idea. They regarded recognition of the Mexican government as a provocation toward Peláez. "I hope Lord Cowdray realizes that if we recognize Carranza we shall have to regard Pelaez as a rebel and withdraw our support for him," said one British diplomat. "Lord Cowdray's cure is recognition of Carranza," replied another.[81] In the end, the Foreign Office realized the difficulties of a pro-Peláez policy: The United States would have to abandon Carranza; Villa must survive in the north of Mexico; Peláez would need "large reinforcements of men"; he would need more munitions; and it would be bad policy to allow the oil company to be involved in an antigovernment movement.[82] What about the British government simply providing arms to Peláez, independent of the companies and the United States? It was an idea that intrigued many a diplomat.

Under the circumstances, was the British import of arms to Mexico possible? Many Mexicans believed it was not only possible but certain that El Aguila and the British government were supplying the Peláez rebellion with arms. Every Constitutionalist commander who could not subdue the *pelaecistas* insisted that El Aguila, in particular, was helping the opposition.[83] In fact, no one knew better the difficulty of getting arms to Peláez than the oil companies. Certainly, arms could not be shipped to the Huasteca just like any piece of equipment: offloaded on freight ships, transported on motor launches through the Tamiahua lagoon, then transferred to the company railway at La Peña. "Notwithstanding the fact that each Bill of Lading is approved by the authorities at [Tampico] before the material leaves," said Body, "it is held up by the local and state authorities at various other points when it enters the State of Vera Cruz."[84] But the British government still explored the possibilities of sending arms to Peláez.

The *pelaecista* foreign policy, simple as it was, was achieving its desired results—or nearly so. Peláez professed himself a devout Ally, persecuted the Germans, and in 1917, played on the heightened fear of German sabotage. Provide me with arms, he said, and the Allies can be assured of oil supplies. Following the interception of the Zimmerman telegram, which suggested a possible alliance between Imperial Germany and Carranza, plans to supply arms to Peláez were actively discussed. Harold Walker of Huasteca expressed some sympathy with the idea, as did Thomas B. Hohler, British chargé d'affaires in Washington. The Foreign Office liked the prospect because it would be the perfect alternative to a U.S. military invasion, which they considered a plan fraught with "great difficulties." When U.S. diplomats suggested that more arms ought to be sent to Carranza to control Mexican banditry, Sir Cecil Spring-Rice, the British ambassador in Washington, D.C., replied, "Perhaps Pelaez had better be allowed to have some too."[85] But El Aguila's Body looked askance on the proposal and considered Walker "absolutely untrustworthy." Cowdray too was dubious. "[If] we were to supply arms to an unsuccessful revolution, not even a British Government could save us," he commented. "We can supply money and that under duresse [sic]. The Americans can do this, as, for them, it does not infringe [on] the Monroe doctrine, also the Americans can probably buy arms, whereas we cannot." Even the British diplomats understood that the Americans had to cooperate in the providing of arms to Peláez.[86]

Finally, after years of inaction, the Foreign Office came to a tortured decision, but not until after the European war was over and concerns for oil supplies greatly diminished. The British government decided that the most prudent policy would be *not* to supply weapons to any Mexican faction. "To send arms to Mexico is merely to add fuel to the fire and it seems a very mistaken policy on the part of the U.S. [to supply arms to Carranza]."[87] In the end, the British formulated no policy toward the Peláez rebellion worthy of the name. In their indecision, divergences of opinion, and inability to help, the British left it up to the United States to handle Peláez.

Did the Americans, in fact, do so? The rebellion in the oil zone also evoked discussion between and among American oilmen and diplomats about what their policy toward Peláez should be. There was also a sharp division of opinion among Americans—only in reverse order from the British. The Wilson administration favored the Carranza government, and the oilmen did not. That made a coordinated, effective policy toward Peláez rather problematic to fashion, let alone implement.

There did exist, however, a contingency plan for the U.S. military occupation of the oil zone. If few Americans wished to use the plan, at least they agreed about what went into it. The oilman and the Wilson administration, especially after the American entry into World War I, shared an equal concern for the continuation of oil supplies. U.S. warships patrolled the Gulf Coast, hovering about the mouths of the Tuxpan and Pánuco rivers. During the Pershing expedition, the warships were the only use of force contemplated, and then only if necessary to rescue the 2,200 Americans in Tampico and the oil fields. Military and diplomatic planners relied on Peláez not to destroy the oil fields. The

State Department justified the lack of plans for an invasion by stating that there was a shortage of marines, who were then occupying the Dominican Republic and Haiti.[88]

Once the United States entered the world war, planning for the security of the Mexican oil fields became more aggressive. Leon Canova of the State Department proposed a military plan having several torpedo boats and destroyers patrolling the coast with enough marines on board to land quickly at both ports and to provide arms for the "loyal" oil workers. Meanwhile, a force of six thousand army troops were to stand by at Corpus Christi to occupy the oil fields, if necessary.[89] Of course, there were some complications. One had to do with the length of time between the initial landing and the actual securing of the oil wells by American troops. Some nervous oilmen and military men suggested that to prevent destruction of the oil fields, the operation had to be completed within two days. The American consul at Tampico said, "If the [Carranza] forces should, unexpectedly, defeat and disperse Pelaez' forces and regain full control of the Huasteca oil fields, the risk of huge damage and loss from willful destruction would be tremendously increased in case of war or intervention."[90]

By 1918, a comprehensive invasion plan was in hand. It called for 207 officers and 5,356 men to be transported to the Gulf Coast on the steam tankers of the oil companies. They were to locate, secure, and hold twenty different objectives throughout the entire oil region, rendering protection to the 2,500 Americans and the approximately 4,000 other foreign residents there.[91] The mere fact of having an invasion plan does not, however, indicate a propensity—or even a remote desire—to use it. Like England, the United States after 1917 had become preoccupied with deploying its troops in France, not Mexico.

That being the case, what planning was made for less drastic measures such as supplying money and arms? These questions provoked conflict between the American oilmen and their home government. For the most part, the Wilson administration clung steadfastly to its policy of supporting Carranza. The British Foreign Office was particularly distressed by the United States' lifting of its embargo on arms shipments to the Constitutionalist government, while still preventing arms shipments to the *villistas* and the *pelaecistas*.[92] The American ambassador to Mexico, Fletcher, had the reply for those who protested the U.S. arms policy. "[I]t was difficult on one hand continually to be asking [the] Mexican Government to protect life and property [which the ambassador had been doing on behalf of the oil companies]," he said, "and on the other to refuse to supply the means of their doing so."[93] In fact, the State Department had always been very careful not to advise the oil companies, at least in an official manner, whether or not they should pay tribute to Peláez. Of course, American diplomats passed along the protests of oilmen, but they scrupulously refused to know the exact amount of these forced loans and who was paying whom.[94] There may have been many different tendencies in U.S. policy toward Mexico—such as aloofness, condescension, occasional disapproval, even disinterest. But support for Peláez was not one of them.

It has already been established that American oilmen—unlike Lord Cowdray—disagreed with the administration's pro-Carranza policy. Does that mean they actually supported Peláez in ways that went beyond the involuntary financial contributions? Never mind their preferences, for they plainly preferred Peláez to Carranza. But in terms of actions, did American oilmen violate the U.S. embargo and send arms to Peláez, as many Constitutionalists had claimed? The American oilmen constantly denied that they aided Peláez with more arms and money than he extorted from them. Doheny admitted that his company had come under pressure, probably from brother Ignacio Peláez, to deliver arms to the rebels in December 1917, when the U.S. government provided Carranza with more arms. "[The company] did not then, it did not before, it has not subsequently ever delivered arms or munitions of any sort to forces in rebellion against the Carranza Government," he told a congressional panel in 1919. Nor had any other company, so far as Doheny knew.[95] The danger of supplying arms to one political faction in the Mexican Revolution was obvious. "From the time General Aguilar occupied Casiano," said Doheny, "its producing fields and its terminal have been controlled by opposing armed factions. It has had to satisfy the exigencies of both, maintaining a neutrality perfect as possible; and it has never in any way favored either side."[96]

Doheny and other executives of the Huasteca Petroleum Company objected strenuously to the U.S. policy of providing arms to Carranza. For one thing, the American oilmen believed that Peláez would take great exception to the U.S. policy, even to the point of increasing his pressure on them—perhaps giving him an excuse for imposing even higher "taxes." They feared that the *pelaecistas* might interrupt the oil supply. Besides, complained Harold Walker, "Peláez has been the friend of Americans from the start. We have never had an American associate even shot at by a Pelaez soldier in the Jungle."[97] Doheny stated that his company opposed the sending of any arms to Mexico, because the fighting threatened harm to Americans there. "[W]e have always opposed sending any arms to any faction in Mexico, so far as our opinion has been asked."[98]

Once again, in the public debate over U.S. policy toward Mexico and Peláez, there was a right and left bank to the mainstream view of Doheny and the oil producers' association. Critics such as Samuel Guy Inman, a missionary, denounced Huasteca and other companies for giving tribute to Peláez, even if under duress. Inman said that Carranza most certainly would have been able to take command of the oil fields, if the companies had not supported Peláez. On the other bank stood William F. Buckley, conservative gadfly of the big U.S. companies. "They are paying Pelaez, not because they want to but because Pelaez compels them to," Buckley said. "Pelaez has given them protection . . . but nevertheless, they are so shortsighted that he has to force them to give him the money to support his troops."[99] Considering the division and acrimony between diplomats and oilmen, it is not surprising that the foreign powers could neither formulate nor implement a pro-Peláez policy. Consequently, the day-to-day relations with the *pelaecista* movement came to be the exclusive work of the managers in the field. We know the local managers had been characteristically interventionist and many had developed colonialist mentalities. Did this mean that the local rebellion, at least, might expect a measure of decentralized assistance from the companies?

For sure, the Americans in the field preferred Peláez to Carranza. American drillers, for example, felt safer with the disciplined, well-paid *pelaecistas* than with the protection of the poorly paid Constitutionalist troops. Peláez may have been a bandit, they said, but he forced his followers to respect agreements with the oil companies. "If some of his men seize provisions or other property," reported some field managers, "he makes due settlement later and if they have acted contrary to his orders he inflicts immediate punishment upon them."[100] Top executives like J. B. Body of El Aguila avoided coming into Peláez territory, for fear either of offending the Constitutionalists by talking to Peláez or of offending Peláez by refusing to see him. The local managers, therefore, carried on the day-to-day task of dealing with their local military chief and his rivals. Even the British government realized that, barring U.S. support, the oil company field managers would have to take care of protecting themselves.[101]

Just as the oil companies, by their very presence, were involved in national politics, so were the local managers involved in regional political affairs. Foreign managers possessed scarce resources, after all.

Both the Constitutionalists and the *pelaecistas* made accusations against the oilmen, if only to keep them pliant and on the defensive. The Constitutionalists never wavered from their charges that the oilmen in the field were supporting the rebels with arms as well as money. It was a standard tactic, evidently, and one that Peláez could not resist using when the occasion demanded. He too found it convenient to play off the companies against each other. He would browbeat one firm and praise the other, then reverse the order when it pleased him.

General Peláez, at least, was shrewd enough not to allow foreign interests to gain advantage from within his ranks. In the fall of 1917, Peláez purged from his ranks a man who had helped him draft his first political pronouncements, Dr. Camilo Enríquez. The apparent reason: an article that appeared in the *Saturday Evening Post*. Playing upon the fear of German sabotage in 1917, the *Post* had sent reporter Carl W. Ackerman to do a series of pieces on the oil industry at Tampico. Ackerman's portrait of Peláez, a man he had not met, was most unflattering. He called the rebel chief "an ignorant Mexican rancher," an "unlimited monarch." If Ackerman did write something positive about Peláez, it was that he had "a teachable mind." On the other hand, Dr. Enríquez was said to be "the so-called brains of the Pelaez Government because he is the only educated man on the rebel leader's staff." Ackerman credited Enríquez, a Tuxpan druggist who had been driven to revolt after being burned out by the Constitutionalists, with being the one who taught Peláez how to collect monthly taxes from the companies.[102] For his story on the oil zone, Ackerman had interviewed Enríquez himself and several unnamed oil managers.

Peláez's reaction was swift and thorough: he banished his subordinate from the Huasteca Veracruzana. The rebel *cabecilla* gave up his plans to install Enríquez in the governorship of the state, a post the druggist's father had once held. He also blamed the oil managers of Huasteca for having planted the story. "I harbour no ill feeling against Green and Galvan of the Huasteca Co. or against the Co. itself," he told the British consul at Tuxpan, "and they can consider me a rough uneducated 'Ranchero' or what they please as I am satisfied that my actions will bear the strictest investigation. After the Ackerman articles in the Saturday Evening Post inspired by that Co. and the way in which they treated Dr. Enriquez, nothing was left to me but to get rid of him and I have told him that he must leave my District."[103] Rumors suddenly spread in the southern fields that Enríquez was plotting with Félix Díaz to ambush William Green. Quite obviously, Peláez himself had started the rumors. From this point onward, he harbored a personal grudge against Green.[104] Yet, El Aguila gained little advantage from Huasteca's involvement in the breach between Peláez and Enríquez. Peláez warned the British not to have any delusions about their alleged hold on him. When he gained good control of the district, Peláez said, he would present El Aguila a heavy bill for damages.[105] Like a whirlpool, political rivalries sucked everything, even the powerful oil companies, into its vortex.

The domestic political intensity enhanced the critical role of the local managers in the companies' affairs. El Aguila and Huasteca each devised a policy toward the Peláez rebellion that gave the local managers the widest possible latitude in handling the rivalry between Constitutionalists and *pelaecistas*. The only instructions were to save the wells and to pay as little as possible. Although Lord Cowdray might have counseled the recognition of Carranza among diplomatic circles, Vaughan at the Potrero camp and Jacobsen at Tampico were repairing water lines and paying *pelaecista* agents as little as possible to keep them from being cut again. While Doheny spent time at the congressional hearings, Huasteca's William Green was repairing railway bridges and attempting to prevent the Constitutionalist forces from entering the oil zone—sometimes even successfully. There is one curious outcome of this policy. Each company maintained the strictest secrecy about its dealings with the Mexican combatants. The cooperation and united front that the oil producers' association was attempting to construct at the executive level did not have a parallel among local managers. All the managers dealt with Peláez in an *ad hoc,* one-on-one fashion. And Peláez preferred it that way.

Peláez's nemesis, William Green, the untutored but sharp-witted manager of Huasteca, became something of a master at oil-camp diplomacy, although it was clear that the Mexicans determined the unfolding of events and the managers merely reacted. Green was close to his employees. He said that he preferred visiting his oil camps often, despite the danger of marauding troops, because he thought "my presence lends moral support to employes who feel nervous."[106] Numerous foreigners in Tampico and Tuxpan considered Green something of a loose cannon. The British consul accused him of angling for a U.S. military invasion and even for serving as Peláez's financial adviser in his business deals in New York and Los Angeles.[107] The Constitutionalists also suspected Green. General Diéguez was convinced that he provided Peláez with arms and in January 1918 considered having Green arrested. In the meantime, while assuring the Constitutionalist commander that no arms were getting through to Peláez, the U.S. naval commander at Tampico called Green a "trickster" who was not otherwise to be believed.[108] Obviously, not everyone agreed with Green's tactics.

On the other hand, William Green was not in a profession for the faint of heart. When the military competition in the oil zone was intensified, as in 1918, Green found himself spending more time placating the Constitutionalists and dealing with Peláez's demands. Green's personal meeting with Peláez elicited a promise that the *pelaecistas* would stop cutting the water pipes.[109] Nonetheless, the disruption continued. The *pelaecistas* returned and threatened to shoot the Huasteca pump man, named Pritchard, if he started the water again. Frustrated, Green contacted General Caballero, the Constitutionalist commander, requesting that he garrison the pump station with enough men to prevent the disruptions of the *pelaecistas*. Green feared that if the oil pipeline were shut down for longer than twenty-four hours, the flow from Huasteca's giant well, Casiano No. 7, would have to be released onto the ground. No sooner had the Constitutionalists under General Lárraga arrived at Tancochín camp, than seven men deserted. They traveled to the Casiano camp and robbed the cashier of five thousand pesos. The incident forced Green to return to Casiano and request Colonel Melgoza, commander of the Santa María Indians, to apprehend the deserters. Melgoza was shown where the men were hiding, but he refused to go after them. Once again, the *pelaecistas* made off with pump parts, and Green gave up on the protection of government troops. Green determined to deal directly with Peláez.

Going to El Aguila's terminal station at La Peña, Green telephoned directly to Peláez and arranged to meet him at the El Aguila camp at Tanhuijo. Peláez denied ordering his troops to cut the water line or burn railway bridges, for that matter. Many among his followers, however, Peláez told Green, had hoped to provoke the United States into invading the oil zone and scattering the Constitutionalist forces. Green informed him that the U.S. government was not likely to invade; it would instead furnish Carranza with enough arms for his men to defeat Peláez. The rebel leader replied coolly that Green had better stay in Tampico for the time being. He believed that Constitutionalist troops might shoot Green "from the bush" and blame it on his men.[110] Preoccupied by these political maneuvers, Green admitted "that the work has not been occupying my mind much lately."[111] So was the affair of the pump station's water line cleared up?

It was not. Back in Tampico, Green received word that the *pelaecis-tas,* under orders from their chief, had disabled the pump station once again. This time, they removed the pipe in the water line at ten different places and prevented the Huasteca crews from fixing it. Green immediately dropped everything, went over to the El Aguila headquarters, and called Peláez at Tierra Amarilla. Peláez evaded Green's complaints and asked him about the "other proposition," the *pelaecista* demand for a fifty-thousand-peso loan. Green told him he was ready to deal, and they agreed to meet again at Tanhuijo. In the meanwhile, Green had been improving his relationship with the Constitutionalist commanders. "There have been no threats of hanging and no insults offered myself or my men for the last couple of weeks," said Green, "and they are more considerate regarding our launches, at least lately they do not demand them at the point of a pistol."[112] Green was selling the Constitutionalists commissary goods at Casiano, which was preferable to their stealing them. With the proceeds, his camp paymasters paid the workers, saving the inconvenience of sending the payroll through the Chijol Canal, where it was frequently held up. Meanwhile, Green needed the cooperation of the Constitutionalist commanders to pass through the checkpoints on his way to meet Peláez, which he obtained by promising not to report General Acosta to his superiors for not having been able to protect the water lines.[113]

Huasteca's William Green negotiated like Metternich and made intricate deals worthy of Bismarck. Although few of his compacts ever stuck for long, he did succeed in "Keeping the Oil Flowing" for the war effort. "Huasteca employees have been practically free of all abuse," Green wrote to Wylie. "I have tried to keep my time honored position on the fence as regards participation in the affairs of the different factions, and I have had to play to both sides as conditions seemed to dictate. I have gone to the extent of conniving with bandits not belonging to either side to avoid the troubles experienced by most companies." Green's problems, perhaps solved for a few months, would crop up again anytime government troops entered the southern fields in force. When fresh troops arrived in September 1918, Peláez once again cut the telephone lines, burned the railway bridges, and broke up the water lines.[114] The *pelaecistas* needed extra money whenever the Constitutionalists threatened.

While handling the emergency of 1918, when Constitutional troops invaded the southern fields, Green finally began to coordinate local policy with Jacobsen of El Aguila. They conferred together nearly by accident, while Green was at El Aguila's Tampico headquarters, phoning

Peláez about the fifty-thousand-peso advance. At any rate, the telephone call gave Jacobsen and Green an opportunity to break their code of silence. Here is Green's description of the chance meeting with El Aguila's Jacobsen:

> I pointed out that we ought to act together in this case, and stated that it would be easy enough for Pelaez to tell me that the Aguila had paid the full amount, which would leave me without an argument, and if he could do the same to me, the same argument could be put to the Aguila; in other words, that he could play one company gainst the other . . . but if we went together and put up a bold front and told him we were authorized to do only so much, I was sure we could bring Pelaez to time. In answer to Jacobsen's questions as to why I was interested in knowing what they did about the matter, I stated that Pelaez needs just so much money to run his business; . . . that if both companies made equal payments, the load would be divided and correspondingly light for both companies; that the Huasteca Petroleum Co. has shown itself ready to pay a reasonable insurance tax, but that we did not intend to pay for the protection afforded the Aguila and the rest of these companies; that it was the Aguila's business if they wanted to pay Pelaez any money for his personal use, but that we did not intend to allow any favor they did him in this respect to operate to our detriment; that we should come to an agreement in regard to this matter, as I did not intend to pay one five-cent piece of the recent demands of Pelaez until I knew the Aguila was paying an equal amount.
> Jacobsen . . . agreed with me regarding the stand we should make with Pelaez; that to supinely come across with the 50,000 [pesos] were nothing more or less than to invite disaster, in that if we paid without a kick, he would be convinced that all he had to do in the future was to ask for other moneys, accompanied by some threat.[115]

The experience of Green and other local managers does not lend itself to an interpretation that the local managers were enthusiastic partisans of the Peláez rebellion. Clearly, the *pelaecistas* had an independent agenda beyond the managers' control, and they extorted financial support from the foreigners. To the companies, Peláez's demands amounted to "oilmail," the disruption of pipeline operations for the purpose of collecting a second tax on the industry. Not fond of paying the first echelon of taxes to the government, these oilmen did not like the second echelon of Mexican taxation any better. No matter what Constitutionalist commanders may have said at the time, I have found no evidence that the oilmen, whether company owners or local managers, imported arms for the movement.

Then how did Peláez acquire enough to stay in the field for six years? First of all, despite the fact that the *pelaecistas* were reasonably well paid, they were not particularly well armed. A rebel group during the Mexican Revolution, however, did not have to be armed to the teeth, so to speak, to carry out guerrilla operations. This was the case of the *zapatistas* as well as the *pelaecistas*. That the government could not subdue either rebel group had more to do with the internal weaknesses of the Constitutionalists than the military effectiveness of the rebels. Esprit de corps did help, and both *zapatistas* and *pelaecistas,* despite their ideological differences, were fighting in their home territory. But government forces suffered because there was too much rivalry between Constitutionalist commanders, too much corruption among their junior officers, and too little pay for government troops.

Various foreign sources, especially American military intelligence, all emphasize the limitations of the weapons available to the Peláez rebellion. Reports estimated that his troops were armed mostly with 30–30 Winchesters and a few Mausers and that they were always short of ammunition. He had no cannon whatsoever. In 1917, facing their first serious Constitutionalist offensive, the *pelaecistas* were said to have only one-third belt of ammunition per man.[116] The British consul at Tuxpan, who often traveled through Peláez's territory, reported, "It is obvious that he has no large supply as he has no regular store, and when he travels has no ammunition mules. The few men I saw carried from 100 to 200 cartridges apiece."[117] The lack of arms certainly explains why Peláez never held terrain, why he did not wish to engage in a pitched battle, why he never mounted a sustained campaign outside *su tierra,* and why Constitutionalist forces wandered through the oil camps at will. His followers remained a lightly armed, mobile guerrilla force.

Not that Peláez had not attempted to create a more formidable force with fresh arms. He certainly had the money to do so, but his rebellion was constrained by the U.S. embargo on all factions but the *carrancistas.* The U.S. decision in 1915 to provide arms only to the Constitutionalists accounted in part for the ultimate defeat of the *villistas.*[118] The halt in the delivery of arms to Carranza in 1916 certainly contributed to giving the *pelaecistas* a reprieve. Carranza had his own munitions industry, modest as it may have been, yet the U.S. government decision of 1917 once again to permit shipments of ammunition to the government forces was a serious blow to Peláez. Given his pro-Allied and anti–Article 27 political positions, Peláez had expected U.S. and British support. He felt double-crossed and threatened the oil fields sufficiently to warrant an explanation from the State Department. The special message, delivered by George Paddleford, the Huasteca superintendent in Tampico, assured Peláez that the arms shipments to Carranza included only 2.8 million rounds of ammunition and no new weapons. Peláez could not have been mollified. The Constitutionalists immediately organized their first serious military campaign against his rebellion, with which we will deal shortly.[119] The Constitutionalists were better armed than Peláez.

The *pelaecistas* also engaged in the smuggling of arms, the exact scale of which cannot be gauged. The word was out that Peláez was prepared to pay up to five hundred dollars for one thousand cartridges of ammunition for his Winchesters, Mausers, and 45-caliber pistols. His agents wanted them dropped off at convenient locations along the Gulf Coast.[120] Brother Ignacio took leave from his legal position at El Aguila and, after the Constitutionalists had mounted their 1918 oil field campaign, traveled to Washington and New York speaking with businessmen and diplomats about Peláez's pro-Allied viewpoints and his need for arms. A sympathetic British ambassador in Washington, Sir Cecil Spring-Rice, listened intently but gave the standard diplomatic put-off: he would think the matter over most carefully.[121] Ignacio may have established contact with arms smugglers in New Orleans who had connections to the Félix Díaz movement. From 1917 to 1920, American military intelligence personnel attempted to track reputed arms shipments aboard oil tankers from New Orleans to Progreso, on the Yucatán peninsula, of all places. Carranza's agents and the Mexican newspapers too reported rumors of arms smuggling, and Mexican consuls throughout the United States reported suspicious ships to be inspected thoroughly by Mexican customs officials.[122] U.S. customs agents were able to seize twenty thousand rounds of small-arms ammunition—but no arms—early in 1920. The problem for smugglers had been that Tuxpan and Tampico were the only major ports in the oil region and both were controlled by the government. Moreover, government patrols regularly searched the small craft of fishermen along the coastline between these ports.[123]

In the final analysis, the U.S. military intelligence agents could not discover a single case of an illegal arms shipment to the Peláez forces. There was also some doubt that the arms going to Progreso were actually destined for the *pelaecistas*. "[I]t should be remembered that Peláez is in the Tampico–Vera Cruz oil districts, where he has a very poorly organized army," reported one of the U.S. agents, "while the shipments in question are destined to Progreso, the Port of Yucatan, which is 450 miles from Vera Cruz and 550 miles from Tampico by water."[124] Smuggling may not have been any answer at all to Peláez's perennial problem of arming his troops.

The steadiest and surest source of arms for the *pelaecistas* was, in fact, the enemy. Peláez was able to capture arms and ammunition by over-running small outlying garrisons, ambushing enemy patrols, and raiding towns like Tamiahua and Pánuco, which he did several times each. An ambush might catch the Constitutionalists off guard, as on one occasion in which enemy troops cut loose the ammunition packs in order to ride the pack mules to safety.[125] A brief roll call of the results of some of the *pelaecista* raids would suffice to indicate how they acquired fresh supplies. Ozuluama fell briefly to Peláez in November of 1916, yielding some fifty rifles and a quantity of ammunition. In November of 1917, his men attacked Tamiahua and took more than eighty rifles and a number of horses. Early in 1920, they attacked Ozuluama again and captured more equipment. Doheny believed that the capture of rifles and ammunition from the enemy had given Peláez enough to equip nearly three thousand men.[126]

Moreover, his access to money taken directly from the oil companies permitted Peláez to take advantage of the enemy's second major weakness—the lack of money. He bought arms and ammunition directly from poorly paid Constitutionalist soldiers and corrupt officers. Best of all, they delivered; no need for transport; no danger of interdiction. Deserters joined the *pelaecistas* with their weapons. When their pay was slow in arriving, they sold their ammunition to local inhabitants.[127] On occasion, the Constitutional officers conspired with *pelaecistas* to sell government arms and ammunition in bulk. In February 1918, government forces advanced to Casiano and engaged the *pelaecistas* in a very brief firefight. They then withdrew, abandoning whole cases of arms and ammunition, the officers exaggerating the severity of the battle to higher-ups. Thus, junior officers earned hard cash "even though a few soldiers have to be sacrificed."[128] A guerrilla leader from first to last, Peláez survived on the weaknesses of his enemy, even though he was never able to broaden his military base of operations.

Every Train Bringing a New Contingent

Nonetheless, despite chronic problems of securing arms, Peláez survived repeated Constitutionalist incursions into his guerrilla domain. Reinforced with new arms and ammunition, a succession of top Constitutionalist commanders—although never the most able,

Gen. Alvaro Obregón—mounted a series of offensives against the *pe-laecistas* beginning in October 1917. None were successful in tracking down the elusive *cabecilla* or in destroying his guerrilla forces. Neither did negotiations work. Apparently the larger political interests of the government commanders diverted their attentions from defeating Peláez. But the pressure of these military incursions brought greater strain on the oil installations and greater demands from Peláez on the resources of the producing companies. This was a desperate time of survival for Peláez, and it was not beneath him to increase the "sacrifice" of the oil companies on his behalf.

A series of campaigns began auspiciously in the fall of 1917, following Carranza's election and the delivery of U.S. ammunition to his armed forces. In September, the newspapers reported that Gen. Heriberto Jara would lead the campaign against Peláez. Instead, Jara spent his entire time in the Huasteca trying to control his unruly troops. They deserted and resorted to brigandage when government payrolls did not arrive. Rather than fight Peláez under these circumstances, Jara attempted to negotiate him into submission. Then reports circulated to the effect that Carranza's representatives had been meeting with the caudillo of the Huasteca Veracruzana. Finally, in October 1917, word arrived that Constitutionalist generals were meeting in San Luis Potosí to plan the campaign against the *pelaecistas*. The diplomatic community remained calm in the belief that neither Peláez nor Carranza wanted to destroy the oil fields.[129] Finally, General Diéguez arrived in the oil district in November, amidst the usual hoopla, accusations of oil company support for the rebellion, and predictions of a short and successful campaign. Even though Diéguez took to the field, mostly moving troops and officers up and down the coastline aboard oil company launches, word soon leaked out that the government was proposing an amnesty for Peláez. He was to give up the rebellion for a large sum of money and the government's recognition of his military rank. Peláez suspected duplicity. After all, Diéguez's commanders were surrounding Peláez's territory with troops, machine guns, and cannons.[130]

The Diéguez offensive continued into January 1918. Every time the Constitutionalist forces approached the oil camps, the Mexican workers, especially from El Aguila, abandoned their work and disappeared, Diéguez's assurances notwithstanding. Soon, it became obvious that the Constitutionalist commander preferred negotiations rather than battle with Peláez. It was said that Diéguez had been angling for Carranza's appointment as secretary of war. Nonetheless, the

Constitutionalist general, confronting Jara's old problem of the lack of discipline of underpaid soldiers, could not consummate the campaign. His Constitutionalist troops turned their hands—and their weapons— to robbery. Peláez slipped out of his hiding place in the rugged mountains astride the oil zone and raided Pánuco and Topila again. On one raid, the *pelaecistas* marched a La Corona employee through the streets of Pánuco with his neck in a noose until he paid them a ransom of one thousand pesos.[131] The attention of Diéguez, in the meanwhile, was diverted by simultaneous military actions against the *cedillistas* in San Luis Potosí and banditry in Tamaulipas.

Another military commander with additional troops and an ambition to win the Tamaulipas gubernatorial election then decided to neutralize Peláez once and for all—and thereby enhance his own political career. Gen. Luis Caballero's first act, in January 1918, was to call together the foreign oilmen and induce them to get Peláez to lay down his arms in exchange for the usual government guarantees and money. The news spread that the Constitutionalists now had six thousand men in the oil zone. Most, however, were still commanded by General Diéguez. Caballero warned the oilmen that the coming campaign might result in the loss of the lives and properties of foreigners, and—who else?—William Green volunteered to take the message to Peláez. Green was particularly concerned about the government's cannons firing into the boilers at the pump houses. Believing the oil fields in grave danger, the managers of El Aguila also decided to do all in their power to convince the *pelaecistas* to lay down their arms.[132] Peláez remained suspicious of government assurances, and the campaign continued quite desultorily. Both sides cut telephone lines in the oil zone, the *pelaecistas* stole horses from government troops near Tuxpan, some government troops deserted to Peláez, and General Acosta was reported to have confiscated cattle belonging to Peláez supporters and selling them in Tampico on his own account. Meanwhile, General Caballero expressed disagreement with a fellow Constitutional officer, Gen. Pablo González, and began to divert his attention to the Tamaulipas gubernatorial contest, in which President Carranza favored General López de Lara.[133]

The large number of government troops tended to increase the payroll robberies and the depredations in the oil zone. By now, it had become clear that Caballero and Peláez seemed to agree not to fight too hard. Some ammunition changed hands as government forces retreated here and there.[134] Caballero led six hundred troops up the Huasteca railway, requisitioning food and supplies from the companies along the way, while the *pelaecistas* were cutting the water lines and burning the railway bridges. Huasteca representatives still attempted to negotiate between Caballero and Peláez.[135] The really juicy piece of information, however, had to do with Constitutionalist politics. Caballero's bid for the governorship was faltering, and he let it be known that he might join with Peláez if he lost the election. Moreover, Caballero became annoyed that Carranza had not been sending him money for his troops. Carranza had a habit of disciplining his military commanders, or at least those out of favor, by denying them supplies. The president reportedly ordered General Caballero to return to Mexico City and Caballero refused, saying that the oil field campaign was too important. It was at this moment that Peláez was renegotiating the oil leases on his properties and making El Aguila pay dearly. Some El Aguila managers, nevertheless, were convinced that Peláez was through.[136] They of all people should have known the Constitutionalists better.

The *pelaecistas* not only held out but even counterattacked, eventually exhausting the Constitutionalist's advance. In fact, Peláez mounted a bold attack on Tampico in March. Huasteca's William Green describes the action:

> The town of Tampico is in an uproar at this moment. Yesterday at noon 350 Pelaezistas [*sic*] arrived at Tampico Alto, just about 15 kilometers from here. They gobbled up the Constitutionalist outpost at La Rivera on their way, having passed at a quarter to twelve through Garrapatas [a Huasteca pump station], where they cut the [telephone] line and told Eddie Price not to repair it until this morning, when they would send him orders. Eddie took a chance and connected the line for a few moments, and called me up to tell me what was going on. . . .
> [T]he Palaezistas have attacked Pueblo Viejo [three miles from Tampico] and . . . lively fighting is now going on. I have also been advised that another bunch of Pelaezistas passed Tankville [a Huasteca tank farm] en route to Pueblo Viejo.
> Some Government troops have been as far south as Cerro Azul. Pelaez cut the water-line again near Tancochin. Government troops have been in Casiano, and Pelaezistas stole their supplies at that camp. Government troops have headquarters in Tampico. Pelaez' men attack Pueblo Viejo, three miles south, occupy Tampico Alto, 9 miles south, and overpower the garrison at Ribera, about 11 miles south. Pelaez' headquarters are at Tierra Amarilla, to which the Aguila Oil Co. has a telephone. Cerro Azul is about six miles away. There is no frontier, no battleline, and the troops of both parties mix up in each other's territory. It is not war.[137]

The Constitutionalist campaign in the oil zone may not have been war, but it was part of a revolution in which military commanders vied among themselves for political advantage. Caballero's gubernatorial ambitions aided Peláez immeasurably in surviving the Diéguez offensive. When the Carranza government denied him the election, Caballero revolted. The catalyst was the assassination of the Tampico garrison commander, General Nafarrete (he was reputedly killed in a whorehouse by an assistant police chief). Diéguez had to divert still more troops, cavalry, artillery, and machine guns to march north and retake Ciudad Victoria from his erstwhile brother-in-arms, General Caballero. There were reports of extravagant promises of money and military assistance from Peláez to Caballero, but none was forthcoming.[138] Caballero's revolt quickly collapsed, but the *pelaecistas* in the meantime attacked the government garrison back in Saladero, killing seventeen and wounding forty-three soldiers. The guerrillas counted only seven dead. A group of seventy-five *pelaecistas* also raided several ranches in southern Tamaulipas and made off with a quantity of cattle and horses. At their wits' end, the oilmen of the northern fields complained that because of the abuses committed by both sides, they could hardly operate in the oil camps.[139]

The scene was equally chaotic in the southern fields, where Peláez traded guerrilla tit for government tat. General Acosta sacked Tierra Amarilla, the family home and headquarters of Peláez, leaving German propaganda everywhere after looting the estate. Acosta also accused El Aguila of warning the *pelaecistas* of the Constitutionalist attack, for his attack had met no resistance and captured no guerrilla fighters. At the same time, Constitutionalist troops pulled out of the southern fields, except for the coast line, and declared that the Peláez rebellion had been crushed.[140] The real truth could not be hidden. The Diéguez campaign of 1917–1918 had not succeeded because of the inability of undisciplined troops to find Peláez in the hills and because of the disruptive political ambitions of the government's commanders.

While Peláez surveyed his burned-out hacienda and the *pelaecistas* regrouped, the government tried again to regain control of the Golden Lane. General López de Lara, fresh from having been deprived of the governorship of Tamaulipas by the Caballero revolt, became the fifth general officer in charge of the oil zone in one year, all under Diéguez, now in Monterrey. López de Lara's outspoken views in favor of the government's position on Article 27 caused the foreign oilmen some jitters, but his troops committed no more than the normal amount of hold-ups. They did not chase Peláez.[141]

López de Lara also suffered from Carranza's neglect. In September 1918, he was left with only three hundred troops with which to garrison the strategic town of Tampico. Peláez decided on a second surprise invasion of this major oil port. As usual, because so many government troops were stationed along the coast, the *pelaecistas* moved north via the overland route. They took Pánuco once again, then headed east straight toward Tampico, cutting telegraph wires and tearing up railway track along the way. Genuinely alarmed, López de Lara called in additional troops, and General Diéguez soon arrived from Monterrey with some four thousand troops. Peláez withdrew his men, complaining later that he could have taken Tampico if the town had done "its part." Perhaps he was anticipating a rebellion of the *tampiqueños*, who might have been given pause by the behavior of the *pelaecistas* on numerous occasions at Pánuco. "The public pulse is just about down to normal in Tampico this morning," reported William Green, "and the gloom becomes more pronounced as the number of government soldiers in Tampico increases. Every train brings some new contingent."[142] The oilmen were gloomy because they knew well the penchant of Constitutionalist soldiers to commit depredations against their properties in the oil zone.

López de Lara now received renewed resources with which to undertake a second coordinated government offensive against Peláez. Among the troops arriving at Tampico were contingents of six hundred Yaqui Indians. The amassing of government troops might have been a propaganda operation rather than actual fact, in order to convince Peláez of the wisdom of a negotiated settlement. The reputation of the Yaquis certainly impressed Green, among others. "They say these Yaqui Indians are bad hombres and conditions might become very interesting," reported Green. "Americans, and especially the employees out in the country, have taken just about all the abuse they can stand, and if these Yaquis are any worse than the ordinary Constitutionalists I say we are in for a hoodlum holiday."[143] Yet, no battles were fought.

Instead, López de Lara sent emissaries to Peláez to negotiate a settlement. Knowing that representatives had been ambushed by one or the other side before in the oil zone, both General López de Lara and General Peláez declined to be present at the negotiations, held at a point on the road from Los Naranjos to Cerro Azul. The details of this particular negotiation merit attention, in view of Peláez's hostility to previous (and subsequent) deals and because of his constituency. The government offered Peláez the rank of general, retention of his present troops, command of the southern fields, and federal equipment and pay for his forces. For his part, Peláez was to agree to recognize the Carranza government, refrain from interfering with the enforcement of the oil decrees, and receive no additional subsidies from the oil companies. The guerrilla chieftain rejected the settlement. He refused to accept Article 27 of the 1917 Constitution.[144] Perhaps one might infer from his refusal that Peláez, in fact, was acting on the advice of the oil managers, who loathed Article 27. Such a conclusion defies logic. The struggle against Article 27 was diplomatic and political, not military. The companies suffered more from the continuation of the Peláez rebellion, in depredations and double taxation—not from his capitulation to the Constitution of 1917. Consider the oilmen's eager participation in earlier negotiations for the end of the rebellion. Peláez represented the landowners and leaseholders of the southern fields, first and foremost. Carranza's tax decrees, especially the as-yet-to-be-enforced measure taxing rent payments and royalties, would have had to be paid by these Mexican landowners too, whether large or small. Anyway, the companies' actual payments to Peláez were equal to what they would have had to pay to Carranza for the land taxes. But they did not pay Carranza, and they were forced to pay Peláez. If the oilmen really had a choice of taxmen, perhaps they would have chosen Carranza. But Peláez was not about to give them a choice; he had more important constituents to satisfy. At any rate, with negotiations at an end, the López de Lara campaign terminated with a whimper.

The government launched yet another campaign in the oil zone beginning in January 1919. General Diéguez returned personally to command and decided once again to surround the Peláez stronghold with strong garrisons in order to starve him out. Tuxpan was reinforced with two thousand government troops; San Gerónimo was guarded by five hundred men; and smaller garrisons were stationed at Ozuluama, Tampico Alto, Pueblo Viejo, Topila, El Higo, Tempal, Tantoyuca, and other locations. Even Tierra Amarilla was held for a short time. As usual, the campaign had more hype than potential, and the *pelaecistas* harassed the garrisons, capturing three machine guns at Tierra Amarilla. The Mexican government claimed its troops in the oil zone, including the Yaquis, numbered between six thousand and ten thousand men. U.S. military intelligence reports placed the real troop strength at three thousand men. The padding of muster rolls and the officers' collection of pay for fictitious soldiers accounted for the difference.[145] Meanwhile, the usual dragged-out Constitutionalist maneuvers and *pe-*

laecista raids now caused little excitement in U.S. and British diplomatic circles. The war in Europe was over, and the flow of Mexican oil no longer seemed all that strategic. "These campaigns have been of such frequent occurrence and hitherto have had so little result," noted one British diplomat, "that there seems no cause at present for undue anxiety."[146] He was right. For the oil companies, business continued in spite of the political standoff. The *carrancistas* collected taxes at the ports, and the *pelaecistas* collected their taxes at the oil camps. Yet, events outside the oil zone soon put an end to the Peláez rebellion.

On 23 April 1920, General Alvaro Obregón, the one-armed hero of the Battle of Celaya, called for an armed rebellion against the regime of President Venustiano Carranza. He happened to be on the run, but his friends at Agua Prieta drafted a political diatribe against Carranza's plan to impose his chosen successor, Ignacio Bonillas, as president in the coming national elections. Eleven months earlier, Obregón had declared himself a candidate for that job. Since then, he had been trailed by Carranza's secret service agents and dogged by summons to Mexico City courts as a witness in the trial for treason of another general. At one point, early in April, Obregón had to escape Mexico City and threats to his safety disguised as a railway worker. The problem for Carranza was that Obregón's candidacy had caught hold of the public's imagination. General Obregón was perceived as being the strong man needed to restore order to a country grown weary of ten years of rebellions, loss of life, military depredations, and economic decline. The Plan of Agua Prieta would split the Constitutionalist army. Some generals, like Diéguez and Cándido Aguila, remained loyal to Carranza, while others, such as Pablo González and Arnulfo Gómez, pledged their support for Obregón. Moreover, the remaining pockets of rebels also declared for Obregón—the *zapatistas* without their fallen leader, the *cedillistas* in San Luis Potosí, Meixueiro in Oaxaca, and Villa in the mountains of Chihuahua.

Manuel Peláez of the Huasteca Veracruzana also decided to cast his support for Alvaro Obregón. Approached by Obregón's emissaries, Peláez agreed to combine his activities with those of General Arnulfo Gómez, garrison commander at Tuxpan, and with those of the twenty-four-year-old Col. Lázaro Cárdenas, the government commander at Papantla. Obregón appointed Peláez as his commander in the oil zone. The game was afoot. Two days before the Agua Prieta declaration, Arnulfo Gómez revolted against Carranza in Tuxpan, taking the three-hundred-man Tuxpan garrison with him. Peláez was more cautious.

Waiting for Obregón's call to rebellion (and then a few days more, perhaps to see which way the political winds were blowing), the *pelaecistas* finally moved into Port Lobos on the national holiday of Cinco de Mayo. The Constitutionalist garrison there also celebrated the nation's holiday by denouncing Carranza. Peláez announced that he was the legitimate authority in the entire oil zone and that, henceforward, the oil companies would pay all their export taxes to him and not to the Constitutionalists. The oil companies now had to choose sides too. They were in a quandary whether to pay the remaining *carrancistas,* in Tampico for example, or the rebels in Port Lobos and Tuxpan. As usual, the U.S. State Department advised everyone to pay whoever had de facto control of customs.[147] The oilmen's discomfiture did not last long.

In confusion appropriate to the crisis, elements of the Tampico garrison revolted on 9 May. Gen. Pablo González, who was close by, had thrown his lot in with the *obregonistas,* although not with the decisiveness that brought Col. Carlos Orozco, the highest-ranking Constitutionalist officer in Tampico, along with him. The Tampico revolt, therefore, was led by a confused lieutenant colonel named Lucas González (no relation to Pablo). The loyal *carrancistas* under Colonel Orozco retreated to the customshouse and awaited their fate. In the meantime, Peláez contacted the lieutenant colonel to inform him he was Obregón's chosen commander in the oil zone. Peláez promoted González to general and the latter, apparently delighted, submitted to the orders of General Peláez. The foreign community received immediate assurances of its safety and property, and the two American gunboats and two destroyers sent to the Pánuco River were relieved of their obligation to remove endangered foreign citizens. The remaining Constitutionalists in the customshouse soon surrendered after their commander, Colonel Orozco, escaped aboard a departing steamer. General Pablo González arrived outside of town with one thousand men to pledge his support for the new order of things. He must have felt considerably abashed that the erstwhile bandit, Peláez, was reinforcing the garrison with seven hundred of his *pelaecistas.* A few unrepentant Constitutionalist troops looted and burned parts of Tuxpan before they cleared out, producing the only destruction of the takeover.[148] The disintegration of Carranza's control of the oil zone had proceeded rapidly and virtually without bloodshed.

The fate of Carranza himself took a bit longer, but the denouement, considered from a national standpoint, proceeded every bit as rapidly. The collapse of his regime and especially his control of the military, always a factious entity, forced Carranza to evacuate the capital. He boarded a train headed for Veracruz, where he thought of holding out once again as he had against Villa in 1914. Forces loyal to Obregón cut the train line, and Carranza and a loyal cavalry troop set off for the rugged mountains of Puebla. There, early in the morning of 21 May, in the village of Tlaxcalantongo, far from Peláez in Tampico, a band of rebels shouting "Viva Obregón!" shot up the houses where the *carrancistas* were sleeping. President Carranza died of his wounds. The rebel band had been led by an associate of Peláez (who was also a follower of Félix Díaz), Rodolfo Herrera, who was operating in the same mountains that had so often given refuge to the *pelaecistas*. Alfredo Peláez, Manuel's younger brother, had reported that Herrera had been ordered to kill the president, but he declined to say by whose orders.

Before concluding the story of Manuel Peláez, it is well to return to the original questions about the complicity of the oil companies in his rebellion against Carranza. Any assumption that the oilmen "created" the Peláez rebellion for their own ends should be laid to rest. In the first place, the rebellion in the southern fields began in November 1914, at a time when the oil companies had been looking forward to the end of turmoil. The Huerta regime had been eliminated. No matter how the oil companies may have liked Huerta's internal policies, they had not appreciated his increased taxation. General Aguilar's imposition of double taxation had already ended, as had the confusion of authority in the oil zone. Moreover, in spite of Governor Aguilar's early manifestations of economic nationalism, the Constitutionalist authorities at the national level had not yet shown themselves inclined to place restrictions on the companies. In November of 1914, the oilmen had little reason to be unhappy with the Constitutionalist regime.

At its inception, it is more likely that the Peláez revolt was a matter of a regionally conservative *serrano* reaction against the imposition of outside authority. The local inhabitants—in particular, the dominant hacendados—had reason to resist the outsiders. The region was prospering. The hacendado class was quite European in social origin and resented the exactions of the mestizo and Indian troops from the mountains and from Central Veracruz. Even to local rancheros, the Constitutionalist troops were outsiders. Late in 1914, it seemed that the Constitutionalists' presence was going to be institutionalized. Their general, Aguilar, was now governor; their troops were still in Tuxpan; and their representatives held public offices in the towns of the Huasteca Veracruzana.

But the local citizens were given an opportunity to strike back in October and November. Villa and Zapata were taking the capital, and the anti-*carrancistas* had established a rival government at Aguascalientes. Never mind that his political programs might have been anathema to the hacendados of the Huasteca Veracruzana, Pancho Villa was far off. The Constitutionalists were close at hand. A local rebellion in alliance with the *villistas,* effected at a moment when the Constitutionalists were vulnerable, had a good chance of succeeding. And success would regain that measure of autonomy that the local notables thought they had recently lost when the Constitutionalists triumphed in their territory. Therefore, Manuel Peláez, veteran rebel in the service of Madero and Félix Díaz, made himself the popular leader, the *cabecilla,* of his home region and of his dominant landowning class.

What complicity did the oil companies have in the origins of the Peláez rebellion? They happened, by chance, to be operating in his area. They were the basis of his region's prosperity, which the rebellion had hoped to protect. They had also shown themselves, as demonstrated during General Aguilar's struggle against the *huertistas,* to be an efficacious source of revenue for a rebellion. But Peláez in 1914 intended to fight over Mexican issues, on Mexican soil. He needed no more permission from the foreigners to begin his important work than did Aguilar a year earlier.

The second hypothesis of the relationship between the oilmen and Peláez has to do with their subsequent encouragement of his rebellion, even if they had not created it. Did the oilmen ultimately support the rebellion because the *pelaecistas* brought peace to the oil zone? Because they prevented the Constitutionalists from enforcing Article 27? No doubt, the reader will have noticed the several instances in which the oilmen cooperated to negotiate a settlement between various government generals and Peláez. There existed very good reason for this: the Peláez rebellion did not bring peace to the oil zone but in fact prolonged and intensified the fighting. If it had not been for the local rebellion, the bulk of the Constitutionalist army, with its regiments of Santa María and Yaqui Indians, would have settled down to the humdrum life of garrisoning Tuxpan and Tampico and the more active life of hunting down rebel *zapatistas, villistas, felicistas, cedillistas,* and dozens of other rebel groups in far-off places. Instead, reinforcements of outside troops were constantly sent through the oil zones after Peláez. Unpaid and alienated, they committed undisciplined acts; ate in the cafeterias of the oil camps; committed payroll robberies; murdered a few foreigners; chased off Mexican workers; hounded weak-kneed foreign workers out of the oil zone; commandeered oil company launches; and took animals, money, and supplies from the oil camps. Peláez himself was not innocent of such tactics. When operating outside of his home district—in the northern fields near Pánuco, for example—he looted and robbed foreigners and Mexicans as if he were a law unto himself. It is not surprising that the depredations increased when the military contest grew most intense, from mid-1917 to mid-1919. And to think that for all this the oil companies paid Peláez close to 1.5 million pesos between January 1915 and May 1920.[149]

Finally, did the Peláez rebellion prevent Carranza from enforcing Article 27 on the oil companies? The answer has to be no. When ordered, Constitutionalist troops could enter the oil camps and shut down the oil wells. If it had been in Carranza's interests to do so, he could have halted all production and export of the northern fields simply by preventing the oil barges from moving crude oil down the Pánuco River. He could have stopped production in the southern fields by closing the oil terminals in Tuxpan and Tampico. Carranza could have shut down the refineries at Minatitlán and Tampico anytime he thought expedient. The truth was simple. If Carranza could not enforce Article 27, it was because his financial straits during a time of extreme political instability did not allow him to forego oil revenues. The Peláez rebellion certainly did not prevent the government from collecting greater increments of taxes from the oil industry. Besides, Peláez made the oil companies pay additional taxes over and above the government's. The greater the government pressure on Peláez, the more the companies were forced to pay him. It is true that Peláez might not have lasted so long and cost the companies so much if they had not had the resources for his taking. The oil companies kept Peláez in the field, but they paid dearly for it—and unwillingly.

A *Pelaecista* Postscript

It will appear odd to the reader that Manuel Peláez came in out of the cold for Alvaro Obregón. After all, back in 1915, Obregón had defeated his ally, Pancho Villa, upon whom Peláez had relied to gain the local autonomy that he and his *serrano* constituents had desired. The hero of Celaya had also been present, though not actually a *constituyente,* at the Constitutional convention that wrote Article 27. Obregón supported the 1917 Constitution, while Peláez still advocated the 1857 model. Of course, if Peláez had really been the puppet of the oil companies, he would not have submitted to Obregón at all. Just what did Peláez expect to gain from this new national leader in 1920? Local autonomy. The agreement under which the *cabecilla* of the Huasteca joined the Plan of Agua Prieta was his appointment as military commander in the oil zone. Peláez had expected that such a position would make him the supreme political arbiter of the region stretching from Tampico to Furbero. And he was willing to give up all his other cherished, though shallow, political ideals to get it. Thus, in a meeting in mid-May with Alvaro Obregón, Peláez accepted the latter's national program in exchange for Obregón's (perhaps reluctant) confirmation of Peláez as zone commander. Peláez had apparently really desired the governorship of Veracruz—like his old rival, Cándido Aguilar.[150] But he did not get it.

It cannot be said that Peláez was an ardent *obregonista.* Even before he traveled to meet Obregón in mid-June 1920, he had voiced reservations about the new regime's "radicalism," which he defined not in terms of its positions on labor and agrarian reform and on economic nationalism but in terms of the appointment of non-*pelaecista* public officials in Tampico and Tuxpan.[151] Already, the zone commander was feeling some constraints on his cherished autonomy. Well he might. Unflattering articles soon began to appear in the nation's newspapers about the money that Peláez had received from the oil companies during his days as a rebel in the Huasteca. The news stories made him appear a venal tool of the foreign interests.[152] Some persons in high places wanted Peláez out of the way. In September 1920, after having faithfully collected for the government the oil taxes at the old *carrancista* levels, General Peláez took leave of his position. He traveled to San Antonio and Los Angeles for the standard political reason: he needed to seek medical attention for an old war wound. He remained in the United States and was feted everywhere he went. Chicago hailed Peláez as "the man who saved the oil industry in Mexico."

Manuel Peláez was not yet discredited with the new regime, but another *serrano* rebellion among his former followers finally vaulted him over the pale. In July 1921, Gen. Daniel Martínez Herrera revolted against the Obregón government in the old *pelaecista* districts around the Potrero del Llano. Obregón ordered Peláez from the United States to Mexico City, where the latter repudiated the rebellion, which had

Ally of the Allies

Man Who Made the Mexican Oil Fields Safe for Democracy Visits Chicago.

GEN. MANUEL PELAEZ.
[TRIBUNE Photos.]

Fig. 13. General Peláez, 1921. This photo of the *cabecilla* of the Huasteca Veracruzana appeared in the *Chicago Tribune* while Peláez toured the United States after another of his periodic retirements. His reputation was greater in the United States than in Mexico, judging from the *Tribune*'s caption. From the Albert B. Fall Collection, courtesy of the Huntington Library, San Marino, California.

embarrassingly invoked his name. Peláez told Mexican journalists that Huasteca's William Green was behind the rebellion, apparently settling a grudge with an old antagonist in the oil industry. Back in the Huasteca, after a brief flurry of taking supplies and money from The Texas Company and the International Petroleum Company, the small rebel force was quickly surrounded by loyal troops under Gen. Arnulfo Gómez. Martínez Herrera gave up, but the harm was done. No one in the Obregón regime would trust Peláez any longer as a military commander. Peláez found it expedient to head back to the United States for additional medical treatment. Obregón's agents tailed him throughout what amounted to a political exile. They linked him with a number of plots with other revolutionary castoffs. Subsequently, Peláez returned at a most inauspicious time—or perhaps he had planned it that way. Peláez moved back to his hacienda at Tierra Amarilla in time for the antigovernment rebellion of Adolfo de la Huerta in December 1923. The government forces immediately imprisoned Peláez, first in Tampico and then in Mexico City. As fate would have it, Carranza's assassin found rehabilitation in the De la Huerta revolt. Rodolfo Herrera, who had lost his military commission after killing the former president, regained his rank and pension by retaking Papantla for the government. With the rebellion subdued, Peláez gained his freedom, retiring to Tierra Amarilla and surviving into his seventies.[153] By the time he died, in 1959, the oil industry had passed from the hands of the foreign interests to the national government. But the Huasteca Veracruzana endured, and so did the dominant families of Spanish heritage that he had represented in his rebellion. Who can say that Peláez lost his struggle?

CHAPTER FIVE

Health and Social Revolution

Of the multiple forces that dictated the nature of producing and marketing oil in Mexico—markets, technology, foreign capital, diplomats, politicians, and military chiefs—the one most often neglected is the worker. What better case exists to ascertain how labor fared before the juggernaut of capitalism if not Tampico and the Golden Lane during the Great Mexican Oil Boom? Contemporaries contended that approximately 90 percent of the work force at Tampico was employed by foreigners, 70 percent by the Americans alone.[1] If capitalism molded the workers into a gray mass of dependent wage-earning proletarians anywhere in Mexico, it would be in Tampico. Here the owners controlled the labor market. Few protective laws enabled local politicos to inspect and regulate the employers. In addition, local government was weakened considerably by the continued political and military turmoil of the Revolution. A long line of military chieftains governed Tampico, most of the time with an eye toward their own survival. Was it not possible for these captains of industry, therefore, to shape the laborers in their own image: hardworking, frugal, dependent, servile, grateful, and obsequious? In short, did not the Tampico workers become a proletarianized class of semiskilled industrial workers, so dependent upon wage work for subsistence that they willingly sacrificed their labor power, at ever decreasing wages, to the owners' profits? If this could have happened anywhere in Mexico, it should have happened in Tampico.

Labor also figures in the outcome of the Revolution. Of late, some historians have tended to reduce the Mexican Revolution to a mere rebellion, because the foreign interests, in alliance with political elites, effectively subverted and "co-opted" demands for land and labor reforms. The word *co-optation* is crucial. Co-optation has come to mean the active deflation of popular demands by the adoption of token reforms and the absorption of popular leaders into the patronage system.[2] Elemental to this view of the Revolution is the assumption that the demands of Mexican peasants and workers between 1910 and 1920 were indeed revolutionary. That is, the popular classes had demanded not only the destruction of the old order, the creation of a revolutionary state, and a redistribution of property (all of which did occur) but also the conversion of the economy from capitalism to socialism. This is a large assumption, indeed.

An analysis of the oil workers at Tampico will indicate several problems with the above interpretations. First of all, to summarize what has already been demonstrated, there was little basis for an alliance between foreign capitalists and Mexican politicians. Their interests diverged more than they converged. The politicians were interested in containing social chaos and the oilmen hated tax hikes and losses of property rights. Did capital and the state disagree over taxes but still cooperate on labor matters? Did the revolutionary armies crush strikes, for example? Occasionally, yes. Most of the time, no. In Tampico, as this chapter will demonstrate, the attitude of the authorities toward workers had more to do with the state's traditional role as mediator of patron-client relationships than with preserving the capitalists' control of the labor market. Indeed, the Constitution of 1917, which reestablished the legitimacy of state mediation, worked against the companies' labor policies.

Those who worked for the oil companies were not hapless. The American workers conspired to resist the inclusion of the Mexicans into the better-paying jobs, it is true. Yet, this did not benefit the companies, which were forced to pay the foreigners higher wages. Anyway, foreign workers were not able to forestall the Mexican takeover of their jobs. Revolutionary turmoil, dangers in the countryside, and the wartime military drafts back in the States hastened the departure of American oil workers from the oil fields in Mexico. Besides, Mexican laborers had had a long tradition of resistance to proletarianization. Indian peasants and mestizo wage earners had preserved their independence and dignity by developing alternating stratagems. They moved from job to job, acquiesced to paternalism, resisted perversely, and even rebelled.[3] Both urbanization and the Revolution enabled the workers to practice old behaviors in new settings. They used traditional forms of social hierarchy to organize and to petition the state. Skilled workers formed trade unions. They assumed leadership of the unskilled in order to reinforce seniority and rank in the workplace. (On the other hand, the companies wanted to promote employees on the basis of efficient work habits, rather than seniority.) When economic conditions threatened to reduce their standard of living, Mexican workers waited for propitious moments of full employment to strike for greater security. Even though the anarchist philosophy of their leaders may have cautioned against political alliances, the workers were politically adept. They knew how to petition—even coerce—the state into taking up their cause.

Finally, were the workers of Tampico revolutionary? Even though they may not have believed entirely in socialism, they did subscribe to ancient traditions of cooperation and order among themselves. Even though few actually fought in revolutionary armies, they did take advantage of the promised social reforms. They supported those politicians who listened to their demands. Even though they may not have actively supported a massive redistribution of property, Tampico workers did demand a more equitable distribution of income. In many ways, they became more nationalistic than socialistic. Their contribution to the ideology of the Revolution had always been "Mexico for the Mexicans," not so much to take property from wealthy Mexicans and foreign owners but to take jobs from American workers. Strikes occasionally had anti-American, though seldom anti-imperialist, overtones. Nevertheless, Mexican workers seized the opportunity of revolutionary turmoil to organize, to strike, and to resist the full implications of proletarianization. Scholars may look askance on their reformism and materialism, but Mexican workers did prevent the companies from converting them into working nonentities, mere sellers of labor power, and wage slaves.[4] Perhaps this was not the revolution that some observers wish they had had, but it was a world that the *tampiqueños* worked tirelessly—and remarkably successfully—to shape. These Mexicans constructed that world, insofar as modernity made it possible, according to their ancient customs.

Refreshing Breezes and Vilest Threats

The Great Mexican Oil Boom accelerated many of those social trends that the exploration and first discoveries had set in motion during the last decade of the Porfiriato. Tampico boomed as the new center of the oil-refining business. Foreigners arrived in large numbers to lay claim to the skilled positions in an industry whose operations were conducted in the English language. Cultural and racial differences exacerbated the relationship between skilled foreigners and less-skilled Mexicans. Among the Mexicans themselves, differences existed. First-generation industrial workers, most of whom were itinerant peasants from the villages of the central plateau, did most of the unskilled lifting and hauling. They were not entirely proletarianized, because most retained some rights to subsistence in their villages. Still, the ravages of revolution, reducing peasant subsistence and mobilizing the rural population, rendered the high wages and work opportunities in the oil zone an attractive alternative. The population of this port and refining town burgeoned in an unprecedented fashion. Before the discovery of the Potrero del Llano well, Tampico was a port and rail terminal of some twenty-five thousand persons. The growth of refining and exporting swelled the population to more than seventy thousand persons by 1918.[5] The size of the city had nearly tripled in less than a decade. The largest contingent of foreigner newcomers were not, in fact, Americans but their Chinese auxiliaries. They had accompanied the new American *conquistadores,* like the sixteenth-century *naboríos* (Indian servants) who attended the Spaniards, as houseboys, cooks, and personal servants. Others became independent traders, shopkeepers, and laundry operators. The breakdown of foreigners in 1915 was as follows:[6]

Chinese	2,000
Spaniards	1,000
Americans	750
Britons	300
Germans	129
Dutch	57
Other	379
TOTAL	4,605

These foreigners owned the choice residential properties, too. Tampico hill was transformed into "neighborhoods of elegant residences where the foreign population lived, enjoying a climate refreshed by the breezes from land and sea."[7]

Migrant workers crowded into makeshift housing along the lowlands and the banks of the lagoons skirting the city of Tampico. In Arbol Grande, site of the Pierce refinery, and Doña Cecilia, site of El Aguila's refinery, workers erected shanties (*casuchas*) elevated on posts over the mud holes. Across the river, alongside the Huasteca refinery at

Mata Redonda, a sizable town of workers developed. It had its own church, market, plaza with gardens and musical kiosk, and sports fields. Closer to the refinery, the supervisory employees, most of whom were foreign, lived in "excellent homes made of wood, forming well-aligned streets and each house having a small garden."[8] The native itinerants suffered the most unhealthful conditions. In one rooming house, 57 persons lived in sixteen rooms. In another, 2,100 persons lived in thirty rooms. Those who decided to stay, allowing themselves to become pro-letarianized, undertook land invasions. Under their own leaders, they seized public and unused lands, divided up the lots among themselves, set aside land for schools, built homes with fences, and petitioned the government for private ownership. Rent was high, space scarce. Mi-grants raised chickens in the city to supplement their diets. The mor-tality rate also rose with the population. In 1910, it was 41 deaths per 1,000 persons, and in 1917, it was 66 per 1,000.[9] Little except the high wages and the expectation someday to move on made up for the un-healthful conditions of living in Tampico's slums.

Not only was the population growing by leaps and bounds through-out the course of the second decade of the twentieth century, but the commercial composition of the city was also being transformed. Petro-leum and American trade gained ascendancy over general and multina-tional commerce. In 1911, mineral and agricultural exports dominated the ships' cargoes. But revolutionary disruption of mining and espe-cially railway connections to the interior forced a decline in mineral shipments by 50 percent. "The roadways leading north and west from Tampico are in disrepair, the rolling stock worn out and grossly inad-equate to the small present day needs," reported the American consul at Tampico, "and the service pitifully bad, unreliable and expensive."[10] Plans to construct rail lines from Tampico north to Matamoros and southwest to Mexico City were abandoned. Banditry and troop depre-dations, in the meantime, disrupted local agriculture. Also, American oil tankers came into prominence in Tampico's shipping. The ore car-riers and general cargo vessels from England, Germany, and Norway arrived less frequently than before.

Meanwhile, the petroleum workers as a group rose to dominate the working class at Tampico. Of course, the oil proletarians did become quite militant. It was not because of their new positions in the export structure but because of the strong heritage of resistance, deriving from the colonial period and from previous worker action at Tam-pico.[11] The skilled workers, as much as anyone, delivered Mexican working-class traditions to Tampico. Mechanics, carpenters, and boiler workers gained their skills in the railway shops and on the trains. These skilled and semiskilled Mexicans brought with them a certain cosmopolitan outlook. They considered themselves the natural leaders of the unskilled Mexicans. The work processes of modern industry, which gave the skilled workers positions of importance in production—running the engines or commanding the valves—reinforced this preindustrial differentiation but did not originate it.

At first, the greatest demand for Mexican laborers existed in the construction trades. Clearing the brush, hauling materials and equipment, swinging machetes and shovels, and driving draft animals used many nonindustrial skills of laborers. As on the hacienda, construction peons worked day-to-day, laying off when the job was completed or when it rained.[12] They built roads, pipelines, pump stations, wharves, terminals, refineries, offices, and houses. Many oil companies secured their unskilled workers through the traditional Mexican contractor, the *enganchador*, much as the hacendados might. Eventually, foreign and national capital established contracting companies in Tampico that specialized in construction work for many oil companies. They were the Petroleum Iron Works Company of Pennsylvania, Jones and Gillegan, and House and Armstrong.

Initially, construction workers existed in Tampico in short supply. In 1913, when Huasteca, El Aguila, and Jersey Standard were constructing refineries at Mata Redonda and Villa Cecilia, wages for unskilled workers soared to 2 and 2.25 pesos per day.[13] As in harvesting wheat or shearing sheep, the peons worked in groups of ten to fifteen under the guidance of a *capataz* (foreman). Also like agricultural work, this kind of toil in Tampico was seasonal, interrupted by the rainy period. El Aguila's department of construction had a payroll that varied between 45 and 1,226 workers, with larger numbers during the dry season. Its regular work force in 1917 was 698 persons, and they worked under the *tarea* (piecework) system as did the first mining workers of the 1880s.[14] Since most of these construction workers were itinerant peasants, there was no loss of skill here. Artisans and skilled workers did not have to take up the unskilled positions. The demand for skilled workers elsewhere in the industry was great enough to prevent veterans of railway and mine work, the real proletarians of Mexico, from having to do the unskilled work. The construction industry hired carpenters and mechanics, as did the marine transport companies and port works. Brickmakers and masons found work in the construction of pump houses and refineries. The wages of the mechanic rose from 2.50 pesos in 1907 to 7 pesos per day in 1914, because the demand was strong.[15]

These skilled workers were the first to organize trade unions. By 1910, the intrepid Mexican railway workers and office workers had established a Tampico branch of the Gran Liga Mexicana de Empleados de los Ferrocarriles. Skilled laborers organized into small groupings among the stevedores in 1911, marine workers in 1913, the laminated iron workers and bank and commercial employees in 1914. As they organized in 1911 and 1912 into a 720-member union, the Gremio Unido de Alijadores harbored great bitterness toward foreigners. Their communiqués "contained vilest threats expressed in the vilest language and stated that if the Americans did not leave this port within twelve hours they would be attacked on March 16 at 4 P.M."[16] The first unions were organized around the trades, cutting across the industries. There were *sindicatos* of carpenters (with 460 members), bricklayers (370), pilots (*paileros*) (320), journeymen (*jornaleros*) (533), and various occupations like clerk (542). Together, these early groups scored some nationalistic victories for themselves. When Casa Rowley, the monopoly freight contractor at the port, brought in West Indian workers to break the Mexican longshoremen's strike in 1911, the latter used nationalism to garner support from fellow power-and-light workers employed by another North American company. Together they won a victory over foreign workers.[17] West Indians, if not Chinese workers, disappeared from the Tampico environment.

In time, these first trade unions federated within their industries to form industrial unions. This was not the idea of the workers in the export industries themselves. It was suggested to them by representatives of the Mexico City labor confederation known as the Casa del Obrero Mundial. These *capitalino* labor organizers had arrived in Tampico in 1915 as elements of the famous Red Battalions, the armed labor contingents that had joined the Constitutionalist cause in 1914, shortly before the peasant armies of Zapata and Villa occupied the capital. As the political influence of the Constitutionalists spread, so did that of the Casa. Urban workers evidently felt little kinship with the peasant revolutionaries. However, their leaders did appreciate their own mission, like that of the Constitutionalist government, to spread their hegemonic influence over the peripheral industrial areas.[18] In the process of Mexican labor organization, the urban skilled workers of Mexico City, the traditional seat of Mexican artisanship and labor hierarchy, spread their influence over the outlying industrial areas.

Workers of Excitable Temperaments

What were the attitude and policies of the foreign employers toward the workers? They were not, after all, like traditional landowning *patrones*. For the most part, company managers treated their workers as any other factor of production: they attempted to control expenses and increase and decrease employment according to demand. Two factors prevented the companies from totally mercenary actions in this regard. They had to take care of their best workers and pay relatively high wages; the growth of the industry made good steady workers a scarce commodity. American managers appreciated the abilities and loyalty of some of the longest-employed Mexican workers. The former manager of the Huasteca topping plant at Tampico admired those who had worked for the company for twenty years. "They [still] need the steadying hand of the American to direct them," he said, "but otherwise there was little to be said against them before the revolution."[19]

But others did not trust the Mexicans. At the El Aguila refinery in Tampico, which employed approximately six hundred men in 1918, the managers regarded the Mexican workmen as dishonest. Only Englishmen and Americans were in charge. "On the whole the management felt no particular obligation toward the workmen," reported an American observer. "[The managers'] main purpose was to make the company pay."[20] The first companies in Mexico had used local authorities to instill labor discipline at their installations. During the Porfiriato, it was common for the companies to acquire the services of the rural police or company policemen appointed by the local *jefe político*. The objective was to prevent the men from drinking on the job; the managers claimed that Mexicans who drank on the job became unruly, surly, and unproductive.[21] Once the Revolution began, however, the use of company police, aside from the watchmen, was not possible. The new governments disapproved.

Oil companies paid high wages during the full employment era of the Great Mexican Oil Boom. But once committed to wages at certain levels, employers were reluctant to increase the pay at the demand of their workers. During the First World War, as we shall see, the workers suffered from the rising cost of living. Were the companies willing to raise wages to offset these price raises? Not at all. Lord Cowdray was probably typical of the other owners. He did not want to raise wages, despite labor's increased suffering, because giving in to demands for higher wages, he said, would only encourage further demands. Cowdray did not believe that he could increase wages, "for the simple reason that wages once increased cannot, in all probability, be lowered."[22] Instead, he preferred to provide a kind of social assistance, in the form of a company store that provided food and clothing below cost. Huasteca was doing the same.[23] In this way, wages would not have to be readjusted later, costing the companies some of their absolute control of the terms of employment.

It was largely to secure workers and not necessarily to pay them more that the companies also undertook additional paternalistic practices. At the Minatitlán refinery of El Aguila, more isolated than the Tampico works and not serviced by a rail line to Mexico City, pay and material standards may have fallen below the level of Tampico. Nonetheless, the demand for labor was quite high. An El Aguila manager, in May 1920, was still bringing as many as 150 workers at a time down from Mexico City. He paid for their transport from the capital by rail to Veracruz, thence by launch to the isthmus. If the climate at Minatitlán was not agreeable to them, he promised to pay their return fare.[24] Foreign oil companies also provided motion pictures; instituted employee savings plans; and furnished housing, medical facilities, and primary schooling for the children of some Mexican workers. The Huasteca terminal and refinery at Mata Redonda provided two- and three-room cottages to native workers but mostly to the "better class of mechanics" rather than "the common peons." The former were more difficult to secure than the latter.[25] The skilled Mexicans lived better than the peons. Both were separated from each other as well as from the much more privileged foreign workers, whose housing, provided by the companies, was far superior. In 1918, during a time of much labor unrest, Huasteca finally built a schoolhouse for the children of its Mexican workers. It hired and paid for three teachers. "So far the work in this school extends only to the first two years of the ordinary course with a few classes belonging to the third grade," observed an American visitor. "Ultimately [the head teacher] plans to have the four grades of the elementary primary with some work in gardening and manual training."[26]

Most large companies also hired nurses and even doctors, Americans and Mexicans. El Aguila's refinery had an extensive medical facility, yet provided separate care for foreign employees, another facility for Mexican skilled workers (*mecánicos, carpinteros,* and *rayadores de tiempo*), and a third for unskilled workers. The 328 patients (out of 900 total employees at the refinery) passing through the clinic during July 1919 were treated for these maladies:[27]

Malaria	80 patients
Minor infection	38
Bronchial inflammation	35
Minor injuries	33
Gassed eyes	27
Boils	21
Intestinal colic	20
Other	64

It is difficult to escape the impression that the companies developed these social amenities not only to increase productivity but also in response to worker unrest.

Yet, the paternalism of the oil employer had its limits. A discharged worker was required to leave company housing and forego company benefits; there was no severance pay. Few men worked on other than short-term, verbal contracts; no collective contract existed at all. Fortunately, high demand for workers meant that jobs were plentiful elsewhere in Tampico and the oil zones. But accidents exposed the worker to insecurity in a labor market controlled by the employers. Jose I. Hernández mutilated his leg installing boilers for Huasteca at Mata Redonda. He received medical treatment and his salary while recuperating in Tampico. But when his leg did not heal properly, Hernández had to seek his own medical treatment in Mexico City. The company did not provide him any financial help there whatsoever.[28] Workers soon realized their vulnerability in the new industrial environment.

A second aspect of the companies' attitude toward its workers—fear of labor radicalism—also stemmed from the employers' jealous defense of their autonomy in the labor market. Oilmen ultimately desired not to give up any control over labor costs, the better to meet volatile international market conditions. Radicals threatened that control. They organized the workers, agitated for higher wages and benefits, and fomented strikes when employers refused. Most of the time, the oilmen considered that the Mexican labor militancy of the war years was attributable to the "very excitable temperament" of the Mexicans or to their susceptibility to be stirred up "by any orator who gets a hearing." As one oil manager said in 1918, "The strikes that have come of recent years have been mostly engineered by men who took advantage of some particular grievance or some local situation in order to gain notoriety."[29] In other words, the employers did not believe the proletarians had any justification for their alienation. Those Mexicans who attempted to gain control over their own conditions of employment were simply victims of emotion.

Such being the case, the oilmen tended to denounce all labor agitation as a plot of the dark, sinister forces of the Industrial Workers of the World, the infamous I.W.W. Or else it was German sabotage. When Tampico workers began a round of strikes in 1917 to offset the rising cost of living, the oilmen cooperated in raising the specter of mindless anarchism. It was nearly pathological. The oilmen's publicists in the American press wrote of I.W.W. agents circulating among the workers at Tampico. The Union of Port Mechanics, which led a port strike in 1917, was called "the I.W.W. in sheep's clothing."[30] When the United States entered the war, these same men advanced the idea that German money financed the strikes. Following the war, the center of international labor agitation shifted from Germany to Soviet Russia. Labor agitators at Tampico in 1919 were now the "Bolsheviks." Foreign employers had only to point out that some Mexican labor leaders published a newspaper called *El Bolsheviki* or had formed a group called the Hermanos Rojos as proof I.W.W. agents now worked for Moscow. Senator Albert B. Fall was collecting a thick dossier on labor agitation in Tampico. Some of his confidential correspondents made the most unfounded connections between labor radicalism and Mexican politics: Plutarco Elías Calles was a "Sonora Radical"; Adolfo de la Huerta was a "rabid socialist."[31] A right-winger named William M. Hanson exposed the links between the I.W.W. and the Mexican labor confederation, the Casa del Obrero Mundial. Writing for William Buckley's American International Protective Association, Hanson connected the I.W.W. and the Casa to President Carranza and his favorite generals.[32] The attitude of the foreigner toward labor unrest at Tampico was neither enlightened nor fraught with understanding.

Men of Judgment and Determination

The reader may ask: What was there to understand? Did not the foreign employers provide Mexicans with high-paying jobs? Was it not true that the oil proletarians willingly entered employment,

Fig. 14. Americans who capped an El Ebano well, 1904. Ten oil-coated
workers pose in front of their dormitory after placing a valve over a
gusher at El Ebano. The Mexicans who assisted are not shown and
lived in a different billet. From the Estelle Doheny Collection,
courtesy of the Archive of the Archdiocese of Los Angeles, Mission
Hills, California.

thereby gaining social status and avoiding the economic consequences
of the Mexican Revolution? Were not the oilmen correct in thinking
that they provided valuable employment opportunities Mexicans might
not otherwise have had without the foreign investment? To all these
queries, the answer is "Yes, but. . . ." Along with the undeniable benefits of industrial employment, especially higher standards of living,
the oil companies also introduced the labor by-products of modern
capitalism: the insecurity and dependency of proletarianization. Moreover, because of the prominent role of foreign capital and technology,
the oil industry reintroduced the old problem of cultural subordination. U.S.-led capitalist change implied that the Mexican workers exchange their cultural heritage for modern social relationships. The tu-
tors of this cultural revolution were skilled American workers. Therein
lay the rub.

    In the United States, the oil field hands were a notoriously hard-
living, mobile, and independent lot, known for moving across the con-

tinent like migratory swallows. They had followed the oil booms from Pennsylvania down through the Mississippi Valley to Texas and Oklahoma. The Great Mexican Oil Boom was like any other. Their peers described the American oil workers as both good men and bad, many of the latter escaping the law in the United States.[33] Their employers in Mexico constantly had to compensate for their often less-than-desirable work habits. They drank, caroused, chased women, and sometimes held up refinery operations while supervisors bailed them out of jail after weekend debaucheries. Other foreign workers spent inordinate amounts of time at sick call. El Aguila had foreign pump station engineers who were always absent from duty for some illness or other. Already, foreigners were receiving the preferential treatment of a week to ten days' worth of paid holiday every three months. If dismissed, the Americans also got one month's severance pay. At any one time, as many as 2,500 Americans and 4,000 other foreigners were working in the oil zone.[34]

Foreign workers retained their penchant to be on the move. A great majority did not stick with any one job for so much as one year. The U.S. consul's record of American workers leaving Mexico because of the revolutionary turmoil of 1913 and 1914 offers a rare statistical glimpse into this mobility. Among the foreign workers choosing to leave the oil zone at this time were rig builders, drillers, tool pushers, electricians, station men, male stenographers, construction engineers, timekeepers, machinists, steam fitters, oil gaugers, pump men, barge men, still men, refining superintendents, auditors, well contractors, pipe men, transmission bosses, stable men, firemen, train engineers, brakemen, and gardeners. Willis Lee, who had his family with him, and A. J. Kelley were long-time well drillers who had been in Mexico since 1903 and 1907, respectively. But most evacuees had been there for less than six months. A survey of the Americans leaving through Tampico in 1913 and the first four months of 1914 indicates the following statistics on the length of stay at their last job:[35]

1 day to 3 months	40 individuals
4 to 6 months	28
7 to 9 months	9
10 to 12 months	4
more than 1 year	1
more than 2 years	1
more than 3 years	6

Many of these men indicated they would not be returning and obtained one-way travel tickets out of Mexico. American workers abandoning mining, smelting, and railway jobs had been generally longer-term employees than those from the oil industry. Few American workers, many of whom had supervisory positions over the Mexicans, had been in the country long enough to learn the culture and language—indeed, if any of them had wanted to.

Differential privileges, hardly a new feature in Mexican life, greatly complicated the relationship between the foreigners and the native-born workers. The Americans received higher pay. As everywhere, drillers got the best pay of all, $250 to $350 per month, paid in drafts drawn on the Chase National Bank in New York or other U.S. banks. In addition, there were allowances for food and housing. Most of the time the foreigners ate at company cafeterias—for free. "When I come back to the United States after working for those Britishers," said a former employee of El Aguila, "my teeth was just about worn down to the gums, I'd eaten so much and so good!"[36] Although Mexican peons hired on for one peso or more per day, the American drillers on twelve-hour shifts were getting up to six dollars, including room and board. Competition for American workers, made scarce by revolutionary depredations, tended to reinforce their wage privileges. "With the several other oil companies operating in the district," observed an El Aguila oil field manager, "the wage invariably paid to foreigners, whether they are Mechanics, Engineers, or Pipe Liners, is $10.00 Mex. gold per day, and outside of Tampico in the Fields they are furnished with free quarters and living. This wage is invariably paid to all [foreigners], many of whom are of a very indifferent class and who drift from place to place filling one job after another." The best Mexican laborer never received more than eight Mexican gold pesos per day.

Housing for the Americans and Britons was separate from that of the natives. In the El Aguila camps, the foreigners' housing had been shipped out from England. Single male foreigners lived in bunkhouses with kitchens in the rear. Chinese workers did the cooking and laundry and waited on tables. At Minatitlán, the Chinese also had their own separate dwellings.[37] "Not only does this difference between the foreigner and the Mexican exist at the refinery," reported a Mexican official, "but also they established another, which is more important for the welfare of the worker, and it is that they pay the foreigner in gold-backed money and the worker in paper money, although they have had to raise the latter by a few percentage points because of the high cost of living."[38] The presence of foreign workers not only created a privileged caste within the oil industry but restricted the upward mobility of the native-born workers. A government petroleum inspector described the consequences of the foreigner's presence at the Minatitlán refinery. He referred to the slow pace of technological transfer:

> The administrative personnel of the refinery is foreign; he who deals directly with economic and administrative matters is English; the technical personnel in charge of the refinery are Austrian, with the exception of the civil engineers, who are Englishmen. All the workers are Mexicans, and it is very rare to see them occupying positions of importance in the refinery, except a few in the offices working as stenographers or doing accounting. The foreigners always show much reserve in their knowledge, whether from personal egotism or at the instructions of the company, but the result is that they never have given the Mexican an opportunity to improve nor do they show him more than absolutely necessary to discharge the task they assign to him, without permitting him to learn the connection that his work has to the other functions within the refinery.[39]

Short-term foreigners were not known for their diplomatic courtesies nor did they demonstrate a high regard for their hosts. American drillers, tool pushers, and "boiler farmers" at the derricks were surrounded by groups of three or four Mexican helpers. "Course they never could learn the technical nature of the business," said one American. The Mexicans had "no curiosity." Said another: "Most of [the Mexican peons] didn't know a drill bit from a tamale shuck."[40] El Aguila restricted the management jobs to Englishmen, especially those with the ability to speak Spanish. They found that the Americans showed little inclination to learn Mexican ways or to practice diplomacy.[41]

The war tended further to disrupt the balance within the group of foreign workers. Many employed in the industry had fled to Mexico so they would not have to serve in the U.S. armed forces. Following the war, a sizable number of American veterans found employment with the oil companies. Among them was L. Philo Maier, a graduate of the Colorado School of Mines, who had served in France as an officer in the U.S. Army Corps of Engineers. E. J. Sadler had recruited him to work in the expanding operations of the Transcontinental Petroleum Company recently purchased by the Standard Oil Company of New Jersey.[42] Other Americans formed a Tampico chapter of the war veterans group, the American Legion. The Legionnaires were not well liked by the Mexicans. The growing number of federal officials in the oil zone especially resented these war veterans. López Portillo remembered them as men imbued with ideas of their national and racial superiority. They failed to recognize his social status, for instance, calling the young oil department technocrat a "Mex," as if he were a common laborer. "I learned my lesson," this son of a former cabinet minister wrote.[43]

The companies attempted to staunch the hemorrhaging of their better foreign workers during war and revolution. Naturally, many left to escape the insecurities of the revolutionary turmoil and robbery, particularly in the oil fields. The popular reaction to the American invasion of Tampico had set many Americans to flight. Most did not return and they were not replaced, a situation that was also true for the mines, railways, and even the Tampico Tramway and Power Company. After World War I began, El Aguila could not prevent its British employees from volunteering for military service. But Lord Cowdray and J. B. Body also considered their work as a patriotic service to the homeland, inasmuch as El Aguila provided at least some of the British fuel requirements during the war. They consulted with British diplomats to exempt their employees from Britain's military draft. Beginning in the summer of 1917, many Americans were also leaving El Aguila for military service, and they could not be replaced.[44] Given their considerable hardships during the Revolution, the American workers became quite reactionary. They complained of insufficient support from their own companies and formed a vocal group advocating U.S. military intervention. Huasteca and The Texas Company had great difficulties getting their American workers to stay on the job amidst the comings and goings of *constitucionalistas* and *pelaecistas*.[45] At Minatitlán, the revolutionary raids made the American technical staff very nervous. They requested that American gunboats be stationed on the Coatzacoalcos River, but it had been insufficiently dredged. There and at Tampico, the Mexican workers had been taking advantage of the fluid political situation to vent antiforeign sentiments. Native workers resented the jobs held by the foreigners.[46] No doubt they also resented much else about the foreigner's presence.

Gradually, the companies had to train the Mexicans to replace those Americans and Britons who departed. It took time. "Regarding the use of Mexicans as Second Engineers," wrote one El Aguila supervisor in 1916,

our experiences in this locality do not seem to have been encouraging; we have at times had Mexican "Seconds" at both Tanhuijo and Tierra Amarilla [pump] stations, but when the plants were enlarged it was no longer considered safe. In past times it was easier, and we hope it will again become so, to get Mexicans of sufficient stamina for those positions. To carry on the operation of the plants according to the standards we have set, to keep up the records in an accurate and reliable manner, and to act promptly in case of occasional emergency require men of training, judgment and determination. Of course, under existing conditions, with the country full of bandits, the change would not be possible; at times all the Mexicans have left our stations and the work has been carried on exclusively by the foreign engineers employed.[47]

El Aguila was not confident about the process. Its managers thought the poor education of the Mexican workers did not make them fit substitutes for American drillers.[48] Although the training of Mexican workers permitted the companies eventually to reduce their labor bill, the circumstances of war and revolution motivated the shift more than did any company policy to promote Mexican workers.

Nevertheless, the shift was made, and the demand for large numbers of skilled and experienced American oil workers declined somewhat. By 1919, Huasteca's workshops had Mexicans doing all the wood-working, steel, and machine activities, and copper and brass fittings. Only one American, the supervisor, remained in each department.[49] Foreign women, no matter what their skills, had never received much encouragement from employers, and by 1919, the American consul at Tampico was also discouraging men from coming to Mexico for work. "The Tampico employment situation is becoming an acute one now to those coming here without previously making arrangements," the consul wrote in response to an inquiry. "Living is very high and you might find yourself considerably embarrassed if you come to Tampico looking for a connection."[50] The general manager of Jersey Standard's Transcontinental also discouraged American workers. "We are glad when possible, to give ex-soldiers and sailors employment," E. J. Sadler said, "but find it disadvantageous to bring men from the States, when it is not absolutely necessary on account of their special training or adaptability for our work."[51] The days when even moderately skilled Americans easily found jobs in the Mexican oil industry were gone forever.

Regretting the Caste System

Years later, when the Mexican state was about to take over the entire industry, Mexican economist Jesús Silva Herzog wrote about the two categories of Mexican oil laborers. The first category consisted of the settled refinery and terminal workers. They were urbanized, skilled or semiskilled, more highly paid, and often had access to company housing. The oil-field workers, on the other hand, were a rather less skilled, more transitory, and poorly housed group.[52] These two groups experienced rather different conditions during the period of oil boom and revolution. Partly based on their place in the production process and partly on the revolutionary turmoil, the oil-field workers suffered insecurities and dangers. Their brethren at the refineries and terminals, however, grew more militant. It may appear a paradox that the most privileged of the Mexican oil proletarians also became the most demanding. But that only highlights the essential ingredient to success in labor organization: militancy begins among those who have the most to lose in the new industrial setting and who are in a position to disrupt production. The skilled refinery worker qualified for the task. The oil-field laborer did not. To a certain degree, this difference was a result of the new industrial setting—or of the production process, as the new labor historians call it.[53] On the other hand, the production process in oil refining that differentiated workers by skill, privilege, and wage also reinforced traditional forms of hierarchy familiar to Mexican workers. Therefore, militant workers too sought to combine old traditions with new opportunities to achieve independence and security in the modern industrial setting.

At the time, few observers doubted the privilege accorded to those Mexicans who worked at the refineries and terminals, at the nexus between the Mexican economy and the international markets. All the pipelines and barge traffic in crude petroleum terminated at the refineries. From these points, the petroleum products and the crude and partially refined oil passed via the on- and off-shore loading facilities to domestic and especially foreign markets. Tampico was the biggest and most important center of refining and shipping. *Tampiqueño* refinery and terminal workers, therefore, performed their duties at the very hub of oil's production process. The employers likewise recognized the central importance of these urban workplaces. They strove to make the refineries the focus of their paternalistic regard for these important workers. "In all the neighborhoods formed around the Tampico refineries, with homes for employees and workers," recalled the geologist Ordóñez, "one always observed cleanliness, hygiene, and order. They gave the clear impression of how one could live immune to the tropical climate with their continuous campaigns against mosquitos and with hospitals, schools, ice factories, drainage systems, etc., etc."[54]

The Huasteca refinery camp at Mata Redonda, on the southern bank of the Pánuco River across from Tampico, boasted a clean slaughterhouse, two motion pictures per week, an elementary school with five teachers, water- and sanitation works, and plumbed homes. At Doña Cecilia, the El Aguila refinery also had a schoolhouse and even a gymnastic society with a membership of fifty Mexicans. Here one found duplexes for the families of Mexican mechanics and nine peons' dormitories with sloping, corrugated tin roofs, all constructed on terrain high enough to escape the 1913 flood.[55] Many workers lived in Tampico and the surrounding suburbs of Doña Cecilia and Arbol Grande. They traveled to work on the trolley cars of the Ferro-carril Eléctrico that ran along the riverbank from Tampico to La Barra. El Aguila had the industry's largest refinery, employing between six hundred and one thousand men.[56] The housing at the older Pierce re-finery at Arbol Grande had not been maintained in as good condition as the newer facilities of Huasteca, El Aguila, Transcontinental, and The Texas Company. In fact, the Pierce compound was dangerous. A fire broke out at the tank farm of the refinery in 1912, burning thirty-five houses in the vicinity and killing a little girl. The Tampico munici-pality was unprepared to battle the blaze. It was put out only after Herbert Wiley and five hundred men from Huasteca arrived to extin-guish the conflagration.[57]

A visit by a labor department bureaucrat early in 1920 revealed the conditions of relative privilege enjoyed by Mexican workers but indi-cated also their clear subordination to foreign personnel. The company housing was divided into two sections. On the highest ground, an ex-clusive neighborhood of "homes made of masonry," there lived the foreigners and the few Mexicans of high authority, such as the assistant engineer to Superintendent Coxon. Although the housing for Mexican mechanics and peons was on the lower ground, Colonia Baja was still healthy and sanitary. "I can assure you that the conditions of hygiene and health of the terrain occupied by the habitations for workers and day laborers are good enough. The Manager of the Colonia, Mr. W. N. Collins, takes special care that they maintain the greatest neatness pos-sible in all the habitations of that place."[58]

An American who spoke good Spanish operated the "Peon Restau-rant." There the Mexican workers paid up to one peso for meals "of good quality and according to reports from those same workers, the price charged is in accord with the quality of food that is pur-chased." The American workers and foreign supervisors, however, ate separately. The cooks for both cafeterias were Chinese. Single men who did not live in town paid fifty pesos per month to obtain room and board at the "Club," as the peons' hotel was called. Cerdán found that the food also was good and the rooms clean and hygienic. He said that the men paid only half of what it would have cost them to have similar accommodations outside the refinery compound. Assuming a beginning peon made sixty pesos per month, he was living close to the margin. The school, inaugurated in 1919 and staffed by three teachers, had only sixty-five boys and fifty-two girls enrolled in grades one through four only. Students wore uniforms, "with the objective that there be no distinctions between children of clerks and those of workers and day laborers." Considering the large number of workers, most Mexicans were not sending their children to the company school.

Did all this privilege translate into a quiet, pliable labor force at the refinery? Cerdán observed that of the 950 Mexican men working at the El Aguila refinery, 820 of them belonged to the Obreros Unidos de la Refinería "El Aguila." The high technological level of plant production placed the refinery workers under constant pressure. Every day, the refinery used more than ten thousand kilowatts of electricity from the (American owned and operated) Compañía de Luz, Fuerza y Tracción de Tampico. Electrical pumps drove the crude oil through the elaboration process and moved the product through the bulk loading facilities into the holds of 750-ton steam tankers. The management constantly renovated the machinery in the can and box plant, to increase both productivity and safety, Cerdán noted. The paraffin plant employed the "Carbondale" system, apparently the cutting edge of refinery technology. Workers at the sulfuric plant lived under the incessant danger of accident, explosion, and fire. "During the entire process of the manufacturing of [sulfuric acid]," Cerdán indicated, "the vigilance that is exercised over the operators is very considerable, with the goal of avoiding an accident that imprudence might originate and that would have fatal consequences for all of them." Although the work could be demanding, one did not find much in the way of coercion. The companies later came under attack for having *guardias blancas,* company police who controlled the labor force. El Aguila's refinery did have special guards, as the labor inspector noted, but "they are limited only to seeing that none of the materials employed there are taken from the place without the express order of some Chief." Mexican workers had not forsworn their tradition of helping themselves to the property of their employer.[59] The work could be demanding, but there appeared to have been no erosion of skill levels among the Mexican employees. If anything, the rapid expansion of the refinery business at Tampico rapidly outstripped the supply of local artisans and trained mechanics.[60] Why else would the companies need to hire expensive, obstreperous foreign workers, when Mexicans would have been cheaper?

Although they afforded the workers a higher standard of living, the refineries nonetheless promoted—or acquiesced to—a hierarchical social structure among their workers. The Texas Company terminal on the south bank of the Pánuco River at Tampico maintained five classes of company housing. At the lower end of the social (and skill) scale, construction workers and part-timers occupied "ordinary thatched huts." No one regulated the sanitary conditions of this community at all. Full-time unskilled peons and their families inhabited two-room wooden cottages with no kitchen. The homes of the families of Mexican mechanics contained three rooms, including a kitchen, and had separate laundry and toilet facilities. Unmarried Americans lived in a clubhouse providing room, board, and recreation, including reading and game areas, billiard tables, tennis courts, and complete bathing facilities. Families of American employees inhabited five-room cottages, "well kept, well cared for and presenting a very attractive appearance," according to one American visitor.[61] The observer had no difficulty at all in understanding why The Texas Company maintained company housing, particularly for the Mexican workers. He said the company acquiesced to laborers' expectations of higher standards of living, "and they can be kept from the worst excesses of the I.W.W." Nonetheless, in the process, a strict hierarchy was established. "The American managers uniformly regret this caste system," the visitor noted, "but find that they have to comply with it."[62] Apparently the skilled Mexicans wished to live separately from the peons, and the Americans, from the Mexicans—a behavior among the working classes having much precedence in Mexico.

In addition, the wage system also reinforced the hierarchy of work traditional to the country. The Americans and Britons were paid in stable foreign currencies, either the U.S. dollar or in Mexican currency according to the exchange rate of what was called the Mexican gold peso. Each Mexican gold peso was worth fifty cents (U.S.). Some Mexican mechanics, the generic term given to skilled and semiskilled native workers, also earned their pay in gold pesos. Most peons and

Table 10. *Wages of Mexican Workers at the El Aguila Refinery in Minatitlán, 1920*

	Minimum Pay (pesos per day)	Maximum Pay (pesos per day)
Carpenter	6.00	10.00
Pilot (*pailero*)	5.00	10.00
Mechanic	5.00	9.00
Blacksmith	6.88	7.50
Mason (*albañile*)	5.00	7.00
Painter	—	6.88
Blacksmith's assistant	3.13	4.00
Carpenter's assistant	3.13	3.75
Pilot's assistant	3.13	3.75
Mechanic's assistant	1.00	3.75
Peon	2.50	3.50

NOTE: This hierarchy of pay was characteristic of all the installations. On the tugboat *Aguila* of El Aguila, for example, the crew of twenty-one men commanded monthly wages ranging from 250 gold pesos for the master to 30 pesos for the "boy." See "Estimate of Monthly Expenditure in Mex Gold-running Tug 'Aguila'" (c. 1916), Pearson, C45.

SOURCE: Cerdán, "Informe," 9 Jan 1920, Ramo de Trabajo, C224, E24, AGN.

part-timers earned wages paid in Mexican script. The problems of Mexican paper money had to do with the great inflation of the revolutionary period. By 1916, for example, the Mexican paper peso was worth 12.50 gold centavos, or a bit more than 6 cents, which occasioned El Aguila's accountants to maintain double and triple entries in their pay books. The foreign personnel earned up to two to four times as much as the highest paid Mexican. At El Aguila's Tampico refinery, the foreign superintendent earned 700 gold pesos per month and the foreign chief of stills got 355 pesos. While foreign administrators earned from 250 to 520 pesos a month, the Mexican supervisors earned from 60 to 200 pesos. At the stills, the foreign chiefs earned 355 pesos and the foreign still men earned between 180 and 300 pesos per month. But the highest paid Mexicans, three sample men, received just 150 pesos. In the pump houses, on the pipelines, and at the terminals, the foreign supervisors got 240 gold pesos per month, while the Mexican workers earned 135 pesos.[63] Among the Mexican workmen themselves, there remained distinct wage differentials. Mexican mechanics started at 5 pesos per day in 1920, and their assistants got only 1 peso (see table 10).

Income differentials such as these separate the modern class society from the caste society. Where once the differences in race and ethnicity had determined one's position in the working class, now the industrial wage accomplished the same task. Yet, there remained some similarities between the caste and class societies in industrial Mexico. Foreign personnel occupied the ranks of privilege, exactly as had the Spaniards in the colonial period. Native-born mestizos occupied the ranks of the semiskilled. Itinerant *campesinos,* many of them Indian, entered the work force at the lowest rank as peons. The educated Mexican disdained the whole lot and disapproved of their high pay in the oil industry. "The extravagance of workers and their families came to be exaggerated," noted the urbane engineer, Ordóñez. "[W]ives of simple peons and foremen dressed ostentatiously in silk stockings, expensive footwear, and silk dresses poorly made and inappropriate to their class and conditions."[64] Actually, this new social hierarchy had many similarities to past Mexican models—except that the non-Spanish speaking, non-Catholic foreign workers were not immigrants and could not be absorbed. The transitory status of foreigners rendered their positions susceptible to erosion.

The increased standards of living notwithstanding, the new industrial environment of Tampico produced a certain degree of alienation among the Mexican workers. It was not so much the rationalization of the work process or the hierarchy, which to a certain extent protected the social status of Mexican skilled workers. Part of the alienation had to do with the privilege of foreigners, which at times amounted to a cultural affront to Mexican laborers.[65] On the one hand, the privileged position of foreign workers blocked the upward mobility of skilled Mexicans. On the other hand, the company's absolute control over hiring, training, and promotion also pressured skilled Mexican laborers from below. They could never be sure that they might not be replaced by lower-paid, less-skilled peons. In spite of their status and material well-being, therefore, the skilled natives were the most insecure and unhappiest of all. As long as the employer controlled the workplace, skilled Mexicans never knew when they might be replaced by workers trained by the company. But they were also in a position to do something about their insecurity. The skilled Mexicans could organize; they could strike; they could exert some control over the unskilled; and they could seek the government's assistance. In the oil refineries at Tampico, they would eventually do all of these. Not their brothers in the oil fields, however.

Withdrawing without Provocation

In general, workers in the oil camps, among the wells and pump stations, were less skilled and less privileged than refinery laborers. More primitive conditions governed their lives in the countryside. Nevertheless, the oil-field workers still enjoyed some of the same opportunities (though restricted by revolutionary depredations) in addition to similar limitations of advancement. Small towns had sprung up throughout the oil zone during the boom. Along the railway lines through Chijol and El Ebano and between the great oil camps of the Faja de Oro, migrants established little population centers quite miserable in their amenities. Geologist Ezequiel Ordóñez, like others of his class, had a somewhat puritanical attitude about workers. He described these small populations as "seedbeds of disorder, abuse, and vice." Ordóñez thought that the prohibition of alcoholic beverages at the numerous cantinas would do wonders to make life respectable. Petty despots there controlled even the necessities of life. Ordóñez described how enterprising persons, without authorization, would tap into the water lines of the companies and sell the water for exorbitant prices to rural inhabitants.[66]

For those workers living inside the compounds of the oil camps, modern technology provided amenities, even if it could not protect them from the shocks of revolution. El Aguila personnel lived in wooden bunkhouses with bathhouses nearby. "These buildings are constructed of rough pine lumber, without any inside boarding, and framed upon hard wooden posts for foundations," as one company official described them:

> All exposed woodwork [receives] two coats of good oil paint. Corrugated iron roofs are used with canvassed ceilings. All window and door openings are properly screened throughout with bronzed gauge screening for protection against mosquitos; for the living quarters, verandahs are built on the most suitable sides of the house.[67]

The camps also provided company stores, which often sold supplies and basic foodstuffs like corn and beans at discount prices. Single men ate at the company restaurant. By the end of the oil boom, the biggest camps had modest schoolhouses for the children of Mexican workers and sanitation and water works. Huasteca's property at El

Fig. 15. Mexican workers' housing, 1920. In the oil field of the Cortez Oil Company, workers and their families lived in one- and two-room units in the same long one-story building in which other families resided. Doors and windows on either side admitted the breezes as well as the insects. From the Ramo del Trabajo, Archivo General de la Nación, Mexico City.

Ebano was a veritable community. At any one time, up to five thousand workmen might have had ten thousand additional family members living with them in the oil camp. At Christmas time, the company entertained its employees with a sumptuous barbecue, in which the Americans served the Mexicans—surely a symbolic gesture only. In 1913, there were games, horse races, and an inspirational speech by Judge Jacobo Váldez.[68]

The small companies and the less productive oil fields, however, could not sustain the amenities of the larger camps like El Aguila's at Potrero del Llano, or Huasteca's at Cerro Azul. In the transitory camps, housing was very rudimentary, and sanitary conditions were often lacking. Still, government labor inspectors often found "very good conditions of security and hygiene" in the smaller camps of the Atlantic and the Cortez companies. Foreigners and Mexicans ate the same food, albeit at different tables. Other camps, at Saladero and Puerto Lobos, separated the housing and mess halls for foreign and Mexican workers, tending to "deepen more the differences," as a government representative reported. At the Atlantic camp, the inspector said, "the treatment of the employees... is always just and on some occasions even venerable."[69] The workers did complain, however, that the Chinese restaurant concessionaire refused to extend breakfast hours from 8:30 to 9 A.M.

Like the refineries, the oil camps gave in to the demands, particularly of its skilled workers, to provide separate housing and maintain the wage hierarchy. The Americans did not want to live or eat with the Mexicans; the Mexican skilled workers did not wish to live the same as the more transitory peons, and no one cared to mingle with the Chinese cooks and servants. Large camps separated the housing and operated segregated mess halls. Wage disparities also remained, especially between the foreign and the native personnel. On the drilling crews, the American drillers and tool dressers made between ten and fourteen gold pesos per day, while the Mexican firemen and helpers earned two and three pesos. The American rig builder worked for fourteen pesos per day and his three Mexican helpers got two to four pesos.[70] The Mexicans themselves earned higher wages than they could have in other lines of work. They even got 30 percent of their wages while on sick call. As the oilmen were fond of pointing out, other Mexican employers such as landowners and businessmen disliked the foreign employer "for spoiling their cheap labor."[71] There also remained a hierarchy of pay among Mexicans. The foremen (cabos) of construction crews received up to 3.00 gold pesos per day; the peons received 1.50 pesos. Carpenters earned 4.00 pesos, blacksmiths and teamsters, 3.50 pesos; watchmen 3.00 pesos, and a camp peon 2.00 pesos.[72] There were almost as many peons in the various oil-field crews as skilled workers—but many more in construction. The wage hierarchy among Mexicans differed little from the colonial mining industry or from traditional hacienda work.

Meanwhile, the companies paid the Chinese workers the lowest wages of all. At the Potrero camp of El Aguila, twenty-five Chinese men were employed in the boarding of the foreign and Mexican employees of the construction and pipeline departments. But their monthly wages averaged less than Mexican workers. The Mexican "stable peon" made as much as the Chinese "kitchen chief" (see table 11). To a certain extent, the workers themselves determined what wages they would work for; no American would accept a Mexican's pay and no Mexican a Chinese wage. Therefore, the capitalist had to ac-

Table 11. *Wages of Mexican and Chinese Workers in El Aguila,*
Potrero Camp, c. 1916

Mexican Employee	Wages (pesos per month)	Chinese Employee
Carpenter	120	
Peon in stables	60	kitchen chief
Peon in construction	40	cook
	40	laundryman
	40	buyer
	30	waiter
Office boy	20	room boy

NOTE: The Chinese "room boy" may have been an adult worker who earned as much as a Mexican "office boy," who may really have been an adolescent.
SOURCE: "Standing Charges, Potrero Camp" (c. 1916), Pearson, C45.

cept the traditional ethnic divisions of labor produced by the multiracial environment. No doubt cost-cutting employers would have preferred paying everyone the Chinese wage. But they could not.

Oil-field workers, however, endured two opposing stimuli during the period of simultaneous revolution and oil boom. On one hand, foreigners, Mexicans, and the Chinese alike all benefited from full employment. On the other, they all suffered from the insecurity caused by military and bandit activity in the countryside. The Mexicans, in particular, already encountered the customary change in time and work discipline when they entered oil-field employment. But the oil camp peons resisted giving their lives over completely to proletarianization, that is, working exclusively for industrial wages. As a labor inspector said, "The majority are from this region who work only in times in which there are no harvests. When harvests come, they leave their work, because some of them are owners of small plots which they sow for their own benefit."[73] The more skilled refinery workers did not have the same alternatives to proletarianization.

Nonetheless, the oil camps offered the Mexicans no security at all from the depredations of the Constitutionalist troops. To rob them, *carrancistas* shot the Mexican peons who were building a tank farm at The Texas Company field on the Obando lease. Eighteen carpenters working on a Huasteca pump station fled for their lives after the Constitutionalists took all their clothes. (The company, by the way, refused to reimburse them. Their loss was termed "a burden of Mexican citizenship.")[74] The managers of company after company complained of the impossibility of keeping men on the job because of the "unsatisfactory and disturbed condition of affairs." Fortunately for the companies, most of the pipelines had already been built when the first outrages began during the Madero revolt. Thereafter, work on tank storage and other facilities had to be delayed from time to time.[75] Both Mexicans and Americans were abandoning the insecurity of the oil camps. "In normal times," reported the manager of the Furbero camp, "the company employes [sic] about 600 men in the oil business and on its pipelines, railways, etc. Since 1914, however, this number has been reduced to 200, most of whom are Mexicans. All Americans have been withdrawn from the field and their places have been taken by Englishmen."[76]

Given the conditions in the countryside, the employers praised their oil-field workers, more so than refinery workers, for their loyalty. Managers often pointed out those instances where Mexican peons showed great fealty in the face of revolutionary despoliation. During the tense final weeks of the Madero revolution, Herbert Wylie said, the Mexicans patrolled the oil camps at night while American residents slept with their doors unlocked. He recalled asking them if they would be prepared to fight. "Si, señor," came the reply. "We will fight or die if necessary to protect you."[77] (They knew just what Wylie wanted to hear. I have found no evidence that Mexican field workers ever placed themselves in the line of fire to save foreign oilmen.)

The test came in 1914. When word spread that the U.S. Marines had landed at Veracruz, the Americans vacated the oil fields in panic. No sooner had the supervisors and skilled workers left than the owners realized the dangers of abandoning the oil fields: runaway wells, burst storage tanks, broken down pumps, equipment theft, destroyed railway rolling stock, and fire. The Mexican workers missed two payrolls during the month's absence of their foreign managers. Yet they stayed on the job, maintaining the oil wells and storing the excess oil in earthen reservoirs. Concluded the American consul at Veracruz:

> The small amount of damage which had been done to vast oil properties which were abandoned thirty days ago is largely due to fidelity of Mexican employees and generally speaking Mexican employees and servants have been very faithful to Americans who left them in charge of property in oil fields and in Tampico without funds for sustenance and in many cases with wages due them. The small losses is [sic] remarkable under the circumstances and great credit is due such employees and servants.[78]

Occasionally, the foreigners overstepped the bounds of their work-ers' loyalty. These instances pertained to the individual Mexican's pen-chant to resist the undesirable aspects of proletarianization and pre-serve traditional individualism and mobility. The Mexicans in the oil industry, especially in construction, still clung to *tarea* (piecework) so that they could take off whenever they pleased. When fired with special indignity, the Mexican workman might round up several friends in or-der to lay an ambush for the offending foreign supervisor.[79] The for-eign employers never did understand the Mexicans' ambivalent attitude about the material improvements, social welfare, and educational op-portunities that the oil companies provided. Just when the company gave him benefits not to be found elsewhere, the individual might walk away from the job. "In spite of these [benefits], the workers show no particular loyalty to the company," reported one informant, "and are ready to sacrifice its interests both by rendering poor service, and by withdrawing without provocation."[80] Many a manager puzzled over the Mexican worker's propensity to preserve his independence. For the most part, the oil-field worker did not subscribe to labor militancy as a remedy to his problems. After all, he was not as dependent as his ur-banized and proletarianized brethren at Tampico. He merely took off for his piece of land.

The refinery workers, however, were different. They depended on factory wages and were more proletarianized. Therefore, they suffered acutely from the greatest problem confronting urban workers dur-ing the oil boom: the cost-of-living rise that afflicted the Mexican econ-omy beginning in 1914. In part, this economic condition obtained throughout the Atlantic world during the First World War, when the arming of the European nations, at the same time that the best workers were conscripted to fight the war, drove commodity prices sky-high. Most Western economies, including those in the Latin Americas, remained at full employment. But rises in the price of foodstuffs and consumer items outstripped wages. Workers through-out the Americas, therefore, threatened additional disruption of the economic system. They demanded higher wages and mounted work stoppages in order to gain some relief from the rising cost of liv-ing. Strikes broke out in Buenos Aires, Santiago, Lima, São Paulo, and Mexico City.[81]

In Mexico, the Revolution compounded the economic stress. After the most violent phases of the Revolution had subsided, experts sur-veyed the agricultural destruction. The population of livestock in

Table 12. *Depletion of Livestock Resources in the State of Veracruz, 1902–1923*

	1902 (head)	1923 (head)
Cattle	392,858	165,325
Goats	19,411	19,512
Sheep	42,754	17,983
Horses	40,914	18,228
Hogs	27,796	24,265
Mules	10,547	6,475

SOURCE: "Mexican Livestock Resources Diminish 60% from Year 1902 to 1923," 20 Feb 1924, State Dept. Decimal Files 812.62/37.

Mexico had been reduced by as much as 60 percent. Veracruz, home of the oil industry, did not escape this disruption (see table 12).

The squeeze on workers' pay also affected the oil industry, but the owners were reluctant to raise wages. They reasoned that once wages were raised, they could not be reduced later when the cost-of-living crisis subsided. Instead, they preferred to increase the nonmonetary benefits like restaurant and company store privileges. Inflation of the Mexican paper peso, nonetheless, threw their pay policies into disarray, forcing employers to combine paper currency, Mexican silver, and American dollars.[82] El Aguila's managers despaired that they could contain worker unrest when the value of the American dollar too began to slip. By the end of 1916, they were finding that the workers would no longer accept their salaries half in silver and half in dollars. The discount on American currency was nearly 15 percent. Mechanics, formerly paid five gold pesos per day, now would not work even for seven pesos. The managers worried about what action the workers might take when the dwindling supply of silver currency dried up completely.[83] What did the workers do? They fought back. Nothing in their labor traditions, neither the outward appearance of servility nor the government's occasional use of repression had taught Mexican workers to accept as final such deteriorating conditions. To the contrary, they had learned that their demands, petitions to the state, and strikes often succeeded in yielding some relief. Oil workers at Tampico were to encounter remarkable successes in this regard, partially because the Mexican Revolution had fostered propitious developments in labor organization and had conditioned the state to be receptive to labor demands.

Just Equilibrium
between Opposing Interests

In November 1911, when a Huasteca paymaster at Tampico was late in distributing the pay, several hundred workers nearly rioted. Four members of the *rurales,* the rural police force, helped calm the crowd. At the time, sixteen *rurales* had also been permanently stationed at the refinery of Waters-Pierce since a 1909 strike to prevent disturbances.[84] If there once might have been a cozy relationship between foreign owners and the state concerning the control of the working class, it was to come to an end with the Mexican Revolution. This monumental upheaval in the social and political life of the nation—despite the relatively lukewarm participation of organized labor—represents a critical watershed. Before the Revolution, labor had little juridical existence. President Porfirio Díaz and local politicians dealt with strikes and workers' demands according to custom, which in Mexico had always dictated the state's protection of the downtrodden. When *ad hoc* state patronage did not restore labor's place in the delicate social order, the Díaz regime applied coercion. Indeed, many of these attitudes toward the working class carried over into the post-Porfirian age.

But the Revolution made possible more significant changes. That is to say, the Revolution itself produced nothing for the workers; it merely offered them the opportunity to act on their own agenda. In Mexico, workers made their own changes.

First and foremost, the incessant competition among the elites over who was to control the state raised labor's political importance. Politicians sought support from the working class in order to outflank competitors. Worker organizations had always been involved in politics; yet much of their participation had been subdued and made unimportant during the long reign of Porfirio Díaz. The Porfirian order of the day was "much administration, little politics," removing opportunities for labor to insert itself into the political process. The Revolution occurred at a moment when the urban, industrial working class was now larger, approximately 16 percent of the economically active population of Mexico.[85] But the clout of the workers was much greater than their number. Although they did not make the Revolution—it had been fought by armies of rancheros and *campesinos*—the workers did help consolidate it. Holding the cities and collecting taxes in the ports became the paramount task of the new revolutionary government.

The state's need for their assistance, therefore, empowered the urban and industrial workers to advance their own agenda. And the agenda of the Mexican workers of the twentieth century was not unlike the artisan's goals of the late eighteenth: to be incorporated juridically into public life in order to assure the individual's security within the economic system.[86] Such a goal violated the tenets of liberal capitalism, because the incorporation of labor into the body politic greatly infringed upon the exercise of private property rights. But even under Porfirio Díaz, Mexico had been an imperfect adherent to liberalism. The desire to tether capitalism became even stronger during the Revolution. In the first place, it provided the bourgeois politicians with a tool to end the social chaos and rebellion from below. In the second place, collective action and social reforms proffered the working class a sense of security and place in society. Unfettered capitalist growth did not.

No sooner had the old regime fallen than the politicians recognized the central role of labor in the new. In 1911, the Madero government established the Office of Labor in order to mediate disputes and "harmonize" capital and labor. Huerta turned the office into a labor department. Later governments expanded the personnel of this new bureaucracy, in recognition of labor's expanded role in revolutionary Mexico and in an effort to extend political control over the industrial and commercial regions, like Tampico, located far from Mexico City. While Carranza was in power, the labor department acquired Constitutional powers of arbitration and established an office of federal labor inspectors in Tampico.[87] The labor bureaucracy served somewhat the same purpose as the petroleum office technocrats. The state expanded both agencies in an effort to gain command over two elements thought to have contributed to the unraveling of Mexico: the excesses of foreign capital and labor unrest.

For these reasons, politicians who sought control of the state openly attempted to win the hearts and minds of the urban and industrial workers. Inhabitants of Tampico, as an important petroleum export center, became particular targets of competing local, state, and national leaders—whether civilian or military. Huerta's new labor department in 1914 assisted the Gremio Unido de Alijadores to win a contract committing the company to hire its members only.[88] Huerta might have won them over. The workers there responded with passivity when Constitutionalist forces besieged the *huertistas* at Tampico—but then Tampico workers, except perhaps as individuals, did not fight for or against any revolutionary faction, ever. Nonetheless, when the *constitu-*

cionalistas took the city, they gained the workers' support by promising land reforms, the eight-hour day, a minimum daily wage of five pesos, and rent reductions.[89] (Urban workers supported land reform because it would presumably keep their country cousins down on the farm.) Carranza himself, however, repudiated some of the more radical promises of his subordinates. The first chief's tepid support of reforms did not prevent his military officers nor the state governors from mediating labor disputes in Tampico. As commander of northeastern Mexico during 1915, Gen. Pablo González involved himself in the negotiations of various labor organizations with El Aguila and the Mexican Light and Power Company in Tampico. González tended to favor Mexican workers in their disputes with foreign-owned enterprises. One of his staff officers even proposed forming "arbitration tribunals," after the Veracruz state model, in which representatives of government, industry, and labor would meet to settle disputes. Only in this way, said González's aide, could the government guarantee stability and gain the support of the majority of its citizens.[90]

General Cándido Aguilar also made initiatives for labor reform in the state of Veracruz. As early as 1914, he proposed state legislation that would have established the nine-hour day and a system of state inspectors and mediators. As governor, he later called for state labor legislation. By 1919, he presented a draft bill to the state legislatures. The state had an obligation to regulate capital and labor, he said, because the strikes that had been occurring since 1915 threatened to "disorganize the active life of the State." The proposed law would "put an end to the anarchy which reigned in the realm of labor." Since conflict between capital and labor was natural, Aguilar stated, this law would provide the "just equilibrium between opposing interest" and would "give to each his share."[91]

Wooing labor became the special objective of those politicians seeking office. Several labor leaders in Minatitlán, in fact, ran for public office. One member of the El Aguila refinery union in 1917 became a local deputy and another the municipal president. In 1919, the young Tamaulipas lawyer Emilio Portes Gil attended the convention of the state's labor organizations in order to help form the Partido Laborista Mexicano, which supported Obregón.[92] The popular general himself came to Tampico in March of 1920. From the balcony of the Hotel Continental, he spoke to a large crowd (fifteen thousand persons, most of them workers, the *obregonistas* claimed) in the Plaza de la Libertad. But the local commanders, Gen. Francisco Murguía and Col. Carlos S.

Orozco, both supporters of Carranza, took several of Obregón's entourage into custody for insulting the president. Seven *pistoleros* confronted Obregón in his hotel room.[93] Mexican politics of the time was a high-stakes game.

The workers' political agitation gained for them recognition in no less than the nation's new Constitution of 1917. For one thing, more workers than peasants were represented among the writers of the constitution (two artisans, a carpenter, a railway mechanic and union leader, and several miners are mentioned). But the bourgeois military leaders and bureaucrats were unhappy with Carranza's weak draft provisions protecting labor. One laborite allowed his inspirational rhetoric to depart from fact. We need labor reforms in the new constitution, said the ex-miner Dionisio Zavala, because "the workers are the ones who have made the Revolution."[94] Several *constituyentes* complained that the states, such as Sonora under Calles and Veracruz under Aguilar, had more progressive labor legislation than Carranza's draft. Among labor's supporters was Gen. Francisco Múgica, the twenty-eight-year-old general from Michoacán, hardly Mexico's industrial heartland. The *constituyentes* relented and wrote a tough, very specific Article 123 into the 1917 Constitution. Pastor Rouaix and a team of bureaucrats had composed the drafts.[95]

No matter how it came about, Article 123 reserved a great role for the state as intervenor in the relationship between workers and employers. "The Congress and the State Legislature shall make laws relative to . . . the labor of skilled and unskilled workers, employees, domestic servants and artisans, and every labor contract in general." The constitution reserved for the state the right to judge strikes to be lawful or unlawful. "Strikes shall be considered unlawful only when the majority of strikers engage in acts of violence."[96] Municipal authorities had to approve all labor contracts between Mexican workers and foreign-owned companies, and disputes were to be settled between arbitration boards made up of representatives of labor, capital, and the state. Government commissions in the states and municipalities were to establish the minimum wage. These provisions made the government the deciding, swing factor in the relationship between the employee and his or her employer. Little in the constitutional debates indicated a purposefully antiforeign meaning to Article 123. Its provisions applied equally to foreign as to domestic employers.

Moreover, the labor article of the constitution detailed the precise responsibilities of employers toward their charges. This had been true of colonial legislation that governed Indian labor.[97] Indebtedness as a method of holding workers was outlawed, and arbitrary discharge was penalized by fines. Article 123 mandated an eight-hour day and limited night work to seven hours. Employers had to pay two times the salary for overtime work, and they could not ask children or women to perform it. Finally, there came the very specific injunctions of Clause XII. "In every agricultural, industrial, mining or any other kind of labor, employers shall be obliged to furnish their workers comfortable and sanitary dwellings, for which they may charge rents not exceeding one-half of one percent per month of the assessed value of the properties. They shall likewise establish schools, dispensaries, and other services necessary to the community."[98] Who assessed property values? Who inspected these educational and medical facilities? The state. The constitution was the perfect compromise between Mexican conservatives, who wanted a strong state to control the impoverished masses, and reformers who wished that the state would ameliorate the distress of the masses. It cannot be forgotten, the *constituyentes* did not devise Article 123 out of thin air. They drew its provisions from petitions that union leaders had been submitting to local officials and military chieftains. In a sense, Mexican workers themselves helped draft the Constitution of 1917.

Although it is true that revolutionary politicians competed for the favor of labor, the workers too found it expedient to exploit the political factionalism of the Revolution in order to gain certain advantages. Such was the case of the Casa del Obrero Mundial. In 1912, during a season of strikes, labor leaders in Mexico City organized the Casa, probably with the backing of American anarchists in the I.W.W. The Casa always represented a small minority of workers. It affiliated 39 unions representing the traditional artisan classes, such as printers, tailors, stonemasons, tramway workers, intellectuals, and students; few factory workers in the city's textile industry joined. Its leaders, like Rosendo Salazar, who later wrote about Mexico's labor history, were highly educated, erudite, and gifted. The skilled workers of the Casa traditionally distrusted two elements of Mexican life, the peasants and religion. Labor leaders blamed Catholic fanaticism for the "ignorance and backwardness" of most Mexican workers; they resented Zapata for taking Mexicans back to the priests and religious processions. In essence, the urbane Casa leadership was competing with these revolutionary leaders for control of the less-skilled workers, most of whom had not forgotten their rural origins.

When the *zapatistas* were about to enter Mexico City in the fall of 1914, leaders of the Casa made their political decision. They threw their support to the Constitutionalists. Dr. Atl, a radical painter and Casa orator whose real name was Gerardo Murillo, and Alberto J. Pani, the lawyer and civil servant, visited the headquarters of General Obregón. A deal was struck. Obregón distributed five hundred thousand pesos to Mexico City's urban workers, who had already begun to suffer from famine. Obregón also donated the Santa Brígida Church as the Casa's first headquarters, a symbolic gesture not lost on the anticlerical labor leadership. Carranza agreed to make laws to improve working conditions and to support labor against capital.[99] In return, the Casa supplied the Constitutional armies with seven thousand volunteers to form six Red Battalions. The famous Red Battalions contributed little to battle, being reserved mostly for guard duty. Nonetheless, the Casa organized twenty-two propaganda missions within these military organizations. They spread the Casa's ideology of a nationally organized and unified proletariat to industrial towns liberated by the Constitutionalist forces.[100] Eventually, a propaganda team of the Casa entered Tampico.

Casa leaders might well have remarked that to live by politics is also to perish by politics, for Carranza eventually broke with the labor confederation. Mexico City's unions had been increasingly resorting to strikes to combat the cost-of-living rises. Finally, in July 1916, the power and light workers shut down the power station, and the tramway employees halted the mass transit system. It was too much for Carranza. He deactivated the Red Battalions, sent Constitutionalist troops against the strikers, and closed down the new Casa headquarters in the House of Tiles.[101] The government considered the general strike in the nation's capital to have challenged the political legitimacy of Carranza.

Tampico came into the Casa's scheme of national labor consolidation in 1915, when members of the Red Battalions entered the Constitutionalist-held port city. These leaders supported—but did not originate—the organizational trends then developing among the city's workers. Trade unions of the more skilled proletarians formed first. The carpenters', bricklayers', and boat pilots' unions had between 320 and 460 members each. The journeymen and day laborers (*oficios varios*) had unions numbering nearly 550 members each. The local labor inspector described them as independent "groups of resistance for the workers' improvement and progress."[102]

The Casa leaders at Tampico were every bit as erudite as their counterparts in Mexico City. Spanish anarchist Ramón Delgado, who in

1917 worked in the paraffin department of the El Aguila refinery, and
Mariano Benítez, an El Aguila boiler mechanic, edited the Casa newspapers that denounced "the bourgeoisie, the clergy and the state." They
dominated the discussion in the workers' assemblies. Always there existed the tension between the imported anarchist ideology attacking
the state and the Mexican labor tradition of cooperating with government. But opposition in Tampico grew against the hegemony of Mexico City labor leaders, just as some state political leaders also resisted
Carranza's national hegemony. Not all workers conformed to the general strike called by the Tampico branch of the Casa in support of its
Mexico City bosses. Therefore, Gen. Emiliano Nafarrete had little
trouble rounding up eight Casa leaders and sending them to Querétaro
and Mexico City prisons.[103] The Casa was undone. Although neither
strikes nor labor organization in the nation were slowed in the least,
the Casa itself could not recover the national hegemony that its political bargaining had once given it. Cracks in working-class solidarity appeared in the Tampico branch of the Casa. Spanish anarchist Jorge D.
Borrán attacked the credentials of Luis Morones, chief of the delegation from Mexico City. Borrán called Morones "a mystificator of the
socialist ideal" and members of his delegation "Allied-ophiles."[104] The
government of Tamaulipas eventually deported Borrán, who was not a
Mexican citizen.

The national disorganization of the Casa finally led to the formation
of yet another national labor confederation, the Confederación Regional Obrera Mexicana, better known as CROM. Its new leaders had
been active members of the Casa. They met in Saltillo, Coahuila, under
the auspices of the state governor. Its top leadership included Morones,
who became its general secretary, and Ricardo Treviño, who became
one of its directors. Another was Andrés Araujo, like Treviño a Casa organizer at Tampico. (In the early 1920s, Araujo would gain appointment as labor inspector at Tampico.) The CROM was organized very
much like the government. Its central committee, like a cabinet, consisted of secretaries of education, interior, exterior, information, and so
forth. The centralization of authority and decision making reflected
very much the rather authoritarian structure of the government.
CROM's leadership also aspired to building a labor hegemony through
political alliance. Treviño communicated to Carranza their goals,
which included "an energetic opposition . . . to the work of intrigue
and falsehoods of foreign capitalists who have interests in Mexico" and
who impeded the implementation of the Constitution.[105] CROM actively sought political protection.

Apparently, Carranza's support did not satisfy its leaders, or perhaps they knew the popularity of his chief rival, General Obregón. Upholding the long labor tradition of political involvement, Morones drew up a secret convention with the presidential candidate in August 1919. Obregón promised to appoint prolaborites to the Department of Labor and the secretariat of industry, and a proagrarian to the secretariat of agriculture. CROM was promised access to decisions on all matters relating to labor in an Obregón government. In return, the CROM leadership participated wholeheartedly in the Partido Laborista, which endorsed Obregón's political candidacy.[106] The labor movement had made great headway in Tampico during the formative era of CROM. By 1920, unions of skilled and semiskilled Mexican workers had formed within the great refineries. Nearly 7,000 workers belonged to formal unions. Among the largest were the unions representing the Transcontinental refinery (1,000 members), the Pierce refinery (932), The Texas Company refinery (850), the El Aguila refinery (820), and the El Aguila terminal (691).[107] In the final analysis, the Revolution may have given Mexico the kind of labor organization and advanced social legislation achieved by strong popular movements in other Latin American nations such as Uruguay, Chile, Argentina, Brazil, Venezuela, and Cuba. Yet Mexican workers gained these benefits sooner. They may not have made the Revolution but Mexican workers did take advantage of it to bargain with the government—not necessarily with their employers. But these achievements do not constitute a sharp break with a long tradition of state intervention in the relationship between employers and employees. They had deep roots in Mexico's history.

Better to Die Free

During the years of the oil industry's expansion from 1911 to 1915, there was very little labor unrest. Workers for the foreign oil companies received salaries superior to any other work in the nation, and they had yet to experience any ill effects of their proletarianization. But beginning in 1915, they quickly perceived the costs of depending upon selling their labor power. Wartime and revolutionary inflation eroded their high standards of living. Ordinarily, workers would not have been motivated to strike if they were being laid off, when those still having jobs became quite conservative. Tampico and

Fig. 16. Laying pipe, c. 1920. Mexican workers of Jersey Standard's Transcontinental Petroleum Company use pipe tongs to assemble an oil pipeline near Tampico. Courtesy of M. Philo Maier.

Minatitlán were full-employment towns during the years of the European war and Mexican Revolution. Workers struck when the terms of employment favored them and when companies could not easily find suitable replacements. Moreover, the so-called labor aristocrats, the relatively privileged workers who had skills and higher pay, could be quite militant.[108] They certainly were in the oil zone. Although oil-field workers suffered the revolutionary depredations, refinery workers led the strikes. What is more, the most skilled of the refinery laborers organized unions, often advised if not led by members of the bourgeoisie like lawyers and school teachers. Also, the workers acted upon their heritage of appealing to political authorities for redress of grievances. New revolutionary politicians responded, so long as the workers did not disrupt the collection of taxes from the foreign companies. This was not particularly revolutionary. The workers never demanded a redistribution of property or the elimination of foreign capital. Instead, they pressed for reforms and a degree of income redistribution to blunt the worst aspects of their new status as proletarians. The Revolution aided them.

The Tampico oil workers began to feel the first pinches of inflation and food scarcity in 1915. On the strength of full-employment expansion in the industry, they responded with demands for higher wages.

The skilled workers had first organized a grouping of "Artesanos Latinos Profesionales" in 1913, under the leadership of a Spanish carpenter and several local teachers. A different group of skilled employees at the El Aguila refinery formed another organization, the Unión de Petroleros Mexicanos. Firemen, still men, carpenters, and mechanics formed its governing council. In April 1915, the workers at Minatitlán carried out a three-day work stoppage, demanding a 100 percent increase in their pay. First Chief Carranza and Governor Aguilar quickly offered protection to the 150 British employees at Minatitlán. Meanwhile, the workers gained a pay increase and the nine-hour day.[109] The strike that broke out on the morning of 27 May at the Standard Oil topping plant in Tampico had as its main objective the eight-hour day. Colonel Espinoza summoned plant superintendent C. O. Meyer to military headquarters and told him to accede to the strikers' demands. "He asked me, too, if it was certain that work had ceased in the plant and if some workers had crossed the strikers' picketline," Meyer reported. The superintendent admitted that he had encouraged a breach of the picket line because the workers had refused to return to work.[110] Meyer was not deported, after all.

The leadership of the Casa del Obrero Mundial also sought to reduce the employer's absolute control of the workplace. One thousand Huasteca workers went out in July to force the company's recognition of their union. Local authorities immediately guaranteed protection of company property, and the American employees kept the plant operating. El Aguila's laborers walked out in sympathy, though neither company would consider recognition of the unions involved. Apparently, wages were not an issue, since the company had just agreed to a 50 to 100 percent pay increase.[111] The struggle aroused the Mexican workers' resentment toward the Chinese and American laborers, none of whom were involved in the Mexican unions. Huasteca strikers demanded that the Chinese cooks be dismissed, but the company refused to give in. Some intimidation of nonstriking Mexican workers occurred. Casa sympathizers "intercepted the few who are working while they were returning to their home for dinner and threatened to kill them."[112] Andrés Araujo, general secretary of the El Aguila union, issued a stern warning to all foreign employees of the company. If the minority of workers do not respect the will of the majority, he said, the strike committee "shall exercise the force of direct action in order to have them comply by means of brute force what they do not and cannot understand by the light of reason."[113]

The labor leaders appealed to national political and military figures. They wrote to Gen. Pablo González, complaining of the "chaos" at the El Aguila plant and how "the bourgeoisie" was violating the general's own "progressive" decrees. He had designated an associate to intervene and mediate a previous dispute, which gained a wage increase for the boatmen. Nevertheless, General González requested advice from Pastor Rouaix, then an assistant secretary of the Ministry of Development, on how to deal with the petroleum companies. He said he wanted to be able to settle future strikes favorably for both parties but especially for the interests of the workers.[114] For the most part, the military authorities wanted to prevent the destruction of property so that the city's economy would not suffer.

Labor used more coercion in November when the Casa-affiliated union of the Colonia Transportation Company struck for the eight-hour day. The Colonia operated the water transport and motor launches under contract to the oil companies. The men on the picket lines intimidated those attempting to cross them and set fire to several company buildings. "Owing to the fact that there are about ten or fifteen thousand workmen and only three or four hundred soldiers in Tampico," reported the American consul, "the situation is a very delicate one and the military forces are afraid to forcibly resist the workmen for fear of creating riots."[115] The year 1915 ended on this distinctive note.

The struggle continued into the next year. In January 1916, the El Aguila workers at Minatitlán once again went on strike over wage issues. The state governor did not favor the strikers and on the sixth day persuaded the men to return to work. They walked off their jobs again in February. The strikers resented being paid in inflated Mexican paper money and demanded gold pesos. The strike spread to the nearby oil fields of Ixhuatlán and Nanchital, and crews on the coastal tank steamers agitated for a 20 percent pay increase. El Aguila's superintendent Gulston reported that the strikes were the result of "the great fluctuations in exchange and the consequent increased cost of living, and to the agitation existing on account of the Unions and their agitators."[116] By April, Tampico unions belonging to the Casa del Obrero Mundial sent ultimatums to employers. They demanded that the wages be paid on the basis of the Mexican gold peso and that the men receive their wages once a week rather than bimonthly. They also wanted an eight-hour day at the same daily (ten-hour) wage. Responding to the breakdown of the Mexico City alliance between the Casa and Carranza,

General Nafarrete sent troops against the strikers. He rounded up several union leaders. Moreover, the general instructed the unions to submit their grievances to him rather than to the employers.[117] State repression was just as ineffective in Tampico as in Mexico City. The workers continued to carry out the strikes, even if the Casa's leadership was thrown into doubt by sudden political disfavor.

General unrest among the workers resulted over wages—not union recognition—in the late spring of 1916. They demanded that the company pay them their wages equivalent in gold. But the companies calculated that the gold value of the peso was thirty cents (U.S.), whereas the workers insisted on the traditional gold value of fifty cents. Companies also resisted giving in to the eight-hour day. Once again, General Nafarrete attempted to negotiate, for he was not willing to permit the workers to riot. He expressed disgust at the recalcitrant attitude of the companies, which had discharged some of the strikers. Nafarrete assembled the workers in a mass meeting and told them to return to work for the pay raise that he had negotiated. The eight-hour day would be discussed later. The military commandant also informed strikers that if they started trouble, he would shoot them. The May unrest did not end with Nafarrete's intervention. Police arrested three foreign workers after an African-American boatman shot several Mexican picketers attempting to prevent the departure of an oil launch.[118]

Not all laborers sympathized with this agitation. It is probable that if authorities had not guaranteed the safety of nonstriking workers, many workers would have joined the strikers out of fear. General Magaña, chief of the local garrison, promptly called in the agitators, however, and warned them that he would not permit the slightest act against the right to work or against property. He held the labor leaders personally responsible for the commission of any such acts. The posting of soldiers around the city—military authorities were already edgy about *pelaecista* activity—calmed the labor situation, even though the companies had not yet endorsed the eight-hour day. Finally, the local military authorities wearied of the labor unrest. They decreed that the army was the supreme arbitrator of all wage and labor matters. They directed foreign businesses to pay all wages on the basis of the Mexican gold standard, regardless of the value of paper money. Any employer not willing to do so was invited to leave Mexico. The oil companies quietly agreed to pay on the gold standard but still refused to accede to the eight-hour day, obviously with the approval of the military.[119] The men were satisfied and returned to work, putting off further demands for a more appropriate time.

Labor agitation continued throughout the summertime. At the end of June 1916, responding to the popular disapproval of Pershing's expedition in Chihuahua, spokesmen at a labor rally denounced the Americans and promised to destroy the refineries if the marines landed. Meanwhile, General Nafarrete moved to repress another anarchist-inspired call for a general strike in Tampico. Nafarrete had just won the local election to attend the constitutional convention in Querétaro. "I speak to you without my commission as general, as I promised", he said following his election, "because political imposition is repugnant to me; today we are instituting a democratic government, and I desire not only to speak democratically, but also to demonstrate with deeds that I am a democrat."[120] Although Nafarrete was not a worker himself, his experience in Tampico informed him well as to the demands of the workers for a minimum wage and for the eight-hour day. These essentially working-class demands—and the state's role as labor mediator—found their way into the constitution, which should not cause surprise.

Even as the *constituyentes* met in December of 1916, labor activities continued in an effort to raise wages again to meet the steady rise in the cost of living. The Minatitlán refinery workers of El Aguila gained the concessions of being paid principally in silver currency and of receiving food tickets to supplement their income. Then the day laborers mounted a two-day strike at the Tampico refinery. They wanted higher wages to offset rising food prices.[121] Some nonstrikers were prevented from crossing the picket lines, and the general secretary of the journeymen's union exhorted all workers to practice self-discipline and mutual support.

> With profound indignation we have seen the villainous tyranny with which the companies treat us and especially El Aguila and Huasteca and others which impose laws that appear that we are in Babylon, without there being anyone to oppose this evil. In view of this, this union has agreed to request a pay increase of 75% over present salaries and that we be paid on the Saturday of each week.

Labor leaders invited their compatriots in other industries to mount a sympathy strike. "Compañeros: To the fight," they said; "do not fear death, because dying free is better than living as a slave."[122] Combative rhetoric for a simple pay raise.

By that time, the local Constitutional authorities had again run out of patience. They received a directive from Carranza to punish with death the acts of inciting to strike and promoting property destruction. Dispatched to the El Aguila refinery, troops apprehended and shot Manuel Rodríguez, thought to be the strike agitator. In fact, the real union leader was named Luis Rodríguez.[123] But the year 1916 ended with several patterns quite well established. Military officers at Tampico had already taken an active role in mediating labor disputes, forcing the companies to pay wage increases while also protecting their property. No constitutional authority as yet had required this intervention—but it was customary in Mexico. Workers had made known to authorities their demands for the eight-hour day and for wages that compensated them for higher prices. As they attempted to reestablish the political order in the final years of the Revolution, the bourgeois politicians could not have failed to understand: the workers were imposing certain economic reforms as a price of industrial peace. If the *constituyentes* intended Article 123 as a palliative—and they probably did—they were mistaken. Buoyed finally by the state's formal recognition of proletarian rights, workers now redoubled their efforts to press their demands. Dependent they may have been, but oil workers were not helpless.

Those Who Are Not with Us . . .

Although it would not go into effect until May 1917, the new constitution became known at the end of January. It lent new stature to the workers' struggle in Tampico, and they reacted with renewed vigor. The combination placed the owners on the defensive; now more than ever, they blamed the labor onslaught on "agitators of the I.W.W." and German provocateurs. El Aguila expanded the workers' nonmonetary benefits in the general stores and reduced the hours of work. By the end of February, the British oil company had pared its original twelve-hour shifts to nine hours for most workers, and to eight hours for pipeline crews. Their wages, however, remained the same as for the longer work day.[124] The laborers, nonetheless, struck again in April. Union officials gave employers twenty-four hours in which to accede to their demands for a 50 percent wage increase. Strikers assaulted two American managers of the firm and halted the loading of steam tankers. Even though Lord Cowdray informed them of rumors that German agents paid the unions to disrupt the oil business, British diplomats acted in the same manner as the Mexican officials. The Foreign Office suggested that Cowdray give in to workers' demands so as to avoid an outbreak that would force U.S. warships at Tampico into action, possibly provoking even further chaos.[125] Employers obviously could not expect much in the way of diplomatic support.

Within three days of the constitution's becoming effective in May, the strike spread to the Pierce refinery. Strikers entered the grounds and drove out the manager and seventeen American employees. Pierce's general superintendent reported that the strike leaders incited the men with their new rights under the constitution. "[T]here was a large congregation of the workmen about the center of our plant and the Agitators were up on pieces of machinery talking to them in their usual manner demanding that the strikers stick up for their rights in accordance with the new Constitution," he wrote, "and that they had the protection of the Government and therefore they were the power."[126] The local military commander declined to interfere with the strikers, who were demanding a 50 percent wage increase and the eight-hour day. "Unhappily," reported the American consul at Tampico, "the Mexican authorities as well as the policemen sent to preserve order have taken sides openly with the strikers and are supporting their actions." Dawson reported that the police took over the refinery and ordered the dismissal of a Mexican chief watchman unpopular with the union. The Americans concluded that strikers and officials alike were in the pay of German agents and the I.W.W.[127]

At any rate, El Aguila's previous settlement induced the workers and the public officials to expect the same of the Pierce refinery. The local municipal president summoned Superintendent Warren to his office. Warren had to explain why his company would not agree to a 25 percent wage increase too, "which was enormous," but the municipal president was not satisfied. According to the Pierce refinery chief:

[H]e said the Aguila had agreed to pay in Oro Nacional and showed me an officio wherein they had agreed to do this on account of an order from the Government of the state of Tamaulipas which stated that ALL PETROLEUM COMPANIES must pay their men in Oro Nacional or the equivalent in American money at the rate established by the Government, which means fifteen percent additional, making a total increase of forty percent.[128]

Superintendent Warren was defeated. The government ordered the Pierce workers back to work on 7 May with a 25 percent wage increase, paid in Mexican gold at the rate of two pesos to the dollar. Government officials, it appeared to the managers, were making common cause with workers.

The Tampico labor confederation apparently coordinated the strike movement from one company to the next, picking on the "soft touches" first, such as the conciliatory British firm of El Aguila. Then they spread the strike into the hard-line American firms like Pierce, Standard Oil, and The Texas Company. Labor leaders expected to achieve from each American employer what they had first gained from El Aguila. They even raised the ante. They demanded that the time spent traveling to and from work be included in the eight-hour day, that companies pay transport costs, and that fired workers receive three months' severance pay.[129]

Minatitlán workers also participated in these strike waves. No sooner had the Pierce strike been settled than the refinery at El Aguila Minatitlán shut down, "owing to absurd demands of workmen," as the British consul said. Having just settled a strike five months earlier with a 20 percent increase, the union demanded an additional 75 percent increase in the basic wage. Refinery superintendent Gulston received authority to give only 35 percent more. Labor-management negotiations before the municipal president broke down when labor leaders would compromise at no less than a 40 percent increase. Meanwhile, the strikers in the marine department also asked for a 90 percent wage hike, halting barge traffic.[130] As the work stoppage entered the second week and picketers began to intimidate those wishing to return to work, the state governor intervened to settle the strike. The governor achieved a sliding scale of wage adjustments. Those workers making two pesos per day received a 55 percent salary hike, those at three pesos per day got 43 percent, and those over three pesos got a 30 percent wage hike. A deadlock developed in the negotiations. As would increasingly become the trend, unmanageable wage disputes were given over to arbitration boards made up of a representative each from capital, labor, and the state.[131]

Finally, the strike wave rolled back to the Huasteca refinery and terminal at Mata Redonda on the Pánuco River. The Mexican workers walked out on 16 June. Huasteca could hardly hold out when other firms had already compromised with both workers and public officials. Huasteca gave in and by 20 June, the men were back at work. The managers were convinced the whole labor movement had been a German conspiracy. They reported that they saw three Germans passing bundles of money to eight Mexicans known to be members of the I.W.W.[132] Whether true or not, the workers had grievances stemming from the wartime bout of inflation. No amount of labor agitation and German

payoffs would motivate hundreds of men to strike, unless their proletarian dependency had not first alienated them.

But solidarity abounded during this time of full-employment inflation. Nowhere was this backing more apparent than in the efforts to extend the labor gains next to the boatmen of Tampico. The July 1917
boatmen's strike gained an extraordinary amount of support from refinery workers who had already won their demands. Known as Local
Branch no. 100 of the I.W.W., the maritime transport union formulated its three-page list of demands at the Tampico headquarters of the
Casa del Obrero Mundial. Their demands appeared to have come
straight from the constitution, which had been derived from earlier
working-class demands. They asked for three eight-hour shifts (which
would have increased the demand for employment), wage increases to
140 pesos monthly for seamen and 360 pesos for engineers and mas-
ters, free rations aboard the boats, prevention of dismissal for union
work, double pay for overtime, and no more than seven-hour overtime
shifts on Sundays, nights, and holidays. Why did these relatively privileged workers make these demands? "[D]ay by day, the rise in cost of
the articles of primary necessity as well as of clothes, housing, and local
transportation are not in balance with the inertia of the wages that we
earn for our personal efforts." A handbill signed by "El Obrero Mundial" circulated among the working class. It exhorted support for the
river boatmen. "From the 15th of this month," the anarchist handbill
warned, "those who are not with us will be our enemies."[133]

By mid-July, the dredgers, motor launches, steamboats, and barges
of twenty-one separate petroleum and marine companies lay idle on the
Pánuco River. In a letter written on stationery of the Philadelphia
I.W.W., union leaders warned the Huasteca Company that workers
would prevent the loading and departure of all steam tankers. The local
garrison commander, on the other hand, had promised free navigation
in the river.[134] When the steam tanker *Panuco* came alongside the Mexican Gulf dock, four union officials showed up to interrupt the loading
of fuel oil. The Gulf manager immediately took his car down to the garrison to complain. Pistol shots were fired at him as he passed the headquarters of the Casa del Obrero Mundial. *Pistoleros* also accompanied a
Portuguese-born strike leader when he prevented nonstriking workers
from boarding their boats for work. He told them they would be paid
if they too went on strike. Other "Spanish and Portuguese" labor leaders boarded a dredger and forced nonstrikers off the boat. The manager
claimed that the I.W.W. in Galveston had sent fifteen thousand dollars

to assist the Tampico boat strike.[135] In other words, the payoffs and coercion provoked the managers to underestimate the motivation of the
working class. "All of our Mexican workmen came to work for wages
with which they were absolutely content when hired," commented one
oilman. "The majority of them do not recognize the I.W.W. and are
quite willing to work, but are prevented from so doing by intimidation
and threats of bodily harm."[136] Collective action and coercion were not
new features of Mexican working-class behavior. Nor were they introduced by Spanish-born anarchists or the American I.W.W.

In fact, the marine workers' strike soon turned into a general strike.
The refinery workers went out again on 24 July. Oil managers appealed to the U.S. gunboats in the river, the U.S. State Department,
and also to Mexican military authorities. The first two parties declined
to intervene, but the latter ordered Mexican soldiers to protect the
refineries.[137] Other groups cooperating with the Casa halted the trams,
but the opposition of the local military authorities prevented the workers from shutting down the power-and-light plant. Strike leaders remained defiant, broadening their rhetorical attacks to include the government itself.[138] After all, they were discovering that civil and military
authorities took exception if the economy was threatened, which this
general strike did.

Negotiations began in earnest before Gen. Alfredo Ricaut, the
governor of Tamaulipas, who happened to be in Tampico. He had
arrived with five hundred soldiers, a contingent that no doubt reinforced his authority among the workers. Five oil managers conferred
with Ricaut. This meeting represented the first occasion in which the
oil companies had united to confront a labor strike. The five local executives may be forgiven if in this novel situation, they disclaimed having sufficient authority to make concessions. Ricaut asked the company
officials to talk with the union men. They refused, saying that they
would deal not with the I.W.W. but with committees of their own employees—after the men came back.[139] In the end, the general strike was
too much for General Ricaut. His forces arrested seventeen I.W.W.
leaders. They also apprehended the Portuguese labor leader Manuel
Almeda and deported him to Laredo, where he was detained by American officials. Meanwhile, the companies remained firm, and when
strike funds ran out, the workers returned to work.[140] The strikers
were more exhausted than broken. The failure of this anarchist-inspired
general strike provided a respite in labor unrest in Tampico. But it did
not stop it.

At the end of September 1917, workers at the Pierce and El Aguila refineries returned to the picket lines. The previous settlement at Pierce had not met several union demands, such as paying in national money at the "official Government rate of exchange." So the labor representatives made new demands for a 50 percent wage increase, recognition of the union, providing a commissary like other companies had, and the observance of Article 123. They insisted "that workmen must not be maltreated nor sworn at, as this is contrary to Law." They also sought the dismissal of three supervisors who apparently violated these rules.[141] Then, workers at El Aguila also declared a strike, demanding wage hikes of 50 to 70 percent. Neither strike lasted for long. Most workers did not leave their work places, a fact that calls into question the ability of labor leaders to make them strike, as many managers tended to believe. Just the same, the local authorities took advantage of the situation and deported two alien anarchist leaders of the Tampico Casa, one a Cuban and the other a Spaniard.[142]

Additional unrest occurred, nonetheless, when the Board of Conciliation announced the final settlement of the previous April's Pierce strike demands. It had been favorable to labor. The president of the board ordered Pierce to pay its workers a salary equivalent to what the workers at El Aguila made. The refinery was to provide a hospital, where injured permanent workers could recover on full salary and temporary workers could convalesce on one-half pay. Moreover, Pierce was to build a commissary, as El Aguila had, and provide workers goods at cost. The Pierce manager came under the board's censure for "notoriously bad faith" for having resisted this latter demand of the workers.[143]

Meanwhile, managers caught rumors about workers planning a "riot" at the Huasteca and El Aguila companies. Nervous military commanders, then outfitting a campaign against Peláez, sent troops to guard the refineries. More labor leaders were arrested.[144] The repression of some of the leadership did not at all end their cost-of-living crisis, nor did it change their full-employment opportunities to do something about it. But government authorities in 1917 had placed the workers on notice. Although they would help the workers negotiate additional benefits from employers, they would not tolerate a major interruption of the oil economy, from which the government obtained important tax revenues. In the process, however, the companies were losing their absolute control over the terms of employment, and their labor expenses were rising.

The Politicization of Labor

The labor unrest that had grown from 1915 to reach a crescendo in 1917 tapered off during the years from 1918 to 1920. International conditions were much the same as they had been since the start of World War I. Domestically, however, perhaps a degree of agricultural recovery in Central Mexico, following the defeat of the Villa faction and the decline of the *zapatistas,* may have brought down the prices of foodstuffs somewhat. Wages were also up 50 percent from what they were earlier, and almost all oil workers, thanks to their own efforts, now enjoyed at least a nine-hour day and rest on Sundays.[145] Workers did not exactly refrain from striking just because their hours and pay were far better than those earned elsewhere in the economy. In times of full employment, workers sought their fair share of capitalist growth. But full employment might not have been the situation in 1918. The labor demand was slackening in the oil industry. Most pipelines, refineries, and terminals had already been constructed, obviating the need for large numbers of semiskilled and unskilled construction workers. The Mexico City newspaper *El Universal* reported that the oil companies were reducing salaries and emoluments because Tampico's labor supply was increasing. Workers were arriving daily aboard trains traveling over the newly repaired line from San Luis Potosí. There was speculation that the companies were curtailing their expansion because of the uncertainty provoked by Carranza's nationalism.[146] This was also a time of known saltwater intrusion in the wells. Creeping unemployment smothered the penchant to strike. No worker would be willing to protest if he could be easily replaced by an eager bumpkin fresh from the farm. Finally, the Constitutionalist authorities were tiring of labor unrest and repressed it.

Whatever the reasons, the will among oil workers to press their demands for greater privileges had been much reduced in 1918. The El Aguila strike in March turned out to be a failure. Workers walked off the job on 20 March, demanding a 75 percent hike in their wages. The managers replied that they would have to reduce the work force by one-half to be able to afford such an increase. Local authorities sent guards to protect the refinery, and no one reported any distasteful disturbances.[147] The government guaranteed the security of those workers wishing to return to work early, and many did. The company did not have to shut down the stills at all. At the time, El Aguila refinery employed 872 men and 48 boys, only some of whom were dismissed for not returning to work. The gleeful manager had noticed the lack of spirit among the strikers. "One has to note," said the company's report to the Labor Department, "that of the 828 workers who took part in this strike, some 500 were disposed to continue working, but the others would not let them. Proof of this is that on 21 [March], 205 operators reported for work; on the 22nd, 286; on the 23rd, 345; on the 24th, 426; the 30th, 651; by 2 [April] all already had returned."[148] Thus passed another year. The oil companies continued to raise exports to new highs, and oil prices climbed even after the armistice of 11 November 1918. The following year brought more of the same. Worker unrest in the oil refineries and terminals of Mexico declined as labor activities became more politicized.

A new round of labor unrest might have been in the offing for 1919, if the Constitutionalist government, with an election approaching, had not taken a dim view of it. Eight hundred out of one thousand workers walked off the job at the Transcontinental refinery at Las Matillas on April 16. Transcontinental kept the refinery operating with the one-fifth of its work force that had not struck. Leaders of the Gremio de Obreros demanded not wages (the average already was five pesos daily) nor the eight-hour day (which they already had). They now pressed for eight days severance pay if laid off. The Board of Conciliation, having been newly set up under the auspices of the 1917 Constitution, ruled against the workers but ordered the company not to fire strikers. Within five days, the workers were back on the job.[149] Transcontinental's stoppage was not so divisive as the other plainly political strike that followed.

Workers of the Pierce refinery went out on the biggest strike of 1919, supported by the political forces backing General Obregón. Does this suggest that oil strikes might have been politically inspired? Yes and no. No doubt the Pierce oil workers still harbored a number of grievances against the oldest operating refinery in Mexico. But union leaders also sought the advantage of cooperating with the faction that promised to be the winner in the national political contest. Backing a successful politician gained a union enormous advantages in bargaining with the employer. It also enabled union leaders to move into the bureaucracy.

Four hundred Pierce workers began their strike at a propitious time, the end of May. It was the beginning of the electoral season. Obregón had just declared for the presidency, and his local supporter, Emilio

Portes Gil, had formed the newspaper *El Diario* in Tampico. Portes Gil had also represented labor in the formation of the Partido Laborista, which supported Obregón, whereas members of the Casa del Obrero Mundial of Tampico formed the Comité Antimilitarista. Its purpose was to "avoid the militarization of the children in the Public Schools."[150] No doubt the organization rankled the local military commanders, who were all ardent *carrancistas*. The political overtones of this strike could hardly have pleased the authorities.

At any rate, the local labor organizations all indicated support for the strikers. Many workers in El Aguila, Huasteca, La Corona, Gulf, and The Texas Company supported the demands of the Trabajadores Unidos de la Pierce. As a member of the Federación de Sindicatos Casa del Obrero Mundial, its slogan was "Salud y Revolución Social," identical to that adopted by CROM. The union had made five principal demands: that a fired worker be reinstated; that the company recognize the union; that pay be increased by 25 percent; that the decrepit commissary be closed down; and that striking workers not be fired. They could not count on the support of Carranza's military officers, however. It was said that even Gen. Diéguez, who as office clerk had led the Cananea mining strikes of 1906, was loyally guarding against "Bolsheviki" laborers. General Magaña jailed four of the strike leaders in one of the secondary sympathy strikes and posted dozens of soldiers conspicuously in several of Tampico's plazas.[151] Pierce officials offered to settle the strike by distributing five thousand pesos to workers through the Board of Conciliation and to build a new commissary. But the company refused to increase the pay, which they said equalled that of other companies, and would not pay the workers' wages for the time they were on strike. The strike leaders repudiated the intervention of Carranza's labor department. They called the Board of Conciliation a tool of the Pierce Oil Company. Instead, the workers appealed to Gen. López de Lara, who at the time was disputing the governorship of Tamaulipas with a Carranza favorite.[152] The whole strike was hopelessly caught up in the whirlwind of Mexican politics.

When the Pierce Oil Company rejected the workers' demands, tensions rose. The labor confederation called a general strike to support the Pierce workers, conspicuously using force. Pierce's managers said that many "old" workers were afraid to return to work because agitators were threatening them. Gen. Ricardo González, the garrison commander, warned the strike leaders not to interfere with laborers who chose to work. A labor organizer died in a confrontation with soldiers

at the railway station. Next, several meetings between the strike delegates and the mayor failed to reach a compromise amidst mutual re-
crimination. The workers accused the *carrancista* mayor of committing
"a political error, giving himself over to snatching supremacy."[153] Concluded the Pierce superintendent:

> In general terms I can say that the strike is due to the common unrest in the
> work places caused by the evolution of one condition to another, this unrest
> having been taken advantage of and augmented, for their own personal ad-
> vancement, by professional agitators and local leaders of the Casa del Obrero
> Mundial and by bosses of local factions of political parties. There is no doubt
> that the most powerful force in this movement was that of a political faction in
> the region that was using the agitators of the Casa del Obrero Mundial for its
> own ends and was encouraging workers to provoke difficulties not only for us
> but also for the Government.[154]

Still, El Aguila's refinery operated with the staff only, because the
workers were staying away. It was but a matter of time before a spark
ignited the volatile situation.

It ignited on 16 June. Local labor leaders resolved to perfect the general strike. Their assembly adjourned from the Casa headquarters and
poured into the streets surrounding the Plaza Libertad, where some four
hundred strikers and sympathizers boarded the trolley cars and stopped
traffic. Several streetcar drivers were persuaded to abandon their trol-
leys. The commander of the military police, Maj. Martínez Cuadras, resolved to get one trolley running again. He personally drove it to the
plaza, where it was promptly surrounded by strike sympathizers. The
major drew his pistol and fired but soon fell from a mortal stab wound.
General González himself led a mounted troop to clear the Plaza Libertad, and eight strikers also died. Days afterward, the authorities closed
down the Casa del Obrero Mundial and arrested several of the politicians, lawyers, and labor leaders who had supported the strike. They
locked them up in a railway hog car and shipped them to a penitentiary
in Chihuahua. Among the detainees were Emilio Portes Gil, the state's
leading *obregonista* and future president; Andrés Araujo, a Casa organizer and future labor inspector; one school teacher; and two members
of the Pierce union.[155] If the strike had political overtones, so did its
repression. By 24 June, the workers returned from their month-long
strike, saying, "They reserved their rights for a better opportunity."[156]
No other strikes marred the rest of this year of record petroleum exports.

In fact, the era of strikes had come to an end for the time being. The
mechanics' strike of January 1920, which agitated for a salary raise to

Fig. 17. El Aguila's can and case factory at Tampico, 1920. Canning was one of the more labor-intensive processes in the refinery. Here migrant men (and boys) found employment filling the tin containers in which kerosene was marketed in Mexico. The well-dressed man operating the canning machine had skill and experience and became a leader on the shop floor. El Aguila used a swastika-like logo before the rise of German fascism. From the Pearson Photograph Collection, British Science Museum Library, London, courtesy of Pearson PLC.

8.80 pesos per day to all first-class mechanics, ended quickly when Huasteca's William Green convinced the other companies to compromise with the union. The failure of the Pierce strike, however, motivated the labor leadership to await the resolution of national political events. Despite at least five years of militant labor activity in the city, it was characteristic of the Tampico labor scene that most workers were not unionized. A majority of the unskilled workers, calculated to consist of some thirty-five thousand *obreros,* still remained outside the union movement. They had contributed to the success of their skilled brethren in the mechanics union, for example, by respecting their picket lines and acting as scabs (*esquiroles*) only under military protection.[157] A second characteristic of this labor movement pertained to its leadership. The oil companies maintained that the leaders of these skilled workers had not themselves been employees. They were always willing to negotiate with their own workers, who were the best remunerated in all of Mexico, company officials said.[158] Lawyers, journalists, and teachers provided much of the union leadership.

In May of 1920, momentous events transpired in Tampico. A barracks revolt broke out against the *carrancista* military officers who had repressed the Pierce strike one year before, and General Peláez took charge of the city in Obregón's name. The militant workers who had once gone out on general strike, however, now sat on their hands. They did not attack the discredited *carrancista* military men. Nor apparently did they see this political transition as the "better opportunity" to exercise their rights, as their leaders had indicated when the Pierce strike fizzled. The oil workers stayed on the job throughout the political events of May 1920. They had their reasons. The cost-of-living crisis had abated, the demand for labor continued to decline somewhat as the migration of unskilled workers from the central plateau swelled the ranks of job seekers, and workers in the oil industry had already won benefits. Therefore, laborers were not motivated to risk their jobs in a dispute between politicians. They may indeed have been happy at the victory of General Obregón. But the rank-and-file workers at Tampico contributed little to it.

What can be concluded from this catalogue of sometimes contradictory evidence about the making of the oil proletariat? The first thing is that modern capitalism brought both opportunities and uncertainties to the Mexican working class. On the one hand, the companies paid higher wages and offered a degree of social prestige to the Mexican employee. The more skilled who "lent their services," as the saying went, to the oil companies enjoyed company housing and other prerogatives, especially differential pay scales, which affirmed their exalted positions within the traditional hierarchy of the Mexican working class. Inasmuch as the companies continued to operate in a fashion that supported these goals, the individual worker developed a loyalty toward the foreign owners—and toward capitalism itself. They were indeed led by leaders who were avowed anarchists. But workers did not subscribe to any behavior that threatened to destroy capitalism or smash the state. They intended for their strikes merely to force the state to take their side against the companies over a narrow range of economic issues.

If their militant activity intended to do anything, it was surely meant to redress those elements introduced by the foreign companies that violated Mexican traditions. Workers especially fought the worst consequence of proletarianization: the insecurity. Working for the oil companies, except perhaps in the oil fields themselves, had demanded that employees give up all ties to other means of subsistence. For Mexicans born to the hacienda and village agriculture of the central plateau, the move down to Tampico signified entry into a new regime in which high wages gradually replaced security and mobility. New unskilled migrants entered the job market in construction, working from one day to the next, in large work gangs. They graduated to work at the port under the same conditions, signing on a day at a time. Thus far, Mexican peons who worked in the urban environment did not have to change any of their strategies for articulating between traditional village agricultural and modern modes of production. They could return to their villages whenever they desired. But to continue to take advantage of opportunities at Tampico, workers sought more permanent employment.

Perhaps the Revolution itself pressured workers into such behavior, for the disruption of agricultural production in the more populated central states prevented a return to the soil for many. Therefore, workers aspired to more permanent employment at the oil companies. This represented a very real change in their time and work discipline.[159] At the beginning of the Revolution, oil companies desired twelve-hour days and six-day weeks. The new employers seldom distinguished between day or night work or between weekdays, Sundays, and holidays. No longer could employees simply take a day off, as they did in construction and the port works. Oilmen demanded maximum utilization of their skills. To become an oil worker during the Great Mexican Oil

Boom was to become proletarianized. As long as high wages compensated them for the loss of their cherished independence, Mexicans were willing to accept proletarianization—their dependence in the new industrial order.

But dependence also brought vulnerability to economic conditions beyond the workers' control. They became the victims of periodic economic depressions that impelled capitalists to cut back on wages and workers. Such had not been the case during the Great Mexican Oil Boom, when demand for work remained relatively high from 1911 to 1920, because both prices and exports of Mexican petroleum tended to rise. What afflicted the workers most was the cost-of-living crisis. In Mexico, the revolutionary depredations of the countryside, throwing the nation into near famine and raising the prices of foodstuffs and basic commodities, compounded the more general world phenomenon of rising commodity prices attendant upon World War I. During times of price inflation, workers on fixed wages discovered that they could afford fewer and fewer of the basic commodities of life, let alone the modest luxuries to which industrial workers had become accustomed.

Working for the oil companies also placed pressure on the traditional prerogatives of the skilled Mexicans. For one thing, their security in the labor hierarchy was limited by the power of the employers over the workplace. Oil executives could hire, fire, and promote workers according to their own dictates of rewarding skill and efficiency and punishing labor militancy. The skilled worker was pressured from below by unskilled workers aspiring to rise into the better-paying jobs. At the same time, an upper stratum of foreign workers prevented the skilled Mexican from rising to the highest rungs of the labor hierarchy. Many proletarians had previously encountered these very same phenomena at the beginning of the century in the foreign-owned railway and mining industries. The evidence shows that many Mexicans advanced as the Americans left Mexico.

The logical outcome of the insecurities of proletarianization in the oil industry was labor militancy. The skilled used their command over the work process and their traditional authority over unskilled workers to form unions and to strike. They requested higher wages and eight-hour days for all workers, meeting the needs of the unskilled as well as widening the number of workers in the industry. Reduction of the twelve-hour day to nine or eight implied that the companies would have to increase their labor force by up to one-third if they operated around the clock.[160] Labor leaders, representing the skilled more than the unskilled, still maintained the wage differentials that gave the skilled workers their traditional hegemony. They also demanded resolution of issues of security: recognition of unions, severance pay, and promotion of Mexican workmen into positions held by foreigners. The war helped the latter problem, for the military conscription removed many Americans and Britons from the work force. All Mexicans resented it when the Americans, now proud and victorious Legionnaires, tried to return in 1919. But by this time, the companies discovered that they did not have to rehire rather indifferent American workers at inflated wages. Mexicans sufficed—at lower pay.

Meanwhile, however, Mexican workers continued to exercise their traditional prerogative of appealing to political authorities. That they conferred perquisites of leadership upon well-connected and politically astute bourgeois leaders, the new *caciques* of the twentieth century, did not at all violate customary behaviors of the Mexican working class. Many school teachers and lawyers provided the early leadership of oil workers in Tampico and Minatitlán. One found *caciquismo* (petty bossism), an ancient Mexican phenomenon, at all social levels. Everyone expected that the *cacique* would contribute a degree of coercion among his minions, to make the system function—so that strikes were effective. Furthermore, the new labor *caciques* afforded workers the protection and patronage of their political contacts. Labor activities, magnified out of proportion to the weight of the urban and industrial workers in the Mexican population and far exceeding the role of the workers in the revolutionary violence, eventually paid off great dividends. Politicians wrote the demands of workers into the constitution, hoping thereby to revalidate traditional social controls for the changing economic times.

But workers did benefit from the Revolution. "The spirit of revolution has bred a feeling of hostility to any restraint on the part of the men," observed the oilman Herbert Wylie, "and they are consequently less easily handled than formerly."[161] Yet neither labor bosses nor politicians could make the workers strike against their collective volition. No well-connected labor leader could ever convince workers to join worker militias or fight the local garrison. The most the labor leaders could deliver, besides the short-lived Red Battalions of 1915, was labor neutrality. In a showdown, when the *constitucionalistas* besieged the *huertistas* in Tampico in 1914, and when the *obregonistas* wrested the city from the *constitucionalistas* in 1920, labor neutrality was worth something. At least, thousands of workers did not assist the defenders.

The behavior of the workers and the bourgeoisie in the revolutionary turmoil of Mexico responded to traditional customs and norms.
Each class within the new social order imposed by rapid capitalist transformation resolved to rearrange their lives according to traditional values. Mexicans understood this. The foreign employers did not. They attributed any demand for curtailing the foreign companies' absolute
control of the labor market to German agents, radical agitators, "Bol-
shevikis," or conniving politicians. During the Revolution, however,
the Mexicans were merely taking charge of their own destiny. They
were not rejecting capitalism so much as shaping it to fit the Mexican
mold. Even though they called themselves social revolutionaries, neither the politicians nor the labor leaders viewed that destiny as being
such an abrupt departure from the past. If anything broke decisively
with the past, unbridled capitalism did. Therefore, Mexicans sought to
bridle it.

Conclusion: The Ambivalence toward Modernization

"I do not understand the Mexicans," the foreign oilman might have said repeatedly. "We brought them our capital, our technology, our management. We contributed more taxes and paid higher wages than they could have accomplished without us. They themselves invited us. And they still treated us shabbily." True, the Mexicans had desired the benefits of modern capitalism. They anticipated the profits, the contributions to the building of the nation state, the ability to renew social controls, and the alternatives to work in low-wage agriculture. But the capitalism envisioned by the Mexicans was not that of the unfettered free market. Nor one of unbridled individualism.

What the foreign companies introduced, however, was the capitalism of the Anglo-American world, which had been relatively free of the rigid social structure of a delicately balanced, postcolonial, multiracial society. Indeed, Anglo-America uniquely had fewer obstacles to change and could accept rapid economic transformation as a permanent condition of life. In Mexico, however, economic change implied cutting across the racial and class antagonisms that authoritarian structures were created to hold in check. Industrialization created a spirited and rambunctious working class that challenged their new dependency through popular actions such as strikes and participation in politics. Modernization brought the elites great wealth. But it also contributed its own set of social dangers. Elites in Mexico, aware of the hatred of the subjugated masses and the antagonism of the have-nots, had always feared rebellion from below. The Mexican Revolution merely confirmed what the Porfirian elites were beginning to suspect: foreign-led capitalism had gone too far.

For the Mexican working class, modernization held out both benefits and pitfalls. Foreign employers proffered opportunities for workers to gain higher wages, more prestige, and a degree of social mobility. Workers could escape the orbit of the hacendados and *jefes políticos*. Thousands of Mexican peons moved from predominantly agricultural to urban and industrial lifestyles. The children of workers now might wear shoes, attend a school, and learn a valuable trade. On the other hand, the Mexican working class had to pay the price: its own proletarianization. Mexican laborers were gradually separated from access to the means of production. They left the fields, which already suffered from increasing population pressure and later from revolutionary turmoil. They worked on the owner's property and with the owner's tools. They increasingly labored the the owner's hours and under his conditions. Of course, it did not mean that all workers were compressed into a faceless, deskilled mass. The familiar hierarchy of the Mexican working class was created anew by industrialization.

But Mexican workers had been born to the struggle against proletarianization early on. They acceded to the process of proletarianization under their own conditions, forcing employers to maintain the wage scale and acting collectively when the need arose. Indeed, it did arise. Foreign investment of such an advanced nature—railways and oil wells were the beginning of modernization in Mexico, whereas they had culminated a long period of economic change in the United States—brought a new layer of *conquistadores*. Foreign capitalists required, especially at first, large numbers of foreign workers and supervisors who were familiar with the latest technology. Their pay and benefits from the very beginning far exceeded the salary of the Mexicans. These English-speaking, white laborers did not much care for the brown-skinned, black-haired Mexicans to whom they were supposed to transfer their technological skills. They refused to conduct business in Spanish and live with the native workers. In fact, as a privileged minority, the American workers conspired to keep the Mexicans from taking their jobs and from advancing in rank. They brought in Chinese workers who extended to them personal services at low wages.

Proletarianization also implied that the urban and industrial workers became vulnerable to international economic depression. Inflation might reduce their incomes, and when laid off, industrial proletarians had little to fall back on. Industrialists were first and foremost businessmen. They had to balance the books and show a profit for the shareholders. Workers were expendable. To combat the menace of the foreign worker and to cope with the layoffs and cost-of-living crises— in short, to make their proletarianization bearable—workers resorted to the traditions of collective action. They gave up some authority to the new *caciques,* the labor bosses, many of whom, like their ancient leaders, were from among the most skilled, highest paid, and most privileged of their class or were members of the bourgeoisie. Politicized and sometimes coercive unionism proved an appropriately Mexican solution to remedy the worst effects of proletarianization.

Of these precedents and these effects, the foreigners were only dimly aware. Henry Clay Pierce and Edward L. Doheny had not entered Mexico as philanthropists. They participated in the spillover of industrial activity from within the United States, replicating their domestic successes abroad in order to make a buck. Mexico's economy was booming and consuming more petroleum products. Pierce fulfilled the role of developing Mexico's appetite for oil by profiting from what he did best in the United States: transporting and selling U.S. products manufactured from oil and technologies provided by his patron, the Standard Oil Company. Making profits also motivated Doheny. He opened up Mexico's petroleum production based upon the lessons he had learned, with profit, in developing oil fields in California.

British capital contributed to oil pioneering at the behest of the Mexican government. Wary of the economic clout the Americans were acquiring, the Porfirian elite encouraged the formation of a British oil operation by an entrepreneurial engineer who was not an experienced oilman. Sir Weetman Pearson warmed to his task, importing technology and expertise from the American and European oil fields. Eventually, he reproduced in Mexico the strategy that had made a few big oil firms successful in the United States: he achieved vertical integration. Pearson's new company, El Aguila, undermined Pierce's import business by combining production, refining, transport, and marketing, all within the Mexican market. Finally, together, El Aguila and Doheny's Mexican firm, Huasteca, brought in the great oil wells that set off the Great Mexican Oil Boom of the 1910s.

Seemingly oblivious to the revolutionary political ferment around them, the oil companies now entered a period of rapid organizational growth that propelled them to become more integrated into the world petroleum economy. They did so by continuing the Americanization of their economic structure. The legal basis of their industry, as in the United States, was the private property contract, which minimized state regulation of the industry. In selling their excessive production, the Mexican-based firms of Huasteca and El Aguila sold to the big international companies such as Standard Oil of New Jersey and sought additional security in developing their own refining and marketing capabilities abroad. Demand for oil was burgeoning. The erstwhile giants of the industry, Jersey Standard and Shell, felt compelled to enter Mexican production as a defensive measure. They did not wish to have their world market shares completely overwhelmed by the growth of independent competitors like Huasteca and El Aguila. Thus far, the foreign capitalists in Mexico were behaving as if they operated in the United States.

At the same moment, however, Mexico was undergoing its most intensive self-examination since the mid–nineteenth century. The Revolution forced those who fought it and those who survived it to define the parameters of the new social order. Although the oilmen believed that the Mexican Revolution did not concern them, the Mexicans thought otherwise. The very presence of foreigners in Mexico was a political act, and even political enemies like Carranza and Peláez agreed that the prosperous oil companies owed them. Increased taxation and forced loans for the revolutionary leaders and robbery and depredations for the common soldiers all followed in due course. Mexican politicians jockeyed for power, dragging the companies into the political struggle. Engaged in their own business struggles, oilmen were unable to fashion a united response and their home governments offered little assistance. More than anyone, Peláez reminded the companies of their unavoidable involvement in Mexican affairs. Yet he followed well-established Mexican customs in insisting that the foreign companies subordinate themselves to *his* political requirements, not the reverse.

During the Revolution, the nation also reexamined the precise relationship between the state, the economy, and the social order. Economic entities from colonial times had always had their social functions, to keep people in line and to provide for their minimum security. Whenever conflict between landlords and peasants, and employers and employees, threatened social breakdown, the state had been ready to step in. The Porfirians also wielded political power to generate capitalist development, even if in the end they could not control it. So it was during the widespread rebellions of the Mexican Revolution that the state felt obligated to increase the taxation, regulation, and social obligations of the foreign interests. Economic nationalism and statism were not conditions born merely of twentieth-century complexities. When faced with upheaval from below, the revolutionary leadership sought to reestablish and reinforce the customary role of the state in both the economy and society.

The Mexican Revolution did not challenge capitalism itself. In the petroleum industry, workers did not participate significantly in revolutionary violence. None sought to smash capitalism; no one was consistently anti-American. Few political and labor leaders were outright anarchists; none, Marxist-Leninists. Despite what the oilmen may have believed, up to 1920 neither the bourgeois politicians nor the urban and industrial workers had ever attacked private ownership of the means of production in industry. That is, not yet.

Some readers, knowing that Mexico expropriated the private foreign oil companies in 1938, may believe that I have needlessly tormented my clientele by not referring to that denouement. Not at all. The story of the foreign oil companies in Mexico from 1880 to 1920 is sufficiently instructive when viewed in the context of Mexico's panoramic history. The international oil companies were among the greatest business organizations of their time. They were powerful harbingers of economic and social change—of modern capitalist society. Their activities carried enormous economic and social implications. Few Mexicans ever forgot—and those that did were reminded by the Revolution—that the nation's volatile, postcolonial heterogeneous society imposed strict limitations on how much it could imitate the economic and social patterns of the United States. That is why Mexican workers and politicians alike sought to remake capitalism. The potential of capitalism to generate growth and material comforts for a rapidly growing population of Mexicans might have been impossible had not every generation from the time of Porfirio Díaz, nay before, worked to incorporate modernization into time-honored and comfortable patterns of social relationships.

Postscript

Capitalism did not introduce equity to an inequitable society, and it may even have made Mexican society more inequitable.

Therefore, one might say that the Mexicans of the Revolution displayed extraordinary genius in not falling into the abyss of rigid state socialism. They could still count on new industrial growth, within malleable parameters, to provide for a rapidly growing population, even if it failed to distribute the benefits of growth equitably throughout its still diverse population. But postrevolutionary industrial growth did not come in the oil industry, a condition that added new, significantly different elements to the story.

Up to 1920, there had been little in Mexico's oil history to suggest that the ultimate nationalization of the oil industry was inevitable. The conditions that led to expropriation were products of the subsequent history of foreign oil companies in Mexico. Nineteen twenty was a watershed year. Not only did Carranza fall, but petroleum prices began to break and production also commenced to decline. President Obregón consolidated political control of the state to a degree not enjoyed by a Mexican president since Díaz, allowing him and his successor, President Calles, to impose new taxes and regulations upon the industry. But in reality, there was much less to tax in the mid-1920s. Production had declined by a factor of four-fifths. The companies, still endeavoring to remain competitive in international markets, laid off thousands of workers in 1921 and 1922. When the oil economy once again reached an equilibrium, the workers responded to the widespread social dislocation by organizing larger unions and fashioning a durable alliance with the state. Wage increases, improved benefits, and collective contracts followed in due course during the economic recovery from 1923 to 1925. The concentration of ownership in the industry preserved a measure of the companies' former autonomy, although British oilmen often broke with their American counterparts on labor and governmental issues.

Yet in the 1920s, the Mexican petroleum industry was but a shell of its former robust self. The companies retreated before the exhaustion of the oil fields, international competition, growing domestic demand, the resurgent Mexican state, and continuing labor militancy. Private foreign capital was forced to concede some of its exclusive property rights and to yield to workers' demands for more security and reward. The companies' exclusive command of the Mexican oil industry was further constrained. Although the depression and political turmoil of the early 1930s rendered labor and the state unable to capitalize on the industry's weaknesses, these precedents remained to be acted upon later.

In 1934, Mexico and the oil companies entered a new age, strengthening one and weakening the other. Both labor and the state renewed the centralization begun in the early 1920s but now in ways even more mutually reinforcing. The Mexican oil industry became increasingly marginalized in the international market, as the foreign companies raised their production in Colombia, Peru, and especially Venezuela. An early Mexican rebound from worldwide depression enhanced the domestic market for petroleum products and multiplied the mechanisms by which labor and the state could make new impositions. For all of this, it remains difficult to state that the oil companies were doomed in Mexico. No one could have predicted the oil expropriation.

The formation of the national petroleum union in 1936 brought great pressure on the companies. The refinery unions from Tampico and Minatitlán brought together some twenty-one separate unions representing seventeen different foreign interests to form the Sindicato de Trabajadores Petroleros de la República Mexicana (STPRM). The new petroleum workers union joined the newly formed Confederación de Trabajo de México, which had wrested power from the CROM in the early 1930s. The STPRM subsequently presented the companies a lengthy collective contract that would have equalized pay and benefits across the industry, bringing workers of smaller companies up to the standard of those of the bigger concerns. Most importantly, the companies would lose many of their managers and supervisors to the union. Employers were gradually losing control over the workplace. Many foreign workers had been laid off during the 1920s and 1930s and not replaced. At the same time that Mexicans were gaining ascendency in the workplace, the union itself was extending its control over the workers. By January 1938, only three thousand of the eighteen thousand laborers in the industry remained outside the STPRM.

More than anything, the demands of organized petroleum workers brought an end to the operations of the private foreign oil companies in Mexico. Having suffered severely for their proletarianization in the 1922 and 1930 layoffs, workers willingly conferred enormous power on their leaders in exchange for security. In fact, when the oil companies bristled at the idea of union control of personnel matters and resisted all government mediation, the union leaders demanded that the state expropriate the industry. The companies wanted to force President Cárdenas to intervene and discipline the oil workers. Moreover, Jersey Standard and other American executives did not want Mexico to establish a precedent that other countries would be tempted to emulate.

These considerations prompted the companies to repudiate the Supreme Court decision of 1 March 1938, which favored labor. Moreover, the foreign executives did not believe the Mexicans were capable of running their own oil industry.

These actions placed the companies on a collision course with labor and the state. The British and Dutch managers of El Aguila wished to reach a last-minute compromise but failed. Days before Cárdenas decreed the oil expropriation, the oil workers had begun to seize control of the oil installations. Under the circumstances, given the uncompromising attitude of both the companies and the labor unions, Cárdenas had no choice but to expropriate. He did so during a dramatic nationwide broadcast on 18 March 1938, a date many Mexicans associate with the economic independence of Mexico. The foreign oilmen were stunned. They had not believed that the state would move so decisively just to reestablish the equilibrium between capital and labor. But the Mexican state resolved that it was in the interests of the nation's social welfare to operate this basic industry directly rather than to allow the resistance of the oil proletariat from threatening the economic health of a nation that since 1880 had grown to depend on petroleum energy. In a manner of speaking, the expropriation culminated a long process by which Mexico absorbed this modern economic function, the production of petroleum products, while at the same time preserving the fragile domestic social and political peace.

The process continues today. Notwithstanding the fact that the state in Mexico and throughout much of Latin America now seeks to solve the problems of economic stagnation and social unrest by inviting in the private interests (as did the Porfirians in the 1880s), this economic restructuring neither reverses nor invalidates the lessons learned in Mexico's historical experiences with the foreign oil companies. Significantly, the politicos have for now ruled out the return of Pemex to private capital. Labor apparently will support—or at least not oppose— the selling of other parastate industries to private foreign and domestic interests as long as it does not injure their interests in worker security. Mexican workers will also welcome new private industries. But a faltering of the process might once again bring forth the economic nationalists and union militants. As in everything, time will tell.

Notes

Introduction

1. As told to the author by Santiago Roel, Austin, Texas, 17 Aug 1988.
2. *El Universal*, 25 Mar 1938.
3. Raúl Prebisch, *Towards a Dynamic Development Policy for Latin America* (New York, 1963); André Gunder Frank, *Capitalism and Underdevelopment in Latin America: Historical Studies of Chile and Brazil* (New York, 1969); E. Bradford Burns, *The Poverty of Progress* (New York, 1980); Fernando Henrique Cardoso and Enzo Faletto, *Dependency and Development in Latin America,* trans. Marjory Mattingly Urquidi (Berkeley, 1979); Emmanuel Wallerstein, "The Rise and Future Demise of the World Capitalist System: Concepts for Comparative Analysis," *Comparative Studies in Society and History* 16 (1974): 387–415; Arghiri Emmanuel, *Unequal Exchange: A Study of the Imperialism of Trade,* trans. Brian Pearce (London, 1972); V. I. Lenin, "Imperialism, the Last Stage of Capitalism," in *Imperialism, The State and Revolution* (New York, 1926); Harry Braverman, *Labor and Monopoly Capital: The Degradation of Work in the Twentieth Century* (New York, 1974); W. W. Rostow, *The Stages of Economic Growth,* 2d ed. (Cambridge, Eng., 1971).
4. Octavio Paz, *The Labyrinth of Solitude: Life and Thought in Mexico* (New York, 1961), 20.
5. Barrington Moore, Jr., *Social Origins of Dictatorship and Democracy: Lord and Peasant in the Making of the Modern World* (Boston, 1966), especially chap. 9.

Chapter One

1. John H. Coatsworth, "Obstacles to Economic Growth in Nineteenth-Century Mexico," *American Historical Review* 83 (1978): 81, 84; Laura Randall, *A Comparative Economic History of Latin America, 1500–1914* (Ann Arbor, 1978), 1:162, 180; Christopher Armstrong and H. V. Nelles, "A Curious Capital Flow: Canadian Investment in Mexico, 1902–1910," *Business History Review* 58 (1984): 179–80; Daniel Cosío Villegas et al., *Historia moderna de México,* vol. 7, pt. 2 (Mexico City, 1965), 642, 1154; Esperanza Durán de Seade, "Mexico's Relations with the Powers During the Great War" (D.Phil. thesis, St. Antony's College, Oxford University, 1980), 7–11; Clifton B. Kroeber, *Man, Land, and Water: Mexico's Farmlands Irrigation Policies, 1885–1911* (Berkeley and Los Angeles, 1983), 12; Stephen H. Haber, *Industry and Underdevelopment: The Industrialization of Mexico, 1890–1940* (Stanford, 1989), 91–93, 100.

2. Richard Guenther to Dept. of State, 11 October 1890, U.S. Consular Despatches, Mexico City, no. 32, Record Group 59, National Archives, Washington, D.C.; and ibid., 1 December 1903, U.S. Consular Despatches, Tampico, no. 181, Record Group 59, National Archives. See also Cosío Villegas et al., *Historia moderna de México,* vol. 7, pt. 1 (Mexico City, 1965), 245, 517, 624, 628, 695; Chitraporn Tanratanakol, "Threats to Subsistence: Regional Economy and the 1869 Mezquital Peasant Rebellion in Mexico" (Ph.D. diss., Northern Illinois University, 1987), chap. 4.

3. Representative works include Randall, *Comparative Economic History of Latin America;* D. C. M. Platt, ed., *Business Imperialism, 1840–1930: An Inquiry Based on British Experience in Latin America* (Oxford, 1977); and Marshall C. Eakin, "Business Imperialism and British Enterprise in Brazil: The St. John d'el Rey Mining Company, Limited, 1830–1960," *Hispanic American Historical Review* 66 (1986): 697–742. Also see Mark Wasserman, "Enrique C. Creel: Business and Politics in Mexico, 1880–1930," *Business History Review* 59 (1985): 645–62; Armstrong and Nelles, "A Curious Capital Flow."

4. Sahagún, *Historia de las cosas de Nueva España* (c. 1569), tenth book, chap. 24, as quoted by Ezequiel Ordóñez, "El petróleo en México: bosquejo histórico," part 1, *Revista Mexicana de Ingeniería y Arquetectura* 10, no. 3 (15 March 1932): 135. Also see Gabriel Antonio Menéndez, *Doheny El Cruel: episodios de la sangrienta lucha por el petróleo mexicano* (Mexico City, 1958), 17–19; Alexander von Humboldt, *Political Essay on the Kingdom of New Spain* (London, 1811), 4:38, 47; untitled memo in English, Aug 1938, Archivo de la Secretaría de Relaciones Exteriores, Mexico City, L-E-555.

5. Quoted by Francisco Alonso González, *Historia y petróleo. México: el problema del petróleo* (Mexico City, 1972), 55. See also Mexico, Secretaría de Industria, Comercio y Trabajo, *Documentos relacionados con la legislación petrolera mexicana* (Mexico City, 1919), 36–37.

6. Alonso González, *Historia y petróleo,* 135; Ordóñez, "El petróleo de México," 143–44.

7. Quoted in José Domingo Lavín, *Petróleo: pasado, presente y futuro de una industria mexicana* (Mexico City, 1976), 23.

8. *Prospectus of "The Boston and Mexican Oil Co." of Portland, Maine* (Boston, 1882), Cleland, box 2.

9. E. DeGolyer, "History of the Petroleum Industry in Mexico," 11 Mar 1914, DeGolyer, file 5347; "The Petroleum Industry of Mexico," [c. 1920,] ibid., file 5220; Lavín, *Petróleo: pasado, presente y futuro*, 22, 25–26.

10. Menéndez, *Doheny El Cruel*, 17–19.

11. Paul H. Giddens, *The Beginnings of the Petroleum Industry: Sources and Bibliography* (Harrisburg, Pa., 1941), 5–9; Giddens, *Early Days of Oil: A Pictorial History of the Beginnings of the Industry in Pennsylvania* (Princeton, 1948), 10.

12. See Ralph W. Hidy and Muriel E. Hidy, *Pioneering in Big Business, 1882–1911: History of the Standard Oil Company, New Jersey* (New York, 1955), 49, 200, 259; Alfred D. Chandler, Jr., *The Visible Hand: The Managerial Revolution in American Business* (Cambridge, Mass., 1977), 424; Daniel Yergin, *The Prize: The Epic Quest for Oil, Money, and Power* (New York, 1991), chap. 2.

13. On Pierce's early career, see Bruce Bringhurst, *Antitrust and the Oil Monopoly: The Standard Oil Cases, 1890–1911* (Westport, Conn., 1979), 40–41; Frederick U. Adams, *The Waters Pierce Case in Texas* (St. Louis, 1908).

14. U.S. Supreme Court, *Transcript of Record, Waters-Pierce Oil Company v. Texas,* October term, 1908, no. 356 (Washington, D.C., 1909), 441.

15. Allen Nevins, *John D. Rockefeller: The Heroic Age of American Enterprise* (New York, 1940), 1:657–58; and Hidy and Hidy, *Pioneering in Big Business,* 49, 122.

16. At least, this was the charge of the Texas attorney general. See *Waters-Pierce Oil Company v. Texas,* no. 1, 212 U.S. 86 and no. 2, 212 U.S. 112 (1898).

17. Waters-Pierce Oil Co. to A. Gilmer, 10 Mar 1894, Waters-Pierce Oil Co. Records, OHTOR, Box 3K10 F2.

18. "Interview with Mr. S. W. Smith of the Mexican Petroleum Company," 11 May 1918, interview no. 596, Doheny. The biographer of Rockefeller, Allan Nevins, finds price cutting morally reprehensible, but he claims that often Rockefeller had no control over the activities of his marketers like Pierce. Nevins, *John D. Rockefeller,* 2:92. Ida Tarbell was also appalled at the business practices of Waters-Pierce. Ida M. Tarbell, *The History of the Standard Oil Company* (1904; reprint, New York, 1950), 2:41–42, 46–47. For price cutting, see the testimony of several Brownsville merchants like Miguel Fernández in U.S. Supreme Court, *Transcript of Record, Waters-Pierce Oil Company v. Texas,* October term, 1898, no. 177, U.S. 28 (Washington, D.C., 1889).

19. *Waters-Pierce Oil Company v. Texas,* 44 S.W. Rep 936 (1898); U.S. Supreme Court, *Waters-Pierce Oil Company v. Texas* (1898).

20. U.S. Supreme Court, *Waters-Pierce Oil Company v. Texas* (1908), 442.

21. Marquis James, *The Texaco Story: The First Fifty Years, 1902–1952* (n.p., 1953), 6–8, 11–13, 21–22; Joseph A. Pratt, *The Growth of a Refining Region* (Greenwich, Conn., 1980), 34–35; Martin V. Melosi, *Coping with Abundance: Energy and Environment in Industrial America* (Philadelphia, 1985), 40–46;

Alfred A. Glasier to Am. consul, 10 Apr 1906, U.S. Consular Records, Tampico, Misc. Letters Rec'd, Record Group 84, National Archives.

22. *Waters-Pierce Oil Company v. Texas,* no. 1, 103 S.W. Rep. 836 (1907); ibid., no. 2, 106 S.W. Rep. 918 (1907); U.S. Supreme Court, *Waters-Pierce Oil Company v. Texas* (1908), 20.

23. Salary Book A, 1 Jan 1887, Secy's Dept., SONJ; Hidy and Hidy, *Pioneering in Big Business,* 5.

24. Thomas C. Manning to Mariscal, 30 May 1887, Despatches from U.S. Ministers to Mexico, no. 144, Record Group 59, National Archives; Hidy and Hidy, *Pioneering in Big Business,* 514.

25. "Interview with Mr. S. W. Smith," 11 May 1918, Doheny; *Mexican Herald,* 1 Nov 1903; Alan Knight, *The Mexican Revolution* (Cambridge, Eng., 1986), 1:80.

26. U.S. Supreme Court, *Waters-Pierce Oil Company v. Texas* (1908), 466.

27. Ibid., 448, 506, 671; Hidy and Hidy, *Pioneering in Big Business,* 128, 258, 363. The California exports to Mexico began as early as 1878. See Gerald T. White, *Formative Years in the Far West: A History of the Standard Oil Company of California and Predecessors Through 1919* (New York, 1962), 56, 97, 122, 145.

28. "Interview with Mr. S. W. Smith," 11 May 1918, Doheny.

29. Six of the wagons were not operating at one point in 1902, awaiting spare parts from St. Louis. U.S. Supreme Court, *Waters-Pierce Oil Company v. Texas* (1908), 1108; U.S. Supreme Court, *Transcript of Record, Standard Oil Company et al. v. U.S.,* October term, 1909, 221 U.S. 1 (Washington, D.C., 1910), 1095–96.

30. Calculated at 42 gallons to the barrel from 11,905,618 gallons of crude oil, lubricants, illuminants, naphthas, and 3,902 barrels of residual products and tar. See table 1; U.S. Supreme Court, *Waters-Pierce Oil Company v. Texas* (1908), 445; and Hidy and Hidy, *Pioneering in Big Business,* 528–29.

31. U.S. Supreme Court, *Waters-Pierce Oil Company v. Texas* (1908), 510.

32. Lord Cowdray to Sir Edmund Holden, 13 Aug 1912, Pearson, C44 F7; Bringhurst, *Antitrust and the Oil Monopoly,* 57; Hidy and Hidy, *Pioneering in Big Business,* 609, 633; and U.S. Supreme Court, *Waters-Pierce Oil Company v. Texas* (1908), 472. Two other Standard marketing companies, Iowa Standard and Consolidated, also made large profits. See White, *Formative Years in the Far West,* 193–94, 323.

33. U.S. Supreme Court, *Waters-Pierce Oil Company v. Texas* (1898); U.S. Supreme Court, *Waters-Pierce Oil Company v. Texas* (1908), 666–67, 874–75.

34. U.S. Supreme Court, *Waters-Pierce Oil Company v. Texas* (1908), 1095; and U.S. Supreme Court, *Standard Oil Company et al. v. U.S.* (1909), 667.

35. U.S. Supreme Court, *Waters-Pierce Oil Company v. Texas* (1908), 471, 666–67, 1105–6, 1115.

36. Ibid., 606.

37. Cosío Villegas et al., *Historia moderna de Mexico,* vol. 7, pt. 1, 211.

38. Hidy and Hidy, *Pioneering in Big Business,* 514.

39. Ibid., 448–51; U.S. Supreme Court, *Waters-Pierce Oil Company v. Texas* (1908), 463, 465, 880–82, 897, 1089–90.

40. Nevins, *John D. Rockefeller,* 1:659.

41. Ibid., 2:531–33, 571. See also testimony of William A. Morgan in U.S. Supreme Court, *United States of America, petitioner, v. Standard Oil Company of New Jersey, et al., defendants* (Washington, D.C., 1909), 3:1006–7.

42. "Interview with Mr. S. W. Smith," 11 May 1918, Doheny.

43. As quoted in Charles K. Smith to David E. Thompson, 27 Aug 1908, State Dept. Numerical and Minor Files, 15351/1–4, Record Group 59, National Archives.

44. *The Mexican Herald,* 3 Nov 1908, as quoted in State Dept. Numerical and Minor Files, 11770/13–15.

45. "Interview with Mr. S. W. Smith," 11 May 1918, Doheny.

46. As quoted in Ward Ritchie, *The Dohenys of Los Angeles* (Los Angeles, 1974), 15–16. Doheny in 1920 recreated the Los Angeles oil strike from the site of this first well, and repeated with raised arm what he said was his 1892 proclamation of a new day for the economy of Los Angeles. See William Rintoul, *Spudding In: Recollections of Pioneer Days in the California Oil Fields* (San Francisco, 1976), 83, 88.

47. White, *Formative Years in the Far West,* 152–53; Caspar Whitney, *Charles Adelbert Canfield* (New York: private printing, 1930), 110–11, 128, 140; Ritchie, *The Dohenys of Los Angeles,* 18–19; Edmund Burke to Doheny, 18 Nov 1900, AALA; *Sign of the 76: The Fabulous Life and Times of the Union Oil Company of California* (Los Angeles, 1976), 105–6.

48. Burke to Doheny, Washington, D.C., 18 Nov 1900, AALA; Whitney, *Charles Adelbert Canfield,* 129–30; Fritz L. Hoffman, "Edward L. Doheny and the Beginnings of Petroleum Development in Mexico," *Mid-America* 24 (April 1942): 97–98; and White, *Formative Years in the Far West,* 154, 198, 229, 234, 312, 351–52. Additional information about Doheny can be found in Gene Z. Hanrahan, *The Bad Yankee—El Peligro Yankee: American Entrepreneurs and Financiers in Mexico,* 2 vols. (Chapel Hill, 1985); Menéndez, *Doheny El Cruel.* The latter two books are rather critical.

49. "Report on Kern Co. Field to W. G. Nevin of Atchison, Topeka and Santa Fe," n.p., n.d., AALA.

50. William E. McMahon, *Two Strikes and Out* (Garden City, 1939), 26–27.

51. Hanrahan, *The Bad Yankee,* 1:6; Clarence W. Barron, *The Mexican Problem* (Boston, 1917), 95; affidavit of E. L. Doheny, n.d., Cleland, box 2.

52. R. G. Cleland, interview with E. L. Doheny, 15 Jan 1918, interview no. 45, Doheny. Arguínzoniz lived in Ciudad del Maís in the state of San Luis Potosí. During the Revolution, he lived in exile in San Antonio, Texas.

53. Ibid.

54. See Doheny's Senate testimony in U.S. Congress, Senate Committee on Foreign Relations, *Investigation of Mexican Affairs,* 66th Congress, 1st sess. (Washington, D.C., 1920), 1:209–12.

55. Ibid., 1:212, 218–19, 225.

56. Walter Sharp to unnamed correspondent, 21 Sept 1901, in Walter Benona Sharp, "Letters, Excerpts from," OHTO, Box 33K11.

57. Interview with Doheny, 20 Apr 1918, Doheny.

58. *Investigation of Mexican Affairs,* 1:213–14, 227–29; Pan American Petroleum Corporation, *Mexican Petroleum* (New York, 1922).

59. *Investigation of Mexican Affairs,* 1:214, 241, 269. On drilling technology, see Mexican Oil Corporation, Ltd., *Mexico Today: The Mexican Petroleum Industry* (London, 1905), 13–15.

60. Barren, *The Mexican Problem,* 122.

61. Ordóñez, "El petróleo en México: bosquejo histórico," part 2, *Revista Mexicano de Ingeniería y Arquetectura* 10, no. 4 (15 Apr 1932): 154–61; McMahon, *Two Strikes and Out,* 29. Menéndez attributes greater Mexican participation than Ordóñez's report does. He states that Doheny would have given up had it not been for the financial backing of a Mexican banker, Gerardo Meade of San Luis Potosí. See Menéndez, *Doheny El Cruel,* 21–22. The story is repeated by James D. Cockcroft, who places the loan at fifty thousand pesos (twenty-five thousand dollars). Cockcroft, *Intellectual Precursors of the Mexican Revolution, 1900–1913* (Austin, 1968), 24–25. The Stanford University geologist was Ralph Arnold. See his entry for 31 July 1911 in Field Books, 1911–1912, Trinidad & Mexico, Arnold, Box 129.

62. "Interview with Mr. H. Wylie," 15 May 1918, interview no. 597, Doheny.

63. Herbert G. Wylie to Charles E. Harwood, Ebano, 13 Jan 1903, AALA.

64. Body to Pearson, 28 June 1904, Pearson, A4; "R. G. Cleland, second interview with Mr. E. D. [*sic*] Doheny," 20 May 1918, Doheny; Hanrahan, *The Bad Yankee,* 1:3; F. B. McKercher to Doheny, 16 Dec 1902, AALA.

65. R. C. Kerens to Doheny, Chicago, 20 July 1902, AALA.

66. Wylie to Doheny, Ebano, 22 and 23 Jan 1902, AALA.

67. Cleland, interview with Doheny, 15 Jan 1918, interview no. 45, Doheny.

68. Martin R. Ansell, "Pouring Oil on Troubled Waters: Edward L. Doheny and the Mexican Revolution" (M.A. thesis, University of Oregon, 1985), 11; Harold Walker to Oscar D. Bennett, 28 Oct 1909, AALA; E. L. Doheny, "A Few Comments on the Report Submitted to You by Mr. R. A. on August 26, 1911," 7 Sept 1911, AALA.

69. E. Ordóñez to Doheny, 6 Oct 1902, AALA.

70. *Investigation of Mexican Affairs,* 1:214–16; President Díaz's message to Congress, *The Mexican Herald,* 2 Apr 1906, in David E. Thompson to sec. of state, 2 Apr 1906, State Dept. Numerical and Minor Files, 16.

71. Walker to Doheny, 28 Oct 1909, AALA.

72. Barron, *The Mexican Problem,* 62–63.

73. Fairchild & Gilmore to Doheny, 1 July 1902, AALA.

74. Wilbur Carr to C. Piquette Mitchel, Washington, 5 Mar 1909, State Dept. Numerical and Minor Files, 18125; República de México, "Resumen de la importación y de la exportación, 1908–09," FO, 368–308/35907.

75. C. H. Smith to Doheny, St. Louis, 30 Mar 1903, AALA.

76. Cleland, second interview with Doheny, 20 May 1918, Doheny; *Investigation of Mexican Affairs,* 1:225–26; Mexican Oil Corporation, *Mexico Today,* 19–21.

77. Mexican Petroleum Co., *Los impuestos sobre la industria de petróleo* (Mexico City, 1912), 1; Barron, *The Mexican Problem,* 131.

78. Cosío Villegas et al., *Historia moderna de Mexico,* vol. 7, pt. 1, 233–34, 520; Great Britain, Foreign Office, *Consular Report for Mexico, 1902* (London, 1903), Tampico consul, no. 3285, 21; *Consular Report for Mexico, 1904* (London, 1905), Tampico consul, no. 932, 11 Mar 1904; *Consular Report for Mexico, 1906* (London, 1907) Tampico consul, no. 240, report dated 8 May 1906.

79. Cleland, second interview with Doheny, 20 May 1918, Doheny. After the government purchased the Mexican Central and merged it into the National Railways system, it continued to purchase fuel oil from Doheny.

80. *Investigation of Mexican Affairs,* 1:216; "E. Richards, counsel for H. Clay Pierce, Summary of Correspondence," J. B. Body to L., 22 Aug 1908 in "Summary of Correspondence: Negotiations with WPO Co.," Pearson, C44 F7; Reports, 6, 13 Apr 1907, Ramo de Hacienda, Fomento y Obras Públicas, Secretaría de Comunicacion y Obras Públicas, 1907–26, 2/226, Leg. 1, 1907, AGN.

81. Ordóñez to Doheny, 6 Oct 1902, AALA.

82. Martínez del Río to Doheny, 23 Oct 1902, AALA.

83. F. B. McKercher to Doheny, 5 June 1903, AALA.

84. Pan American Petroleum Corporation, *Mexico Petroleum,* 28–29.

85. *Investigation of Mexican Affairs,* 1:226–27, 299; Clarence A. Miller to R. W. Grant, 17 Dec 1910, U.S. Consular Records, Tampico, Misc. Letters Rec'd.

86. See the correspondence relating to the dispute in despatches dating from 26 Nov to 8 Dec 1908, State Dept. Numerical and Minor Files, 1728.

87. Cleland, interview with Doheny, 15 Jan 1918, interview no. 45, Doheny.

88. *Investigation of Mexican Affairs,* 1:217; Pan American Petroleum Corporation, *Mexico Petroleum,* 26–27.

89. McKercher to Doheny, 16 Dec 1902, AALA.

90. Cleland, second interview with Doheny, 20 May 1918, Doheny. See also Ansell, "Pouring Oil on Troubled Waters," 33, 49.

91. Contract, 22 May 1908, Ramo de Hacienda, Fomento y Obras Públicas, Minas y Petróleo, 1916, C194, E23/324.6–452/2, AGN.

92. Ronald MacLeay to Foreign Office, Mexico, 18 Mar 1909, FO, 12924; Mexican Petroleum Co., *Los impuestos sobre la industria de petróleo,* 4.

93. Cleland, interview with Doheny, 15 Jan 1918, interview no. 45, Doheny.

94. C. M. Leonard to asst. sec. of state, 3 Sept 1908, State Dept. Numerical and Minor Files, 11770/5.

95. Doheny to Estelle Doheny, Buena Vista Station, 29 Dec 1906, AALA.

96. Ezequiel Ordóñez, "El petróleo en México," part 2, 193.

97. Doheny to Estelle Doheny, 1 May 1910, AALA; Pan American Petroleum Corporation, *Mexico Petroleum*, 31–32; *Investigation of Mexican Affairs*, 230–32, 242; Barron, *The Mexican Problem*, 38.

98. Sam T. Mallison, *The Great Wildcatter* (Charleston, W.V., 1953), 33–37.

99. Mexican Petroleum, *The Oil Industry in Mexico*, 35–38; Doheny to Wm. Salomon & Co., 7 Sept 1911, Arnold, box 201.

100. Ralph Arnold et al., *The First Big Oil Hunt: Venezuela, 1911–1916* (New York, 1960), 63, 91.

101. Mallison, *The Great Wildcatter*, 238–41.

102. Mexican Petroleum, *The Oil Industry in Mexico*, 35; McMahon, *Two Strikes and Out*, 39.

103. Ordóñez, "El petróleo en México," part 2, 196–97.

104. Hanrahan, *The Bad Yankee*, 1:9; White, *Formative Years in the Far West*, 152.

105. The following information comes from J. A. Spender, *Weetman Pearson: First Viscount Cowdray, 1856–1927* (London, 1930; reprint, New York, 1977); Desmond Young, *Member for Mexico: A Biography of Weetman Pearson, First Viscount Cowdray* (London, 1966); Robert Keith Middlemas, *The Master Builders: Thomas Brassey, Sir John Aird, Lord Cowdray, Sir John Norton-Griffiths* (London, 1963).

106. See especially Cathryn Thorup, "La competencia económica británica y norteamericana en México (1887–1910): El caso de Weetman Pearson," *Historia Mexicana* 31 (1982): 599–641.

107. Middlemas, *The Master Builders*, 171–72, 175, 180; President Díaz's message to congress, *Diario Oficial*, 28 Feb 1889, in Reinsen Whitehouse to sec. of state, 28 Feb 1889, Despatches from U.S. Ministers to Mexico, no. 268. Spender, *Weetman Pearson*, 286–90, lists the company's contracts from 1854 to 1926.

108. Middlemas, *The Master Builders*, 183.

109. Ryan to sec. of state, 7 Feb 1890, 4 March 1890, Despatches from U.S. Ministers to Mexico, nos. 239, 253.

110. Clayton to sec. of state, 18 Aug 1902, 26 November 1902, ibid., nos. 1532, 1634.

111. As quoted in Young, *Member for Mexico*, 107–8. On the Tehuantepec railway, see Middlemas, *The Master Builders*, 194–99; *The Mexican Daily Record*, 14 May 1906, in D. E. Thompson to sec. of state, 25 May 1906, Despatches from U.S. Ministers to Mexico, no. 69; *Mexican Herald*, 1 Dec 1902.

112. *The Mexican Herald*, 24 Jan 1907; Thompson to sec. of state, 5 Mar 1907, State Dept. Numerical and Minor Files, 1639/13.

113. As quoted in Spender, *Weetman Pearson*, 149–50.

114. B. to P., 29 May 1903, Body to Pearson, 23 June 1905, Pearson, "Memo for Mr. J. B. Body," 28 April 1908, Pearson, A4.

115. As quoted by E. DeGolyer, "Anthony Francis Lucas (1855–1921)," 1951, DeGolyer, file 1074.

116. Body to Pearson, 23 Aug 1904, Pearson to Body, 26 Jan 1906, B. to P., 29 May 1903, Body to Pearson, 29 May 1905, 23 June 1905, Pearson, "Memo for Mr. J. B. Body," 28 Apr 1908, Pearson, A4.

117. Bryan Cooper, ed., *Latin American and Caribbean Oil Report* (London, n.d. [c. 1980]), 136.

118. Purdy went on to become a director of Shell-Mex Petroleum, Ltd., the London holding company, in the 1920s. *The Pipeline,* 3:57 (1923): 51; Ryder to Body, 8 Apr 1906, Pearson, A4.

119. P. to B., 1 May 1906, B. to P., 21 Jan 1909, Pearson, A4; "History: The Mexico Eagle Oil Company, Limited," ibid., C43 F1.

120. "Memorandum by Lord Cowdray," 10 May 1915, Pearson, A3; P. to B., 6 Oct 1906, 3 Dec 1908, "Memo for Mr. Body," 21 Apr 1907, ibid., A4.

121. "History, The Mexican Eagle Oil Company, Limited," Pearson, C43 F1.

122. "Memorandum by Lord Cowdray," 10 May 1915, Pearson, A3.

123. B. to P., 19 Dec 1905, 8 Jan 1906, 22 Jan 1906, Pearson, A4; Middlemas, *The Master Builders,* 186, 220, 222.

124. B. to P., 9 Nov 1905, 30 July 1908, Pearson, A4; Thorup, "La competencia económica," 616.

125. "Contrato entre Secretaría de Fomento y la Compañía S. Pearson & Son, Ltd.," 12 May 1906, State Dept. Decimal Files, 812.6363/126, Record Group 59, National Archives; I. H. MacDonald to Major Cassius E. Gillette, 13 Oct 1916, Pearson, A4.

126. B. to P., 8 Jan 1906, Pearson, A4; Thorup, "La competencia económica," 622.

127. See the testimony in *Revolutions in Mexico,* Hearing before a Subcommittee of the Committee on Foreign Relations, U.S. Senate, 62d Congress, 2d sess. (Washington, 1913), 263–65.

128. Both Doheny and Pearson were impelled toward integration by the same incentives identified by Alfred Chandler as motivating U.S. firms to begin foreign operations. Pearson and Doheny wished "to reduce costs by exploiting the economies of throughput" and "to assure a constant flow of materials into processing and manufacturing plants on a precise schedule and to precise specifications." Alfred Chandler, Jr., "Technological and Organizational Underpinnings of Modern Industrial Enterprise: The Dynamics of Competitive Advantage," in *Multinational Enterprise in Historical Perspective,* ed. Alice Teichova, Maurice Lévy-Leboyer, and Helga Nussbaum (Cambridge, Eng., 1986), 52.

129. "Second Interview with Mr. Arthur C. Payne," 20 May 1918, Doheny.

130. Percy Norman Furber, *I Took Chances: From Windjammers to Jets* (Leicester, 1953), 129–30, 139–41. Apparently the Royal Dutch–Shell also rejected an offer to buy Furbero. See Gerretson, *History of the Royal Dutch* (Leiden, 1953), 4:264.

131. Anonymous, Daily Field Book, 1908, entry for 22 Feb, OHTOR, Box 3K10 F6.

132. Furber, *I Took Chances,* 125, 141–142; "Oil Fields of Mexico Co." *The Joint Stock Companies' Journal,* 14 Aug 1912, Shell International Petroleum Co. archives, London, press clippings.

133. "Anglo-Mexican Oilfields Limited" [log book], 1908–9, OHTO, box 3K10 F6; Furber, *I Took Chances,* 127–30, 140–45.

134. "Mexico Oil Fields: Some Well Logs," n.d., DeGolyer, file 5300; Guillermo de Landa y Escandón to Pearson, 8 June 1910, Pearson, A4.

135. See correspondence of A. J. Lespinasse to David E. Thompson, 6 Oct 1906 to 2 Oct 1908, State Dept. Numerical and Minor Files, 1854.

136. Body, "Notes for Sir Weetman," 15 May 1909, Pearson, "Memo for Mr. Body," 9 Mar 1909, Pearson, A4.

137. As quoted in Spender, *Weetman Pearson*, 155.

138. Merrill Griffith to asst. sec. of state, 15 Aug 1908, State Dept. Numerical and Minor Files, 14453/2.

139. Merrill Griffith to Thompson, 6 July 1908, ibid., 14453. Also see *The Pipe Line* 3, no. 63 (23 May 1923): 126; R. P. Brousson, "The Oil Industry of Mexico," Pearson, C43 F1.

140. Doheny, "A Few Comments on the Report Submitted to You by Mr. R. A. on August 26, 1911," 7 Sept 1911, Arnold; Merrill Griffith to asst. sec. of state, 8 Sept 1908, State Dept. Numerical and Minor Files, 14453/3; C. Reed, "History of S.P. & S's Interests in Mexico," Aug 1928, Pearson, C43 F1.

141. B. to P., 30 Nov 1907, "Aguila/Waters-Pierce Oil Co. Agreement," 15 May 1908, Pearson, C44 F7.

142. L. to G. W., 16 May 1908, Pearson, C44 F7.

143. P. to B., 23 Dec 1907, Cowdray, "History of the Fight with the Waters Pierce Oil Co.," Aug 1928, Cowdray, "Private Memo re negotiations with Mr. Clay Pierce," 8 Mar 1909, Pearson, C44 F7.

144. "Memo to Mr. W. re Agreement with C. P." 30 Jan 1908, L. to H. C. P, 8 Feb 1908, C. to H. J., 20 Oct 1909, and L. to Japp, 8 Nov 1909, Pearson, C44 F7.

145. From Cowdray's private papers, as quoted in Middlemas, *The Master Builders*, 216.

146. Ronald MacLeay to Sir Edmund Gray, 18 June 1909, FO, 368–309/25272; "History: The Mexican Eagle Oil Company, Ltd.," Pearson, C43 F1; Julian Barlow to asst. sec. of state, 31 Dec 1897, U.S. Consular Despatches, Mexico City, no. 65. Gerretson, *History of the Royal Dutch*, 4:260, claims that El Aguila incorporated in 1908.

147. *Diario Oficial*, 4 Feb 1904, 1 Apr 1904 in Clayton to sec. of state, 11 Apr 1904, Despatches from U.S. Ministers to Mexico, no. 2235.

148. As quoted in Gerretson, *History of the Royal Dutch*, 4:261; Pearson to Dr. M., 16 Apr 1909, "Summary of Correspondence: Negotiations with W. P. O. Co.," Pearson, C44 F7.

149. Thorup, "La competencia económica," 633; Ordóñez, "El Petróleo en México," part 1, 158; *Revolutions in Mexico*, 263–65.

150. Benjamin Ridgely, "A Great Oil Fight in Mexico," 18 July 1908, State Dept. Numerical and Minor Files, 11770/2–3.

151. "Extract from letter to Senor Guillermo Landa," 30 July 1909, Pearson, A4; *Mexican Herald*, 27 Mar 1909.

152. See contracts dated 26 Nov 1908, Pearson, C43 F2; *The Mexican Herald*, 23, 29 Oct 1908; document dated 18 Oct 1908, Ramo de Hacienda, Fomento y Obras Públicas, Secretaría de Comunicación y Obras Públicas, 82/118–1, AGN.

153. "Extract from letter to Senor Guillermo Landa," 30 July 1909, Pearson, A4.

154. "Report of Secretary of Interior in Response to Senate Res. No. 53, Statement of Dr. C. W. Hayes respecting the Petroleum Fields of Mexico," 5 June 1909, DeGolyer, file 1591; Pearson, "General Memo for Mr. Body," 16 May 1909, Pearson, A4.

155. Lon Tinkle, *Mr. De: A Biography of Everette Lee DeGolyer* (Boston, 1970), 6–39; B. to P., 21 Jan 1909, Pearson, "Memo for Mr. Body," 24 Mar 1909, Pearson, A4.

156. Tinkle, *Mr. De,* 15.

157. For a detailed description of the scene at Potrero, see Tinkle, *Mr. De,* chap. 3; A. E. Chambers, "Potrero No. 4: A History of One of Mexico's Earliest and Largest Wells," *Journal of the Institution of Petroleum Technologists* 37, no. 9 (1923): 141–64.

158. See DeGolyer's notes dating from Dec 1910 to Jan 1911, DeGolyer, file 1439.

159. Chambers, "Potrero No. 4," 164.

160. *Oil Weekly* 59, no. 11 (28 Nov 1930): 26.

161. Comments of Robert Stirling in Chambers, "Potrero No. 4," 163–64.

162. Spender, *Weetman Pearson,* 157–58.

163. Pearson to Body, 8 June 1909, B. to C., 28 June 1911, Body to Cowdray, 10 May 1911, Pearson, A4; Young, *Member for Mexico,* 131.

164. México, Departamento de la Estádistico Nacional, *Resumen del censo general de habitantes de 30 de noviembre de 1921* (Mexico City, 1928), 187–88, 190; México, Secretaría de Economía, Dirección General de Estadística, *Estadísticas sociales del Porfiriato, 1877–1910* (Mexico City, 1956), 11; Carlos González Salas, "Sub-cultura laboral en Tampico (1877–1924)" (unpublished ms., 1988), 9–10; S. Lief Adleson G., "Historia social de los obreros industriales de Tampico, 1906–1919" (doctoral thesis, El Colegio de México, 1982), 4.

165. México, Secretaría de Fomento, *Censo y division territorial del Estado de Tamaulipas verificados en 1900* (Mexico City, 1904).

166. Historically, Veracruz had always dominated Mexican foreign trade. In 1828, for example, 276 ships departed from Mexico, of which 110 departed from Veracruz, 69 from Tampico, 7 from Tuxpan, and 4 from Coatzalcoalcos. Inés Herrera Canales, *Estadística del comercio exterior de México (1821–1875)* (Mexico City, 1980), 237, 245–46, 262, 287–92.

167. H. S. Gilbert to Magill, 1 Oct 1902, U.S. Consular Records, Tampico, Misc. Letters Rec'd; Salas, "Sub-cultura laboral en Tampico," 11; Cosío Villegas et al., *Historia moderna de México,* vol. 7, pt. 2, 95.

168. Cosío Villegas et al., *Historia moderna de México,* vol. 7, pt. 2, 10, 247, 520, 544; Adleson, "Historia social de los obreros," 14–15.

169. México, Secretaría de Fomento, *Censo y division territorial del Estado de Vera Cruz verificados en 1900* (Mexico City, 1904); *Censo de Tamaulipas* (Mexico City, 1904).

170. Cosío Villegas et al., *Historia moderna de México,* vol. 7, pt. 2, 115–16, 135, 147.

171. México, Secretaría de Economía, *Estadísticas sociales del Porfiriato*, 41. For all of Mexico between 1877 and 1910, the number of haciendas grew from 5,869 to 8,431 and ranchos from 14,705 to 48,633.

172. See Frans J. Schryer, *The Rancheros of Pisaflores: The History of a Peasant Bourgeoisie in Twentieth-Century Mexico* (Toronto, 1980), 7.

173. W. E. Lucas to S. E. Magill, 31 Jan 1907, U.S. Consular Records, Tampico, Misc. Letters Rec'd.

174. Ordóñez, "El petróleo en México," part 1, 159.

175. Powell Clayton to sec. of state, 27 May 1898, Despatches from U.S. Ministers to Mexico, no. 443.

176. Andrés Molina Enríquez, *Los grandes problemas nacionales (1909)* (Mexico City, 1978), 158–59.

177. México, Secretaría de Fomento, *Censo de Vera Cruz* and *Censo de Tamaulipas*.

178. Cosío Villegas et al., *Historia moderna de México*, vol. 7, part 2, 747.

179. Merrill Griffith to Thompson, 1 June 1908, State Dept. Numerical and Minor Files, 14054.

180. Thomas Ryan to sec. of state, 2 Jan 1890, Despatches from U.S. Ministers to Mexico, no. 197; *Mexican Herald*, 2 Apr 1904, in Clayton to sec. of state, 11 Apr 1904, Despatches from U.S. Ministers to Mexico, no. 2235.

181. A. J. Lespinasse to Loomis, 28 Apr 1905, U.S. Consular Despatches, Tuxpan, no. 52, Record Group 59, National Archives; Lespinasse to Robert Bacon, 7 Feb 1906, ibid., no. 62; Lespinasse to David J. Hill, 21 Aug 1902, 9 Mar 1904, 5 Jan 1903, 11 Mar 1903, 11 May 1904, ibid., nos. 9, 40, 19, 23, 44.

182. Lespinasse to Hill, 25 Feb, 20 Apr, 18 May 1904, ibid., nos. 38, 41, 46; Cosío Villegas et al., *Historia moderna de México*, vol. 7, part 2, 14, 545, 963.

183. Samuel E. McGill to Francis Loomis, 5 July 1904, Despatches from U.S. Ministers to Mexico, no. 201; Horace M. Reeve to Powell Clayton, 13 Oct 1904, ibid., no. 2486; McGill to Loomis, 18 Feb 1903, 31 Oct 1905, U.S. Consular Despatches, Tampico, nos. 159, 221; Magill to Herbert H. D. Pierce, 27 July 1903, ibid., no. 172; Mordelo L. Vincent, Jr., *A Man Remembers* (Chapel Hill, 1985), 9–12.

184. 28 June, 4 Aug 1906, U.S. Consular Despatches, Tampico, nos. 245, 251; John A. Nelson to Magill, 16 Apr 1906, U.S. Consular Records, Tampico, Misc. Letters Rec'd.

185. H. H. Harder to Magill, 20 Feb 1906, William Hollis to Magill, 24 Apr 1905, ibid.

186. C. A. Miller to F. C. Tompkins, 14 June 1911, U.S. Consular Records, Tampico, General Correspondence.

187. Neill E. Pressley to Mr. G. W. Sigler, 17 Sept 1907, U.S. Consular Records, Tampico, Misc. Letters Rec'd.

188. 6 Dec 1903, U.S. Consular Despatches, Tuxpan, no. 35; Edwin R. Wells to Alvey A. Adee, 30 August 1901, 14 Nov 1902, ibid., nos. 5, 14; unnamed correspondent to Loomis, 5 Dec 1904, 2 May 1903, ibid., nos. 51, 25; 29 Sept 1903, ibid., no. 34.

189. Testimony of William A. Horton, *Investigation of Mexican Affairs,* 2:1710. See ibid., 2:1036–37 and 1708–12 for additional information about the American farmers in Mexico.

190. "Labor Conditions on Banana Plantations near Tampico," 11 June 1918, interview no. 545, Doheny.

191. "Interview with Mr. S. W. Smith," 11 May 1918, ibid.

192. Jorge Basurto, *El proletariado industrial en México (1850–1930)* (Mexico City, 1975), 49.

193. Mexico, Departamento de la Estadística Nacional, *Resumen del Censo General de Habitantes,* 190; Viviane Brachet de Márquez, *La población de los estados mexicanos en el siglo xix (1824–1895)* (Mexico City, 1976), 95, 141. The population density of Veracruz increased from 6.99 persons per square kilometer to 15.69 between 1877 and 1910. México, Secretaría de Economía, *Estadísticas sociales del Porfiriato,* 68.

194. Ralph W. Hutchinson to Magill, 4 July 1903, U. S. Consular Records, Tampico, Misc. Letters Rec'd.

195. Ralph W. Hutchinson to Magill, Pánuco, 25 Apr 1904, ibid.

196. W. W. Smith to Magill, 9 Apr 1906, ibid. The eastern region of San Luis Potosí gained a reputation for peasant revolts, and historians identify uprisings in 1849, 1856, 1879, 1882, 1905, and 1910. Cockcroft, *Intellectual Precursors of the Mexican Revolution,* 51–52.

197. S. E. Cross to Magill, San Luis Potosí, 18 Aug 1905, U.S. Consular Records, Tampico, Misc. Letters Rec'd. For the "moral economy," see E. P. Thompson, "The Moral Economy of the English Crowd in the Eighteenth Century," *Past & Present* 50 (1971): 76–136; and James Scott, *The Moral Economy of the Peasant: Rebellion and Subsistence in Southeast Asia* (New Haven, 1976).

198. Ordóñez, "El petróleo de México," part 1, 148.

199. [Affidavit of E. L. Doheny], n.d. [c. 1918], Cleland; Furber, *I Took Chances,* 125; "Second Interview with Mr. Arthur C. Payne," 20 May 1918, Doheny; Jesús Silva Herzog, *El petróleo de México* (Mexico City, 1940), 50.

200. [Affidavit of E. L. Doheny], Cleland.

201. "Interview with Mr. H. Wylie," 15 May 1918, Doheny.

202. Cleland, second interview with Doheny, 20 May 1918, ibid.

203. "Interview with Mr. H. Wylie," 15 May 1918, Doheny.

204. Ibid.

205. "Second Interview with Mr. Arthur C. Payne," 20 May 1918, Doheny; L. W. Prunty to American consul, 10 Sept, 11 Dec 1910, U. S. Consular Records, Tampico, General Correspondence.

206. Doheny to Estelle Doheny, 29 Dec 1906, Pablo P. Juárez to Carlos E. Shillaber, 28 Aug 1907, Shillaber to Doheny, 12 Sept 1907, AALA.

207. "Interview with Mr. H. Wylie," 15 May 1918, Doheny.

208. Body to Pearson, 25 July 1902, Pearson to Body, 30 June 1905, Pearson, A4.

209. Julio Valdivieso Castillo, *Historia del movimiento sindical petrolero en Minatitlán, Veracruz* (Mexico City, 1963), 25; Silva Herzog, *El petróleo de México,* 50.

210. *Investigation of Mexican Affairs,* 219; anonymous, Daily Field Book, 1908, OHTOR, Box 3K10 F6; Adleson, "Historia social de los obrero," 76, 104.

211. Pearson Photographic Albums, p. 14, PR; Valdivieso Castillo, *Historia del movimiento sindical petrolero,* 21.

212. D. S. McAlister to U.S. consul, 18 Sept 1910, U. S. Consular Records, Tampico, General Correspondence.

213. Body to Pearson, 4 July, 23 July 1910, Pearson, A4.

214. L. D. Archer to sec. of state, 30 Nov 1907, U.S. Consular Records, Tampico, Misc. Letters Rec'd.

215. Wylie to Magill, 11 Oct 1906, ibid.; Diana Davids Olien, *Oil Booms: Social Change in Five Texas Towns* (Lincoln, 1982), 110; Pratt, *Growth of a Refining Region,* 155. Also see various interview typescripts in the Oral History of the Texas Oil Industry, University of Texas Barker History Center, Austin. The Americans established a similar hierarchical social system in the Panama Canal Zone, retaining native Panamanians and West Indians in the unskilled, low-paying, and unprivileged positions. European gang laborers, who frequently worked no more efficiently than the most seasoned West Indians, still received greater privileges. A Canal Zone policeman once commented on the social attitudes of New Englanders in Panama: "Any northerner can say 'nigger' as glibly as a Carolinian, and growl if one of them steps on his shadow." David McCullough, *The Path Between the Seas: The Creation of the Panama Canal, 1870–1914* (New York, 1977), 475–77, 575–76.

216. Anonymous, Daily Field Book, 1908, entry for 19 Mar, OHTOR, Box 3K10 F6.

217. For discussions of these issues, see Friedrich Katz, *The Secret War in Mexico: Europe, the United States and the Mexican Revolution* (Chicago, 1981), x; G. M. Joseph, *Revolution from Without: Yucatán, Mexico, and the United States, 1880–1924* (Cambridge, Eng., 1982), xiv, 45, 82; Mark Wasserman, *Capitalists, Caciques, and Revolution: The Native Elite and Foreign Enterprise in Chihuahua, Mexico, 1854–1911* (Chapel Hill, 1984), 6, 93–94, 173n; John Mason Hart, *Revolutionary Mexico: The Coming and Process of Mexican Revolution* (Berkeley and Los Angeles, 1987), 87, 109; Steven Topik, "The Economic Role of the State in Liberal Regimes: Brazil and Mexico Compared, 1888–1910," in *Guiding the Invisible Hand: Economic Liberalism and the State in Latin American History,* ed. Joseph L. Love and Nils Jacobsen (New York, 1988), 117–44.

218. David W. Walker, *Kinship, Business, and Politics: The Martínez del Río Family in Mexico, 1824–1867* (Austin, 1986), 23.

219. "Interview with Mr. S. W. Smith," 11 May 1918, Doheny.

220. Alexander Gerschenkron, *Economic Backwardness in Historical Perspective: A Book of Essays* (Cambridge, Mass., 1962), 25, 28. There remains the question about whether the Díaz policies were conducive to economic growth or whether those policies increased the instability of the Mexican economy. For instance, Laura Randall criticizes Porfirian decision-makers for faulty economic policies that unbalanced agricultural production and provoked foreign exchange problems that eventually undermined the Mexican economic growth of

the Porfiriato. See Laura Randall, *A Comparative Economic History of Latin America,* 1:2, 190.

221. Cosío Villegas et al., *Historia moderna de México,* vol. 8, part 2 (Mexico City, 1972), 842.

222. Marvin D. Bernstein, *The Mexican Mining Industry, 1890–1950: A Study of the Interaction of Politics, Economics, and Technology* (Albany, 1964), 11, 18–19, 27–28.

223. Carleton Beals, *Porfirio Diaz: Dictator of Mexico* (Philadelphia, 1932), 328.

224. Detailed discussions of the various laws affecting the petroleum industry are found in Merrill Rippy, *Oil and the Mexican Revolution* (Leiden, 1972), 7–26; Antonio J. Bermúdez, *The Mexican National Petroleum Industry: A Case Study in Nationalization* (Stanford, 1963), 2–3.

225. Don M. Coerver, *The Porfirian Interregnum: The Presidency of Manuel González of Mexico, 1880–1884* (Fort Worth, 1979), 64, 71–72.

226. José Yves Limantour, *Apuntes sobre mi vida pública [1872–1911]* (Mexico City, 1965), 91.

227. Furber, *I Took Chances,* 95–100.

228. Pearson to Dr. M., 16 Apr 1909, "Summary of Correspondence: Negotiations with W.P.O. Co.," Pearson, C44 F7.

229. Walker, *Kinship, Business, and Politics,* chap. 10; Cosío Villegas et al., *Historia Moderna de México,* vol. 8, part 2, 359, 371–72, 409. A Mexican historian suggests that Manuel Calero and Jorge Vera Estañol also served as legal advisors to Doheny. See Menéndez, *Doheny El Cruel,* 35.

230. Beals, *Porfirio Diaz,* 379; Cosío Villegas et al., *Historia Moderna de México,* vol. 8, part 2, 130, 169, 373, 387, 424.

231. Ibid., 363, 365, 400, 416, 596, 858.

232. Cowdray to Manuel Zamacona, New York, 26 Apr 1911, Pearson, A3 (this letter informed the Mexican government of Cowdray's interview); W. B. Hohler to Grey, 17 May 1911, FO, 371–1147/20781.

233. Cable, Doheny to W. H. Taft, New York City, 5 May 1911, State Dept. Decimal Files, 812.00/1666.

234. H. C. Folger, Jr., "Standard Oil Company and Mexico," 4 Apr 1911, State Dept. Decimal Files, 812.00/1796.

235. S. W. Finch to the Attorney General, 26 Apr 1911, ibid., 812.00/1503.

236. This report, sent by the special agent for El Paso, Texas, was forwarded by the attorney general to the sec. of state, 2 May 1911, ibid., 812.00/1593.

237. Report quoted verbatim in attorney general to sec. of state, 9 May 1911, ibid., 812.00/1679.

238. See C. R. Troxel to John D. Archbold, 13 Jan 1910; Archbold to Troxel, 14 Jan 1910; William H. Libby to attorney general, 11 May 1911; J. D. Archbold to P. C. Knox, 15 May 1911, ibid., 812.00/1796. Several historians of the Revolution also question the authenticity of the Standard Oil–Madero connection. See especially Knight, *The Mexican Revolution,* 1:184–87; Peter A. R. Calvert, *The Mexican Revolution, 1910–1914: The Diplomatic Anglo-American*

Conflict (Cambridge, Eng., 1968), 78–84. Madero's biographer points out that Standard Oil never received a thing from the Madero government. See Stanley R. Ross, *Francisco I. Madero: Apostle of Mexican Democracy* (New York, 1955), 142–43.

239. Calvert, *The Mexican Revolution*, 84. Stanley Ross lends credence to this view. Ross, *Francisco I. Madero*, 141–42.

240. J. B. Body to Cowdray, 20 May, Cowdray to Sebastian de Mier, 9 June 1911, Pearson, A3.

Chapter Two

1. Mexico, *El petróleo de México: Recopilación de documentos oficiales* (Mexico City, 1940; reprint, Mexico City, 1963), 14; Francisco Martín Moreno, *México negro: Una novela política* (Mexico City, 1986).

2. Anglo Mexican Petroleum Products Co., *Mexican Fuel Oil* (London, 1914), 68–71, 77, 79; testimony of Doheny, *Investigation of Mexican Affairs*, 1:236.

3. *Mexican Fuel Oil*, 17; document dated 17 Feb 1917, Carranza, carpeta 12601.

4. *Mexican Fuel Oil*, 80; Harold Walker, Memorandum, 22 Feb 1918, State Dept. Decimal Files, 812.6363/397.

5. Robert Adamson to Sen. William N. Calder, 2 Feb 1920, State Dept. Decimal Files, 812.6363/642; *Mexican Fuel Oil*, 132–33.

6. Harold F. Williamson et al., *The American Petroleum Industry* (Evanston, Ill., 1963), 2:115; B. W. Smith, "The Story of Royal Dutch/Shell Up to 1945," undated ms., Shell, 166.

7. Calvert, *The Mexican Revolution*, 173; Contract: The Admiralty and Anglo Mexican Petroleum Products Co., Ltd., 7 Jan 1914, Pearson, C49 F2; Cowdray to Thomas J. Ryder, 31 Aug 1914, Pearson, A3; *Mexican Fuel Oil*, 3–4. The view that the British navy depended upon Mexican oil for up to 75 percent of its fuel supplies is not corroborated elsewhere. Those (including oilmen) who wished to portray the Carranza government as hindering the Allied war effort propagated this erroneous assumption. See Leon Canova, "Memorandum," 18 Feb 1918, State Dept. Decimal Files, 812.6363/401.

8. U.S. Congress, Senate, Committee on Public Lands, *Leasing of Oil Lands*, 65th Congress, 1st sess. (Washington, D.C., 1917), 125.

9. *Mexican Fuel Oil*, 62–63; "Mexican Eagle Oil Company, Ltd.," New York, 1921, DeGolyer, file 6142.

10. These contacts loomed large for El Aguila, for they gave Cowdray's Mexican company access to U.S. petroleum technology and equipment. Body, "Memo on Mr. Body's Departure," 1 Nov 1916, Pearson, A4; "New Notes from Mexican News Bureau," 26 July 1917, State Dept. Decimal Files, 812.6363/294.

11. "The Sulphur and Oxygen Compounds of Petroleum and the Synthesis of Asphaltenes," 1920, DeGolyer, file 5267; Williamson et al., *The American Petroleum Industry,* 2:267.

12. Dawson, "Tampico District Oil Report for March, 1920," State Dept. Decimal Files, 812.6363/672; Williamson et al., *The American Petroleum Industry,* 2:29.

13. Lloyd Burlingham, "Prices of Fuel Oil Increased," Salina Cruz, 1 May 1920, State Dept. Decimal Files, 812.6363/681.

14. Ralph Arnold, "Appraisal of the Physical Properties of the Mexican Petroleum Co. Ltd. of Delaware," 26 Aug 1911, Arnold, Box 201; E. T. Dumble, "The Occurrence of Petroleum in Eastern Mexico as Contrasted with Those in Texas and Louisiana," American Institute of Mining Engineers, *Bulletin,* no. 104 (August 1915): 1627. The presence of water in the limestone supported the oil in large quantities in one level, whereas the oil sands of Texas held deposits of oil at various levels.

15. DeGolyer, "The Significance of Certain Mexican Oil Field Temperatures," n.d., DeGolyer, file 5141; W. E. Weather to E. DeGolyer, Wichita Falls, 8 July 1916, ibid., file 5262.

16. Testimony of Michael A. Spellacy, *Investigation of Mexican Affairs,* 1:939–41; Body to Cowdray, 23 Aug 1912, Pearson, A4; W. F. Buckley to P. Merrill Griffith, 11 Aug 1909, U.S. Consular Records, Tampico, General Correspondence.

17. Testimony of Spellacy, *Investigation of Mexican Affairs,* 1:942. The opinion of López Portillo y Weber that the whole of the Huasteca had been an "Indian" region with no traditions of private property is inaccurate. He relates how lease agents lured "Indians" to Tampico's red light district and got them to sign oil leases while they reveled in a drunken stupor. I have not seen these stories corroborated elsewhere. José López Portillo y Weber, *El petróleo de México: su importancia, sus problemas* (Mexico City, 1975), 102–5.

18. Testimony of Britt, *Investigation of Mexican Affairs,* 1:1007, 1009–10.

19. "Memorandum re. Aguila Company Leaseholds in Northern Mexico," [circa 1920], DeGolyer, file 5244.

20. "Minutes of Meeting Held in Tampico," 15 May 1917, DeGolyer, file 5166.

21. Testimony of C. H. Rathbone, *Investigation of Mexican Affairs,* 1:546. This condition was also prevalent in U.S. booms, where the leasetakers had to be cautious, as one of their number said, for "many leases [were] given by phoney owners." W. L. Connelly, *The Oil Business As I Saw It: Half a Century with Sinclair* (Norman, 1954), 51.

22. "Minutes of Meeting Held in Tampico," 15 May 1917, DeGolyer, file 5166.

23. Testimony of Doheny, *Investigation of Mexican Affairs,* 1:237; José Vázquez Schiaffino et al., *Informes sobre la cuestión petrolera* (Mexico City, 1919), appendix; testimony of Rathbone, *Investigation of Mexican Affairs,* 1:545. One Mexican source estimated that the oil companies paid approximately 6.4 million pesos yearly in rent on 1.6 million hectares of leased land. Mexico, Secretaría de Industria, Comercio y Trabajo, *Proyecto de la ley de petróleo de los*

Estados Unidos Mexicanos (Mexico City, 1918), 33. *Tal vez* is Spanish for "perhaps" or "maybe."

24. "Minutes of Meeting Held in Tampico," 15 May 1917, DeGolyer, file 5166.

25. U.S. Bureau of Foreign and Domestic Commerce, *Commerce Reports* (13 Sept 1920), 11–12.

26. "The Petroleum Industry in Mexico" (circa 1921), State Dept. Decimal Files, 812.6363/882; Kenneth C. Phipps, "The Petroleum Industry of Mexico" (M.A. thesis, The University of Texas, 1922), 12. Also see V. R. Garfías, "The Oil Region of Northeastern Mexico," *Economic Geology* 10, no. 3 (1915): 195–224.

27. Hudson returned to Texas, invested his capital in an oil well in Wallaceville in 1916, and lost it all. See interview with W. M. Hudson, 16, 18 Sept 1952, OHTO, T79, T81.

28. "Matters Testified to by Clinton D. Martin," (circa 1932), Arnold, Box 131.

29. E. J. Nicklos, 8 July 1953, OHTO, T103, T104.

30. Ibid.

31. Hudson interview, 16 Sept 1952, OHTO, T79.

32. Ezequiel Ordóñez, "El petróleo en México," part 2, 194–95.

33. See "Mexican Oil Fields: Some Well Logs," DeGolyer, folder 5300.

34. Ralph Arnold, "Basis of Appraisal," (circa 1932), Arnold, Box 131.

35. Ibid.

36. "Matters Testified to by Clinton D. Martin," Arnold, Box 131.

37. Vincent, *A Man Remembers*, 20–22.

38. "The Petroleum Industry in Mexico," (circa 1921), State Dept. Decimal Files, 812.6363/882.

39. W. A. Thompson, Jr., to sec. of state, 1 May 1914, State Dept. Decimal Files, 812.6363/67.

40. Ordóñez, "El petróleo en México," part 2, 197; Gerretson, *History of the Royal Dutch*, 4:259.

41. "The Petroleum Industry in Mexico," (circa 1921), State Dept. Decimal Files, 812.6363/883. Also see U.S. Bureau of Foreign and Domestic Commerce, *Commerce Reports* (13 Sept 1920), 1215; Phipps, "The Petroleum Industry of Mexico," 8; W. A. Thompson, Jr., to sec. of state, 1 May 1914, State Dept. Decimal Files, 812.6363/67.

42. "Minutes of a Meeting Held in Tampico," 15 May 1917, DeGolyer, file 5166.

43. Bureau of Foreign and Domestic Commerce, *Commerce Reports* (13 Sept 1920), 1214–15; "The Petroleum Industry in Mexico," (circa 1921), State Dept. Decimal Files, 812.6363/882; *Commerce Reports* (13 Sept 1920), 1214.

44. J. Vázquez Schiaffino, "Mexico," *Petroleum* 7, no. 4 (Aug 1919), 106; "The Petroleum Industry in Mexico," (circa 1921), State Dept. Decimal Files, 812.6363/882.

45. Ben C. Belt, "Survey of the Limantour Lands," 16 Nov 1913, DeGolyer, file 5395.

46. Cummins to Foreign Office, 30 May 1919, FO, 371–3830/95153; Charles H. Cunningham, "Investigations of Petroleum Conditions in Mexico," 6 May 1919, State Dept. Decimal Files, 812.6363/458; B. F. Yost, "Oil Prospecting in Sonora and Lower California," 14 Apr 1920, ibid., 812.6363/664; Fletcher to sec. of state, 10 July 1918, ibid., 812.6363/405.

47. Kyle Kinney to U.S. consul, 14 Nov 1919, State Dept. Decimal Files, 812.6363/610.

48. Gaylord March to sec. of state, 4, 10 May 1919, ibid., 812.6363/459, 812.6363/675; Lloyd Burlingham to sec. of state, 2 Feb, 10 Mar 1920, ibid., 812.6363/644, 812.6363/658.

49. U.S. Bureau of Foreign and Domestic Commerce, *Commerce Reports* (13 Sept 1920), 1217; E. Dean Fuller, "The Oil Situation in Mexico in Relation to American Investments," 1916, State Dept. Decimal Files, 812.6363/255; Vázquez Schiaffino et al., *Informes sobre la cuestión petrolera*, appendix.

50. "List of British Oil Properties," 21 Nov 1916, FO, 371–2706/235235; J. E. Lucey to sec. of state, 11 May 1914, State Dept. Decimal Files, 812.6363/60.

51. A. L. Patterson to sec. of state, 8 Aug 1917, ibid., 812.6363/297; Chambers to Body, 3 June 1917, Pearson, A4; Edith T. Penrose, *The Large International Firm in Developing Countries: The International Petroleum Industry* (London, 1968), 117.

52. Clarence A. Miller to sec. of state, 29 Jan 1911, State Dept. Decimal Files, 812.6363/1; R. H. Rose to Brodix, 3 Sept 1917, Lansing to Sen. Morris Sheppard, 18 Sept 1917, ibid., 812.6363/304.

53. Mallison, *The Great Wildcatter,* 242.

54. Ibid., 251–52; 258–59.

55. George F. Summerlin to sec. of state, 8 Jan 1921, State Dept. Decimal Files, 812.6363/791.

56. Williamson et al., *The American Petroleum Industry,* 2:262.

57. Jack Logan, "Mexico's Future Petroleum Possibility," *Oil Weekly* 59, no. 11 (28 Nov 1930): 26. Pan American Petroleum Corporation, *Mexican Petroleum,* 33. Ordóñez places its total production at more than 71 million bd. See Ordóñez, "El petróleo en México," part 2, 194.

58. Ralph Arnold to Salomon Bros., New York, 26 Aug 1911, "Appraisal of the Physical Properties," Arnold, Box 200.

59. "Digest of Deposition of William Green," [circa 1932], Arnold to Salomon Bros., 26 Aug 1911, Arnold, Box 200.

60. Also see Pan American Petroleum Corporation, *Mexican Petroleum,* 36–38. The date of the statement is not clear, but the book was published in 1922.

61. Ibid., 40–45.

62. Ordóñez, "El petróleo en México," part 2, 202.

63. I. C. White, "Third Report," March 1916, DeGolyer, file 5300.

64. Ordóñez, "El petróleo en México," part 2, 202–4.

65. Body to Cowdray, 12 Feb 1916, Pearson, A4.

66. Ordóñez, "El petróleo en México," part 2, 204; Logan, "Mexico's Future Petroleum Possibility," 26.

67. "Digest of Deposition of William Green," 9 Dec 1932, Arnold, Box 200.

68. Arnold, "Appraisal of the Physical Properties," Arnold, Box 200; Doheny testimony, U.S. Senate, Committee on Public Lands, *Leasing of Oil Lands*.

69. *Annual Report of the Mexican Petroleum Co. Ltd. of Delaware* (n.p., 1917); Doheny testimony, *Investigation of Mexican Affairs*, 1:233, 243; G. H. Hewitt to E. Paget Thurston, 31 Oct 1918, Pearson, A3.

70. Arnold, "Appraisal of the Physical Properties," Arnold, Box 20; Pan American Petroleum Corporation, *Mexican Petroleum*, 52; Barron, *The Mexican Problem*, 26; Doheny testimony, *Investigation of Mexican Affairs*, 1:233.

71. Body to Cowdray, 18 Dec 1912, Pearson, A4.

72. Pan American Petroleum Corporation, *Mexican Petroleum*, 35.

73. See E. T. Brown to S. B. Brooks, 8 Mar 1913, and statements of C. L. Wallis, Doheny, and George C. Greer, "S.O. Suit: Relating to Federal Matter," n.p., n.d. [circa 1913], Law Library Archives, University of Texas at Austin; Hopkins testimony, *Investigation of Mexican Affairs*, 2:2568–71. After the 1911 dissolution, however, Magnolia was a part of Standard Oil Company of New York (Socony), not Standard Oil Company of New Jersey (Jersey Standard). See James A. Clark and Michel T. Halbouty, *Spindletop* (New York, 1952), 181–82.

74. See Pan American Petroleum Corporation, *Mexican Petroleum*, 35, 111, 117, 123, 127–68, 180–82; Doheny testimony, U.S. Senate Hearing, *Leasing of Oil Lands*, 126–27; Barron, *The Mexican Problem*.

75. Documents dated 9 Sept 1916, 2, 19 Oct 1916, Ramo de Hacienda, Fomento y Obras Públicas, Minas y Petróleo, C194, esp. E23/324.6–452-/2, part 1, AGN.

76. Doheny testimony, *Investigation of Mexican Affairs*, 1:249, *Annual Report of the Mexican Petroleum Company of Delaware*; *Annual Report, Pan American Petroleum & Transport Co.* (n.p., 1920).

77. Ordóñez, "El petróleo en México," part 2, 204; Pan American Petroleum Corporation, *Mexican Petroleum*, 33.

78. "Digest of Deposition of William Green," 9 Dec 1932, Arnold, Box 200.

79. López Portillo y Weber, *El petróleo de México*, 100.

80. Ibid., 99.

81. Ordóñez, "El petróleo en México," part 2, 155–57. Although a teetotaler, Doheny is depicted by the novelist Francisco Martín Moreno as constantly drinking whiskey at the businessmen's club while he and other Yankee robber barons decided Mexico's fate. See Moreno, *México negro*.

82. Ordóñez, "El petróleo en México," part 2, 155–57.

83. U.S. Senate, Committee on Public Lands, *Leasing of Oil Lands*, 125–26.

84. Ibid., 176; James L. Bates, *The Origins of Teapot Dome: Progressives, Parties, and Petroleum, 1909–1921* (Champaign-Urbana, 1962; reprint Westport, Conn., 1978), 12–13, 40–41, 119.

85. U.S. Congress, Senate, Committee on Commerce, *Regulation of Ocean Freight Rates, Requisitioning of Vessels, and Increasing the Powers of the Shipping Board.* 65th Congress, 2d sess. (Washington, D.C., 1918), 26–43.

86. Barron, *The Mexican Problem,* 12, 14.

87. Body to Cowdray, 17 Sept, 5 Oct 1912, 3 Aug 1916, Pearson, A4.

88. Body to Cowdray, 18 Dec 1912, Body, "Memo on Mr. Body's Departure," 1 Nov 1916, Pearson, A4.

89. Body to Cowdray, 3, 30 Aug, 21 Sept 1912, Pearson, A4.

90. See *General Reports of the Suit against the Mexican Eagle Petroleum Co.,* (Mexico, 1934–35); *The Amatlán Suit* (Mexican Eagle Oil Co., 1934), both found in Pearson, C44 F5.

91. Body to Cowdray, 23 Aug, 13 Sept, 14, 18 Dec 1912, Pearson, A4.

92. Body to Cowdray, 23 Dec 1915, 19 Dec 1916, Pearson, A3; Foreign Office to Spring-Rice, 14 Oct 1915, FO, 371–2403/151159.

93. Lord Reading to Foreign Office, Washington, D.C., 9 July 1918, FO, 371–3246/120387; "Memorandum of Agreement," 16 Dec 1918, Pearson, C43 F2. A similar dispute between El Aguila and Mexican Gulf over Lot 146, Amatlán, was settled nearly in the same manner. Gulf and El Aguila simply split the lot between them. A. Jacobsen to T. J. Ryder, 21 Feb 1920, DeGolyer, file 5145.

94. Body to Cowdray, 1 Apr 1913, Pearson, A4. This Waters-Pierce well at the Hacienda Santa Fe did not last.

95. See "Report on Accounts," 7 Feb 1917, Pearson, C-43, file 6; Body to Cowdray, 27 Jan 1916, Pearson, Box A-4.

96. Logan, "Mexico's Future Petroleum Possibilities," 26.

97. Chambers to Body, 27 May 1917, Pearson, A4; *Boletín de Petróleo* (Feb 1916), 137–38.

98. Body to Cowdray, 25 Oct, 30 Nov 1912; Cowdray to Thomas J. Ryder, 31 Aug 1914, Cowdray to Escandón, 11 Oct 1914, Pearson, A3.

99. Body to Cowdray, Tampico, 16 Feb, 1 Mar 1917, Pearson, A4.

100. A. Jacobsen to T. J. Ryder, 21 Feb 1920, DeGolyer, file 5120.

101. Paul F. Lambert and Kenny A. Franks, eds., *Voices from the Oil Fields* (Norman, 1984), 43.

102. See E. DeGolyer, "Reconnaissance Geological Examination of Hacienda San Felipe," 1912, DeGolyer, folders 5211, 5129.

103. Lambert and Franks, *Voices from the Oil Fields,* 43; DeGolyer to Hayes, n.d., Hayes to DeGolyer, 1914, T. Wayland Vaughn to DeGolyer, 25 Feb 1920, DeGolyer, folders 696, 5129.

104. Body to Cowdray, 4 May 1916, Pearson, A4.

105. Cowdray to Body, 13 May 1918, Pearson, A3; Anglo Mexican Petroleum Products Co., *Mexican Fuel Oil,* 9.

106. Cowdray to Directors of Aguila, 20 July 1914, Pearson, C45 F1; Furber, *I Took Chances,* 178–79.

107. *Mexican Eagle Oil Co., Ltd.* (New York, 1921) DeGolyer, folder 6142.

108. "Escritura complentaria [*sic*] a la de aportación otorgada por el Señor Lic. Don Luis Riba," 3 Feb 1913, Ramo de Hacienda, Fomento y Obras

Públicas, Minas y Petróleo, AGN; "Oil Fields of Mexico Co." *The Joint Stock Companies' Journal,* Aug 1912.

109. A. Jacobsen to T. J. Ryder, 2 Feb 1920, DeGolyer, folder 5120; "Estimate of Cost of a Barrel of Oil," [1916], Pearson, C45.

110. Body to Cowdray, 13 May 1913, Pearson, A4.

111. Body, "Memo on Mr. Body's Departure," 1 Nov 1916, Body to Cowdray, 22 Feb 1917, Pearson, A4; *Mexican Fuel Oil,* 11.

112. Cowdray to Body, 24 Mar 1916, Body to Cowdray, 4 May 1916, Body to Cowdray, 22 Feb 1917, Pearson, A4; *Mexican Fuel Oil,* 9.

113. Body to Cowdray, 10 Feb 1916, Pearson, A4.

114. Pearson Photographic Albums, Pearson, P/1.

115. Cowdray, "Refineries Programme," 31 Dec 1917, Cowdray to José Y. Limantour, 19 Jan 1916, Pearson, C45, F7, A4; *Mexican Fuel Oil,* 11.

116. Body to Cowdray, 8 Aug 1914, Pearson, A3; F. M. Davies to H. J. Seymour, London, 7 Dec 1920, FO, 371–4499/A8644.

117. Pearson, C48 F8, F9.

118. *Mexican Fuel Oil,* 13; C. Pearson, "Memo to Chief," 25 Nov 1915, Pearson, C48 F1; Durán de Seade, "Mexico's Relations with the Powers During the Great War," 52.

119. Body, "Memorandum," 6 Sept 1915, Pearson, A3.

120. "Anglo Mexican's Proposal," 19 May 1916, "The Eagle Oil Transport Co., Ltd., Accounts, 1918," Pearson, C49 F2, F4.

121. Body to Cowdray, 17 Aug, 24 Oct 1912, Pearson, A4.

122. Letter to Ryder, 8 Nov 1912 in "Waters Pierce Oil Co. Competition," Ryder to Chief, 10 May 1913, Pearson, C44 F7.

123. "Ltr. from Ryder," 23 June 1918, Chief to Hugh Schere, 13 Mar 1913, Chief to Body, 13 Mar 1913, Chief to Ryder, 10 Feb 1914, Pearson, C44 F7.

124. Cowdray, "History of the Fight w/ the Waters Pierce Co.," August 1928, Pearson, C44 F7; Robert S. Israel, "Deposits of Fuel Oil," 4 Oct 1919, Military Intelligence Division, Correspondence, 10640–1695/6, Record Group 165, National Archives.

125. Body to Cowdray, 6 May 1913, Pearson, A4; Body to Ryder, 3 Nov 1914, Ryder to Chief, 19 Oct 1914; Letter from Ryder, 16 Oct 1912 in "Competition: Waters Pierce & Co.," Pearson, C44 F7.

126. Cowdray to Sir Edward Holden, Dunecht, 13 Aug 1912, Pearson, A4.

127. Cowdray to Harold, New York, 4 Aug 1911, Pearson, C44 F2.

128. See contract, 4 Apr 1912, Pearson, C43 F2.

129. H. W. M., "Memorandum: Standard Oil Company," 14 Oct 1914, Pearson, C49 F2.

130. Cowdray to Body, 22 Mar 1916, Body to Cowdray, 4 May 1916, Pearson, A4.

131. Cowdray to Holden, 13 Aug 1912, Hutchinson to Macdonald, 16 Feb 1914, Pearson, C44 F7, C49 F2.

132. *Mexican Fuel Oil,* 15–16; "Extracts from letter and statement to Sir Thomas Bowring," 1 Sept 1913, Pearson, C49 F2; "The Bowing Petroleum Co., Ltd.," May 1918, ibid., C43 F2; Contract, Aguila and Port of Pará, 1 Nov

1912, Cowdray, "Private Memorandum for Mr. Kindersley," 13 April 1916, ibid., C44 F9.

133. The gold peso equaled 24.5 pence or 49.75 cents. Statistics for 1921 represent the fiscal year. See "Summary of Balance Sheet for Years 1919 to 1926 Inclusive," n.d., Cowdray to Foreign Office, 3 Feb 1915, "Report on Accounts," 7 Feb 1917, Pearson, C43 F5, F6.

134. Cowdray to J. B. Body, 29 Dec 1916, Pearson, A4.

135. Cowdray, "Memorandum re. the Aguila Co.," 13 Jan 1919, Pearson, C44 F3.

136. "Mr. Corwin's Trip to Mexico—1911, Reports," Production Dept., Transcontinental Petroleum Co., SONJ. I would like to acknowledge my gratitude to the late Henrietta M. Larson for allowing me to see materials she culled from the Jersey Standard archives. I understand the company has since destroyed the historical files for lack of storage space.

137. W. C. Teagle to Arthur Corwin, 11 Aug 1911, "Corwin's trip to Mexico—1911," ibid. At the time, Arthur Corwin was general manager of South Penn, the only producing property in the United States still retained by Jersey Standard after the dissolution. Corwin to sec. of state, 10 May 1914, State Dept. Decimal Files, 812.6363/68.

138. Cowdray, "Private & Confidential Memo for Mr. Bedford," 28 Mar 1913, Cowdray, "Memo re. Interview with Mr. J. D. Archbold," n.d.; T. H. Bedford to Cowdray, 16 Apr 1913, Pearson, C44, F2.

139. J. J. Carter, "Reports on London & Pacific Properties and Lobitos," 22 Apr, 15 July 1913, Imperial Oil Co. archives, file 157.

140. John Archbold to Cowdray, New York, 17 Oct 1913, Pearson, C44 F2.

141. "Memo on Negotiations with Standard Oil New Jersey," Pearson, C44 F2; Durán de Seade, "Mexico's Relations with the Powers," 255, 257.

142. J. L. Hirth to Pearson & Son, Ltd., 29 Apr 1918, John Cadman to Foreign Office, 17 Dec 1917, Pearson, C44 F2.

143. "Memorandum to the Chief," 5 May 1915, Cowdray to Sir George Barnes, 6 Dec 1915, Cowdray, "Private Memorandum for Mr. Kindersley," 13 Apr 1916, Pearson, C52 F1, C44 F9.

144. Body to C. Reed, New York, 19 Jan 1917, C. Reed to Body, London, 8 Feb 1917, Pearson, A4; Middlemas, *The Master Builders,* 134–37.

145. Maurice de Bunsen, "Foreign Office Memorandum on British Oil Interests in Mexico," 26 Mar 1917, FO, 371–2964/203294; Foreign Office to Spring-Rice, 27 June 1917, ibid., 371–2964/128411; "Memo on Pearson's Oil Interests in Mexico," 1917, ibid., 371–2964/230821; Cowdray, "Brief Statement on the Importance of This Country Having Their Own Sources of Petroleum," 5 Dec 1918, Pearson, C44 F9.

146. C. G. Hyde to Treasury, 6 May 1918, Pearson, C44 F2.

147. Jean Meyer, "Los Estados Unidos y el petróleo mexicano: Estado de la cuestión," *Historia Mexicana* 18 (1968): 79–96; Enrique Mosconi, *El petróleo argentino, 1922–1930, y la ruptura de los trusts petrolíferos inglés y norteamericano* (Buenos Aires, 1936); Frank C. Hanighen, *The Secret War* (New York, 1934); Adelberto J. Pinelo, *The Multinational Corporation as a Force in Latin American Politics: A Case Study of the International Petroleum Company in Peru* (New

York, 1973). For a comprehensive treatment of the oil industry in Latin America, see George Philip, *Oil and Politics in Latin America: Nationalist Movements and State Companies* (Cambridge, Eng., 1982).

148. Rory Miller, "Small Business in the Peruvian Oil Industry: Lobitos Oilfields Limited Before 1934," *Business History Review* 56 (1982): 400–23; Carl E. Solberg, *Oil and Nationalism in Argentina: A History* (Stanford, 1979); Jonathan C. Brown, "Jersey Standard and the Politics of Latin American Oil Production, 1911–1930," in *Latin American Oil Companies and the Politics of Energy,* ed. John D. Wirth (Lincoln, 1985), 1–50.

149. Penrose, *The Large International Firm,* 46–47. Also see Mira Wilkins, "Multinational Oil Companies in South America in the 1920s: Argentina, Bolivia, Brazil, Chile, Colombia, Ecuador, and Peru," *Business History Review* 48 (1974): 414–46; Chandler, "Technological and Organizational Underpinnings of Modern Industrial Multinational Enterprise," 30–54.

150. U.S. Supreme Court, *Standard Oil Company et al. v. U. S.* (1909), 221 U. S. 1, 1147–52; Bennett H. Wall and George S. Gibb, *Teagle of Jersey Standard* (New Orleans, 1974).

151. Sadler to S. B. Hunt, 5 Mar 1917, Directors' files, Sadler Papers, SONJ.

152. Ibid.

153. George Sweet Gibb and Evelyn H. Knowlton, *The Resurgent Years, 1911–1927: History of the Standard Oil Company (New Jersey)* (New York, 1956), 182, 198–99.

154. "Memorandums," 23 July 1920, 6 Aug 1920, Directors' files, Sadler Papers, SONJ.

155. Hidy and Hidy, *Pioneering in Big Business,* 404, 711–12; Nevins, *John D. Rockefeller,* 2:611–12; Bringhurst, *Antitrust and the Oil Monopoly,* 134. Beginning in 1907, the government prosecutors spent eighteen months collecting testimony of 444 witnesses. The final record extended to 14,495 printed pages in twenty-three volumes.

156. "Notes on Conversation with Mr. Burton W. Wilson," 27 Oct 1949. Courtesy of the late Henrietta M. Larson.

157. S. B. Hunt to Swain, 4, 23 Dec 1913, 15 Jan 1914, Swain to E. Arredondo, 7 May 1915, Esso Standard, Legal Dept., file 117, SONJ. Arredondo was the representative in the United States of the revolutionary leader and future Mexican president, Venustiano Carranza. C. O. Swain of Jersey's legal department met with Arredondo in 1915 to inform him of the company's business activities in Mexico. Arredondo to Swain, 8 May 1915, ibid.

158. "Notes on conversation with Mr. Burton W. Wilson," 27 Oct 1949.

159. Copy of 1912 testimony of Hopkins, *Investigation of Mexican Affairs,* 2:2569–70.

160. Flanagan to Teagle, 8 July 1914, Imperial Oil Co. archives, Teagle Papers, Correspondence with Flanagan.

161. Flanagan to Teagle, 4 Dec 1914, ibid.

162. Flanagan, "Memo Relative to Moyutla hacienda," 6 July 1916, ibid.

163. Skoien & Smith to Flanagan, Tampico, 2 Jan 1915, ibid.; "Notes on conversation with Mr. Burton W. Wilson"; C. O. Swain to C. T. White, 26 March 1915, Esso Standard, Legal Dept., file 117, SONJ.

164. "List of Leases Protocolized in the name of John Kee," 19 Apr 1917, ibid.; Gibb and Knowlton, *The Resurgent Years,* 87. At least one of Kee's leases, Chinampa Lot 163, later became the subject of legal dispute by Mexican Gulf. See *Mexican Gulf v. Transcontinental: Plaintiffs and Defendants Exhibition* (n.p., n.d.), 6–7. The case was tried in U.S. District Court in New York in 1921–22.

165. Sadler to S. B. Hunt, 18 Feb 1918, Directors' Files, Sadler Papers, SONJ. Apparently in 1912 Teagle had had an opportunity to acquire Penn-Mex with its 160,000 acres of leases but failed to do so. Gibb and Knowlton, *The Resurgent Years,* 85.

166. Transcontinental Consolidated Oil Co., Ltd., no. 7, 24 Aug 1917, J. A. Brown to F. D. Asche, 23 June 1917, Production Dept., Contract Files, Transcontinental Petroleum Co., SONJ; Gibb and Knowlton, *The Resurgent Years,* 87.

167. Sadler to S. B. Hunt, 18 Feb 1918, Directors' Files, Sadler Papers, SONJ.

168. Sadler to Northrop Clarey, 26 Feb 1925, Production Dept., Sadler's Mexican Files, SONJ.

169. "Reports of Transcontinental, 1918–28," Controller's Dept., SONJ; "Reports on Mexico-General," Sadler to S. B. Hunt, 31 July 1918, Production Dept., Sadler's Mexican Files, SONJ; "News Notes from Mexican News Bureau," 26 July 1917, State Dept. Decimal Files, 812.6363/294; Vázquez Schiaffino et al., *Informes sobre la cuestión petrolera,* appendix.

170. Gibb and Knowlton, *The Resurgent Years,* 41.

171. J. A. Brown to A. F. Corwin, 27 Oct 1920, Production Dept., Sadler's Mexican files, SONJ; J. A. Brown to C. O. Swain, San Antonio, 3 Dec 1919, State Dept. Decimal Files, 812.6363/1603.

172. Gerretson, *History of the Royal Dutch,* 1:383–86; 3:55.

173. As quoted from 1920 annual report of the Royal Dutch Co. in U.S. Federal Trade Commission, *Foreign Ownership in the Petroleum Industry* (Washington, D.C., 1923), 12–13.

174. Gerretson, *History of the Royal Dutch,* 3:4, 4:268–72, 276, 278, 280; Jonathan C. Brown, "Why Foreign Oil Companies Shifted Their Production from Mexico to Venezuela during the 1920s," *American Historical Review* 90 (1985): 377.

175. Gerretson, *History of the Royal Dutch,* 4:251.

176. Anonymous note, 1914, note received, 20 Dec 1919, Tweede Afdeling, Archief van het Ministerie van Buitenlandse Zaken, B–Dossiers, Betreffende Consulaire en Handels-Aangelegenheden, 1871–1940, [1955], Inv. nos. 1686, 1681, AR; Gerretson, *History of the Royal Dutch,* 4:266–68; F. C. Gerretson, *Geschiedenis de Koninklijke Nederlandsche Petroleum Maatschappij,* vol. 5 (Baarn, Neth., 1973), 281, 306–7.

177. Gerretson, *Geschiedenis,* 308–10.

178. Ibid., 310, 321.

179. "Memoranda Interviews between Gulbenkian and L. Cowdray," 7 Oct 1918 to 2 Dec 1918, Pearson, C44 F3.

180. "Letter of Undertaking: S. Pearson & Son, Ltd., to the Royal Dutch Company and the 'Shell' Transport and Trading Company, Ltd.," 26 Mar 1919, Pearson, C44 F3; U.S. Consul General to sec. of state, London, 10 Dec 1920,

State Dept. Decimal Files, 812.6363/774; Gerretson, *Geschiedenis,* 317. Gulbenkian apparently earned a 20 percent profit for his brokerage in the sale. Cowdray, "Memo for Mr. Tanner: The R. D.-Shell Agreement," 21 Mar 1919, Pearson, C44 F3.

181. Smith, "The Story of Royal Dutch/Shell," 174.

182. Deterding to Cowdray, 25 Mar 1919, Pearson, C44 F3; J. M. Cadman to Lord Cowdray, 27 March 1919, ibid.; Cable, Foreign Office to Cummins, 29 Mar 1919, FO, 371–3827/44166; H. G. Hilton, "Memorandum," Washington, D.C., 21 Apr 1919, State Dept. Decimal Files, 812.6363/449.

183. Lord Cowdray, "Memorandum re. the Aguila Co.," 13 Jan 1919, Pearson, C44 F3; Gerretson, *Geschiedenis,* 317–19.

184. Federal Trade Commission, *Foreign Ownership,* 16–17, 132.

185. "Total Production of Potrero No. 4," 26 Feb 1920, DeGolyer, file 5300; James D. McLachlan, "Report upon the Situation in Mexico," 17 Dec 1918, FO, 371–3836/472.

186. Ralph Arnold, "Appraisal of the Physical Properties of the Mexican Petroleum Co. Ltd. of Delaware," 26 Aug 1911, Arnold, box 200; "Digest of Deposition of William Green," Los Angeles, 9 Dec 1932, ibid., box 201.

187. *Mexican Eagle Oil Company,* 2.

Chapter Three

1. See especially John Womack, Jr., "The Mexican Revolution, 1910–1920," *The Cambridge History of Latin America,* vol. 5, ed. Leslie Bethel (Cambridge, Eng., 1984), 81–153; Hart, *Revolutionary Mexico;* Adolfo Gilly, *La revolución interrumpida: México, 1910–1920, una guerra campesina por la tierra y el poder,* 5th ed. (Mexico City, 1975).

2. See Steven Topik, *The Political Economy of the Brazilian State, 1889–1930* (Austin, 1987); George Philip, *Oil and Politics in Latin America;* Solberg, *Oil and Nationalism in Argentina;* George M. Ingram, *Expropriation of U.S. Property in South America* (New York, 1974); Stephen J. Randall, *The Diplomacy of Modernization: Colombian-American Relations, 1920–1940* (Toronto, 1977); John D. Wirth, *The Politics of Brazilian Development, 1930–1954* (Stanford, 1970).

3. Anton Mohr, *The Oil Wars* (New York, 1926), 209.

4. Testimony of Manuel A. Estera, testimony of Sloan W. Emery, *Investigation of Mexican Affairs,* 1:1362, 2:2222–23. See also John Kenneth Turner, *Barbarous Mexico* (Chicago, 1912; reprint Austin, 1969).

5. ["Al Pueblo Mexicano,"] n.p., n.d., in Marion Fletcher to State Dept., 12 Apr 1912, Chihuahua, State Dept. Decimal Files, 812.00/3539; Phillip E. Holland to State Dept., Saltillo, 17 July 1912, as quoted in Gene Z. Hanrahan, ed., *Counter-Revolution along the Border* (Salisbury, N.C., 1983), 115–16; Michael C. Meyer, *Mexican Rebel: Pascual Orozco and the American Revolution, 1910–1915* (Lincoln, 1978), 62, 64; Calvert, *The Mexican Revolution,* 106–7.

6. *El Diario,* 4 June 1912; "Memorandum by Lord Cowdray," 10 May 1915, Pearson, A3.

7. Testimony of Shelburne G. Hopkins, *Investigation of Mexican Affairs,* 2:2524–35, 2550–61.

8. Albert B. Fall to Senator Bacon, 9 Apr 1913, Fall, box 72 F4.

9. Body to Cowdray, 27 May, Thomas J. Ryder to Cowdray, Mexico, 4 Nov 1911, Pearson, A3.

10. Body, "Memorandum," 29 Aug 1911, Pearson, A3.

11. B. C. P. to W. B., 3 Jan 1912, Body to Cowdray, 15 Apr, 22 Mar 1912, Pearson, C55 F29, A4.

12. Enrique Creel to James Bryce, 13 Mar, Body to Cowdray, 10 Apr 1912, Pearson, A3.

13. Body to Cowdray, 15 Apr, Cowdray to Body, 16 Apr 1912, Pearson, A4.

14. Body to Cowdray, 28 Nov 1912, Pearson, A4.

15. Body to Cowdray, 3 Jan, Cowdray to Body, 5 Feb 1913, Pearson, A4.

16. Testimony of Doheny, *Investigation of Mexican Affairs,* 1:234.

17. *Annual Report of the Mexican Petroleum Co., Ltd., of Delaware,* n.p.; Knight, *The Mexican Revolution,* 1:447–48, 456, 465–66.

18. Body to Cowdray, 8 June 1912, 15 June 1912, 6 July, 11 July, 23 July, 23 Aug 1912, Pearson, A4.

19. Harold Walker, "Protest of Taxes," in Miller to State Dept., 18 July, 27 July 1912, State Dept. Decimal Files, 812.6363/6, /7.

20. Mexican Petroleum Company, *Los impuestos sobre la industria de petróleo,* 3–4; testimony of Doheny, *Investigation of Mexican Affairs,* 1:233.

21. Testimony of William F. Buckley, *Investigation of Mexican Affairs,* 1:831; Body to Cowdray, 30 Nov, 7 Dec 1912, Pearson, A4; Mexican Petroleum Company, *Los impuestos sobre la industria de petróleo.*

22. Body to Cowdray, 2 Feb 1914, Pearson, A3.

23. A. E. Chambers to J. B. Body, 8 Mar, Body to Cowdray, 11 Mar 1912, Pearson, A4; Francis Stronge to Sir Edward Grey, 20 Apr, 23 Apr 1912, FO, 371–1672/21531.

24. J. A. Sharp to Clarence A. Miller, 19 Apr, Miller to State Dept., 15 June, Miller to El Aguila, 25 May 1912, Miller to Matías Guerra, 6 May, Miller to Col. R. Guerra Martínez, 14 June 1912, U.S. Consular Records, Tampico, General Correspondence.

25. Body to Cowdray, 22 Feb, 26 Feb, Cowdray to Body, 28 Mar 1913, Pearson, A4.

26. Body to Cowdray, 28 Feb, 1, 5 Mar, Frederick Adams to Cowdray, 28 July 1913, Pearson, A4, A3.

27. In his memoirs, British oilman Percy Furber says that early in 1914, he accompanied a group of executives from Jersey Standard, Texas, Gulf, Sinclair, and Mexican Eagle to the White House. But they found that their support for Huerta was useless because President Wilson harbored a visceral loathing for the man. See Furber, *I Took Chances,* 174–75.

28. Cowdray to F. Díaz, 3 Sept, E. Madero to Cowdray, 25 Oct, Cowdray to Sir Walter Langley, 11 Nov, Cowdray to Madero, 11 Nov 1913, Pearson, A3.

402   NOTES TO PAGES 181–87

29. Body, "Confidential Memo to the Chief," 25 Feb, Huerta to Cowdray, 2 Feb, Body to Cowdray, 22 Oct 1914, Pearson, A3.

30. Michael C. Meyer, *Huerta: A Political Portrait* (Lincoln, 1972), 119, 181; Knight, *Mexican Revolution,* 2:129–33.

31. Body to Cowdray, 1 Apr, Cowdray to Limantour, 10 Apr 1913, Cowdray to Am Hub [?], 30 June 1915, Pearson, A3, A4; Calvert, *The Mexican Revolution,* 183–85, 231. Meyer, *Huerta,* 186–87, states that the commission was forty-one million pesos, or nearly four million pounds.

32. Meyer, *Huerta,* 184, Body to Cowdray, 9 Apr 1913, Pearson, A4; E. L. Doheny, "Memorandum of Facts Presented by the Huasteca Petroleum Co.," 5 Nov 1917, Military Intelligence Division, Correspondence, 10640–246/284.

33. Body to Cowdray, 22 Apr, 6 May 1913, Pearson, A4; Clarence A. Miller, "Report on Oil Taxation," Tampico, 2 July 1914, State Dept. Decimal Files, 812.6363/124.

34. Canada to State Dept., 28 June 1914, Miller to State Dept., 12 Nov, Bryan to U.S. consul, 21 Nov 1913, State Dept. Decimal Files, 812.6363/532, /14. The information about Huerta's oil nationalization plan is from Meyer, *Huerta,* 170–71, and *El Imparcial,* 26 Sept 1913.

35. Meyer, *Huerta,* 188.

36. Derived from "Summary of Press Attacks During 1913–1914," 3 Mar 1915, Pearson, A4.

37. Cowdray to editors, 12 Nov, 17 Nov 1913, Pearson, A3; Larry D. Hill, *Emissaries to a Revolution: Woodrow Wilson's Executive Agents in Mexico* (Baton Rouge, 1973), 102–3; Kenneth J. Grieb, *The United States and Huerta* (Lincoln, 1969), 132–34.

38. Cowdray to T. J. Ryder, 22 Nov, Body to Cowdray, 1 Dec, Cowdray, "Memo to Dr. Hayes and Mr. Ryder," 25 Nov 1913, Pearson, C44 F7, A4. One unconfirmed report from Villa's agents at the time states that a Pierce agent had contacted Pancho Villa in order to secure Tampico concessions. Cobb to State Dept., El Paso, 22 Aug 1914, State Dept. Decimal Files, 812.6363/129.

39. Doheny, "Memorandum of Facts," 5 Nov 1917, Military Intelligence Division, Correspondence, 10640–246/284.

40. T. J. Ryder to Cowdray, 24 Nov, Dr. Hayes to Cowdray, 25, 28 Nov 1913, Pearson, A3; James D. McLachlan, 17 Dec 1918, "Report upon the Situation in Mexico," FO, 371–3826/472; Calvert, *The Mexican Revolution,* 275, 282.

41. Canada to State, 3 June 1914, State Dept. Decimal Files, 812.6363/90; Doheny, "Memorandum of Facts," 5 Nov 1917, Military Intelligence Division, Correspondence, 10640–246/284; testimony of Doheny, *Investigation of Mexican Affairs,* 1:276–77.

42. H. C. Pierce to State Dept., 2 Dec 1913, State Dept. Decimal Files, 812.6363/19; Garretson, *Geschiedenis,* 185–87.

43. Cowdray, "Interview and Exchange of Views with Am. Ambassador," 9 Jan, Cowdray to Clive Pearson, 13 Mar, Cowdray to Body, 14 Mar 1914, Pearson, A3; Miller to State Dept., 4 Dec 1913, State Dept. Decimal Files, 812.6363/21.

44. Covarrubias to Fabela, 15 May, Body to Cowdray, 27 May, Body to George Owens, 19 June, Luis Riba to Cowdray, 27 July 1914, Pearson, A3.

45. W. J. Payne to State Dept., 5, 7 Sept, State Dept. Decimal Files, 812.6363/133, /134; Silliman to State Dept., 14 Sept 1914, ibid., 812.6363/136.

46. Bevan to State, 7 Feb 1915, ibid., 812.6363/171.

47. Testimony of Doheny, *Investigation of Mexican Affairs,* 1:178–79.

48. L. van der Wal, "Report," 19 July 1914, Tweede Afdeling, Archief van het Ministerie van Buitenlandse Zaken, B–Dossiers, 1686, AR.

49. Van Rappard to foreign minister, 28 Jan, J. H. Scheltema to W. L. F. C. Ridder van Rappard, 25 Mar, Scheltema to Foreign Office, 31 Mar 1914, Tweede Afdeling, Kabinetsarchief van het Ministerie van Buitenlandse Zaken, Betreffende Politieke Rapportage door Nederlandse Vertegenwoordigers in het Buitenland, 1871–1940, (1.05.18), 115(49), AR.

50. Cowdray to Capt. Hugh Watson, n.d., [circa 1913], Walter H. Page to Cowdray, 20 Nov 1913, Pearson, A3; Van Rappard to Foreign Office, 15 May 1914, Tweede Afdeling, Kabinetsarchief van het Ministerie van Buitenlandse Zaken, 115(49), AR.

51. Payne to State Dept., 29 Sept 1914, State Dept. Decimal Files, 812.6363/140.

52. Body, "Memo for Cpt. Arthur Murray relative to conditions in Mexico," 30 July 1913, Pearson, A3.

53. H. W. Wilson to Stronge, 22, 26 Feb 1913, FO, 371–1671/13165.

54. Fletcher to Navy, 22 Nov, 12, 13 Dec 1913, Daniels, file 536.

55. H. T. Mayo to Rear Admiral F. F. Fletcher, 28 Mar, 7 Apr 1914, Naval Records Collection, WE–5 (Mexico), Record Group 45, National Archives; R. A. Liske to State, Washington, D.C., 9 Apr 1914, State Dept. Decimal Files, 812.6363/103.

56. Fletcher to Navy, 11 Apr 1914, Daniels, file 536.

57. Daniels to Navy Radio Station, San Diego, 15 Apr 1914, Daniels, file 536; Robert E. Quirk, *An Affair of Honor: Woodrow Wilson and the Occupation of Veracruz* (Lexington, Ky., 1962), 19–26; Edith O'Shaughnessy, *A Diplomat's Wife in Mexico* (New York, 1916), 266.

58. As quoted in Quirk, *Affair of Honor,* 18.

59. Ibid., 46–48; 71–72.

60. Clarence A. Miller to Admiral Mayo, 3 May 1914, Naval Records Collection, WE–5.

61. Daniels to Fletcher, 21 Apr 1917, Daniels, file 536.

62. Badger to Navy, 21 Apr 1917, Edw. L. to Daniels, Washington, 24 Oct 1935, Daniels, files 536, 537; Quirk, *Affair of Honor,* 98–99; 151.

63. "Statement of Facts Given to the People of the United States by 372 Tampico Refugees aboard the S.S. Esperanza," 30 Apr 1914, Daniels, file 536.

64. Ibid.; testimony of Spellacy, *Investigation of Mexican Affairs,* 1:945–47.

65. Badger to Navy, 9 May 1914, Daniels, file 536. Badger implied that the decision had not been his but that of Rear Adm. H. T. Mayo, who had been commanding the *Dolphin, Des Moines,* and *Chester* and five other vessels at Tampico.

66. Badger to Navy, 30 Apr 1914, Daniels, file 536; Anglo-Saxon Petroleum Co., Ltd., to Foreign Office, 16 May, 1 July 1914, FO, 371–2036/22392, /29872.

67. Navy Department, "Bulletin no. 125," 28 Apr 1914, Daniels, file 536; Van Rappard to Foreign Office, 6 May 1914, Tweede Afdeling, Kabinetsarchief van het Ministerie van Buitenlandse Zaken, 115(49), AR.

68. E. J. Nicklos, 8 July 1953, OHTO, T104.

69. His claim was later transferred to the joint claims commission, which in 1925 awarded him a check for $165. But no one could find the claimant eleven years after his loss. G. H. Kelly to Navy, Shreveport, 26 Dec 1914, Thomas H. Bevan to State Dept., 17 Apr 1915, Henry W. Anderson to G. H. Kelly, 17 Mar 1925, U.S. Consular Records, Tampico, 312.114 K29/1; N. A. Harris to State Dept., 17 Sept 1914, ibid. 312.114 H241.

70. J. F. Lucey to William J. Bryan, 19 Apr 1914, State Dept. Decimal Files, 812.8363/34; Franklin D. Roosevelt to State Dept., 1 Mar 1915, U.S. Consular Records, Tampico, 312.114 K29.

71. [Refugees] to President Wilson, 12 May 1914, Daniels, file 536; *Chicago Tribune,* 8 May 1914.

72. Testimony of Buckley, *Investigation of Mexican Affairs,* 1:783.

73. Bryan to U.S. consul, 12, 20 May, Canada to State, 18 May 1914, State Dept. Decimal Files, 812.6363/55, /70a, /69; Cecil Spring-Rice to Robert Lansing, 29 May 1914, Tweede Afdeling, Archief van het Ministerie van Buitenlandse Zaken, B–Dossiers, 3060, AR.

74. Sir Edward Grey to R. de Marees van Swinderen, 21 July 1914, Tweede Afdeling, Archief van het Ministerie van Buitenlandse Zaken, B–Dossiers, 1686, AR; Cowdray to Spring-Rice, Pearson, A3; Cecil Spring-Rice to Grey, 25 May 1914, FO, 371–2037/24535; Spring-Rice to Bryan, 29 May 1914, State Dept. Decimal Files, 812.6363/96.

75. E. T. Duble to State Dept., 4 May 1914, State Dept. Decimal Files, 812.6363/44.

76. W. A. Thompson, Jr., to Bryan, 1 May 1914, Daniels, file 536.

77. Digest of Deposition of William Green, Arnold, box 200.

78. Boaz Long to Charles T. de Ganahl, 4 May, Canada to State Dept., 6 May, David T. Warden to U.S. consul, 26 May 1914, State Dept. Decimal Files, 812.6363/33, /51, /77.

79. Bryan to George C. Carothers, 28 Apr, J. Daniels to State Dept., 30 Apr, C. Carothers to State, 1 May 1914, ibid., /29a, /39g, /32.

80. Body to Cowdray, 11 May 1914, Pearson, A3.

81. Cowdray to U.S. Ambassador, 29 Apr, "Precis of Report of Mr. J. B. Body to Lord Cowdray," 23 Apr to 26 May, Cowdray to Spring-Rice, 5 May 1914, Pearson, A3.

82. Warden to State Dept., 25 May, Robert Lansing to Warden, 18 June, Frank Wilson to State Dept., 24 June 1914, State Dept. Decimal Files, 812.6363/77, /84, /114.

83. Lansing to J. L. de Saulles, 17 June, Canada to State Dept., 29, 30 June 1914, ibid., 812.6363/119.

84. Testimony of P. W. Warner, *Investigation of Mexican Affairs,* 1:1038.

85. Testimony of Doheny, ibid., 1:239, 245; "Digest of Deposition of William Green," Arnold, box 200; Linda B. Hall and Don M. Coerver, *Revolution on the Border: The United States and Mexico, 1910–1920* (Albuquerque, 1988), 101.

86. Joaquín Meade, *Historia de Valles: Monografía de la Huasteca Potosina* (San Luis Potosí, 1970), 181.

87. F. A. Adams to Body, 2 Jan 1915, Pearson, A3.

88. Commanding Officer, USS *Sacramento* to Commanding Officer, USS *Washington,* 17 May 1915, Naval Records Collection, WE–5.

89. "Memorandum of Chester O. Swain," 25 May 1916, ibid.

90. Commanding Officer, USS *Marietta* to Commanding Officer, USS *Kentucky,* Tampico, 16 May 1916, ibid. None of the tension had dissipated when later that same month the military chief of Tuxpan closed the offices of all the lease-takers. Haff et al., to State Dept., 29 May 1916, State Dept. Decimal Files, 812.6363/234.

91. Body to Cowdray, 13 May 1916, Pearson, A3.

92. Hohler to Foreign Office, 18, 19 June, Spring-Rice to Grey, 9 June 1916, FO, 371–2701/117822, /118573, /118840.

93. Pulford to Hohler, 13 June 1916, FO, 371–2702/142126.

94. Dawson to State Dept., 23 June 1916, State Dept. Decimal Files, 812.6363/227; testimony of Levi Smith, *Investigation of Mexican Affairs,* 1:300; Hewitt to Hohler, 20, 27 June 1916, FO, 371–2703/153433; Barron, *The Mexican Problem,* 132.

95. Hewitt to Hohler, 27 June 1916, FO, 371–2703/153433.

96. Hohler to Foreign Office, 30 June 1916, FO, 371–2702/127440; Foreign Office to Lord Cowdray, 30 Mar 1916, Pearson, A3; Ray C. Gerhardt, "Inglaterra y el petróleo mexicano durante la Primera Guerra Mundial," *Historia Mexicana* 25 (1975): 124.

97. "Precis of Confidential Memoranda by Mr. Body to the Chief, re. Am-Mex. Crisis," n.d. [1914], Body to Cowdray, 15 Nov 1916, Pearson, A3.

98. Furber, *I Took Chances,* 172; Cowdray to J. B. Body, 11 May 1911, Pearson, A3.

99. Cowdray to Body, 25 May 1911, Pearson, A3.

100. Body to Cowdray, 9 Apr, 10, 17 Aug, 24 Oct 1912, Pearson, A4.

101. Some of the Americans began to organize the foreign and native workers in defense of the oil wells. Speculation of American armed intervention also arose for the first time. "If America does intervene, the conditions in Mexico are going to be infinitely worse than they are," Cowdray speculated, "and I feel that it would necessitate our shutting down, perhaps not entirely, but very largely, our operations there." Cowdray to Herbert J. Carr, 9 Aug 1913, Pearson, A3.

102. Cowdray to Guillermo de Landa y Escandón, 14 Nov, Hayes to Chief, 5 Sept, Chief to Hayes, 24 Sept, A. E. Chambers to Cowdray, 16 Nov 1913, Pearson, A3; Garretson, *Geschiedenis,* 281–82.

103. Hall and Coerver, *Revolution on the Border,* 101–2; "Mexican Revolutionary Claims, 1918–1920," Production Dept., Transcontinental Petroleum Co., SONJ.

104. Mayo to Navy, 30 June 1914, Naval Records Collection, WE–5.

105. Green to George Paddleford, 1 Mar 1918, FO, 371–3243/A47338.

106. G. H. Hewitt to Hohler, 3 Aug 1916, FO, 371–2703/173269; testimony of Spellacy, *Investigation of Mexican Affairs,* 1:945.

107. A. S. Gulston to Body, 12 July 1917, Pearson, A3.

108. Cowdray to Body, 13 May 1918, Pearson, A3; Cowdray to Foreign Office, 6 May 1918, FO, 371–3244/81898. An American report differed on the details. It said the rebels numbered four hundred, the number of *carrancistas* killed was twenty-five, and the amount taken from El Aguila was forty thousand pesos in currency and thirty thousand pesos in goods. D. W. Fowler, "Attack upon Minatitlán," 28 May 1918, Military Intelligence Division, Correspondence, 10640–481/1. Many also differ as to the date. Fowler says 7 May, but Cowdray had notified the Foreign Office of the event on 6 May. The biographer of Félix Díaz places the raid on 4 May. Peter V. N. Henderson, *Félix Díaz, the Porfirians, and the Mexican Revolution* (Lincoln, 1981), 139.

109. Green to Paddleford, 1 Mar 1918, FO, 371–3243/A47338.

110. Dr. Weston to Body, 19 May 1917, Pearson, A4; Green to Paddleford, 1 Mar 1918, FO, 371–3243/A47338; "Report on Political Situation," 23 Apr, in Cowdray to Foreign Office, 30 Apr 1919, FO, 371–2829/78566.

111. [Report,] 1916, p. 75, Pearson, C45; Vincent to State Dept., 19, 26 May 1916, Wilber J. Carr to James Linn Rodgers, 20 May 1916, State Dept. Decimal Files, 812.6363/231–33; Green to Paddleford, 1 Mar 1918, FO, 371–3243/A47338.

112. Testimony of Spellacy, *Investigation of Mexican Affairs,* 1:949–50; T. E. King to J. J. Slayton, Tampico, 7 Nov 1915, U.S. Consular Records, Tampico, 312.114 K581.

113. "Estimate of the Situation Covering Protection of Life and Property at Tampico, Mexico," 16 Oct 1916, Naval Records Collection, WE–5; Barron, *The Mexican Problem,* 132; Hewitt to Cummings, 14 Nov 1917, FO, 371–3241/5107.

114. Testimony of Amos Beaty, *Investigation of Mexican Affairs,* 1:530–31; William Green to Herbert Wylie, 25 June 1918, Naval Records Collection, WE–5.

115. William Green to Herbert G. Wylie, 25 Aug 1918, Military Intelligence Division, Correspondence, 10640–164–40.

116. Ibid.; testimony of Beaty, *Investigation of Mexican Affairs,* 1:529–30.

117. A. C. Bedford to Board Chairman, 7 Feb 1919, in Daniels, file 537.

118. *Tampico Tribune,* 23 Aug 1919; Beaty, appendix B, *Investigation of Mexican Affairs,* 1:574.

119. Green to Herbert Wylie, 25 June 1918, Military Intelligence Division, Correspondence, 10640–164/11; O. W. Fowler, "Conditions in Tampico District, Mexico," 22 May 1918, Military Intelligence Division, Correspondence, 10640–580/1; interview of E. J. Nicklos, 8 July 1953, OHTO, T103.

120. Testimony of Britt, *Investigation of Mexican Affairs,* 1:1011; "Descriptive Statement of Bandit Outrages and Hold-ups throughout the Tampico Oil Fields," n.d., FO, 371–3246/169532.

121. "Descriptive Statement of Bandit Outrages"; "Relations of the Oil Companies with the Mexican Authorities," interview 683, Doheny; testimony

of Williams, *Investigation of Mexican Affairs*, 1:599; Sadler to S. B. Hunt, 31 July 1918, SONJ, Prod. Dept., Sadler's Old Mexican files.

122. Testimony of Harry C. Donoho, *Investigation of Mexican Affairs*, 2:2132–38; "Report on Political Situation," 23 Apr 1919, FO, 371–3829/78566.

123. Green to Wylie, 25 Aug 1918, Military Intelligence Division, Correspondence, 10640–164–40.

124. "Relations of the Oil Companies with the Mexican Authorities," interview 683, Doheny.

125. Herrera to González, 4 Dec, González to Herrera, 9 Dec 1915, González, leg. 7, exp. 68, reel 33.

126. J. T. Burns to González, 5 Apr, González to Burns, 9 May 1916, González, leg. 2, exp. 64, reel 33.

127. Commanding Officer, USS *Annapolis* to Navy, 31 Aug 1917, Naval Records Collection, WE–5.

128. Buckley to Ira W. Williams, 18 Dec 1919, Fall, box 73 F35.

129. "Memorandum of Chester O. Swain," 25 May 1916, Naval Records Collection, WE–5.

130. Pastor Rouaix, *Génesis de los artículos 27 y 123 de la constitución política de 1917,* 2d ed. (Mexico City, 1959), 47.

131. Katz, *The Secret War in Mexico,* 139–41; Knight, *The Mexican Revolution,* 2: 413–14; Womack, "The Mexican Revolution," 94, 100, 107.

132. Spanish version in *Boletín del petroleo* 1, no. 1 (1916): 15; an English version in Fall, box 88 F11; synopsis in Bevan to State Dept., 14 Aug 1914, State Dept. Decimal Files, 812.6363/130.

133. "Decree of Gen. Aguilar" in Bevan to State Dept., 27 Aug 1914, State Dept. Decimal Files, 812.6363/132.

134. Mayo to Navy, 6 Sept 1914, Naval Records Collection, WE–5.

135. Order of Carranza, 15 Sept 1914, Ramo de Hacienda, Fomento y Obras Públicas, Minas y Petróleo, C48, AGN.

136. "Translation of Decree by V. Carranza," 7 Jan 1915, FO, 371–2396/13311; Canada to State Dept., 8 Jan 1914, Bevan to State Dept., 10 Jan 1915, State Dept. Decimal Files, 812.6363/146, /149.

137. Frederick R. Kellogg to State Dept., 13 Jan 1914, State Dept. Decimal Files, 812.6363/150; Hohler to Grey, 14 Jan, Cowdray to Sir Arthur Nicolson, 16 Jan 1915, FO, 371–2395/5673, /6427; "Chief Memorandum of Interview with Sir R. Paget," 15 Jan 1915, Pearson, A3; Everbusch to Dutch Ambassador, 18 Jan 1915, Tweede Afdeling, Archief van het Ministerie van Buitenlandse Zaken, B–Dossiers, 3060, AR.

138. "Mexico Political—Precis of Correspondence," 9 Jan to 6 Feb 1915, Vaughan to Body, 19 Jan 1915, Pearson, A3.

139. Cowdray to Limantour, 19 Jan, Cowdray to Foreign Office, 30 Jan, Pearson, A3; Bevan to State Dept., 22 Jan, State Dept. Decimal Files, 812.6363/160; J. S. Hutchinson to Hohler, 6 Feb 1915, FO, 371–2397/26990.

140. Bevan to State Dept., 25 Jan 1915, State Dept. Decimal Files, 812.6363/156.

141. Dawson to State Dept., 16 Mar 1916, ibid., 812.6363/227.

142. Spring-Rice, "Memorandum, 12 June 1915, ibid., 812.6363/196; Rouaix, "Decretos sobre el petroleo, expedidos por el Gobierno Constitucionalista," 15 Nov 1915, ibid., 812.6363/200.

143. *El Dictamen*, 16 Jan 1916, as translated in ibid., 812.6363/211.

144. Foreign Office to Hohler, 11 Feb 1916, FO, 371–2698/27641. James L. Rodgers to Aguilar, 11 Aug 1916, Archivo Histórico "Genaro Estrada" de la Secretaría de Relaciones Exteriores, Mexico City, L–E–533; Bevan to State Dept., 25 Jan, Silliman to State Dept., 27 Jan, Parker to State Dept., 4 Nov 1916, State Dept. Decimal Files, 812.6363/205, /209, /251.

145. Joseph A. Vincent to State Dept., 7 Jan, John R. Silliman to State Dept., 18, 25 Jan, Vincent to State Dept., 8 Mar 1916. State Dept. Decimal Files, 812.6363/218, /205, /206, /221.

146. Decree of Venustiano Carranza, 13 Apr 1917, in ibid., 812.6363/275.

147. López Portillo y Weber, *El petróleo de México,* 35.

148. Ibid., 35, 37–38.

149. *Boletín del Petróleo* 1, no. 1 (1916): 2.

150. Ibid., 1, no. 5 (1916): 408.

151. Van H. Manning to Julius G. Lay, 5 Feb 1920, State Dept. Decimal Files, 812.6363/686.

152. Joaquín Santaella, "Intervención oficial," *Boletín del Petróleo* 1, no. 4 (1916): 328.

153. López Portillo y Weber, *El petróleo de México,* 75, 85, 93.

154. Ibid., 58–59, 128–130.

155. William Green to Herbert G. Wylie, 25 June 1918, Military Intelligence Division, Correspondence, 10640–164.

156. López Portillo y Weber, *El petróleo de México,* 25.

157. Manuel A. Chávez, 3 Aug 1917, Carranza, carpeta 115; Vincent to Lansing, 7 Jan 1916, "Petroleum Code as Submitted to Congress on Nov. 23, 1918," Summerlin to State Dept., 1 Oct 1919, State Dept. Decimal Files, 812.6363/218, /558, /568.

158. Bevan to State Dept., 18 Jan 1918, State Dept. Decimal Files, 812.6363/210; P. W. to A. Jacobsen, 26 Feb 1920, DeGolyer, file 5300.

159. Body to Cowdray, 19 Dec 1916, 22 Feb, 14 Apr, Chambers to Body, 3 June 1917, Pearson, A3, A4.

160. Green to Wylie, 25 June 1918, Military Intelligence Division, Correspondence, 10640–164.

161. On the Constitution and the constitutional convention, see Rouaix, *Génesis de los artículos 27 y 123;* E. V. Niemeyer, Jr., *Revolution at Querétaro: The Mexican Constitutional Convention, 1916–1917* (Austin, 1974); Knight, *The Mexican Revolution,* 2:469–77; Charles C. Cumberland, *Mexican Revolution: The Constitutionalist Years* (Austin, 1972), 2:320–60; Douglas W. Richmond, *Venustiano Carranza's Nationalist Struggle, 1893–1920* (Lincoln, 1983), 308–9; Frank Tannenbaum, *The Mexican Agrarian Revolution* (New York, 1929), 183–84, 189–203.

162. Rouaix, *Génesis de los artículos 27 y 123,* 47.

163. McMahon, *Two Strikes and Out,* 35. For other assessments of the colonial legal precedence of Article 27, see Rouaix, *Génesis de los artículos 27 y 123,*

38; Leslie Byrd Simpson, *The Ejido: Mexico's Way Out* (Chapel Hill, 1937), 64; Niemeyer, *Revolution at Querétaro,* 139. Given the strong historical precedence, perhaps Tannenbaum is too grandiose in calling Article 27 a "new theory of property, neither capitalistic nor socialistic." Frank Tannenbaum, *Mexico: The Struggle for Peace and Bread* (New York, 1950), 112.

164. *Diario de los debates del Constituyente, 1916–1917* (Mexico City, 1960), 2:1083–84.

165. From Niemeyer, *Revolution at Querétaro,* 250–51, 256–57. Spanish version in Rouaix, *Génesis de los artículos 27 y 123,* 217–18.

166. H. N. Branch, "The Mexican Constitution of 1917," Supplement to the *Annals of the American Academy of Political and Social Science* 71 (May 1917): 15–19.

167. Ibid., 7; McMahon, *Two Strikes and Out,* 35.

168. Vázquez Schiaffino, "Mexico," 20.

169. Rouaix, *Génesis de los artículos 27 y 123,* 44.

170. Aguilar to Carranza, 2 July 1919, Archivo Histórico "Genaro Estrada" de la Secretaría de Relaciones Exteriores, L–E–533.

171. Body to Cowdray, 17 Feb, F. Adams to Body, 1 June 1917, Pearson, A4.

172. Dutch Consul-General for Mexico, "Political and Economic Report on Mexico," Mar 1917, Tweede Afdeling, Archief van het Ministerie van Buitenlandse Zaken, B–Dossiers, 1686, AR; Garretson, *Geschiedenis,* 293–94.

173. Eugenio Méndez to Cándido Aguilar, 3 Oct 1917, Carranza, carpeta 13314.

174. Cowdray to Foreign Office, 24 Mar 1916, Pearson, A3; Decree of C. Aguilar, 14 Dec 1917, State Dept. Decimal Files, 812.6363/326.

175. Robert P. Hoover to State Dept., 3 May 1919, State Dept. Decimal Files, 812.6363/461.

176. Summerlin to State Dept., 20 Feb 1918, ibid., 812.6363/356.

177. Joaquín Santaella, "Informe del Jefe de la Comisión Técnica," 29 Jan 1918, "Proyecto de ley del petróleo," n.d., Carranza, carpeta 13653.

178. U.S. Senate, *Senate Document 272,* 66th Congress, 2d sess. (Washington, D.C., 1919), 15; Bermúdez, *The Mexican National Petroleum Industry,* 7–8.

179. Sadler to S. B. Hunt, 31 July 1918, SONJ, Prod. Dept., Sadler's Mexican Files.

180. Cowdray, "Memo for Mr. Stewart," 5 Mar, Body to Cowdray, 9 May 1918, Pearson, A3; Departamento del Petróleo, "Petróleo crudo producido por los pozos de las cías que operan en el país . . . ," n.d. (c. 1919), Carranza, carpeta 14683; *Mexican Review* 3 (7 October 1919): 12, 34.

181. Anon. to Aguilar, 15 Apr 1918, Carranza, carpeta 23731.

182. Matthew E. Hanna to sec. of state, 16 Apr 1918, State Dept. Decimal Files, 812.6363/668.

183. See testimony of Beaty, *Investigation of Mexican Affairs,* 1:536–40; J. Jordan to Carranza, 21 June 1917, Carranza, carpeta 12992.

184. Walker to Long, 3 Apr 1919, State Dept. Decimal Files, 812.6363/438.

185. Polk to U.S. Embassy, 11 Apr, Summerlin to State Dept., 16 Apr, H. N. Branch to State Dept., 16 Apr 1919, Williams to Fletcher, 24 Apr 1919 ibid., 812.6363/444–45, /447, /450.

186. Polk to Fletcher, 16 Apr 1919, ibid., 812.6363/448; John N. Denny to A. J. Balfour, 23 Jan 1919, FO, 371–3826/13558.

187. Summerlin to State Dept., 2 June, Ernesto Garza Pérez to George T. Summerlin, 29 May 1919, State Dept. Decimal Files, 812.6363/463, /469.

188. Sir Cecil Spring-Rice to Grey, 23 Dec 1915, William J. Pulford to Spring-Rice, 11 Dec 1915, Cowdray to Foreign Office, 20 Jan 1916, FO 371–2697/3244, /5997, /12993; Body to Cowdray, 14 Apr 1917, Pearson, A4.

189. W. G. de Kanter to Foreign Office, 7 Apr 1917, Tweede Afdeling, Archief van het Ministerie van Buitenlandse Zaken, B–Dossiers, 1686, AR; Page to State Dept., 11 Nov, Cobb to State Dept., 8 Dec 1917, State Dept. Decimal Files, 812.6363/317, /323.

190. Francis B. Loomis to William A. Carr, 8 May, Walker to Long, 23 July 1919, State Dept. Decimal Files, 812.6363/ 494, /560.

191. Polk to U.S. Embassy, 9 Apr 1919, ibid., 812.6363/433.

192. Vázquez Schiaffino to War Dept., 16 May, Stephen V. Graham to Navy, 14 June 1919, ibid., 812.6363/476, /478; testimony of Williams, *Investigation of Mexican Affairs,* 1:592–93.

193. Manuel Sánchez Ponton to Aguilar, 10 Jan 1919, Aguilar to A. M. González, 24 Jan 1919, Carranza, carpetas 14736, 14785.

194. Summerlin to State, 29 Jan, Summerlin to State Dept., 20 Aug 1919, State Dept. Decimal Files, 812.6363/426, /535.

195. Fletcher to State Dept., 20 July, Williams to State Dept., 28 Aug, Fletcher to State Dept., 18 Sept 1917, ibid., 812.6363/293, /300, /310.

196. See "Proyecto de ley del petróleo"; Swain to Fletcher, 18 Dec 1918, State Dept. Decimal Files, 812.6363/568.

197. "Memorandum on Conference," 12 Nov, James R. Garfield to Walker, 19 Dec 1918, ibid., 812.6363/415, /568.

198. Summerlin to State Dept., 6, 13 Aug, 16, 21, 29 Oct, 30 Dec, Fletcher to State, 8 Oct 1919, ibid., 812.6363/523, /525, /564, /573, /578, /617, /646.

199. Secretaría de Industria, Comercio y Trabajo, *Legislación petrolera* (Mexico City, 1922), 154; Summerlin to State Dept., 21 July 1919, León Salinas, "Circular número 9," 1 Aug 1919, State Dept. Decimal Files, 812.6363/ 486, /519.

200. C. O. Swain to State Dept., 25 Oct, Alvey Adee to Swain, 5 Nov 1919, Esso Standard, Legal Dept. file 117, SONJ; U.S. Department of State, *Papers Relating to the Foreign Relations of the United States* (Washington, D.C., 1919), 2:605.

201. See, especially, testimony of Doheny, *Investigation of Mexican Affairs,* 1:243.

202. F. Watriss to State Dept., 15 Nov, Sausing to U.S. Embassy, 18 Nov, Brown to Swain, 3 Dec 1919, State Dept. Decimal Files, 812.6363/581, /603.

203. Mayo to Navy, 2 Aug 1914, Naval Records Collection, WE–5.

204. Ryder, "Memorandum of Interview with Lic. Luis Cabrera," 21 Dec 1915, Pearson, A3.

205. W. F. Buckley et al. to Woodrow Wilson, 22 May, Body to Cowdray, 28 Nov 1916, ibid.

206. A. L. Beaty et al. to Association members, 16 Oct 1919, State Dept. Decimal Files, 812.6363/572.

207. Feb 1919, FO, 371–3831/105884.

208. Sen. Morris Sheppard to Lansing, 10 Dec 1919, State Dept. Decimal Files, 812.6363/597.

209. M. L. Requa to Polk, 12 Aug 1918, ibid., 812.6363/375.

210. Swain to Fletcher, 3 Dec 1919, ibid., 812.6363/603.

211. *Oil and Gas Journal*, 2 May 1919, 54–55; Williamson, *The American Petroleum Industry*, 2:300–301; Joseph P. Annin to Daniels, 13 Dec 1919, Daniels, file, 537.

212. Frederick Adams to Body, 10 June 1917, Pearson, A3; Alvey A. Adee to Albert B. Fall, 27 Oct 1919, State Dept. Decimal Files, 812.6363/532.

213. Body to T. B. Hohler, 5, 7, 14 July 1917, Pearson, A4; Franklin K. Lane to Doheny, 6 Jan 1917, Fall, box 108 F20.

214. E. L. Doheny, *The Mexican Question: Its Relation to Our Industries, Our Merchant Marine, and Our Foreign Trade* (Los Angeles, 1919).

215. Statement dated 7 May 1918, Cleland, box 2a; Mexican Consulate, San Francisco to Aguilar, 29 July 1918, Carranza, carpeta 13952; Frank William Peterson, "The Promise and Failure of the Doheny Research Foundation," typescript, 8 June 1965, Doheny.

216. Summerlin to State Dept., 25 Mar, Walker to Reynoso, 9 Apr, Walker to Long, 10 Apr 1919, State Dept. Decimal Files, 812.6363/435, /446.

217. *Los Angeles Herald*, 24 Jan 1919; "Los decretos mexicanos serán llevados a la Conferencia de Paz," 22 Jan 1919, Archivo Histórico "Genaro Estrada" de la Secretaría de Relaciones Exteriores, L–E–533.

218. H. G. L. Hilton to Lord Curzon, 18 Apr, 1 May 1919, FO, 371–3828/65764.

219. See oil executives to Furnifold M. Simmons, 8 Dec, Simmons to Lansing, 10 Dec, C. W. Whitehead to Charles A. Culbertson, 30 Dec 1919, Culbertson to Lansing, 2 Jan 1920, Allison Mayfield to State, 5 Jan, State Dept. Decimal Files, 812.6363/598, /614, /621.

220. "Extracts from letter Received from our Washington Representative," 21 June 1917, Pearson, A3; David H. Stratton, "Albert B. Fall and the Teapot Dome Affair" (Ph.D. diss., University of Colorado, 1955), 52–53, 110. Also see chap. 7.

221. The details of their testimony have appeared throughout this book. Perhaps there was some substance to the fear of reprisals. Buckley believed that the *carrancistas* shut down one of his wells as a result of his testimony before the Fall committee. Buckley to F. J. Kearful, 30 Dec 1919, Fall, box 73 F35.

222. Doheny to Swain, 6 Feb 1920, Fall, box 106 F1a.

223. Statement of Kellogg, *Investigation of Mexican Affairs*, 2:3278; testimony of Corbin, ibid., 1:1453; Williams to Polk, 19 Mar 1919, State Dept.

Decimal Files, 812.6363/432; Cowdray, "Memo: Interview and Exchange of Views with American Ambassador," 9 Jan 1914, Pearson, A3; Commanding Officer to Navy, 31 Aug 1917, Naval Records Collection, WE–5; Walker, "Memorandum of Conference," 8 Jan 1920, State Dept. Decimal Files, 812.6363/641; "Relations of the Oil Companies with the Mexican Authorities," n.d. [c. 1918], interview 683, Doheny; Swain to Fletcher, 9 Dec 1919, Swain, "Memorandum," 8 Jan 1920, State Dept. Decimal Files, 812.6363/641, /645; S. Casillas Cruz to Ernesto Garza Pérez, 25 July 1917, Archivo Histórico "Genaro Estrada" de la Secretaría de Relaciones Exteriores, L–E–533.

224. Cowdray, "Memo: Interview and Exchange of Views with American Ambassador," 9 Jan 1914, Pearson, A3.

225. *Bulletin of the National Association for the Protection of American Rights in Mexico* 1, no. 5 (20 September 1919); C. H. Boynton to Fall, 18 Sept 1919, Fall, box 89 F11b; testimony of Williams, *Investigation of Mexican Affairs,* 1:605.

226. Green to Wylie, 25 June 1918, Naval Records Collection, WE–5.

227. Testimony of Buckley, *Investigation of Mexican Affairs,* 1:830.

228. Ibid.; Buckley to Fall, 5 Feb 1920, Fall, box 73 F35.

229. J. B. Yzaguirre to Carranza, 23 Dec 1918, Carranza, carpeta 128.

230. E. Hutchins to Sheppard, 25 Sept 1918, State Dept. Decimal Files, 812.6363/413.

231. *El Universal,* 5 Feb 1920; *Excélsior,* 5 Feb 1920; *El Heraldo,* 16 Oct 1920; Summerlin to State Dept., 17 Feb 1920, State Dept. Decimal Files, 812.6363/645.

232. R. E. Dodson to State Dept., 16 Jan 1915, ibid., 812.6363/155.

233. Commanding Officer, USS *Annapolis* to Navy, 31 Aug 1917, Naval Records Collection, WE–5.

234. Notes of R. S. on Cowdray to Maurice de Bunsen, 9 Oct 1915, FO, 371–2402/147780.

235. J. B. Body, "Memorandum," 20 Sept, Cowdray to Vincent Yorke, 19 Oct 1915, Pearson, A3; Ray C. Gerhardt, "Inglaterra y el petróleo mexicano," 132.

236. "Notes re. Mr. Body's Visit to Washington," 18 May, Body, "Memorandum to Lord Cowdray," 18 Sept 1917, Pearson, A4, A3; Minutes, 19 Nov 1917, FO, 371–2963/219811; Durán de Seade, "Mexico's Relations with the Powers," 216, 224, 233, 241.

237. Foreign Office to Thurstan, 27 Jan, Foreign Office to Spring-Rice, 21 Feb, Thurstan to Foreign Office, 17 Feb 1917, FO, 371–2958/19330, –2959/37114, /37714; Cowdray to Sir Maurice de Bunsen, 19 May 1917, Cowdray, "Memo for Mr. Steward," 5 Mar 1918, Pearson, A3.

238. Cowdray to Balfour, 7 Dec 1917, Cowdray to Sir Eric Drummond, 17 Jan, Vivian Smith et al. to Balfour, 29 Jan, Body to Cowdray, 9 May 1918, Pearson, A3.

239. RSS, "Minutes on Recognition of Carranza," 28 May 1919, FO, 371–2820/82356.

240. Aguilar to Carranza, 15 Aug 1919, Archivo Histórico "Genaro Estrada" de la Secretaría de Relaciones Exteriores, L–E–533.

241. Cummings to Curzon, 20 Feb 1920, FO, 371–4491/A1811; Walker, "Memorandum of Conference," 8 Jan 1920, State Dept. Decimal Files, 812.6363/641.

242. George F. Summerlin to State Dept., 29 July, Walker to State Dept., 13 Dec, Williams to State Dept., 31 Dec 1919, State Dept. Decimal Files, 812.6363 /509, /608, /613.

243. Ryder to Jacobsen, 7 Jan 1920, DeGolyer, file 5145.

244. Montes to Ryder, 3 Jan 1920, State Dept. Decimal Files, 812.6363/636.

245. Jacobsen to Ryder, 20 Jan 1920, DeGolyer, file 5145.

246. Cummins to Foreign Office, 12 Jan 1919, Ryder to Montes, 14 Jan 1920, FO, 371–4498/A132, /593; Walker to State Dept., 15 Jan, Oil Producers' Association to Carranza, 13 Jan 1920, State Dept. Decimal Files, 812.6363/624, /623; Carranza to Foreign Oil Producers, Summerlin to State Dept., 22 Jan 1920, ibid., 812.6363/628; Cummins to Foreign Office, 17, 22 Jan 1920, FO, 371–4498/A269.

247. López Portillo Y Weber, *El petróleo de México*, 133–34.

248. Corwin and J. A. Brown to S. Bunt, 10 Nov 1919, Esso Records, Legal Dept., file 117, SONJ.

249. F. M. Davies to Foreign Office, 8 Apr, John Dalton Venn to V. Carranza, 20 Apr, Cowdray to Curzon, 21 Apr 1920, FO, 371–4498/A2046, –4499/A2474; De Bataafsche Petroleum Maatschappy to Foreign Office, 26 Apr 1920, Tweede Afdeling, Archief van de Directie Economische Zaken van het Ministerie van Buitenlandse Zaken, 1919–41, 1800, AR.

Chapter Four

1. "Memorandum re Revolutionary Activity," 10 Dec, H. W. Wilson to Hohler, 10 Dec, Pulford to Hohler, 21, 29 Dec, Peláez to El Aguila, El Aguila to Peláez, 27 Dec, S. A. Grahame to Hohler, 23 Dec 1914, FO, 371–2395/046919, /2445, 371–2396/9797, 371–2397/23925; Testimony of E. L. Doheny, *Investigation of Mexican Affairs*, 1:284.

2. Heather Fowler Salamini, "Caciquismo and the Mexican Revolution: The Case of Manuel Peláez," paper presented at the 6th Conference of Mexican and United States Historians, 1981; Dennis J. O'Brien, "Petróleo e intervención: relaciones entre los Estados Unidos y México, 1917–1918," *Historia Mexicana* 27 (1977): 103–40; Durán de Seade, "Mexico's Relations with the Powers," 283–301; Lorenzo Meyer, *Mexico and the United States in the Oil Controversy, 1916–1942* (Austin, 1977), 48–51; Bermúdez, *The Mexican National Petroleum Industry*, 5; Silva Herzog, *El petróleo de México*, 17; Katz, *The Secret War in Mexico*, 463, 467, 487. For a typically uncomplimentary view of Peláez, see the introduction to a reedition of *El petróleo de México: Recopilación de documentos oficiales* (Mexico City, 1940; reprint, 1963), 14. Peter Linder provides a more balanced interpretation, emphasizing the complexity of the

relationship between Peláez and the oil industry, not that he was just a lackey. Peter S. Linder, "Every Region for Itself: The Manuel Peláez Movement, 1914–1923" (M.A. thesis, University of New Mexico, 1983), v.

3. *El Universal*, 19 Mar 1938; Lazaro Cardenas, *Messages to the Mexican Nation on the Oil Question* (Mexico City, 1938): 5–12.

4. Commanding Officer, USS *Des Moines*, "Notes Concerning Present Situation—Mexico East Coast," 12 Oct 1920, Naval Records Collection, WE-5.

5. Linder, "Every Region for Itself," 7, 15; Menéndez, *Doheny El Cruel*, 75–76; Fowler Salamini, "Caciquismo," 7.

6. Henderson, *Félix Díaz*, 56; Linder, "Every Region for Itself," 18–19.

7. Menéndez, *Doheny El Cruel*, 77–82; Linder, "Every Region for Itself," 20–25.

8. "Production of Petroleum in Mexico by Fields and Years," n.d., De-Golyer, file 5342; "Status of Rentals of the Aguila," 1 June 1917, ibid., file 5166; "Mexican Oilfields," 1916, Pearson, C46 F7.

9. Body to Cowdray, 4 Mar 1918, ibid., A3.

10. "Manifesto of General M. Peláez," 31 Dec 1917, Military Intelligence Division, Correspondence, 10640–164/9. Also see *New York Times*, 31 Dec 1917.

11. Doheny, "Memorandum of Facts Presented by the Huasteca Petroleum Co.," Military Intelligence Division, Correspondence, 10640–246/284.

12. Ibid.; testimony of Spellacy, *Investigation of Mexican Affairs*, 1:943–44; O. W. Fowler to Naval Intelligence, 12 Apr 1918, State Dept. Decimal Files, 812.6363/387.

13. "Manifesto of General M. Pelaez," 31 Dec 1917, Military Intelligence Division, Correspondence, 10640–164/9; Cummins to Foreign Office, 14 Nov 1917, FO, 371–3241/47338.

14. Body to Foreign Office, 9 June, Vaughan to Pulford, 7 June, Robert W. Hillcoat, "Report on the Attack at Tuxpan," 6 June, Body to Foreign Office, 7 July 1915, FO, 371–75455/ 371–2400/80398, /89400, 371–2401/91337.

15. Body to J. W. Hutchinson, 7 June, Montes to Carranza, 11 June, 14 June 1915, Pearson, A3; Body to Foreign Office, 11, 22 June, FO, 371–2398/ 77362, 371–2400/83410.

16. Foreign Office to Hohler, 14 June, Body to Foreign Office, 24 July, "Report of Evidence," 8 July, "Evidence of Thomas Mallard, 13 July, Vaughan to Carranza, 19 July 1915, FO, 371–2398/75455, 371–2401/95423, /97550, 371–2402/114218/ 122438.

17. Vaughan to W. J. Pulford, 14 June, Body to Foreign Office, 14 July 1915, FO, 371–2401/92927, /95401, /95523.

18. Hewitt to Hohler, 18 Jan 1916, FO, 371–2699/45960; Body to Cowdray, 12 Feb 1916, Pearson, A4.

19. T. C. Vaughan to C. Aguilar, 16 Jan 1915, Pearson, A3.

20. Pulford to Hohler, 7 Jan 1915, Hohler to Grey, 26 Jan 1915, FO, 371–2396/18728, /23923.

21. Body to Cowdray, 24 Jan 1917, Pearson, A3; Hewitt to Cummins, 14 Nov 1917, FO, 371–3241/5107.

22. Cummins to Foreign Office, 14 Nov 1917, FO, 371–3241/47338.

23. P. M. Bennett to Body, 9 Feb 1916, Pearson, A3; Hewitt to Hohler, 7 Feb 1916, FO, 371–2699/53951.

24. Vaughan to Body, 23 Oct 1916, FO, 371–2706/238952.

25. Hewitt to Foreign Office, 7 Dec 1916, Pearson, A3; Hewitt to Foreign Office, 6 June, 17 Oct 1917, FO, 371–2962/158778, 371–3242/201251.

26. Spring-Rice to Foreign Office, 17 Feb, Hewitt to Hohler, 14 Feb 1916, Hewitt to Cummins, 23 Jan 1918, FO, 371–2698/31720, 371–2699/53951, –3242/41500; Commanding Officer, USS *Annapolis* to Naval Operations, 11 Nov 1917, State Dept. Decimal Files, 812.6363/319.

27. Hewitt to Foreign Office, 17 Oct 1917, Hewitt to Cummins, 23 Jan 1918, FO, 371–3242/20251, /41500; testimony of Buckley, *Investigation of Mexican Affairs,* 1:840.

28. Unidentified to Carranza, 3 Oct 1917, Carranza, carpeta 13315; Hewitt to Foreign Office, 12 Sept 1917, FO, 371–2963/205098.

29. Hewitt to Thurstan, 7 Dec 1916, Hewitt to Foreign Office, 17 Oct 1917, FO, 371–2958/17254, 371–3242/201251; Thurstan to Foreign Office, 23 Dec 1916, Pearson, A3.

30. Hewitt to Hohler, 5 July, Hewett to Cummins, 19 Aug 1917, FO, 371–2962/158778, 371–2963/205095.

31. Hewitt to Thurstan, Tuxpan, 10 Nov 1916, FO, 371–2706/262143.

32. Thurstan to Foreign Office, 27 Apr 1917, FO, 371–2706/86909.

33. Hewitt to Cummins, 12 Sept 1917, FO, 371–2963/205095.

34. Report of U.S. War College, Barclay to A. J. Balfour, 14 Feb 1918, FO, 371–3243/34422.

35. Testimony of Smith, *Investigation of Mexican Affairs,* 1:303–4.

36. Hewitt to Hohler, 3 Aug 1916, FO, 371–2703/173269; "Strength of Rebel Forces in Mexico, 1919," Records of the Office of the Chief of Naval Operations, Office of Naval Intelligence, Naval Attaché Reports, 98–12099, Records Group 38, National Archives. For the personal identification between leader and follower in the Revolution, see John Reed, *Insurgent Mexico* (New York, 1969), 79.

37. Pulford to Hohler, 18 June 1917, FO, 371–2962/143982.

38. Ordóñez, "El petróleo en México," part 2, 226.

39. "Conditions in Mexico, 1919," MID, 98–12450, RG 165, NARS.

40. Hewitt to Hohler, 10, 14 Feb 1916, FO, 371–2699/53951; testimony of Spellacy, *Investigation of Mexican Affairs,* 1:944; Clarence L. Hay, "Situation of Forces in Tampico Region," 15 June 1918, Military Intelligence Division, Correspondence, 10640–240; John Womack, Jr., *Zapata and the Mexican Revolution* (New York, 1968), 229–35; Raymond Th. J. Buve, " 'Neither Carranza nor Zapata!': The Rise and Fall of à Peasant Movement that Tried to Challenge Both, Tlaxcala, 1910–19," in *Riot, Rebellion, and Revolution: Rural Social Conflict in Mexico,* ed. Friedrich Katz (Princeton, 1988), 338–75; Romana Falcón, "Charisma, Tradition, and Caciquismo: Revolution in San Luis Potosí," in *Riot, Rebellion, and Revolution,* 417–47.

41. "Translation of Proclamation of May 5th, 1917," Pearson, A3.

42. "Conditions in Mexico 1919," MID, 98/12450.

43. Cowdray to Landa y Escandón, 30 Mar 1916, Pearson, A3.

44. Pulford to Hohler, 18 June 1917, FO, 371–2962/143982.

45. Walker to Doheny, 4 Feb 1916, introduced by Doheny, *Investigation of Mexican Affairs,* 1:280.

46. Document, n.d., introduced by Doheny, *ibid.,* 1:281.

47. Hewitt to Cummins, 14 Nov 1917, FO, 371–3241/47338.

48. *El Dictamen,* 4 Aug 1921.

49. Testimony of Doheny, *Investigation of Mexican Affairs,* 1:282–83.

50. J. A. Brown to Sadler, 29 Apr 1920, "Mexico, 1920," Production Dept., Sadler's Mexican files, SONJ.

51. Testimony of Levi Smith, *Investigation of Mexican Affairs,* 1:196–97; H. E. Yarnell to USS *Nashville,* 26 Jan 1917, State Dept. Decimal Files, 812.6363/259.

52. Hewitt to Hohler, 10, 14 Feb 1916, FO, 371–2699/53951; Dawson to State Dept., 6 Mar, Walker to Doheny, 8 Mar 1918, Alvey A. Adee to James G. McDonald, 15 Aug 1919, State Dept. Decimal Files, 812.6363/357, /372, /508.

53. Martínez Herrera to Paddleford, 1 Feb 1916, document introduced by Doheny, *Investigation of Mexican Affairs,* 1:281; "Memorandum of Facts Presented by the Huasteca Petroleum Co.," Military Intelligence Division, Correspondence, 10640–246/284.

54. Body to Cowdray, 12 Feb 1916, Pearson, A4; Pulford to Hohler, 10 Feb 1916, Hohler to J. Acuna, 19 Feb 1916, FO, 371–2699/63825.

55. Testimony of Beaty, *Investigation of Mexican Affairs,* 1:533.

56. Walker to George Marvin, 9 Sept 1917, State Dept. Decimal Files, 812.6363/312; Testimony of Doheny, *Investigation of Mexican Affairs,* 1:289. The combined total of $30,000 is not specified in U.S. or Mexican currency.

57. Dawson to State Dept., 11 Mar 1918, State Dept. Decimal Files, 812.6363/357.

58. Fowler Salamini, "Caciquismo and the Mexico Revolution," 9. All figures used in the oil zone were in gold pesos, pegged at two per the American dollar, not in the troublesome Mexican peso or in Villa's Monclova script or Carranza's *peso infalsificable.* The oil zone, like Panama and other small Caribbean and Central American countries then and now, used American currency as the basic monetary unit.

59. Edgar L. Field to Intelligence Office, 20 Nov 1917, Military Intelligence Division, Correspondence, 9700–608.

60. Peláez, "To the Mexican People," 31 Dec 1917, Pearson, A3.

61. Knight, *The Mexican Revolution,* 1:368–69; 2:56, 243–44.

62. "Manifesto of General M. Pelaez," 27 June 1918, Military Intelligence Division, Correspondence, 10640–164/9; Peláez, "To the Mexican People," 31 Dec 1917, Pearson, A3.

63. Hohler to Foreign Office, 29 June 1916, FO, 371–2701/125937; Commanding Officer, USS *Marietta* to Commanding Officer, USS *Dixie,* 17 July 1916, Naval Records Collection, WE-5; "Informe rendido a este Consulado," New York, 7 May 1918, Carranza, carpeta 13766; Field to Intelligence Office, 20 Nov 1917, Military Intelligence Division, Correspondence, 9700–608.

64. [Peláez], Document Translation of 1918, Fall, box 91, file 33.

65. Cummins to Foreign Office, 19 Oct 1917, FO, 371–2963/201368.

66. "Translation of Proclamation of May 5th, 1917," Pearson, A3.

67. "Conference between General López de Lara and General Pelaez, 22 Oct 1918," Military Intelligence Division, Correspondence, 10640–579.

68. Spring-Rice to Foreign Office, 4 Dec 1917, FO, 371–2964/231353; Body, "Memorandum to Lord Cowdray," 6 Dec 1917, Pearson, A3.

69. Robert E. Quirk, *The Mexican Revolution, 1914–1915: The Convention of Aguascalientes* (Bloomington, Ind., 1960), 40, 42, 232; Womack, *Zapata and the Mexican Revolution,* 217–18; Katz, *The Secret War in Mexico,* 139–45; Knight, *The Mexican Revolution,* 2:119–20.

70. Spring-Rice to Hohler, 3 May, Spring-Rice to Foreign Office, 4 May 1915, FO, 371–2399/53733.

71. Hewitt to Hohler, 14 Mar, Vaughn to Body, 23 Oct 1916, FO, 371–2700/81954, 371–2706/238952.

72. Hewitt to H. A. Cunard Cummins, 7 June 1917, FO, 371–2962/148210.

73. Hewitt to Cowdray, 14 June 1918, FO, 371–3245/128549; Henderson, *Félix Díaz,* 123–24, 134, 441.

74. Edgar L. Field to Intelligence Office, 20 Nov 1917, Military Intelligence Division, Correspondence, 9700–608; Falcón, "Charisma, Tradition, and Caciquismo," 420, 438.

75. As quoted in C. H. Boynton to Fall, 23 Sept 1919, Fall, box 89, file 11b.

76. Womack, *Zapata and the Mexican Revolution,* 310, 325, 346–47.

77. R. S., "Internal Memo," 15 Nov 1916, FO, 371–2705/228882.

78. Barclay to Foreign Office, 9 Nov 1917, Thurstan, "Memorandum," 30 Apr 1918, FO, 371-2963/215442, 371–3244/82133; Body to Cowdray, 7 May, Cowdray to Body, 7 May 1917, Pearson, A4.

79. See correspondence in Foreign Office, 371–2700/95698. The Foreign Office had made such a request to pay bribes to protect British citizens from *zapatistas* if they returned to Mexico City again after the late 1914 occupation. They did not.

80. "Protection of Oil Fields in Mexico," 23 Nov 1916, Spring-Rice to A. J. Balfour, 1 Mar 1917, FO, 371–2706/237221, 371–2959/60106.

81. "Minutes, 12 Nov, Cummins to Foreign Office, 12 Dec 1917, Stewart to Maurice de Bunsen, 6 Apr 1918, FO, 371–2964/236485, 371–3243/63332.

82. Thurstan to Spring-Rice, 18 April, Thurstan to Foreign Office, 28 Apr 1917, FO, 371–2960/80733.

83. *El Dictamen* (Veracruz), 5 Aug 1915.

84. Body to Cowdray, 3 Mar 1916, Pearson, A3.

85. Foreign Office to Spring-Rice, 17 Apr, Thurstan to Foreign Office, 17 Apr, Naval Intelligence to Foreign Office, 10 Dec, Cummins to Foreign Office, 10 Dec 1917, FO, 371–2959/77834, /79679, 371–2964/234127, /234835; "Interview between Sir Maurice de Bunsen and Mr. Stewart," 11 July 1917, Pearson, A3.

86. Hohler, "Memorandum," 17 Feb, PCHS, "Memo to Lord Cowdray," 2 Mar, Spring-Rice to Foreign Office, 13 Mar, Cummins to Foreign Office, 7

Dec 1917, FO, 371–2959/60106, /52269, 371–2964/233404; Herbert J. Carr to Body, 2 Mar, Body to Carr, 5 Mar 1917, Pearson, A3.

87. Alex Flint to Foreign Office, 17 Mar 1918, J. E. Shuckburgh to Foreign Office, 22 July, R. S. S., [Minutes], 25 July 1919, FO, 371–3827/40183, 371–3831/106894.

88. Spring-Rice to State Dept., 18 Mar, Polk to Spring-Rice, 22 Mar, Polk to Byrd, 22 July 1916, Walker, "Memorandum," 12 Apr 1917, State Dept. Decimal Files, 812.6363/226, /228, /240, /296; Body to Cowdray, 28 Nov 1916, Pearson, A3; Hohler to Foreign Office, 25 Mar 1916, FO, 371–2699/56928.

89. Canova, "Memorandum," 14 Apr 1917, State Dept. Decimal Files, 812.6363/308.

90. Dawson to State Dept., 11 Aug 1916, ibid., 812.6363/245; Commanding Officer, USS Annapolis to Navy, 5 Jan 1918, Naval Records Collection, WE-5; Spring-Rice to A. J. Balfour, 17 Nov 1917, Hewitt to Thurstan, 8 Oct 1918, FO, 371–2964/244107, 371–2247/207236.

91. Naval Operations, "Occupation of Mexican Oil Fields—Tampico and Tuxpam [sic]," 22 Apr 1918, in Naval Records Collection, WE-5, Tampico—1914 file; O'Brien, "Petróleo e intervención," 127–30.

92. Spring-Rice to Foreign Office, 21 Oct 1915, Alex Flint to Foreign Office, 17 Mar 1918, FO, 371–2403/154593, 371–3827/40183; Commanding Officer, USS Annapolis to Navy, 5 Jan 1918, Naval Records Collection, WE-5.

93. Fletcher to State Dept., 19 Apr 1918, State Dept. Decimal Files, 812.6363/384; Lord Reading to Foreign Office, 18 Mar 1919, FO, 371–3827/43604.

94. Alvey A. Adee to James G. McDonald, 9 Sept 1919, State Dept. Decimal Files, 812.6363/522.

95. Testimony of Doheny, Investigation of Mexican Affairs, 1:286.

96. E. L. Doheny, "Memorandum of Facts," 5 Nov 1917, Military Intelligence Division, Correspondence, 10640–246/284.

97. Walker to Auchincloss, 28 July 1917, Military Intelligence Division, Correspondence, 10640–164/29; Walker to Lansing, 7 Aug, Walker to Gordon Auchincloss, 9 Sept 1917, State Dept. Decimal Files, 812.6363/303, /312.

98. Testimony of Doheny, Investigation of Mexican Affairs, 1:286.

99. Testimonies of Inman and Buckley, ibid., 1:67, 839.

100. Testimony of Spellacy, ibid., 1:945; "Relations of the Oil Companies with the Mexican Authorities," [c. 1918], Doheny, interview no. 683.

101. Body to Cowdray, 1 Mar 1917, Pearson, A4; W. J. Pulford to Hohler, 23 Feb, A. N. "Minutes," 6 July 1916, FO, 371–2699/63825, 371–2700/109289.

102. Carl W. Ackerman, "Germany's Ally at Tampico," Saturday Evening Post, 13 Oct 1917. The title referred not to Peláez but to the International Workers of the World, then instigating strikes in Tampico.

103. Cummins to Foreign Office, 14 Nov 1917, FO, 371–3241/47338; Claude I. Dowson to State, 20 Nov 1917, Military Intelligence Division, Correspondence, 9700–684.

104. Green to Wylie, 25 June 1918, Military Intelligence Division, Correspondence, 10640–164.

105. Hewitt to Cummins, 1 Nov 1917, FO, 371–3241/16046.

106. George E. Paddleford to E. L. Doheny, 12 Nov 1917, Military Intelligence Division, Correspondence, 9700/556.

107. Hewitt to Foreign Office, 13 Feb 1918, FO, 371–3243/58867; Louis C. Richardson, Commanding Officer, USS *Annapolis* to Navy, 15 Jan 1917, Naval Records Collection, WE-5.

108. Louis C. Richardson, Commanding Officer, USS *Annapolis* to Navy, 18 Dec 1917, 1 Jan 1918, ibid.

109. Green to Wylie, 25 Feb 1918, FO, 371–3243/47338; Linder, "Every Region for Itself," 101–3.

110. Green to Wylie, 28 Feb 1918, FO, 371–3243/47338; Green to Paddleford, 1 Mar 1918, State Dept. Decimal Files, 812.6363/373. Also see Hall and Coerver, *Revolution on the Border,* 102.

111. Green to Paddleford, 1 Mar 1918, FO, 371–3243/47338.

112. Green to Wylie, 18 Mar 1918, Military Intelligence Division, Correspondence, 10640–164/4.

113. Ibid.

114. Green to Wylie, 13 Sept 1918, Military Intelligence Division, Correspondence, 10640–164/41.

115. Green to Wylie, 18 Mar 1918, ibid., 10640–164/4.

116. Hay, "Situation of Forces in Tampico Region," 15 June 1918, Military Intelligence Division, Correspondence, 10640–240; Commanding Officer, Mexican Patrol, to Navy, 4 Nov 1917, Office of Naval Intelligence, "Conditions in Mexico, 1919," WE-5.

117. Hewitt to Cummins, 14 Nov 1917, FO, 371–3241/5107.

118. Hohler to Foreign Office, 27 Mar 1915, FO, 371–2406/61586.

119. Hay, "Situation of Forces in Tampico Region"; "Memo from H." 16 Jan 1919, Military Intelligence Division, Correspondence, 10640–240.

120. Office of Naval Intelligence, "Conditions in Mexico, 1919," WE-5.

121. Spring-Rice to Foreign Office, 4 Dec 1917, FO, 371–2964/231353.

122. Linder, "Every Region for Itself," 111–13.

123. Anon. to Carranza, 30 May 1918, Carranza, carpeta 13817; *El Dictamen,* 20 July 1919; Commanding Officer, USS *Annapolis* to Navy, 17 Nov 1917, A. A. Seraphic to Naval Intelligence, 22 Oct 1919, in Naval Attaché Reports, WE-5; "Gun-running, New Orleans to Mexico," n.d., Le Roy Lutes, "Mexican Activities in Ammo. Smuggling," 12 Mar 1920, Edmund A. Buchanan, "Arms and Ammo Smuggling from New Orleans to Mexico," 24, 27 Apr 1920, R. G. Skamp to J. M. Nye, 24 Oct 1918, Military Intelligence Division, Correspondence, 9343–306/3, /5, /12, /14, 10640–1485.

124. Buchanan, 19 Apr 1920, Military Intelligence Division, Correspondence, 9343–306/10, RG 165; "Mexico, Arms and Ammunition," n.d., [located in file dated 1918–1919], Naval Records Collection, WE-5; Menéndez, *Doheny El Cruel,* 89.

125. Hewitt to Thurstan, 5 Feb 1917, FO, 371–2959/60674.

126. Linder, "Every Region for Itself," 46; Cummins to Foreign Office, 14 Nov 1917, FO, 371–3241/47338; Russell C. Snyder, "Pelaez Activities," 19 Apr 1920, Military Intelligence Division, Correspondence, 10640–2003. Doheny, "Memorandum of Facts Presented by the Huastecan Petroleum Co.," Military Intelligence Division, Correspondence, 10640–246/284.

127. Cowdray to Foreign Office, 23 Mar 1918, FO, 371–3243/53462; Commanding Officer, Mexican Patrol, to Navy, 4 Nov 1917, Naval Records Collection, WE-5; Hay, "Situation of Forces in Tampico Region."

128. Hewitt to Cummins, 1 Feb 1918, FO, 371–3243/58867; William Green to Paddleford, 2 Feb 1918, State Dept. Decimal Files, 812.6363/389.

129. Dawson to State Dept., 6 Sept 1917, ibid., 812.00/21272; Cummins to Foreign Office, 22 Sept, Foreign Office to Spring-Rice, 20 Oct, Spring-Rice to Foreign Office, 21 Oct, FO, 371–2963/184427, /201118, /202679; Linder, "Every Region for Itself," 76.

130. Cummins to Foreign Office, 7, 9 Nov, 9 Dec 1917, FO, 371–2963/ 213296, /233707.

131. Dawson to State Dept., 20 Nov 1917, Military Intelligence Division, Correspondence, 9700–684; Foreign Office to Cowdray, 15 Nov 1917, Pearson, A3; Hewitt to Cummins, 23 Jan 1918, FO, 371–3242/41500; Linder, "Every Region for Itself," 73–81. Linder presents a detailed description of this and subsequent military campaigns in the oil zone.

132. Spring-Rice to Foreign Office, 6 Jan, Hewitt to Cummins, 8 Jan 1918, FO, 371–3241/3749, 371–3242/41473; Body, "Memorandum to the Chief," 8 Jan, Foreign Office to Lord Cowdray, 15 Jan 1918, Pearson, A3; Dawson to State Dept., 24 Jan 1918, State Dept. Decimal Files, 812.6363/332.

133. Hewitt to Pulford, 18 Jan 1918, FO, 371–3244/108160; Phillip O. Hanna to State Dept., 29 Jan 1918, State Dept. Decimal Files, 812.6363/336; Linder, "Every Region for Itself," 81–84; Durán de Seade, "Mexico's Relations with the Great Powers," 298.

134. Hewitt to H. A. Cunard Cummins, 13 Feb 1918, State Dept. Decimal Files, 812.6363/356; Cummins to Foreign Office, FO, 371–3242/32675.

135. Lord Reading to Foreign Office, 19 Feb, Cummins to Foreign Office, 20 Feb 1918, FO, 371–3241/31978, /33420; Doheny to State Dept., 17 Feb 1918, Walker to Auchincloss, 18 Feb, Dawson to State Dept., 19, 20 Feb, State Dept. Decimal Files, 812.6363/342, /345–46, /397.

136. Body to Cowdray, 24 Feb, Cowdray to De Bunsen, 28 Feb 1918, Pearson, A3.

137. Green to Wylie, 18 Mar 1918, Military Intelligence Division, Correspondence, 10640–164/4.

138. Cummins to Foreign Office, 20 Mar, 12 Apr 1918, FO, 371– 3242/46189, 371–3243/66510; Linder, "Every Region for Itself," 84–87.

139. Lord Reading to Foreign Office, 11 Mar 1918, FO, 371–3242/46189.

140. O. W. Fowler to Naval Operations, 12 Apr 1918, letter to William J. Pulford, n.d., State Dept. Decimal Files, 812.6363/387, /392; Cummins to Foreign Office, 19 Apr, Barclay to Foreign Office, 12 Apr, Hewitt to Cummins, 1 Apr 1918, FO, 371–3243/69928, /75698, 371–3244/82631.

141. Linder, "Every Region for Itself," 129–30.

142. Green to Wylie, 13 Sept 1918, Military Intelligence Division, Correspondence, 10640–164/41; Pulford to Hohler, 5 Sept, Barclay to Foreign Office, 5 Sept, Thurstan to Foreign Office, 7, 10 Sept, Hewitt to Thurstan, 9 Oct 1918, FO, 371–3246/174256, /153178, /153910, /154791, 371–3247/ 191661; Linder, "Every Region for Itself," 131–33.

143. Green to Wylie, 13 Sept 1918, Military Intelligence Division, Correspondence, 10640–164/41. Heather Fowler Salamini has suggested that López de Lara did not fight Peláez because he had received a bribe of ten thousand pesos by the oil companies. Fowler Salamini, "Caciquismo and the Mexican Revolution," 27. I have seen no evidence one way or the other.

144. "Conference between General de Lara and General Pelaez," 22 Oct 1918, Military Intelligence Division, Correspondence, 10640–579/2; Hewitt to Thurstan, 31 Oct 1918, Pearson, A3.

145. U.S. Military Intelligence, "Mexico," 10 Mar 1919, FO, 371–3828/51282; Linder, "Every Region for Itself," 135–37; Barclay to Foreign Office, 4 Apr 1919, FO, 371–3828/58627.

146. Minutes of RS, 27 Feb, Cummins to Foreign Office, 12 Mar, Pulford to Norman King, 14 Apr 1919, FO, 371–3827/40284, 371–3829/77275.

147. U.S. Consul to State Dept., 5 May 1920, in East Coast Situations, 1918–1921, Naval Records Collection, WE-5; Dawson to State Dept., 5 May 1920, Colby to U.S. Consul, 8 May 1920, State Dept. Decimal Files, 812.6363/673, /673; Linder, "Every Region for Itself," 156.

148. Sir. A. Geddes to Foreign Office, 10, 13 May, Pulford to Cummins, 11 May 1920, FO, 371–4492/A2980, /A3039, /A3486; Linder, "Every Region for Itself," 156–58; Dawson to State Dept., 8 May 1920, State Dept. Decimal Files, 812.00/23896.

149. Reports of Sosthenes Behn, 16, 23 Jan 1920, ibid., 812.00/26462.

150. Ibid.; "Political Situation, General Discussion," 5 July 1920, Military Intelligence Division, Correspondence, 10640–2307/1.

151. Dawson to Colby, 30 May, Colby to State Dept., 3 June 1920, State Dept. Decimal Files, 812.00/24142; *El Dictamen*, 31 May 1920.

152. The fodder for these articles is found in the archives of President Obregón. See Fondo Presidentes Alvaro Obregón y Plutarcho Elías Calles, 101-P-6, AGN.

153. See especially Linder, "Every Region for Itself," chap. 6; Menéndez, *Doheny El Cruel*, 100–109; John W. F. Dulles, *Yesterday in Mexico: A Chronicle of the Revolution, 1919–1936* (Austin, 1972), 110, 223.

Chapter Five

1. W. J. Pulford to Hohler, Tampico, 13 June 1916, Pulford to King, 23 Aug 1919, FO, 371–2702/142126, 371–3833/134861.

2. Ramón Eduardo Ruiz, *Labor and the Ambivalent Revolutionaries: Mexico, 1911–1923* (Baltimore, 1976), 2. See also Gilly, *La revolución interrumpida;* Arnaldo Córdoba, *La ideología de la Revolución Mexicana: la formación del nuevo régimen* (Mexico City, 1973); Hart, *Revolutionary Mexico;* Nora Hamilton, *The Limits of State Autonomy: Post-Revolutionary Mexico* (Princeton, 1982); Katz,

The Secret War in Mexico; Adolfo Gilly et al., *Interpretaciones de la revolución mexicana,* 10th ed. (Mexico City, 1987).

3. For example, see Moises González Navarro, *Las huelgas textiles en el Porfiriato* (Puebla, 1970); Rodney Anderson, *Outcasts in Their Own Land: Mexican Industrial Workers, 1906–1911* (DeKalb, Ill., 1976); Lorena M. Parlee, "The Impact of United States Railroad Unions on Organized Labor and Government Policy in Mexico (1880–1911)," *Hispanic American Historical Review* 64 (1984): 443–75; Marcelo Rodea, *Historia del movimiento obrero ferrocarrilero* (Mexico City, 1944); Barry Carr, *El movimiento obrero y la política en México, 1910–1929* (Mexico City, 1981); *El Trabajo y los trabajadores en la historia de México,* ed. Elsa Cecilia Frost, Michael C. Meyer, and Josefina Zoraida Vásquez (Mexico City and Tucson, 1979); Torcuato S. Di Tella, "The Dangerous Classes in Early Nineteenth-Century Mexico," *Journal of Latin American Studies* 5 (1973): 79–105; Carr, *El movimiento obrero y la política en México;* Jorge Basurto, *El proletariado industrial en México,* 25.

4. As Alan Knight observes, "Given half a chance, the organized working class opted for unionism and reformism (sometimes camouflaged under revolutionary rhetoric); only when it was brusquely and brutally denied the chance did it entertain risky thoughts of revolution. Historically, the workers have not been born revolutionaries, but have had revolutions thrust upon them." Knight, "The Working Class and the Mexican Revolution, c. 1900–1920," *Journal of Latin American Studies* 16 (May 1984): 71.

5. Claude I. Dawson, "Economic Changes Since the Beginning of the War," Tampico, 17 June 1918, U.S. Consular Records, Tampico, 850.4. Adleson, "Historia social de los obreros," 4, indicates a population increase from 13,452 persons in 1910 to 40,192 in 1917. E. L. Doheny said the population rose from 8,000 in 1900 to 50,000 or 60,000 in 1919, *Investigation of Mexican Affairs,* 1:236; Ordóñez placed the number of inhabitants at 9,000 in 1900 and more than 100,000 in 1922. Ordóñez, "El petróleo en México," part 2, 221. These figures lack precision because of the government's inability to carry out the scheduled census of 1920 because of political unrest.

6. "Estimate of the Situation Covering Protection of Life and Property at Tampico, Mexico," 16 Oct 1916, Naval Records Collection, WE–5.

7. Ordóñez, "El petróleo en México," part 2, 221.

8. Ibid., 223.

9. Adleson, "Historia social de los obreros," 108, 126, 329, 345–48.

10. Dawson, "Economic Changes Since the Beginning of the War," 17 June 1918, U.S. Consular Records, Tampico, 850.4.

11. Charles Bergquist suggests that those Latin American workers in the predominant export industries generated a new militancy and a new perspective because of their position at the nexus between the national (and so-called dependent) economy and the international market. The oil workers' militancy at Tampico, however, seems based on their traditions of resistance rather than on their knowledge of and opposition to international capitalism. Charles Bergquist, *Labor in Latin America: Comparative Essays on Chile, Argentina, Venezuela, and Colombia* (Stanford, 1984), 8, 376.

12. Adleson, "Historia social de los obreros," 144.

13. Nicklos, 8 July 1953, T103, OHTO; "Potrero—Tuxpam 8" Pipe Line, Pump Stations—Labour" [c. 1916], Pearson, C45.

14. Adleson, "Historia social de los obreros," 146–49; 417, 420–23. Like many mine owners during the Porfiriato, Doheny claimed that the Mexicans themselves preferred *tarea* work. It permitted the mine workers to complete a job at times of their own choosing rather than at prescribed times. Perhaps laborers might accomplish two *tareas* in one day, so that they could take off the next day. Testimony of Doheny, *Investigation of Mexican Affairs*, 1:234. Also see Bernstein, *The Mexican Mining Industry*, for mining labor during the Porfiriato.

15. Adleson, "Historia social de los obreros," 147.

16. Clarence A. Miller to Col. Martínez, 15 March 1912, U.S. Consular Records, Tampico, Correspondence—Mexican Officials; Adleson, "Historia social de los obreros," 170, 172, 174.

17. Enrique S. Cerdán, 29 Jan 1920, Ramo de Trabajo, Departamento de Trabajo, 1911–1930, C224, E23, AGN; Adleson, "Historia social de los obreros," 188, 192–95.

18. Enrique S. Cerdán, 29 Jan 1920, Ramo de Trabajo, C224, E23. Skocpol notes that the function of labor was to reinforce the state during the time of postrevolutionary consolidation. See Theda Skocpol, *States and Social Revolutions: A Comparative Analysis of France, Russia, and China* (Cambridge, Eng., 1979), 112, 236.

19. "Interview with Mr. S. W. Smith of the Mexican Petroleum Company," 11 May 1918, interview no. 596, Doheny.

20. Interview no. 696, n.d. [circa 1918], Doheny. The observer can be accused of pro-American, pro-Huasteca, anti-British, anti–El Aguila biases, because the research foundation of E. L. Doheny paid the observer's expenses in Tampico.

21. E. J. Nicklos, 8 July 1953, OHTO, T-104.

22. Cowdray to Mr. Kemsley, 30 Apr 1915, FO, 371–2399/53060; Cowdray to J. B. Body, 29 Dec 1916, Pearson, A4.

23. Interview no. 401, Doheny.

24. *El Dictámen*, 23 May 1920; Silva Herzog, *El petróleo de México*, 50.

25. Interview no. 401, Doheny.

26. Ibid.; McMahon, *Two Strikes and Out*, 42.

27. Enrique Cerdán, "Informe," 9 Jan 1920, Ramo de Trabajo, C224, E24.

28. "José Hernández, mutilado al prestar sus servicios en la Huasteca Petroleum Co.," 1919, Ramo de Trabajo, C170, E2.

29. "Interview with Mr. S. W. Smith," 11 May 1918, interview no. 596, Doheny.

30. Carl W. Ackerman, "Germany's Ally at Tampico," *The Saturday Evening Post*, 13 Oct 1917.

31. James D. McLachlan, "Report on Bolshevism in Mexico," 20 May 1919, FO, 371–3830/83812; Anon. to Fall, 24 Jan 1919, Fall, box 72, file 49.

32. W. M. Hanson to Fall, 17 Sept 1916, Anon. to Fall, 18 Oct 1918, 7 July 1919, Fall, box 84, file 2, box 72, box 49.

33. O. G. Lawson, 29 July 1952, OHTO, T31; E. J. Nicklos, 8 July 1953, ibid., T104.

34. "Aguila Co. 1916, Estimates Northern and Southern Fields Navigation Department and O.F.M.," Pearson, C45 F6; Office of Naval Operations, Planning Section, "Occupation of Mexican Oil Fields—Tampico and Tuxpam [*sic*]," 22 Apr 1918, in "Mexico: Tampico—Firing on U.S. Naval Forces, 1914," Naval Records Collection, WE–5; Dawson to M. C. Hutchinson, 7 Mar 1919, U.S. Consular Records, Tampico, 850.4.

35. "Data re. American Refugees from Mexico, 1913–1914," ibid.

36. Dawson to Earle W. Jopp, 16 Apr 1919, ibid.; Lambert and Franks, *Voices from the Oil Fields*, 44.

37. Nicklos, 8 July 1953, T103, OHTO; "Plan of Minatitlan Oil Refinery," 31 Oct 1922, Pearson, C46 F5.

38. Germán García Lozano, "Estadio descriptivo de la refinería de petróleo en Minatitlán, Ver.," *Boletín del Petróleo* 1, no. 3 (1916): 266–67.

39. Ibid.

40. O. G. Lawson, 29 July 1952, T31, OHTO; Lambert and Franks, *Voices from the Oil Fields*, 46.

41. Cowdray to Thomas J. Ryder, 31 Aug 1914, Pearson, A3.

42. Dawson to El Aguila, 13 Aug 1918, Dawson to George A. Chamberlain, 14 Aug 1918, Dawson to U.S. consul, Nuevo Laredo, 21 Aug 1918, U.S. Consular Records, Tampico, 850.4/822; author's interview with Maier, Coral Gables, Florida, 30 Dec 1982. Maier later managed the Tropical Oil Company of Colombia.

43. López Portillo y Weber, *El petróleo de México*, 135–37; testimony of James J. Britt, *Investigation of Mexican Affairs*, 1:995, 1002; Hall and Coerver, *Revolution on the Border*, 99.

44. Body to Cowdray, 16 Jan, 3 July 1917, Pearson, A4; Foreign Office to consular officers, Mexico, 12 July 1917, FO, 371–2962/138423; Cowdray to Body, 28 Apr 1914, Pearson, A3; Cowdray to Board of Trade, 10 Oct 1914, ibid.

45. Testimony of Spellacy, *Investigation of Mexican Affairs*, 1:952–53; Green to Paddleford, 1 Mar 1918, FO, 371–3243/A47338.

46. Thomas J. Ryder to Colville Barclay, 26 Aug 1919, FO, 371–3833/134146; Wilson to Hohler, 24 Nov 1914, FO, 371–2397/23934.

47. "Potrero—Tuxpam 8" Pipe Line, Pump Stations—Labour," Pearson, C45.

48. Cowdray to Ryder, 31 Aug 1914, Pearson, A3.

49. Testimony of Dr. Bruce Baker Corbin, *Investigation of Mexican Affairs*, 1:1459.

50. War Department to F. J. Collins, 20 Oct 1919, W. Milligan to Capt. George S. Frickes, 16 Dec 1918, U.S. Consular Records, Tampico, 850.4.

51. Sadler to Dawson, 19 Feb 1919, ibid.

52. Silva Herzog, *El petróleo de México*, 50.

53. Some historians, like Roberto Korzeniewicz, place the labor process at the center of any interpretation of labor unrest. "Insofar as the position of different groups of workers in the labor market was itself shaped by the nature of the labor process and workplace relations, the transformation of these spheres constitutes an important analytical point of departure for explaining the central features of the emerging labor movement." Roberto P. Korze-

niewicz, "Labor Unrest in Argentina, 1887–1907," *Latin American Research Review* 24 (1989): 71.

54. Ordóñez, "El Petróleo en México," part 2, 223.

55. Testimony of Corbin, *Investigation of Mexican Affairs,* 1:1459; "Pearson Photographic Albums," 1, 44; G. H. Coxon to R. D. Hutchinson, 21 Jan 1919, Pearson, P/1.

56. Interview no. 696, Doheny.

57. Miller to sec. of state, 25 May 1912, State Dept. Decimal Files, 812.6363/4.

58. Enrique S. Cerdán, "Informe," 9 Jan 1920, Ramo de Trabajo, C224, E24.

59. Ibid.

60. Here the theoretical work of Harry Braverman can be taken too far by historians of early industrialization. The Braverman thesis implies that machinery reduces work to routine and separates work into specific tasks, such that technological advancement leads to a deskilling of the labor force. The application of the Braverman thesis to early Mexican industrial development, because of the importance of foreign skilled workers, does not seem reasonable. See Braverman, *Labor and Monopoly Capital,* 149; John Womack, Jr., "The Historiography of Mexican Labor," in Frost, Meyer, and Vásquez, *El Trabajo y los trabajadores en la historia de México,* 739–56; Adleson, "Historia social de los obreros," 405, 535.

61. "The Texas Company of Mexico" [circa 1918], Doheny, LJC-DS, file 3467.

62. Ibid. On the hierarchy of the Mexican working class, see Di Tella, "The Dangerous Classes in Early Nineteenth-Century Mexico," 79–105.

63. "Estimated Monthly Expenditures and Receipts," 1 Jan to 30 June 1916, "Navigation Department," and "Tampico and Minatitlán Refinery Estimates" [c. 1916], Pearson, C45 F4; "Schedule of wages," Mexican Petroleum Company, 31 May 1918, Doheny, files 3717–3718.

64. Ordóñez, "El petróleo de México," part 2, 224.

65. Adleson, "Historia social de los obreros," 161, 166.

66. Ordóñez, "El petróleo de México," part 2, 220. The practice of selling purloined water recalls the testimony of Carolina Maria de Jesús, who described how unscrupulous entrepreneurs of the *favelas* of São Paulo would tap into the public electricity system, without permission, and sell power to the residents. See *Child of the Dark: The Diary of Carolina Maria de Jesus,* tr. David St. Clair (New York, 1962), 35.

67. "Erection of Camp Buildings," [c. 1916], Pearson, C45.

68. Testimony of Doheny, *Investigation of Mexican Affairs,* 1:234–35; Eberstadt Photo Collection, Box 3S1, Mexico Petroleum Co., c. 1913, Barker Texas History Center Photograph Collection, University of Texas at Austin.

69. "Se trasmite informe de la Agencia del Petróleo en Tuxpan, Ver.," 12 Jan 1920, Ramo de Trabajo, C114, E27.

70. "Estimate for 2,000 Foot Wells," [c. 1916], Pearson, C45.

71. Testimony of Doheny and Spellacy, *Investigation of Mexican Affairs,* 1: 234, 940, 942; "Standing Charges, Potrero Camp," [c. 1916], Pearson, C45 F6.

72. Wage data from "Standing Charges, Potrero Camp," "Estimate Monthly Expenditures and Receipts," "Southern Fields," "Aguila Co., 1916—Estimating

Northern & Southern Fields Navigation Department and O.F.M." [c. 1916], Pearson, C45 F6.

73. Pérez Ruiz to Jefe, 18 Sept 1920, Ramo de Trabajo, C220 E6.

74. Testimony of Beaty, *Investigation of Mexican Affairs,* 1:532–33; William Green to George E. Paddleford, 17 Feb 1918, State Dept. Decimal Files, 812.6363/389.

75. Body to Cowdray, 10 May 1911, Body to Cowdray, 3 Mar, Vaughn to Anglo-Mex, 4 Dec 1916, Pearson, A4; Pulford to Hohler, 18 June 1917, Green to Paddleford, 1 Mar 1918, FO, 371–2962/143982, -3243/A47338.

76. "Interview with Arthur Coyle Payne, General Manager, Oil Fields of Mexico Co.," interview no. 588, 13 May 1918, Doheny.

77. "Interview with Mr. H. Wylie," 15 May 1918, interview no. 597, Doheny.

78. Miller to Canada, Canada to sec. of state, 21 May 1914, State Dept. Decimal Files, 812.6363/72; testimony of Doheny, *Investigation of Mexican Affairs,* 1:237; Canada to sec. of state, Bryan to Miller, 4 May, W. A. Thompson to Robert Lansing, 29 May 1914, State Dept. Decimal Files, 812.6363/42, /51a, /85; Silva Herzog, *El petróleo de México,* 83.

79. Testimony of Doheny, *Investigation of Mexican Affairs,* 1:234; Nicklos, 8 July 1953, OHTO, T103.

80. Interview no. 75, 26 July 1918, Doheny.

81. David Rock, "Lucha civil en la Argentina: La Semana Trágica de enero de 1919," *Desarollo Económico* 114 (1971–72), 165–215; Peter DeShazo, *Urban Workers and Labor Unions in Chile, 1902–1927* (Madison, 1983); Ronaldo Munck, "Cyclers of Class Struggle and the Making of the Working Class in Argentina, 1890–1920," *Journal of Latin American Studies* 19 (1987): 19–39; Andrew Patrick Boeger, "Mexican Workers and Their Struggles, 1910–1918" (M.A. thesis, the University of Texas at Austin, 1989), 69–71.

82. "Potrero—Tuxpam 8" Pipe Line. Pump Stations—Labour" [c. 1916], Pearson, C45; "Programs 1916," Pearson, C45 F5.

83. Body to Chief, 22 Dec 1916, 20 Jan 1917, Pearson, A4.

84. Miller to sec. of state, 16 Nov 1911, U.S. Consular Records, Tampico, 812.504.

85. Ruiz, *Labor and the Ambivalent Revolutionaries,* 5.

86. For the Mexican artisan, see Manuel Carrera Stampa, *Los gremios mexicanos: La organización gremial en Nueva España, 1521–1861* (Mexico City, 1954); John E. Kicza, *Colonial Entrepreneurs: Families and Business in Bourbon Mexico City* (Albuquerque, 1983), 208–239; Frederick J. Shaw, "The Artisan in Mexico City (1824–1853)," in Frost, Meyer, and Vásquez, *El Trabajo y los trabajadores en la historia de México,* 399–418; Dorothy Tanck de Estrada, "La abolición de los gremios," in ibid., 311–31.

87. The debate about whether the Department of Labor succeeded in reducing strikes and deflecting labor militancy, as Ruiz asserts, is taken up throughout this chapter. See Ruiz, *Labor and the Ambivalent Revolutionaries,* 2, 31, 41, 57–58.

88. Knight, "The Working Class and the Mexican Revolution," 75; Adleson, "Historia social de los obreros," 209.

89. Ibid., 69–70; H. T. Mayo to sec. of navy, 2 Aug 1914, Naval Records Collection, WE–5.

90. Sindicato de Empleados de Comercio, 3 Sept, Mexican Light and Power Company to González, 2 Dec, Sindicato de Artes Gráficos, 18 Dec 1915, Sindicatos de Empleados de la Compañía de Tranvíos, Luz y Fuerza de Puebla, 17 Jan 1916, Luis Pateño, "El Depto. Jurídico del Cuerp de Ejército de Oriente en 1915 . . . ," González, L13, E135, E136, L13, E306.

91. Valdivieso Castillo, *Historia del movimiento sindical*, 26; "News Notes from Mexican News Bureau, 9 Aug 1917, State Dept. Decimal Files, 812.6363/309; C. Aguila, "Declaraciones a la prensa con motivo del conflicto obrero," 8 Jan 1919, Carranza, carpeta 129.

92. Valdivieso Castillo, *Historia del movimiento sindical*, 27; Ciro R. de la Garza Treviño, *La Revolución Mexicana en el Estado de Tamaulipas* (Mexico City, 1975), 2:280, 284–85.

93. De la Garza Treviño, *La Revolución Mexicana*, 2:293–95.

94. *Diario de los debates*, 1:984, as quoted by Niemeyer, *Revolution at Querétaro*, 108. Zavala was engaging in hyperbole. The workers had done very little compared to the peasants. Knight, "The Working Class and the Mexican Revolution," 71.

95. Rouaix, *Génesis de los artículos 27 y 123*, 127–41; Linda B. Hall, *Alvaro Obregón: Power and Revolution in Mexico, 1911–1920* (College Station, Tex., 1981), 178–79; Niemeyer, *Revolution at Querétaro*, chap. 4.

96. As quoted in Niemeyer, *Revolution at Querétaro*, Appendix C.

97. See especially Silvio Zavala and María Castelo, *Fuentes para la historia del trabajo en Nueva España*, 8 vols. (Mexico City, 1939–1945); Woodrow Borah, *Justice by Insurance: The General Indian Court of Colonial Mexico and the Legal Aides of the Half-Real* (Berkeley, 1983).

98. As quoted in Niemeyer, *Revolution at Querétaro*, Appendix C.

99. Hall, *Alvaro Obregón*, 100–101, 110–11; 140–41; Richmond, *Venustiano Carranza's Nationalist Struggle*, 73; Carr, *El movimiento obrero y la política en México*, 64–74; Barry Carr, "Organized Labour and the Mexican Revolution, 1915–1938," Oxford University Occasional Papers, No. 2 (1972), 4, 9.

100. Barry Carr, "The Casa del Obrero Mundial, Constitutionalism and the Pact of February 1915," in Frost, Meyer, and Vásquez, *El Trabajo y los trabajadores en la historia de México*, 603–32; John Mason Hart, *Anarchism and the Mexican Working Class, 1860–1931* (Austin, 1978), 150; Ruiz, *Labor and the Ambivalent Revolutionaries*, 47, 54–57.

101. Hart, *Anarchism and the Mexican Working Class*, 155; Richmond, *Venustiano Carranza's Nationalist Struggle*, 125–26; Carr, "The Casa del Obrero Mundial," 628. Today home to Sanborn's Restaurant, the House of Tiles once belonged to the Conde de Regla, owner of the Real del Monte mines, which was the scene of Mexico's first labor strike in 1769.

102. Cerdán, 29 Jan 1920, Ramo de Trabajo, C224, E23.

103. Adleson, "Historia social de los obreros," 264, 352, 355, 358, 363, 430, 436, 439, 456, 458; De la Garza Treviño, *La Revolución Mexicana*, 2:233–34.

104. De la Garza Treviño, *La Revolución Mexicana*, 2:255–56.

105. Ricardo Treviño et al. to Carranza, Saltillo, 1 May 1919, Carranza, carpeta 15197; Adleson, "Historia social de los obreros," 435; Hart, *Anarchism and the Mexican Working Class,* 157–58.

106. This secret convention was not known until 1930, when Morones himself, under suspicion of having had Obregón assassinated two years before, divulged it. Hall, *Alvaro Obregón,* 217–18; Ruiz, *Labor and the Ambivalent Revolutionaries,* 59–61, 70.

107. Cerdán, 29 Jan 1920, Ramo de Trabajo C224, E23.

108. On the labor aristocracy, see Eric Hobsbawm, *Workers: Worlds of Labor* (New York, 1984), 185.

109. J. B. Body to Foreign Office, 22 Apr, 23 Apr 1915, FO, 371–2398/48597, /48598; Valdivieso Castillo, *Historia del movimiento sindical,* 25, 27.

110. C. O. Meyer to Thomas H. Bevan, 27 May 1915, U.S. Consular Records, Tampico, 850.4/235.

111. Bevan to sec. of state, 20 July, 30 July 1915, ibid., 850.4/233–34; Bevan to sec. of state, 30 July, 3 Aug 1915, State Dept. Decimal Files, 812.504/9.

112. J. C. Evans to Bevan, 14 June 1915, U.S. Consular Records, Tampico, 850.4/242; Commanding Officer, USS *Wheeling* to Commanding Officer, USS *Sacramento,* 25 July 1915, Naval Records Collection, WE–5.

113. A. Araujo to foreign employees, 1 Aug 1915, "Mexico: Conditions in Tampico, 1915–1916," Naval Records Collection, WE–5.

114. Sindicato de Empleados de Comercio to González, 3 Sept 1915, Emilio A. Quiñones et al. to González, 3 Nov 1915, González to Rouaix, 13 Nov 1915, González, L13, E135.

115. Bevan to sec. of state, 1 Dec 1915, U.S. Consular Records, Tampico, 850.4/243.

116. Body to Cowdray, 10 Feb 1916, Pearson, A4.

117. Dawson to sec. of state, 6 Apr 1916, State Dept. Decimal Files, 812.504/46.

118. Commanding Officer, USS *Marietta* to Commanding Officer, USS *Kentucky,* 3, 7, 8, 10 May 1916, "Mexico: Conditions in Tampico, 1915–1916," Naval Records Collection, WE–5.

119. W. F. Buckley, et al. to Woodrow Wilson, 22 May 1916, Pearson, A3; Commanding Officer, USS *Marietta* to Commanding Officer, USS *Kentucky,* 27 May 1916, Naval Records Collection, WE–5; Pulford to Hohler, 13 June 1916, FO, 371–2702/142126.

120. As quoted in De la Garza Treviño, *La Revolución Mexicana,* 2:238; Hohler to Foreign Office, 26 June 1916, FO, 371–2701/123687.

121. Gulston to Anglo-Mex, Body to Cowdray, 4 Dec 1916, Pearson, A4.

122. As quoted in De la Garza Treviño, *La Revolución Mexicana,* 2:240.

123. Ibid., 2:241.

124. Body to Cowdray, 20 Jan, 24 Feb 1917, Pearson, A4.

125. Thurstan to Foreign Office, 24, 25 Apr 1917, Thurstan to Spring-Rice, 29 Apr 1917, FO, 371–2960/84125, /85616, /88278; Dawson to sec. of state, 23, 24 Apr 1917, U.S. Consular Records, Tampico, 850.4.

126. Warren to H. C. Pierce, 30 Apr 1917, Naval Records Collection, WE–5.

127. Dawson to sec. of state, 16 Apr, 2 May 1917, Josephus Daniels to sec. of state, 2 May 1917, State Dept. Decimal Files, 812.504/85, /89, /95; Claude I. Dawson to P. Symington, 28 Apr 1917, U.S. Consular Records, Tampico, 850.4.

128. Warren to H. C. Pierce, 30 Apr, Naval Records Collection, WE–5; Warren to H. C. Pierce, 8 May 1917, State Dept. Decimal Files, 812.504/97.

129. "Report on Conditions at Tampico," in Barclay to Lord Robert Cecil, 26 May, FO, 371–2961/116927; USS *Tacoma* to sec. of navy, 30 Apr 1917, State Dept. Decimal Files, 812.504/91.

130. Cummins to Foreign Office, 30 May 1917, FO, 371–2961/108766; "Weekly News Summaries," in Body to C. Reed, 4 June, and F. M. Davies to C. Reed, 11 June 1917, Pearson, A4.

131. "Weekly News Summary," in Body to C. Reed, 25 June 1917, Pearson, A4; Canada to sec. of state, 30 June 1917, State Dept. Decimal Files, 812.504/113.

132. McHenry to sec. of state, 18, 20 June 1917, State Dept. Decimal Files, 812.504/107, /110; W. J. Stork to Dawson, 5 May, Dawson to sec. of state, 14 May 1917, U.S. Consular Records, Tampico, 850.4.

133. Document signed by F. Gamallo and Ramón Parreño, 12 July 1917, and El Obrero Mundial al ciudadano, n.p., n.d., ibid.

134. F. Gamallo to Oficina Huasteca, 13 July 1917, Cortina to Huasteca et al., 13 July 1917, ibid.

135. "Declaración hecho por el Señor A. W. Turner," n.d., J. B. River, affidavit, 16 July 1917, ibid.; Dawson to sec. of state, 12, 16 July 1917, State Dept. Decimal Files, 812.504/114, /117.

136. Frank C. Laurie to Dawson, 17 July 1917, U.S. Consular Records, Tampico, 850.4.

137. E. Richards to Frank C. Polk, 24, 26 July 1917, State Dept. Decimal Files, 812. 504/116, /120; Pearson to Lord Solum Stuart, 27 July 1917, FO, 371–2962/149925.

138. Cummins to Foreign Office, 24, 27 July 1917, FO, 371–2962/146802, /147660.

139. C. Hamilton et al., to Dawson, 25 July 1917, Dawson to sec. of state, 25 July 1917, U.S. Consular Records, Tampico, 850.4; Paddleford to Mex. Petrol. Co., 26 July 1917, State Dept. Decimal Files, 812.504/121.

140. USS *Annapolis* to Opnav, 28 July 1917, State Dept. Decimal Files, 812.504/124; Polk to sec. of state, 30 July, Dawson to sec. of state, 30 July; J. E. Trout to U.S. consul, 11 Sept 1917, U.S. Consular Records, Tampico, 850.5; Cummins to Foreign Office, 29 July, 7 Aug, to Pearson & Sons, 1 Aug 1917, FO, 371–2962/149406, /155641.

141. G. Arriyaza et al. to Pierce Oil Co., n.d., Dawson to sec. of state, 25 Sept 1917, U.S. Consular Records, Tampico, 850.4.

142. Commanding Officer, Mexican Patrol to Navy, 4 Nov 1917, Naval Records Collection, WE–5; Cummins to Foreign Office, 2, 5, 11 Oct 1917, FO, 371–2963/190753, /191742, /195778.

143. A. Salín ["Pierce Oil Accord"], 17 Nov 1917, Ramo de Trabajo, C169, E40.

144. Spring-Rice to Foreign Office, 19 Nov 1917, FO, 371–2964/220249; Edgar L. Field to Dept. Intell. Officer, 20 Nov 1917, Military Intelligence Division, 9700–608.

145. "Estimates 1st July to 31st December 1918," Pearson, C45 F1.

146. *El Universal,* 10 Aug 1918; "Separación de Obreros por varias Cías petroleras," Ramo de Trabajo, C126, E18; U.S. Military Intelligence Dept., "Mexico," 10 Mar 1919, FO, 371–3828/51282.

147. Dawson to sec. of state, 20 Mar 1918, U.S. Consular Records, Tampico, 850.4; Cowdray to Foreign Office, 21 Mar 1918, FO, 371–3243/53461.

148. "Informes de Huelga declarada en la Cía Mexicana Petrolera 'El Aguila,' Tamps., 1918," Ramo de Trabajo, C118, E7; Foreign Office to Cowdray, 29 Mar 1918, Pearson, A3.

149. "Informes de huelga en la Cía. Petrolera Transcontinental," 1919, Ramo de Trabajo, C169, E39.

150. Anonymous to Fall, 24 Jan 1919, Fall, box 72, file 49.

151. "Huelga de la negociación petrolera Pierce Oil Corporation," 1919, Ramo de Trabajo, C169, E40; *El Excélsior,* 24 Jan 1919; W. A. Ward to Dawson, 7 May 1919, U.S. Consular Records, Tampico, 850.4; De la Garza Treviño, *La Revolución Mexicana,* 2:282–83.

152. E. Pérez Arce, 2, 25 June, Pierce Oil Co. to F. Flores Santos, 21 June 1919, Ramo de Trabajo, C169, E40.

153. As quoted in Adleson, "Historia social de los obreros," 521.

154. W. Mealy to León Salinas, 22 July 1919, Ramo de Trabajo, C169, E40.

155. Stephen V. Graham to sec. of navy, 14 June 1919, State Dept. Decimal Files, 812.6363/478; Graham to sec. of navy, 19 June 1919, Naval Records Collection, WE–5; U.S. consul to sec. of state, n.d., U.S. Consular Records, Tampico, 850.4, W. J. Pulford to Norman King, 17 June 1919, FO, 371–3831/103005; De la Garza Treviño, *La Revolución Mexicana,* 2:282–83; Emilio Portes Gil, "15 Years in Mexican Politics," unpub. translated typescript, vol. 13, p. 3, Daniels. De la Garza Treviño dates the violence on 16 May 1919, whereas American naval and British consular sources at the time reported it to have been on 16 June. The most complete description of the strike is Adleson, "Historia social de los obreros," 513–24.

156. As quoted in Adleson, "Historia social de los obreros," 522.

157. "Tampico Huelga," 1920, Ramo de Trabajo, C213, E29; Enrique S. Cerdán, 29 Jan 1920, Ramo de Trabajo, C224, E23.

158. H. A. Ellis et al. to P. E. Calles, 17 Feb 1920, Ramo de Trabajo, C213, E30.

159. E. P. Thompson, "Time, Work-Discipline, and Industrial Capitalism," *Past and Present* 38 (1967): 56–97.

160. Valdivieso Castillo, *Historia del movimiento sindical,* 25.

161. "Interview with Mr. H. Wylie," 15 May 1918, interview no. 597, Doheny; Carr, "Organized Labor and the Mexican Revolution," 2.

Selected Bibliography

Abbreviations

AALA	Estelle Doheny Collection, Archive of the Archdiocese of Los Angeles, Mission Hills, California
AGN	Archivo General de la Nación, Mexico City
AR	Algemeen Rijksarchief, The Hague
Arnold	Ralph Arnold Collection, Huntington Library
Buckley	William Buckley Archive, University of Texas at Austin
Carranza	Archivo del Presidente Venustiano Carranza, Centro de Estudios de Historia de México, Condumex, Mexico City
Cleland	Robert Glass Cleland Research Collection, Huntington Library
Daniels	Papers of Josephus Daniels, Library of Congress
DeGolyer	Papers of E. L. DeGolyer, Sr., Southern Methodist University
Doheny	Doheny Research Foundation Collection, Occidental College Library
Fall	Albert B. Fall Collection, Huntington Library
FO	Foreign Office General Correspondence, Public Record Office, London
González	Pablo González Archive, University of Texas at Austin
OHTO	Oral History of the Texas Oil Industry, University of Texas at Austin
OHTOR	Oral History of the Texas Oil Industry Records, University of Texas at Austin
Pearson	Records of S. Pearson & Son, Ltd., British Science Museum Library, London

431

Shell   Shell International Petroleum Company, London
SONJ   Records of Standard Oil Company (New Jersey), New York

Archival Sources

Algemeen Rijksarchief, The Hague
Tweede Afdeling
    Archief van de Directie Economische Zaken van het Ministerie van
       Buitenlandse Zaken, 1919–41
    Archief van het Ministerie van Buitenlandse Zaken, A-Dossiers
    Archief van het Ministerie van Buitenlandse Zaken, B-Dossiers, Betref-
       fende Consulaire en Handels-Aangelegenheden, 1871–1940
    Kabinetsarchief van het Ministerie van Buitenlandse Zaken, 1871–
       1940
    Kabinetsarchief van het Ministerie van Buitenlandse Zaken, Betref-
       fende Politieke Rapportage door Nederlandse Vertegenwoordigers
       in het Buitenland, 1871–1940
    Documenten Betreffende de Buitenlandse Politiek van Nederland, 1919–
       45. Deel V. 1 Oktober 1923–31 Augustus 1924. Bewerkt door Dr. J.
       Woltring. 's-Gravenhage: Martinus Nijhoff, 1985.
Archivo General de la Nación, Mexico City
    Fondo Presidentes Alvaro Obregón y Plutarco Elías Calles, 1920–28
    Ramo de Hacienda, Fomento y Obras Públicas
       Minas y Petróleo, 1916
       Industrias Nuevas, 1908–15
       Secretaría de Comunicación y Obras Públicas, 1907–26
    Ramo de Trabajo, Departamento de Trabajo, 1911–30
Archivo Histórico "Genero Estrada" de la Secretaría de Relaciones Exterio-
    res, Expropriación de la Industria del Petróleo Mexicana, Mexico City
Archive of the Archdiocese of Los Angeles, Mission Hills, California
    Estelle Doheny Collection, Miscellaneous Correspondence, 1900–1913
British Science Museum Library, London
    Records of S. Pearson & Son, Ltd., 1879–1945
Centro de Estudios de Historia de Mexico, Condumex, Mexico City
    Archivo del Presidente Venustiano Carranza
Huntington Library, San Marino, California
    Ralph Arnold Collection, 1875–1961
    Robert Glass Cleland Research Collection
    Albert B. Fall Collection
Imperial Oil Company, Ltd., Toronto

Teagle Papers
Library of Congress, Manuscript Division, Washington, D.C.
　　Papers of Josephus Daniels
National Archives and Record Service, Washington, D.C.
　　Record Group 38, Office of the Chief of Naval Operations, Office of Naval Intelligence, Naval Attaché Reports, 1887–1939
　　Record Group 45, Naval Records Collection, 1911–27, WE-5 (Mexico)
　　Record Group 59, General Records of the Department of State
　　　　Despatches from U.S. Ministers to Mexico, 1823–1906
　　　　Numerical and Minor Files of the Department of State, 1906–10
　　　　State Department Correspondence, 1910–29, Decimal File 812 (Mexico)
　　　　U.S. Consular Despatches to the Department of State, 1822–1906
　　Record Group 84, Post Records of the U.S. Consulates, 1900–1937
　　Record Group 165, Military Intelligence Division, Correspondence, 1889–1941
Occidental College Library, Los Angeles, California
　　Doheny Research Foundation Collection
Public Record Office, London
　　Foreign Office General Correspondence, 1906–38
Shell International Petroleum Company, London
　　Group History, Country Series, Mexico Management, 1919–31
Southern Methodist University, Dallas, The DeGolyer Library
　　Papers of E. L. DeGolyer, Sr.
Standard Oil Company (New Jersey), New York
The University of Texas at Austin
　　Barker Texas History Center
　　　　Eberstadt Photograph Collection
　　　　Oral History of the Texas Oil Industry
　　　　Oral History of the Texas Oil Industry Records, 1952–58
　　Law School Library Archives
　　Nettie Lee Benson Latin American Collection
　　　　Pablo González Archive
　　　　William Buckley Archive

Primary Sources

Anglo Mexican Petroleum Products Co. *Mexican Fuel Oil.* London, 1914.
The Amatlán Suit. Mexican Eagle Oil Co., 1934.
Annual Report of the Mexican Petroleum Co., Ltd., of Delaware. N.p., 1917.
Annual Report, Pan American Petroleum & Transport Co. N.p., 1920.
Barron, Clarence W. *The Mexican Problem.* Boston, 1917.
Boletín de Petróleo. 1916–20.

Branch, H. N. "The Mexican Constitution of 1917." Supplement to the *Annals of the American Academy of Political and Social Science* 71 (May 1917): 2–31.

Bulletin of the National Association for the Protection of American Rights in Mexico 1, no. 5 (20 September 1919).

Bulnes, Francisco. *El verdadero Díaz y la Revolución.* Mexico City, 1921.

Cárdenas, Lázaro. *Messages to the Mexican Nation on the Oil Question.* Mexico City, 1938.

Chambers, A. E. "Potrero No. 4: A History of One of Mexico's Earliest and Largest Wells," *Journal of the Institution of Petroleum Technologists* 37, no. 9 (1923): 141–64.

Doheny, E. L. *The Mexican Question: Its Relation to Our Industries, Our Merchant Marine, and Our Foreign Trade.* Los Angeles, 1919.

Furber, Percy Norman. *I Took Chances: From Windjammers to Jets.* Leicester, 1953.

García Lozano, Germán. "Estudio descriptivo de la refinería de petróleo en Minatitlán, Ver." *Boletín del Petróleo* 1, no. 3 (1916): 260–68.

Garfías, V. R. "The Oil Region of Northeastern Mexico." *Economic Geology* 10, no. 3 (1915): 195–224.

General Reports of the Suit against the Mexican Eagle Petroleum Co. Mexico City, 1934–35.

Great Britain, Foreign Office. *Diplomatic and Consular Reports: Mexico, 1880–1910.* London, 1881–1911.

Hamilton, Charles W. *Early Day Oil Tales of Mexico.* Houston, 1966.

Lambert, Paul F., and Kenny A. Franks, eds. *Voices from the Oil Fields.* Norman, 1984.

Limantour, José Yves. *Apuntes sobre mi vida pública [1892–1911].* Mexico City, 1965.

López Portillo y Weber, José. *El petróleo de México: Su importancia, sus problemas.* Mexico City, 1975.

Lynch, Gerald. *Roughnecks, Drillers, and Tool Pushers: Thirty-Three Years in the Oil Fields.* Austin, 1987.

McMahon, William E. *Two Strikes and Out.* Garden City, 1939.

Madero, Francisco I. *La sucesión presidencial en 1910: El partido nacional democratico.* San Pedro, Coahuila, 1908.

Mexican Eagle Oil Co., Ltd. New York, 1921.

Mexican Gulf v. Transcontinental: Plaintiffs and Defendants Exhibition. n.p., n.d.

Mexican Oil Corporation, Ltd. *Mexico Today: The Mexican Petroleum Industry.* London, 1905.

Mexican Petroleum Company, *Los impuestos sobre la industria de petróleo.* Mexico City, 1912.

México, Departamento de la Estadística Nacional. *Resúmen del censo general de habitantes de 30 de noviembre de 1921.* Mexico, 1928.

México, Secretaría de Economía, Dirección General de Estadística. *Estadísticas sociales del Porfiriato, 1877–1970.* Mexico City, 1956.

México, Secretaría de Fomento. *Censo y división territorial del Estado de Tamaulipas verificados en 1900.* Mexico City, 1904.

———. *Censo y división territorial del Estado de Vera Cruz verificados en 1900.* Mexico City, 1904.

México, Secretaría de Industria, Comercio y Trabajo. *Documentos relacionados con la legislación petrolera mexicana.* Mexico City, 1919.

———. *Legislación petrolera.* Mexico City, 1922.

———. *Proyecto de la ley de petróleo de los Estados Unidos Mexicanos.* Mexico City, 1918.

"Oil Fields of Mexico Co." In *The Joint Stock Companies' Journal.* August 1912.

Ordóñez, Ezequiel. "El Petróleo en México: Bosquejo histórico." 2 parts. *Revista Mexicana de Ingeniería y Arquetectura* 10, no. 3 (15 March 1932): 154–61, and 10, no. 4 (15 April 1932): 187–230.

El petróleo de México: Recopilación de documentos oficiales. Mexico City, 1940, reedition, 1963.

Pan American Petroleum Corporation, *Mexican Petroleum.* New York, 1922.

Prospectus of "The Boston and Mexican Oil Co." of Portland, Maine. Boston, 1882.

Rouaix, Pastor. *Génesis de los artículos 27 y 123 de la constitución política de 1917.* 2d edition. Mexico City, 1959.

U.S. Bureau of Foreign and Domestic Commerce. *Commerce Reports.* 13 September 1920.

U.S. Congress, Senate, Committee on Commerce. *Regulation of Ocean Freight Rates, Requisitioning of Vessels, and Increasing the Powers of the Shipping Board.* 65th Congress, 2d sess. Washington, D.C., 1918.

U.S. Congress, Senate, Committee on Foreign Relations. *Investigation of Mexican Affairs.* 66th Congress, 1st sess. 2 vols. Washington, D.C., 1920.

U.S. Congress, Senate, Committee on Public Lands. *Leasing of Oil Lands.* 65th Congress, 1st sess. Washington, D.C., 1917.

U.S. Congress, Senate, *Report of Secretary of State to Senate.* Senate Document 330. 65th Congress, 1st sess. Washington, D.C., 1917.

U.S. Congress, Senate. *Senate Document 272.* 66th Congress, 2d sess. Washington, D.C., 1919.

U.S. Congress, Senate, Subcommittee of the Committee on Foreign Relations. *Revolutions in Mexico.* 62d Congress, 2d sess. Washington, D.C., 1913.

U.S. Department of State. *Papers Relating to the Foreign Relations of the United States.* Washington, D.C., 1919.

U.S. Supreme Court. *Transcript of Record, Standard Oil Company et al. v. U.S.* October term, 1909, 221 U.S. 1. Washington, D.C., 1910.

———. *Transcript of Record, Waters-Pierce Oil Company v. Texas.* October term, 1898. 177 U.S. 28. Washington, D.C., 1889.

———. *Transcript of Record, Waters-Pierce Oil Company v. Texas.* October term, 1908, no. 356. Washington, D.C., 1909.

———. *United States of America, petitioner, v. Standard Oil Company of New Jersey et al., defendants,* 22 vols. Washington, D.C., 1908–11.

Vázquez Schiaffino, José, et al. *Informes sobre la cuestión petrolera.* Mexico City, 1919.

Vincent, Mordelo L., Jr. *A Man Remembers.* 1919. Reprint. Chapel Hill, 1985.

Waters-Pierce Oil Co. v. Texas. No. 1, 212 U.S. 86, and No. 2, 212 U.S. 112 (1898).
Waters-Pierce Oil Co. v. Texas. No. 1, 103 S.W. Rep. 836, and No. 2, 106 S.W. Rep. 918 (1907).

Secondary Sources

Adams, Frederick U. *The Waters Pierce Case in Texas.* St. Louis, 1908.

Adams, Richard Newbold. *The Second Sowing: Power and Secondary Development in Latin America.* New York, 1967.

Adleson G., S. Lief. "Historia social de los obreros industriales de Tampico, 1906–1919." Doctoral thesis, El Colegio de México, 1982.

Anderson, Rodney. *Outcasts in Their Own Land: Mexican Industrial Workers, 1906–1911.* DeKalb, Ill., 1976.

Ankerson, Dudley. "Some Aspects of Economic Change and the Origins of the Mexican Revolution, 1876–1910." Mimeograph, Center of Latin American Studies, Cambridge University, 1975.

Ansell, Martin R. "Pouring Oil on Troubled Waters: Edward L. Doheny and the Mexican Revolution." M.A. thesis, University of Oregon, 1985.

Armstrong, Christopher, and H. V. Nelles. "A Curious Capital Flow: Canadian Investment in Mexico, 1902–1910." *Business History Review* 59 (1984): 178–203.

Baker, George. *Mexico's Petroleum Sector: Performance and Prospect.* Tulsa, 1984.

Basurto, Jorge. *El proletariado industrial en México (1850–1930).* Mexico City, 1975.

Bazant, Jan. *Historia de la deuda exterior de México (1823–1946).* Mexico City, 1968.

Beals, Carleton. *Porfirio Diaz: Dictator of Mexico.* Philadelphia, 1932.

Beezley, William H. *Judas at the Jockey Club and Other Episodes of Porfirian Mexico.* Lincoln, 1987.

Bergquist, Charles. *Labor in Latin America: Comparative Essays on Chile, Argentina, Venezuela, and Colombia.* Stanford, 1984.

Bermúdez, Antonio J. *The Mexican National Petroleum Industry: A Case Study in Nationalization.* Stanford, 1963.

Bernstein, Marvin D. *The Mexican Mining Industry, 1890–1950: A Study of the Interaction of Politics, Economics, and Technology.* Albany, N.Y., 1964.

Braverman, Harry. *Labor and Monopoly Capital: The Degradation of Work in the Twentieth Century.* New York, 1974.

Bringhurst, Bruce. *Antitrust and the Oil Monopoly: The Standard Oil Case, 1890–1911.* Westport, Conn., 1979.

Brown, Jonathan C. "Why Foreign Oil Companies Shifted Their Production from Mexico to Venezuela during the 1920s." *American Historical Review* 90 (1985): 362–85.

Bryant, Keith L., Jr. *History of the Atchison, Topeka and Santa Fe Railway.* New York, 1974.

Calvert, Peter A. R. *The Mexican Revolution, 1910–1914: The Diplomatic Anglo-American Conflict.* Cambridge, Eng., 1968.

Carr, Barry. *El movimiento obrero y la política en México, 1910–1929.* Mexico City, 1981.

Chandler, Alfred, Jr. *The Visible Hand: The Managerial Revolution in American Business.* Cambridge, Mass., 1977.

———. "Technological and Organizational Underpinnings of Modern Industrial Enterprise: The Dynamics of Competitive Advantage." In *Multinational Enterprise in Historical Perspective,* edited by Alice Teichova, Maurice Lévy-Leboyer, and Helga Nussbaum. Cambridge, Eng., 1986.

Chapman, John Greshman. *La construcción del ferrocarril mexicano (1837–1880).* Mexico City, 1975.

Clark, James A., and Michel T. Halbouty, *Spindletop.* New York, 1952.

Coatsworth, John H. *Growth Against Development: The Economic Impact of Railroads in Porfirian Mexico.* DeKalb, Ill., 1981.

———. "Características generales de la economía mexicana en el siglo xix." In *Ensayos sobre el desarrollo económico de México y América Latina, 1500–1975,* edited by Enrique Florescano. Mexico City, 1979.

———. "Obstacles to Economic Growth in Nineteenth-Century Mexico." *American Historical Review* 83 (1978): 80–100.

———. "Railroads and the Concentration of Land Ownership in the Early Porfiriato." *Hispanic American Historical Review* 54 (1974): 48–71.

Cockcroft, James D. *Intellectual Precursors of the Mexican Revolution, 1900–1913.* Austin, 1968.

Coerver, Don M. *The Porfirian Interregnum: The Presidency of Manuel González of Mexico, 1880–1884.* Fort Worth, 1979.

Connelly, W. L. *The Oil Business As I Saw It: Half a Century with Sinclair.* Norman, 1954.

Cooper, Bryan, ed. *Latin American and Caribbean Oil Report.* London, n.d. [c. 1980].

Córdova, Arnaldo. *La ideología de la Revolución Mexicana: La formación del nuevo régimen.* Mexico City, 1973.

Cortés Conde, Roberto. *The First Stages of Modernization in Latin America.* New York, 1974.

Cosío Villegas, Daniel, et al. *Historia moderna de México.* 8 vols. Mexico City, 1965–72.

Cumberland, Charles C. *Mexican Revolution: The Constitutionalist Years.* 2 vols. Austin, 1972.

De la Garza Treviño, Ciro R. *La Revolución Mexicana en el Estado de Tamaulipas.* 2 vols. Mexico City, 1975.

Dealy, Glen Caudill. *The Public Man: An Interpretation of Latin American and other Catholic Countries.* Amherst, Mass., 1977.

Di Tella, Torcuato S. "The Dangerous Classes in Early Nineteenth-Century Mexico." *Journal of Latin American Studies* 5 (May 1973): 79–105.

Díaz Dufoo, Carlos. *Limantour.* Mexico City, 1911.

———. *México y los capitales extranjeros*. Mexico City, 1918.

Dolson, Hildegarde. *The Great Oildorado: The Gaudy and Turbulent Years of the First Oil Rush, Pennsylvania, 1859–1880*. New York, 1959.

Dulles, John W. F. *Yesterday in Mexico: A Chronicle of the Revolution, 1919–1936*. Austin, 1972.

Durán de Seade, Esperanza. "Mexico's Relations with the Powers during the Great War." D. Phil. thesis, St. Antony's College, Oxford University, 1980.

Emmanuel, Arghiri. *Unequal Exchange: A Study of the Imperialism of Trade*. Translated by Brian Pearce. London, 1972.

Evans, Peter. *Dependent Development: The Alliance of Multinational, State, and Local Capital in Brazil*. Princeton, 1979.

Fowler Salamini, Heather. "Caciquismo and the Mexican Revolution: The Case of Manuel Peláez." Paper presented at the 6th Conference of Mexican and United States Historians, 1981.

Frost, Elsa Cecilia, Michael C. Meyer, and Josefina Zoraida Vásquez, eds. *El trabajo y los trabajadores en la historia de México*. Mexico City and Tucson, 1979.

Gerhard, Peter. *A Guide to the Historical Geography of New Spain*. Cambridge, Eng., 1972.

———. *The North Frontier of New Spain*. Princeton, 1982.

Gerhardt, Ray C. "Inglaterra y el petróleo mexicano durante la Primera Guerra Mundial." *Historia Mexicana* 25 (1975): 118–42.

Gerretson, F. C. *History of the Royal Dutch*. 4 vols. Leiden, 1953.

———. *Geschiedenis de Koninklijke Nederlandsche Petroleum Maatschnappij*, vol. 5. Baarn, Neth., 1973.

Gibb, George Sweet, and Evelyn H. Knowlton. *The Resurgent Years, 1911–1927: History of the Standard Oil Company (New Jersey)*. New York, 1956.

Giddens, Paul H. *The Beginnings of the Petroleum Industry: Sources and Bibliography*. Harrisburg, Pa., 1941.

———. *Early Days of Oil: A Pictorial History of the Beginnings of the Industry in Pennsylvania*. Princeton, 1948.

Gilly, Adolfo. *La revolución interrumpida: México, 1910–1920, una guerra campesina por la tierra y el poder*. 5th ed. Mexico City, 1975.

Glade, William. "Latin America and the International Economy, 1870–1914." *Cambridge History of Latin America*, edited by Leslie Bethel. Vol. 4. Cambridge, Eng., 1986.

González, Francisco Alonso. *Historia y petróleo, México: El problema del petróleo*. Mexico City, 1972.

González Navarro, Moisés. *Las huelgas textiles en el Porfiriato*. Puebla, 1970.

Grieb, Kenneth J. *The United States and Huerta*. Lincoln, 1969.

Gunder Frank, André. *Capitalism and Underdevelopment in Latin America: Historical Studies of Chile and Brazil*. New York, 1969.

Gutman, Herbert G. *Work, Culture and Society in Industrializing America: Essays in American Working-Class and Social History*. New York, 1976.

———. "Work, Culture, and Society in Industrializing America, 1815–1919," *American Historical Review* 78 (1972): 531–88.

Haber, Stephen H. *Industry and Underdevelopment: The Industrialization of Mexico, 1890–1940*. Stanford, 1989.

Hall, Linda B. *Alvaro Obregón: Power and Revolution in Mexico, 1911–1920*. College Station, Tex., 1981.

Hall, Linda B., and Don M. Coerver. *Revolution on the Border: The United States and Mexico, 1910–1920*. Albuquerque, 1988.

Hamilton, Nora. *The Limits of State Autonomy: Post-Revolutionary Mexico*. Princeton, 1982.

Hanighen, Frank C. *The Secret War*. New York, 1934.

Hanrahan, Gene Z. *The Bad Yankee: El Peligro Yankee: American Entrepreneurs and Financiers in Mexico*. 2 vols. Chapel Hill, 1985.

——, ed. *Counter-Revolution along the Border*. Salisbury, N.C., 1983.

Hanson, Roger D. *The Politics of Mexican Development*. Baltimore, 1971.

Hart, John Mason. *Anarchism and the Mexican Working Class, 1860–1931*. Austin, 1978.

——. *Revolutionary Mexico: The Coming and Process of the Mexican Revolution*. Berkeley and Los Angeles, 1987.

Henderson, Peter V. N. *Félix Díaz, the Porfirians, and the Mexican Revolution*. Lincoln, 1981.

Hidy, Ralph W., and Muriel E. Hidy. *Pioneering in Big Business, 1882–1911: History of the Standard Oil Company, New Jersey*. New York, 1955.

Hill, Larry D. *Emissaries to a Revolution: Woodrow Wilson's Executive Agents in Mexico*. Baton Rouge, 1973.

Hobsbawm, Eric. *Workers: Worlds of Labor*. New York, 1984.

Hoffman, Fritz L. "Edward L. Doheny and the Beginnings of Petroleum Development in Mexico." *Mid-America* 24 (April 1942).

Hymer, Stephen. *The International Operations of National Firms: A Study of Direct Foreign Investment*. Cambridge, Mass., 1976.

James, Marquis. *The Texaco Story: The First Fifty Years, 1902–1952*. N.p., 1953.

Joseph, G. M. *Revolution from Without: Yucatán, Mexico, and the United States, 1880–1924*. Cambridge, Eng., 1982.

Katz, Friedrich. *The Secret War in Mexico: Europe, the United States and the Mexican Revolution*. Chicago, 1981.

——, ed. *Riot, Rebellion, and Revolution: Rural Social Conflict in Mexico*. Princeton, 1988.

Kennedy, James Harrison. *A History of the City of Cleveland, 1796–1890*. Cleveland, 1896.

Keremitsis, Dawn. *La industria textil mexicana en el siglo XIX*. Mexico City, 1973.

Kindleberger, Charles P. *American Business Abroad: Six Lectures on Direct Investment*. New Haven, 1969.

Knight, Alan. *The Mexican Revolution*. 2 vols. Cambridge, Eng., 1986.

——. *U.S.-Mexican Relations, 1910–1940: An Interpretation*. San Diego, 1987.

——. "El liberalismo mexicano desde la reforma hasta la revolución (una interpretación)." *Historia Mexicana* 35 (1985): 59–91.

———. "The Political Economy of Revolutionary Mexico, 1900–1940." In *Latin American Economic Imperialism and the State,* edited by Christopher Abel and Colin M. Lewis. London, 1985.

———. "The Working Class and the Mexican Revolution, c. 1900–1920." *Journal of Latin American Studies* 16 (1984): 51–97.

Krause, Enrique. *Historia de la revolución mexicana.* Mexico City, 1972.

Kroeber, Clifton B. *Man, Land, and Water: Mexico's Farmlands Irrigation Policies, 1885–1911.* Berkeley and Los Angeles, 1983.

Lavín, José Domingo. *Petróleo: pasada, presente y futuro de una industria mexicana.* Mexico City, 1976.

Lenin, V. I. "Imperialism, the Last Stage of Capitalism." In *Imperialism: The State and Revolution.* New York, 1926.

Linder, Peter S. "Every Region for Itself: The Manuel Peláez Movement, 1914–1923." M.A. thesis, University of New Mexico, 1983.

McCullough, David. *The Path Between the Seas: The Creation of the Panama Canal, 1870–1914.* New York, 1977.

Mallison, Sam T. *The Great Wildcatter.* Charleston, W.V., 1953.

Marichal, Carlos. *A Century of Debt Crisis in Latin America: From Independence to the Great Depression, 1820–1930.* Princeton, 1989.

Martínez Sobral, Enrique. *La reforma montaria.* Mexico City, 1909.

Meade, Joaquín. *Historia de Valles: Monografía de la Huasteca Potosina.* San Luis Potosí, 1970.

Melosi, Martin V. *Coping with Abundance: Energy and Environment in Industrial America.* Philadelphia, 1985.

Menéndez, Gabriel Antonio. *Doheny El Cruel: Episodios de la sangrienta lucha por el petróleo mexicano.* Mexico City, 1958.

Meyer, Jean. "Los Estados Unidos y el petróleo mexicano: Estado de la cuestión." *Historia Mexicana* 18 (1968): 79–96.

Meyer, Lorenzo. *Mexico and the United States in the Oil Controversy, 1916–1942.* Austin, 1977.

Meyer, Michael C. *Huerta: A Political Portrait.* Lincoln, 1972.

———. *Mexican Rebel: Pascual Orozco and the American Revolution, 1910–1915.* Lincoln, 1978.

Meyer, Michael C., and William L. Sherman. *The Course of Mexican History.* New York, 1983.

Middlemas, Robert Keith. *The Master Builders: Thomas Brassey, Sir John Aird, Lord Cowdray, Sir John Norton-Griffiths.* London, 1963.

Miller, Richard Ulric. "American Railroad Unions and the National Railways of Mexico." *Labor History* 15 (1974): 242–59.

Mohr, Anton. *The Oil Wars.* New York, 1926.

Molina Enríquez, Andrés. *Los grandes problemas nacionales.* 1909. Reprint Mexico City, 1978.

Moore, Barrington, Jr. *Social Origins of Dictatorship and Democracy: Lord and Peasant in the Making of the Modern World.* Boston, 1966.

Moreno, Francisco Martín. *México negro.* Mexico City, 1986.

Mosconi, Enrique. *El Petróleo argentino, 1922–1930, y la ruptura de los trusts petrolíferos inglés y norteamericanos.* Buenos Aires, 1936.

Nevins, Allen. *John D. Rockefeller: The Heroic Age of American Enterprise.* 2 vols. New York, 1940.

Niemeyer, E. V., Jr. *Revolution at Querétaro: The Mexican Constitutional Convention, 1916–1917.* Austin, 1974.

O'Brien, Dennis J. "Petróleo e intervención: Relaciones entre Los Estados Unidos y México, 1917–1918." *Historia Mexicana* 27 (1977): 103–40.

O'Donnell, Guillermo. *Modernization and Bureaucratic-Authoritarianism: Studies in South American Politics.* Berkeley and Los Angeles, 1973.

Parlee, Lorena M. "The Impact of United States Railroad Unions on Organized Labor and Government Policy in Mexico (1880–1911)." *Hispanic American Historical Review* 64 (1984): 443–75.

Parkes, Henry Bamford. *A History of Mexico.* 3d ed. Boston, 1966.

Paz, Octavio. *The Labyrinth of Solitude: Life and Thought in Mexico.* New York, 1961.

Penrose, Edith T. *The Large International Firm in Developing Countries: The International Petroleum Industry.* London, 1968.

Perry, Laurens Ballard. *Juárez and Díaz Machine Politics in Mexico.* De Kalb, Ill., 1978.

Philip, George. *Oil and Politics in Latin America: Nationalist Movements and State Oil Companies.* Cambridge, Eng., 1982.

Phipps, Kenneth C. "The Petroleum Industry of Mexico." M.A. thesis, University of Texas, 1922.

Platt, D. C. M., ed. *Business Imperialism, 1840–1930: An Inquiry Based on British Experience in Latin America.* Oxford, 1977.

Pletcher, David M. *Rails, Mines, and Progress: Seven American Promoters in Mexico, 1867–1911.* Ithaca, 1958.

Poulson, Barry W. *Economic History of the United States, 1867–1960.* New York, 1963.

Pratt, Joseph A. *The Growth of a Refining Region.* Greenwich, Conn., 1980.

Prebisch, Raúl. *Towards a Dynamic Development Policy for Latin America.* New York, 1963.

Quirk, Robert E. *An Affair of Honor: Woodrow Wilson and the Occupation of Veracruz.* Lexington, Ky., 1962.

———. *The Mexican Revolution, 1914–1915: The Convention of Aguascalientes.* Bloomington, 1960.

Ramos Escandón, Carmen. *La industria textil y el movimiento obrero en México.* Mexico City, 1988.

Randall, Laura. *A Comparative Economic History of Latin America, 1500–1914.* 3 vols. Ann Arbor, 1978.

———. *The Political Economy of Mexican Oil.* New York, 1989.

Reynolds, Clark W. *The Mexican Economy: Twentieth Century Structures and Growth.* New Haven, 1970.

Richmond, Douglas W. *Venustiano Carranza's Nationalist Struggle, 1893–1920.* Lincoln, 1983.

Rintoul, William. *Spudding In: Recollections of Pioneer Days in the California Oil Fields.* San Francisco, 1976.

Rippy, J. Fred. *Latin America and the Industrial Age.* New York, 1947.

Rippy, Merrill. *Oil and the Mexican Revolution*. Leiden, 1972.

Ritchie, Ward. *The Dohenys of Los Angeles*. Los Angeles, 1974.

Rodea, Marcelo. *Historia del movimiento obrero ferrocarrilero*. Mexico City, 1944.

Ross, Stanley R. *Francisco I. Madero: Apostle of Mexican Democracy*. New York, 1955.

Rostow, W. W. *British Economy of the Nineteenth Century*. Oxford, 1948.

———. *How It All Began: Origins of the Modern Economy*. New York, 1975.

———. *The Stages of Economic Growth*. Cambridge, Eng., 1971.

Ruíz, Ramón Eduardo. *The Great Rebellion: Mexico, 1905–1924*. New York, 1980.

———. *Labor and the Ambivalent Revolutionaries: Mexico, 1911–1923*. Baltimore, 1976.

———. *The People of Sonora and Yankee Capitalists*. Tucson, 1988.

Salazar, Rosendo, and José G. Escobedo. *Las pugnas de la gleba, 1907–1922*. Mexico City, 1923.

Schryer, Frans J. *The Rancheros of Pisaflores: The History of a Peasant Bourgeoisie in Twentieth-Century Mexico*. Toronto, 1980.

Scott, James C. *The Moral Economy of the Peasant: Rebellion and Subsistence in Southeast Asia*. New Haven, 1976.

Scott, James C., and Benedict J. Tria Kerkvliet, eds. *Everyday Forms of Peasant Resistance in South-East Asia*. London, 1986.

Sign of the 76: The Fabulous Life and Times of the Union Oil Company of California. Los Angeles, 1976.

Silva Herzog, Jesús. *El petróleo de México*. Mexico City, 1940.

Smith, B. W. "The Story of Royal Dutch/Shell up to 1945." Unpublished manuscript. Shell International Petroleum Co. archives, London, 1961.

Smith, Robert Freeman. *The United States and Revolutionary Nationalism in Mexico, 1916–1942*. Chicago, 1972.

Spender, J. A. *Weetman Pearson: First Viscount Cowdray, 1856–1927*. London, 1930. Reprint. New York, 1977.

Stratton, David H. "Albert B. Fall and the Teapot Dome Affair." Ph.D. diss., University of Colorado, 1959.

———, ed. *The Memoirs of Albert B. Fall*. El Paso, 1966.

Tannenbaum, Frank. *Mexico: The Struggle for Peace and Bread*. New York, 1950.

———. *The Mexican Agrarian Revolution*. New York, 1929.

Tanratanakol, Chitraporn. "Threats to Subsistence: Regional Economy and the 1869 Mezquital Peasant Rebellion in Mexico." Ph.D. diss., Northern Illinois University, 1987.

Tarbell, Ida M. *The History of the Standard Oil Company*. 2 vols. New York, 1950.

Tenenbaum, Barbara. *The Politics of Penury: Debts and Taxes in Mexico, 1821–1856*. Albuquerque, 1986.

Thompson, E. P. *The Making of the English Working Class*. New York, 1973.

Thorup, Cathryn. "La competencia económica británica y norteamericana en

México (1887–1910): El caso de Weetman Pearson." *Historia Mexicana* 31 (1982): 599–641.

Tinkle, Lon. *Mr. De: A Biography of Everette Lee De Golyer.* Boston, 1970.

Tobler, Hans Werner. *Die Mexikanische Revolution: Gesellschaftlicher Wandel und Politischer Umbruch, 1876–1940.* Frankfurt-am-Main, 1984.

Turlington, Edgar. *Mexico and Her Foreign Creditors.* New York, 1930.

Tutino, John. *From Insurrection to Revolution in Mexico: Social Bases of Agrarian Violence, 1750–1940.* Princeton, 1986.

Valdivieso Castillo, Julio. *Historia del movimiento sindical petrolero en Minatitlán, Veracruz.* Mexico City, 1963.

Vanderwood, Paul J. *Disorder and Progress: Bandits, Police, and Mexican Development.* Lincoln, 1981.

Voss, Stuart F. *On the Periphery of Nineteenth-Century Mexico: Sonora and Sinaloa, 1810–1877.* Tucson, 1982.

Walker, David W. *Kinship, Business, and Politics: The Martínez del Río Family in Mexico, 1824–1867.* Austin, 1986.

Wallerstein, Emmanuel. "The Rise and Future Demise of the World Capitalist System: Concepts for Comparative Analysis." *Comparative Studies in Society and History* 16 (1974): 387–415.

Wasserman, Mark. *Capitalists, Caciques, and Revolution: The Native Elite and Foreign Enterprise in Chihuahua Mexico, 1854–1911.* Chapel Hill, 1984.

―――. "Enrique C. Creel: Business and Politics in Mexico, 1880–1930." *Business History Review* 59 (Winter 1985): 645–62.

Werner, M. R., and John Star. *Teapot Dome.* New York, 1959.

White, Gerald T. *Formative Years in the Far West: A History of the Standard Oil Company of California and Predecessors Through 1919.* New York, 1962.

Whitney, Caspar. *Charles Adelbert Canfield.* New York: Private Printing, 1930.

Wilkie, James W. *The Mexican Revolution: Federal Expenditure and Social Change Since 1910.* Berkeley and Los Angeles, 1970.

―――, ed. *Statistical Abstract of Latin America.* Vol. 24. Los Angeles, 1985.

Wilkins, Mira. *The Emergence of Multinational Enterprise: American Business Abroad from the Colonial Era to 1914.* Cambridge, Mass., 1981.

―――. *The Maturing of Multinational Enterprise: American Business Abroad from 1914 to 1970.* Cambridge, Mass., 1974.

―――. "Multinational Oil Companies in South America in the 1920s: Argentina, Bolivia, Brazil, Chile, Colombia, Ecuador, and Peru." *Business History Review* 48 (1974): 414–46.

Williamson, Harold F., et al. *The American Petroleum Industry.* 2 vols. Evanston, 1959–63.

Womack, John, Jr. *Zapata and the Mexican Revolution.* New York, 1968.

―――. "The Mexican Economy during the Revolution, 1910–1920." *Marxist Perspectives* 1 (1978): 80–123.

―――. "The Mexican Revolution, 1910–1920." In *The Cambridge History of Latin America,* edited by Leslie Bethel. Vol. 5. Cambridge, Eng., 1984.

Yergin, Daniel. *The Prize: The Epic Quest for Oil, Money, and Power.* New York, 1991.

Young, Desmond. *Member for Mexico: A Biography of Weetman Pearson, First Viscount Cowdray.* London, 1966.

Zea, Leopoldo. *Apogeo y decadencia del positivismo en México.* Mexico City, 1944.

———. *The Latin American Mind.* Translated by James H. Abbott and Lowell Dunham. Norman, 1963.

Index

Ackerman, Carl W., 285
Acosta, Emilio, 206, 294, 296
Adams, Frederick, 200, 229
El Aguila. *See* Compañía Mexicana del Petróleo El Aguila, S.A.
Aguilar, Cándido, 186, 191, 235, 261; attempts to influence Supreme Court, 234; and Constitution, 228; denounces El Aguila, 260, 261; labor policies, 339, 340; leads rebellion in oil zone, 204–5; as nationalist, 214–15, 216, 219, 230; in Tuxpan, 198, 258, 301; views on oil contracts, 218. *See also* Peláez, Manuel
American Association of Mexico, 245, 317
Americans. *See* Immigrants, U. S.
Araujo, Andrés, 343, 346, 359
Archbold, John D., 62, 97, 98, 152, 157
Arnold, Ralph, 43, 106, 114, 127, 163
Arredondo, E., 270, 398n.157
Asphalt, 33–35. *See also* Walker, Harold W.
Assheton, J. A., 167
Association of Foreign Oil Producers, 238–41, 244, 246, 247; policy of, 248, 249
Atchinson, Topeka, and Santa Fe Railroad, 26, 33
Azuela, Mariano, 252

Badger, Charles T., 194, 403n.65
Barron, Clarence W., 136

Beaty, Amos, 239, 242
Benedum, Michael, 43, 44–45, 123, 124
Bergquist, Charles, 422n.11
Body, J. B., 128, 138, 143, 149, 166, 176, 177; blames Constitutionalists, 261; early career with Pearson, 49, 51, 53, 62, 64, 69, 85; on intervention, 190, 279; and Madero, 204; on Peláez, 281, 284; relations with Carranza, 180–81, 182, 187, 198, 239, 246
Branch, Hilarión, 134, 221
Braverman, Harry, 425n.60
Brown, J. A., 201, 236
Bryan, William Jennings, 184, 189, 196
Buckley, William, 107, 239, 242, 317, 411n.221; on bribery, 211; criticizes big companies, 179, 245; criticizes Wilson, 196; on Peláez, 284. *See also* National Association for the Protection of American Rights in Mexico

Caballero, Luis, 191, 287, 294; falls out with Carranza, 295–96
Cabrera, Luis, 216, 220, 237, 239
Calero, Manuel, 176, 178, 389n.230
California oil strike. *See* Doheny, Edward L.
Calles, Plutarco Elías, 235, 317, 372
Canfield, Charles, 26, 27, 133
Canova, Leon, 282

Compositor:	BookMasters
Text:	10/13 Galliard
Display:	Galliard
Printer:	Thomson-Shore, Inc.
Binder:	Thomson-Shore, Inc.